LEGAL RESOURCE

for

SCHOOL HEALTH SERVICES

A reference regarding legal issues impacting school health. The book provides information on over 50 topics that school health services programs and school nurses encounter, addresses legal implications and presents legal resources and references that can be applied to practice and policy development.

Editors
Cheryl A. Resha, EdD, MSN, RN, FNASN
Vicki L. Taliaferro, BSN, RN, NCSN

Legal Consultant
Erin D. Gilsbach, Esquire

SchoolNurse.com
P.O. Box 150127
Nashville, TN 37215

LEGAL RESOURCE FOR SCHOOL HEALTH SERVICES
Copyright © 2017 SchoolNurse.com

ISBN-13:   978-0-9792497-6-1
ISBN-10:   0-9792497-6-7

Phone: 615-370-7899
Fax: 615-370-9993

DISCLAIMER

Many hours of research went into the creation of this book, and the authors worked diligently to provide information that is accurate and up-to-date. Laws change on a regular basis, however, and interpretations of law can vary significantly. This publication is intended to provide a comprehensive overview of a wide variety of legal topics related to the practice of school nursing. The information in this book should not be considered to be legal advice, and readers should understand that court decisions and legislative actions that occur every day may render particular laws or legal concepts invalid or outdated. In addition, legal analysis depends very heavily upon the fact patterns to which a law or legal concept is applied, and sometimes even the smallest change in fact can result in a completely different finding of law.

The jurisdiction in which an issue occurs also plays a large role in the applicability and/or interpretation of any particular law or legal concept. Thus, this work is not intended to replace case-specific research or legal counsel, and no representations, warranties, or guarantees, express or implied, are made as to the accuracy, adequacy, reliability, currentness, completeness, suitability, or applicability of the information found within. All information should be independently verified before being relied upon.

SchoolNurse.com, the editors, legal consultant, authors, or reviewers do not assume responsibility for or liability regarding any error, omission, or inaccuracy of law or fact in the information contained within this work. Readers should seek independent legal counsel before relying on any part of this work. To the maximum extent permitted by law, SchoolNurse.com, its editors, legal consultant, and contributing authors and reviewers also do not assume any responsibility for or liability regarding any loss, damage or injury, financial or otherwise, suffered by any person acting or relying on information contained in or omitted from this work.

This publication provides links to a number of 3rd party websites. These links have been provided for convenience only and may be subject to updates, revisions or other changes by the entities controlling or owning those sites. The inclusion of the link does not imply that the publisher, editors, legal consultant, authors, or reviewers endorse the content or the site operator. Likewise, this publication cites a large number of reference materials. Endorsement of such works, their authors, publishers, or organizations with which they are affiliated should not be implied.

This work is subject to copyright, and SchoolNurse.com reserves all rights regarding its use. No portion of this work may be copied, reproduced, and/or distributed without written permission by an authorized representative of SchoolNurse.com. All materials contained within this work that have been re-printed from other publications have been used with permission.

FOREWORD

I am honored to have been invited to write the foreword for this valuable resource for school nurses, administrators and attorneys. As legal counsel for the National Association of School Nurses, I have been involved in legal issues related to school nursing and school health services for over 30 years.

The legal landscape associated with healthcare has become increasingly complex over the past several decades, and even more so in the school setting. Once our legal system recognized the rights of medically complex students to receive education in the least restrictive environment and receive the supportive services they need to do so, the responsibilities of the licensed professionals who provide those services expanded.

Those professionals must be knowledgeable about a myriad of laws and regulations, both state and federal, that pertain to the services they provide. Those laws are scattered throughout the federal and state codes and administrative rules—not simply located in the sections of the law directly related to professional licensure or education. And, at times, the school district policies and procedures adopted to comply with the mandates of those various laws conflict with those governing nursing practice, creating ethical and legal dilemmas for school nurses.

The challenge of providing school health services within tight budget constraints creates pressure to delegate to unlicensed assistive personnel responsibilities that might otherwise be provided by licensed school nurses. Because nurse practice acts and related regulations differ from state to state with respect to delegation, school nurses must make sure that school district delegation policies do not require actions that violate those practice acts.

Because of the complexity involved, few of the many legal dilemmas that arise in the school health setting lend themselves to black and white answers. When working through the many shades gray, those involved should seek input from trusted advisors and turn to reliable resources. The *Legal Resource for School Health Services* is a valuable asset and much-needed addition to that collection of resources.

Katherine J. Pohlman, MS, JD, RN
Nurse Attorney and Consultant

ABOUT THIS BOOK

School nursing services are comprehensive and uniquely address health and safety needs of students individually and also in populations, as a component of their role incorporates community/public health nursing. School nurses' work focuses directly on three areas: health services, health education, and the healthy school environment. Their services require diverse knowledge including, but not limited to, pediatric/ adolescent health, infectious diseases, mental health, chronic diseases, and emergency care. School nurses can influence health and safety aspects of schools and can provide leadership to a district's or campus' whole school, whole child, whole community model that in addition to health services, health education, and the healthy school environment addresses mental health and social services, nutrition services, physical activity, family and community involvement, and staff health promotion/services.

Inherent in providing these services and in the daily activities of school nurses and school health programs are legal issues that school health services' personnel must address in order to provide care to children safely and safeguard the schools' accountability for student well-being and the individual school nurse's professional licensure. This resource serves as a reference for school nurses and can assist them, their administrators, school boards and consulting attorneys to identify legal topics, develop policies and procedures, and implement strategies for safe student care. This manual offers brief summaries of a variety of legal considerations that schools and school nurses encounter but is not intended to substitute for any legal consultation nor serve as the sole resource on legal topics.

Legal Resource for School Health Services was developed through cooperative efforts of school nurse experts, nurse attorneys and education attorneys. Compliance with health, education and employment law is of utmost importance for school health services programs but can often be complicated and layered with state and local district laws and policies. It is our hope that this reference provides information, explanations and resources that can assist school health services programs to meet their legal obligations, provide safe care, respect the rights of children while protecting schools and school nurses. It is important to note that in some situations/content areas there is no legal guidance or laws that direct safe practice. In those situations, the authors present "best practices" based on acceptable clinical guidelines or practice models.

LAWS

As depicted in the algorithm below, the legal framework for practice begins with the federal and state constitutions, federal and state laws, federal and state regulations, caselaw, and finally non-regulatory guidance, such as recommendations from state departments of health and education.

SOURCES OF LAW

Erin D. Gilsbach, Esquire

1st Amendment – Free Speech, Freedom of Religion, Free Association

4th Amendment – Prohibits Unreasonable Search and Seizure by Govt. (incl. public schools)

5th Amendment – Due Process Rights

14th Amendment – "Equal Protection Clause" – Equal Opportunities & Equal Treatment

State constitutions establish right to free public education

Includes such statutes as:
- IDEA
- PPRA
- FERPA
- ESSA/ESEA
- Section 504
- McKinney-Vento
- Civil Rights Act of 1964

Includes State Nurse Practice Act (or the equivalent) – statutes regulating the practice of nursing

Rules promulgated by federal agencies pursuant to statutory authority – provides more detailed rules re: compliance with federal statutes, such as those listed, above

Rules promulgated by state agencies pursuant to statutory authority – includes state Dept. of Health / state Board of Nursing (or their equivalents) – requirements for licensure / standards of nursing practice

Interprets law based upon specific facts in a case

Interprets law based upon specific facts in a case

- Office of Civil Rights (OCR) Letters
- Family Policy and Compliance Office (FPCO) Letters
- Office of Special Education Programs (OSEP) Letters

Guidance issued by agencies such as:
- State Dept. of Health
- State Dept. of Education
- State Dept. of Public Welfare

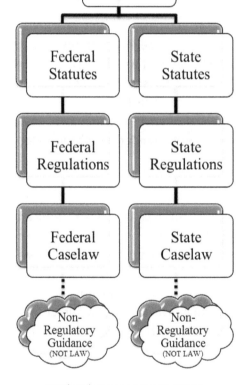

U.S. Constitution

State Constitution

Federal Statutes

State Statutes

Federal Regulations

State Regulations

Federal Caselaw

State Caselaw

Non-Regulatory Guidance (NOT LAW)

Non-Regulatory Guidance (NOT LAW)

Not law, but persuasive to courts

Often issued by same agency tasked with enforcing the law

DESCRIPTION OF LEGAL RESOURCE FOR SCHOOL HEALTH SERVICES

The book is divided into 6 sections:

School Nurse Practice Issues

Laws/Policy

Nursing Care

Nursing Coordination

Staff Services

Beyond the Public School

Each chapter follows a prescribed format:

Description of the Issue

Background

Implications for School Nurse Practice

Conclusion

Resources

References

In some cases, the authors provided additional information which is included in chapter appendices. In other chapters, outside authors provide some practical tips on the topic and are included as addendum with credit to the outside author noted.

The process for developing a chapter included recruiting and selecting authors who have expertise in the area through specialized practice, as presenters, authors on the topic, or as instructors. Authors provided drafts of their chapters to the editors who reviewed and made suggestions for changes throughout the development of the chapter. Each chapter went through blind reviews by both school nurse and legal content experts (school nurses, state school nurse consultants, school nurse educators, health educators, education attorneys, health-related attorneys or nurse attorneys). Final chapters were once again reviewed and finalized by the editors and the legal consultant.

TERMINOLOGY

Child Find: The term "child find" is not formally identified in Section 504 of the Rehabilitation Act of 1973; however, Section 504 does call for the need to identify and determine eligibility for children with disabilities; therefore "child find" in quotes is used not as a formal term but as a way to express the intent to find children in need of services.

Healthcare Provider: This term is used to address all terms used for healthcare providers-physicians, practitioners, doctors, dentists, those with prescriptive authority, etc.

IDEA/IDEIA: The IDEA has undergone multiple amendments and reauthorizations in the decades since its initial passage. Most recently, the IDEA was reauthorized as the Individuals with Disabilities Education Improvement Act (the "IDEIA") in 2004. The original acronym continues to be used colloquially and, for practical purposes, we refer to the legislation in its most recent form as the IDEA throughout the book; however, on occasion, IDEIA is also used.

School(s): The term school in this book refers to "public" schools. When the term is related to private or parochial schools, it will be specifically identified as such.

School District: Different terms are used throughout the country to describe school entities, i.e. school system, school jurisdictions, school campus. Throughout this book will use the term "school district".

School Nurse: For this book, the term school nurse is used for a licensed registered nurse (RN). Under some state laws, school nurses are required to obtain special certification by their state departments of education which may mean additional credits and/or experience. Licensed Nurse Practitioners and RNs without school nurse certification may assist "school nurses," but they cannot replace them, and they do not count towards the state minimum for school nurses. Licensed Practical Nurses (LPNs) or Licensed Vocational Nurses (LVNs) often are hired as school nurses and in most states, are required to work in a team relationship with a RN. The differences vary across states, so for simplicity we have used the term broadly.

We welcome your suggestions for future editions and wish you success in safely caring for our nation's children. You may contact us at *www.schoolnurse.com*.

Cheryl A. Resha, EdD, MSN, RN, FNASN, Editor
Vicki L. Taliaferro, BSN, RN, NCSN, Editor
Erin D. Gilsbach, Esquire, Legal Consultant
Robert Andrews, Publisher
SchoolNurse.com
P.O. Box 150127
Nashville, TN 37215
(866) 370-7899
www.schoolnurse.com

ACKNOWLEDGEMENTS

As editors, we would like to extend our sincere gratitude to the authors and reviewers of this book. Each spent many hours researching the topic, writing, and reviewing materials which significantly contributed to the development of this resource. As you review this book, it will become obvious that each chapter was authored by experts who were both passionate and knowledgeable about their subject matter. Not unlike other large endeavors, this work is clearly one that was successfully completed due to the collective efforts of many.

We would also like to take this opportunity to thank our publisher, Robert Andrews, for his support and commitment to providing school health services personnel with needed resources.

Finally, we would like to thank our families, especially Bonnie and Mike, for their support during this process.

CONTRIBUTORS

AUTHORS AND EDITORS

Andrea Adimando, DNP, MS, APRN, PMHNP-BC, BCIM

Dr. Andrea Adimando is an Assistant Professor of Nursing at Southern CT State University (SCSU). In addition to her teaching responsibilities, Dr. Adimando practices as a Board-Certified Family Psychiatric & Mental Health Nurse Practitioner (PMHNP-BC) in various outpatient and acute care settings in Connecticut, specializing in the care of children and adolescents with psychiatric and behavioral disorders. Prior to becoming a certified nurse practitioner, Dr. Adimando worked as a pediatric nurse on a school-aged medical/surgical unit at Yale New Haven Children's Hospital. Throughout her 12+ years of practice, she has worked collaboratively with school systems, including therapeutic and residential schools, as part of her mental health evaluations and comprehensive treatment planning for her clients.

Alyce L. Alfano, JD, BA

Alyce Alfano focuses her practice in the area of School Law. She has experience with special education, regular education, bullying, residency and disciplinary issues. Additionally, as a consultant for the Connecticut State Department of Education, she served as a mediator for special education disputes between boards of education and families, as well as investigating and responding to special education complaints. At the State Department of Education, Alyce also participated in the management and coordination of the special education due process unit. Alyce regularly speaks on the topic of special education law for various organizations in Connecticut and nationally, including the Connecticut Bar Association, the Hartford County Bar Association and the Connecticut Council of Administrators of Special Education. She has also presented on the legal rights of students as they relate to disciplinary proceedings and bullying. She is a partner with Shipman and Goodman, Hartford, CT.
BAR ADMISSIONS: Connecticut
COURT ADMISSIONS: U.S. District Court, District of CT

Lawrence J. Altman, Esquire

Lawrence J. Altman is an attorney and an adjunct professor at Avila University in Kansas City, Missouri. Until he retired in January of 2016, Mr. Altman was the Special Education Lead Attorney and Compliance Officer for Kansas City Public Schools and the Title IX Coordinator for the Kansas City School District. Prior to that position, he was a practicing attorney in St. Louis County for 34 years. In addition to membership in his state and local bar, he is a valued member of the National School Board Association's Counsel of School Attorneys, and he has earned a number of awards and honors for his service to public schools and his dedication to the law. Mr. Altman continues to write and present on current topics, including assistance and compliance with federal and state laws affecting educational venues. He currently serves on the Missouri Department of Elementary and Secondary Education 's Legislative Workgroup for the Prevention of Student Bullying and Suicide, as chair for the committee tasked with developing model policies to prevent student bullying.

Patricia K. Bednarz, RN, MN, FNASN

Patricia Bednarz is a health and education consultant. She received her Bachelors in Nursing from the University of Illinois Medical Center and her Masters in Nursing from Michigan State University. Patricia had a 25+ year career of diversified, progressive experience as a school nurse, project manager and nursing educator in Lansing School District and Michigan State University. She has expertise in managing state and federal grants (over 8 million in funded awards) that included writing and contributing to proposals, implementation, fiscal management and evaluation. In 2010, Patricia was named a Fellow in the National Academy of School Nurses. Patricia was a member of the Michigan State School Nurse Task Force and continues to lead the development of guidelines and resource documents for school nurses. Her goal is to improve the health and safety of school populations. Patricia has published articles in peer-reviewed journals; presented at state and national school nurse conferences; and was a contributor and reviewer for the School Nurse Resource Manual, 9th ed. School Health Alert (publisher).

Martha D. Bergren, DNS, RN, NCSN, APHA-BC, FNASN, FASHA, FAAN

Martha Dewey Bergren is nationally certified in school nursing and advanced public health nursing, and her areas of expertise include legal issues, leadership, population health, nurse sensitive outcome indicators, and informatics. She is currently the Director of Advanced Population Health, Health Systems Leadership and Informatics Doctor of Nursing Practice programs at the University of Illinois-Chicago College of Nursing. She has served on the National Quality Forum Child Health Outcomes and Pediatric Measures Steering Committees. She has multiple publications in peer reviewed journals and book chapters on legal issues and privacy. She is a fellow in the American Academy of Nursing, the National Association of School Nurses and the American School Health Association. Dr. Bergren teaches health promotion behavior interventions and evidence based practice to doctoral nursing students and develops, measures and disseminates the evidence that school nurses are a cost effective and prudent investment in the health of our nation's children.

Mary Blackborow, MSN, RN, NCSN

Mary Blackborow is a school nurse at North Brunswick Township High School with 17 years' experience as a school nurse. Ms. Blackborow's school nursing experience includes middle and high school students as well as special needs students from three to 21. Ms. Blackborow has held leadership positions in school nursing organizations at the county, state and national levels. She has collaborated on several of the National Association of School Nurses positions documents. Currently, she serves on the editorial advisory board of the NASN School Nurse and in 2015 became a Johnson & Johnson School Health Leadership Fellow.

Edie Brous, MS, MPH, BSN, JD, RN

Edie Brous is a Nurse Attorney in private practice in New York City where she concentrates in professional licensure representation, medical malpractice defense, and nursing advocacy. She has practiced in major litigation law firms representing nurses, physicians, hospitals and pharmaceutical companies. Edie is admitted to practice before the bars of the state courts of New York, New Jersey and Pennsylvania, the Southern and Eastern Districts of the New York Federal Courts and the United States Supreme Court. She is a member of many bar associations and nursing organizations and was the 2011 president of The American Association of Nurse Attorneys.

Ms. Brous has an extensive clinical and managerial background in OR, Emergency and Critical Care Nursing. In addition to her law degree, she holds masters degrees in Public Health and in Critical Care Nursing from Columbia University. She has been part time faculty at Columbia University, and has held adjunct faculty positions at several universities teaching legal aspects of nursing. Ms. Brous has lectured and published extensively on legal issues for nurses and co-authored the textbook *Law and Ethics for Advanced Practice Nurses*. She is the 2008 recipient of the Outstanding Advocate Award from The American Association of Nurse Attorneys.

Linda Caldart Olson, MS, RN, FASHA

Linda Caldart-Olson is currently retired from her position as the State School Nurse Consultant for the state of Wisconsin. Since her retirement, she has done independent consulting for school nursing and health services projects, and authored chapters in Selekman's *School Nursing*, and Costante's *School Nurse Administrators: Leadership and Management* in addition to other publications regarding school nursing. With over 40 years' experience as a registered nurse, Ms. Caldart-Olson has been active in many professional organizations and served on many boards and committees in a leadership capacity. Her clinical specialty is occupational health/ community health nursing.

Tia Campbell, MSN, RN, NCSN, FNASN

Tia Campbell is currently the Director of School Health Services for Chesterfield County Public Schools. Mrs. Campbell received her diploma in nursing from Richmond Memorial Hospital School of Nursing in 1983. In 1985, she received her bachelor of science in nursing from the Medical College of Virginia and completed her master of science in nursing, with a concentration in nursing education from Walden University in 2008. Mrs. Campbell joined Chesterfield County Public Schools in 2016 as the Director of School Health Services. She oversees the provision of health services to 59,000 students. Prior to coming to Chesterfield County, she was the school health specialist at the Virginia Department of Education from 2005-2016. Tia is a National Board Certified School Nurse and currently serves as President of the National Board for Certification of School Nurses. She served as Vice President of the National Association of School Nurses from 2010-2014. She received the 2012 Walden University Outstanding Alumni Award for promoting social change and in 2014 she was inducted as a Fellow in the National Academy of School Nursing.

Elizabeth Chau, SRN (UK), RN

Elizabeth Chau worked as a school nurse at the National Cathedral School for Girls in Washington, DC for 14 years. During that time, she held various positions in the Private and Parochial School Nurse (PPSN) Special Interest Group (SIG) of NASN, including three years as Chairperson. During her term as NASN Director representing the District of Columbia, she was elected to the NASN Executive Committee, overseeing the Governance and Ethics Advisory Committees. Elizabeth has also authored six articles for the NASN School Nurse publication.

Sandra Clark, RN, ADN

Sandra (Sandi) Clark, RN, is currently an Investigator and Compliance Case Manager at the Kentucky Board of Nursing. Previously, Ms. Clark worked as a school nurse for over 14 years in both private and public settings, worked eight years as the State School Nurse Consultant at the Department for Public Health in Kentucky, and also as Pediatric Section Supervisor. Professionally, Ms. Clark served two terms on the National Association of School Nurses Board of Directors, served two terms as President of the Kentucky School Nurse Association, and served on the Governor's task force to create a School Nurse Consultant Position in the Department of Education for the Commonwealth of Kentucky. Ms. Clark has presented on school health related issues at local, state and national levels. She has authored and contributed to school nursing articles, position papers, publications, state and local guidelines, manuals and protocols related to school nursing.

Elizabeth Clark, MSN, RN, NCSN

Elizabeth Clark is the School Medicaid Coordinator for Boulder Valley School District in Boulder, Colorado. She has over 20 years of experience in school-based nursing practice and has been a School Medicaid Consultant since 2002. She received her Master's Degree in the Nursing Care of Children from the University of Colorado, Health Science Center in 1991. She has served as adjunct faculty for the University of Northern Colorado, School of Nursing. She was elected to the National Association of School Nurses Board of Directors and served from 2013 to 2017. Ms. Clark is a member of the American Nurses Association, and a Past President of the Colorado Association of School Nurses. She is a nationally certified school nurse.

Steve M. Cohen, EdD, MPH, BS

Steve M. Cohen, Ed.D., is President and the managing partner of the Labor Management Advisory Group located in the Kansas City Metro area. Dr. Cohen has his Doctorate in Educational and Industrial Psychology, his Masters in Public Administration, and his Bachelors in Speech communications and human relations. He also went to DePaul University Law School's Alternative Dispute Resolution (ADR) Program, where he became a certified mediator. He has a Certificate in Health Care Labor Relations from the Wharton School of Business, University of Pennsylvania. He has 15 years' experience as a hospital administrator, nursing home administrator, physician clinic practices, and retirement center CEO and an additional 25 years' experience as a management consultant. His consultancy consists of working with for profit organizations and not for profit agencies. Steve manages difficult personnel situations like sexual harassment, terminations, and employee / employer conflicts. He also manages & mediates partner to partner conflicts as well as family dynamics within the business setting.

Additionally, he works in turn around, interim, and startup business situations. He conducts management training, sets up human resources systems like crisis plans, job descriptions, performance appraisals, policy manuals, and conducting wage & salary surveys and setting up compensation plans. He provides litigation support and acts as an expert witness. He has published three books entitled: *Mess Management: Lessons from a Corporate Hitman, Ministry Mess Management: Solving Leadership Failures* and *From Bullying to Sexual Violence: Protecting Students and Schools Through Compliance*. His wife and his sister are both nurses.

Laurie Combe, MN, RN, NCSN

Laurie G. Combe has been a Klein ISD school nurse for 24 years, serving Intermediate and High School students prior to moving to her current role as Health Services Coordinator in 2005. Ms. Combe is responsible for the supervision of over 100 Licensed, Certified and Unlicensed Assistive Personnel providing healthcare to students both in school clinics and in classrooms. Professionally, Ms. Combe has been a registered nurse for 41 years with experience in psychiatric and hospice nursing as well as nursing education. Ms. Combe is an active member of the Texas School Nurse Organization as well as the National Association of School Nurses where she serves on the Board of Directors and Executive Committee. Ms. Combe has authored and contributed to articles and publication regarding school nursing practice and is a frequent presenter of Nursing Jurisprudence and Ethics for Texas School Nurses.

Mariann F. Cosby, DNP, MPA, RN, PHN, CEN, NE-BC, LNCC, CLCP, CCM, MSCC

Dr. Mariann F. Cosby is a California Credentialed School Nurse with over 37 years of experience in a variety of nursing specialties. As the owner of MFC Consulting, since 1991 she has provided legal nurse consulting services including expert witness testimony for medical malpractice and school nursing cases. Dr. Cosby is an Assistant Professor for California State University, Sacramento school nurse credential program. She is published in peer reviewed journals and textbooks regarding children and school health such as the past and upcoming edition of the National Association of School Nurses: *School Nursing: A Comprehensive Text*. She is the senior editor and one of the authors for the upcoming fourth edition of the American Association of Legal Nurse Consultants, *Legal Nurse Consulting Principles and Practices* that will include new content on school health. She is an active member in many professional organizations and functions in leadership roles in several organizations including California School Nurses Organization.

Linda Davis-Alldritt, MA, BSN, RN, FNASN, FASHA

Linda Davis-Alldritt is Past President of the National Association of School Nurses, and is currently an independent school health services consultant. Linda was educated in California. She has a Master's Degree in Sociology from California State University Long Beach, a Baccalaureate Degree in Nursing from California State University Sacramento, and a Baccalaureate Degree in Sociology from the University of California Davis. She holds credentials from the California Commission on Teacher Credentialing in school nursing, administrative services, and community college teaching. She has been a nurse for 38 years, including 10 years as a school nurse administrator, and 16 years as the State School Nurse Consultant for the California Department of Education. Linda is a past president of the California School Nurses Organization (CSNO) and a past president of the National Association of State School Nurse Consultants (NASSNC). She has received several awards, including CSNO School Nurse of the Year, NASSNC Outstanding State School Nurse Consultant, and California Public Health Association Public Health Leadership Award. Linda is a fellow of NASN and the American School Health Association (ASHA). She is a published author, including journal articles and the chapter on school health funding for both editions of the NASN textbook: "School Nursing: A Comprehensive Text."

Nancy L. Dube, MPH, BSEd, RN

Nancy Dube is a retired school nurse consultant for the Maine Department of Education. Prior to retirement, Ms. Dube worked for twenty years as a school nurse and consultant and has over 40 years' experience as a nurse. Ms. Dube continues to be active in state and national organizations including the National Association of State School Nurse Consultants (NASSNC), past-president and the National Association of School Nurses (NASN). She has authored and contributed articles related to H1N1, the role of unlicensed personnel serving in schools as well as the concussion chapter in this manual.

Teresa DuChateau, DNP, RN, CPNP

Teresa DuChateau has been a nurse for the past 19 years and has worked in the area of school nursing for over 13 years. In Teresa's most recent position as Director WISHeS (Wisconsin Improving School Health Services) Project she successfully cultivated and sustained collaborative partnerships with critical statewide stakeholders that resulted in highly effective grassroots school district policy change initiatives. Teresa has experience with developing and implementing a statewide school health services assessment along with providing school districts with guidance on providing services to students with chronic health conditions.

Prior to her work on the WISHeS Project, Teresa was the Director of Aurora Healthcare's School Based Health Program and the Pediatric Home Health Program in Milwaukee, WI. In her role as Director of School Based Health, she was responsible for managing 12 school based health centers in Milwaukee, Wisconsin. In 2011, Teresa received her doctorate in nursing practice, focused on school nursing and nursing leadership. Teresa is currently a Clinical Assistant Professor in the College of Nursing at the University of Wisconsin-Milwaukee.

Ingrid Hopkins Duva, PhD, RN

Dr. Ingrid Duva is currently an instructor for Emory University and a school nurse in Gwinnett County, Georgia. Dr. Duva's research focus is health services, improvement work, and the contributions of nursing to care quality. Previously funded by the AHRQ, Veteran›s Health Administration and Sigma Theta Tau, Dr. Duva led studies examining nurse care coordination in a variety of settings, the nurses› role in diabetes care and changing scope of registered nurse practice in primary care. After more than 25 years as a nurse, Dr. Duva's prior roles include operations leadership, administration, and regulatory compliance within the healthcare system. For two years, Dr. Duva served as a national Director of EMTALA Compliance for Tenet Healthcare. An active member of several professional organizations, Dr. Duva previously authored a chapter on leadership for the American Nurses Association (ANA) publication: *Care Coordination: The Game Changer - How nursing is revolutionizing quality care* (2014).

In addition to several local and national professional committees, Dr. Duva is a member of the Endocrine Standing Committee for the National Quality Forum (NQF), which reviews and endorses quality measures for our entire healthcare industry.

Karen Erwin, MSN, RN

Karen Erwin is the Kentucky Education School Nurse Consultant. For the past thirteen years, Ms. Erwin has provided consultation and technical assistance to state and local school boards of education, individual public schools and local and state health departments on the delivery of school health services. Ms. Erwin was instrumental in revising of state regulations for school health services, which now require standardized training for unlicensed assistive school personnel. Ms. Erwin is an executive board member of the National Association of State School Nurse Consultants and a member of the National Association of School Nurses and the Kentucky School Nurses Association. Ms. Erwin has nationally and locally presented on school health services and has been an author of school health services articles, publications, state guidelines, protocols and manuals.

Laura A. Fisher, JD, BA

Laura A. Fisher is an associate attorney with Shipman & Goodwin, LLP. She focuses her practice on the evolving legal matters confronting both private and public educational institutions. Laura received her J.D. *summa cum laude* from Western New England University and her B.A. from Smith College. She is admitted to the bar in Massachusetts and Connecticut.

Melika S. Forbes, JD, BA

Melika Forbes is a member of the School Law practice group at Shipman & Goodwin LLP. Melika represents public school districts and independent schools in all areas of school law. Prior to practicing law, Melika worked as a public school teacher in the New York City Department of Education for six years. In particular, Melika served as a Teach for America corps member at an under-resourced school in the South Bronx, where she taught 6th and 7th grade Math, before serving as the Director of College Placement at the Bronx Lab School. Melika's experience also includes working with education-related national organizations such as Let's Get Ready, an organization that provides free SAT preparation to low income students and serving as a member of the Screening and Selection Committee for Math for America. While in law school, Melika served as a student attorney with the Child and Family Advocacy Clinic and completed an internship at the Vera Institute of Justice, where her research spawned the formation of Be More, a non-profit organization devoted to reducing implicit bias. Additionally, Melika interned at the Truancy Bureau of the Kings County (Brooklyn) District Attorney's Office. Melika earned her B.A. from Syracuse University and her J.D. from the Washington University in St. Louis School of Law.

John E. Freund, III, Esquire

Attorney Freund is the chairman of the Education Law Practice Group at King Spry Herman Freund & Faul in Bethlehem, PA.

Erin D. Gilsbach, Esquire

Erin Gilsbach is the Director of Professional and Policy Development with King Spry Herman Freund & Faul, and the Greyfriars Institute. She is also CEO of EdLaw Interactive, a unique online learning tool designed to provide educators, school nurses, and school leaders with access to high-quality, low-cost training in the area of school law. Atty. Gilsbach is an experienced speaker at the state and national levels, and she works with schools throughout Pennsylvania and nationwide, consulting on legal issues, assisting in the development of legally-defensible policies and procedures, and providing professional development in the area of school (education) law. In her practice, she frequently provides professional development for school nurses and school nurse organizations on current and high-liability issues related to school law and nursing. Atty. Gilsbach is the President of the PA School Boards Association (PSBA)Solicitors Association, and she is a frequent author and presenter with the National School Boards Association (NSBA), NSBA's Council of School Attorneys (COSA), the National Business Institute, the Pennsylvania School Boards Association, and the Pennsylvania Bar Institute. She began her career as a public high school English teacher. Prior to entering private practice, she served for over two years at the Pennsylvania Department of Education's Office of Chief Counsel.

Timothy E. Gilsbach, Esquire, JD, BA

Timothy E. Gilsbach is an attorney with King Spry in Bethlehem, Pennsylvania and concentrates his practice in the area of special education and other areas of education law. For the last ten years, Mr. Gilsbach has defended school districts, intermediate units and charter schools in all phases of special education litigation and advised clients on a wide variety of other educational law issues, including FERPA, student records, student services, and employment matters. Mr. Gilsbach earned a Juris Doctor from the Pennsylvania State University's Dickinson School of Law and a Bachelor of Arts from Messiah College. Mr. Gilsbach is admitted to the bars of Pennsylvania, New Jersey, the United States District Courts for the Eastern District of Pennsylvania, the Middle District of Pennsylvania, and the District of New Jersey, the United States Court of Appeals for the Third Circuit, and the United States Supreme Court. Mr. Gilsbach was selected as a Pennsylvania Rising Star in the area of school law from 2012 through 2014 and a Pennsylvania Super Lawyer in the area of school law in 2017.

Shirley Countryman Gordon, PhD, RN, NCSN, AHN-BC

Dr. Shirley Countryman Gordon is currently a Professor of Nursing at Florida Atlantic University (FAU) where she founded and has continuously directed the Head Lice Treatment and Prevention Project since 1996. Professionally, Dr. Gordon has over 40 years' experience as a registered nurse and nurse educator. Dr. Gordon is an active member in many professional organizations, including the National Association of School Nurses and is an invited member of the International Phthiraptera Congress of lice experts. Dr. Gordon has authored national and international articles and publications regarding school nursing and student health. She was the first to define and focus attention on persistent head lice infestations, conceptualize head lice as a family phenomenon, and identify early nursing interventions.

Jenny M. Gormley, MSN, RN, NCSN

Jenny Gormley is currently Director of the Northeastern University School Health Academy (NEUSHA), which provides standards-based, face to face and online learning opportunities for school nurses and their colleagues to support student health and achievement. She has 30 years of experience as a registered nurse, with the last 17 years in school health. Prior to NEUSHA, she worked for the Hudson Public Schools as Director of Health, Nursing and Safety, where she completed and developed training with local law enforcement and administrators on planning for and responding to a violent intruder. In this role, she also coordinated the Youth Risk Behavior Survey, using results to plan curriculum and programs to address student reports of violence and mental health risk behaviors. Ms. Gormley serves on the Massachusetts School Nurse Organization board as Data Co-Champion for Step Up and Be Counted, the national uniform data collection joint initiative by the National Association of School Nurses and the National Association of State School Nurse Consultants. Ms. Gormley anticipates graduating from the Northeastern University Doctor of Nursing Practice (DNP) program in May 2018.

Lorali Gray, MEd, BSN, RN, NCSN

Lorali Gray is the northwest regional administrator for the Washington State School Nurse Corps Program. In her current position, she provides funding and oversight for nursing services in 13 rural school districts and school health services consultation to all 35 school districts in her five-county region. She is a member of Sigma Theta Tau International Honor Society of Nursing; the American Nurses Association; the National Association of School Nurses, serving on the NASN School Nurse editorial board; and, the School Nurse Organization of Washington where she received the 2011 State School Nurse Administrator of the year award. Lorali has been a contributing author for numerous school health manuals, school nursing and university publications. She believes in promoting a safe and healthy learning environment that fosters integrity, dignity, and respect for the wellbeing of all school aged children and youth.

Lee-Ann Halbert, JD, EdD(c), MSN, RN, CNM, NCSN

Lee-Ann Halbert is currently an Assistant Professor in the Health Sciences Department of New Jersey City University. The primary focus of her responsibilities is in the area of school nursing. Her present research is directed at the topic of supervision of school nurses. Ms. Halbert was a school nurse in all grade levels from pre-k through 12 for 10 years and was the school district lead nurse during her tenure in clinical practice. She is a Nationally Certified School Nurse and a member of the National Association of School Nurses. Ms. Halbert has spoken at state and national conferences on the topic of legal issues for school nurses. Previously, she was a Certified Nurse-Midwife and practicing attorney.

Kathleen A. Hassey, MEd, BA, BSN, RN

Kathy Hassey received a BA in Biology, then her Bachelor of Science in Nursing from Boston University. She has been a Registered Nurse for 35 years and initially worked at Mount Auburn Hospital and Deaconess Waltham Hospital. She moved into the school health specialty in 1999 as the Director of Health Services for the Hudson Public School system until 2005 and she received her Master's in Education in 2001. Ms. Hassey was the Director of the NEU School Health Institute at Northeastern University and is now the Director of the Northeastern University School Health Academy, providing conferences and continuing education for School Nurses. She has taught graduate courses such as *"Legal and Ethical Issues in School Nursing"* and *"Leadership Skills for School Nurses"* since 2003 and presently teaches *Leadership in School Health* for Cambridge College *and Leadership Skills in School and Community Health and Health Impacts on Academics* for Canisius College. She was President of the Massachusetts School Nurse Organization (MSNO) 2007-2009 and is was the MSNO NASN Director for Massachusetts (2014-2016) and served on the NASN Executive Committee. Ms. Hassey is now in a 3-year DNP program at Northeastern University with graduation in May 2018.

Kathleen H. Johnson, DNP, RN, NCSN, FNASN

Dr. Katie Johnson is currently a Clinical Assistant Professor in Community Health Nursing at the University of Washington (UW). Prior to joining UW, Dr. Johnson worked as the Manager of Student Health Services in Seattle Public Schools supervising 90 nurses serving 54,000 students. She briefly served as Interim State Consultant for WA while completing her DNP in Community Health Systems Nursing. She is currently a RWJ Executive Nurse Fellow, 2014 Cohort and was a Johnson & Johnson School Health Fellow. She served on the National Board for Certification of School Nurses and is a founding member of the Step Up! Be Counted data collection program. Katie presents and has published on school health records systems and data to support advocacy for students and to advance school nursing practice.

Pamela Kahn, MPH, RN

Pamela Kahn is currently the Coordinator for Health and Wellness for the Orange County Department of Education in California. In this capacity, she acts in an advisory position regarding health programs and healthcare to the 28 public school districts in the county. She works closely with the school nurses as well as many community and private agencies to provide the 500,000 students in Orange County with the health services that they need in order to be successful in school.

She belongs to many professional organizations, including the National Association for School Nurses and is the 2017-19 President-Elect for the California School Nurses Organization. She has been published in Nursing World magazine, the Journal of School Nursing, Congenital Cardiology Today and has contributed a chapter to the 2nd edition of "School Nursing: A Comprehensive Text". She received the Nurse.com 2012 Nursing Excellence Award in the area of Advancing and Leading the Profession, and was named the 2013 Cypress College Alumni of the Year.

Linda S. Kalekas, MSN, RN, NCSN

Linda Kalekas has over 41 years of acute care hospital, ambulatory care, and school health experience. She is currently employed as a nursing administrator for the Clark County School District, the fifth largest school district in the country. Ms. Kalekas maintains a business providing expert legal and educational nursing consultant services. She is a national instructor for School Emergency Triage Training (SETT) program sponsored by the National Association of School Nurses (NASN) and served as secondary author in the revision of the SETT manual.

Ms. Kalekas graduated from Muhlenberg Hospital School of Nursing and Union County College in New Jersey where she earned a Diploma in Nursing and an Associate in Science Degree in 1977. She is an honors graduate of Arizona State University receiving a Bachelor of Science in Nursing, cum laude, in 1987. She is an honors graduate of the University of Nevada, Las Vegas receiving a Master of Science in Nursing (MSN) degree, with an emphasis in nursing education in 2008. She earned post-graduate certifications in School Safety: Emergency Preparedness in Schools in 2010, and Educational Technology in 2011 from Southern Utah University. She maintains professional certifications including NCSN, ACLS, PALS, TNCC, and PHTLS. Ms. Kalekas is an active member of the National Association of School Nurses, Nevada State Association of School Nurses, and Clark County School Nurses Association.

Rebecca King, MSN, RN, NCSN

Rebecca King is currently the Director of Nursing for the Delaware Department of Public Health. Professionally, Rebecca has 36 years of experience as a registered nurse. For 18 years, as a nationally board-certified school nurse, she worked in schools serving populations from kindergarten through 12th grade. Additionally, she is adjunct faculty at Immaculata University, Immaculata, PA. She is an active member of the Delaware School Nurses Association (DSNA) and the National Association of School Nurses (NASN) where she has held multiple leadership roles. She is the co-author of the NASN position document on naloxone (2015) and a member of the NASN naloxone workgroup that created the Naloxone Toolkit for School Nurses (2016). She is a 2012 Fellow from the Johnson & Johnson School Health Leadership Institute at Rutgers University Center of Alcohol and Drug Abuse Studies. Rebecca is a board member of the Delaware grassroots organization "atTAcK addiction". Former Delaware Governor Jack Markell appointed her in 2016 to the Delaware Overdose Fatality Review Commission. Rebecca spends time locally and nationally presenting on the topic of substance use disorder and use of naloxone in communities.

Rebecca was the Delaware School Nurse of the Year in 2007. Other awards include the 2014 Caron Medical Professionals Award for the Greater Philadelphia area, the 2008 Delaware Nurses Association Excellence in Nursing Award for Community Nursing, and the 2006 Nemours Vision Award Winner for Excellence in Child Health Promotion and Disease Prevention. Rebecca received two Governor's Volunteer awards (2004 for community education and 2014 with "atTAcK addiction").

Stephanie Knutson, MSN, RN

Stephanie Knutson is an accomplished nurse leader and educator with over 20 years of experience in diverse nursing and educational settings advocating for nurses, children and families. As the School Health Administrator and Educator Consultant for School Nursing and School Health for the Connecticut State Department of Education (CSDE), as well as President of Connecticut Nurses' Association, she provides state-wide leadership in the areas of school health, students' physical and mental health and education and nursing in general. She is responsible for state-level policy development, resource development and informing legislation in the areas of nursing practice, health promotion and wellness.

Julia Lecthenberg, MSN, RN, NCSN

Julia Lechtenberg has over 17 years of experience as a school nurse. She is a member of several professional organizations including the National Association of School Nurses and Sigma Theta Tau International. She is a nationally certified school nurse and a Johnson and Johnson School Health Leadership Fellow. Julia's school nursing experience includes district level consultative services in an urban school district, preschool through 12th grade. Julia has authored and contributed to articles regarding school nursing and student health. She is committed to providing quality health services in the academic setting and actively advocates for safe school nurse practice and quality school health programs at the national and state level.

Suzanne Levasseur, MSN, APRN, CPNP, NCSN

Suzanne Levasseur is currently The Supervisor of Health Services for Westport Public Schools in Westport CT, and is also on staff in the Department of Pediatrics at Danbury Hospital where she works as an APRN. Professionally, Suzanne has over 25 years' experience as a registered nurse and an Advanced Practice Registered Nurse and is currently the President of the Association of School Nurses of Connecticut. Suzanne has authored and contributed to articles and publications regarding Pediatric and Perinatal Nursing as well as school nursing and student health.

Kathleen Maguire, DNP, RN

Dr. Kathleen Maguire is currently the District Nurse Coordinator for Wissahickon School District (WSD). Prior to WSD, Dr. Maguire worked for the Philadelphia School District as Coordinator of Nursing Services and a Certified School Nurse for almost nineteen years. Dr. Maguire also served on the PA. Governor's Commission on Children & Families. Professionally, Dr. Maguire has over 37 years of registered nurse experience and continues to remain active in the National Association of School Nurses (NASN) and the Pennsylvania Association of School Nurses and Practitioners (PASNAP). Dr. Maguire has received both the Certified School Nurse of the Year and Administrator of the Year awards from PASNAP. Dr. Maguire will be recognized May 2017 as Gwynedd Mercy University School of Nursing Excellence Award. Dr. Maguire has presented numerous school and public health conference presentations for NASN, PASNAP, and the American Public Health Association.

Carol Marchant, Esquire

Carol Marchant is the Assistant Division Counsel with the Fairfax County Public Schools in Fairfax, VA.

Lisa Minor, EdD, MSN, RN

Dr. Lisa Minor currently reside in Mechanicsville, Virginia which is just outside of Richmond and has been a registered nurse for a little over 29 years. She is currently an Assistant Professor in the department of nursing at Longwood University where she teaches pharmacology and maternal –newborn nursing while providing clinical assistance in the fields of community health and psychiatric nursing. She graduated from Radford University in 1987 with a Bachelor of Science in Nursing. I received my Master of Science in Nursing Education in 2007 from Walden University and my Doctorate in Higher Education and Adult Learning in 2012 also from Walden University. Dr. Minor has held numerous positions in nursing including orthopedics, OB, pediatrics, community health, and school nursing. She entered school nursing in 1999 until 2013 when I moved to her current position at Longwood University. During my time with Hanover County I have given numerous presentations in school nursing, community health, coordinated school health, supervising and evaluating school nurses. I also assisted the School Nurse Institute Partnership (SNIP) on the development of a school nurse evaluation tool. My doctoral dissertation revolved around school nursing, coordinated school health, the role of the school nurse and school nurse supervisor in enhancing the academic success of students in the school setting.

Mary Newell, PhD, MSN, RN, NCSN

Dr. Mary E. Newell is currently the Nursing and Health Services Coordinator for the Kent School District located in Kent, Washington. Professionally, Dr. Newell has over 30 years of experience as a registered nurse primarily in school settings. She is an active member in many professional organizations, including the National Association of School Nurses. She was a fellow during the 2006-2009 Robert Wood Johnson Executive Nurse Follow Program. In 2014, Dr. Newell was the first nurse to receive the "Leader to Learn From" award from Education Week magazine.

Kathleen Patrick, MA, RN, NCSN

Kathleen Patrick has been the Assistant Director of Student Health Services in the Health and Wellness Unit at the Colorado Department of Education since 2006. Kathleen started her career in school nursing in 1994 and received her Master's in Educational Counseling in 1999. Her prior job experience was in public health nursing. She works with the school districts and school nurses around the state of Colorado by providing professional development and technical assistance. She is active in both the National Association of School Nurses and the National Association of State School Nurse Consultants.

William (Bill) Patterson Jr., MPA, RN

Bill Patterson is currently the Program Manager of the Skilled Nursing Services Program for the State of Hawaii, Department of Education (HIDOE). Prior to joining the HIDOE, Bill worked for the State of Hawaii Department of Health as a Supervisor of the Children with Special Health Needs Program and a field Public Health Nurse. Through Public Health Nursing, Bill first encountered school health and school nursing which became his "cause" or passion. Professionally, Bill has over twenty (20) years of experience in the medical and nursing fields and is an active member of both the National Association of School Nurses (NASN) and the National Association of State School Nurse Consultants (NASSNC).

Katherine J. Pohlman, MS, JD, RN

Katherine J. Pohlman has served as legal counsel to the National Association of School Nurses since 1986. She has practiced healthcare law, medical malpractice defense litigation, professional licensure defense and served as risk manager and in-house counsel at healthcare and insurance companies. Over the years, Katherine also served in a variety of nursing positions, including clinical, management and faculty. As a nurse attorney, coach, and consultant, Katherine's passion is advocating for, counseling, and coaching healthcare providers regarding their legal rights, practice, and professional & personal well-being. She's an integrative practitioner who works within a holistic perspective, taking into consideration body, mind and spirit. Find more at katherinejpohlman.com

Jessica R. Porter, BSN, RN, NCSN

Jessica R. Porter is currently a school nurse in Lexington School District One in Lexington, South Carolina. Ms. Porter has over 30 years' experience as a registered nurse and 17 years' experience as a school nurse. She has worked as an elementary school nurse, a school nurse supervisor, and as a float school nurse in a variety of school nurse settings. She has served as a state director and an elected executive committee member for the National Association of School Nurses. She has written and contributed to position statements, articles, and social media campaigns in the field of school nursing.

Suzanne Putman, MEd, BSN, RN

Suzanne Putman is a Nurse Consultant-Special Education in Michigan and earned her bachelor of science degree in nursing from Oakland University and her master of education specializing in school nursing from Cambridge College. She has over 30 years of maternal-child nursing experience including 20 years of experience as a school nurse consultant for students with moderate-severe cognitive and physical impairments.

Kathy L. Reiner, MPH, BSN, RN

Kathy Reiner is currently a School Nurse Consultant and member of the Health Services Management Team for the Aurora Public School District in Aurora, CO. Previously, she worked in the public health arena in the study of communicable diseases and injury epidemiology. In that role, Ms. Reiner authored and contributed to articles regarding head injury and infectious diseases. Professionally, Ms. Reiner has 20 years' experience as a school nurse and 10 years as a public health researcher. She is currently the Colorado Director to the National Association of School Nurses and has been actively involved in her State School Nurse organization, serving on the Executive Board and as the Legislative chair for 2010-15.

Cheryl Resha, EdD, MSN, RN, FNASN

Dr. Cheryl Resha is currently a Professor of Nursing at Southern Connecticut State University (SCSU). Prior to joining SCSU, Dr. Resha worked for the Connecticut State Department of Education as a manager and state school nurse consultant. Professionally, Dr. Resha has over 30 years' experience as a registered nurse and is an active member in many professional organizations, including the National Association of School Nurses (NASN). Dr. Resha has authored and contributed to articles and publications regarding school nursing and student health, and is currently the co-editor of School Health Alert, the School Nurse Resource Manual, and was chair of the 3rd edition of *School Nursing: Scope and Standards of Practice* (2017). Dr. Resha continues to remain active in school nursing, consulting to local school districts, providing professional development, and is currently the state director for Connecticut on the NASN Board of Directors. Dr. Resha was also inducted as an NASN Fellow in 2012.

Sara Rigel, MPH, CHES

Sara Rigel is currently a Program Manager at Public Health - Seattle & King County - leading and coordinating services, supports and local investments in school based health centers and child care health consultation. The King County network includes more than 30 school based clinics. Sara has been active in the advancement of school-based health centers (SBHC) throughout her career, and is currently a board member of the Washington School Based Health Alliance. She holds a Masters of Public Health from Tulane University in Maternal and Child Health and Health Education.

William J. Roberts, Esquire

William J. Roberts (Bill) is a Partner at Shipman & Goodwin LLP and practices out of the firm's Hartford, Connecticut office. Bill is a member of the firm's Health Law Practice Group and chairs the firm's Privacy + Data Protection Group. Businesses and organizations, including public and independent schools and colleges and universities, seek Bill's advice and counsel on a full range of healthcare and data privacy matters. Bill is a frequent author and speaker on and privacy topics, both nationally and internationally.

Wendy L. Sellers, RN, MA

Wendy L. Sellers is a national author and trainer, the founder of Health4Hire, Inc., and a prevention consultant with Eaton Regional Education Service Agency. Wendy has been a passionate advocate for health promotion for children and youth for more than 30 years. Ms. Sellers authored and published *Puberty: The Wonder Years*, a curriculum for 4th, 5th and 6th graders. She also co-authored the nationally recognized *Michigan Model for Health*, a K-12 comprehensive health curriculum that is on the prestigious National Registry of Evidence-based Programs and Practices. Wendy has served as president of the Michigan School Health Coordinators' Association and was their Legislative Committee Chair for 10 years. Wendy was named 2014 National Health Coordinator of the Year by the American School Health Association (ASHA). She recently began serving on the ASHA Board of Directors and co-chairs their Advocacy Committee.

Vicki L. Taliaferro, BSN, RN, NCSN

Vicki L. Taliaferro is a school nurse consultant and editor of *School Nurse Digest* (weekly electronic newsletter for school nurses) and *Administrator's Risk Alert* (bi-monthly electronic newsletter for school nurses, school administrators and school attorneys). She is the lead editor for the *School Nurse Resource Manual* - 2010, 2013, and 2016. She has authored articles, school nurse text chapters, position papers and state and local guidelines on school health topics and initiatives. She currently serves as a consultant to the National Association of School Nurses and works as their coordinator of professional practice documents. As a consultant to various agencies and professional organizations she provides reports, assists in developing policies, and conducts school health services program needs assessments. She has been a speaker at various school nurse conferences. As State School Nurse Consultant with the Maryland State Department of Education for 10 years, she provided technical advice to state school nursing leadership; developed state guidelines & policies and assisted with the development of Board of Nursing curriculums for delegation and medication administration. She served on numerous commissions and coordinated an annual School Health Interdisciplinary Program – a multi-state professional development weeklong training for school staff. Additionally, she is a member of the National Assn. of State School Nurse Consultants having served as president and in other officer positions.

Antoinette Towle, EdD, PNP-BC, SNP-BC

Dr. Towle is an Associate Professor at Southern Connecticut State University, New Haven CT, USA. She is an American Nurse Credentialing Center (ANCC) Board Certified Advanced Practiced Registered Nurse (APRN) in the specialty areas of Pediatric and School Health. Dr. Towle has worked as a professional nurse for over 30 years, in a variety of capacities (Administrator, Manager, Director, Case Wrker, APRN, RN, and Educator) and within a wide variety of healthcare setting (schools, residential settings for children and the elderly, veterans' hospitals, Insurance companies, federal and privately funded medical offices and hospitals, and community healthcare agencies). Presently, teaching full time both graduate and undergraduate nursing students, with focus on nursing leadership, understanding, respecting, appreciating cultural diversity, health promotion, and integration of these key components in to clinical practice. Dr. Towle is the first to create and continues to lead nursing study abroad program for students at the University to Jamaica, China, and Armenia.

Cameron Traut, MS, BSN, RN, PEL-IL, NCSN

Cameron Traut is a school nurse at Libertyville High School in Libertyville, Illinois. Her professional experience includes 21 years in school nursing, and prior to that, 9 years in pediatric intensive care. Cameron serves in a variety of leadership roles in both the Illinois Association of School Nurses and as Director to NASN from Illinois. She led development of her school's concussion protocol 7 years ago and currently is leader of the concussion oversight committee at Libertyville High School. She has consulted with local concussion specialists and presented on concussion management in schools at a number of Illinois school nursing conferences, as well as for her own school staff, the Lake County School Counselor Association, and will co-present at the NASN 2017 annual conference in June.

Sharonlee Trefry, MSN, RN, NCSN

Sharonlee Trefry is a State School Nurse Consultant who came to the State School Nurse Consulting role in 2012 after 18 years as a school nurse in public and private schools. In she has an additional 24 years involving child care settings, children with special healthcare needs, and the Migrant Education Program (Title I, Part C). The greatest joy in her current job is to watch and support school nurses as they thrive. When school nurses thrive, students thrive!

Perry A. Zirkel, PhD, JD, ML

Perry A. Zirkel is university professor of education and law at Lehigh University, where he formerly was dean of the College of Education and more recently held the Iacocca Chair in Education for its five-year term. He has a Ph.D. in Educational Administration and a J.D. from the University of Connecticut, and a Master of Laws degree from Yale University. He has written more than 1,475 publications on various aspects of school law, with an emphasis on legal issues in special education. He writes regular columns for *Principal* magazine and NASP's *Communiqué*, and did so previously for *Phi Delta Kappan* and *Teaching Exceptional Children*. Past president of the Education Law Association (ELA) and co-chair of the Pennsylvania special education appeals panel from 1990 to 2007, he is the author of the Council for Exceptional Children (CEC) monograph *The Legal Meaning of Specific Learning Disability*; the more recent books, *A Digest of Supreme Court Decisions Affecting Education* and *Student Teaching and the Law*; and the two-volume reference *Section 504, the ADA and the Schools*, now in its fourth edition. In 2012, he received Research into Practice Award from the American Educational Research Association (AERA) and the Excellence in Research Award from AERA's Division A (Administration, Organization & Leadership). In 2013, he received the University Council for Educational Administration's Edwin Bridges award for significant contributions to the preparation and development of school leaders. In 2016, he received the ELA's Steven S. Goldberg Award for Distinguished Scholarship in Education Law. In April 2017, Dr. Zirkel received the Council for Exceptional Children's Special Education Research Award.

Gwen J. Zittoun, Esquire

Gwen Zittoun is counsel with Shipman & Goodwin LLP and practices in the area of school law. She represents boards of education and school districts in relation to special education, Section 504, ADA, student discipline, Title IX, restraint and seclusion, student data privacy and general education matters. Ms. Zittoun frequently supports school districts in special education mediations, due process hearings, and federal court actions, and provides legal counsel on a variety of special education issues. She also supports schools in Office for Civil Rights complaints and Title IX investigations. In addition, Ms. Zittoun is an adjunct professor at the University of Connecticut's Neag School of Education and is a frequent speaker on education issues.

REVIEWERS

Lisa Albert, MSN, RN, CSN
Instructor, Division of Nursing
Pennsylvania College of Health Sciences
Pennsylvania

Eric Barba, JD, BA
Associate, Berchem, Moses & Devlin, P.C.
Bar Admissions: Connecticut, 2016; California,
2011
U.S. District Court Northern District of California,
2012
Member of the American Bar Association, the
Connecticut Bar Association, the National School
Boards Association (NSBA) Council of School
Attorneys, and the Connecticut Council of School
Attorneys
Connecticut

Patricia Bednarz, RN, MN, FNASN
Health and Education Consultant
PKB Strategies LLC
Michigan

Brenda M. Bergeron, Attorney
Principal Attorney
Division of Emergency Management and
Homeland Security
Connecticut Department of Emergency Services
and Public Protection
Connecticut

**Martha D. Bergren, DNS, RN, NCSN, APHA-
BC, FNASN, FASHA, FAAN**
Director of Advanced Population Health
Health Systems Leadership and Informatics
Doctor of Nursing Practice
University of Illinois-Chicago College of Nursing
Illinois

Edie Brous, MS, MPH, BSN, JD, RN
Nurse Attorney
Edith Brous, Esquire, PC
New York

Alfred Bruno, JD, BA
Senior Counsel, Berchem, Moses & Devlin, PC
Bar Admissions: United States District Court for
the District of Connecticut
Licensed to practice law in Connecticut
Member of the American Bar Association, the
Connecticut Bar Association, the National School
Boards Association (NSBA) Council of School
Attorneys, and the Connecticut Council of School
Attorneys
Connecticut

Margo Bushmiaer, MNSc, BSN, NCSN
Coordinator of Health Services
Little Rock School District
Arkansas

Sarah Butler, MS, RN, CDE, NCSN
Director, Education and Training Programs
National Breast Cancer Coalition
Maryland

Joan Cagginello, MS, BSN, RN
School Nurse, Area Cooperative Educational
Services
Connecticut

Shelia Caldwell, BSN, RN, CSN-NJ
School Nurse
New Jersey

Tia J. Combs, Esquire
Attorney at Law
Mazanec, Raskin & Ryder, Co., L.P.A.
Kentucky

Mariann F. Cosby, DNP, MPA, RN, PHN, CEN, NE-BC, LNCC, CLCP, CCM, MSCC
MFC Consulting
California

Julia Muennich Cowell, PhD, RN, APHN-BC, FAAN
Professor Emerita
Rush University College of Nursing
Chicago, IL
Executive Editor
The Journal of School Nursing
Illinois

Leigh E. Dalton, Esquire, PhD
School Law Attorney
Stock and Leader, Attorneys at Law
Pennsylvania

Linda Davis-Alldritt, MA, BSN, RN, FNASN, FASHA
Past President, National Association of School Nurses
School Nurse & School Health Services Consultant
California

Marie DeSisto, MSN, RN, NCSN
District 504 Coordinator
Waltham Public Schools
Massachusetts

Andrea Dillon, RNC, MEd
Director – Student Health Center
American School for the Deaf
Connecticut

Carolyn Dolan, JD, MSN, RN, PCPNP, FNP
Professor
University of South Alabama, Baldwin Campus
Alabama

Rosemary Dolatowski, MSN, RN
Director, School Health Services - retired
Past Wisconsin Director to NASN
Burlington Area School District
Wisconsin

Janice Doyle, MSN, RN, NCSN, FNASN
Clinical Faculty, Pacific Lutheran University
Lead Nurse, Bethel School District
Washington

Carolyn Dugas, JD, BA
Associate, Berchem, Moses & Devlin, P.C.
Admitted to practice law in Connecticut
Member of the American Bar Association, the Connecticut Bar Association, the National School Boards Association (NSBA) Council of School Attorneys, and the Connecticut Council of School Attorneys
Connecticut

Joan Edelstein, DrPH, MSN, RN
Instructor
School Nurse Credential Program, California State University, Sacramento
California

Bonnie J. Edmondson, EdD
Education Consultant, Program Manager, School Health Education
Connecticut State Department of Education
Office of Student Support and Organizational Effectiveness
Bureau of Health/Nutrition, Family Services and Adult Education
Connecticut

Margaret T. Eighan, RN, JD, MSN
Pennsylvania

Karen Flanagan, JD
Retired
Vermont

Mary Ann Gapinski, MSN, RN, NCSN
Director of School Health Services
MA Department of Public Health
Massachusetts

Gilbert R. Garcia, JD, BSN, ADN, RN
Practiced critical care nursing primarily in the
cardiac care unit.
Licensed to practice law in Nevada (2004) and
Texas (2012). Have practiced school law from July
2013 to present.
Assistant General Counsel, Dallas Independent
School District
Texas

Marlene S. Garvis, JD, MSN, BSN, BA
Marlene S. Garvis, LLC
Minnesota

Stephanie Geremia RN, BSN, MPH
Associate Director of Health & Human Services
Meriden Health Department
Connecticut

**Jessica Gerdes, MS, RN, NCSN, IL Licensed
School Nurse**
State School Nurse Consultant
Principal Consultant, School Nursing and Health
Illinois State Board of Education
Illinois

Timothy E. Gilsbach, Esquire, JD, BA
King, Spry, Herman, Freund & Faul, LLC
Pennsylvania

Lorali Gray, MEd, BSN, RN, NCSN
School Nurse Corps Administrator
Northwest Educational Service District 189
Washington

**Lee-Ann Halbert, JD, EdD(c), MSN, RN, CNM,
NCSN**
Assistant Professor, Health Sciences Department
New Jersey City University
New Jersey

Karen Hollowood, MSEd, BSN, RN
State School Nurse Consultant
Associate in School Nursing
Office of Student Support Services
New York State Education Department
New York

Barb Johnson, PhD
Educational Consultant
Michigan

John Khalil, JD, BA
Associate, Berchem, Moses & Devlin, P.C.
Bar admission: Connecticut 2016
Member of the American Bar Association, the
Connecticut Bar Association, the National School
Boards Association (NSBA) Council of School
Attorneys, and the Connecticut Council of School
Attorneys
Connecticut

Linda Khalil, MSEd, BSN, RN
State School Nurse Consultant
New York

Justin Knight, Attorney
Perry, Guthery, Haase & Gessford, P.C., L.L.O.
Nebraska

Patricia Krin, MSN, RN, FNP-BC, NCSN, FNASN
School Health Consultant
Connecticut

Dawn Lambert, PhD, MSN, RN
Assistant Professor and School Nurse Program Coordinator
Eastern Mennonite University at Lancaster
Pennsylvania

Michelle C. Laubin, JD, BA
Senior Partner, Berchem, Moses & Devlin, P.C.
Bar Admissions: Connecticut (1996), New York (1997)
United States District Court for the District of Connecticut, United States Court of Appeals for the Second Circuit, Member of the American Bar Association, the Connecticut Bar Association, the National School Boards Association (NSBA) Council of School Attorneys, and the Connecticut Council of School Attorneys
Past president of the Connecticut Council of School Attorneys
Connecticut

Sandra Leonard, DNP, RN, FNP-BC
Health Education Specialist/Program Consultant
CDC Division of Adolescent and School Health
Georgia

Suzanne Levasseur, MSN, APRN
Supervisor of Health Services
Westport Public Schools
Connecticut

Phyllis Lewis, MSN, BSN, RN, FNP, FCN, FASHA
Adjunct Faculty, IUPUI; School board member
Indiana

Kerri Mahoney, RN, Esquire
Nurse/Attorney
The Law Office of Keri Mahoney, PLLC
New York

Abbey J. Marr, Esquire
Member, New York Bar, No. 5325154
State Policy Analyst
Advocates for Youth
Washington, DC

Linda Meeder, MS, FNP, RN, NCSN
State School Nurse Consultant
Michigan

Dianne Mennitt, DNP, MS, BSN, RN, PHCNS-BC, AE-C, NCSN
School Nurse Consultant
University of South Florida
Student Support Services Project
Florida Department of Education
Florida

Lindsey Minchella, MSN, RN, NCSN, FNASN
NASN Board of Directors; Indiana Director
NASN Special Needs School Nurse Sig Chair
Indiana

Judith Morgitan, MEd, BSN, RN, CSN
Health Services Department Chair
Perkiomen Valley School District
Pennsylvania

Sandra Moritz, MEd, BS, RN, CSN
School Nurse Consultant
New Jersey

Lisa S. Morse, JD, BSN, RN
Law Offices of Lisa S. Morse, P.C.
Colorado

Bill Patterson, MPA, RN
State School Nurse Consultant
Program Manager, Skilled Nursing Services Program
State of Hawaii, Department of Education
Hawaii

Katherine J. Pohlman, MS, JD, RN
Nurse Attorney and Consultant
Minnesota

Deborah J. Pontius, MSN, RN, NCSN, FNASN
Heath Services Coordinator
Pershing County School District
Lovelock, NV
Nevada

William J. Roberts, Esquire
Shipman & Goodwin LLP
Partner
Connecticut

Kathleen C. Rose, MHA-N, BS, RN, NCSN-E
Consulting School Nurse
National Association of School Nurses
Florida

Brooke E.D. Say, Esquire
School Law Attorney
Stock and Leader, Attorneys at Law
Pennsylvania

Sally Schoessler, MSEd, BSN, RN
Director of Education, Allergy & Asthma Network
Virginia

Wendy L. Sellers, MA, RN
Health Education Consultant
Health 4 Hire, Inc.
Michigan

Christine Sullivan, PhD, BA, JD
Senior Counsel, Berchem, Moses & Devlin, P.C.
Licensed to practice law in Connecticut
Member of the American Bar Association, the Connecticut Bar Association, the National School Boards Association (NSBA) Council of School Attorneys, and the Connecticut Council of School Attorneys
Connecticut

Gail Trano, BSN, RN, CSN
SCHOOL HEALTH HELP Consulting
School Nurse/ Health Educator Pre-K - 12
PPSN Discussion List Monitor
NYS Epinephrine Resource Nurse
SCHOOL HEALTH HELP Consulting
New York

Sharonlee Trefry, MSN, RN, NCSN
State School Nurse Consultant
Maternal and Child Health Division
Vermont Department of Health
Vermont

Jo Volkening, MSEd, BSN, RN, PEL/IL-CSN, NCSN
Certified School Nurse
Illinois

JoAnne von Kostka, MSN, RN
Credentialed School Nurse
California

Melissa Walker, BSN, RN
State School Nurse Consultant
Iowa Department of Education
Iowa

H. Estelle S. Watts, DNP, RN, NCSN

State School Nurse Consultant
Office of Healthy Schools
Mississippi Department of Education
Mississippi

Susan Westrick, JD, MS, RN, CNE

Professor of Nursing
Southern Connecticut State University
Department of Nursing
Connecticut

Louise Wilson, MS, BSN, RN, NCSN

School Nursing and Health Services Consultant
WI Department of Public Instruction
Wisconsin

Gail Wold, BSN, RN

RN Coordinator
State School Nurse Consultant
Coordinator
New York State Center for School Health
New York

Linda C. Wolfe, EdD, RN, NCSN, FNASN

Independent School Nurse Consultant
Delaware

Leah Wyckoff, MS, BSN, RN, NCSN

School Nurse Consultant
Diabetes Nurse Educator
Colorado

Regina Wysocki, MS, RN

Clinical Information Analyst
Memorial Hermann Health System
Texas

Cathy Young-Jones, MSN, RN, RN

Deputy Division Director II - School Health
Mecklenburg County Health Department
North Carolina

Susan Zacharski, MEd, BSN, RN

School Nurse Consultant
Michigan

TABLE OF CONTENTS

TABLE OF CONTENTS by subject

SCHOOL NURSE PRACTICE ISSUES

Chapter 1

PROFESSIONAL LICENSURE

Edith Brous, MS, MPH, JD, RN

Each licensed nurse is responsible and accountable for practicing nursing within a legally defined scope of nursing practice based upon the parameters set forth in law and rules, and consistent with his/her own education, knowledge, skills and abilities. (National Council of State Boards of Nursing [NCSBN], 2015)

DESCRIPTION OF ISSUE

School nurses face unique challenges because they are employed by academics, administrators, or educators who commonly do not appreciate professional licensure regulations or scope of practice restrictions. Unlike nurses who work in most other settings, school nurses are likely to report to a person who is not another nurse so often does not understand clinical standards of care or legal aspects of nursing practice. For this reason, it is essential that school nurses be fully familiar with the Nurse Practice Act (NPA) or other nursing regulations in the states in which they practice and take adequate steps to protect their licenses.

Many nurses have misinformation about licensure or the steps they should be taking to safeguard their livelihoods. School nurses are particularly vulnerable to this knowledge deficit because they work in isolation and are less likely to have continuous interaction with other nurses. It is never an effective defense to argue that you did not understand that your actions were considered unethical or illegal, or that they constituted professional misconduct (i.e., ignorance of the law is never a defense). Nursing boards issues licenses and renewal certificates with the expectation that nurses have familiarized themselves with the state's standards of professional conduct and hold them accountable for violations.

BACKGROUND

Nurses are more likely to be disciplined by the board of nursing than they are to be sued in malpractice. Healthcare professionals are reported to the National Practitioner Data Bank (NPDB) – an electronic repository that tracks information on medical malpractice payments and adverse actions such as licensure discipline or the loss or privileges or credentials (U.S. Department of Health and Human Services [USDHHS], 2015a). In the years 2004 through 2014, a total of 129,571 registered nurses were reported to the NPDB. Of those, only 3,781 were reported for medical malpractice payments. The remaining 106,645 were reported for adverse actions. Contrast this with physicians reported to the NPDB during the same time period. Of the 185,332 physicians reported to the NPDB, 120,272 were reported for malpractice payments, and only 56,952 for adverse actions (USDHHS, 2015b). Disciplinary action on a license can be more damaging to a career than a lawsuit because it can separate a nurse from practice, result in collateral consequences, or even permanently terminate one's livelihood and permission to hold oneself out as a nurse. It is important to understand how nursing regulation works and separate common misperceptions from reality regarding licensure:

Common Misperceptions

Someone else is "working under my license" or "working on my license"

Licenses are not transferrable. The state issues a professional nursing license to one person and only that person is authorized to practice using that license. School nurses might supervise others but the people they supervise are not working under or on the school nurse's license. School nurses might delegate to others but the people to whom they delegate are not working under or on the school nurse's license. Only the school nurse is working on the school nurse's license. The school nurse is responsible for what and to whom he or she delegates, but is not responsible for anyone else's practice but his or her own.

A state cannot discipline my license if I don't renew it.

A license, once issued, is good for the lifetime of the licensee. It is accompanied by a registration certificate which must be renewed periodically to continue in practice. It is the registration certificate that lapses or expires, but the license itself remains valid unless it is surrendered or revoked. Some states retain jurisdiction over the licensee indefinitely, regardless of the registration status. This means the state can continue to discipline a license even if the nurse has not renewed the registration.

I am covered to do something as long as a doctor or my supervisor orders me to do it

Nurses are responsible for adhering to their legal scope of practice and standards of care. Physicians cannot override the NPA and order a nurse to exceed the lawful scope of practice. Principals or school administrators cannot override state regulations and order a school nurse to violate the law. They also cannot mandate that nurses violate acceptable standards of nursing care or ethical codes of conduct.

School nurses who violate state practice acts or nursing standards cannot defend themselves to the nursing board by saying the healthcare provider ordered it or the school told them to do so. Nurses are held responsible for adhering to legal and ethical requirements as stated in the American Nurse's Associations' (ANA) Standard 14 of the Standards of Professional Nursing Practice, "[T]the registered nurse evaluates her or his own nursing practice in relation to professional practice standards and guidelines, relevant statutes, rules, and regulations" (ANA, 2010b, p. 19).

IMPLICATIONS FOR SCHOOL NURSE PRACTICE

Each state has its own set of laws and regulations. Many states incorporate nursing regulations under a single statute called the NPA. Other states imbed nursing law in health law, business law, or other regulatory schemes. This chapter will refer to nursing law as the NPA. The board of nursing is responsible for enforcing the NPA by investigating and disciplining nurses who are in violation of the law. It is important to not only know what the law says, but how the nursing board interprets that law. For instance, the NPA might specifically state that a nurse must possess moral character. It is important to know that the board of nursing considers a criminal conviction to be a reflection of a nurse not meeting that moral character requirement. The following are some specific implications for school nurses based on laws and BON interpretations.

Scope of Practice and Delegation

The National Association of School Nurses (NASN) considers delegation to be a valuable tool but states that it must be based upon nursing's definition of delegation and compliant with state laws and nursing board regulations (NASN, 2014). Nursing boards (not education departments) regulate nursing practice and state practice acts (not school districts) determine what nurses can and cannot delegate (NCSBN, 2005).

The legal definition of nursing practice varies considerably from state to state. The school nurse must know what is within the scope of practice not only for his or her own role, but also for anyone to whom he or she delegates. What a school nurse can or cannot delegate to another Registered Nurse, to a Licensed Practical or Vocational Nurse, or to unlicensed personnel also varies considerably from state to state.

Compare, for example, some of the language addressing delegation and supervision in Pennsylvania with that in North Dakota and Utah to see how wide the variation is. Pennsylvania specifically does not permit school nurses to delegate nursing functions to unlicensed persons and spells out that school administrators do not have the authority to delegate nursing functions such as medication administration. North Dakota, on the other hand, does permit a nurse to delegate the administration of insulin but offers no guidance. Utah permits school nurses to delegate medication administration but with specific criteria.

Pennsylvania states:

> Registered Nurses licensed in Pennsylvania may NOT delegate nursing functions to unlicensed persons... School administrators do not have the authority to delegate nursing functions, such as medication administration.... An educator holding a valid Pennsylvania certificate as a K-12 Principal is qualified to perform the following: ... Supervision and direction of certified and non-certified staff persons required for school operation **exclusive of directing health services controlled by the Nurse Practice Act**." ... Paraprofessionals serving as health room aides or other non-professional school district employees shall not be directed to engage in health-related activities reserved exclusively for licensed professionals and controlled by the Nurse Practice Act or other medically related laws" (Pennsylvania Department of Health, 2015).

Contrast this with North Dakota, which simply states, "[I]f a diabetic student is stable and has specific parameters, an insulin injection may be delegated by the licensed nurse using the rules for specific delegation" (North Dakota Board of Nursing, 2014).

Utah, on the other hand gives specific direction:

> Before a registered nurse may delegate a task that is required to be performed within a school setting, the registered nurse shall:
>
> (a) develop, in conjunction with the applicable student, parent(s) or parent surrogate(s), educator(s), and healthcare provider(s) an IHP; and
>
> (b) ensure that the IHP is available to school personnel.
>
> (2) Any task being delegated by a registered nurse shall be identified within the patient's current IHP.

(3)(a) A registered nurse shall personally train any unlicensed person who will be delegated the task of administering routine medication(s), ... to a student.

(b) The training required... shall be performed at least annually.

(c) A registered nurse may not delegate to an unlicensed person the administration of any medication:

(i) with known, frequent side effects that can be life threatening;

(ii) that requires the student's vital signs or oxygen saturation to be monitored before, during or after administration of the drug;

(iii) that is being administered as a first dose:

(A) of a new medication; or

(B) after a dosage change; or

(iv) that requires nursing assessment or judgment prior to or immediately after administration.

(d) In addition to delegating other tasks pursuant to this rule, a registered nurse may delegate to an unlicensed person who has been properly trained regarding a diabetic student's IHP:

(i) the administration of a scheduled dose of insulin; and

(ii) the administration of glucagon in an emergency situation, as prescribed by the practitioner's order or specified in the IHP. (Utah Board of Nursing, 2016).

It is essential that school nurses know what the nursing board's position is in the state in which they practice and only delegate what is within a lawful scope of practice to delegate. In states where school nurses are permitted to delegate some nursing functions to others, the nurse will be held accountable not for the practice of those to whom he or she has delegated, but for his or her own sound delegation practices. A principle offered by the ANA and National Council of State Boards of Nursing (NCSBN) is the use of critical thinking and professional judgment in following the "Five Rights of Delegation." The assignment is the:

1. Right task;
2. Under the right circumstances;
3. To the right person;
4. With the right directions and communications; and
5. Under the right supervision and evaluation (ANA/NCSBN, 2013).

Delegation decision trees can assist the school nurse in the thinking process. The NCSBN provides a decision tree using four steps:

1. Assessment and planning;
2. Communication;

3. Surveillance and supervision; and

4. Evaluation and feedback (NCSBN, 2011).

At the outset, it is critical to know if the law permits the delegation. If such delegation is not within the legal scope of practice for the school nurse's license, the analysis ends and the school nurse does not perform the delegation. If the law does permit the delegation, the school nurse proceeds with the analysis. The complete decision tree is provided in *APPENDIX- Decision Tree – Delegation to Unlicensed Personnel*.

It is essential that the school nurses maintain training records for those to whom you are delegating to document evidence of adequate education and competency assessment. School district policies must be in place to support the delegation and the school nurse must have the ability to supervise the delegatee. While the delegatee is responsible for his or her own performance, the school nurse is legally and ethically responsible for the decision to delegate to that person. The ANA Code of Ethics Provision Four states, "[T]the nurse is responsible and accountable for individual nursing practice and determines the appropriate delegation of tasks consistent with the nurse's obligation to provide optimum patient care" (ANA, 2010a).

Conflict Between School District and Professional Obligations

The school nurse can have conflicting responsibilities. On one hand, the nurse is an employee who reports through a chain of command in the workplace. On the other hand, the nurse is a licensed professional who is responsible to a regulatory agency that oversees his or her practice. When the expectations of the school district are at odds with what the nursing board would find acceptable, the school nurse can be placed in a challenging situation.

School administrators do not always understand the standards of practice to which the nurse will be held. Nor do they always appreciate the rules of professional conduct by which nursing licenses can be disciplined. When school nurses are told to do something that violates the NPA, or that is inconsistent with acceptable nursing practice, or with the ethical code of conduct for nursing, they must explain why they cannot follow those directives. This can create conflict with the employer, but such conflict is preferable to engaging in professional misconduct or unsafe practice.

"My boss told me to", "That's what we have always done" or "The healthcare provider said so" are not effective defenses in a nursing board investigation. The mission of the nursing board is to protect the public. If a nursing board believes a school nurse has engaged in unsafe or unethical practice, it will impose discipline on that nurse's license regardless of the fact that the school nurse was following healthcare provider's orders or a school administrator's directions. (*Please see Chapter 47 for more information on employee conflict resolution*).

Privacy Issues

School nurses may be employed in schools that subject to federal laws - either the Family Educational Rights and Privacy Act (FERPA) or the Health Insurance Portability and Accountability Act (HIPAA) or both, as well as state privacy laws. Generally, FERPA applies to agencies and institutions that receive federal funds under programs administered by the U.S. Department of Education. Most public schools are covered by FERPA.

Schools subject to FERPA cannot disclose *education* records or personally identifiable information from education records without parental or eligible student's written consent. (An eligible student is one who is at least 18 or who attends a postsecondary institution at any age.) *Education* records under FERPA include student health records, however *treatment records* of eligible students are not available to anyone other than professionals providing treatment to the student (Electronic Code of Federal Regulations, 2016). Generally, *education* records are those that are shared outside of the treatment context such as immunization or Individuals with Disabilities Act (IDEA) records. *Treatment* records are used only for treatment, such as medical and psychological treatment, and are not shared. School nurses should seek guidance when unsure if the records can be shared as educational records, or must be protected as treatment records.

Private and religious schools generally do not get U.S. Department of Education funds, and are therefore not subject to FERPA. Schools not subject to FERPA can be subject to HIPAA. HIPAA can apply to a school if the school employs healthcare professionals or provides a health clinic, therefore becoming a *healthcare provider* and if it conducts electronic transactions related to health care, making it a *covered entity*. Like FERPA, schools subject to HIPAA cannot disclose protected health information without written consent (*Please see Chapter 11 for more information on FERPA/HIPAA*).

Privacy and confidentiality are also addressed by IDEA and individual state law. Faculty and school staff other than healthcare providers should only have the ability to access healthcare material if they have a legitimate need to know specific information and this must be determined on a case by case basis. Some specific information such as anaphylactic allergies or dietary restrictions can be communicated without sharing the health record itself.

In all cases, school nurses must be cautious in disclosing student health information. The NASN Code of Ethics recognizes the importance of privacy in the school nurse's role, "[S]chool nurses maintain client confidentiality within the legal, regulatory and ethical parameters of health and education" (NASN, 2016, pp. 9). Nurses who violate patient privacy rights can face disciplinary action by the nursing board.

Nurses who misuse social media expose themselves to misconduct charges for privacy as well as professional boundary violations. It is not acceptable to discuss a student on any of these platforms, even when redacting student-identifiers. Personal relationships outside of the provider/patient relationship are viewed with suspicion. The nurse/student relationship exists solely for the benefit of the student. "Friending," "following," or otherwise connecting with students on social media platforms can create the appearance of unhealthy boundaries and lead to licensure discipline. Texting medical information or taking photographs with personal devices can also lead to charges of privacy violations. (*Please see Chapter 43 for more information on social media*).

Field Trips

Field trips require planning and coordination, particularly for students with health needs. Federal laws provide students with special needs the right to participate in these experiences. The school nurse must play an active role in assessment and planning the health needs of students during times when they will not be on school premises.

Some states permit unlicensed personnel to administer medications. The school must have clear policies on who the qualified personnel are, how they are trained, how they are supervised, what medications can be administered, and how parental or guardian written consent is obtained. These policies must be consistent with the state's NPA. In states that do not permit nurses to delegate this function, or in cases where such delegation cannot be safely performed, a nurse might be required to accompany the student on the trip (NASN, 2013).

If the field trip is planned for a state in which the school nurse is not licensed, the nurse must contact that state board of nursing to receive permission to practice in that state. When in another state, the school nurse must know and abide by the scope of practice and laws of that state, regardless of what is permitted in the nurse's home state. Nurses who practice in states that participate in the Nursing Licensure Compact (NLC) can practice in other compact states but still must do so within that state's regulations.

Some students might be able to self-administer medications. The school must also have clear policies regarding the self-administration of medications that is consistent with the student's individual medication plan and the written orders of a licensed prescriber.

(*Please see Chapter 51 for more information on school-sponsored trips*).

LICENSURE PROTECTION STRATEGIES

Professional Liability Insurance

School nurses should not fall prey to the many false claims about malpractice insurance:

- I don't need it because my employer covers me;
- I am more likely to be sued if I have a policy;
- Juries give higher awards if they know you are insured;
- It's too expensive;
- I have immunity so I can't be sued;
- I'm retired or not currently in practice so I don't need it.

These reasons are all inaccurate. As stated earlier, the greater risk for nurses is in being disciplined by licensing boards than in being sued for malpractice. In general, employer policies do not cover nurses for disciplinary defense so school nurses need policies that offer that coverage. Employer policies also do not cover nurses for anything that happens off the job.

It is not true that nurses are more likely to be named in lawsuits if they have malpractice policies. Plaintiff's lawyers do not have malpractice insurance information when they file complaints. They will obtain that information in the discovery phase of the lawsuit and there might be strategic reasons to keep a party in or let a party out of a lawsuit based upon insurance coverage, but it does not determine if a person is named in the suit. Juries do not have insurance information so having a policy does not figure into deliberations.

Insurance premiums for registered nurses (RNs) are quite inexpensive for the coverage they provide and are business expenses that might be deducted during tax preparation. The rates for nurse practitioners (NPs) are higher than for RNs because NPs have additional risk exposure from diagnosis and prescription, but still remain substantially lower that the rates for physicians. Immunity doesn't apply in many circumstances and even when it does, the legal arguments have to be made by counsel so the nurse will still incur attorney expenses.

There is no immunity for nursing board investigations. Even when retired or not working, the standard school nurses will be held to is different from the standard a lay person will be held to. The nursing board does not care if the nurse is retired or not currently in practice. The mission of the nursing board is to protect the public and that can result in discipline on a license in any case.

When nurses are investigated by the board of nursing, they should be represented by attorneys who are experienced in licensure defense. Being uninsured can make that financially difficult or impossible. Nurses spend a great deal of time, money and energy obtaining their credentials and experience. They need to protect that investment.

Portfolio

When defending against board of nursing allegations of professional misconduct, it can be helpful to provide evidence of a history of safe practice and ethical conduct. Nurses should ask for copies of any performance appraisals or evaluations that they receive along with copies of letters of reference or recommendation, thank you letters from students and their families, awards, publications, public speaking, volunteer or public interest work, or anything else that speaks to professional accomplishments. Membership in professional organizations and subscriptions to professional journals, as well as certificates of completion for continuing education and specialty certifications can demonstrate a commitment to continuing education and competency. Keeping all of those documents in a folder along with licenses, registration certificates, insurance policies and records will make them accessible should a defense become necessary.

Stay Informed About Nursing Law

Nursing boards have web sites which publish advisory opinions, practice alerts, frequently asked questions, and position papers. Discipline of a licensed professional is public information so charges and penalties against nurses are also published on nursing board web sites. School nurses should go to the web sites periodically to review the NPA in their state. Knowing the law and regulations is essential to being compliant. It is important to be familiar with the Code of Ethics as published by professional nursing organizations as well.

Review the definitions of professional misconduct and the scope of practice for all providers. Keeping a copy of the regulations in the school nurse's office can be convenient as a reference when having disputes with school administration about what is and is not permitted. When conflict arises, seek the opinion of the nursing board or a licensure attorney in your state. If the conflict between what the school district wants you to do and what the nursing board allows you to do cannot be resolved, you must abide by the nursing board's definition of professional conduct. School nurses need to explain that they are not being insubordinate, but cannot follow a certain directive without violating the law or exposing the student to unsafe nursing practice. Put such concerns in writing and maintain a copy for your own files.

Keep Records

Maintain copies of correspondence with administrators where safety issues are addressed or concerns are voiced about conflict between job expectations and nursing law or standards. Keep records of education provided to people you train in medication administration, seizure precautions, response to asthma attacks or allergies or anything else related to health care. The records should include the information that was imparted, materials used, an assessment of proficiency, return demonstrations and periodic supervision. Keep copies of any correspondence with the nursing board where you have sought clarification or an advisory opinion or have requested permission to attend an out of state field trip.

If You Are Investigated by The Board of Nursing

Nursing boards generally advise licensees that they are under investigation by either calling the nurse on the telephone or by sending the nurse a letter. In some states, the investigator might physically come to the nurse's home or place of employment. Nurses should tell investigators that they will cooperate in the investigation but cannot make statements or answer questions without an attorney being present. Obtain counsel immediately and refrain from having direct contact with the board. Investigations are adversarial proceedings and nurses do not have the presumption of innocence or the due process rights they assume are in place. Having an attorney from the beginning of the process is preferable to trying to hire one after the case in in progress or after damage has been done.

Inform your professional liability insurance company of the investigation as soon as you receive notice. Notification is required to trigger coverage. The insurance company can provide a referral to a licensure defense attorney. Do not use a lawyer without specific experience in licensure defense before the nursing board. It is an area of practice that requires specific expertise and attorneys who practice in other arenas are not equipped to represent you adequately. Licensure defense attorneys can also be found through The American Association of Nurse Attorneys (TAANA, 2016) local or state bar associations, collective bargaining units, and professional nursing organizations.

Do not apply for licensure in another state until the matter is fully resolved in your home state. Disciplinary action in one state does cause *reciprocal discipline* or discipline in other states. Receiving a license in another state can lead to discipline in that other state as well. Make sure the licensure defense attorney representing you knows of any other licenses you have ever held in any other states so reporting requirements can be met in those states. The requirement to report out of state discipline might still be in place, even if your registration lapsed years ago.

Take care of yourself emotionally. The experience of being investigated by the nursing board is stressful. If you are employed during the process, it can be difficult to function safely at work if you are sleep-deprived or distracted by anxiety. Get stress counseling if necessary and engage in whatever sleep hygiene measures are effective so you are well-rested. The American Holistic Nurses Association (AHNA, 2016) offers resources for self-care and stress management.

CONCLUSION

A nursing board investigation is a stressful experience, even if no charges are ultimately filed. Having good practice habits, maintaining competency in current, evidence-based standards, keeping accurate records, understanding the Nurse Practice Act, scope of practice, definitions of professional misconduct, and state regulations can reduce your exposure to being placed under investigation. Having a professional liability insurance policy, keeping a portfolio, and obtaining counsel immediately if you are the subject of a complaint, can increase your chances of a good outcome if that does happen.

RESOURCES

Blum, Cynthia A. (2014). Practicing Self-Care for Nurses: A Nursing Program Initiative, American Nurses Association *Online Journal of Issues in Nursing*, Vol. 19, No. 3, September, 2014, Retrieved from http://www.nursingworld.org/MainMenuCategories/ANAMarketplace/ANAPeriodicals/OJIN/TableofContents/Vol-19-2014/No3-Sept-2014/Practicing-Self-Care-for-Nurses.html

Electronic Code of Federal Regulations (2016) Title 34, Education, Subtitle A, Chapter 1, Part 99, The Family Educational Rights and Privacy Act (FERPA). Retrieved from http://www.ecfr.gov/cgi-bin/text-idx?c=ecfr&sid=11975031b82001bed902b3e73f33e604&rgn=div5&view=text&node=34%3A1.1.1.1.33&idno=34

NCSBN Delegation Decision Tree https://www.ncsbn.org/Preceptor-DelegationProces.pdf and see APPENDIX.

REFERENCES

American Holistic Nurses Association. (2016). *Holistic stress management for nurses*. Retrieved from http://www.ahna.org/Resources/Stress-Management

American Nurses Association. (2010a). *Guide to the code of ethics for nurses: Interpretation and application, 2010 reissue.* Silver Spring, MD: Nursesbooks.org.

American Nurses Association. (2010b). *Nursing scope and standards of practice, 2nd edition*, Silver Spring, MD: Nursesbooks.org.

American Nurses Association and National Council of State Boards of Nursing. (2013*). Joint statement on delegation.* Retrieved from https://www.ncsbn.org/Delegation_joint_statement_NCSBN-ANA.pdf

Electronic Code of Federal Regulations. (2016). *Title 34, Education, Subtitle A, Chapter 1, Part 99, The Family Educational Rights and Privacy Act* (FERPA). Retrieved from http://www.ecfr.gov/cgi-bin/text-idx?c=ecfr&sid=11975031b82001bed902b3e73f33e604&rgn=div5&view=text&node=34%3A1.1.1.1.33&idno=34

National Association of School Nurses. (2013). *School-sponsored trips, role of the school nurse* (Position Statement). Retrieved from http://www.nasn.org/PolicyAdvocacy/PositionPapersandReports/NASNPositionStatementsFullView/tabid/462/smid/824/ArticleID/567/Default.aspx

National Association of School Nurses. (2014). *Nursing delegation to unlicensed assistive personnel in the school setting* (Position Statement). Retrieved from https://www.nasn.org/PolicyAdvocacy/PositionPapersandReports/NASNPositionStatementsFullView/tabid/462/ArticleId/21/Delegation-Nursing-Delegation-to-Unlicensed-Assistive-Personnel-in-the-School-Setting-Revised-June-2

National Association of School Nurses. (2016*). Code of ethics*. Retrieved from https://www.nasn.org/RoleCareer/CodeofEthics

National Council of State Boards of Nursing. (2011). *Decision tree: Delegation to nursing assistive personnel.* Retrieved from https://www.ncsbn.org/Preceptor-DelegationProces.pdf

National Council of State Boards of Nursing. (2015). *What you need to know about nursing licensure and boards of nursing.* Retrieved from https://www.ncsbn.org/Nursing_Licensure.pdf

National Council of State Boards of Nursing. (2005). *Working with others: A position paper.* Retrieved from https://www.ncsbn.org/Working_with_Others.pdf

North Dakota Board of Nursing. (2014). *School nursing medication administration.* Retrieved from https://www.ndbon.org/RegulationsPractice/Practice/SchoolNsgMedAdmin.asp

Pennsylvania Department of Health. (2015). *Nurse practice issues in the school setting: Caseload/delegation.* Retrieved from http://www.health.pa.gov/My%20Health/School%20Health/Pages/Quick%20Links/School%20Nurse%20Practice%20Issues/CaseloadDelegation.aspx#.V2rKA2grKUk

The American Association of Nurse Attorneys (TAANA). (2016). *Attorney referral.* Retrieved from http://taana.org/referral

United States Department of Health & Human Services. (2015a). *NPDB national practitioner data bank,* Retrieved from https://www.npdb.hrsa.gov/topNavigation/aboutUs.jsp

United States Department of Health & Human Services. (2015b) *NPDB research statistics.* Retrieved from https://www.npdb.hrsa.gov/resources/npdbstats/npdbStatistics.jsp

Utah Board of Nursing. (2016). *R156. Commerce, Occupational and Professional Licensing.*

Rule R156-31b. Nurse Practice Act Rule. R156-31b-701a. Delegation of tasks in a school setting. Retrieved from http://www.rules.utah.gov/publicat/code/r156/r156-31b.htm

APPENDIX

Decision Tree – Delegation to Nursing Assistive Personnel

Step One – Assessment and Planning

Are there laws and rules in place that support the delegation?

NO → If not in the licensed nurse's scope of practice, then cannot delegate to the nursing assistive personnel (NAP). **Authority to delegate varies; so licensed nurses must check the jurisdiction's statutes and regulations.**

YES

Is the task within the scope of the delegating nurse?

NO → Do not delegate.

YES

Has there been assessment of the client needs?

NO → Assess client needs and then proceed to a consideration of delegation.

YES

Is the delegating nurse competent to make delegation decisions?

NO → Do not delegate until evidence of appropriate education available, then reconsider delegation; **otherwise do not delegate.**

YES

Is the task consistent with the recommended criteria for delegation to nursing assistive personnel (NAP)? Must meet **all** the following criteria:

- Is within the **NAP** range of functions;
- Frequently recurs in the daily care of a client or group of clients;
- Is performed according to an established sequence of steps;
- Involves little or no modification from one client-care situation to another;
- May be performed with a predictable outcome;
- Does not inherently involve ongoing assessment, interpretation, or decision-making which cannot be logically separated from the procedure(s) itself; and
- Does not endanger a client's life or well-being.

NO → Do not delegate.

YES

Does the nursing assistive personnel have the appropriate knowledge, skills and abilities (KSA) to accept the delegation?
Does the ability of NAP match the care needs of the client?

NO → **Do not delegate** until evidence of education and validation of competency available, then reconsider delegation; **otherwise do not delegate.**

YES

Are there agency policies, procedures and/or protocols in place for this task/activity?

NO → **Do not proceed** without evaluation of need for policy, procedures and/or protocol or determination that it is in the best interest of the client to proceed with delegation.

YES

Is appropriate supervision available?

NO → Do not delegate.

YES

PROCEED WITH DELEGATION.*

* Nurse is accountable for decision to delegate, to implement steps of the delegation process, and to assure that the delegated task/function/action is completed competently.

The Delegation Decision Tree above represents the first step in the delegation process. The other three steps are summarized below.

Chapter 2

MALPRACTICE/PROFESSIONAL LIABILITY

Edith Brous, MS, MPH, JD, RN

*Many claims develop due to a failure involving core competencies, such as patient assessment, monitoring, treatment and care, practitioner and patient communication, timely and complete documentation, and invocation of the chain of command – all of which are essential to ensure quality patient care in a safe environment. (*CNA HealthPro and Nurses Service Organization[NSO], 2011)

DESCRIPTION OF ISSUE

The fear of liability far exceeds the reality for nurses in all areas of practice. Despite constant rhetoric about a "malpractice crisis" or "runaway juries" or "frivolous lawsuits" most nurses will complete their careers without ever being named in a malpractice lawsuit. This chapter will discuss the elements that are required for nurse to be sued for malpractice and tips for further reducing the low exposure school nurses already have.

As of April 2016, the Kaiser Family Foundation reported that there were a total number of 3,129,452 professionally active Registered Nurses (RNs) in the United States (Kaiser Family Foundation, 2016). If nurses were the frequent target of medical malpractice lawsuits, one would expect a significant percentage of that 3 million or so nurses to be involved in cases that resulted in payments to plaintiffs (persons bringing the suit.) The National Practitioner Data Bank reports for the calendar years of 2004 through 2014, however, indicate that during that ten-year period, only 3,781 RNs in the United States were reported because of a malpractice payment (United States Department of Health and Human Services, n.d.).

For school nurses, in particular, the risk is exceptionally low. The largest medical malpractice insurance provider for nurses - Nurses Service Organization (NSO) – provided a claims study evaluating paid claims for nurses between 2006 and 2010 by specialty and location (CNA & NSO, 2011). School nursing did not even appear as a distinct category. As uncommon as it is for school nurses to be individually named in medical malpractice lawsuits, it is still important to understand the elements of a suit and engage in exposure reduction strategies.

BACKGROUND

It is important to distinguish between *negligence* and *malpractice*. Negligence is a *lay* standard. What would a reasonably prudent *person* have done in same or similar circumstances? A person is negligent if he or she does not exercise the care that a reasonably prudent person would have exercised. Malpractice is a *professional* standard. What would a reasonably prudent *nurse* have done in same or similar circumstances? The distinction is important because procedural requirements to file the lawsuit can differ depending upon whether the suit is in negligence or malpractice. Statutes of limitation can be different as well (the time limit during which the person must bring the suit). Most importantly, the standards by which the defendant (the person accused) is judged depend upon whether the complaint is framed as negligence or malpractice.

While specifics may vary from state to state, for a plaintiff to bring a medical malpractice lawsuit against a school nurse, he or she must successfully demonstrate four elements – duty, breach, cause and harm:

Duty: Duty is the duty of reasonable care. A nurse has a duty to provide care that is consistent with professional standards. The element of duty is established as soon as the nurse/patient relationship is created.

Breach: A nurse breaches his or her duty to a patient by departing from the standards of care. Unlike negligence, which is a lay standard, an expert witness is required to demonstrate this element. The expert witness must testify to the standard of practice and must also testify that the nurse deviated from the acceptable standards of practice by doing something a reasonably prudent nurse in same or similar circumstances would not have done (an act), or by not doing something a reasonably prudent nurse would have done in same or similar circumstances (an omission).

Cause: The plaintiff must demonstrate that the injury he or she sustained was *proximately* caused by the nurse's departure from standards. This can be either a "but for" standard, meaning the injury would not have occurred *but for* the nurse's departure or it can be a "substantial factor" standard, meaning there might have been other, independent forces at play, but the nurse's departure from acceptable standards of practice played a substantial role in causing the patient to be injured.

Harm: The purpose of a lawsuit is to compensate a plaintiff for damages so there must be actual damages to compensate. A nurse cannot be sued for potential or theoretical harm to a patient, but only because a patient was, in fact, injured. Patients can be harmed in ways that cause physical, emotional/psychological, and financial damage.

The elements of duty, breach, cause and harm are demonstrated in a 2006 Iowa case. In *Gray v. Council Bluffs*, the parents of Joshua Gray filed a medical malpractice lawsuit against the school district and the school nurse, alleging that Joshua suffered a prolonged hypoglycemic seizure at school. They claimed that the school nurse failed to properly diagnose and treat the seizure, leading to cognitive decline, behavioral disorders, social regression and depression.

To prevail in their suit, the parents needed to demonstrate that the school nurse had a **duty** to Joshua. This element would be easily demonstrated by establishing the nurse/patient relationship the school nurse had with the students. The duty would be the duty of reasonable care – what a reasonably prudent school nurse would do in same or similar circumstances.

The Grays alleged that the school nurse **breached** this duty by departing from the standards of practice. Defense testimony, however, demonstrated that the school nurse's actions were consistent with Joshua's Individual Health Plan (IHP). All school personnel present that day testified that Joshua experienced a "routine and successful treatment" for hypoglycemia. Blood sugar levels were monitored and documented and no seizure was witnessed. Joshua had returned to class and the mother had been notified.

If the parents had succeeded in proving duty and breach, they would next need to demonstrate, through an expert witness, that Joshua's cognitive decline, behavioral disorders, social regression and depression were **caused by** the school nurse's breach of duty. Expert testimony, however indicated that Joshua had been born prematurely. A board-certified neurologist attributed Joshua's deficits to injury of his brain's right hemisphere at birth. He had also experienced a number of severe diabetic reactions, any one of which could have caused intellectual decline. The expert testified that even if the school nurse had departed from the standards of practice, it would not be possible to attribute Joshua's problems to that breach.

Finally, the Grays would need to prove that Joshua suffered actual **harm** as a consequence of the school nurse's breach of duty. They were unable to do so and the jury returned a verdict in favor of the school and the school nurse. On appeal, the court noted, "[T]he jury found no negligence on the part of the school district or its nurse, … For that reason, it did not have to decide the issues of causation or damages. … Causation and damages are irrelevant if the jury fails to find no underlying breach of duty" (*Gray v. Council Bluffs*, 2006, p. 12).

Because school nurses are employees, most medical malpractice lawsuits will target the school district as the employer. The nurse might be individually named as well. The elements will remain the same – the plaintiff will need to demonstrate that the school and the nurse had a **duty**; that they **breached** that duty by departing from acceptable standards of practice; that the breach was the **cause** of an injury; and that there were actual damages (**harm**).

IMPLICATIONS FOR SCHOOL NURSE PRACTICE

Interpersonal Skills

The single most important action the school nurse can take is to develop good interpersonal communication skills. Multiple studies have indicated that there is no more effective risk-reduction strategy in decreasing liability exposure (Kreimer, 2013). Adverse events are far less likely to result in litigation when there are healthy provider/patient relationships. Students and their families are more reluctant to file lawsuits when they trust the school nurse. Transparency, trust, accountability, respect and apologies can reduce litigation (Crane, 2013).

Professional Liability Insurance

School nurses should maintain personal insurance policies and not rely upon their employers for professional liability coverage. Employer policies do not cover nurses for any actions that arise from events that are unrelated to the scope of their employment. Employer policies also generally do not cover school nurses for licensure defense or other administrative actions. Because school nurses are more likely to be in a position of reporting to a person who does not understand scope of practice limitations or clinical standards of practice, it is particularly important to have adequate insurance protection. In addition to malpractice lawsuits, licensed professionals have liability exposure in other arenas for which they need coverage.

School policies typically name the school district as the insured party, and not the individual school nurse. The school nurse is an employee of the insured party, not the named insured or protected party. School nurses should review the insurance policy to determine if he or she is an additional insured. If the school nurse is not a named insured, he or she will not be protected. It is also important to know if the policy only covers malpractice, or if the school nurse is also protected for administrative and licensure defense. In any case, the school nurse should still maintain his or her own policy.

The attorney who represents the school district in a lawsuit is representing the best interests of his or her client - the *school*, not the nurse. The focus is on dismissing, settling or trying the case, not on protecting the nurse's career. Some malpractice attorneys are not familiar with the administrative and licensure implications to the school nurse. Without individual coverage, the school nurse is not adequately represented or protected.

Immunity

One reason school nurses give for not having their own professional liability insurance is the belief that they are protected from exposure by way of "immunity" because they are employed by a school district. Although each state provides some shelter from liability for public schools, the degree and nature of that legal protection varies widely. Some states offer very narrow protection, while others provider a broader shield. Whether or not immunity applies in a given situation depends on a number of factors that are specific to the case and to the state law.

Legal analysis is necessary to determine if any immunity protection applies. Many questions must be answered. What does the specific state statute say regarding immunity protections? Is the immunity *absolute* or *qualified*? Was the negligence *simple negligence* or *gross negligence*? Was the function *ministerial* or *discretionary*? Are the actions *governmental* or *proprietary*? Do circumstances place the case under one of the exceptions to the immunity statute? What is the school's insurance coverage? Has the school district *waived* immunity? Was the student injured in an area used for educational or recreational activities? Was there malicious intent on the part of the defendants? Was the care rendered in a setting that provided proper and necessary medical equipment? Did the defendant have a duty to render assistance? Was the care rendered in a manner that could be considered the scene of an accident or emergency? The analysis can be complicated and contentious.

It is essential to understand that "governmental immunity" or "sovereign immunity" is a defense which can be asserted in an answer to a complaint, but does not prevent a lawsuit from being filed. Immunity does not mean that a school nurse cannot be sued. The nurse will still have to defend the lawsuit and make the legal arguments that immunity applies. The same is true for charitable immunity, Good Samaritan immunity, Official immunity, or any other form of immunity. There is no immunity from lawsuits. Immunity only provides some protection from the extent to which a school nurse or a school district can be held liable for damages. The expense of defending the suit on immunity grounds, even if successful, can be considerable. **Most importantly for nurses, there is no immunity whatsoever from nursing board investigations that can accompany the lawsuit.**

Maintain Clinical Competency

Unlike nurses who work in hospitals or many other settings, school nurses practice in isolation, without the availability of immediate and on-site consultation. Standards of care change and the school nurse's isolation can result in outdated practices. To further reduce liability exposure, **it is critical that school nurses maintain competency and update their skills to reflect current, evidence-based standards.** Continuing education, membership in professional organizations, subscriptions to professional journals and participation in conferences can assist the school nurse to practice in accordance with the standards of care as they would be judged in a malpractice lawsuit. **Policies and procedures should be updated to reflect practices that are consistent with industry standards.**

Documentation

In a medical malpractice lawsuit, the best evidence, and sometimes the only evidence that can be used to defend against the allegations is found in the medical record. If the student's health record demonstrates that the school nurse adhered to the standards of practice, it is difficult for a plaintiff to prove that he or she breached a duty. As previously discussed, without a breach of duty, the elements of causation and harm become irrelevant. Records that establish compliance with organizational policies, care plans and prescriber's orders can be evidence that the school nurse acted in the way another reasonably prudent school nurse would have acted in same or similar circumstances.

When documenting assessments and interventions, it is important to chart in a manner that allows the re-creation of an accurate sequence of events and picture of the student. Vague terms like "moderate" and "copious" should be avoided when measurable terms can be used instead. Specifically identify people by last name rather than referring to titles such as "MD", "parents", or "teacher." Use entire dates including year and entire times including am or pm. Document all communications or attempts to contact administrators, parents/guardians, or other providers about student concerns. In documenting communication with students, capture the presence of any witnesses to the conversation, the student's level of consciousness at the time, and the student's ability to understand and repeat the information.

Pursue concerns to resolution and document that you engaged the chain of command. As the 2011 CNA claims study notes:

> *Nurses are the patient's advocate, ensuring that the patient receives appropriate care when needed. Advocacy includes the duty of invoking both the nursing and medical staff chains of command to ensure timely attention to the needs of every patient, and persisting to the point of satisfactory resolution. Nurses must be comfortable with utilizing the medical chain of command whenever a practitioner does not respond to calls for assistance, fails to appreciate the seriousness of a situation or neglects to initiate appropriate intervention* (CNA & NSO, 2015).

Documentation must accurately reflect the evaluation and treatment of the student and the records must be maintained in a manner that preserves their credibility. An example of problematic documentation and record-keeping practices is illustrated in *K.R.S. v. Bedford Community School District* (*K.R.S.*, 2015).

K.R.S. was a special education student at the defendant school district in 2012 where he was subjected to bullying. He saw the school nurse with complaints of headaches on several occasions and reported to her that players had thrown footballs at his head. He also demonstrated double vision and expressed concern that he had a concussion. He stated the double vision had started after being hit in the head with the footballs. On one occasion, the school nurse advised K.R.S. to inform his grandmother but she did not notify the football coach. On another occasion, she documented that she spoke with the grandmother who agreed to take K.R.S. to the doctor but, again, she did not notify the football coach.

Four days after his last visit with the school nurse, K.R.S. was taken to the emergency room with balance problems, headache, neck pain and visual problems. An MRI revealed a mass in his head and he was admitted to the hospital where a cavernous malformation was detected. He was advised against contact sports, provided an eye patch, and told to stay out of school for two to three weeks. Less than two weeks later he was readmitted with a recurrence of hemorrhage requiring surgery. He was placed in a medically-induced coma and after two weeks of hospitalization he was transferred to a rehabilitation facility with permanent brain damage.

A lawsuit against the school district was brought on behalf of K.R.S. in which the school nurse was individually named. Several claims were made, including violations of the Rehabilitation Act (§ 504 claims) breach of fiduciary duty, intentional infliction of emotional distress, and failure to remove from athletic competition. The claim against the school nurse was negligence in failing to provide reasonable medical care.

The school nurse was deposed on two occasions. At the first deposition, she testified that it was her practice to keep a spiral notebook which she used as a daily log. She wrote notes about student visits by hand into that notebook, then later transcribed the notes into an electronic medical record (EMR). At the end of the school year she destroyed the spiral notebook. At the end of this particular school year, however, she had kept the pages related to K.R.S. She brought those pages to the deposition and they were marked as exhibits. With one of K.R. S.' visits to her office, she believed she had mistakenly written the wrong encounter date in the log but had not corrected it upon transcribing it into the EMR.

During the discovery period of the lawsuit, it was revealed that what she had provided as "original" records at her deposition, in fact, were records she had re-created from the EMR after losing the original records. This compromised her credibility as a witness and the credibility of the medical records. Most importantly, it harmed the defense in the case. The school district made a *motion for summary judgment*, which is an application to the court asking to have the case dismissed. Such motions are granted when there are no facts in dispute. The court denied this motion because of the school nurse's documentation and record-keeping practices:

> *As for the claim that Nurse Schuelke failed to provide reasonable medical care, it is undisputed that K.R.S. visited her on at least two occasions complaining of headache and double vision which he said started after he was hit in the head with footballs. Because of the credibility issues arising from her duplication of lost notes, however, the dates when Nurse Schuelke saw K.R.S. are disputed, indeed all her testimony at this stage is tarnished by the "lost notes" issue. In resistance to the summary judgment motion, plaintiff has included a report from their nursing expert witness Martha Dewey Bergren which criticizes how Nurse Schuelke responded to K.R.S.'s complaint of headaches in connection with football practice in several respects. The Court cannot determine credibility issues on summary judgment and there is a debate in the record about the adequacy of Nurse Schuelke's practices concerning K.R.S. Based on this summary judgment record the Court finds there are disputed facts which preclude entry of summary judgment in favor of defendants on plaintiff's negligence claims... (K.R.S., 2015, pp.23-24).*

The trial lasted a week and the jurors found both the school and the school nurse negligent for failing to notify the coaches that K.R.S. might have a concussion and for not making sure he saw a physician after being seen by the school nurse (Bleier, 2015). He was awarded $991,832 (Nelson, 2015). About $140,000 of that was for medical expenses and the remainder was for damages for pain and suffering, loss of mind and body, and loss of future earnings (Elliott, 2015).

Note: This case also illustrates why school nurses should not rely upon "immunity" to practice without professional liability insurance and how complicated the analysis of whether or not immunity applies can be. The defendants argued that they were entitled to immunity under state law because they were performing *discretionary* functions which exempted them from claims. The state law defined discretionary functions as those that involved an element of choice or discretion, and provided protection if such discretionary judgment was driven by public policy concerns, social, economic, or political considerations.

The court in this case did say that all defendants met the first part of this test in that they all exercised professional judgment. The school failed, however, to convince the court of the second prong of this analysis:

> *Defendants do not identify any social, economic or political consideration as a basis for the coaches' permitting K.R.S. to participate in football after he complained of a headache (which for purposes of this motion the Court will assume occurred) or for Nurse Schuelke's decision to have K.R.S. report his headaches to his grandmother and to accept his word he was not participating in practices instead of reporting K.R.S.'s complaints to the coaches (K.R.S., 2015, p. 24).*

(Please see Chapter 9 for more information on documentation).

If Named in a Suit

Employers have what is referred to as *vicarious liability* for the actions of their employees. This means a school district can be held responsible for school nurse's acts or omissions within the course of the school nurse's employment. Students who are harmed by a school nurse's negligence can hold the nurse personally responsible, but they can also hold the school district responsible as the school nurse's employer.

Because school nurses are employees, it will generally be the employer who is notified of a lawsuit by being served with a *summons with notice* or a *summons and complaint*. Occasionally, however, employees are directly served with these documents. If notified directly that you have been named in a suit, you should inform your school's legal department immediately so a timely answer can be served on your behalf.

Whether directly served or notified by the school that you have been named in a lawsuit, inform your private insurance company immediately. Your policy is likely to have a clause requiring you to report as soon as you are aware of a claim even if it is the school that will be defending you. Obtain a consultation with an attorney who can advise you as to the licensure and other administrative implications of the lawsuit. Ask your private insurance for a referral to a licensure defense attorney when you notify them of the lawsuit.

Avoid discussing the matter with anyone other than the attorney who will be representing you. Conversations with other people can be discoverable if they are not privileged and can unintentionally create adverse witnesses. Additionally, if you have inadvertently made a statement against your own interest it can be used to damage you. Resist the temptation to make personal copies of records, accident reports, statements or other documents. Doing so can violate school policies, privacy laws and professional conduct rules. Do not keep personal logs, diaries or journals that detail experiences related to student care or adverse events. They can be discoverable in litigation. Even when redacting identifiers, they can also violate privacy laws or professional standards.

CONCLUSION

Most school nurses will complete their entire careers without ever being involved in a medical malpractice lawsuit. Staying insured, maintaining clinical competency, documenting adequately and cultivating healthy relationships with sound interpersonal communication skills can reduce liability exposure even further.

RESOURCES

Cady, Rebecca F. (2016). Understanding Malpractice Liability. In K. G. Ferrell (Ed.) *Nurses Legal Handbook, 6th Edition* (pp. 135-166). New York, NY: Wolters Kluwer.

Case law

Gray v. Council Bluffs Comm. School Dist., 725 N.W.2d 659 (Iowa App. 2006).
Available at https://casetext.com/case/krs-v-bedford-cmty-sch-dist

K.R.S. v. Bedford Community School District, 109 F.Supp.3d 1060 (2015).
Available at https://casetext.com/case/krs-v-bedford-cmty-sch-dist

REFERENCES

Bleier, E. (2015, May 12). Jury awards high school football player who suffered concussion but was allowed to continue practicing $1million in largest high school head injury payout in history. *Daily Mail.com*. Retrieved from http://www.newsjs.com/url.php?p=http://www.dailymail.co.uk/news/article-3078682/Jury-awards-injured-high-school-football-player-1M.html

CNA Healthpro and Nurses Service Organization[NSO]. (2011). *Understanding nurse liability, 2006-2010: A three-part approach.* Retrieved from http://www.hpso.com/Documents/Risk%20Education/individuals/RN-2010-CNA-Claims-Study.pdf

Crane, M. (2013, November 25). Patients who won't sue their doctors — even when they could. *Medscape*. Retrieved from http://www.medscape.com/viewarticle/814876

Crico Risk Management Foundation of the Harvard Medical Institutions Incorporated. (2015). *Malpractice risks in communication failures: 2015 benchmarking report.* Retrieved from https://www.rmf.harvard.edu/~/media/0A5FF3ED1C8B40CFAF178BB965488FA9.ashx

Elliott, D. (2015, May 12). Jury awards H.S. athlete nearly $1 million in head injury case. *Yahoo Sports*. Retrieved from http://sports.yahoo.com/blogs/highschool-prep-rally/jury-awards-h-s--athlete-nearly--1-million-in-head-injury-case-145741413.html

Kaiser Family Foundation. (2016). *State health facts, total number of professionally active nurses.* Retrieved from http://kff.org/other/state-indicator/total-registered-nurses/

Kreimer, S. (2013, December 10). Six ways physicians can prevent patient injury and avoid lawsuits. *Medical Economics.* Retrieved from http://medicaleconomics.modernmedicine.com/medical-economics/content/tags/injury/six-ways-physicians-can-prevent-patient-injury-and-avoid-lawsu

Nelson, A. (2015, May 12). Former Iowa HS Football player nearly $1m; nurse didn't respond properly to concussion-like symptoms. *World Herald.* Retrieved from http://www.livewellnebraska.com/consumer/former-iowa-hs-football-player-nearly-m-nurse-didn-t/article_505471b1-88b9-535a-9685-459b2fc2879a.html

United States Department of Health and Human Services. (n.d.). National practitioner data bank. *NPDB Research Statistics.* Retrieved from http://www.npdb.hrsa.gov/resources/npdbstats/npdbStatistics.jsp#contentTop

Chapter 3

SCOPE, STANDARDS AND COMPETENCIES FOR SCHOOL NURSING: IMPLICATIONS FOR SCHOOL NURSE PRACTICE

Cheryl Resha, EdD, MSN, RN, FNASN
Stephanie Knutson, MSN, RN

DESCRIPTION OF ISSUE

The scope and standards of nursing, and subsequently the related competencies, guide the professional practice for all nursing. For school nurses including school nurse consultants and graduate-level nurses working with school communities, specifically the *School Nursing: Scope and Standards of Practice* (2017) provide the framework for nursing care within schools and school communities. The scope describes who, what, where, when, why, and how of school nursing and the standards are the authoritative statements of nursing practice and professional expectations (American Nurses Association (ANA), 2015). Competencies are objective measures of the standards and are a way to demonstrate nursing knowledge, skill and behaviors regarding particular standards of practice.

School nursing has a social and professional obligation to practice within and to the full extent of the scope and standards of practice. Legally school nurses can and should use the *School Nursing: Scope and Standards of Practice* to guide what they do every day for all healthcare consumers within the school community. For school nurses, the healthcare consumer "includes not only the student, but also those influencing students such as the family, school community, the larger surrounding community, aggregates within the school population, or the entire school population" (ANA & National Association of School Nurses[NASN], 2017, p.11)

Adhering to the scope and standards of practice, along with individual state laws and nurse practice acts, can support safe practice, promote high quality care, guide nurses to successfully meet the various roles and responsibilities of school nursing, and minimize the risk of malpractice claims. The standards of practice can be useful to establish in a legal setting that the standard of care was met; i.e., that another nurse with similar education and experience in similar circumstances would have provided the same care. The scope and standards of practice can also serve as the basis for job descriptions, supervision and evaluation, and direct negotiations for union contracts.

BACKGROUND

History

As stated above, the scope and standards of nursing practice describe nursing practice. In 1973, the American Nurses Association (ANA) published the first standards for the practice of nursing and subsequently invited specialty areas of nursing to develop standards unique to their area of practice within the context of ANA's overarching scope and standards. In the early 1980s, the first standards of school nursing practice were published and now the standards of school nursing practice are on the 6th edition (Proctor, 2013). According to Proctor, despite the view that standards are the "authoritative statements of practice," standards are meant to be "global and general" (Proctor, 2013, p. 50) and need examples and details to make them specific and understandable for nurses. Therefore, in addition to standards, competencies serve as the measures of knowledge, skills and behaviors that become understandable to school nurses and the public.

Educating school nurses about their practice, the standards, and the resources available to them is a priority to promote safe care for students and avoid liability from negligence or deviations from how prudent school nurses would function in a similar situation. According to Laubin, Schwab and Doyle (2013), standards are often used in legal proceedings, especially in the absence or silence of state laws. The question often asked is "Was the standard of care met?" (Laubin, et al., 2013, p. 597).

NASN (2016b) describes the broad and evolving role of the school nurse as including elements of leadership, community/public health, care coordination, and quality improvement. With this expanding and evolving role, the scope and standards of practice are revised every five years to keep up with changing trends. In order to foster high quality care, school nurses need to stay up to date with practice changes, revisions to the scope and standards of practice, and emerging evidence that supports best practices.

Standards of Practice and Professional Performance (ANA & NASN, 2017)

STANDARD 1. ASSESSMENT

The school nurse collects pertinent data and information relative to the student's health or the situation.

STANDARD 2. DIAGNOSIS

The school nurse analyzes the assessment data to determine actual or potential diagnoses, problems, and issues.

STANDARD 3. OUTCOMES IDENTIFICATION

The school nurse identifies expected outcomes for a plan individualized to the student or the situation.

STANDARD 4. PLANNING

The school nurse develops a plan that prescribes strategies to attain expected, measurable outcomes.

STANDARD 5. IMPLEMENTATION

The school nurse implements the identified plan.

STANDARD 5A. COORDINATION OF CARE

The school nurse coordinates care delivery.

STANDARD 5B. HEALTH TEACHING AND HEALTH PROMOTION

The school nurse employs strategies to promote health and a safe environment.

STANDARD 6. EVALUATION

The school nurse evaluates progress toward attainment of goals and outcomes.

STANDARD 7. ETHICS

The school nurse practices ethically.

STANDARD 8. CULTURALLY CONGRUENT PRACTICE

The school nurse practices in a manner that is congruent with cultural diversity and inclusion principles.

STANDARD 9. COMMUNICATION

The school nurse communicates effectively in all areas of practice.

STANDARD 10. COLLABORATION

The school nurse collaborates with key stakeholders in the conduct of nursing practice.

STANDARD 11. LEADERSHIP

The school nurse leads within the professional practice setting and the profession.

STANDARD 12. EDUCATION

The school nurse seeks knowledge and competence that reflects current nursing practice and promotes futuristic thinking.

STANDARD 13. EVIDENCE-BASED PRACTICE AND RESEARCH

The school nurse integrates evidence and research findings into practice.

STANDARD 14. QUALITY OF PRACTICE

The school nurse contributes to quality nursing practice.

STANDARD 15. PROFESSIONAL PRACTICE EVALUATION

The school nurse evaluates one's own and others' nursing practice.

STANDARD 16. RESOURCE UTILIZATION

The school nurse utilizes appropriate resources to plan, provide, and sustain evidence-based nursing services that are safe, effective and fiscally responsible.

STANDARD 17. ENVIRONMENTAL HEALTH

The school nurse practices in an environmentally safe and healthy manner.

STANDARD 18. PROGRAM MANAGEMENT

The school nurse directs the health services program within the school and community that includes evidence-based practice and accountability measures for quality, student health and learning outcomes.

(ANA & NASN, 2017, p. 7-9. Reprinted with permission. All rights reserved).

Use of Standards

The use of the school nursing standards is emerging as the foundation for orientation to the role of school nursing, the development of job descriptions, as well as the guide for an evaluation/job performance system that further validates the significance of those standards as a guide for practice (Connecticut State Department of Education, 2014; McDaniel, Overman, Guttu, & Engelke, 2012; Proctor, 2013). According to McDaniel, et al. (2012), "by implementing an evaluation tool that reflects the standards, nurses become more keenly aware of them and begin to truly realize how the standards are an intrinsic part of their job responsibilities. It follows that they also become directly accountable for meeting them" (p. 19).

The standards have also served to educate others of the role of school nurses. In an environment where school nurses often work as the sole healthcare provider alongside non-healthcare administrators and staff, there are times when conflict occurs regarding what care can be provided and by whom. The scope and standards of school nursing practice have served to help articulate the unique and professional role of the school nurse (Proctor, 2013).

Standards can serve to inform policies and procedures within a school district or at a state level. Policies are broad statements regarding specific activities, such as medication administration, immunization requirements for entrance into school, and care of ill or injured students and approved by a governing board, usually the board of education. Procedures or protocols are the details behind the policy and specifically outline how the policy is operationalized.

Finally, the standards provide a structure for quality improvement to continuously evaluate and promote best practices regarding the overall district or statewide practice of school nursing. If the standards are used to develop the policies and procedures; they are also useful in the evaluation of procedures and overall health services (Proctor, 2013). For example, school district can examine Standard 8: Education, and recommend that a goal for their school nurses would be to have all of their school nurses to become nationally certified.

IMPLICATIONS FOR SCHOOL NURSE PRACTICE

Nursing Preparation

School nurses practice in environments that offer opportunities to make important decisions that may have a lasting impact on the lives of students. School nurses are usually the sole healthcare professional in school environments and contribute significantly to the development of school health policies and programs. Although they enjoy a significant level of autonomy based on their scope of practice, the school nurse: engages with students, families, healthcare providers and the school community; and is involved with decision making, delegation and many other aspects of nursing practice (Levitt & Taylor, 1999). School nurses must therefore ensure that their practices are grounded in professionally recognized standards and best practices, such as those provided by the *School Nursing: Scope and Standards of Practice* (ANA & NASN, 2017).

> *An example of this need to base care on standards is exemplified in the case of Nguyen v. Grain Valley R-5 School Dist., 353 S.W.3d 725 (2011). In this case, the parents of an 11-year old student who died from head injuries sustained when she struck her head in physical education class brought a wrongful death action against the school district, school superintendent, principal,*

teachers, nurses, and nurse supervisor. It was proven that the school nurse involved did not comply with the applicable school district rules, policies or guidelines in her treatment of the student. The Court of Appeals held that the school nurse and school teachers were not entitled to statutory immunity from the wrongful death action, however, the school superintendent, principal, and nurse supervisor were protected by statutory immunity.

Nurses who choose to enter into the specialty of school nursing may not be proficient in all the national school nursing standards (ANA & NASN, 2017). School nurses may initially be surprised by and unprepared for the degree of autonomy their specialty provides them. However, regardless of their prior experiences, educational preparation, or the diverse conditions under which school nurses work, they must understand that they are legally responsible and accountable for practicing and adhering to the school nursing scope and standards of practice. Specifically, *Standard 12, Education*, states that "the school nurse attains knowledge and competence that reflect current nursing practice…" (ANA & NASN, 2017, p. 72). NASN (2016a) further acknowledged that commonality of conduct and gains towards proficiency in competencies must be upheld by all practicing school nurses.

Suggested Strategies

Participating in professional development activities can lead to proficiency in school nursing competencies. Professional development should be intentional and goal-directed, as opposed to random. School nurses who plan and manage such activities to acquire current knowledge and skills are more likely to provide safe and effective nursing care (Learning Nurse Resources Network, 2015). Sound knowledge of the scope and standards that are then implemented in daily school nursing practice is the legal ground upon which school nurses can stand when issues arise that question nursing decisions, actions and outcomes.

In line with the Robert Wood Johnson Foundation's Initiative on *The Future of Nursing* (2011) recommendations, practicing school nurses should continue their education and "engage in lifelong learning" (Institute of Medicine) that leads to exemplary school nursing practice. The NASN also recommends that school nurses engage in scholarship, research and learning in order to advance their professional knowledge and skills, achieve professional competence and improve school nursing practice work environments (NASN, 2016a). Engaging in theoretical as well as clinically focused professional development activities can minimize knowledge deficit and improve student health outcomes. It can also maximize the nurse's potential and job satisfaction. Professional school nurses must therefore engage in self-evaluation to gauge their competences, and self-reflective processes to gain insights that lead to the creation of specific plans to meet their professional development needs.

In addition to self-evaluations, practicing school nurses must take the necessary steps to align their job-related responsibilities, job descriptions and employee evaluations with the *School Nursing: Scope and Standards of Practice* (ANA & NASN, 2017). Continuous preparation to meet competencies, are reinforced when formal documentation of school nursing role and responsibilities (i.e., job descriptions and employee evaluations) are supported with the well-recognized standards of practice. (*Please see Chapter 6 for more information on school nurse evaluation*).

Finally, the use of recommended decision-making processes will assist school nurses to know that are functioning within their scope of practice. In collaboration with other nursing groups, the National Council of

State Boards of Nursing (NCSBN) recently developed a decision-making tool to guide practicing nurses through making informed decisions. The algorithm (APPENDIX) helps practicing nurses provide care within their scopes of practice (Ballard et al., 2016).

Working in Interprofessional Teams

School nurses work in elementary and secondary schools and therefore, must know, understand and abide by relevant education and nursing/health laws and regulations. Federal laws such as the Individuals with Disabilities Education Improvement Act (IDEIA), the Americans with Disabilities Act (ADA), the McKinney-Vento Homeless Assistance Act, as well as state education and health laws, are specific to educational environments. State nurse practice acts and laws specific to school nursing practice must then be considered along with federal and state education laws when creating, implementing and then evaluating nursing and healthcare services provided to students. Laws also vary across states in terms of what nursing and health practices are allowed in school environments. For example, certain medication administration, screening or school enrollment practices permitted in one state may be illegal in another state. Delegation of nursing activities to unlicensed assistive personnel also vary from state to state. (*See Chapter 4 on delegation for more information*).

> *The case of the American Nurses Association (ANA) v. Torlakson, 57 Cal.4th 570 (2013), provides an example of the variations of state laws. In California, unlicensed personnel may administer insulin. This is not the case in other states. The ANA sued the California Superintendent of Public Instruction and Department of Education regarding the authorization of school employees, other than school nurses, to administer insulin to students (citation, p.1). The California Supreme Court, decided that the California Nursing Practice Act and California law did not prohibit school personnel other than licensed healthcare providers to administer medication, therefore unlicensed school personnel could administer insulin to students (ANA v. Torlakson, 57 Cal.4th 570, 2013).*

Educational and health related individualized plans are one way of documenting services provided to students by members of the school interprofessional teams. These teams rely on school nurses to contribute their health and nursing expertise to the development of legally binding student plans, such as Individualized Education Plans (IEP) or Section 504 Plans. Without the knowledge and a clear understanding of how to apply education and nursing/health laws in school environments, boards of education can be placed at risk for legal action.

> *In Begley v. City of New York, 29 Misc.3d 579 (2010), parents of a developmentally delayed student, who died after suffering anaphylactic reaction at a non-public school, failed to establish that the local department of education (DOE) was responsible for the actions of an independently contracted nurse. In this case, the related services agreement documented in the student's IEP expressly stated that it (1) was an agreement between the parent and the independent nurse for nursing services approved by DOE; (2) required the nurse to carry her own professional liability insurance; and (3) further reiterated that current DOE employees could not provide such services under that contract. The court ruled in favor of the DOE due to the language provided in the student's IEP.*

Standard 10 of the *School Nursing: Scope and Standard of Practice*, which is titled Collaboration, emphasizes team and interprofessional interaction and states that the school nurse "partners with all stakeholders to create, implement, and evaluate a comprehensive plan" (ANA & NASN, 2017, p. 68). Not only is participation in interdisciplinary teams a competency benchmark, but according to *Standard 9 on Communication*, it is expected that professional school nurses must also understand regulations so they can be communicated in a responsible manner so as to protect the rights of students, parents and the local DOE.

Suggested Strategies

By participating in mentorships school nurses can gain new knowledge and guidance from experts in their field. Developing a trusting and professional relationship with an expert school nurse can provide a learning and development partnership that closes the knowledge gap, which ultimately benefits students. Transitioning from a nursing/healthcare environment to an educational environment oftentimes requires knowledge and skills that may only be available or acquired through professional relationships with school nurse leaders and colleagues with expertise in school nursing practices.

Mentorship opportunities that include "other aspects of performance not exclusive to the practice of nursing... may be [supported]... by professional colleagues [and] administrators" (ANA & NASN, 2017, p. 32) in the school environment. This additional engagement by school nurses with other disciplines can serve to educate members of the interprofessional team about their valuable role as the health expert in the school community, while building professional relationships.

Joining professional associations is another way of creating professional relationships. The benefits of becoming a member of a local, regional or national nurses' association include opportunities for enhanced networking, access to career resource information, current events and best practice updates, while staying connected to colleagues with similar specialty, such as school nursing.

Aligning School Nursing Practice with School District's Goals and Priorities

Experienced school nurses know and understand the importance of aligning health goals of students with school district goals and priorities. As public health nurses, school nurses may encounter situations and circumstances where the prioritization of health goals outweigh an immediate educational activity. The professional nurse is relied on to apply, abide by, and when necessary, reference appropriate laws and regulations. Boards of Education have a legal duty to educate students, but they also have a legal duty of care to protect students from harm through safe, preventative and direct care measures, and when necessary, provide emergency care in cases of injury or accidents. School nurses, as the primary healthcare professional in the school environment, must be well versed and knowledgeable in applying the scope and standards of school nursing practice that includes:

- communicating with students and parents/guardians;
- conducting health promotion activities;
- collaborating with the appropriate local public health and emergency crisis teams;
- connecting with the school physician;
- knowing and following the chain of command; and
- communicating well thought out information that assists school leaders in making decisions that ensures the health and safety of students.

Disrupting students' educational access or any aspect of a normally functioning school day is noteworthy in school environments. Ramifications may include the need to make up hours of instruction missed by students with IEPs, reallocating staff, rescheduling or cancelling school events, contacting parents/guardians, to name a few. However, there may be occasions that require interruption of the school program, such as to conduct screening tests for students, or in the case of an epidemic. School nurses must then use appropriate competencies such as those outlined in Standards one through six, including assessment, planning, implementation strategies, coordination of care; and then, using critical thinking skills, communicate information that promotes and supports a functioning, healthy and safe learning experience and environment for students.

> One important district goal and priority is school attendance by students. Chronic absence is now recognized as a national crisis as it is directly linked to exacerbating achievement gaps and dropout rates (Attendance Works, 2014). Fortunately, chronic absence may be reduced when school communities, families and community partners work together to remove barriers that inhibit attendance to school by students and engage in effective practices for improved student attendance. School nurses, as members of the school community, can address absenteeism by "outreaching to students/families to meet their individual needs; helping student/family access to needed physical or mental healthcare providers; providing student and family support during the school day; and encouraging utilization of reporting systems for better data collection" (NASN, 2015, p 1). These activities and interventions by school nurses demonstrates how school nursing practice can be aligned with school district goals and priorities.

Suggested Strategies

Engaging in the development of school health policies, protocols, and procedural guidelines that impact student health outcomes and school nursing practice is another important role of the school nurse. When circumstances do not allow for active engagement in the creative process, school nurses must be vigilant in lending their expertise by reviewing policies, etc. that have been developed and revisiting existing student individualized plans. These actions should be ongoing throughout each school year.

Participating on crisis and emergency school teams is another important responsibility of the school nurse. School nurses advocate for safety by participating in the development of school safety plans to address bullying, school violence, and the full range of emergency incidents that may occur at school (Wolfe, 2013). In addition to providing a nursing, medical and healthcare perspective, school nurses "promote health equity, assisting students and families in connecting with healthcare services, financial resources, shelter, food, and health promotion... [As such,] ... the school nurse is often the only healthcare professional aware of all the services and agencies involved in a student's care" (NASN, 2016b, p. 2) and therefore a critical part of the crisis and emergency teams.

CONCLUSION

The scope and standards of practice serve as the guide and provide authoritative statements on standards of care for all school nurses. In the absence of federal, state or local laws, the professional standards become the "standard of care" which can be used to determine if a school nurse (s) acted in a way that reflects best practices, competent care, health promotion and safety for all. Becoming educated on the standards and using them to guide job descriptions, orientation, evaluation, professional development, policies and quality improvement is key in promoting high quality, evidenced-base healthcare services in the school.

RESOURCES

American Nurses Association & National Association of School Nurses. (2017). *School Nursing: Scope and Standards of Practice*. 3rd Ed. Silver Spring, MD: Author.

Costante, C. (2013). Ed. *School Nurse Administrators: Leadership and Management.* Silver Spring, MD: National Association of School Nurses.

National Association of School Nurses. The role of the 21st century school nurse. (Position Statement). http://www.nasn.org/PolicyAdvocacy/PositionPapersandReports/NASNPositionStatementsFullView/tabid/462/ArticleId/87/The-Role-of-the-21st-Century-School-Nurse-Adopted-June-2016

REFERENCES

American Nurses Association v. Torlakson, 57 Cal.4th 570 (2013), 304 P.3d 1038, 160 Cal.Rptr.3d 370, 295 Ed. Law Rep. 688

American Nurses Association & National Association of School Nurses. (2017). *School nursing: Scope and standards of practice (*3rd ed.). Silver Spring, MD: Author.

Attendance Works. (2014). *The attendance imperative: How states can advance achievement by reducing chronic absence*. Retrieved from http://www.attendanceworks.org/wordpress/wp-content/uploads/2013/09/AAM-Policy-Brief-091214-2.pdf

Ballard, K., Haagenson, D., Christiansen, L., Damgaard, G., Halstead, J., Jason, R. ... Alexander, M. (2016). Scope of practice decision-making framework. Journal of Nursing Regulation; 7 (3), 19-21. doi: http://dx.doi.org/10.1016/S2155-8256(16)32316-X

Begley v. City of New York, 29 Misc.3d 579 (2010), 907 N.Y.S.2d 373, 259 Ed. Law Rep. 804, 2010 N.Y. Slip Op. 20339

Connecticut Department of Education. (2014). *Competency in school nurse practice*. Hartford, CT: Author. Retrieved from http://www.sde.ct.gov/sde/lib/sde/PDF/deps/student/health/Nursing_Competencies.pdf

Institute of Medicine. (2011). *The future of nursing: Leading change, advancing health.* Washington, D. C.: National Academies Press. Retrieved from https://www.ncbi.nlm.nih.gov/books/NBK209880/

Learning Nurse Resources Network. (2015). *Professional development for nurses*. Retrieved from http://www.learningnurse.org/index.php/library/pro-development

Levitt, E., & Taylor, S. (1999). An ethical dilemma in school nursing. *Journal of School Nursing, 15(4), 19-24.*

McDaniel, K., Overman, M., Guttu, M. & Engelke, M. (2012). School nurse evaluations: Making the process meaningful and motivational. *The Journal of School Nursing, 29* (1),19-30. doi: 10.1177/1059840512469407

Nguyen v. Grain Valley R-5 School Dist., 353 S.W.3d 725 (2011). 274 Ed. Law Rep. 1089, *N.J.S.A. 59:1–2*

National Association of School Nurses. (2015). *School nurses' role in combating chronic absenteeism.* Retrieved from https://higherlogicdownload.s3.amazonaws.com/NASN/3870c72d-fff9-4ed7-833f-215de278d256/UploadedImages/PDFs/Advocacy/whitepaperabsenteeism.pdf

National Association of School Nurses. (2016a). *Code of ethics*. Retrieved from https://www.nasn.org/RoleCareer/CodeofEthics

National Association of School Nurses. (2016b). *The role of the 21ˢᵗ century school nurse*. (Position Statement). Silver Spring, MD: Author. Retrieved from http://www.nasn.org/PolicyAdvocacy/PositionPapersandReports/NASNPositionStatementsFullView/tabid/462/ArticleId/87/The-Role-of-the-21st-Century-School-Nurse-Adopted-June-2016

Proctor, S. (2013). Standards of practice. In J. Selekman (Ed.), *School nursing: A comprehensive text* (2nd ed.) (pp. 48-78). Philadelphia: F.A. Davis

Wolfe, L. (2013). The profession of school nursing. In J. Selekman (Ed.), *School nursing: A comprehensive text* (2nd ed.) (pp. 25-47). Philadelphia: F.A. Davis

APPENDIX

Scope of Nursing Practice Decision-making Framework

Identify, describe, or clarify the activity, intervention, or role under consideration.

Is the activity, intervention, or role prohibited by the NPA and rules/regulations or any other applicable laws, rules/regulations, or accreditation standards or professional nursing scope and standards? **YES** → **STOP**

NO ↓

Is performing the activity, intervention, or role consistent with evidence-based nursing and health care literature? **NO** → **STOP**

YES ↓

Are there practice setting policies and procedures in place to support performing the activity, intervention, or role? **NO** → **STOP**

YES ↓

Has the nurse completed the necessary education to safely perform the activity, intervention, or role? **NO** → **STOP**

YES ↓

Is there documented evidence of the nurse's current competence (knowledge, skills, abilities, and judgments) to safely perform the activity, intervention, or role? **NO** → **STOP**

YES ↓

Does the nurse have the appropriate resources to perform the activity, intervention, or role in the practice setting? **NO** → **STOP**

YES ↓

Would a reasonable and prudent nurse perform the activity, intervention, or role in this setting? **NO** → **STOP**

YES ↓

Is the nurse prepared to accept accountability for the activity, intervention, or role and for the related outcomes? **NO** → **STOP**

YES ↓

The nurse may perform the activity, intervention, or role to acceptable and prevailing standards of safe nursing care

Chapter 4

PROCESS FOR DELEGATION IN THE SCHOOL SETTING

Cheryl Resha, EdD, MSN, RN, FNASN

DESCRIPTION OF ISSUE

Delegation, as defined by the American Nurses Association [ANA] (2012), is "the transfer of responsibility for the performance of an activity to another, with the former retaining accountability for the outcome" (p. 5). The National Council of State Boards of Nursing [NCSBN] (2016) further states "delegation is allowing a delegatee to perform a specific nursing activity, skill, or procedure that is beyond the delegatee's traditional role and not routinely performed" (p. 6). In school nursing, delegation occurs when the school nurse transfers the nursing activity, skill or procedure to another person, often to another licensed nurse or an unlicensed assistive personnel (UAP), such as an administrator, teacher, paraprofessional or health aide (National Association of School Nurses [NASN], 2016).

To ensure safe practice, and ultimately safe care for all children, school nurses are responsible for the delegation of any nursing care or activity in the school setting and on school-sponsored trips. This requires knowledge and understanding of the profession's guidance on delegation, their specific state's Nurse Practice Act (NPA) related to delegation of nursing activities, other applicable state laws related to unlicensed personnel in schools (e.g., specific medication or screening laws), district policies, and communication and collaboration among all stakeholders (ANA, 2012; NASN, 2014; NCSBN, 2016; & Resha, 2010).

BACKGROUND

It is well documented that the number of children with special healthcare needs attending schools is increasing, in part due to advances in technology and medicine. In addition, the complexity of care required at school and incidence of chronic conditions has also grown (Lineberry & Ikes, 2015; NASN, 2014; Resha, 2010). As the incidence of children with chronic or special healthcare condition grows, so does the legal responsibility of schools to ensure access to a free, appropriate public education (FAPE) for all children under Section 504 of the Rehabilitation Act of 1973 (Section 504), the Americans with Disability Act or Individuals with Disabilities Education Act (IDEA) (Zirkel, Granthom, & Lovato, 2012). Zirkel, et al. (2012) suggest that school nurses are at the forefront of promoting and ensuring FAPE through "child find" (e.g., identifying children for possible Section 504 accommodations by reviewing the records of all children with special healthcare needs or individualized healthcare plans) and determining eligibility for services so that children with healthcare needs are properly identified and accommodated.

According to the NASN School Nurse Survey, there are variations across the country regarding staffing patterns (i.e., one building per school nurse versus school nurses responsible for more than one school building) and the number of students per building (Mangena & Maughan, 2015). The findings indicated that "respondents were most likely to work in one building (51.3%) with 251 to 500 students (21.7%), although the average of responses indicated an average of three buildings and with an average of 924 to 1,072 students" (Mangena & Maughan, 2015, p. 332). In addition, 36.2% of the school nurses in the survey indicated having a registered nurse as a supervisor. These staffing patterns, workloads, and availability of a nursing supervision can, at times, impede the delivery of health services.

The growing healthcare needs and staffing patterns coupled with the need to ensure FAPE and provide the health services to students on and off campus makes delegation a valid consideration to meet the health needs of children in schools. However, delegation comes with challenges. Overcoming the challenges and successfully using delegation to provide health care in schools requires a clear understanding of the key definitions, one's state NPA and any associated state Board of Nursing (BON) regulations or Declaratory Rulings. Other pertinent federal and state laws (e.g., Section 504, IDEA, and state medication laws), and acceptable standards of care for delegation from professional nursing organizations, such as ANA (2012), NASN (2016), and NCSBN (2016) must also be considered. If students are traveling out of state on school-sponsored trips, school nurses should also be familiar with the destination state's NPA and regulations on delegation to UAPs (NASN, 2013).

Definitions

Accountability: "to be answerable to oneself and others for one's own choices, decisions and actions as measured against a standard..." (ANA, 2015, p. 41)

Assignment: "the routine care, activities, and procedures that are within the authorized scope of practice of the RN, LPN/LVN or part of the routine function of the UAP" (NCSBN, 2016, p. 6)

Delegatee: the person accepting the responsibility to perform a specific nursing activity (NCSBN, 2016).

Delegation: the transfer by a registered nurse to an unlicensed person the responsible to perform a specific nursing activity, skill, or procedure that is beyond that person's traditional role and not routinely performed (ANA, 2012; NCSBN, 2016)

Delegator: the person (APRN, RN, or LPN/LVN, if allowed by state NPAs) training and supervising another licensed nurse or UAP in performing a nursing activity that is not within their tradition role (NCSBN, 2016).

Licensed Nurse: an advanced practice registered nurse (APRN), a registered nurse (RN), a licensed practical or vocational nurse (LPN/LVN) (NCSBN, 2016, p.7).

Responsibility: having the duty to carry out the nursing activity, skill or procedure (ANA, 2012; NCSBN, 2016).

Unlicensed assistive personnel (UAP): an unlicensed person trained to perform a nursing activity. In the school setting, an UAP is often an administrator, teacher, or paraprofessional (teacher or health aide) (NASN, 2014; NCSBN, 2016).

Case Review

> The case of Mitts vs. Hillsboro Union High School (1987) is one of the most well documented opinions regarding delegation and school health services, and in some ways, has set the stage for current practices. In the Mitts vs. Hillsboro case, the paraprofessional (in this case Ms. Mitts) sued the school in court after she was directed by the school principal to perform clean intermittent catheterization (CIC) on a student with spina bifida. The paraprofessional was initially trained by the parent. After carrying out the duty for a period of time, she was provided additional

training and supervision on a monthly basis by the school nurse. The essence of the suit was the paraprofessional's claim that she was not competent to perform the CIC.

*The case was heard in the Oregon court system; however, the court then asked the Oregon Board of Nursing for a ruling in the case. The key outcomes of the ruling set the groundwork for current practices in school nursing. First, depending on state law, CIC can be delegated to a UAP **only** after the licensed nurse has assessed the healthcare needs, the stability of the client, the competency of the UAP to perform the activity and deemed it safe for the UAP to carry out the nursing activity. Second, the principal did not have the authority to delegate a nursing activity to a UAP. Third, because he assessed the health needs and delegated care, he was practicing nursing without a license. Finally, although the school nurse had the authority to delegate after an appropriate assessment, the court also found that the nurse neglected to conduct the initial assessment and assumed a supervisory role after the delegation occurred which is not an acceptable standard of practice (Mitts vs. Hillboro, 1987; NASN, 2014; & Spriggle, 2009).*

It is evident that delegation is an acceptable practice in nursing. However, it is the nurse, and not administrators, other school personnel or directives, that guides the process and is accountable for the outcomes of the nursing care provided.

Delegation Model

The national guidelines for nursing delegation, including a Delegation Model presented by NCSBN (2016), includes dynamic and overlapping concepts of delegation.

The Delegation Model (Figure 1) outlines the employer/nurse leader responsibilities along with those for the delegating nurse and delegatee. The employer/nurse leader role in school nursing might be the school nurse supervisor (who is a registered nurse) or the lead school nurse for the district or building when there is no nursing supervisor. Because of the autonomous role of school nursing and the varying staffing patterns for school health services, the lead school nurse often holds a dual role as the employer/nurse leader and the nurse delegating to UAPs.

In addition to the overlapping spheres depicting the responsibilities of these three roles are the key concepts of two-way communication, the delegation process and UAP competency, and training and education with the ultimate goal of public protection. Inherent in this model continues to be the *Five Rights of Delegation* (task, circumstance, person, direction and communication, and supervision and evaluation) (NCSBN, 2016).

Figure 1

Delegation Model

Figure 1. NCSBN (2016). Delegation Model. ©2016 National Council of State Boards of Nursing. Reprinted with permission. All rights reserved.

Although there are national guidelines developed by an expert panel outlining the delegation process of nursing activities to other licensed nurses and UAPs, there is not a universal law governing delegation. The individual state NPAs and state laws continue to address to whom and, in some cases, what, nursing activities, skills and procedures may be delegated (NCSBN, 2016).

School nurses often use delegation as an effective tool to ensure FAPE and access to needed healthcare services for students. However, there is still concern among school nurses regarding what a school nurse can and cannot delegate; what is recommended for safe delegation practices; and who can assume responsibility for nursing activities, and who is liable if there is an error. The following section outlines implications for school nurses and suggested strategies to use when school nurses delegate nursing care to other licensed nurses or UAPs in the school setting.

IMPLICATIONS FOR SCHOOL NURSE PRACTICE

State Nurse Practice Acts and Other Pertinent State Laws

School nurses have the responsibility to themselves, other school staff who assume responsibility for nursing activities and students to be knowledgeable of state laws regarding delegation of nursing activities to other licensed nurses (i.e., LPN/LVNs) and UAPs. Most states include delegation laws, regulations, and declaratory rulings under the auspice of the state BON and the state NPAs. The NCSBN provides a link to every state BON on their website for easy access in finding this information at https://www.ncsbn.org/contact-bon.htm

Some states' NPAs are very specific and identify which activities may be delegated to UAPs; while other state NPAs may only outline what aspects of the nursing process may be delegated rather than provide a list of tasks. For example, the Connecticut BON issued a *Declaratory Ruling* on delegation to unlicensed personnel (1995) which clearly identifies that only nursing tasks, skills or procedures that do not require nursing judgment are allowed to be delegated and these activities would fall under the implementation phase of the nursing process. This might include blood glucose monitoring for a stable student with type 1 diabetes, where a school nurse would train and supervise a UAP conducting blood glucose testing for a young student. However, the UAP would not be able to determine next steps after obtaining the blood glucose reading without a written protocol or care plan (Connecticut Board of Examiners for Nurses [CT BON], 1995).

National guidelines, most state NPAs, and declaratory rulings also emphasize that only the delegating nurse can determine what may be delegated, that the nurse is responsible to determine competency of the UAP to carry out the nursing activity, and that no other aspect of the nursing process may be delegated, i.e., assessment, diagnosis, planning or evaluation may not be delegated (ANA, 2012; NASN, 2016; & NSCBN, 2016).

Some state BONs are silent on delegation within the NPA. In these situations, school nurses will need to review other state laws that may inform their decisions and follow acceptable standards of care, such as the delegation process outlined by school nursing's professional organizations (ANA, 2012; NASN, 2016; & NCSBN, 2016).

Finally, as mentioned above, school nurses also need to be knowledgeable of other state laws that may allow or prohibit certain nursing activities or procedures that can be delegated to other licensed nurses or UAPs. Some examples of these state laws, outside of the BON rulings or NPAs, include individual state educational or health laws on medication administration, administration of emergency epinephrine or inhalers, and blood glucose monitoring. For example, many states allow UAP in schools to administer medication to students in the absence of the school nurse.

Delegation versus Assignment

As mentioned earlier in the definition section, delegation is the transfer of responsibility for a nursing activity, skill or procedure from a licensed nurse to another licensed nurse or UAP and that the activity is beyond the traditional and routine role for this person. In this situation, the nurse retains accountability for the activity. The delegatee is responsible to carry out the task properly and according to the direction provided by the nurse (ANA, 2012; NASN, 2014). For example, in many states the administration of an epinephrine auto-injector (aka: EpiPen™) to a child identified with a life-threatening food allergy may be delegated to an UAP in school or for off campus events (Asthma and Allergy Network, n.d.). The UAP is trained by the school nurse, the UAP is determined by the school nurse to be competent to perform the activity by return demonstration with a trainer injector and accurate understanding of the emergency care plan indicating when to administer the auto-injector. The UAP is also able to verbalize when to contact EMS and what information should be communicated back to the school nurse following every off-campus event.

One common question that arises from retaining accountability for the activity is the question of liability (i.e., allegations of malpractice or discipline by the BON) if the delegatee makes an error in performing the activity. If the delegating nurse followed all the acceptable practices of delegation (see delegation process section) and has documentation of those practices, the school nurse would not be responsible for the error. If, however, the school nurse did not conduct a comprehensive assessment, provide adequate training, supervision, evaluation and documentation, both the school nurse and the delegatee would be responsible for the error (ANA, 2012; NCSBN, 2016).

Assignment is the transfer of the responsibility and accountability of the activity from the licensed nurse (APRN or RN) to another licensed nurse (e.g., LPN/LVN) or UAP and the activity is part of their traditional role. For example, the RN may assign the LPN/LVN to perform a routine gastrostomy tube feeding after the RN conducted the assessment and developed the IHP. In this case, the LPN/LVN is likely to have had training/ education on this activity as part of their basic education or certification (NCSBN, 2016). Another example is when a licensed nurse can assign a health assistant (UAP) that works routinely in the school health office to take a temperature on all students who come in with the chief complaint of stomach ache or sore throat. The health assistant is responsible for obtaining the temperature, competently carrying out the task, and reporting the results to the school nurse.

While there is no argument that both delegation and assignment require supervision and assurance by the registered nurse that the task is completed correctly, the key difference is if the activity (i.e., assignment) is within their scope of practice for an LPN/LVN or routine responsibilities as a UAP (NCSBN, 2016). If it is, then the person carrying out the activity is both responsible and accountable for the activity. For many school nurses, this distinction is important, particularly if they are not on-site for daily supervision and evaluation of the activity.

Delegation Policies

Policies are effective tools to provide clarity to an issue, ensure effective decision making, standardize care, and education to those less familiar with the intent and purpose of the issue and in this case, delegation (Hootman, 2012; Krin & Taliaferro, 2013; NASN, 2014; NCSBN, 2016; Resha, 2010; & Spriggle, 2009). According to Spriggle (2009), "without a policy to guide delegation, school nurses may be forced to choose between following standards of school nursing practice and following a directive from a school administrator who may be delegating based upon educational standards of delegation [rather than his/her understanding of delegation in nursing]" (p. 103).

The school nurse or school nurse supervisor is a critical member of the team developing and continuously reviewing any policies related to student health. Policy statements are broad statements of the issue and guide what is expected of the organization (Krin & Taliaferro, 2013; NCSBN, 2016). For example, a policy on delegation may state that:

- the school nurse initiates and guides delegation of nursing activities;
- the school nurse follows procedural guidelines set forth by the professional organizations responsible for nursing licensure, nursing care and the safety of care delivery;
- the school nurse is responsible for the supervision of the delegation of care; and

- the school nurse may terminate the delegation of nursing activities at any time if there is a concern for safety for the student or delegatee or it is ineffective in meeting the student's healthcare outcomes.

Policies are substantiated with legal references and should be reviewed at least every three years and any time a new law or regulation is enacted. Finally, policies should not be confused with procedures or protocols that are much more detailed and may include all the necessary steps in the delegation process (Krin & Taliaferro, 2013).

Delegation Process

After reviewing the applicable laws and district policy and determining that delegation is an option in the particular state and for the school nurse, the delegation process would begin with an assessment of the student's health plan and needed health services. Using the nurse's critical thinking, decision-making skills, and nursing judgment, the school nurse considers some key questions:

- does the activity require nursing judgment?
- is there potential for harm?
- what is the complexity of care?
- what is the predictability of the outcome? (Mueller & Vogelsmeier, 2013)

If the answers to these beginning questions lead the school nurse to feel delegation is a safe option; the nurse would then begin a more formal assessment process using the decision-making tree (APPENDIX, ANA & NCSBN, 2012) and the *Five Rights of Delegation* (ANA, 2012, ANA & NCSBN, 2006; Mueller & Vogelsmeier, 2013; NCSBN, 2016; NASN, 2016) to determine if delegation for a specific situation/activity is safe and appropriate.

Assessment

The assessment would include a thorough review of the student's health needs and IHP to determine what nursing activities or procedures may need to be delegated in order to ensure the student is safe and his/her healthcare needs are met during the school day and school-sponsored trips. Following this review, the school nurse would then review the *Five Rights of Delegation* (Table 1- ANA & NCSBN, 2006; NASN, 2016; NCSBN, 2016).

Table 1   Five Rights of Delegation

Right Task	Is the activity within the designee's job description? Is it allowed by law and in your policy? Can the necessary training be provided?
Right Circumstance	Is the student's condition stable? Is the care predictable?
Right Person	Does the delegatee have the skills and knowledge to carry out the task? Does the delegatee demonstrate the competencies needed to carry out the task?
Right Direction and Communication	Is there a specific Individualized Healthcare Plan (IHP) or emergency care plan (ECP) that outlines the care for the student? Is there specific communication for both the initial instructions and ongoing opportunities for two-way communication? Is the delegatee willing to accept the responsibility? How will data on the student's condition be collected and shared with the delegator? Does the delegatee understand that they cannot make any decisions and must consult with the delegating nurse for additional guidance?
Right Supervision and Evaluation	How will supervision occur? What frequency and mode of evaluation? How will the delegatee communicate any immediate or emergency concerns? Is the delegating nurse able to respond as needed? Is all information related to the activity documented?

Adapted from ANA & NCSBN, 2006; NASN, 2016; & NCSBN, 2016

In addition to the *Five Rights*, the school nurse needs to consider what documents are available to guide safe care and would provide written direction of the delegated tasks, such as IHPs, ECPs, and nursing protocols.

Communication

Communication is a critical link in safe delegation from a school nurse to other licensed nurses and UAPs. Gordon and Barry (2009) identified trust, achieved through open and ongoing communication, as one of the most important variables in effective and safe delegation.–Clear verbal and written directions when delegating activities to others are essential (ANA, 2012; NASN, 2014). In a recent publication, the use of checklists was presented as an effective tool for both initial documentation of training and competency as well as the **usefulness** in ongoing instruction for the delegatee (Adair Shannon & Kubelka, 2013b).

Following the initial communication and direction, ongoing two-way communication is needed to maintain open lines of communication between the delegating nurse and the delegatee for questions, reinforcement, and supervision. The school nurse and the delegatee should establish the frequency and methods of communication for routine supervision and evaluation of the activity; and particularly how changes or emergencies in the student's condition will be communicated to the delegating nurses. (Mueller & Vogelsmeier, 2013; NCSBN, 2016).

Supervision/Evaluation

Supervision and evaluation of the delegation process vary depending on the student's condition, complexity and stability. Variabilities also occur based on the delegatee's skill, the proximity to the nurse, and need for additional training and supports (ANA & NCSBN, 2012; Mueller & Vogelsmeier, 2013). For example, the delegation of blood glucose monitoring may have two very different supervision and evaluation plans based on the fluctuations in their daily blood glucose numbers; their age; and their cognitive abilities. It may also vary based on the delegatee's prior knowledge and education of the activity. A delegatee who is familiar and performed blood glucose monitoring for another student in the past, may be more comfortable implementing this particular student's plan than someone who has never performed blood glucose monitoring before. Regardless of these variations, every supervision and evaluation plan should include the following elements for all delegatees:

- frequency of supervision, based on complexity, predictability, proximity to the nurse, and setting;
- method of supervision (e.g., on-site, direct observation, review of the student's record);
- setting for supervision;
- evaluation of competency performing task/activity;
- evaluation of student's condition;
- evaluation of student's expected outcomes;
- evaluation of communication plans;
- assessment of responses to emergencies or urgent situations; and
- evaluation of ongoing training, supports or resources for the delegatee (ANA & NCSBN, 2006; Mueller & Vogelsmeier, 2013; NASN, 2016).

Documentation

Documentation of the delegation process is another aspect that helps protect the school nurse if his/her actions are ever called into question. Legally, in a court of law, it can be argued if it was not documented it was not done. This concept, which is true in-patient care, is also true in documentation of the delegation process.

According to Attorneys Scott and Bubert (2012), documentation should include:

1. the rationale for determining that a particular nursing activity could be safely delegated to another licensed nurse or UAP;
2. the rationale used to determine the competency of the other person that will allow for safe care and delegation based on the client's condition;
3. how the activity, task or procedure was taught;
4. the teaching outcome;
5. the content and materials provided to the delegatee;
6. evidence that the delegatee understood any risks in performing the activity and what to do should any adverse events occur;
7. evidence that the delegatee understands that they are only allowed to perform the task on the specific client and is not intended to be transferred to another client;
8. how frequently the client should be assessed regarding continued delegation; and
9. how frequently the delegatee should be evaluated on performing the task. (p.214)

In addition to documentation of the delegation process and training provided, the delegating nurse should have a written IHP and ECP (if appropriate) for the student and a nursing protocol for the activity. Adair Shannon

& Kubelka (2015a; 2015b) also recommend the use of procedural checklists as a teaching and documentation tool. By using a checklist, it becomes clear the steps needed to complete the activity as well as the sequence of the steps to complete it and document it appropriately.

Finally, documentation of the supervision and evaluation should be included in the process. Notations should be made regarding the student's condition and response to the intervention (e.g., stability of condition, tolerance of activity, etc.) and the delegatee's performance and comfort with the activity. The checklist could serve as a documentation tool assessing for continued competence and proper technique (Adair Shannon & Kubelka, 2015a; ANA & NCSBN, 2006; NASN, 2016).

Education and Training

Delegation is a complex process that necessitates comprehensive knowledge and training for all parties, i.e., the school community, the delegating nurse and the delegatee (Gordon & Barry, 2009; Resha, 2010; Mueller & Vogelsmeier, 2013).

Delegation doesn't simply go from one person to another.   Developing and documenting policy is the first step to avoid conflicts in the process. The second step is determining who this policy will affect, educating them and educating the entire school community that the policy exists (e.g., there is a policy about who can administer medications. All teaching staff need to know this policy so they do not unwittingly accept a medication from a parent who tells the teacher, "Susan needs to take this at lunch."). This will help avoid unnecessary conflict between parents, school administrators, delegatees and nurses (NCSBN, 2016; Resha, 2010).

Education of the delegating nurses ideally begins in basic nursing education and continues throughout their careers (ANA & NASN, 2017). To effectively delegate, school nurses need knowledge of all the areas previous outlined (e.g., state laws, national guidelines, district policies, etc.). Nurses can obtain this knowledge through their professional organizations, their direct **nursing** supervisor (if available), formal education, such as webinars and conferences, as well as developing networks and mentors of more experienced or seasoned nurses (Gordon & Barry, 2009; Resha, 2010; Mueller & Vogelsmeier, 2013; Spriggle, 2009).   Mueller & Vogelsmeier (2013) state it best, "mastering the skill and art of delegation is a critical step on the pathway to nursing excellence" (p. 24).

The delegating nurse is directly responsible for the education of another licensed nurse or UAP. Although parents/guardians may provide insight into unique needs or techniques for their child, the lead nurse (in this case, the school nurse) is responsible for the training of the delegatee in accordance with acceptable standards of care (Adair Shannon & Kubelka, 2015b; Mitts v. Hillsboro, 1987; NCSBN, 2016). The education of the delegatee includes the steps needed to carry out the nursing activity, perhaps through the use of a checklist or procedural guideline (Adair Shannon & Kubelka, 2015b), demonstration of competency to carry out the activity; and a communication plan for routine supervision and evaluation as well as what to do in the event of an urgent or emergency situation.

One acceptable strategy for observing competency is the use of the _teach-back_ or return demonstration method where the delegating nurse demonstrates the activity and then the delegatee performs the activity under the direct supervision of the delegating nurse. This method allows for accurate and direct observation of the skill, the opportunity for immediate feedback and correction if needed, and questions and answers that the delegatee may have in performing the skill/activity (Adair Shannon & Kubelka, 2015b; NCBSN, 2016).

Strategies to Safely Delegate in Schools

1. Know your state Nurse Practice Act and other pertinent state and federal laws that would inform your decision to delegate.

2. Advance your knowledge and confidence regarding delegation.

3. Develop or participate in the development of a school district policy on delegation and procedural guidance.

4. Participate in ongoing review of the policy.

5. Follow the delegation process, including the use of the decision-making tree and five rights of delegation.

6. Provide necessary and ongoing training, including the use of teach-back methods to document the competency of the UAP.

7. Implement and follow a two-way communication plan (between the delegating nurse and the delegatee) for routine questions and supervision as well as emergency situations.

8. Establish and follow a clear method for supervision and evaluation, including the competency and accuracy of the performed task/activity by the UAP as well as the stability and outcomes of student's health condition.

9. Document, document, document.

CONCLUSION

Delegation is needed in all healthcare delivery systems, including school health. Adequate preparation at all levels (organization, nurse, delegatee, and student) is required for delegation to be a safe and effective tool in providing health care to students in schools. Furthermore, delegation should be based on standards of care, state laws and national evidence-based guidelines. Mueller and Vogelsmeier (2013) state that "delegation decisions must be based on the fundamental principle of public protection. The RN cannot delegate responsibilities requiring nursing judgments, such as patient assessment, care planning, and evaluation of care" (p. 22). Delegation should never be used as a substitute for the school nurse; but may be a complementary practice that allows all students access to an education and allows the school nurse to provide more complex nursing care that requires critical thinking and nursing judgement.

RESOURCES

Please also see Chapter 1 for more information regarding professional licensure.

American Nurses Association. (2012). *Principles of Delegation*. Silver Spring, MD: Nursesbooks.org.

National Association of School Nurses. (2016). *Principles for Practice: Nursing Delegation to Unlicensed Assistive Personnel in the School Setting*.

National Association of School Nurses. (2014). *Nursing Delegation to Unlicensed Assistive Personnel in the School Setting.* (Position Statement). Silver Spring, MD: Author.

National Council of State Boards of Nursing. (2016). Delegation. https://www.ncsbn.org/1625.htm

State Board of Nurses: The National Council of State Boards of Nursing provides a link to each state's Board of Nursing at https://www.ncsbn.org/contact-bon.htm

Legal Cases

Mitts, Carol v. Hillsboro Union High School district 3-8 Jt et al., Washington County Circuit Court Case 87-1142C (1987).

REFERENCES

Adair Shannon, R. & Kubelka, S. (2013a). Reducing the risks of delegation: Use of procedure skills checklist for unlicensed assistive personnel in schools, part 1. *NASN School Nurse*; July 2013, 178-181. doi: 10.1177/1942602X13489886

Adair Shannon, R. & Kubelka, S. (2013b). Reducing the risks of delegation: Use of procedure skills checklist for unlicensed assistive personnel in schools, part 2. *NASN School Nurse*; September 2013, 222-226. doi: 10.1177/1942602X13490030

American Nurses Association. (2012). *Principles of delegation*. Silver Spring, MD: Nursesbooks.org.

American Nurses Association. (2015). *Code of ethics with interpretive statements*. Silver Spring, MD: Nursesbooks.org.

American Nurses Association & National Association of School Nurses. (2017). *School nursing: Scope and standards of practice* (3rd ed.). Silver Spring, MD: Author.

American Nurses Association & National Council of State Boards of Nursing. (2006). *Joint statement on delegation.* Retrieved from https://www.ncsbn.org/Delegation_joint_statement_NCSBN-ANA.pdf

Asthma and Allergy Network. (n.d.). *School stock epinephrine laws.* Retrieved from http://www.allergyasthmanetwork.org/advocacy/current-issues/stock-epinephrine/

Connecticut Board of Examiners for Nursing. (1995). *Delegation by licensed nurses to unlicensed assistive personnel* (Declaratory Ruling). Retrieved from http://www.ct.gov/dph/lib/dph/phho/nursing_board/guidelines/unlicensed_ap_dec_rul.pdf

Gordon, S. & Barry, C. (2009). Delegation guided by school nursing values: Comprehensive knowledge, trust, and empowerment. *The Journal of School Nursing*, *25*(5), 352-360. doi: 10.1177/1059840509337724

Hootman, J. (2012). Staff management. In J. Selekman (Ed.), *School nursing: A comprehensive text* (2nd ed.) (pp. 1290-1321). Philadelphia, PA: F. A. Davis Company.

Lineberry, M. & Ikes, M. (2015). The role and impact of nurses in American elementary schools: A systematic review of the research. *The Journal of School Nursing*, *31*(1), 22-34. doi: 10:1177/1059840514540940

Krin, P. & Taliaferro, V. (2013). Establishing policies and procedures: The core of school nursing practice. In Costante, C. (Ed.), *School nurse administrators: Leadership and management* (pp. 339-362). Silver Spring, MD: National Association of School Nurses.

Mangena, A. & Maughan, E. (2015). The 2015 NASN school nurse survey: Developing and providing leadership to advance school nursing practice. *NASN School Nurse*, November 2015, 329-335. doi: 10.1177/1942602X15608183

Mitts, Carol v. Hillsboro Union High School district, Washington County Circuit Court Case 87-1142C (1987)

Mueller, C. & Vogelsmeier, A. (2013). Effective delegation: Understanding responsibility, authority, and accountability. *Journal of Nursing Regulation*, *4*(3), 20-27. doi: http://dx.doi.org/10.1016/S2155-8256(15)30126-5

National Association of School Nurses (2013). *School-sponsored trips- Role of the school nurse* (Position Statement). Silver Spring, MD: Author.

National Association of School Nurses. (2014). *Nursing delegation to unlicensed assistive personnel in the school setting* (Position Statement). Silver Spring, MD: Author. https://www.nasn.org/PolicyAdvocacy/PositionPapersandReports/NASNPositionStatementsFullView/tabid/462/ArticleId/21/Delegation-Nursing-Delegation-to-Unlicensed-Assistive-Personnel-in-the-School-Setting-Revised-June-2

National Association of School Nurses. (2016). *Principles for practice: Nursing delegation to unlicensed assistive personnel in the schools setting*. Silver Spring, MD: Author.

National Council of State Boards of Nursing. (2016). National guidelines for nursing delegation. *Journal of Nursing Regulation*, *7*(1): 5-14. Retrieved from https://www.ncsbn.org/NCSBN_Delegation_Guidelines.pdf

Resha, C. (2010). Delegation in the school setting: Is it a safe practice? *OJIN: The Online Journal of Issues in Nursing*, *15*(2), 5. doi: 10.3912/OJIN.Vol15No02Man05

Scott, L. R., & Bubert, J. S. (2012). Legal issues related to school nursing practice: The foundation. In J. Selekman (Ed.), *School nursing: A comprehensive text* (2nd ed., pp. 196–224). Philadelphia, PA: F. A. Davis Company.

Spriggle, M. (2009). Developing a policy for delegation of nursing care in the school setting. *The Journal of School Nursing*, *25*(2), 98-107. doi: 10.1177/1059840508330756

Zirkel, P. A., Granthom, M. F., & Lovato, L. (2012). Section 504 and student health problems: The pivotal position of the school nurse. *The Journal of School Nursing*, *28*(6), 423–432. doi:10.1177/1059840512449358

APPENDIX

Decision Tree for Delegation by Registered Nurses

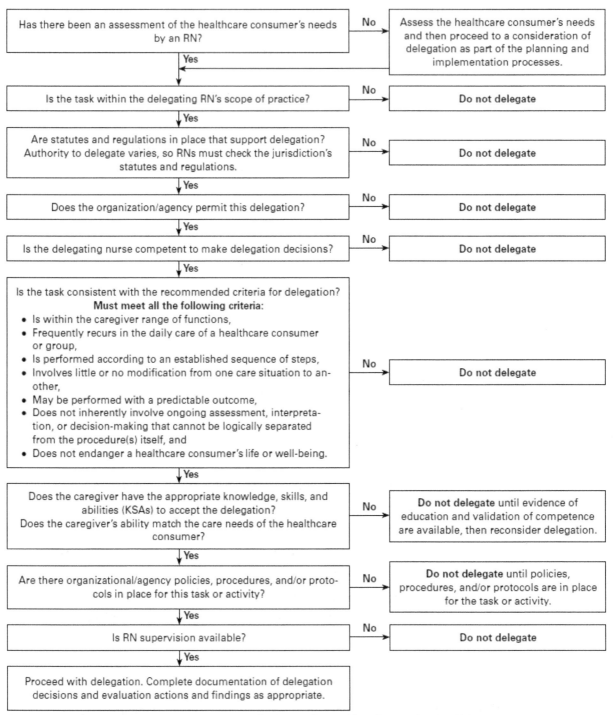

Reprinted with permission, © American Nurses Association and The National Council of State Boards of Nursing, 2012.

Chapter 5

SUPERVISION OF SCHOOL NURSES

Tia Campbell, MSN, RN, NCSN, FNASN
Lisa Minor RN, MSN, EdD

DESCRIPTION OF ISSUE

Schools throughout the United States are recognizing the need for better healthcare for children and are striving to promote a healthier environment for them in which to grow, learn, and thrive. This is one of the primary reasons that many school systems throughout the United States are employing registered nurses to provide health services and assistance in the school setting. "School nursing is a specialized practice of nursing that advances the well-being, academic success, and lifelong achievement and health of students. Keeping children healthy, safe, in school, and ready to learn should be a top priority for both healthcare and educational systems." (National Association of School Nurses (NASN), 2016, p.1). School nurses are often the sole healthcare provider in a school setting. The school nurses function within the nursing standards of care and routinely follow orders that have been provided by a physician or other healthcare provider. However, although school nurses are the trained and licensed healthcare provider in the school setting, they are most often supervised by non-medical personnel which could have legal implications. The National Association of School Nurses (NASN) also identified this concern in a recent position paper which states "...school nurses may be supervised and evaluated by school administrators who have little or no knowledge and understanding of the school nurse role" (NASN, 2013, p.1). It is not uncommon for school nurses to be supervised by the school principal or have non–nursing supervisors with no medical knowledge at all.

BACKGROUND

Having someone with sound clinical knowledge and a strong clinical background supervise the professional school nurse in the school setting is relevant to quality, safe practice in the school nursing community. It is the school nurse's professional responsibility to ensure the safety and well-being of the students in our care. The impact for employers is multifactorial; they may be liable for retention of unsatisfactory employees or negligent in the supervision of staff because the school administrator lacks the clinical expertise to know if a nursing task is being done correctly or incorrectly. This also holds true for school administrators who designate an employee to serve in the role of unlicensed assistive personnel (UAP). Because most school administrators have no medical or clinical knowledge, they cannot be sure that the school nurse overseeing the task being delegated to the UAP is appropriate, is being taught properly or if the UAP is competent. If the school administrator designates someone to perform a task and does not allow time for proper training by the school nurse, there can be legal ramifications for the school system and staff members involved.

In Trebatoski, Chris, Lindman, Eric, Lindman, Nichole v. Ashland School District (2013), an elementary school Type I diabetic student's parents had worked with the Ashland school system to develop a Section 504 Plan for their son's care during the school day. One of the requirements included that three staff members along with the school nurse be trained in the care of this diabetic student and to fully understand what was to be done with his medical needs. According to the case, the school division only had one fully trained individual for the student and that was the school nurse. One on occasion, the school nurse had to be out for the day and the school nurse supervisor, who had not been trained for this particular student's needs, took over for the day. Even though the school nurse tried to explain what was expected for this student, the supervisor ignored the nurse's recommendations. The school nurse supervisor, on the day in question, made several inappropriate decisions and did not adequately follow the plan of care. The student's blood sugars became elevated and proper measures were not taken to correct the hyperglycemia. When the school nurse returned, she questioned the school nurse supervisor about the inappropriate decisions. The school nurse supervisor informed the principal about having been questioned by the school nurse. The principal reacted by reprimanding the school nurse because he did not understand the seriousness, ramifications and concerns that were presented on behalf of the school nurse. As time progressed, there still were no measures made on behalf of school administration to train 2 more individuals to meet the requirements listed in the Section 504 Plan. Because the principal, as the school administrator and ultimate supervisor of the school nurse when in the school setting, did not have proper clinical knowledge, he allowed the problems to continue which put the student at risk. The principal did not understand the importance of following through with the Section 504 requirement to have three individuals trained to care for the student and did not intervene when inappropriate decisions were made in the care of the student which resulted in legal action on the part of the student's parents.

This case, although ultimately overturned and found in favor of the school district, supports the fact that non-clinical administrators lack the professional nursing/medical knowledge needed to supervise school nurses or make sound clinical decisions based on the health needs of students which could lead to legal implications.

Supervision of Registered Nurses by Non-Clinical Personnel

Years ago, prior to the passage of Section 504 of the American's with Disabilities Act (Section 504) and Individuals with Disabilities Education Act (IDEA), many school health offices were covered by UAPs or at times a parent volunteer who would provide very basic first aid and occasionally administer medication to students. In these situations, it was common and more acceptable for non-clinical personnel to supervise these UAPs or volunteers because neither the clinic attendant nor parent volunteer was a licensed healthcare provider. Ironically the use of these unlicensed personnel still holds true in some cases in school systems where a registered nurse is not present. However, based on the requirements of Section 504 of the Rehabilitation Act, students with more significant health needs are now attending public school which requires determining who is skilled enough to care for those students with special needs and health issues. Even with more specialized nursing care needed in the school setting, school nurses are not mandated in most states. "More than half of American public schools don't have a full-time nurse, and the situation is getting worse as school systems further cut budgets" (Tomsic, 2012). Although it is not a law in most states, many school systems have decided to employ registered nurses in the schools to meet the needs of those requiring that level of care when in the school setting. "Although school nurses are often seen as people who deliver first aid at school, their role is much deeper and has such breadth that only a registered professional nurse has the skill set to provide this profoundly needed health aspect to the school setting" (Schoessler, 2011, p. 12).

Registered nurses in the school setting are unique because they are often the only health professional in a building that focuses on academics and instruction. School nurses are therefore often supervised by non-clinical personnel with administrators who do not understand that they are not qualified to oversee the school nurse. It is essential that school administration understand that even though non-clinical personnel are able to legally supervise school nurses regarding skills related to their professionalism, communication, and work ethic; they are not able to effectively supervise clinical skills or determine safe practice while in the school setting. They not only lack the clinical knowledge; they also lack the professional license (Beirne, 2009).

Because school administrators may not fully understand the legal scope of practice of the school nurse, they may ask school nurses to complete tasks or divulge confidential information which is not within, and many times beyond, the scope and standards of practice for a school nurse which could put the school system at increased risk for legal ramifications. According to Laubin, Schwab & Doyle (2013) "liability for school districts can be increased when educational administrators are expected to provide clinical direction or make clinical decisions for which they have no professional or legal authority" (p. 501).

School nurses' clinical performance should be supervised by a nurse professional with the knowledge and skill to effectively oversee the clinical qualifications of the school nurse as well as have the legal authority to supervise by way of a nursing license. "Clinical supervisors of school nurses should be experienced nursing professionals with knowledge and skills both in the nursing care of children and youth and in the application of relevant ethical principles, rules and regulations, and professional standards related to the practice of nursing in school settings" (Laubin et al., 2013, p. 501).

Supervision of School Nurses

Adequate supervision of school nurses is essential to ensure that the school nurse is appropriately meeting the scope and standards of practice whether it is providing direct care to a student or supervising UAP. When there is no nurse supervisor, the challenges can prove to be detrimental to the student. Practice guidelines are based on state boards of nursing; therefore, the nurse must be clear when explaining his/her role to school administration. The school nurse must also be clear on what they can and cannot delegate to UAP and what they are allowed to supervise in order to avoid litigation or more importantly, harm to the student. School nurses must also be very careful to document any training given to UAP and document what has been observed when supervising a particular procedure. There can be increased liability for all school systems due to failure to show competence because the role of the school nurse is often poorly understood by the educational sector and administration. "Although some principals may want to control all facets of the school nurse's role, the school nurse must explain the parameters of licensure and state board of nursing regulations" (Wold & Selekman, 2013, p. 106). It may also prove to be dangerous when a principal or other non-clinical personnel supervising the school nurse states that the nurse is competent to make proper judgement calls or provide appropriate direction to the UAP when the nurse may lack competency in his/her role as a school nurse or necessary skills for safe delegation. *(See Chapter 4 for more information on delegation).*

Potential Strategies to Promote Supervision of the School Nurse

To address the challenge of non-nurses supervising the clinical practice of a school nurse, educating the non-medical administrator on the scope of practice of the school nurse and possible legal implications (negligent supervision, practicing without a license and the liability of retaining unsatisfactory employees) is a beginning.

In addition to educating administrators, possible solutions for supervision include:

- Conduct peer review.
- Allow self-evaluation with provision of the evidence of meeting clinical standards of practice.
- Contract with someone with a clinical background to provide supervision of the school nurse (such as experienced school nurse or school nurse administrator).
- Partner with a clinical supervisor (school nurse administrator if available) to evaluate and supervise the clinical component and support the school administrator in the evaluation or supervision the professional component of the school nurse's performance.

CONCLUSION

When school systems employ a registered nurse in the school, there are certain parameters that must be addressed and adhered to in an effort to avoid legal ramifications. Because school nurses are often the sole health professional in the building, they must be held accountable for their actions and supervised in a way that ensures that accountability. It is most important that legally authorized and clinically sound supervision be in place for the school nurse. If the nurse is being supervised by a non-medical or non-nurse school administrator, it is essential that there be additional input from a nursing professional or a process for peer review or self-evaluation. Without ensuring that the registered nurses in the school setting are clinically sound and competent in their own actions as well as in their supervision of UAP, the administrator could be held liable for unsafe care and, if engaging in nursing supervision, practicing nursing without a license.

It is essential that school nurses advocate for themselves and be accountable for their own actions. School nurses must also ensure that their administrators understand the scope and standards of practice for school nurses as well as individual state laws and educate administrators as to what can and cannot be delegated to UAP. It is also of utmost importance that school nurses explain to school administration why they cannot effectively supervise the clinical knowledge and skill of the nurse. "It is important to remember that every state has specific laws and regulations to guide school district policy and nursing practice. Every school principal and every school nurse must be well versed in their own state's laws and regulations "(Schoessler, 2011, p. 13). If school nurses, school administration, and school systems work together by putting proper clinical supervision in place, school districts can be more confident that they are meeting the health needs of students and by effectively keeping them healthy, it can help them excel academically.

RESOURCES

Trebatoski, Chris, Lindman, Eric, Lindman, Nichole v. Ashland School District. United States District Court for the Western District of Wisconsin, Case No. 13-1790 (2013).

National Association of School Nurses (NASN). (2013). *Supervision and evaluation of the school nurse* (Position Statement). Retrieved from http://www.nasn.org/PolicyAdvocacy/PositionPapersandReports/NASNPositionStatementsFullView/tabid/462/ArticleId/51/Supervision-and-Evaluation-of-the-School-Nurse-Revised-June-2013

NC Board of Nursing. (2015, Winter). *Who's your supervisor or manager? Nursing practice: The management and supervision of nursing services.* Nursing Bulletin, Winter 2015,*11*(2). Retrieved from http://www.ncbon.com/myfiles/downloads/news-resources/bulletin/2015/winter-2015.pdf

REFERENCES

Beirne, M. (2009). Using a professional portfolio to enhance school nursing practice. *NASN School Nurse, 24* (5), 212-214. Retrieved from http://hdl.handle.net/10822/1026952

Laubin, M., Schwab, N.C., & Doyle, J. (2013). Understanding the legal landscape. In C.C. Costante (Ed.). *School nurse administrators: Leadership and management*, (pp. 459-519), Silver Spring, MD. National Association of School Nurses.

National Association of School Nurses (2016). The role of the 21st century school nurse (Position Statement). Retrieved from http://www.npr.org/2012/01/03/144615747/no-the-school-nurse-is-not-in.

National Association of School Nurses. (2013). *Supervision and evaluation of the school nurse* (Position Statement). Retrieved from http://www.nasn.org/PolicyAdvocacy/PositionPapersandReports/NASNPositionStatementsFullView/tabid/462/ArticleId/51/Supervision-and-Evaluation-of-the-School-Nurse-Revised-June-2013

Schoessler, S. (2011, September/October). More than first aid. *Principal* 91 (1), 10-13. Alexandria, VA: National Association of Elementary School Principals.

Selekman, J. & Wolfe, L.C. (2010). *School nursing certification review*. Silver Spring, MD: National Association of School Nurses.

Tomsic, M. (2012). No, the school nurse is not in. *Around the Nation*. Retrieved from http://www.npr.org/2012/01/03/144615747/no-the-school-nurse-is-not-in.

Trebatoski, Chris, Lindman, Eric, Lindman, Nichole v. Ashland School District United States District Court for the Western District of Wisconsin, Case No. 13-1790 (2013).

Wold, S.J. & Selekman, J. (2013). Frameworks and models for school nursing practice In J. Selekman (Ed.), *School nursing: A comprehensive text* (2nd ed.) (p.106). Philadelphia, PA. F.A. Davis Company.

ADDENDUM

Practical (and Tactful) Solutions to Problematic Employment Request

Erin D. Gilsbach, Esquire

There may be times when a school nurses' superior is doing something or asking the school nurse to do something that the school nurse believes is in violation of nursing laws or nursing standards of care. This can be a very difficult situation, and the manner in which the school nurse handles the situation can make all the difference. Attorney John E. Freund, III, chairman of the Education Law Practice Group at King Spry Herman Freund & Faul in Bethlehem, PA, has represented schools for over 35 years and offers some advice on the issue. " School nurses need a balanced approach in these types of matters. If a school nurse perceives violation of the nurse practice act, they should make their concerns known to the building and/or district-level administration. If the matter is serious enough that it poses a risk of harm to students that is not mitigated by informing the administration, the nurse may have an ethical and/or legal duty to report the violation to the state nursing authorities."

Steve M. Cohen, Ed. D, President and Managing Partner of the Labor Management Advisory Group located in Kansas City, who has an extensive background in both education and business, and whose wife and sister are both nurses, has some practical advice regarding how nurses could approach this sensitive topic with their employers. "The school nurse should advise, in polite and professional terms, that the official has wandered into an area where the official is unauthorized to operate. The nurse should provide the administrator with documentation that supports the position that it is inappropriate and perhaps illegal to do what has been or is attempting to be done." Dr. Cohen further advises, "I would point out that by taking this action, the administrator is incurring liability for him/herself and for the District that is unnecessary and could be a job killer or even a career killer." Importantly, he urges school nurses to come prepared not only with a message of potential liability but also potential solutions that will demonstrate that, while the school nurse's foremost concern is for the safety of the students, they are also committed to finding practical solutions. "My suggestion is to not simply say 'no' but, rather, to seek to deploy a course of action that achieves a win / win. Any one can say no and appear irksome and unaccommodating. The person who works toward getting to 'yes' without violating fiduciary obligations demonstrates that they are trying to accommodate." This approach is both practical and positive, and it achieves the desired goal: ensuring g the safety and security of the students and preventing the unauthorized practice of nursing. Attorney Freund reminds nurses that, at the end of the day, "the most important factor in this decision-making is the health and safety of the students. All legal, regulatory, and employment requirements should be interpreted in light of their needs."

Chapter 6

PERFORMANCE EVALUATION OF SCHOOL NURSES

Tia Campbell, MSN, RN, NCSN, FNASN

Lisa Minor RN, MSN, EdD

DESCRIPTION OF ISSUE

In conversations with school nurses across the United States and abroad, concern is expressed due to the lack of evaluation or evaluation by personnel unqualified to assess nursing skills. Many are evaluated utilizing tools that are used for unlicensed school personnel that simply address attendance, dress, punctuality and the like. School nurses express frustration that they are not viewed as professionals for evaluation purposes.

McDaniel, Overman, Guttu & Engelke (2013) note," because of the wide range of duties, it is challenging for administrators to fully understand the professional role of the school nurse, yet they have the responsibility of assuring competence of the nurses" (p. 19). Clinical nursing supervisors are often not employed by school districts, especially those with a smaller total student population. In districts without clinical nursing supervisors, it is particularly difficult to receive clinically based feedback in the form of an evaluation.

BACKGROUND

While there are more recent school nursing articles and information in textbooks regarding the need for, and development of, standards based evaluation tools and clinical supervision and evaluation, there appears to be a gap in the literature related to the specific legal implications posed for school nurses and school systems on the topic of school nurse evaluations.

According to the American Nurses Association (ANA) and the National Association of School Nurses (NASN) (2017), evaluation is a standard of professional performance. The school nurse is responsible for ensuring that her/his practice meets standards for safety, is based in evidence and current best practice. Redshaw (2008), suggests that for an evaluation system to be successful it must have clear objectives, be able to be fairly implemented, and have relatively simple documentation. In addition, there must be the opportunity for structured feedback, action planning, and follow-up at set intervals. The ultimate goal of the evaluation process is to ensure competence, provide a plan for correcting any deficiencies, and to support staff in performing and achieving to their full potential.

In some states, such as California, the Board of Registered Nursing, has determined that only medical personnel may evaluate the clinical performance of the school nurse. "Competence in nursing practice must be evaluated by the individual nurse (self-assessment), nurse peers, and nurses in the roles of supervisor, coach, mentor, or preceptor" (ANA, 2010, p. 40).

The literature is clear that evaluation tools should be standards-based. The school nurse should be aware of the scope of practice and professional performance for the specialty. Evaluation tools should address specific competencies within the scope of practice. "An evaluation system serves to document that an individual's performance meets standards and competencies, develop a plan for improvement, and provide the opportunity for the supervisor to guide professional development opportunities" (Resha, 2009, p.241). Lacking the educational background, understanding of health laws, licensure requirements, and practice issues of school nurses, educational administrators are not qualified to evaluate the clinical practice of the school nurse. "In organizations where the leader of the health services program is not a nurse, it is essential to designate a professional registered nurse as the lead nurse to provide clinical input into the performance management process" (Somerville, 2013, p. 233). It is best practice to have a registered nurse, in a leadership position, to assist with determining the core responsibilities of the school nurse role, to develop an evaluation tool which reflects the job description and competencies, and provide clinical evaluation of the school nurses' practice (NASN, 2013).

IMPLICATIONS FOR SCHOOL NURSE PRACTICE

Documenting Competence

Evaluations provide the organization with documentation that the employee is meeting stated job standards. Therefore, it is important for the school nurse evaluation tool to be specific to school nurse standards of practice. Nurse supervisors would be able to establish specific competencies based upon a job analysis, job description, professional standards and organizational goals (Somerville, 2013). When school districts fail to utilize a standards-based evaluation tool, they miss the opportunity to document that their nurse meets established criteria. If litigation were to ensue, the district would have no "proof" that the nurse was competent to perform job related duties. "Accurate job descriptions and an evaluation process that includes both an administrative and a clinical nursing component are essential and should be based on the standards of practice and professional performance for school nurse practice" (NASN, 2013, paragraph 4).

Ensuring Quality Practice

Evaluation serves to ensure quality practice in the school setting. Performance appraisals offer opportunities to evaluate nursing practice in relation to school nursing standards and to develop a plan of action to improve any noted deficits. According to Somerville (2013), "The evaluation process should provide the school nurse with valuable feedback on strengths, and a discussion of the written evaluation gives the manager and the school nurse the opportunity to identify and discuss personal, professional, and program growth" (p. 244).

Standards-Based Evaluation Tools

For districts who do not employ a nurse supervisor, The ANA and NASN have developed standards of practice and professional performance for school nurses. Available from Nursebooks.org, every school nurse should base her/his practice on these standards. In addition, a number of states or localities have developed standards based evaluation tools. Following are three examples. The State Department of Education in Connecticut revised its' Competency in School Nurse Practice in 2014. It is closely aligned with the ANA/NASN School Nursing: Scope & Standards of Practice, 2nd edition (Connecticut State Department of Education, 2014). The School Nurse Institute Partnership in Virginia has developed a standards-based evaluation tool that closely mirrors the mandated state teacher's evaluation tool. This approach promotes ease of use by non-clinical administrators and allows the school nurse to provide concrete evidence of having met the standards of practice. The Shaker Heights City School District redesigned their evaluation tool as part of the Race to the Top initiative in an effort to provide evidence of school nurses impact on academic performance (Haffke, Damm, & Cross, 2014).

Impact on Employers

"Evaluation also impacts on employers, who may be liable for retention of unsatisfactory employees or negligent supervision (i.e., failure to reasonably monitor the actions of an employee)" (Hootman, 2013, p. 1299). It behooves the school system to ensure that the school nurse is providing safe and effective care to students that conforms to state laws governing the practice of nursing, local policy, and established clinical guidelines. "The employer's interest is to ensure that all school nurses are competent" (Somerville, p. 240).

The most common challenges to acceptable evaluation practices are the lack of a clinical supervisor and educational administrators who don't understand that they don't possess the skills to evaluate school nursing practice. Educating the non-medical administrator on the scope of practice of the school nurse and possible legal implications (negligent supervision, practicing without a license, and the liability of retaining unsatisfactory employees) is a beginning. Advocating for a standards-based evaluation tool and the ability provide evidence of having met the standards of practice is certainly within the power of the individual nurse.

Smaller school systems may address the lack of a nurse supervisor by utilizing peer review, professional portfolios, regional supervision or "designating a professional registered nurse as the lead nurse to provide clinical input into the performance management process" (Somerville, 2013, p. 233). Robust school nurse evaluation methods should include both a clinical and an educational component.

Strategies

To ensure annual school nurse evaluation:

- Read and understand the *School Nursing: Scope and Standards of Practice.*
- Provide ongoing education for non-clinical school nurse administrators on the scope of practice, licensure, and laws guiding school nursing practice.
- Advocate for a clinical nurse supervisor or a designated lead nurse to provide clinical input on evaluations.
- Contribute to a standards-based evaluation tool if one does not exist in your district (search the internet for existing tools and seek permission to modify if you need a place to start).
- Document annual personal and professional goals.
- Conduct an annual self-evaluation of practice based on the *School Nursing: Scope and Standards of Practice,* especially if you do not receive a formal evaluation.
- Engage in peer review if no formal evaluation is provided.
- Work to establish policies for the annual evaluation of school nurse practice by a registered professional school nurse based on the job description and scope and standards of practice.

CONCLUSION

The legal implications of the evaluation of school nursing practice include ensuring a competent workforce, avoiding non-nurse administrators practicing nursing without a license, and negligent supervision. School nurses, like all school employees deserve the opportunity to discuss their clinical performance based on laws and acceptable standards. If the nurse is being evaluated by a non-medical administrator, additional input is needed from an evaluator with clinical expertise. Without clinical input from a licensed practitioner, the administrator runs the risk of being found guilty of practicing without a license. In addition, without knowledge of nursing practice, the administrator may unknowingly breech the state nurse practice act when making assignments or designating medical tasks to unlicensed personnel.

The school nurse has a responsibility to evaluate her/his professional practice. It is the school nurse's responsibility to educate administrators on the laws that govern nursing, and the scope and standards of school nursing practice. Furthermore, the school nurse must advocate for a professional-level evaluation process. Using a standards-based evaluation tool and advocating for a clinical evaluator to contribute to the evaluation process will help to ensure that appropriate feedback is received to ensure the safe and effective care of children in the school setting. This can also document the attainment of professional goals, outcome measures, and benchmarks for the school nurse.

RESOURCES

Connecticut State Department of Education: Competency in School Nurse Practice, 2nd ed. (2014). http://www.sde.ct.gov/sde/lib/sde/PDF/deps/student/health/Competency_in_School_Nurse_Practice.pdf.

NASN Position Document: Supervision and Evaluation of the School Nurse (Rev. 2013). http://www.nasn.org/PolicyAdvocacy/PositionPapersandReports/NASNPositionStatementsFullView/ tabid/462/ArticleId/51/Supervision-and-Evaluation-of-the-School-Nurse-Revised-June-2013

Shaker Heights City School District: School Nurse Evaluation Process (Rev. 2013). https://www.google.com/webhp?sourceid=chrome-instant&ion=1&espv=2&ie=UTF-8#q=shaker%20 heights%2C%20ohio%2C%20school%20nurse%20evaluation%20form

Virginia School Nurse Institute Partnership: Standards Based School Nurse Evaluation Tool (2013). http://www.doe.virginia.gov/support/health_medical/index.shtml

REFERENCES

American Nurses Association. (2010). *Nursing: Scope and standards of practice* (2nd ed.) Silver Spring, MD: Nursebooks.org.

American Nurses Association & National Association of School Nurses. (2017). *School nursing: Scope and standards of practice* (3rd ed.). Silver Spring, MD: Author.

Connecticut State Department of Education. (2014). *Competency in school nurse practice (2nd ed.).* Retrieved from: http://www.sde.ct.gov/sde/lib/sde/PDF/deps/student/health/Competency_in_School_Nurse_Practice.pdf

Haffke, L., Damm, P. & Cross, B. (2014). School nurses race to the top: The pilot year of how one district's school nurses revised their evaluation process. *The Journal of School Nursing, 30*(6), 404-410. doi: 10.1177/1059840514536581

Hootman, J. (2013). Staff management. In J. Selekman (Ed.), *School nursing: A comprehensive text, (2nd ed.)* (pp. 1290-1321). Philadelphia, PA: F.A. Davis Company.

McDaniel, K., Overman, M., Guttu, M. & Engelke, M. (2013). School nurse evaluations: Making the process meaningful and motivational. *The Journal of School Nursing, 29*(1), 19-30. doi: 10.1177/1059840512469407

National Association of School Nurses. (2013). *Supervision and evaluation of the school nurse* (Position Statement). Retrieved from http://www.nasn.org/PolicyAdvocacy/PositionPapersandReports/NASNPositionStatementsFullView/tabid/462/ArticleId/51/Supervision-and-Evaluation-of-the-School-Nurse-Revised-June-2013

Redshaw, G. (2008). Improving the performance appraisal system for nurses. *Nursing Times*. Retrieved from www.nursingtimes.net/roles/nurse-managers/improving-the-performance- appraisal-system-for-nurses/1314790.fullarticle.

Resha, C. (2009). School nurse competencies: How can they assist to ensure high-quality care in the school setting? *NASN School Nurse, 24*(6), 240-241. doi: 10.1177/1942602x09348226

Somerville, D.C. (2013). Managing school nurse performance for success. In C.C. Costante (Ed.), *School nurse administrators: Leadership and management,* (pp. 231-255). Silver Spring, MD. National Association of School Nurses.

Chapter 7

CONSIDERATIONS WHEN DETERMINING SAFE SCHOOL NURSE STAFFING

Laurie G. Combe, MN, RN, NCSN

DESCRIPTION OF ISSUE

School nurse staffing models vary greatly in the United States. Some states provide a legal mandate for certified school nurses, while others do not. For states without a legal mandate for certified school nurses, staffing models range from all registered nurse (RN) staff, a blend of RN and licensed vocational/practical nurse (LVN/LPN) staff, RN and Unlicensed Assistive Personnel (UAP), LVN/LPN only staffing, to UAP only staffing (Mangena & Maughan, 2015; Sensor, 2007). Table 1 demonstrates results of the National Association of School Nurses (NASN) (2015) survey related to school nurse models of practice. These data do not take into account unlicensed personnel who function in a school clinic with no registered nurse or other medical supervision.

Table 1: School Nurse Staffing Models (Mangena & Maughan, 2015)

RN in 1 building	RN in greater than 1 building	RN supervises LPN in more than 1 building	RN oversees UAP/aide/clerk in greater than 1 building
51%	9%	5%	33%

Regardless of the staffing model selected by schools or school systems, student safety is always the primary concern. Policies and procedures that protect against inadequate staffing protect the student as well as the nursing staff charged with providing in-school health care (American Nurses Association [ANA], 2015).

BACKGROUND

Ratios of school nurses to students were originally recommended based on multiple federal mandates, including the Rehabilitation Act of 1973; Section 504 (2000); and Public Law 94-142, the Education for All Handicapped Children Act (1975) reauthorized in 2004 as the Individuals with Disabilities Education Improvement Act (IDEIA). These laws guarantee all students' access to a free and appropriate public education and the health services necessary for those students with complex health needs to access the educational process. Beginning in the 1970s, NASN (2015), the American Academy of Pediatrics (AAP) (2016), and Healthy People 2020 (U.S. Department of Health and Human Services [USDHHS], 2014) supported school nurse to student ratios of 1:750 for healthy children, 1:225 for students requiring daily nursing services, 1:125 for students with complex health needs, and 1:1 for students requiring continuous nursing services. Most recently, the Every Student Succeeds Act (ESSA) of 2015 cites school nurses as Specialized Instructional Support Personnel who are responsible for leading student chronic disease management.

When taking into account the complex health needs of students including 1) health co-morbidities, 2) the supports available in the communities where students live, learn and play, and 3) social determinants of health, such as economic, political and environmental factors (Combe et al., 2015; NASN, 2015; Schwab & Gelfman, 2001/2005), it is now evident that one school nurse's assignment to 750 students may present greater workload considerations than another school nurse's 750 student assignment. NASN (2015) recommends that school nurse staffing models take a multi-faceted, workload approach that considers student acuity; community needs assessment; and social determinants of health.

IMPLICATIONS FOR SCHOOL NURSE PRACTICE

For the purposes of this discussion, the term *school nurse(s)* will be used to designate both school nurses practicing on school campuses and school nurses with dedicated administrative duties. School nurses are expected to meet practice standards as set forth by federal education and disability laws, national professional nursing organizations, state Boards of Nursing (BON), and employer policy and procedure (Schwab & Gelfman, 2001/2005). School nurses serve as the bridge between health care and education, and encounter *"legal, policy, funding and supervisory issues that may also have ethical dimensions"* (NASN, 2016, para. 3). It is each nurse's professional and legal responsibility to be familiar with laws, standards and ethical considerations that impact their practice.

National Standards and Law

National standards of practice for school nurses are set forth in *School Nursing: Scope & Standards of Practice, 3rd ed.* (ANA & NASN, 2017), *Nursing Administration: Scope & Standards of Practice* (ANA, 2016), the *Code of Ethics for Nurses with Interpretative Statements* (ANA, 2015), *and the NASN Code of Ethics* (NASN, 2016). The aforementioned documents note the obligation of nurses to: 1) promote a culture of safety in their workplace; 2) advocate for the health and safety of patients; and 3) assign and accept only those responsibilities for which the nurse possesses skill, competence and workload capacity (ANA, 2015; ANA & NASN, 2017; ANA, 2016). These foundational documents establish that "the standard of care is what an ordinary prudent professional would provide under the same or similar circumstances" (Scott & Bubert, 2013, p. 214), and may be called into evidence during board of nursing or legal proceedings surrounding the delivery of school nursing care (National Council of State Boards of Nursing [NCSBN], 2007). Therefore, it is incumbent upon school nurses to familiarize themselves with the tenets of these documents and to use them as a guide for continuous improvement of nursing practice.

Equally important is that school nurses have an understanding of the impact that federal educational law, rules, and regulations have on school nurse practice. School nurses serve as advocates for student access to the education guaranteed by Section 504 of the Rehabilitation Act of 1973 and IDEIA (2004).

As such, school nurses are essential team members who serve several functions:

    1) identify and assess students for qualifying health status;

    2) develop Individualized Healthcare Plans (IHP) and Emergency Care Plans (ECP);

    3) recommend accommodations and services;

    4) inform the Individualized Education Plan/Programs (IEP) or Section 504 Plan;

    5) mitigate health related barriers to learning;

    6) train staff in management of the IHP;

    7) provide nursing care within the school setting;

    8) delegate nursing care within the school setting; and

9) evaluate effectiveness of IEP health components.

(Zirkel, Granthom, & Lovato, 2012; Gibbons, Lehr, & Selekman, 2013)

State Statutes and Nurse Practice Acts

Some state statutes afford sovereign immunity to public entities and their employees. This immunity protects public employees from liability, unless their actions "constitute gross negligence or are construed as willful or wanton" (Schwab & Gelfman, 2001/2005, p. 76). In *Spring Independent School District v. C. A. Hopkins (1987)* a parent brought suit against the school district and its employees when a student with cerebral palsy sustained a head injury after being pushed into a stack of chairs. Immediately following the incident, the student exhibited convulsions, sweating and incoherence. The teacher did not send the student to the school nurse. Later in the day, another employee brought the student to the school nurse, who returned the student to class without calling the parent. While on the bus ride home, the student experienced a convulsion. The bus driver requested a school nurse at the next stop, none was provided, and the driver was instructed to continue to the student's daycare. The parent claimed that as a result of the school's negligence the student's life expectancy was shortened. Based on the principle of sovereign immunity, the Texas court found the school district and its employees not liable for negligence.

Other state statues allow for discretionary function immunity, providing protection from liability for employees who act in good faith. A 1986 Illinois case found school district employees liable for willingly and wantonly delaying emergency treatment when a student sustained a head injury on the school playground (*Barth v. Board of Education*). In this case, a child sustained a head injury during a PE class head collision with a fellow student. The student

> Even though employed by a school district, school nurses can be held accountable and liable by Boards of Nursing and the courts for failure to act in accordance with standards of nursing practice (Lechtenberg, 2009).

exhibited pain, drowsiness and nausea as a result of the injury and was subsequently found to have an orange-sized subdural hematoma. The court found that although the school had called 911, they should have exercised the principle of *in loco parentis* and transported the student to the hospital directly across the street from the school when emergency medical services were delayed by 50 minutes. The school's failure to act swiftly in response to this injury resulted in the student's permanent disability. The concept of *in loco parentis* indicates that, when sending their children to school, parents confer to school personnel the power to discipline as well as the responsibility to protect the child (DeMitchell, n.d.).

All nursing practice within the United States is further guided by legal constructs delineated in individual state Nurse Practice Acts (NPA) and the associated Rules and Regulations set forth to interpret the NPA (NCSBN, 2016). While carrying equal weight under the law, NPAs and the Rules and Regulations authorize formation and composition of Boards of Nursing; protect nursing titles; set forth requirements for nursing education and licensure; outline nursing scope and standards of practice; define parameters for safe practice; and provide the grounds for violations, disciplinary action and remedies (Russell, 2012). School nurses' duty to their patients supersedes sovereign and discretionary function immunities; therefore, even though employed by a school district, school nurses can be held accountable and liable by Boards of Nursing and the civil courts for failure to act in accordance with standards of nursing practice (Lechtenberg, 2009).

Local School Policy

Quality school health program policies and procedures provide structure for school nursing activities, define expectations for quality practice, create a local standard of care for school communities, and provide legal protection for school systems and their employees (Costante, 2013).

> Adherence to employer policy is considered prudent as long as the policy does not supersede patient protections afforded by the state NPA (Schwab & Gelfman, 2001/2005).

Schluessler v. Independent School District (1989) found in favor of the plaintiffs (the student) in determining that school policy created a standard of care that the school nurse failed to follow. In this case, a student died of an asthma attack. The court found that the nurse was negligent for failure to properly assess the student's condition and summon emergency care. In conflict with district policy, the school nurse did not notify school administration or the parents that the student had used another student's inhaler.

In *Lunsford v. Board of Nurse Examiners* (1983), Nurse Lunsford, a nurse in a rural emergency room (ER), referred a man in acute cardiac distress to another hospital 24 miles away. The man suffered a fatal heart attack five miles from Nurse Lunsford's facility. Nurse Lunsford held that the ER physician, who had not examined the patient, directed her to refer the man elsewhere. The court found in favor of the BON to affirm that the nurse's first duty is to the patient and that this duty cannot be superseded by institutional policy or procedure.

Provision of Safe Student Care

It is well documented that advances in health care have contributed to the increasing number of children attending school with complex health needs. Ascertaining student health acuity is essential to determining appropriate models of staffing and school nurses must take into consideration whether a student requires:

- Continuous care provided by a RN or LPN;
- Daily intervention and/or monitoring by an RN for unstable health conditions; or
- Periodic monitoring for a stable & predictable health condition (Costante, 2013).

Nursing Delegation

As allowed by state law, the school nurse may decide that delegation to an UAP is a tool that can be utilized to meet student healthcare needs (NASN, 2014). The ANA (2012) defines delegation as "the transfer of responsibility for the performance of an activity to another with the former retaining accountability for the outcome" (p. 5). *School Nursing: Scope and Standards of Practice* (ANA & NASN, 2017) defines delegation as "the assignment of the performance of a nursing activity to a non-nurse. Accountability remains with the registered nurse; state laws and regulations must be followed; and standards of nursing practice must be upheld" (p. 88). While delegation of some nursing functions can extend the reach of the school nurse, the nurse must be cautious in their application of the delegation process, taking into consideration the Five Rights of Nursing Delegation as demonstrated in Table 2.

Table 2: Five Rights of Nursing Delegation

Delegation Principle	Delegation Considerations
1. Right Task	• Nursing process cannot be delegated, including nursing judgment, clinical reasoning, critical decision making • Within job description of UAP delegatee • Established written policies and procedures • Expectations and limits described
2. Right Circumstance	• Patient condition is stable and predictable • Changes in patient condition must be communicated to and reassessed by the nurse delegator
3. Right Person	• Patient specific training may not be transferred to another patient by the delegatee • The delegatee may not assign the nursing task to another UAP • Nurse delegator must ensure the skills, knowledge and competency of the delegatee
4. Right Direction & Communication	• Nurse delegator provides specific written and verbal instructions on necessary data collection surrounding the delegated task • Delegatee understands and accepts the delegation • Delegatee cannot modify nursing care provided without consultation of nurse delegator • Nurse delegator establishes clear written emergency action procedures, including actions to be taken when school nurse substitute is not available
5. Right Supervision & Evaluation	• Nurse delegator is available to the patient and delegatee within reasonable proximity (same building, close proximity, in-person, by phone) as determined by stability and predictability of the student's health • Nurse delegator provides periodic supervision of delegatee performance of assigned nursing tasks • Nurse delegator establishes processes to ensure accurate documentation. • Nurse delegator documents all steps of the delegation process

Local school policy and procedure must provide procedural guidance to school nurses and UAPs related to nursing delegation and unfilled school nurse absences. The UAP must have unlimited access to nurse consultation regarding delegated tasks. This may be accomplished through the use of onsite school nurses, school nurse administrators, experienced lead school nurses, or assignment of "buddy" campuses where school nurses share information about the health needs of their students. Regardless of the support system provided, clear lines of communication must be established and documented in a readily accessible format. When school nurses who provide care for students with the potential for emergency outcomes are absent and a nurse substitute cannot be secured, it is a prudent practice to contact the student's parent to make them aware of the lack of a school nurse for the duration of the uncovered absence. This critical communication allows the school nurse to collaborate with the parent to develop a plan for safe care at school during the school nurse absence. The Texas Board of Nursing (2013) provides guidance via the Delegation Resource Packet, including the document *Rule 225: Professional Nursing*

Assessment Grid and Case Examples

School systems and school nurses must exercise caution when assigning UAPs to perform nursing procedures. For example, in one case, an Oregon principal directed the UAP to perform clean, intermittent catheterization for a new student. The parent trained the UAP while the school nurse was present to answer questions. The school nurse did not provide written direction to the UAP, but did provide periodic supervision as directed by the school district. The court consulted the Oregon Board of Nursing (BON) to determine if the nursing procedure could be legally delegated to a UAP (_Mitts, C. v. Hillsboro Union High School District, 1987_). The BON found that in making the assignment of a nursing procedure to the UAP, the principal had practiced nursing without a license. The BON also disciplined the school nurse for accepting the principal's assignment and failing to comply with BON regulations related to delegation, including nursing assessment to determine the rightness of the delegation (Schwab & Gelfman, 2001/2005). _(Please see Chapter 4 for more information on delegation)._

Staffing Concerns

School nurses may encounter staffing situations that they consider unsafe or that do not align with their legally defined scope of practice. When school nurses accept an assignment, they are obligated to provide nursing care that aligns with the aforementioned standards (Singh, 2015). If confronted with unsafe staffing or scope of practice concerns, the school nurse must advocate for safe patient care, report unsafe staffing situations, and request assistance in writing (ANA, 2015; Schwab & Gelfman, 2001/2005). Scope of practice, staffing and other client safety concerns must be addressed directly and through appropriate organizational channels.

The Texas NPA (2013) and the Texas Administrative Code (TAC), Rule 217.20 (2012), allow a nurse who determines that an assignment is unsafe to declare _safe harbor_ and request Peer Review of the practice concern. A good faith declaration of _safe harbor_, made in writing before the nurse begins the assignment, provides the following protections to the nurse:

(1) may not be disciplined or discriminated against for making the request;

(2) may engage in the requested conduct pending the peer review;

(3) is not subject to the mandatory reporting requirement for unsafe practice; and

(4) may not be disciplined by the board for engaging in that conduct while the peer review is pending (TX NPA, 2013).

Safe harbor protection is unique to nurses in Texas (Zolnierek, 2012). In other states school nurses may be subject to employer discipline for failure to accept an assignment (Singh, 2015). These situations create ethical and professional dilemmas as the school nurse weighs duty to client, impacts on nursing licensure and future employment. If the school nurse is unable to secure the changes needed for a safe healthcare environment, the duty to resign may be the only resort (ANA, 2016; ANA, 2015). Resignation must be given with adequate notice in order for the school nurse to avoid a charge of abandonment. For example, the North Dakota BON defines abandonment as "accepting a patient assignment and then disengaging from that assignment without providing reasonable notice to a person responsible for securing a replacement" (2012, para. 1). Connecticut and Oregon also provide specific guidelines to assist nurses and their employers to determine if abandonment occurred (Connecticut Board of Examiners for Nurses, 2002). Nurses should consult their individual state NPA for determining actions that may constitute patient abandonment.

Civil and Criminal Liability

Primary causes of school nurse *civil liability* include:

- Failure to conduct a thorough nursing assessment;
- Failure to respond to emergency situations in an acceptable manner;
- Inadequate documentation of nursing care;
- Failure to keep up to-date records;
- Not abiding by district policy;
- Failure to work and perform safely; and
- Failure to inform parents about their child's condition (Nursing Schools, 2011).

Primary causes of school nurse *criminal liability* include:

- Stealing controlled drugs from the school;
- Having inappropriate contact with a child; or
- Practicing medicine without a license.

Criminal convictions may result in probation, incarceration and/or surrender of one's nursing license (Texas Administrative Code, 2012).

Job Assignment Not Congruent with Licensure

Schools may offer employment to registered nurses (RN) in jobs that are intended for LVN/LPN or UAP. Similarly, LVN/LPN may be offered jobs as UAP. While the state NPA requires the nurse to practice to the full extent of their licensure, the employer job description may limit the nurse's ability to function as a RN or an LVN/LPN. To fulfill the standard of the NPA may require the nurse to violate the standard as set forth by the employer, and vice versa (Schwab & Gelfman, 2001/2005). Nurses who practice under these circumstances receive compensation that is well below that expected for licensed nurses, and perpetuate employer expectation of a high level of care for less than adequate pay. Nurses in these situations should consult their state BON for guidance about use of their credentials in the documentation of care and exposure of the nurse's license to liability.

Addressing School Healthcare Concerns

Zolnierek (2012) holds that nurses are often the last healthcare providers to stand between safety and error. Clear, direct and specific communications between all stakeholders are essential to sustaining a culture of safety in schools. School nurses should follow the chain of command when communicating concerns about student safety. Depending on employer organizational structures, the school nurse's immediate chain of command may be an educational, medical or nursing administrator. School nurses must be cognizant of the fact that education and medical administrators may not have a full and clear understanding of nursing education preparation or the legal constraints of the NPA and its associated Rules and Regulations. Organizational policies and procedures should provide a structure through which nurses can express safety concerns without fear of retaliation, as well as a method to test proposed strategies for staffing improvement.

The **Situation, Background, Assessment, Response (SBAR)** model is one method of communication that provides a proactive process to address critical situations before error and inadequate care occur. SBAR allows presentation and discussion of problems and potential solutions in an objective, measured manner, thereby allowing all parties to seek solution (Safer Healthcare, 2016; Zolnierek, 2012). SBAR delivers concise communication with the goals of promoting collaborative relationships with key stakeholders and influencing policy decisions (Olson, 2016). Utilized to deliver information in a rapid manner, the SBAR method can serve to standardize communication, promote critical thinking by the nurse, increase collaboration, and enhance perception of the nurse's validity (Cornell, Townsend Gervis, Yates, & Vardaman, 2014). Table 3 demonstrates the steps of the SBAR communication model.

Table 3: SBAR Communication Model (Horgan, 2013)

Situation	Brief statement of the current concern
Background	Set the scene with a concise review of the current practice concern, including relevant student/situation data, historical data
Assessment	Statement of interpretation of situation and professional conclusions
Response	Offer recommendation(s) for resolution of the practice concern

When staffing concerns do not present a pressing safety issue for students or legal concern for the school nurse, the Plan-Do-Study-Act model, as demonstrated in Table 4, can be utilized to explore possible staffing improvements (U.S. Department of Health and Human Services: Agency for Healthcare Research and Quality, 2014).

Table 4: Plan-Do-Study-Act Model (USHHS: AHRQ, 2014; Institute for Healthcare Improvement, 2017)

Plan	Develop a plan to test a scenario and collect the data
Do	Pilot the plan on a small sample
Study	Analyze the data
Act	Create an action plan based on modifications identifies during the test.

School nurses must be proactive in developing and adopting formal procedures for addressing practice concerns related to staffing. These processes require training and case study testing so that school nurses are familiar with the process, have an opportunity to role play crisis communication with administrative stakeholders, and anticipate critical staffing situations that may arise. School nurse list serves, such as those provided by the National Association of School Nurses can help school nurses to identify and anticipate school nurse staffing practice issues (Lechtenberg, 2009).

CONCLUSION

Nursing codes of ethics, scope & standards of nursing practice, and state NPA outline nurses' professional responsibility to protect the safety of their patients. Because unsafe staffing conditions result in nursing error and ineffective care, it is incumbent upon the school nurse to advocate for improved staffing conditions via the established chain of command, institutional practices, and respective NPA statutes/rules (ANA, 2015; Zolneirek, 2012). School nurses must familiarize themselves with problem resolution models in order to facilitate rapid response in times of staffing crises.

School nurses are responsible to have a working knowledge of statutes, laws, rule, regulations, policies, standards and codes of ethics governing their practice and to keep abreast of changes to these documents. Continuous improvement of nursing skill and knowledge is essential to safe, competent care and is the responsibility of every school nurse.

RESOURCES

Legal References

Connecticut Board of Examiners for Nurses (2002). *Patient abandonment guidelines for APRN's, RN's, and LPN's.* Retrieved from http://www.ct.gov/dph/lib/dph/phho/nursing_board/guidelines/patient_aband.pdf

Education for All Handicapped Children Act of 1975, Pub. L. No. 94-142

Every Student Succeeds Act of 2015, Pub. L. No. 114-95 § 114 Stat.

Individuals with Disability Education Improvement Act (2004), 20 U.S.C. 1400 et seq.

Rehabilitation Act of 1973, 29 U.S.C. § 504.

Texas Administrative Code, Title 22, Part 11, Chapter 217, Rule § 217.20. (2012). *Safe harbor peer review for nurses and whistleblower protections.* Retrieved from http://www.bon.texas.gov/rr_current/217-20.asp

Texas Board of Nursing (2013). *Nurse practice act, nursing peer review, & licensure compact Texas occupations code and statutes regulating the practice of nursing.* Retrieved from http://www.statutes.legis. state.tx.us/Docs/OC/htm/OC.301.htm

Case Law

Barth v. Board of Education, 490 N.E. 2d 77 (Ill. App. 1 Dist. 1986)

Lunsford v. Board of Nurse Examiners, 648 S.W. 2d 391 (Tex. App.--Austin, 1983)

Mitts, Carol v. Hillsboro Union High School District No. 3, et al., Washington County Circuit Court, Case No. 87-1142C. (1990)

Schluessler v. Independent School District No. 200 et al. (April 27, 1989), Dakota County District Court Case No. NM89-14V.

Spring Independent School District v. C. A. Hopkins, 736 S.W.2d 617 (Texas 1987)

Other Resources

American Academy of Pediatrics (AAP). (2016). *The role of the school nurse.* 137(6), 34-39. *doi.org/10.1542/peds.2016-0852*

National Association of School Nurses. (2014). *Nursing delegation to unlicensed assistive personnel in the school setting* (Position Statement). Silver Spring, MD: Author.

National Association of School Nurses. (2015). *School nurse workload: Staffing for safe care* (Position Statement). Silver Spring, MD: Author.

REFERENCES

American Academy of Pediatrics. (2016). The role of the school nurse. *Pediatrics, 137*(6), 34-39. *doi.org/10.1542/peds.2016-0852*

American Nurses Association. (2012). *Principles of delegation.* Silver Spring, MD: nursebooks.org.

American Nurses Association. (2015). *Code of ethics for nurses with interpretative statements.* Silver Spring, MD: Nursesbooks.org.

American Nurses Association. (2016). *Nursing administration: Scope and standards of practice.* Silver Spring, MD: Nursesbooks.org.

American Nurses Association & National Association of School Nurses. (2017). *School nursing: Scope and standards of practice (3rd ed.).* Silver Spring, MD: Author.

American Nurses Association & the National Council of State Boards of Nursing. (2006). *Joint statement on delegation.* Retrieved from https://www.ncsbn.org/Delegation_joint_statement_NCSBN-ANA.pdf

Barth v. Board of Education, 490 N.E. 2d 77 (Ill. App. 1 Dist. 1986)

Combe, L. G., Bachman, M. B., Dolatowski, R., Endsley, P. E., Hassey, K., Maughan, E., Minchella, L., Shanks, B., Trefry, S. & Zeno, E. (2015). School nurse workload: Students are more than just numbers. *NASN School Nurse, 30*(5), 283-288. doi: 10.1177/1942602X15596582

Connecticut Board of Examiners for Nurses (2002). *Patient abandonment guidelines for APRN's, RN's, and LPN's.* Retrieved from http://www.ct.gov/dph/lib/dph/phho/nursing_board/guidelines/patient_aband.pdf

Cornell, P., Townsend Gervis, M., Yates, L., & Vardaman, J. M. (2014). Impact of SBAR on nurse shift reports and staff rounding. *MEDSURG Nursing, 23(5), 334-342.*

Costante, C. C. (Ed.). (2013). *School nurse administrators: Leadership and management.* Silver Spring, MD: National Association of School Nurses.

DeMitchell, T. A. (n.d.). Education law: In loco parentis. Retrieved from http://usedulaw.com/345-in-loco-parentis.html

Every Student Succeeds Act of 2015, Pub. L. No. 114-95 § 114 Stat.

Gibbons, L. J., Lehr, K., & Selekman, J. (2013). Federal laws protecting children and youth with disabilities in the schools. In J. Selekman (Ed.), *School nursing: A comprehensive text* (2nd ed.) (pp. 257-283). Philadelphia, PA: F. A. Davis & Co.

Horgan, M. (2013). *Communication is key.* World of Irish Nursing & Midwifery, 21(1), 46-47. Retrieved from https://www.inmo.ie/tempDocs/ISBAR_PAGE46-47%20feb13.pdf

Individuals with Disability Education Improvement Act (2004), 20 U.S.C. 1400 et seq.

Institute for Healthcare Improvement. (2017). *How to improve: Science of improvement-testing change.* http://www.ihi.org/resources/Pages/HowtoImprove/ScienceofImprovementTestingChanges.aspx

Lechtenberg, J. (2009). Legal aspects of school nursing. *School Health Alert.* Retrieved from http://www.schoolnurse.com/public/images/Legal%20Aspects%20of%20School%20Nursing%2004-2009.pdf

Lunsford v. Board of Nurse Examiners, 648 S.W. 2d 391 (Tex. App.--Austin, 1983)

Mangena, A. S. & Maughan, E. D. (2015). The 2015 NASN school nurse survey: Developing and providing leadership to advance school nursing practice. *NASN School Nurse, 30*(6), 328-335. doi: 10.1177/1942602X15608183

Mitts, Carol v. Hillsboro Union High School District No. 3, et al., Washington County Circuit Court, Case No. 87-1142C. (1990)

National Association of School Nurses. (2014). *Nursing delegation to unlicensed assistive personnel in the school setting* (Position Statement). Silver Spring, MD: Author. Retrieved from https://schoolnursenet.nasn.org/blogs/nasn-profile/2017/03/13/unlicensed-assistive-personnel-their-role-on-the-school-health-services-team

National Association of School Nurses. (2015). *School nurse workload: Staffing for safe care* (Position Statement). Silver Spring, MD: Author. Retrieved from https://schoolnursenet.nasn.org/blogs/nasn-profile/2017/03/13/school-nurse-workload-staffing-for-safe-care

National Association of School Nurses. (2016). *Code of ethics.* Silver Spring, MD: Author. Retrieved from http://www.nasn.org/RoleCareer/CodeofEthics

National Council of State Boards of Nursing. (2007). *Guiding principles of nursing regulation.* Retrieved from https://www.ncsbn.org/Guiding_Principles.pdf

National Council of State Boards of Nursing. (2016). National guidelines for nursing delegation. *Journal of Nursing Regulation, 7*(1). Retrieved from https://www.ncsbn.org/1625.htm

North Dakota Board of Nursing. (2012). *Abandonment* (Practice Statement). Retrieved from
https://www.ndbon.org/RegulationsPractice/PracticeStatements/Abandonment.asp

Olson, K. (2016). Influence through policy: four steps you can take. *Reflections on Nursing Leadership, 42(2),*
1-3. Retrieved from http://www.reflectionsonnursingleadership.org/pages/Vol42_2_Olson_Policy.aspx

Rehabilitation Act of 1973, 29 U.S.C. § 504

Russell, K. A. (2012). Nurse practice acts guide and govern nursing practice. *Journal of Nursing Regulation,*
3(3), 36-40. Retrieved from https://www.ncsbn.org/2012_JNR_NPA_Guide.pdf

Safer Healthcare. (2016). *Why is SBAR communication so critical?* Retrieved from
http://www.saferhealthcare.com/sbar/what-is-sbar/

Schluessler v. Independent School District No. 200 et al. (April 27, 1989), Dakota County District Court Case
No. NM89-14V.

Schwab, N.C. & Gelfman, M.H.B. (Eds.). (2001). *Legal issues in school health services.* Sunrise River Press.
North Branch MN.

Scott, L. R. & Bubert, J. S. (2013). Legal issues related to school nursing practice: The foundation. In J.
Selekman (Ed.), *School nursing: A comprehensive text* (2nd ed.) (pp. 196-224). Philadelphia, PA: F. A. Davis
& Co.

Sensor, C. S. (2007). School nursing: Managing a small city. *NSNA imprint.* Retrieved from
http://www.nsna.org/Portals/0/Skins/NSNA/pdf/Imprint_Jan07_SchoolNurse.pdf

Singh, T. L. (2015). Avoid malpractice & protect your license: The truth about refusing unsafe assignments &
patient abandonment. *Nevada RNformation*, 24(3), 10-11. Retrieved from http://www.nursingald.com/
articles/13782-unsafe-patient-assignments-a-professional-dilemma

Spring Independent School District v. C. A. Hopkins, 736 S.W.2d 617 (Texas 1987)

Texas Administrative Code, Title 22, Part 11, Chapter 217, Rule § 217.20. (2012). *Safe harbor peer review for*
nurses and whistleblower protections. Retrieved from http://www.bon.texas.gov/rr_current/217-20.asp

Texas Board of Nursing. (2013). *Nurse practice act, nursing peer review, & licensure compact Texas*
occupations code and statutes regulating the practice of nursing. Retrieved from
http://www.statutes.legis.state.tx.us/Docs/OC/htm/OC.301.htm

Texas Board of Nursing. (2013). *Rule 225: Professional nursing assessment grid and case examples*. Retrieved
from http://www.bon.state.tx.us/pdfs/delegation_pdfs/225grid2.pdf

U.S. Department of Health and Human Services. (2014). *Healthy People 2020, educational and community-*
based programs. Retrieved from http://healthypeople.gov/2020/topicsobjectives2020/objectiveslist.
aspx?topicId=11

U.S. Department of Health and Human Services: Agency for Healthcare Research and Quality. (2013). *Plan-do-study-act (PDSA) cycle.* https://innovations.ahrq.gov/qualitytools/plan-do-study-act-pdsa-cycle

Zirkel, P. A., Granthom. M. F., & Lovato, L. (2012). Section 504 and student health problems: The pivotal role of the school nurse. *The Journal of School Nursing, 28*(6), 423-432. doi: 10.1177/1059840512449358

Zolnierek, C. (2012). Speak to be heard: Effective nurse advocacy. *American Nurse Today, 7*(10). Retrieved from https://www.americannursetoday.com/speak-to-be-heard-effective-nurse-advocacy/

Chapter 8

RESEARCH IN SCHOOL HEALTH

Ingrid Hopkins Duva, PhD, RN

DESCRIPTION OF ISSUE

The school setting offers a ripe opportunity for health research. School health covers a myriad of issues, the services and scope of school health is rapidly increasing, and students in schools represent a significant cross section of our nation. Nurses are uniquely positioned at the crux of this intersection between school services and health research. The nurse's role in research may have many different variations, and all are important. School nurses are in an ideal position to lead their own investigations, collaborate with other researchers and facilitate the management of research studies, or even be the participant in studies led by others, such as public health researchers. At the very least, school nurses are accountable for evidence-based practice and therefore should be able to access research findings and translate those findings into practice.

Legal issues arising from the conduct, participation in, or use of research by nurses in schools are rare. If documented disputes exist, the legal cases are difficult to locate, much less to interpret. However, the school setting is subject to both the federal regulations governing ethical research and the safe treatment of children in an educational, or school setting. Understanding how these regulations affect informed consent, privacy, and parental oversight is a must for the nurse involved in research in this setting. The school, as a research setting, is complex but can be navigated. This chapter provides a review of the basic legal obligations that accompany research to enhance the school nurse's ability to protect those in their care and at the same time to contribute more fully to the future health and wellness of this population.

BACKGROUND

Ethical conduct is a consideration for all types of research experiments or studies, just as it is in any type of nursing practice. Ethical considerations in the conduct of school health research meet a high standard of obligations, particularly if the research involves students as participants. Basic human subjects' protection is required. According to the U.S. Department of Health and Human Services (USDHHS) regulations at 45 CFR 46, students are considered a vulnerable population if they are under the age of 18 (Protection of Human Subjects, 2009). Students are also vulnerable because a school is considered an institutional setting, so their participation in research may be influenced by authority figures (National Institute of Health [NIH], 2009). Legal guidelines exist so that at least minimal ethical standards of behavior are upheld. At minimum, these essential protections assure autonomous decision-making (respect for persons), beneficence, and justice for all research participants (USDHSS, 1979).

Current legal protections for research participants arose from decidedly poor ethical conduct by researchers dating back to the early 20th century. The Nuremberg war crime trials in Germany (1945-1947) judged physicians and scientists unethical conduct. Biomedical experiments on concentration camp prisoners included various tests of human endurance, fully expecting that death and disability may be the outcome for the participants. These inhumane acts led to the Nuremberg Code, providing international and national guidelines for the ethical treatment of research subjects (Houser, 2012). The Nuremberg Code was the prototype for current legal protections in the form of specific informed consent requirements to participate in research experiments (USDHHS, 1979).

The Tuskegee Study began in 1932 to follow the natural disease progression of syphilis. Participants in this study were not fully informed of their diagnoses or the intent of the study. This study continued until 1972. As a result, new treatments for syphilis were withheld for approximately 400 black men participating in the study (Houser, 2012). Soon after the conclusion of this study, the federal government commissioned a report to outline the basic ethical principles and to provide guidance for research involving human subjects. Referred to as the Belmont Report (named after the conference center hosting the majority of the meetings deliberating this issue), it outlines the basic ethical principles of autonomy, beneficence and justice. The Belmont report was published in the Federal Register on April 18, 1979 and was meant to serve as a guide for resolving ethical problems associated with research involving human subjects (USDHHS, 1979).

Unfortunately, ethical violations in research are not limited to historical cases. Examples of more recent ethical transgressions can easily be found with a quick scan through the ethics chapter of a current nursing research textbook. To address ongoing concern that all biomedical or behavioral research studies involving human subjects meet legal and ethical requirements, institutions that conduct or host research are required to have a human subjects review committee (also referred to as an Institutional Review Board [IRB]) approve and monitor research activities (Protection of Human Subjects, 2009). Proposed research must be submitted to the institution's IRB (for public schools, research approval occurs most likely at the district level) and /or the partnering academic research institution's IRB, prior to initiation of the study. This process is in place to further promote ethical compliance, functioning as another layer of oversight for the ethical conduct of studies. Informed consent and IRB approval are legal protections for research supported or conducted by a Federal Department or Agency in any way (e.g. all public schools meet this requirement, unless the research meets one of the exemptions outlined in the regulations, such as de-identified educational testing data). These same principles of protection should still be applied in school research regardless of whether a formal approval process is in place.

Further federal guidelines exist to protect the civil rights of students in public education settings. In depth discussion of those laws and statutes go beyond the scope of this chapter, but a cursory introduction helps frame the context for the additional complexities and nuances unique to research in the school setting. First, the Family Educational Rights & Privacy Act (FERPA) protects the rights and privacy of student information and education records (FERPA, 1974). FERPA applies to all schools that receive federal funds under an applicable program of the U.S. Department of Education. FERPA is similar to the Healthcare Insurance Portability and Accountability Act (HIPAA) passed in 1996, which addresses the documentation, sharing, and privacy of health information (HIPAA, 1996). Only persons with a legitimate interest should access student information, whether health or education information, and this access should be documented (FERPA, 2012, HIPAA, 1996). Additionally, the Protection of Pupils Rights Act (PPRA) may also be relevant to research (PPRA, 2001). This law allows for parents to preview student education materials (in eight specific areas noted later in this chapter), and may be interpreted to mean that any survey instruments, interviews, or assessments in these specific areas included in a study should be accessible to the parents. Because parents typically need to provide informed consent (discussed in more detail below) for children 18 years of age or under, compliance with PPRA may be accomplished through the informed consent process. However, the researcher should recognize these as two separate and distinct requirements.

Private schools generally do not fall under these same legal obligations, unless it is a federally funded research project. Still, the school nurse in the private setting should also assure appropriate school approvals are obtained and student protections are in place. Typically, approval processes that must be executed by the school board or authorized administration would be outlined in the school's policies or operational regulations. A student/parent (guardian) handbook, or similar documentation, expresses these as a contract between the school and the students and governs what student information is shared with parents/guardians.

IMPLICATIONS FOR SCHOOL NURSE PRACTICE

To date the research conducted on the practice of school nursing is minimal (Krause-Parello, 2013). School nurses initiating a research question and leading a formal study in the school setting is also lacking (Fleming, 2013). Still, there are knowledge gaps to fill, and so the likelihood that the school nurse will become more involved in research is high. Several factors contribute to this projection. To name a few; the healthcare environment is changing so more health care responsibilities fall on the school as a community provider and health system safety net (National Association of School Nurses [NASN], 2015); the characteristics of students are changing; up to 25% have a documented chronic illness requiring more services (Halfon & Newacheck, 2010); and the Every Student Succeeds Act (ESSA) encourages funding toward support roles, such as nurses, to create healthier school environments for greater student success (ESSA, 2016). Finally, as the breadth of services provided by school nurses increases, so does the need for the most current, reliable data from high quality research to guide school nurses in every day clinical decision making, care planning, and best practice care.

Research Determination

According to the National Association of School Nurses (NASN, 2016), "School nurses utilize research data as they advocate and illustrate the impact of their role on meaningful health and academic outcomes. Formal school nursing research is needed to ensure that delivery of care to students and school communities by the school nurse is based on current evidence" (NASN, 2016, p.49). Differentiating informal and formal research is important. The **first step** to determining any legal obligations related to a research study and use of data is to determine whether a study is really formal research. Systematic inquiry using disciplined methods to answer questions or solve problems is the scientific method, or research. But, what distinguishes formal research is the purpose: to generate new or validate existing knowledge (Grove, Burns, & Gray, 2013). For example, data collected during the routine examination of a student to improve the process of providing daily health services locally to group of students does not qualify, necessarily, as formal research (Fleming, 2013). This data obtained during the course of practice can and should be used to improve practice. Investigation into published research findings and improved outcomes, if applicable to the local context, can and should be implemented. However, even if these activities were approached in a systematic manner, they may not be considered formal research if the conclusions are not intended to be generalized or applied universally. The purpose of a study, therefore, is critical to establishing the necessary threshold for applying the legal research considerations discussed here. This poses a learning curve for most nurses. Partnering with experts i.e. health scientists or nurses with PhDs from local hospitals, health or universities will benefit the process.

Differentiating research used for quality improvement in individual practice from formal research, which is intended for broader application is a first step to understanding legal obligations.

Practice example:

> *A survey collecting information on dietary habits within the school setting may not meet the research threshold: If the intent of the study is to improve internal school process (such as self-serve lunch lines), it may directly benefit the survey participant (improved food choices), and the results are only planned to be shared locally (within the school itself or with district administrators). This survey could be part of an improvement initiative, not a formal research study.*
>
> *Alternately, a survey collecting information on dietary habits within the school setting (either provided alone or as part of a larger or more comprehensive study) could be could meet the research threshold: If the intent of the study is to gain knowledge, knowledge gained will not benefit the participating student, and the results of the study will be shared with a broad audience, the basic legal obligations accompanying research may apply.*

Institutional Review Board (IRB)

The **second step** for the school nurse is to contact the local IRB or obtain a copy of the research protocol with IRB approval. Most research studies in schools, unless strictly limited to unidentifiable data, will fall under the category of human subjects' research. The IRB is comprised of a group of individuals charged with protecting the rights, safety and welfare of these human subjects. This group provides an added layer of oversight to "human subjects" research, assuring on-going safety for all participants (Protection of Human Subjects, 2009). The IRB stamp of approval is a requirement for funding agents of research studies. Larger school districts may have their own IRB in place and a policy directing the researcher through an approval process with the school district and/ or collaborating academic institution. Smaller or independent schools may rely on collaborating organizations to provide an IRB. When no IRB is available because a study is small, unfunded, or not sponsored by the federal government, there should be a local research review process in place to assure the appropriate ethical considerations. Nurses conducting studies will submit their proposal directly to the applicable review process or oversight committee. School nurses working solely as collaborators or data collectors of a study (conducted by a person or entity within or outside of the school district) should ask to have a copy of the study's protocol and documentation of IRB approval. Documentation of approval should be easily identified on any research study announcements and consent forms.

Informed Consent Requirements

Most research studies in schools, unless strictly limited to unidentifiable data, will fall under the category of human subjects and require informed consent. Through the human subjects review process, the IRB will determine the type and extent of consent required from research participants. There can be exceptions to the informed consent requirement, particularly in educational settings. For example, research involving normal education practices or the use of standard educational test scores may not need documented consent. In some of these cases the study will be exempt from the requirement or the consent requirement will be waived. There are also instances where a waiver of a documented consent may be appropriate. For some research studies an implied consent may be justified, meaning that after becoming informed, participation is sufficient to indicate agreement on the part of the participant. For example, an implied consent process may be approved if obtaining documented consent will present a barrier to student participation (therefore limiting the benefit of the research to a certain population of students). This need for implied consent has been documented by investigators, particularly in alternative school environments that may have more transient students or less contact with parents and guardians (Johnson, Morris, Rew & Simonton, 2016). Keep in mind that the decision to waive consent for a research study is not up to the individual investigator, that an implied consent maintains the requirement to meet the basic elements of informed consent, and for either an exemption or a waiver, documentation of the approval will need to be on record.

Formal research studies requiring student participation will likely be categorized as research including children. Children are a special class of research participants, with unique considerations and protections. For the purposes of human subjects research, regulation defines children as "persons who have not attained the legal age for consent to treatment or procedures involved in the research, under the applicable law of the jurisdiction in which the research will be conducted "(Protection of Human Subjects, 2009, 45 CFR 46.402(a)). The age determination for adulthood may vary in some states or locales, or depending on medical treatment under consideration, but typically is 18 years or older. The most recent NIH update, effective in January 2016, classified children as ages 18 or younger (NIH, 2016). The process for consenting students, particularly those who are children, may have the most implications for a collaborating school nurse. For a child to participate in research, one or more parent/ guardian(s) must consent. Additionally, for the school-age child who is capable, assent is required. This means that the child must also be informed of the basic elements of consent and agree to participate in the research. Cases in which a child would typically not be required to agree to research include those where the risk is minimal, or where there may be a direct personal benefit to the child. Need for this documented agreement from the child is determined based on a sliding scale, weighing the risk (harm, discomfort, or threat to well-being) of participating against the benefit that may be experienced. Again, the need for documented consent and/ or student assent is governed by federal regulation and approved locally by the IRB.

Practice example:

> *Consider again the dietary survey. If deemed research by the IRB informed consent will be required. However, if the risk of participation is low, and/or requiring signed/witnessed consent may limit participation, then consent may be implied through the students' voluntary participation. Study participants are informed of the study purpose, risks and how to withdraw participation and this process is documented.*
>
> *In other cases, such as a study with an intervention or a survey that might impose some determined risk to a participant, the informed consent process will be documented and each participant's consent will be required in writing. In the school setting, this means that students may need to document assent, and the parent/legal guardian would sign consent. This process is documented and approved by the IRB or local research review authorities. Informed consent is required to meet human subject research requirements.*

Privacy and Confidentiality

Participating in a research study should not compromise student privacy rights. Therefore, organization of documents pertaining to any ongoing or recently concluded research study is another important step to consider. Storing sensitive data, and the study documents that include this data, must be addressed. These plans are included in the study protocol, which is submitted with the research proposal for IRB for approval. Any forms and data collected from study participants must be kept locked or safeguarded when not in use. Electronic data should be encrypted and stored in a password-protected file.

Students' educational and health information is confidential. Only those school staff with a job-related purpose should have access to those documents, either educational or health data. For example, a school nurse (regardless of the employer) would need parental (for minors) and school permission to use test score or healthcare data.

Diligent access logs need to be kept. Even the approved school staff persons, who access documentation, or raw data, need to log their access including their name, title, date and need to know (Magnushealth, 2016). When school staff access a student's health or education data, because of their need to know, their legal access is still limited to just that portion of information or data that applies. Student data may not be shared outside of the "need to know" without prior approval, informed consent, and, if applicable, an approved data use or data sharing agreement (FERPA, 2012).

Surveys, Instruments or Assessments

The Protection of Pupils Rights Act (PPRA) found at 20 U.S.C.A. § 1232h contains an inspection and consent requirement of instructional materials. Again, this federal statute applies to any educational institution receiving federal funds. It may implicate student health studies using surveys or educational material and adds another layer of legal oversight, unique to research in student health settings. Under the Act, all instructional materials, in the eight categories below, used in conjunction with any survey, evaluation or analysis as part of any applicable program must be made available for inspection by the minor's parent or guardian (20 U.S.C.A. 1232h(a)). The Act then goes further and mandates an additional informed consent requirement on eight categories of sensitive information (20 U.S.C.A. 1232h(b)). Those categories are:

1. Political affiliations or beliefs of the student or the student's parent;
2. Mental or psychological problems of the student or the student's family;
3. Sex behavior or attitudes;
4. Illegal, anti-social, self-incriminating, or demeaning behavior;
5. Critical appraisals of other individuals with whom respondents have close family relationships;
6. Legally recognized privileged or analogous relationships, such as those of lawyers, physicians, and ministers;
7. Religious practices, affiliations, or beliefs of the student or student's parent; or
8. Income (other than that required by law to determine eligibility for participation in a program or for receiving financial assistance under such program).

Any survey, evaluation, or analysis of any information covered by these eight categories requires informed parental consent, not just the right to inspect the actual material. Without the informed parental consent, the minor student is not required to submit to any analysis, evaluation or survey covering any material involving information dealing with these eight categories.

The Act includes a list of policies that must be set forth by the local educational agency to protect student privacy, parental access to information and physical examinations. If the state or local educational agency had policies that meet the Act's specifications in place as of January 8, 2002, then the agency simply needs to provide parents with notification of these policies in accord with the notification provision contained in the statute.

Importantly, the Act does not provide a private cause of action for individuals who feel that their rights under the Act have been violated. That means that an individual cannot use the Act itself as a tool to sue the entity or individual who violates the Act. The federal government enforces compliance with the Act, and the Act itself expressly states that in order for assistance under the Act to be terminated there must be a finding that there was a failure to comply with the Act and that compliance cannot be gained through voluntary means. Assuming that the violating agency simply agrees to comply, it is therefore unlikely that an enforcement action could do any real harm to the local or state agency (the school or school nurse). Just the same, compliance with the Act is an important piece of properly administered school based research. Therefore, in addition to assuring IRB approval, the school nurse should confirm the district policy and that it complies with the PPRA.

Practice example:

> *Under PPRA, the survey regarding dietary habits within the school setting intended to improve internal school process, could require parent notification even though it does not serve the purpose of education or research. Parent notification letters offer the parent or legal guardian an opportunity to take action with a written statement to "opt –out" their student, with no justification and assure no ramifications to the student.*
>
> *Likewise, a student survey about daily dietary habits within the school setting provided as part of a comprehensive research study on student performance may require that the school notify parents/ legal guardians of their right to request prior viewing of any invitation to participate, survey instruments being used or other accompanying information given to the student related to the study.*

> *The Center for Disease Control's "Youth Risk Behavior Surveillance" is an example of a survey high school students complete that includes questions about their diet, but is part of a comprehensive study. According to the CDC (2016), their own IRB approved the protocol for the national survey, but local parental permission procedures were followed (UDHHS/CDC, 2016). This implies that, because there is sensitive information collected, not only were parent notification letters sent to all students asked to complete this survey but informed consent was needed. The local IRB or research board may have approved an implied consent because student participation in the survey is voluntary and anonymous. The school nurse can and should access the locally approved protocol prior to administration of the survey and assure compliance with parent permission procedures prior to initiation of data collection.*

CONCLUSION

The scope of nursing research in a public education setting has not been extensively discussed in our courts. Limitations on the number of student participants, the appropriate level of consent, the types of studies that can or cannot be conducted, or even the length of studies, has not spawned enough litigation to give us any clear guidance on these issues. In order to conduct or facilitate a legally "compliant" formal research study, the school nurse must therefore abide by basic research principles of informed consent, protection of private health and academic information, and any other fundamental research controls. In order to use any data to improve individual practice or student outcomes, the school nurse needs to abide by all applicable guidelines to protect student privacy, confidentiality and, if sensitive information is involved, appropriate informed consent. In order to conduct or facilitate a legally "compliant" formal research study, the school nurse will need IRB approval and further follow basic research principles of informed consent, protection of private health and academic information, and any other fundamental research controls. While school nurses may have a qualified immunity for discretionary actions taken in the course and scope of their nursing care duties, the law is less clear on what liability protection a school nurse may have in the context of conducting or facilitating a research study, particularly an unauthorized or non-consented study.

Therefore, before the study begins, the school nurse should make sure the school district has not only authorized the study but has also agreed to indemnify and hold harmless the research team from and against any lawsuits, claims or damage demands that arise out of the performance of the study. The nurse should make absolutely certain that the research team is covered by insurance as an additional insured under the insurance policy issued to the school district not only for any school related medical care being provided but also for any claims arising out of the research study itself. In most instances, this insurance coverage is handled through the school's legal department and is documented via a contract between the school and the collaborating research institutions.

In summary, the general legal considerations for the school nurse involved in research are:

1. Determination of the research as formal research.
2. In the private setting, just as in the public setting, the school nurse will need to investigate applicable school policies before initiating, or participating in any way, in the conduct of research.
3. Obtain a copy of the research proposal; including a protocol for participant recruitment, consent and document/ data management and dissemination plan with IRB approval documented.
4. Knowledge of the proper consenting procedures, assuring necessary parental notifications.
5. Depending on the age of the research subjects and the nature of the study, the school nurse may be responsible for obtaining assent from the subjects themselves (even though as minors they cannot give informed consent).
6. Protection of student confidentiality and privacy by securing student data and meeting all school health documentation rules.
7. Compliance with any data management, storage or sharing plan including all study materials and documentation after conclusion of the study.

Also, see Table 1.

Table 1

Legal Consideration	Resource
Determination of formal research	Expert consultation e.g. Doctoral prepared RNs or Health Services Researchers
Protection of Human Subjects	Collaborating institution IRB. Local school, district, university or state IRB regarding protocol approval.
Compliance with federal regulations governing the school's protection of students.	The local school, district and state policies and administrative team.
Compliance with private school rules, regulations and parent contracts.	Private school policies, administration and governing board.
Respect for students and consideration for equal, representative access to study participation.	Collaborating institution IRB. Local school, district, university or state IRB regarding consent/assent procedures.
Privacy and confidentiality for students (including documentation management).	Collaborating institution IRB. Local school, district, university or state IRB regarding consent procedures. The local school, district and state policies and administrative team

RESOURCES

Mosca, N.W. (2007). Research tidbits: When research involves human subjects: The institutional review board. *NASN Newsletter, 22*(2), 8-9.

National Association of School Nurses. Research agenda and research grants. https://www.nasn.org/Research/ResearchPrioritiesforSchoolNursing

National Institutes of Health (NIH). *Research involving human subjects*. https://humansubjects.nih.gov

National Institute of Nursing Research (NINR). Grant development and management resources. https://www.ninr.nih.gov/researchandfunding

National Research Act, Pub. Law 93-348 (1974).

U.S. Department of Health and Human Services (HHS). Office for human research protections. http://www.hhs.gov/ohrp/regulations-and-policy/guidance/faq/children-research/index.html

REFERENCES

Every Student Succeeds Act of 2015, Pub. L. No. 114-95 § 114 Stat. 1177 (2015-2016).

Family Educational Rights and Privacy Act, 20 U.S.C. § 1232g; 34 CFR Part 99 (1974).

Fleming, R. (2013). Demystifying the differences in using data to improve individual practice versus publishing research findings. *School Nurse, 28*(5), 237-238. doi: 10.1177/1942602X13494847

Grove, S.K., Burns, N., & Gray, J. (2013). *The practice of nursing research: Appraisal, synthesis, and generation of evidence* (7th ed). St. Louis, MO. Saunders Elsevier.

Halfon, N., & Newacheck, P. (2010). Evolving notions of childhood chronic illness. *Journal of The American Medical Association, 303*(7), 665-666. doi:10.1001/jama.2010.130

Health Insurance Portability and Accountability Act, P.L. No 104-191, 110 Stat. 1938 (1996).

Houser, J. (2012). *Nursing research: Reading, using and creating evidence*. Sudbury, MA: Jones & Bartlett Learning.

Johnson, K.E., Morris, M., Rew, L., & Simonton, A.J. (2016). A systematic review of consent procedures, participation rates, and main findings of health-related research in alternative high schools from 2010 to 2015. *The Journal of School Nursing 32*(1), 20-31.

Krause-Parello, C.A. (2013). An overview of nursing research and relevance to school nursing practice. *NASN School Nurse, 28*(6), 294-296. doi: 10.1177/1942602X13502675

National Association of School Nurses. (2015). *The Patient Protection and Affordable Care Act: The role of the school nurse* (Position Statement). Silver Spring, MD: Author.

National Association of School Nurses (2016). Framework for 21st century school nursing practice. *NASN School Nurse, 31*(1), 45-53. doi: 10.1177/1942602X15618644

National Institutes of Health (2016). *NIH Policy and Guidelines on the Inclusion of Children as Participants in Research Involving Human Subjects* (NOT-OD-16-010). Retrieved from https://grants.nih.gov/grants/funding/children/children.htm

Protection of Human Subjects, 45 CFR § 46 (2009). Retrieved from https://www.hhs.gov/ohrp/regulations-and-policy/regulations/45-cfr-46/index.html

Protection of Pupils Rights Act, 20 U.S.C.A. § 1232h (1978, 2001). Retrieved from https://www.gpo.gov/fdsys/granule/USCODE-2010-title20/USCODE-2010-title20-chap31-subchapIII-part4-sec1232h/content-detail.html

U.S. Department of Health and Human Services/ Centers for Disease Control and Prevention (2016). Youth risk behavior surveillance- United States, 2015. *Morbidity and Mortality Weekly Report*. 65 (6), 1-175. doi: http://dx.doi.org/10.15585/mmwr.ss6506a1

U.S. Department of Health and Human Services, Office for Human Research Protections. (1979). National
Commission for the Protection of Human Subjects of Biomedical and Behavioral Research. *The Belmont
Report: Ethical Principles and Guidelines for the Protection of Human Subjects of Research*. Retrieved
from https://www.hhs.gov/ohrp/regulations-and-policy/belmont-report/index.html

Chapter 9

SCHOOL HEALTH DOCUMENTATION AND IMPLICATIONS FOR DATA COLLECTION

Kathleen H. Johnson, DNP, RN, NCSN, FNASN

DESCRIPTION OF ISSUE

Documentation of the health care provided in the school setting is essential for the communication of the safe, effective care of students, continuity across the care continuum, and the student's school career, as well as the legal protection of the nurse and the school district. Aggregated data developed from nursing documentation has the power to develop evidence for practice, create effective policy, and drive quality of care. The following describes guidance on elements of documentation, documentation formats, quality standards, and reporting of school health data.

Wang, Hailey, and Yu (2011) define nursing documentation as "the record of nursing care that is planned and given to individual patients and clients by qualified nurses or by other caregivers under the direction of a qualified nurse" promoting "structured, consistent, and effective communication between caregivers" (p. 1859). Effective documentation promotes safe, legal, individualized care that is coordinated across caregivers and settings.

The primary purposes of documentation are to describe the clinical history of the student's care and treatment, to allow for continuity of care, and to provide evidence that the nurse has discharged their duties of care (Griffith, 2016). Effective reporting of documentation supports the development of evidence for practice and advocacy.

Effective documentation requires attention to a variety of standards, including nursing standards of care; accurate, adequate and timely recording of care; and effective use of the information collected in the student record.

BACKGROUND

Importance of Documentation

Nursing documentation has been described as defining "the nature of nursing itself" and being a "repository of knowledge" that supports the visibility of the work, decision-making and outcomes of nursing care (Jefferies, Johnson, & Griffiths, 2010, p. 113). British legal expert, Richard Griffith, states, "in litigation, the outcome is not based on truth, but on proof" supporting the nursing adage that "if it isn't documented, it wasn't done." Griffith reminds nurses that "records are never neutral – they will either support you or condemn you" (2016, p. 408). Legal experts describe the success or failure of litigation based on the completeness, timeliness and accuracy of the health practitioner's documentation. The importance of documentation is further emphasized in the many ways in which it is used to support safe, legal care of students. Effective documentation provides:

- a legal record of care;
- the history of care and the student's needs;

- supports communication with other members of the school team;
- supports continuity of care; and
- allows for the evaluation of care.

When aggregated and analyzed, it also supports the:

- development of evidence for effective practice;
- understanding of population health needs; and
- identification of critical nursing sensitive student outcomes which hold implications for policy, research and resource allocation.

What to Document

Prudent documentation reflects the nursing process and communicates application of nursing judgment in: 1) assessment and identification of a nursing diagnosis, 2) nursing interventions, and 3) outcomes of nursing care demonstrating adherence to nursing regulations, professional practice and performance standards. Nurses should document:

- abnormalities;
- changes in condition;
- adverse findings;
- changes in the plan of care and reason for the change;
- student outcomes after the intervention;
- family responses;
- relevant social issues;
- care declined by clients;
- the health status of the patient; and
- the patient's perspective of their health (Blair & Smith, 2012; Griffith, 2007; Jefferies, Johnson, & Griffith, 2010; Koch, 2014; Prideaux, 2011).

Complete documentation also includes dissent with other team members about the care provided. The recorded note of the dissent contains factual accounting of the events leading to the dissent, the nurse's rationale for disagreement, and subsequent action taken (Griffith, 2015). This would include the nurse's accounting of their communication regarding dissent with those in authority.

The Family Educational Rights and Privacy Act (FERPA) allows parents "the right to request that inaccurate or misleading information in his or her child's education records be amended," however "this right cannot be used to challenge a grade, an individual's opinion, or a substantive decision made by a school about a student" (U.S. Department of Education [USDE], 2015, p. 1). Nursing documentation is a legal record that cannot be altered without the risk of appearing to conceal misconduct (Cornell University Law School, n.d.). The USDE (2015) further advises that if there is a dispute about the accuracy of the nurse's documentation, the parent may submit an amendment to the note that includes the parent's comments, parent's name, relationship, the section of notes disputed and the date submitted. (*See Chapter 11 for more information on FERPA/HIPAA).*

Standardized Nursing Languages

Standardized nursing languages allow nurses to describe and document their care using common terminology that aligns with and supports the nursing process. Most nursing languages have been "mapped" or aligned with standards of computer codes used in medical, billing and other health services that allow similar concepts to be machine (computer) aggregated (American Nurses Association [ANA], 2014). Machine aggregation supports the seamless exchange of data between healthcare systems, as well as a broader analysis of the patient's care - integrating data from many providers for a holistic view of the patient's care. Standardized nursing languages facilitate "interoperability between different concepts, nomenclatures, and information systems" (ANA, 2014, p. 11). The Nursing Informatics: Scope and Standards of Practice (ANA, 2014) provides a list of nursing languages. Norma Lang described the importance of standardized variables to collect nursing data in 1992: "...if we cannot name it, we cannot control it, finance it, teach it, research it, or put it into public policy" (Clark & Lang, p. 109).

Documentation Formats

There are many formats available to promote clear, accurate and intelligible documentation. These include a chronological narrative of the events of student care, an orderly review of body systems, or a problem-oriented approach based on the nursing process (Blair & Smith, 2012). The nursing process provides the most widely accepted structure for nursing documentation assuring a full description of the student's condition, the nursing interventions addressing the reason for care, and the outcomes related to those interventions (Blair & Smith, 2012). The most commonly recommended format is SOAPIER –

- Subjective data – statements of the student or family;
- Objective data – what the nurse observes or measures;
- Assessment – the nurse's conclusion in the form of a nursing diagnosis based on the data available;
- Plan – of the expected outcomes and actions to achieve those outcomes;
- Implementation of the plan;
- Evaluation of the outcomes of the plan; and
- Revision of the plan based on any differences between the plan and the outcomes.

Focus charting promotes improved accessibility and data flow around specific problems. Documentation using focus charting uses the DAR technique:

- Data – subjective and objective information that includes the assessment, signs and symptoms, and nursing diagnosis;
- Action – describing the nursing interventions that includes planning and implementation; and
- Response – describing the student's response to interventions corresponding to the nurse's evaluation of the outcomes of interventions (Blair & Smith, 2012).

Standards and Quality

Quality of documentation is essential both to ensure effective communication of the student's care across caregivers and settings, and that the records afford legal protection to the nurse and the district in the event of a dispute over care. Griffith (2016) recommends that nurses:

- document care as close to the time of rendering as possible (contemporaneously);
- document risks or problems and the nurse's intervention in response;
- ensure accuracy of record without falsification;
- ensure all notes are appropriately attributed or linked to the author of the note;
- ensure notes are clear with the date and time of entry included, and contain no unnecessary jargon or abbreviations;
- ensure notes are fact based – not speculative; and
- secure.

Poor documentation is affected by workload, inefficient documentation forms, use of local abbreviations or terminology that are not well-understood, inadequate resources, and workplace culture (Okaisu, Kalikwani, Wanyana, & Coetree, 2014). Recommendations to improve nursing documentation included appropriate forms to support nursing workflow and a healthy work culture that included "authentic leadership, meaningful recognition, skilled communication, and appropriate staffing" as well as professional development in documentation (Okaisu et al., 2014, p. 5).

The importance of quality in documentation is evidenced by the volumes of literature addressing it (Wang et al., 2011). Findings from a systematic review on quality of nursing documentation included incomplete documentation on psychosocial, cultural and spiritual aspects of care; patient teaching, and nursing assessment of the patient's quality of life, knowledge deficits, and pain. Other deficits included the inaccurate use of nursing diagnoses and interventions, and a lack of coherence in the steps of the nursing process. Recommendations to address these issues included the use of electronic documentation systems (EDS), use of standardized terminology, prompts in the EDS to improve comprehensiveness, as well as education in documentation of the nursing process (Wang et al., 2011).

To support quality, Bruylands, Paans, Hediger, and Muller-Staub, (2013) summarized the literature on the value of diagnostics on the quality and quantity of documentation. They identified a need for a structure that describes the nursing process and endorsed the value of professional development in documentation to improve quality. Their research examined the value of "Guided Clinical Reasoning" as a tool to promote quality documentation (p. 164). The guide focused on integration of critical thinking and reflection on the nursing process using clinical case studies. They recommended that professional development in documentation include guided clinical reflection, electronic documentation systems, and support in standardized terminologies. Professional development in documentation for new nurses focused on documenting the critical thinking behind their care.

Wang et al. (2011) identified audit tools that addressed three dimensions of documentation: 1) structure, 2) process, and 3) content. The authors noted that the quality of the content of nurse's documentation is interpreted to align with the quality of nursing care provided. They also note that thorough documentation of the nursing process demonstrates nursing knowledge and skill in the application of clinical reasoning. Blair

& Smith (2012) noted as a deficit the frequent absence of documentation that demonstrated nurse's critical thinking. The Nursing and Midwifery Content Audit Tool (NMCAT) demonstrated both content and interrater reliability. It focused on both legal components of documentation as well as content (Johnson, Jefferies, & Langdon, 2010).

Reporting School Health Information

Documentation – particularly that developed in electronic systems - holds great value in reporting on student health both at the individual and population level. Effective reporting:

- tracks progress and trends;
- is actionable;
- accountable;
- asset focused;
- important;
- has a plausible theory;
- is reliable and valid;
- accessible; and
- is values based (Flores, Davis, & Culross, 2007).

The meaningful use of patient information from documentation is an outgrowth of healthcare reform and is designed to address the poor outcomes of U.S. health care identified by the Institute of Medicine (IOM) (2000; 2010a; 2010b; 2012). Meaningfully using the information contained in nursing documentation to report on and analyze health care and systems enhances the value of the information it contains, allowing its value to move beyond a static electronic file cabinet (Johnson & Bergren, 2010). When the information is aggregated and analyzed over time for an individual or across populations, it becomes knowledge that drives evidence for practice (ANA, 2014). According to the Office of the National Coordinator for Health Information Technology (ONC) using records meaningfully "will

- improve quality, safety, efficiency, and reduce health disparities;
- engage patients and family;
- improve care coordination, and population and public health; and
- maintain privacy and security of patient health information" (HealthIT.gov, 2015, para. 1).

Accomplishing meaningful use requires the use of electronic documentation systems as well as the use of standardized terminology to effectively aggregate similar data points. Standardized terminology supports the machine (computer) aggregation of like data elements. Data elements can then be reported and analyzed to develop evidence for practice. "Standardized nursing languages provide common definitions of nursing concepts and allow theory-based and comparable nursing data to emerge" from the record (Wang et al., 2011, p. 1859). A variety of standardized nursing languages exists including NANDA, NOC and NIC, Omaha, and Clinical Care Classification (American Nurses Association [ANA], 2014).

IMPLICATIONS FOR SCHOOL NURSE PRACTICE

Appropriate documentation protects the student, the nurse and the organization. The importance of complete and accurate documentation is reinforced in the frequency with which it is identified in the *School Nursing: Scope and Standards of Practice* – the professional and legal standard to which all school nurses are held (ANA & NASN, 2017) as well as the broader *Nursing: Scope and Standards of Practice* (ANA, 2015). Additionally, the nursing *Code of Ethics* implies the importance of documentation in its references to accountability, communication, and contributions to research and practice standards (Fowler, 2015).

Failure to document according to standards can put the student at risk for poor outcomes from inadequate communication as well as put the nurse and the school district at risk for litigation. State Nurse Practice Acts and Medical Records Acts, the *School Nursing: Scope and Standards of Practice* (ANA & NASN, 2017) and billing requirements drive standards for documentation. Nurses should ensure that their documentation provides evidence of the critical thinking that directed their care and demonstrates that the nurse has discharged their duty of care. School nurses should be familiar with their scope and standards of practice, as well as the nurse practice act and medical records acts in the state in which they practice. For example, the Washington Nurse Practice Act states that documentation "shall communicate significant changes in the client's status to appropriate members of the healthcare team... in a timely manner... the nursing care given and the client's response to that care" (Washington Administrative Code, 246-840-700 §§ (3) (b) 2004). In the event of a question about the outcomes of care, documentation that reflects those standards will provide the supporting evidence of quality care.

Documentation that occurs contemporaneously with care enhances the perception of accuracy, quality and reliability (Griffith, 2016). Documentation should be completed by the individual providing the care – this includes care provided by unlicensed persons - unless the information in that record is clearly attributed to the person providing care. However, documentation created directly by the person providing care holds more credibility in legal questions than second hand reports. Griffith also points out that any alteration of a record after the fact would be taken as a cover-up of wrongdoing. A single line through a paper entry that allows the error to be legible, with the word "error" and nurse's initials is an appropriate method to correct errors. Records are dated and signed and follow the previous entry. Document changes or additions made after the initial entry a "late entry" with the writer's signature and date. With any changes to a record - it must be clear who made the changes, what the changes were, and when they were made. Electronic documentation systems should provide overwrite protection that does not allow entries to be deleted but supports correction of errors (Johnson & Guthrie, 2012).

Standardized Language and Formats

Using standardized languages and formats that are universally accepted and which reflect standards of care allow integration of school health information into the student's broader health record, reflects the professional care provided in schools, and allows for effective aggregation and reporting across systems. Particularly for the population level data collection that is available in student health documentation, there are robust opportunities to "promote research, inform policy, and identify best practice" when standardized languages are used (ANA, 2014, p. 54). Standardized languages that use the nursing process have the added benefit of providing nurses with a "cognitive map" to support critical thinking and effective care (Von Krough,

Dale, & Nadin, 2005, p. 276). For instance, when a student presents to the health room, the nurse assesses the student symptoms and identifies a nursing diagnosis. That diagnosis leads to a set of desired outcomes for the student which appear in the EDS in a dropdown menu. The selection of the outcomes by the nurse further prompts the selection of appropriate interventions to achieve those outcomes that appear in a dropdown menu. Further, when the medical diagnosis of asthma is entered, additional decision support is triggered in the EHR, prompting reminders to enter rescue inhalers, peak flow measures and symptom triggers for the student. As population level research on related to student health matures, clinical decision support using standardized languages can be built into the electronic health record. Using standardized languages allows student health data that is contained in nursing records to be used meaningfully – to support policy, evidence for practice, research, and resource allocation.

SOAPIER and problem oriented (focused) documentation methods have been used across healthcare disciplines and thus are formats that can be readily utilized across the care continuum including acute and ambulatory care. An editorial in the *Annals of Internal Medicine* (Sequist, 2015, p. 315) promotes the value of "longitudinal management of conditions across settings and providers" suggesting the importance of the accessibility of all child health records into one record of care – a concept that aligns with the longitudinal nature of school health records. Promoting access by the student's medical provider to the records that are kept at school ensures that the full picture of the student's health is available for care planning. It would also clearly identify those students whose only access to a health professional is at their school (Johnson, Bergren, & Westbrook, 2012).

Focus charting may be an effective documentation rubric for school nurses in that it reflects the reasons for interventions, which in the school setting are often focused on a specific student health problem. Blair's team (2012) modified the DAR focus to AIE – Assessment, Intervention, and Evaluation, in which the documentation is focused around a specific, identified problem. The authors found that this method allowed rapid aggregation of specific problems within an individual record or across many patients in a practice. They found that AIE focus charting was easily understood and quickly adopted by the majority of hospital nursing staff. This method proved its value in the timeliness of a response to an infectious disease outbreak allowing infections to be quickly and easily identified across the patient population, and documentation of the course of the infection more readily tracked within an individual patient record. Given the longitudinal and population based aspects of school nursing, focus charting may allow rapid analysis of both the individual student and the school or district health issues.

Data Ethics

Nurses and their administrators who use data based on their documentation have a duty to use that data ethically (ANA, 2014; ANA, 2015; ANA, 2016). This includes attention to privacy, confidentiality and security of the data collected. They should review the *Forum Guide to Data Ethics* on the U.S. Department of Education website to ensure ethical use. Care should be taken to ensure that reported totals are large enough that individual students cannot be identified in the data. This ensures that student privacy is maintained and records are held confidentially. The Forum guides educators in using data in a manner that supports student well-being, is valid (accurately represents the true events), reliable (is consistent), accurate, timely and cost effective (National Forum on Education Statistics, 2010). The Family Educational Rights and Privacy Act (FERPA) requires consent of the parent/guardian to release personally identifiable information on students except in certain situations. Aggregated, de-identified data does not require consent to release (U.S. Department of Education [USDE], n.d.).

The quality of documentation is important not only to demonstrate the quality of school nursing care, but to ensure effective and accurate communication of the student's concerns, nursing interventions and the outcomes of care. Audit tools could be used to not only measure the quality of nursing documentation, but when used in a timely manner, can also support feedback to the nurse to improve the quality of their care. Glasper (2011) recommends the use of the CIA Standard to ensure that records that are Clear, Intelligible, and Accurate. Griffith (2015 & 2016) recommends that nurses perform a 5-minute personal audit of their records addressing:

- Completeness – duty of care discharged, all care documented including consent, immunizations, and explanation of risk;
- Accuracy – details of the factual basis of any opinion; and
- Clarity – understandable by non-health readers, avoidance of abbreviations and jargon, detailed enough to clearly represent the status of the student and the care given.

Meaningful Use of Data

The variety of conditions, large caseloads and longitudinal data collected over the years of a student's school attendance produce volumes of data that are too broad and complex for the human mind to effectively process (Amatayakul, 2009). However, using standardized languages (or information coding formats) that are collected and stored electronically, and using software that allows the data to be reported (queried) from multiple perspectives allows it to be analyzed for deeper meaning to promote child health and standards of care. Nurses can then process the data into manageable chunks to provide the individual student's care, and further aggregated it into population level data at the school, district, state or national level. Using data collected in the day-to-day documentation of school nurses in this way provides a unique population level view of the health of school-age children (Johnson & Bergren, 2011).

Aggregating these large amounts of data and reporting them in meaningful ways reflects the standards of school nursing practice by providing information for research; evidence based practice; collaboration; advocacy; and communication across silos of care (ANA & NASN 2017). The Family Educational Rights and Privacy Act (FERPA) permits use of aggregated data as long as an individual cannot be identified in the data (USDE, n.d.). Aggregating the data in their documentation allows the nurse to use it meaningfully. It becomes more than a static record of care to become information, knowledge and wisdom (ANA, 2015). It allows the information entered into the record once to be used many times to support care and build evidence for practice. For example, immunization dates entered and analyzed at the individual student level are used to determine that student's immunization compliance. In a meaningful use environment, immunization dates are then aggregated with school level data to determine what vaccine preventable illnesses the school may be at risk for. They can be further aggregated to monitor the history of immunization compliance over several years to understand district immunization patterns. The dates that represent data on an individual's immunization status hold additional power when combined and analyzed in this way. The same concept can be applied to data on chronic conditions, playground injuries and other health issues routinely managed by school nurses.

Because the clear majority of school-age children attend school, and school nurses' documentation represents not only students with chronic health conditions, but also screening and episodic care of well students, the data collected by school nurses daily in the course of their normal documentation represents true population data. It provides a window into prevalence of chronic conditions of childhood and the health status of children (NASN & National Association of State School Nurse Consultants [NASSNC], n.d.). Every school nurse can identify their students with Type I Diabetes and describe the parameters of their care. Every school nurse can identify their students with life threatening allergies, and describe every dose of epinephrine they have administered to save lives. Despite this, the true prevalence of these conditions among school aged children, and many other low frequency but potentially life-threatening conditions can only be estimated in current child health databases. The documentation of school nurses provides the only evidence of the prevalence of these conditions for children and youth attending school – making these records invaluable to promote child health.

Collecting data meaningfully positions a student's school health data to be integrated into the broader universe of their electronic health record in acute and ambulatory care settings thus maximizing the coordination of care and minimizing silos of information. Electronic transfer of data minimizes human error through transcription errors and is particularly useful for the precision of medication orders and immunization dates. It contributes to efficient and safe care of students across systems and ensures that students outside the traditional healthcare systems have their needs equitably represented. It promotes the visibility of school nursing interventions and holds implications for resource allocation.

To that end, the NASN and the National Association of State School Nurse Consultants (NASSNC) have collaborated to develop a nationally standardized school health dataset called *Step Up! Be Counted* that uses aggregated, de-identified data collected from the daily documentation of school nurses across the United States. The data is used to describe student health needs, the resources to address those needs and the nursing sensitive student outcomes of nursing interventions (NASN & NASSNC, n.d.). Resources to support data collection and reporting are included on the NASN website.

Impact of Effective Documentation

Effective reporting of school health data is student focused, organized for easy understanding and considers the audience perspective when reported. Considerations for effectively framing reports using nursing data may include:

- A description of the resources available for student care vs. the size of a school nurse's caseload.
- Data reports can be organized along the NASN's Framework for 21st Century School Nursing Practice (NASN, 2016), focused on elements of school nursing practice such as Care Coordination, Risk Management, Health Promotion and Episodic care (Johnson, Bergren, & Westbrook, 2012), or a chronological account of an individual student's care to another provider or the student's parent/ guardian.
- When used within the confines of proper consent and confidentiality standards as outlined in The Forum's Data Ethics guidance, aggregated data can provide information to advocate for student health for a variety of stakeholders (National Forum on Education Statistics, 2010).

o For instance, the school board may be interested in how documentation supports compliance with federal and state statutes or district policy.

o Medical providers will be interested in an individual student's progress

o The principal of a school may be interested in the academic impacts of a nurse's health program – how instruction in respiratory hygiene or handwashing has reduced absenteeism.

o Risk management, legal and budget departments will be interested in documentation to support their missions.

o Federal and community stakeholders may be interested in documentation that describes equity, resource distribution, and academic impact of nursing work.

CONCLUSION

Documentation in school nursing practice is essential to ensure continuity of care over the student's school career and to support the nurse in demonstrating that appropriate care was delivered. It is the foundation for data that supports research, child health policy, and evidence for practice. Quality documentation describes the school nurse's critical thinking as the nursing process is applied to the care of students.

Documentation of the nursing process is important for legal, research, and care coordination purposes. A variety of formats supports effective documentation including SOAPIER and problem oriented methods. Data from documentation in electronic records using standardized variables supports the meaningful use of records and holds potential to create evidence for practice, inform policy and improve care coordination across settings and over time. School nurses particularly benefit from electronic systems and standardized variables to improve the visibility of school nursing interventions and promote the health of school-age children.

RESOURCES

- The Forum Guide to Data Ethics http://nces.ed.gov/pubs2010/2010801.pdf

- Step Up Be Counted http://www.nasn.org/Research/StepUpBeCounted

- Framework for 21st Century School Nursing http://www.nasn.org/Framework

- NASN Documentation Resources https://www.nasn.org/ToolsResources/DocumentationinSchoolHealth

- Washington State Standardized Health Codes https://www.nwrdc.net/getattachment/78174083-5a91-4c1d-b2ff-7a89ffc2964a/Health-Codes

REFERENCES

Amatayakul, M. K. (2009). *Electronic healthcare records: A practical guide for professionals and organizations* (4th ed.). Chicago: American Health Information Management Association.

American Nurses Association. (2010). *Nursing: Scope and standards of practice* (2nd ed.). Silver Spring, MD: American Nurses Association.

American Nurses Association. (2014). *Nursing informatics: Scope and standards of practice* (2nd ed.). Silver Spring, MD: American Nurses Association.

American Nurses Association. (2015). Provision 3. In *Code of ethics for nurses with interpretive statements* (pp. 9-13). Silver Spring, MD: Author.

American Nurses Association. (2016). *Nursing administration: Scope and standards of practice* (2nd ed.). Silver Spring, MD: Author.

American Nurses Association and National Association of School Nurses. (2017). *Scope and standards of school nursing practice* (3rd ed.). Silver Spring, MD: Authors.

Blair, W., & Smith, B. (2012, June). Nursing documentation: Frameworks and barriers. *Contemporary Nurse*, *41*(2), 160-168. doi: 10.5172/conu.2012.41.2.160

Bruylands, M., Paans, W., Hediger, H., & Muller-Staub, M. (2013, October). Effects on the quality of the nursing care process through an educational program and use of electronic nursing documentation. *International Journal of Nursing Knowledge, 24*(3), 163-170. doi: 10.1111/j.2047-3095.2013.01248.x

Clark, J., & Lang, N. (1992). Nursing's next advance: An internal classification for nursing practice. *International Nursing, 4*, 109-112109-112.

Cornell University Law School. (n.d.). 18 U.S. Code § 1519 - Destruction, alteration, or falsification of records in Federal investigations and bankruptcy. Retrieved from https://www.law.cornell.edu/uscode/text/18/1519

Flores, L. M., Davis, R., & Culross, P. (2007). Community health: A critical approach to addressing chronic diseases. *Preventing Chronic Disease, 4*(4), 1-6. Retrieved from http://www.cdc.gov/pcd/issues/2007/oct/07_0080.htm

Fowler, M. D. (Ed.). (2015). *Code of ethics for nurses with interpretive statements*. Silver Spring, MD: American Nurses.

Glasper, A. (2011). Improving record keeping: Important lessons for nurses. *British Journal of Nursing, 20*(14), 886. doi:10.12968/bjon.2011.20.14.886

Griffith, R. (2007). The importance of earnest record keeping. *Nurse Prescribing, 5*(8), 364. doi: http://dx.doi.org/10.12968/npre.2007.5.8.363

Griffith, R. (2015, October). Understanding the code: Keeping accurate records. *British Journal of Community Nursing, 20*(10), 511-514. doi: http://dx.doi.org/10.12968/bjcn.2015.20.10.511

Griffith, R. (2016). For the record: Keeping detailed notes. *British Journal of Nursing, 25*, 408 - 409. doi:10.12968/bjon.2016.25.7.408

HealthIT.gov. (2015). *Meaningful use definition & objectives: Meaningful use defined*. Retrieved from https://www.healthit.gov/providers-professionals/meaningful-use-definition-objectives

Institute of Medicine. (2000). *To err is human: Building a safer health system* (Institute of Medicine). Retrieved from http://www.nationalacademies.org/hmd/Reports/1999/To-Err-is-Human-Building-A-Safer-Health-System.aspx

Institute of Medicine (2010a). *The future of nursing: Leading change, advancing health*. Retrieved from http://books.nap.edu/openbook.php?record_id=12956&page=R9

Institute of Medicine. (2010b). *For the public's health: The role of measurement in action and accountability* (Institute of Medicine). Retrieved from http://www.nationalacademies.org/hmd/Reports/2012/For-the-Publics-Health-Investing-in-a-Healthier-Future.aspx

Institute of Medicine. (2012). *Health IT and patient safety: Building safer systems for better care* (National Academy of Sciences). Retrieved from http://www.nap.edu/catalog/13269/health-it-and-patient-safety-building-safer-systems-for-better

Jefferies, D., Johnson, M., & Griffiths, R. (2010). A meta-study of the essentials of quality nursing documentation. *International Journal of Nursing Practice, 16*, 112-124. Retrieved from http://dx.doi.org/10.1111/k.1440-172X.2009.01815.x

Johnson, K. H., & Bergren, M. D. (2011). Meaningful use of school health data. *The Journal of School Nursing, 27*, 102-110. doi:http://dx.doi.org/10.1177/1059840510391095

Johnson, K. H., Bergren, M. D., & Westbrook, L. O. (2012). The promise of standardized data collection: School health variables identified by states. *Journal of School Nursing, 28*(2), 95-107. doi: http://dx.doi.org/10.1177/1059840511426434

Johnson, K. H., & Guthrie, S. (2012, January). Harnessing the power of student health data: Selecting, using, and implementing electronic school health documentation systems. *NASN School Nurse, 27*(1), 26-33. doi: 10.1177/1942602X11429828

Johnson, M., Jefferies, D., & Langdon, R. (2010, June). The Nursing and Midwifery Content Audit Tool (NMCAT: A short nursing documentation audit tool. *Journal of Nursing Management, 18*, 832-845. doi: http://dx.doi.org/10.1111/j.1365-2834.2010.01156x

Koch, G. (2014). Going back to basics: Documentation. *Oregon Board of Nursing Sentinel, 33*(2), 14-15. Retrieved from http://epubs.democratprinting.com/publication/?i=214579

National Association of School Nurses. (2016). Framework for 21st century school nursing practice. *NASN School Nurse, 31*(1), 45-53. doi: 10.1177/1942602X15618644

National Association of School Nurses & National Association of State School Nurse Consultants. (n.d.). *Step Up Be Counted: A nationally standardized school health data set.* Retrieved from http://www.nasn.org/Research/StepUpBeCounted

National Association of School Nurses & National Association of State School Nurse Consultants. (n.d.). *Uniform national data set: Step up and be counted!* Talking points. Retrieved from https://www.nasn.org/Research/StepUpBeCounted/TalkingPoints

National Forum on Education Statistics. (2010). *The Forum guide to data ethics* (NFES 2010-801). Retrieved from http://www.edpubs.org

Okaisu, E. M., Kalikwani, F., Wanyana, G., & Coetree, M. (2014). Improving the quality of nursing documentation: An action research project. *Curationis, 38*(1). doi:http://dx.doi.org/10.4102/cyratuibus,v37i1.1251

Prideaux, A. (2011). Issues in nursing documentation and record-keeping practice. *British Journal of Nursing, 20*(22), 1450-1454. doi:10.12968/bjon.2011.20.22.1450

Sequist, T. D. (2015, February). Clinical documentation to improve patient care. *Annals of Internal Medicine, 162*(4), 315-316. doi: 10.7326/M14-2913

U.S. Department of Education. (2015). FERPA general guidance for parents. Retrieved from http://www2.ed.gov/policy/gen/guid/fpco/ferpa/parents.html

U.S. Department of Education. (n.d.). FERPA: Frequently asked questions. Retrieved September 5, 2016, from http://familypolicy.ed.gov/faq-page#t89n440

Von Krough, G., Dale, C., & Nadin, D. (2005, Third Quarter). A framework for Integrating NANDA, NIC, and NOC in electronic patient records. *Journal of Nursing Scholarship, 37*(3), 275-281. doi: 10.1111/j.1547-5069.2005.00047.x

Wang, N., Hailey, D., & Yu, P. (2011). Quality of nursing documentation and approaches to its evaluation: A mixed-method systematic review. *Journal of Advanced Nursing*, 1858-1875. doi: 10.1111/j.1365-2648.2011.05634.x

Washington Administrative Code 246-840-700 §§ (3) (b) (2004). Standards of nursing conduct or practice, art. Retrieved from http://app.leg.wa.gov/wac/default.aspx?cite=246-840-700

Chapter 10

SCHOOL HEALTH RECORDS

Kathleen H. Johnson, DNP, RN, NCSN, FNASN

DESCRIPTION OF ISSUE

School health records are comprised of the documentation developed and collected by school nurses in the course of their work with students. They are comprised of health-related documents and files that address a variety of purposes, contained in a variety of formats, and are often subject to multiple federal, state and local regulations. The complexity of school health records is reflected in the wide variety of management requirements. This chapter will address the types of records, the formats they may be contained in, and the common requirements for privacy, storage, access and reporting.

School nurses manage a wide variety of school health records, including the following:

- documentation of healthcare;
- individualized healthcare and emergency care plans;
- communication with other providers, parents/guardians and students;
- screening test records;
- immunization records;
- medication records;
- special education records;
- Section 504 disability records;
- billing records; and
- accident/injury records.

Records are increasingly being contained in electronic formats that allow information to be entered once and used many times, allow access to a variety of persons who have a need to know about the student's health issues, and facilitate reporting and analysis from a wide variety of perspectives to improve student health and well-being. In addition, school health records in paper and electronic formats provide legal protection for the nurse and the district in documenting the specific care given to students.

School nurses are bound ethically and legally to balance protection for student records related to privacy, security, and loss and while advocating for student health needs by effectively using records to communicate with student care teams. Federal and state statutes and rules protect student and family rights to confidentiality, access, and correction. Statutes also drive the kinds of information that need to be kept in student records – especially to demonstrate compliance with the Individuals with Disabilities in Education Act (IDEA – special education) (U.S. Department of Education [USDE], n.d.), the Americans with Disabilities Act Amendment Act (ADAAA – Section 504) (USDE, Office for Civil Rights [OCR], 2016), and state nurse practice acts. School districts may also have requirements for records as directed in school board policies and procedures, and in school district department protocols.

The variety and complexity of school health records, and the role of the school nurse as the expert on health records in an educational environment require that school nurses have knowledge of those requirements and the ways to demonstrate compliance.

BACKGROUND

Privacy, Confidentiality and Security of School Health Records

Assuring the privacy, confidentiality and security of student health information is a duty upheld by both nursing code of ethics (American Nurses Association [ANA], 2015) and the scope and standards of nursing practice (ANA & National Association of School Nurses [NASN], 2017). **Privacy** is the right of an individual to determine which information they disclose (Hunter, 2002). **Confidentiality** is a duty of healthcare professionals to assure that disclosed information will not be shared without permission of the originator (Hunter, 2002). **Security** addresses the "policies procedures, software and/or hardware designed to ensure that data in information systems are protected against accidental or inappropriate destruction, alteration, or access" (Chou & Sengupta, 2008, p. 37). All three areas must be considered when addressing the collection and storage of student health information regardless of the method used to manage information.

Highly sensitive records such as standardized testing, psychological and psychiatric examinations, reproductive health and records disclosed by other agencies often require a higher level of confidentiality. Access should be limited to those persons who have a *"need to know,"* which can include the school nurse, the nurse's clinical supervisor, a substitute nurse, the school medical advisor, the parent/guardian and/or student, and a university nursing student (with faculty supervision) (Gelfman & Schwab, 2001/2005). Security of records requires physical security – locked from access by unauthorized persons, maintained in a manner that keeps records intact, shielded from inadvertent review by others, and inclusion of an audit log (system to track who accessed the record, any changes made to the record, who made those changes, and when the changes were made) (Griffith, 2016). Security of school health records is important to assure compliance with federal and often state requirements. Fundamental safeguards include:

- not sharing passwords;
- not leaving student records unattended;
- logging off when the student information system is not in use;
- maintaining locked records for confidential and personally identifiable information;
- assuring that consent to share records is obtained and that the individual providing consent understands what information is being kept and with whom it will be shared;
- assuring that private information is disclosed only to those who have a legitimate "need to know";
- ensuring that records are accurate;
- maintaining knowledge of and compliance with local and federal statutes and policies regarding information sharing and data management; and
- assuring data is used as it was intended (Beach & Oates, 2014, p. 48).

Electronic records should be equipped with features that ensure confidentiality and security. This includes the strategies discussed below in Table #1.

Table #1 Strategies for Security and Confidentiality (Bergren, 2001/2005, cited by Johnson & Guthrie, 2012, p.32. Reprinted with permission).

System Elements	
Partitioning	Separates sections of the record from other sections (ex. health from food service)
Rejection	Refuses access to a user who attempts to log on with an incorrect password too many times
Audit of access	Records a user's trail of access through the system to limit unnecessary viewing of the record
Overwrite protection	Assures that there is no unauthorized alteration of the record
Password Security	Secure requirements i.e. must contain symbols, be a certain length, use capital and lower-case letters, and need to maintain secrecy
Business Practices	
Security policy	Written policy on compliance with confidentiality and roles associated with access; and responsibilities of various roles.
Access	Limited to specific individuals
Employee Education	Regarding appropriate management of security and confidentiality
Confidentiality Agreement	Related to use of the data
Communication with the IT department	Regarding security requirements for healthcare records
Legal Issues	
Authentication	Legally recognized electronic signature of the entry into the record – often a log of the user name
Durability	Appropriate retention and maintenance of the data
Secure storage	Protects the data from loss or damage due to disaster or theft
Admissibility	The record can be verified as being produced in the normal course of business with a log of the date and time the record was entered or changed
Audit log	Log of changes to the data that provides evidence that the record is the original entry and has not been changed or manipulated

For more information, the U.S. Department of Education (USDE) has created a Privacy Technical Assistance Center (PTAC) to support school personnel in assuring the privacy, confidentiality, and security of school data. The USDE has identified a variety of technical and non-technical threats to security, and recommends features of a strong security network along with suggested mitigation measures. PTAC also has training videos available to support security of school information systems (USDE, n.d.).

While the privacy and security of student health and education records are protected by federal statutes – primarily the Family Educational Rights and Privacy Act (FERPA), schools interface with other entities that are subject to other federal privacy acts. The healthcare privacy act known as the Health Insurance Portability and Accountability Act (HIPAA), does not apply directly to health records kept by federally funded K-12 public school because they are considered education records under HIPAA and already have protection under FERPA (U.S. Department of Health and Human Services [USDHHS], 2000; USDHHS & USDE, 2008). However, HIPAA does impact the exchange of information from other health systems as well as private schools that do not receive federal funding. A more detailed description of each law is discussed below.

Family Educational Rights and Privacy Act (FERPA)

The FERPA was enacted in 1974 (predating the HIPAA by more than two decades). It addressed the rights of parents/guardians and eligible students to (1) inspect and review student records; (2) request a correction to records; and (3) require consent before releasing any information from an educational record. FERPA "applies to all schools that receive funds under an applicable program of the U.S. Department of Education" (USDE, 2015, p. 1; USDHHS & USDE, 2008, p. 1).

The right to limit disclosure does not include school directory information, provided that parents/guardians are notified of the potential release of directory information and have a reasonable opportunity to refuse release of this information on their child. Directory information includes "the student's name, address, telephone listing, date and place of birth, major field of study, participation in officially recognized activities and sports, weight and height of members of athletic teams, dates of attendance, degrees and awards received; and the most recent previous educational agency or institution attended by the student" (USDE, 2004, p. 3). Schools may also release de-identified data without permission, if the size of the reported data is large enough to **not allow** an individual to be identified (USDE, n.d.).

FERPA specifically addresses students' education records. Education records are defined as being those that are "(1) directly related to a student, and (2) maintained by an educational agency or institution or by a party acting for the agency or institution" (USDHHS & USDE, 2008, p. 1). This includes immunization and records "maintained by a school nurse" (USDHHS & USDE, 2008, p. 2), as well as special education records – even if that nurse is employed by another entity (such as a Department of Health) but acting as an agent of the school district (USDE, 2015).

Exceptions to the prior written consent rule include:

- School officials with a legitimate educational interest;
- Other schools to which a student is transferring;
- Specified officials, for audit or evaluation purposes;
- Appropriate parties in connection with financial aid to a student;
- Organizations conducting certain studies for or on behalf of the school;
- Accrediting organizations;
- To comply with a judicial order or lawfully issued subpoena;
- Appropriate officials in cases of health and safety emergencies; and
- State and local authorities, within a juvenile justice system, pursuant to specific state law (USDE, 2015a, p. 1).

Private schools that do not accept funds from the USDE are not subject to FERPA, but may be subject to HIPAA if they transmit health data electronically. However, records for a student from a FERPA covered entity receiving services from a private school are subject to FERPA even if the records of their classmates are not covered under FERPA (USDHHS & USDE, 2008). Records maintained by a post-secondary institution are also subject to different rules under FERPA (USDE, n.d.).

(See *Chapter 11 for more information on FERPA*).

Health Insurance Portability and Accountability Act (HIPAA)

As described previously, education records in public elementary and secondary schools include those maintained by school nurses – even if they have been created by nurses who are employees of a hospital or public health agency. Because the records of school nurses are education records, they are explicitly subject to FERPA (USDHHS & USDE, 2008). While HIPAA does not apply directly to student records, it is helpful to have a fundamental understanding of this federal statute, as most healthcare providers who provide information to schools will be required to comply with its regulations. HIPAA was enacted in 1996 and has undergone several revisions since that time (HIPAA Journal, n.d.). Its goals were to adopt national standards for electronic healthcare transactions and to protect the privacy of health information (USDHHS/OCR, n.d.).

There are three elements to HIPAA:

1) Privacy Rule;
2) Security Rule; and
3) Breach Notification Rule (Office of the National Coordinator for Health Information Technology [ONC], 2015).

HIPAA addresses "protected health information" (PHI) held by "covered entities" and consists of information on an individual's physical or mental health condition, provision of care, and payment information by which an individual can be identified (USDHHS/OCR, 2010). Covered entities include healthcare providers that conduct business electronically, a healthcare clearinghouse, or a health plan (USDHHS/OCR, n.d.).

HIPAA allows healthcare providers to share information with other healthcare providers without consent for treatment purposes including administration of medication (USDHHS/OCR, 2008; ONC, 2015). While FERPA predates electronic communication of student information, HIPAA's Security Rule requires a secure method to communicate information – including email or texting – that is certified "under the ONC's 2014 Certification Rule" (ONC, 2015, p. 31). The ONC Guide provides information for the analysis of security risk as well as measures to improve security measures.

The HIPAA security rule provides guidance on standards that protect electronic PHI which include:

- Encryption;
- Auditing functions;
- Backup and recovery routines;
- Unique user IDs and strong passwords;
- Role- or user-based access controls;

- Auto time-out;
- Emergency access; and
- Amendments and accounting of disclosures (ONC, 2015, p. 29).

Meaningful use of health information also falls under HIPAA and focuses on:

- Electronically capturing health information in a structured format;
- Using that information to track key clinical conditions and communicating that information for care coordination purposes (whether that information is structured or unstructured, but in structured format whenever feasible; i.e. standardized languages are preferred);
- Implementing clinical decision support tools to facilitate disease and medication management;
- Using electronic health records (EHRs) to engage patients and families; and
- Reporting clinical quality measures and public health information – including immunizations (ONC, 2015, p. 33).

(Please see Chapter 11 for more information on HIPAA).

Disclosure of Student Immunizations to Schools

HIPAA allows healthcare entities to share information electronically and requires certain provisions to protect the privacy, confidentiality and security of protected health information (PHI). Under both HIPAA and FERPA, parents must consent in writing to the exchange of PHI; however, modifications to HIPAA effective in 2013 reduced the barriers to HIPAA-covered entities sharing immunization data with schools. The final rule allows HIPAA covered entities to "disclose proof of immunization to a school where State or other law requires the school to have such information" (NASN Weekly Digest, 2013, p. 4). HIPAA covered entities must obtain agreement from the parent/guardian to provide the information. It can be an oral (including via phone) agreement from the parent, guardian or other person in loco parent; or from the individual, or the student themselves if they are an adult or emancipated minor. No signature of the permission is required. Parents/guardians may request that their provider disclose immunization data in the future as well – for instance when there is a series of vaccines that needs to be completed. The permission is considered effective until the parent/guardian revokes the permission (NASN Weekly Digest, 2013).

While the oral agreement must be documented by the HIPAA-covered entity, the details of the documentation are left to the healthcare providers' administration. The appropriate person to receive the immunization information is left up to the school's discretion. The 2013 Privacy Rule does not prohibit or require authorization for disclosure of immunization where it is mandated by State law. The Privacy Rule also allows disclosure of PHI without authorization for public health activities which includes State immunization registries (Modifications to the HIPAA Privacy, Security, Enforcement, and Breach Notification Rules under the Health Information Technology for Economic and Clinical Health Act and the Genetic Information Nondiscrimination Act; Modifications to the HIPAA Rules, 2013.).

(See Chapter 37 for more information on immunizations).

Public Health Access to Student Health Data

Recognizing the importance of school health data to effective public health surveillance, intervention, and prevention activities, the Association of State and Territorial Health Officials (ASTHO) (2016) has developed FERPA and HIPAA guidance on the exchange of personally identifiable information (PII) from student records. Areas which ASTHO has identified that school data has the potential to impact public health include: (1) outbreaks of infectious illness, (2) immunization tracking, (3) prevalence of chronic and environmental conditions, (4) success of injury prevention activities, (5) trending of health status such as obesity rates, (6) surveillance of toxic environmental exposures such as lead, and (7) identification of disease outbreaks related to disasters or emergencies. The complexity of data sharing between schools and public health has value yet is subject to complex and sometimes challenging regulations. ASTHO outlines the following areas where data can be shared:

1) Schools may disclose without consent to law enforcement, public health officials, and trained medical personnel in health and safety emergencies with an "articulable and significant threat" (p. 4);
2) Studies conducted on behalf of the school by "federal, state, and local agencies, and independent organizations" (p. 4);
3) To comply with a judicial order or lawfully issued subpoena;
4) To a school where a student is transferring – which can include disciplinary actions
5) As part of a request by the student for financial aid;
6) To accrediting organizations; and
7) To juvenile justice authorities (ASTHO, 2016).

Rights of Minors to Consent

In general, parents have a right to access and make decisions about their minor child's care except in three circumstances where the minor has authority to control their health information:

- "when state or other law does not require the consent of a parent or other person before a minor can obtain a particular healthcare service, and the minor consents to the healthcare service;
- when a court determines or other law authorizes someone other than the parent to make treatment decisions for a minor; or
- when a parent agrees to a confidential relationship between the minor and the healthcare provider" (Pritts, Kayne, & Jacobson, 2009, p. 3-11)

The ONC developed a report that outlines state regulations on access of minors to their healthcare records. This report addressed access by minors to their own records acknowledging that there are complications related to the age of consent for confidential care (including care for substance abuse, sexual health and mental health) (Pritts et al., 2009). The reports differentiated between the rights of parents to be notified vs. have access to their minor child's records related to confidential care. The guidance did not address the issues of parental access to their child's education record as protected by FERPA. The paper identified the complexity of parental access to records related to confidential care for minors and the impact of electronic records on that issue. Generally, "when a minor lawfully consents to healthcare without the permission of the minor's parents, the HIPAA Privacy Rule defers to state laws with respect to whether the healthcare provider must or may notify the parents...or provide access to health information related to such treatment" (Pritts et al., 2009, p. 1-2). HIPAA and FERPA both protect the right of the individual to access and amend records kept by the institution on the patient or student (Pritts, et al., 2009).

HIPAA describes where it defers to state law with regard to disclosure responsibilities including where it permits, prohibits or is silent on disclosure (Pritts et al., 2009). The inexactness of the guidance from HIPAA on rights of minors requires that school nurses be familiar with and have resources regarding HIPAA and minor consent rules in their state. In order to address the variability in access to their minor child's records, the American Academy of Pediatrics recommends the EHR systems reflect the child's age in regards to system privacy protection features (Pritts et al., 2009).

(See Chapter 14 for more information on rights of minors).

Records Retention

Rules related to the retention of healthcare records are governed by state statutes (Pritts et al., 2009). A summary is available on the ONC website at https://www.healthit.gov/sites/default/files/appa7-1.pdf. Records retention requirements of states are generally linked to statutes of limitations related to negligence. Similar consideration for the retention of school health records is prudent given the potential for minors' rights to access their records after they reach the age of 21 years. Nurses are advised to check their state statutes for the most current guidance on records retention–which may be managed by their individual Secretaries of State.

Management of School Health Records

Student health records may be managed on paper or electronic systems – although the convenience and security of electronic records make them the increasingly common choice of nurses and school districts. Paper records may be state, district, or nurse-developed forms that act as a prompt for complete documentation. Electronic records can be self-developed in software programs such as Microsoft Word, Excel or Access; stand-alone school nursing software; or as a health module in a student information system (SIS) (Johnson & Guthrie, 2012). Each method has benefits and risks (See *Table 2* below for Comparison of Documentation Systems).

Table #2 Comparison of Documentation Systems (Johnson & Guthrie, 2012, p. 30. Reprinted with permission).

System	Opportunities	Threats
Paper	Inexpensive, simple to use, high control over access	Records can be easily lost; only one user at a time; record can be inaccessible for remote documentation; does not allow for rapid, systematic entry of data, lacks the ability to aggregate, sort, or query data, and does not identify who has accessed the health information.
Self-developed files in Microsoft Word, Excel or Access	Less expensive; little training required.	Can be destroyed if computer crashes or corrupted; questionable legal protection related to admissibility; only one user at a time; doesn't authenticate who entered data or identify who accessed information.
Health module in a school-wide student information system (SIS)	Benefits of electronic documentation; access to education data; uses database technology to analyze and report on data; can allow direct communication with education staff; no extra training for non-health staff required	Often do not use nursing languages; requires technical support; requires training; may not address nursing specific documentation needs.
Commercial school nursing software	Often use nursing languages; benefits of electronic documentation; uses database technology to analyze and report on data.	Difficult to compare health interventions with education outcomes; requires technical support; requires training; may not allow direct communication with education staff; increases the number of programs to purchase & train for, using a separate system for health decreases communication of data between users of the systems.

Electronic Documentation Systems

In 2004, the increasing cost and complexity of healthcare in the U.S. prompted the government to establish the Office of the National Coordinator for Health Information Technology (ONC). The ONC is managed by the Centers for Medicare and Medicaid (CMS) and was designed as a bi-partisan effort to improve the U.S. healthcare system through technology – including EHRs (Blumenthal, 2009). The goal was to implement "an interoperable health information technology infrastructure to improve the quality and efficiency of health care" (HiTech Answers, n.d., p. 1). An infrastructure that allows communication across systems of care providers was thought to be fundamental to coordination of care.

The ONC has determined that electronic health records (EHRs) will promote (1) complete and accurate health information on patients, (2) improve access to a patient's record for those providing care, (3) improve coordination of care across systems and providers, and (4) improve access by patients to their health record (ONC, n.d.). Benefits of EHRs over paper records include:

- Providing accurate, up-to-date, and complete information about patients at the point of care;

- Enabling quick access to patient records for more coordinated, efficient care;
- Securely sharing electronic information with patients and other clinicians;
- Helping providers more effectively diagnose patients, reduce medical errors, and provide safer care;
- Improving patient and provider interaction and communication, as well as healthcare convenience;
- Enabling safer, more reliable prescribing;
- Helping promote legible, complete documentation and accurate, streamlined coding and billing;
- Enhancing privacy and security of patient data;
- Helping providers improve productivity and work-life balance;
- Enabling providers to improve efficiency and meet their business goals; and
- Reducing costs through decreased paperwork, improved safety, reduced duplication; of testing, and improved health (ONC, n.d., p. 1).

The American Nurses Association supports the use of electronic records as it allows the nurse to collaborate with other members of the student team to "collect, categorize, interpret, manage, evaluate and share relevant information" to promote quality, safety, and improved outcomes (ANA, 2014, p. 187). The National Association of School Nurses (NASN) takes the position that EHRs are "essential ... to provide efficient and effective healthcare in schools and to monitor the health of the entire student population" (NASN, 2014, p. 1).

Elements of EHRs recommended by the Institute of Medicine (IOM) include:

- Complete, accurate data;
- Integration of data from multiple sites;
- Strong protection for confidentiality & data security;
- Continuous access to record;
- Easy access by patient/family;
- Ease of use;
- Inclusion of reminders/alerts;
- Clinical decision support systems;
- Standardized codes/formats;
- Standardized & customized reporting;
- Link to evidence based data; and
- Outcomes analysis (Englebardt & Nelson, 2002, p. 213).

Just like the rights for medication administration and delegation, there are five rights for EHR systems. These include:

- Right Clinical Data – complete; accurate; meaningful;
- Right Presentation – human computer interface is efficient & effective in capturing & displaying data, information, and knowledge;
- Right Decision – clinical decision support that is context sensitive, tailored to the user, based on current evidence and allows documentation of override reasons;

- Right Work Processes – efficient and effective processes and work flows; and
- Right Outcomes – value driven, quality, and cost (Amatayakul, 2009, p. 175).

Interoperability is the ability of electronic "systems to work together" through the adoption of standards for language and protocols (Amatayakul, 2009, p. 499). Critical to the use of and interoperability between systems is the use of standardized languages or coding systems to improve data entry and assure that data can be used appropriate across systems of care. The IOM indicates that the use of standardized languages enhances safety by assuring that care providers have the information they need to coordinate care (IOM, 2012). Described as "essential" by nursing researchers and leaders they "provide names for the clinical phenomena of concern to the nursing profession" (Jones, Lunney, Keenan, & Moorhead, 2010, p. 253).

Standardized nursing languages facilitate "interoperability between different concepts, nomenclatures, and information systems" (ANA, 2014, p. 11). A list of nursing languages can be found in the Nursing Informatics: Scope and Standards of Practice (ANA, 2014). Electronic methods using standardized nursing languages allows for decision support and a "cognitive map" (Von Krough, Dale, & Nadin, 2005, p. 276) for the provision of care prompting nurses to consider the entire nursing process when providing and documenting care and integrated evidence-based practice.

Implementation of electronic health systems is improved with training on the use of the system. A hybrid training model that incorporates online learning, face to face instruction and support from super users – early adopters of technology - can guide integration of the new system by their colleagues. Technical support in the implementation of electronic records improved nurses' knowledge and attitudes toward use of electronic systems as well as compliance with documentation requirements, completeness, and accuracy (Evatt, Ren, Tuite, Reynolds, & Hravnak, 2014). Training for use of the EHR demonstrates an organization's commitment to safe and effective use of the system.

Providing much of the technical support and training in the use of EHRs are nurse informaticists. Nurse informaticists specialize in information and records management in nursing care. They describe the components of health records as a continuum of data, information, knowledge and wisdom. **Data** are "discrete entities ...described objectively without interpretation." Data is interpreted, then organized or structured into **information**. Relationships between bits of information are synthesized by the nurse into **knowledge**. Finally, **wisdom** results when that knowledge is used to "manage and solve human problems" (ANA, 2014, p. 2-3). For example, discrete data points such as 12, 200, 27 and 7.1 are merely a string of numbers. It becomes information when the context is added: 12 noon; 200 mg/dL of blood sugar; 27 grams of carbohydrate; and 7.1 A1c. When set in the context of the nurse's knowledge of diabetes, a plan of care can be developed for the student. When the nurse synthesizes the knowledge about this individual student's diabetes care with their knowledge of the student's past history and the nurse's experience providing care for other students with diabetes, wisdom emerges to support effective nursing care of students and the development of evidence for practice.

Electronic documentation systems allow school nurses to aggregate and report on the data in student health records to better understand not only the history of the student's health needs but to also understand the population of students they serve – regardless of whether that population is special education students, students with special healthcare needs, or district and state level populations of students. In fact, the volume and complexity of data that school nurses collect on students in their large caseloads over the many years of a student's school career make it a challenge to use that data effectively to promote individual and population health unless electronic documentation systems are used.

Using electronic documentation systems that are built to store data in an organized fashion, and retrieve reports of that data, allow school nurses to "bridge the gap between the complexity of medical data and decision-making and the limitations of unaided human cognition" (Amatayakul, 2009, p. vii). Particularly for the population level data that is available in student health documentation, there are robust opportunities to use that information to "promote research, inform policy, and identify best practice" (ANA, 2014, p. 54), thus creating knowledge and wisdom. As population level research related to student health matures, clinical decision support can be built into the EHR. For example, when the diagnosis of asthma is entered, decision support prompting reminders to enter rescue inhalers, peak flow measurement and symptom triggers for the student can be generated by the EHR. Prompts and decision support mechanisms inherent in electronic documentation systems demonstrate the nursing judgement behind the care provided and promote the efficient and thorough documentation required to demonstrate appropriate healthcare.

In order to create an electronic health information system that meets the needs of its constituents, assures compliance with legal requirements, and promotes sustained use after installation, foundational elements need to be in place to assure adoption is most effective:

- an advisory committee that represents end users;
- data points, and vendor selection standards developed by end users;
- an information technology infrastructure;
- a competitive selection process;
- training for staff;
- a strong on-site vendor presence during implementation;
- involved partners (project champions) that are required to be on-site during key implementation points; and
- sustainability of training resources for new staff (Robert Wood Johnson Foundation [RWJF], 2011).

IMPLICATIONS FOR SCHOOL NURSE PRACTICE

Types of School Health Records

School nurses maintain many records to describe student health and the care that is provided. These include:

- records of care;
- individualized healthcare and emergency care plans;
- communication with other providers, parent/guardian(s) and students;
- medication records;
- screening results;
- immunization records;

- special education records;
- staff training records;
- incident/accident/injury records; and
- billing records.

Healthcare records should reflect the nursing process, standards of care and the critical thinking that went into that care. The care should be documented contemporaneously (at the time that care is given) and by the person providing the care. Appropriately documenting care assures that all members of the health and/or educational team can coordinate to deliver student-centered healthcare, and that the nurse and the district demonstrate that they have discharged their duty for care. *(See Chapter 9 for more information on school health documentation).* The record of healthcare also includes communication with students, parent/guardian(s) and other members of the school/healthcare team; and the individualized health plans (IHPs) developed by the nurse.

IHPs, including emergency care plans, contain important information on the guidance the school nurse provides to school staff on the care to be given for a student's health condition. The IHP demonstrates the nurse's discharge of their duty of care in the event that any questions arise. Updates to the care plan should be documented with the date and reasons any change in the care plan was made. Zimmerman (2013) identified the value of electronic systems in monitoring and documenting outcomes of care.

Medication records are especially important parts of the school health record. As with medication administration in any setting, the importance of documentation is reflected in the Agency for Healthcare Research and Quality's "Six Rights of Medication Administration:"

- RIGHT Patient;
- RIGHT Medication;
- RIGHT Dose;
- RIGHT Route;
- RIGHT Time; and
- RIGHT Documentation (Agency for Healthcare Research and Quality [AHRQ], 2006).

The *right documentation* includes the requirement to promptly document medication as it is administered to prevent double dosing. Documentation of administered medications is required of all caregivers – licensed providers or unlicensed assistive personnel (UAP), who are delegated to administer medications.

Screenings that may include vision, hearing, dental, body mass index (BMI), scoliosis, lead or other health measures are often required by state statutes. Appropriate record management demonstrates compliance with those statutes. When managed in electronic systems, the reports produced from the aggregated data of the screenings provide the opportunity to better understand student health status, care needs and population health issues. Screening records should include the date of the screening, the results, and completion status of screening referrals – such as a completed physical examination by a professional and any treatment prescribed, e.g., glasses, etc.

Immunization records demonstrate compliance with state school attendance requirements related to the spread of vaccine-preventable illness. Records should be maintained over the student's school career to allow assessment of risk of illness individually and in the overall school population in the event of an outbreak. Complex algorithms to determine compliance with state statutes and the guidelines of the Advisory Committee on Immunization Practices (ACIP) make electronic management of immunization data more efficient. Many states maintain immunization registries that collect immunization administration data, organize it by patient, analyze it for compliance with recommended immunization schedules, and report on recommendations for due dates to complete an immunization series. Using electronic systems in this way promotes effective population level care and the efficient use of vaccine supplies, through the accurate and timely records that can be accessed as needed to manage care, demonstrate compliance with statutes, and monitor population health in the event of an outbreak.

Health components of special education records may include vision and hearing screening results, recommendations by the student's medical provider, health and developmental history, nursing assessment of the student's health and current needs, and the indication for any nursing or health services required to allow the student to access their federally protected right to a free and appropriate education (FAPE). Electronic programs document compliance with the procedural rules for IDEA. Billing records are most often associated with nursing or health services that are provided as part of a student's special education. Nursing documentation is often a component of that billing record.

Records describing training of school staff for medication delegation and individual student emergency care planning should include the date, contents of the training, and the names and signatures of the trainer and the trainee(s). Documentation of staff training is required to demonstrate appropriate delegation processes and compliance with statutes. Ongoing supervision of delegated tasks must also be documented and describe the trainee's verbal, demonstrated understanding of the skill of administering medications and/or individual student emergency care, and the dates of ongoing supervision.

Accident and injury records comprise factual documentation of an accident or injury that occurs while the student is in the custody of the school. The report is completed by the person who witnessed the injury and/or provided first aid. If this person was not the school nurse, the nurse may also include their documentation of any follow-up care or contact with the student's parent/guardian(s) or medical providers.

Personal notes – those "maintained by and for a sole individual as a memory aid and not made available to any other faculty or staff" have long been considered to be exempt from FERPA protections; however, nurses should be aware that their notes have the potential to be subpoenaed (Boston College Office of Student Services, 2016, p. 1).

Electronic Documentation Systems

Electronic documentation systems hold great value in helping school nurses organize and report the volumes of information they create in the course of their daily care of students.

Using EHRs meaningfully – using standardized languages with the ability to be interoperable with other systems – improves the safety and efficiency of care for children. Interoperability with a children's hospital and clinic records, for example, can improve communication of critical details to reduce hospital readmissions, improve continuity of care, and facilitate medication management. The outcomes of care coordinated across school and clinic include improved school attendance for students, reduced interruptions in employment for parents/guardians, reduced cost of child healthcare for society, and improved academic outcomes (Basch, 2009; Wang et al., 2014). Some acute and ambulatory healthcare systems allow school nurses to access their student's electronic health record with the permission of the student's parent/guardian(s) which can also support coordinated care.

The Triple Aim is a foundational concept in healthcare reform developed by the Institute for Healthcare Improvement (IHI). It is a systems approach to the improvement in healthcare delivery that focuses on three elements:

- Improving the patient experience of care (including quality and satisfaction);
- Improving the health of populations; and
- Reducing the per capita cost of health care (Institute for Healthcare Improvement [IHI], n.d., para. 1)

The IHI endorses the use of EHRs to achieve the Triple Aim. It is important that school nurses also promote the use of electronic school health documentation systems that are interoperable with the student's other healthcare records to assure that the "breadth, depth and pervasiveness of school health data" (Johnson & Guthrie, 2012, p. 104) is available to support the Triple Aim. This allows coordination care with providers in the acute and ambulatory care settings. Interoperable records improve the accessibility of care records, and reduce the expense, and risk of error from multiple human data entry events.

Privacy, Confidentiality and Security of School Health Records

School nurses have an ethical and a legal obligation to assure the privacy, confidentiality and security of the information they collect on student health (ANA, 2015; ANA & NASN, 2017; USDE, 2015a).

While paper systems limit direct access to the healthcare information, electronic systems can improve the confidentiality and security of healthcare records through a variety of measures as described in Table 1 above (page 3). For example, EHRs can partition access to the various parts of the system based on role-specific permissions. This means that the system can be set to only allow those staff identified as nurses to access health records, or to only allow only dietary specialists to access student lunch accounts. In addition, an audit log, where the system keeps track of who accesses the record and the date and time that any changes are made, can result in tighter control over access to student records. The log of who accesses the record meets FERPA requirements to maintain a record of where education records were disclosed. For these reasons, knowledge of fundamental security measures needed for health records, and participation in the processes to select and implement an electronic documentation system are important responsibilities of school nurses.

While many districts have an information technology (IT) department, their expertise is primarily in education records, and the school nurse must be aware of and support requirements for privacy and security of health information as well. School nurses must assure that their IT professionals have the information they need to assure that electronic school health records meet health documentation requirements including "types, maintenance, protection, access, retention, destruction, and confidentiality" (NASN, 2014, p. 1). These features should be clearly discussed as part of the negotiations when purchasing an electronic system.

Another benefit of electronic systems is in logging health room visits. Parents technically have a right to review any records kept on their child – including a log of health room activity. Health room logs that contain information on multiple students may not adequately protect another student's privacy, if the log is requested by another parent to obtain access to information on their own student. If a record is subpoenaed, it may be required to be presented without redacting the private health room visits of other students. An individual student's privacy may be at risk even if no other information than the student's name and reason for visit is kept on a health room log of visits. It is problematic and a likely violation of confidentiality if other students see the names and reasons for a health visit by students who came before them that day.

Individual records of health room care should be used to assure the privacy of individual students. Electronic health records can enhance privacy by allowing an individual student to log themselves into the health room, capturing the date and time and potentially the reason for their visit, through the use of the student's unique student ID and password. Electronic documentation systems that aggregate student log-ins on a screen seen only by the nurse can allow the nurse to triage students for care, yet maintain the privacy of an individual student's reason for the visit.

For all student records, a parent's right to access their child's healthcare records may be complicated by minor's rights to assent to care – rights which vary from state to state. School nurses should be familiar with their state's laws related to parental access to records for confidential student healthcare.

In the healthcare setting, EHRs are required to be certified for compliance with the ONC to assure they meet the standards for privacy, and security as well as interoperability and safety standards (ONC, 2016). No similar certification process for electronic school health records has been identified at this time.

As in other healthcare settings, the use of electronic records by school nurses is important to support efficient documentation of compliance with legal standards of care. Documentation of care is enhanced with appropriate electronic systems that are built to support the nursing process and evidence-based practice. Using school health data to support care decisions assures the inclusion of real time entry of medication use, description of student symptoms and response to care, and the professional assessment by a school nurse to establish a data driven treatment plan. Screens for data entry in electronic health records can be set up to prompt data entry and even require that data be entered in specific fields to efficiently support complete and timely documentation.

CONCLUSION

School nurses stand at the intersection of both the health and education sectors. As such, they generate records that must consider the requirements of both sectors. Federal statutes, such as FERPA and HIPAA, protect the privacy and security of student information that must be balanced against the legitimate educational "need to know" of school staff providing direct healthcare to students. The maintenance of records to appropriately document healthcare delivery is an important aspect of the role of the school nurse.

RESOURCES

General

- Agency for Healthcare Research and Quality: National Guideline Clearinghouse: Guideline for Medication Management, https://www.guideline.gov/summaries/summary/39268

- IDEA – Building the Legacy, http://idea.ed.gov/explore

- National Association of School Nurses (NASN) & National Association of State School Nurse Consultants (NASSNC) School Nursing Services Data; Standardized Documentation, Collection, and Utilization Joint Resolution

- Parent and Educator Resource Guide to Section 504 in Public Elementary and Secondary Schools, https://www2.ed.gov/about/offices/list/ocr/docs/504-resource-guide-201612.pdf

Electronic Documentation Systems

- Institute for Healthcare Improvement and the Triple Aim, https://www.ihi.org/engage/initiatives/tripleaim/pages/default.aspx

- Health IT.gov Guide to Privacy and Security of Electronic Health Information https://www.healthit.gov/sites/default/files/pdf/privacy/privacy-and-security-guide.pdf

- NASN Position Statement: *School Nurse Role in Electronic School Health Records* http://www.nasn.org/Portals/0/positions/2014psehr.pdf

- Office of the National Coordinator for Health Information Technology (ONC) https://www.healthit.gov/

- Privacy and Security Solutions for Interoperable Health Information Exchange https://www.healthit.gov/sites/default/files/290-05-0015-state-law-access-report-1.pdf

- Summary of Privacy and Technical Assistance Center Topics and Services http://ptac.ed.gov/sites/default/files/PTAC%20Service%20Offerings_4-13-16_508.pdf

- Washington State Staff Training Records http://www.k12.wa.us/BulletinsMemos/memos2012/M064-12Attach3.doc

Privacy, Confidentiality & Security

- Comparison of FERPA and HIPAA Privacy Rule for Accessing Student Health Data http://www.astho.org/programs/preparedness/public-health-emergency-law/public-health-and-schools-toolkit/comparison-of-ferpa-and-hipaa-privacy-rule/

- Data Security: Top Threats to Data Protection http://ptac.ed.gov/sites/default/files/Issue%20Brief%20Data%20Security%20Top%20Threats%20to%20Data%20Protection.pdf

- Disclosure of Student Immunizations to Schools
  http://www.nasn.org/Portals/0/digest/20130822_5616_Federal_Register_Immunization_Disclosure.pdf

- SECTION 164.512(B)—DISCLOSURE OF STUDENT IMMUNIZATIONS TO SCHOOLS
  https://www.federalregister.gov/documents/2013/01/25/2013-01073/modifications-to-the-hipaa-privacy-security-enforcement-and-breach-notification-rules-under-the

- FERPA: Frequently Asked Questions
  http://familypolicy.ed.gov/faq-page#t89n440

- FERPA: Postsecondary
  https://www2.ed.gov/policy/gen/guid/fpco/pdf/ferpafaq.pdf

- Health Insurance Portability and Accountability Act (1996) – HIPAA
  https://www.hhs.gov/hipaa/for-professionals/privacy/

- HHS - FERPA & HIPAA
  http://www.hhs.gov/hipaa/for-professionals/faq/ferpa-and-hipaa

- Joint Guidance on the Application of the Family Educational Rights and Privacy Act (FERPA) and the Health Insurance Portability and Accountability Act of 1996 (HIPAA) to Student Health Records
  http://www2.ed.gov/policy/gen/guid/fpco/doc/ferpa-hipaa-guidance.pdf

- Protection of Pupil Rights Amendment
  http://familypolicy.ed.gov/ppra

- Public Health Access to Student Health Data: Authorities and Limitations in Sharing Information Between Schools and Public Health Agencies
  http://www.astho.org/Programs/Preparedness/Public-Health-Emergency-Law/Public-Health-and-Schools-Toolkit/Public-Health-Access-to-Student-Health-Data/

- State Laws Expressly Granting Minors the Right to consent to Health Care Without Parental Permission and Addressing Disclosure of Related Information to Parents. Table A-8a Overview
  https://www.healthit.gov/sites/default/files/appa8-1.pdf

REFERENCES

Agency for Healthcare Research and Quality. (2006). *National guideline clearinghouse: Medication management guideline*. Retrieved from https://www.guideline.gov/summaries/summary/39268

Amatayakul, M. K. (2009). *Electronic healthcare records: A practical guide for professionals and organizations* (4th ed.). Chicago: American Health Information Management Association.

American Nurses Association. (2014). *Nursing Informatics: Scope and standards of practice* (2nd ed.). Silver Spring, MD: Nursesbooks.org.

American Nurses Association. (2015). *Code of ethics for nurses*. Silver Spring, MD: Author.

American Nurses Association & National Association of School Nurses. (2017). *School nursing: Scope and standards of* practice (3ʳᵈ ed.). Silver Spring, MD: Author.

Americans with Disabilities Act of 1990 (ADA) (2000), 42 U.S.C. §§ 12101-12213

Association of State and Territorial Health Officials. (2016). *Public health access to student health data: Authorities and limitation in sharing information between schools and public health agencies*. Retrieved from http://www.astho.org/Programs/Preparedness/Public-Health-Emergency-Law/Public-Health-and-Schools-Toolkit/Public-Health-Access-to-Student-Health-Data/

Basch, C. E. (2011). Healthier students are better learners: High quality, strategically plans, and effectively coordinated school health programs must be a fundamental mission of schools to help close the achievement gap. *The Journal of School Health, 81*, 650-662. doi: 10.1111/j.1746-1561.2011.00640.x

Beach, J., & Oates, J. (2014, May 7). Maintaining best practice in record-keeping and documentation. *Nursing Standard, 28*(36), 45-50. http://dx.doi.org/10.7748/ns.29.15.61.s49

Bergren, M. D. (2005). Electronic records and technology. In N. C. Schwab & M. C. Gelfman (Eds.), *Legal issues in school health services,* (pp. 317-334). New York, NY: Authors Choice Press.

Blumenthal, D. (2009, December 30). Launching HITECH. *New England Journal of Medicine*. doi: 10.1056/ NEJMp0912825

Boston College Office of Student Services. (2016). *FERPA: What faculty and staff members need to know*. Retrieved from http://www.bc.edu/offices/stserv/ferpa_faculty.html

Chou, D., & Sengupta, S. (2008). Infrastructure and security. In T. H. Payne (Ed.), *Practical guide to clinical computing systems* (pp. 37-78). Boston, MA: Academic Press.

Englebardt, S. P., & Nelson, R. (2002). *Health care informatics: An interdisciplinary approach*. New York: Authors Choice Press.

Evatt, M., Ren, D., Tuite, P., Reynolds, C., & Hravnak, M. (2014, March-April). Development and implementation of an educational support process for electronic nursing admission assessment documentation. MedSurg Nursing, 23(2), 89-95. MEDLINE Info:PMID: 24933785 NLM UID: 9300545

Gelfman, M. H., & Schwab, N. C. (2005). School health records and documentation. In M. H. Gelfman & N. C. Schwab, *Legal issues in school health services* (pp. 298-316). New York: Authors Choice Press.

Griffith, R. (2016). For the record: Keeping detailed notes. *British Journal of Nursing, 25*, 408 - 409. doi: http://dx.doi.org/10.12968/bjon.2016.25.7.408

HIPAA Journal. (n.d.). *HIPAA history*. Retrieved from http://www.hipaajournal.com/hipaa-history/

HiTech Answers. (n.d.). *The quest for EHR adoption*. Retrieved from http://www.hitechanswers.net/ehr-adoption-2/history-of-ehr-adoption/

Hunter, K. M. (2002). Electronic health records. In S. P. Englebardt, & R. Nelson (Eds.), *Health care informatics: An interdisciplinary approach* (pp. 209-230). St. Louis, MO: Mosby.

Individuals with Disability Education Improvement Act (2004), 20 U.S.C. 1400 et seq.

Institute for Healthcare Improvement. (n.d.). *The IHI triple aim*. Retrieved from http://www.ihi.org/engage/initiatives/tripleaim/pages/default.aspx

Institute of Medicine. (2012). *Health IT and patient safety: Building safer systems for better care* (National Academy of Sciences). Retrieved from http://www.nationalacademies.org/hmd/Reports/2011/Health-IT-and-Patient-Safety-Building-Safer-Systems-for-Better-Care.aspx

Johnson, K. H., & Guthrie, S. (2012). Harnessing the power of student health data: Selecting, using, and implementing electronic school health documentation systems. *NASN School Nurse, 27*(1), 27-33. doi: 10.1177/1942602X11429828

Jones, D., Lunney, M., Keenan, G., & Moorhead, S. (2010). Standardized nursing languages: Essential for the nursing workforce. In *Annual review of nursing research* (pp. 253-294). http://dx.doi.org/10.1891/0739-6686.28.253

NASN Weekly Digest. (2013, August 22). *Modifications of the HIPAA Privacy, Security, Enforcement, and Breach Notification Rules under the Health Information Technology for Economic and Clinical Health Act the Genetic Information Nondiscrimination Act; Modifications to the HIPAA Rules, 78*(1), 5616 *Federal Register § 164.512(b)*. Retrieved from https://www.nasn.org/Portals/0/digest/20130822_5616_Federal_Register_Immunization_Disclosure.pdf

National Association of School Nurses. (2014). *School nurse role in electronic school health records* [Position Statement]. Retrieved from http://journals.sagepub.com/doi/abs/10.1177/1942602X14534391

Office of the National Coordinator. (2015). *Guide to privacy and security of electronic health information*. Retrieved from https://www.healthit.gov/sites/default/files/pdf/privacy/privacy-and-security-guide.pdf

Office of the National Coordinator. (2016). *Health IT certification program overview*. Retrieved from https://www.healthit.gov/sites/default/files/onc-healthit-certification-program-overview.pdf

Office of the National Coordinator. (n.d.). *Benefits of EHRs*. Retrieved from http://www.hitechanswers.net/ehr-adoption-2/history-of-ehr-adoption/

Pritts, J., Kayne, K., & Jacobson, R. (2009). *Privacy and security solutions for interoperable health information exchange: Report on state medical record access laws* (0209825.000.015.100). Washington, DC: Government Printing Office.

Rehabilitation Act of 1973, 29 U.S.C. § 504

Robert Wood Johnson Foundation. (2011). *School health connection goes electronic: Developing a health information management system for New Orleans' school-based health centers*. Retrieved from http://www.rwjf.org/content/dam/farm/reports/program_results_reports/2011/rwjf71528

U.S. Department of Education. (2004). *Legislative history of major FERPA provisions*. Retrieved from
http://www2.ed.gov/policy/gen/guid/fpco/ferpa/leg-history.html

U.S. Department of Education. (2015a). *Family Educational Rights and Privacy Act (FERPA)*. Retrieved from
http://www2.ed.gov/policy/gen/guid/fpco/ferpa/index.html

U.S. Department of Education. (2015*b*). *FERPA general guidance for parents*. Retrieved from
http://www2.ed.gov/policy/gen/guid/fpco/ferpa/parents.html

U.S. Department of Education. (n.d.). *Frequently asked questions about FERPA*. Retrieved from
http://familypolicy.ed.gov/faq-page#t89n440

U.S. Department of Education. (n.d.). *FERPA: Frequently asked questions*. Retrieved from
http://familypolicy.ed.gov/faq-page#t89n440

U.S. Department of Education. (n.d*.). Individuals with disabilities in education*. Retrieved from
http://idea.ed.gov/explore/search?search_option=all&query=documentation&GO.x=0&GO.y=0

U.S. Department of Education. (n.d.). *Privacy and technical assistance center.* Retrieved from
http://ptac.ed.gov/

U.S. Department of Education, Office for Civil Rights. (2016). Parent and educator resource guide to Section
504 in public elementary and secondary schools. Retrieved from https://www2.ed.gov/about/offices/
list/ocr/docs/504-resource-guide-201612.pdf

U.S. Department of Health and Human Services, Office for Civil Rights. (2008). *Health information privacy:
Student Immunizations*. Retrieved from http://www.hhs.gov/hipaa/for-professionals/faq/student-
immunizations

U.S. Department of Health and Human Services, Office for Civil Rights. (2010). *Protected health
information*. Retrieved from http://www.hhs.gov/hipaa/for-professionals/privacy/special-topics/de-
identification/#protected

Department of Health and Human Services (2000). Standards for Privacy of Individually Identifiable Health
Information; Final Rule, 65 Federal Register § 160.

U.S. Department of Health and Human Services, Office for Civil Rights. (n.d.). *Covered entities, business
associates, and PHI.* Retrieved from http://www.hhs.gov/hipaa/for-professionals/index.html

U.S. Department of Health and Human Services & U.S. Department of Education. (2008). *Joint guidance
on the application of the Family Education Rights and Privacy Act (FERPA) and the Health Insurance
Portability and Accountability Act of 1996 (HIPAA) to student health records.* Retrieved from
http://www2.ed.gov/policy/gen/guid/fpco/doc/ferpa-hipaa-guidance.pdf

Von Krough, G., Dale, C., & Nadin, D. (2005, Third Quarter). A framework for integrating NANDA, NIC, and
NOC in electronic patient records. *Journal of Nursing Scholarship, 37*(3), 275-281. doi: 10.1111/j.1547-
5069.2005. 00047.x

Wang, L. Y., Vernon-Smiley, M., Gapinski, M. A., DeSisto, M., Maughan, E., & Sheetz, A. (2014, Jul). Cost-benefit study of school nursing services. *JAMA Pediatrics*, *168*, 642-648. http://dx.doi.org/10.1001/jamapediatrics.2013.5441

Zimmerman, B. (2013). Student health and education plans. In J. Selekman (Ed.), *School nursing: A comprehensive text* (2nd ed.) (pp. 284-314). Philadelphia, PA: F.A. Davis.

LAWS/POLICIES

Chapter 11

FAMILY EDUCATIONAL RIGHTS AND PRIVACY ACT ("FERPA")/HEALTH INSURANCE PORTABILITY AND ACCOUNTABILITY ACT ("HIPAA")

Attorney William J. Roberts
Attorney Gwen J. Zittoun
Shipman & Goodwin LLP

DESCRIPTION OF ISSUE

The confidentiality of student records within the educational environment is a topic fraught with legal and practical implications that present a constant struggle for school nurses, administrators and other school personnel. While the importance of maintaining the confidentiality of personally identifiable information (PII) cannot be emphasized enough, it must be balanced in the school environment with the need for educational professionals to have access to information necessary to appropriately and effectively educate students and the right of parents/guardians and eligible students to access education records.

The two major federal laws addressing the confidentiality of student records are the Federal Educational Rights and Privacy Act (FERPA) and the Health Insurance Portability and Accountability Act (HIPAA). While state laws may also address confidentiality requirements, state law cannot conflict with federal law. Federal law serves as the base for building these state requirements. HIPAA is widely known and understood to be the law governing all medical records, while FERPA serves to protect the confidentiality and integrity of student's education records. **What is surprising to many, however, is that, as a general rule (to which there is always an exception) FERPA governs the confidentiality and access to all education records, which includes student health records once those records are created or received and maintained by a school district.**

BACKGROUND

FERPA - At A Glance

Congress enacted FERPA in 1974 for the purposes of protecting the confidentiality of, and providing access to, education records of students (34 CFR § 99.2). FERPA requires that educational institutions in receipt of federal funding maintain the confidentiality of PII within education records and permit parental access to inspect and correct such records. An educational institution that does not receive federal funding is not subject to the requirements of FERPA. Private elementary and secondary schools, which do not receive federal funding may not be required to comply with FERPA, may be guided by state laws and principles of contract and negligence in their management of student records (34 C.F.R. § 99.1).

FERPA is administered by the Family Policy Compliance Office (FPCO) in the United States Department of Education (20 U.S.C. § 1232g). The FPCO accepts complaints related to the application of FERPA and issues letters to interested parties explaining the law's applicability to individual factual scenarios. While schools risk loss of federal funding for failure to comply with FERPA's requirements, a parent or eligible student does not have the right to sue an educational institution for an alleged violation of FERPA (*Gonzaga University v. Doe* (2002) holding that parent/guardian(s) and eligible students have no private right of action to enforce FERPA).

Simply put, FERPA contains two explicit provisions: first, it mandates the confidentiality of PII in education records, subject to limited exceptions for disclosure (20 U.S.C. § 1232g(b)); and second, it grants to parents (parents include "a natural parent, a guardian, or an individual acting as a parent in the absence of a parent or a guardian", 34 C.F.R. § 99.3) the right to inspect and review education records of their students and make corrections where the records are inaccurate, misleading, or otherwise in violation of privacy rights of students (20 U.S.C. § 1232g(a)(2)). This parental right of access applies to both custodial and non-custodial parents. Both parents have full access rights under FERPA unless and until the school district is provided evidence of the revocation of that right by a court order, state statute, or legally binding document (34 C.F.R. § 99.4). These rights of access and amendment transfer to the student upon attainment of the age of eighteen or enrollment in a postsecondary institution (making the student an "eligible student" under FERPA, 20 U.S.C. § 1232g(d)).

Importantly, FERPA's confidentiality provision is limited to education **records**, which are defined rather broadly as records that are directly related to a student and maintained by an educational agency or institution or by a party acting for the agency or institution, which may include a health department providing school nurse services (34 C.F.R. § 99.3). If the student information is not actually documented (for example, if information is provided verbally or by observation and is not otherwise included in a document), it is not covered by FERPA. Education records do not include records that are kept in the sole possession of the maker, which are only used as a personal memory aid and which are not accessible or revealed to any other person except an individual serving as a temporary substitute. However, if the document is revealed to any other individual, it may be considered an education record if it meets the other criteria contained in the definition (34 C.F.R. § 99.3).

Interestingly, it is not the education records themselves that FERPA protects, but the PII included within those records. Indeed, under some circumstances, schools may be required to produce education records pursuant to a state's public records law; however, any PII must be redacted from those records prior to disclosure unless an exception applies. Under FERPA, PII includes what one might expect: a student's name, birth date, address, parents' names, and mother's maiden name. Maybe more surprisingly, PII also includes information that is linked or linkable to a specific student that would lead a reasonable person within the school community to know the identity of the student (34 C.F.R. § 99.3). Finally, PII also includes student-specific information relating to a "targeted request." A school district is prohibited from releasing documents, even if cleaned of identifying information, to an individual the school "reasonably believes knows the identity of the student to whom the education record relates" (34 C.F.R. § 99.3, See the definition of "personally identifiable information" at (g)). For example, if two students are involved in a school incident, the school may be prohibited from releasing certain information to each of the students' parents, as both families know the identity of the other student involved.

HIPAA - At A Glance

HIPAA is a federal law that, among other things, governs the use, disclosure, maintenance and safeguarding of patient health information. In the context of HIPAA, patient information (also referred to as protected health information or "PHI") is defined broadly to include virtually any record an individual or entity maintains about a person's past, present or future health care, health status or payment for healthcare services (45 C.F.R. §

160.103). However, HIPAA does not apply to every entity in the healthcare field. Instead, HIPAA applies to only two sets of individuals and entities known as *"covered entities"* and *"business associates."* A covered entity is a healthcare provider, health insurance plan or a healthcare clearinghouse that conducts certain transactions, such as electronic billing for patient services (45 C.F.R. § 160.103). A business associate is a vendor of a covered entity that creates, uses, discloses or maintains PHI for or on behalf of the covered entity during the course of the services it provides (45 C.F.R. § 160.103). For example, a physician's practice may provide PHI to a lawyer or consultant for compliance work or may utilize a cloud storage company to maintain patient records. In these examples, the lawyer, consultant and cloud storage company would be business associates of the physician and thus subject to HIPAA. A healthcare clearinghouse is an entity, including a billing service, repricing company, community health management information system or community health information system, and "value-added" networks and switches, that performs certain functions relating to the processing of health information (45 C.F.R. § 160.103).

It is important to note that unless a person or entity meets the (very technical) definitions of covered entity or business associate, they are not subject to HIPAA and are not required to comply with its voluminous rules and regulations.

For those that are subject to HIPAA, the law's rules and requirements can be grouped into three categories. The first is the *"Privacy Rule,"* which is an extensive set of regulations that establish how covered entities and business associates may use and disclose PHI and the rights individuals have to access, amend, restrict access to and obtain information about their PHI. The *"Security Rule"* establishes the physical, technical and administrative safeguards a covered entity and business associate must utilize in order to protect the confidentiality and integrity of the electronic PHI it maintains. The third component is the *"Breach Notification Rule."* This regulation defines when an inadvertent or authorized use or disclosure of PHI constitutes a data breach and sets forth how a covered entity or business associate must react when such a breach is discovered, including providing notice to affected individuals, the media and/or governmental authorities (45 C.F.R. §§ 164.400-414).

In the normal course, HIPAA's privacy, security and breach notification rules do not apply to the healthcare records created or maintained by schools. This may be because the school is not a HIPAA covered entity (i.e., it does not perform HIPAA transactions, such as electronically billing an insurer) or because the student health records it maintains are not PHI. Specifically, HIPAA does not apply to any information that is also student health information in education records protected by FERPA. In other words, if FERPA applies to a particular record, HIPAA does not. That said, Section 3 will discuss several instances in which HIPAA may come into play in the public school setting.

IMPLICATIONS FOR SCHOOL NURSE PRACTICE

The management of student records impacts the daily practice of school nurses. While school nurses must keep in mind the need to maintain confidentiality, they must also address the need for other school professionals and parents to have access to those same records under certain circumstances. School personnel are encouraged to review their school district policies concerning student confidentiality and student records and to review the specific procedural requirements of FERPA relating to the confidentiality of education records. The vast extent of this law runs beyond the scope of this Chapter. However, simply put, for schools to disclose PII from education records that are within the purview of FERPA, either a parent or an eligible student must consent explicitly in writing to the disclosure, or one of several statutory exceptions to the consent requirement must apply (20 U.S.C. §§ 1232g(b)(1) -(2)). As with many laws, the exceptions under FERPA are extensive and -- whether or not it is realized, impact the day to day work of every school nurse.

Confidentiality

1. *No Access by Third Parties without Parental Consent*

   Under FERPA, disclosure of PII within education records is authorized only when parents or eligible students provide written consent to the disclosure or a statutory exception applies (20 U.S.C. § 1232g (b)(1) -(2); 34 C.F.R. § 99.30). The signed, dated, written consent must specify which records may be disclosed, the purpose of the disclosure, and the party to whom the disclosure may be made (34 C.F.R. § 99.30(b)).

   As related to this limitation on disclosure, FERPA requires schools to institute security protections to prevent unauthorized release of PII (34 C.F.R. § 99.31(1)(ii)). Schools must, either physically or electronically, prevent access to third parties and school professionals who do not have a legitimate educational interest in the PII. Practically, this means securing paper records in locked or otherwise restricted locations and including password protection or other security measures on electronically-stored information. School nurses should take further steps to protect PII, specifically as related to discussing or reviewing confidential information in areas where third parties may be present, whether while on the telephone, using the computer or providing treatment to students.

2. *Exceptions to Parental Consent*

   FERPA includes a variety of narrowly tailored exceptions to the general confidentiality requirement. If an exception applies, parental consent is not required prior to the release of PII contained within education records, although some exceptions require parental notification or review of records being disclosed. As will be seen, education professionals would find everyday functions difficult without the use of FERPA exceptions. Some of these exceptions include disclosure to another school where the student seeks or intends to enroll; in connection with financial aid applications; to a state official pursuant to statute; pursuant to a court order or subpoena; to accrediting institutions; and to organizations conducting studies for or on behalf of educational agencies to develop, validate, or administer predictive tests, administer student aid programs, or improve instruction (34 C.F.R. § 99.31). Below, explanations and examples of the most commonly used exceptions for school nurses are provided, (**note:** a complete explanation of the entire list of exceptions goes beyond the scope of this Chapter and may require reviewing resources provided or consultation with the school district administration and board attorneys).

   a. Legitimate Educational Interest

      The first and most commonly used exception is disclosure to school officials, including teachers, within the school whom the school has determined to have legitimate educational interests in the PII (34 C.F.R. § 99.31(a)(1)(i)(A)). The term *school official* is not defined by the applicable statute or regulations; however, the FPCO generally interprets the term to include parties such as professors, instructors, administrators, health staff, counselors, and others. Contractors, consultants, volunteers, or other parties to whom the school has outsourced institutional services may also be considered school officials, if they meet additional elements provided by the regulations (34 C.F.R. § 99.31(a)(1)(i) (B)). School officials are generally deemed to have legitimate educational interests when they need to review an education record as part of their professional responsibilities (FPCO, Letter to Davis,2005). Care must be taken to ensure that such officials obtain access only to those education records in which they have a legitimate educational interest (34 C.F.R. § 99.31(a)(1)(ii)).

Most importantly, this exception allows a teacher, administrator, counselor, school nurse or other school professional access to a student's PII if that individual has a legitimate, professional interest in viewing the information. For example, a teacher attending a meeting pursuant to Section 504 of the Rehabilitation Act ("Section 504") for a student with a peanut allergy may have a legitimate educational interest in reviewing that student's health information, as that teacher would be required to participate in the meeting and understand the nature of the student's health issues relative to the student's educational needs. Also, members of an individualized education program team may have a legitimate education interest in reviewing a psychiatric evaluation for a student identified with an emotional disturbance. Schools and individuals working within the school should ensure that appropriate safeguards are used to protect education records; however, all school professionals must be aware that other professionals within the school are able to access education records, without parent consent, if such access is legitimately related to the performance of the individual's professional responsibilities.

While recognizing the importance of monitoring proper access to and disclosure of students' education records, pursuant to laws such as FERPA and HIPAA, it is also necessary to balance those interests in complying with other education laws. Specifically, while we must ensure the confidentiality of student information, we must also comply with laws such as the Individuals with Disabilities Education Act, Section 504, and the Americans with Disabilities Act. Compliance with these laws generally requires implementation of educational programs and accommodation plans specific to the unique needs of students. Schools must ensure that appropriate staff have access to the student-specific information necessary to effectively implement a student's plan.

b. Parents of Dependent Students

Once a student reaches age eighteen or attends a postsecondary institution, that student becomes an eligible student under FERPA and all the rights that are conveyed to parents transfer to the eligible student. This includes the right to access (and request amendment of) his or her education records. Significantly, however, Congress recognized that with this shift in rights, comes serious concern by parents about losing access to educationally-related information concerning their children. Thus, another exception. FERPA expressly permits disclosure of education records to parents of dependent students, as defined by the Internal Revenue Code (34 C.F.R. § 99.31(a)(8)). If a parent claims a child on his or her tax returns after the student turns eighteen, the school may release to that parent and the parent not claiming the student the student's education records without the student's written consent. As a practical matter, most students at the secondary level are still claimed as dependents by their parents, so although the student can access and request amendment of their record, parents may continue to have access to the records.

c. Health and Safety Emergencies

FERPA has always generally included an exception for the disclosure of PII in the case of a health or safety emergency, which was previously narrowly construed (34 C.F.R. § 99.31(a) (10)). In 2008, however, FERPA was amended to clarify that an educational agency or institution may disclose PII from an education record to appropriate parties, including parents of an eligible student, in connection with an emergency, if knowledge of the information is necessary to protect the health or safety of the student or other individuals (34 C.F.R. § 99.36(a)). In making a determination as to whether such disclosure is necessary for health or safety reasons, the school may consider the totality of the circumstances pertaining to a threat to the health or safety of a student or other individuals (34 C.F.R. § 99.36(c)). If it is determined that there is an articulable and significant threat to the health or safety of a student or other individuals, the school may make the disclosure necessary to protect the health or safety of those involved (34 C.F.R. § 99.36(c)). Significantly, as long as there is a rational basis for the school's determination of an articulable and significant threat, and the school has documented the articulable threat, the Department of Education will not substitute its own judgment for the educational agency with regard to the decision to release PII (34 C.F.R. § 99.36(c)). Additional confirmation of this is discussed by the FPCO in guidance letters and by the U.S. Department of Education commentary on the federal regulations (See FPCO, Letter to Anonymous, 2008 stating emergency exists when there is a significant, articulable threat to individual's health or safety; and73 Fed. Reg. 74.838, 2008statinghreat need not be verbal, but must be articulable by institution when it makes and records the disclosure).

The importance of this exception cannot be underscored enough. A health and safety emergency may include, for example, a significant medical issue concerning an individual student. School officials may inform emergency responders, police, and fire personnel of any appropriate PII for the health and safety of that student. This may include the student's medical information (allergies, chronic conditions, etc.), parent(s) name(s), address, etc. This exception may also be applicable in a school-wide crisis or significant threat where the health and safety of all students is at issue. Schools should be cautious, however, to ensure that emergency personnel receive PII only if this or another exception are applicable, rather than as a convenience.

d. Directory Information

Provided that the district has designated certain types of information to be directory information, a school is permitted to release such information to a third party without parent consent. Directory information is information contained in a student's educational record that would not generally be considered to be harmful or an invasion of privacy if disclosed (34 C.F.R. § 99.3). Examples of directory information include a student's name, address, telephone listing, electronic mail address, photograph, place and date of birth, major field of study, grade level, enrollment status, dates of attendance, participation in officially recognized activities and sports, weight and height of members of athletic teams, degrees, honors, and awards received, and the most recent educational agency or institution attended (34 C.F.R. § 99.3). Directory information does not generally include a student's social security number or student identification number (But see 34 C.F.R. § 99.3 under definition of directory information (c)(1) and (2)).

Importantly, the school must provide proper notice to parents of the designation of information as directory information and allow parents the opportunity to opt-out of such release (34 C.F.R. § 99.37). Thus, for example, while a school may publish student names and awards received in the town newspaper without parent consent (think of an honor roll list), the school is prohibited from putting the name and award of a student in the newspaper if the student's parent has opted-out of the release of such information (FPCO, Letter to Jett, 2012, which outlined procedures for designation and parental opt-out provisions with regard to directory information).

Access

Under FERPA, parents or eligible students have the right to access the student's education records upon request. The school must provide the requesting party the opportunity to inspect and review the education records within 45 calendar days of receiving a request, being mindful that shorter timelines may apply for special education records under state law (34 C.F.R. § 99.10(a)and(b)). The educational agency must also respond to reasonable request for explanations and interpretations of the educational records (34 C.F.R. § 99.10(c)). This provision, in practice, generally requires a school district to provide access to parents to any document that directly relates to the student and is maintained by the school district. This includes a student's health records. The access and confidentiality rights under FERPA belong to the parents or eligible students; and, as discussed earlier, a parent may continue to have the right to access student records even after a student turns eighteen, under certain circumstances. Of note, FERPA does not apply to information observed by a school official that is not otherwise documented in a student's education record (FPCO, Balancing Student Privacy and School Safety: A Guide to the Family Educational Rights and Privacy Act for Elementary and Secondary Schools, 2007). In those instances, FERPA would not protect the release of information about a student that was obtained through the school official's personal knowledge or observation.

Similarly, FERPA does not include any provisions concerning the role of a school professional in maintaining confidentiality of information received directly from a student. Codes of ethics may spell out a professional's obligation to maintain as confidential some information relayed from a student. School nurses and other school health-related professionals must balance the need to maintain the confidence of, and build relationships with, students, with the requirements of FERPA, mandatory reporting obligations relative to abuse and neglect, as well as standards of practice and liability. While state laws and certain privacy rights (e.g., legal rights of minors) may come into play, FERPA does not require that a school professional maintain as confidential from a parent information provided from a student. For example, if a student were to inform a school nurse that she intends on running away from home, FERPA does not prohibit the school nurse from informing the student's parents, even if the information is included in an education record.

If the education records at issue contain information pertaining to more than one student, the parent or eligible student may inspect and review only the specific information about his or her student (34 C.F.R. § 99.12(a)). School professionals may be required to redact education records before sharing them with the parents of a second student, as those parents only have the right to see the information relevant to their child, absent consent from the other parent. Under some circumstances, when a reasonable person within the school community would have knowledge of a student's PII, even redaction will not suffice, and the school may be prohibited from releasing the education record entirely.

Amendment

Parents and eligible students also have the right to request amendment of education records where those records are inaccurate or misleading or are a violation of the student's rights of privacy (34 C.F.R. § 99.20(a)). The school must consider a request to amend and if it decides not to amend in accordance with the request, must inform the parents or eligible student of their right to a hearing on the issue within a reasonable time (34 C.F.R. § 99.20(c)). If the educational agency, as a result of the hearing, deems the information to be inaccurate, misleading, or otherwise in violation of the privacy rights of the student, it shall amend the record accordingly and inform the parent or eligible student of such amendment in writing (34 C.F.R. § 99.21(b)(1)). If, after the hearing, the school affirms its decision not to amend the records, the parents or student have the right to insert into the record a statement outlining their views (34 C.F.R. § 99.21(b)(2)). If such a statement is placed into the records, it must be maintained as long as the record is maintained, usually in accordance with state statute or regulation concerning record retention (34 C.F.R. § 99.21(c)). The school district must then disclose the parent statement with the associated educational record whenever that educational record is disclosed (34 C.F.R. § 99.21(c)(2)).

When Does HIPAA Come into Play?

As discussed previously, the practice of the traditional school nurse is not subject to HIPAA and thus the school nurse is not required to comply with its rules and regulations. However, there are instances in which school nurses must be aware of HIPAA's requirements and, in some instances, may even be subject to them.

1. Interactions with Healthcare Professionals

    The most common instance in which school nurses interact with HIPAA is when medical records of a student are to be provided by a healthcare provider to the school. Generally, a healthcare provider may disclose a patient's medical records to a third party only upon receipt of a HIPAA-compliant authorization from the patient (45 C.F.R. § 164.508). State laws may also require specific consent for certain types of information, including behavioral health, venereal disease (i.e., sexually transmitted diseases or infections), genetic, or substance abuse information. To facilitate the disclosure and receipt of student health records from a provider, schools should consider adopting their own authorization form in compliance with HIPAA and applicable state law which can be distributed to students, families and healthcare providers.

    Despite the general rule, there are two instances in which a healthcare provider may disclose a student's PHI to a school nurse without receipt of a HIPAA-compliant authorization. **First, HIPAA permits a healthcare provider to disclose a student's health information to school nurses, physicians or other healthcare providers for purposes of treating the student**, unless state law (as noted above) requires consent, even for treatment purposes (45 C.F.R. § 164.506(c)(2)). HIPAA defines treatment broadly and this exception would permit, for example, a healthcare provider to discuss a student's medication regime with the school nurse who will administer the medications without first obtaining an authorization (45 C.F.R. § 164.501). School nurses familiar with this exception can remind healthcare providers of their treatment role at the school and work to educate providers on their right to disclose student information without an authorization - doing so may save valuable time when information is needed quickly but an authorization cannot be obtained.

The second exception relates to school immunization records. HIPAA permits a healthcare provider to disclose immunization records of a student directly to a school without a HIPAA compliant authorization if the school is required by law to have such records prior to admitting the student and the student's parent or guardian agrees to the disclosure (45 C.F.R. §164.512(b)(1)(vi)). If the student is an adult or emancipated minor, the agreement of the student is required. Although typically a written authorization is required by HIPAA, the agreement in the context of immunization records may be verbal and does not need to be signed or include the numerous elements necessary to constitute a HIPAA-compliant authorization (45 C.F.R. §164.512(b)(1)(vi)). When disclosing immunization records pursuant to this exception, the healthcare provider may disclose the records to whomever the parent or school designates. Unlike with disclosures for treatment purposes, the immunization records need not be provided to a specific healthcare provider within the school.

Schools wishing to take advantage of the flexibility offered by the immunization records exception may consider the development of educational materials for healthcare providers to inform them of the exception and its relationship to information needed by schools (i.e. the school is required by law to have such records prior to admitting the student). Schools may also develop a protocol to assist in obtaining the "agreement" required by the exception or forms that would allow a healthcare provider to document such agreement.

2. School-Based Health Centers

In the typical school-based health center arrangement, a healthcare provider (often a community clinic or hospital) establishes healthcare services on school premises in order to treat or provide specific services to students. These arrangements often present several HIPAA-related challenges for school nursing staff.

Most importantly, school staff must be cognizant of the center's status as a distinct entity that is permitted to share a student's PHI only in accordance with HIPAA and state law, as discussed above. Accordingly, a school-based health center's disclosures of PHI to the school will be limited to instances of treatment or when an authorization has been executed.

In addition, the school must carefully consider the administrative services it will provide in support of the school-based health center. Specifically, a school must be aware that providing certain services may make the school a HIPAA "business associate" and thus subject to HIPAA's privacy, security, and breach notification rules. For example, if a school were to volunteer to maintain the center's medical records in a school closet, the school would be a business associate. Further, if the school agreed to shred documents containing PHI from the center (e.g. lab test results, billing information), the school would be a business associate. The ease with which a school may be deemed a business associate in this context calls for caution when establishing and operating such arrangements.

3. Schools as Covered Entities

While unusual, it is important to acknowledge that as schools expand beyond their traditional healthcare functions and extend the healthcare services they provide to a broader population, it is possible that such schools will be, in part, subject to HIPAA. This is most likely to occur when a school provides healthcare services to non-students and bills a third-party payer for reimbursement for such services. For example, if a school were to operate a mental health clinic or audiology program that is open to members of the public and the school were to bill Medicaid for the services provided, the school would be a HIPAA "covered entity" with respect to that particular program and would need to comply with all of HIPAA's requirements with respect to the health information of non-students that it creates. Schools contemplating providing services in this manner should consider the implications of compliance with HIPAA and strategies for minimizing the application of HIPAA to the school's operations. Such strategies may include designation as a hybrid entity or carving out HIPAA covered components in school policies and procedures (45 C.F.R. § 164.105(a)(1)).

CONCLUSION

The maintenance of student confidentiality must be a priority within the school environment. FERPA, and HIPAA under limited circumstances, provide sets of rules on the manner in which schools must handle student education records. School nurses should use these rules to guide their practice, understanding that state law and school district policies and procedures may also come into play in the management of student education records.

RESOURCES

See ADDENDUM #1: School Nurse Strategies for Protecting Student Privacy; and
ADDENDUM #2: Exceptions to Education Records under FERPA.

Family Policy Compliance Office. http://www2.ed.gov/policy/gen/guid/fpco/index.html

Family Policy Compliance Office, Frequently Asked Questions: FERPA for School Officials, available at http://familypolicy.ed.gov/faq-page/ferpa-school-officials#t69n51

United States Department of Education. Protecting Student Privacy. Available at https://studentprivacy.ed.gov/?utm_content=&utm_medium=email&utm_name=&utm_source=govdelivery&utm_term=

United States Department of Health and Human Services, Health Information Privacy, available at http://www.hhs.gov/hipaa/

Wright's Law. Special Education Caselaw. http://www.wrightslaw.com/caselaw.htm

REFERENCES

Family Educational Rights and Privacy Act, 20 U.S.C. § 1232g; 34 C.F.R. § 99.1 et seq.

Family Policy Compliance Office. (2007). *Balancing student privacy and school safety: A guide to the family educational rights and privacy act for elementary and secondary schools*. Retrieved from https://www2.ed.gov/policy/gen/guid/fpco/brochures/elsec.pdf

Family Policy Compliance Office. (2008). Letter to Anonymous, 109 LRP 59140

Family Compliance Office. (2005). Letter to Davis, 106 LRP 43600

Family Policy Compliance Office. (2012). Letter to Jett, 112 LRP 58495

Gonzaga University v. Doe, 122 S. Ct. 2268 (2002)

Health Insurance Portability and Accountability Act of 1996, 45 C.F.R. § § 160, 162 and 164

HIPAA Omnibus Rulemaking, 78 Fed. Reg. 5566 - 5702 (January 25, 2013). Retrieved from www.gpo.gov/fdsys/pkg/FR-2013-01-25/pdf/2013-01073.pdf

HIPAA Privacy Rule, 65 Fed. Reg. 82462 – 82829. (December 28, 2000). Retrieved from www.hhs.gov/sites/default/files/ocr/privacy/hipaa/administrative/privacyrule/prdecember2000all8parts.pdf

HIPAA Privacy Rule Modifications, 67 Fed. Reg. 53182 – 53273. (August 14, 2002). Retrieved from www.hhs.gov/sites/default/files/ocr/privacy/hipaa/administrative/privacyrule/privrulepd.pdf

HIPAA Security Rule, 68 Fed. Reg. 8334 – 8381. (February 20, 2003), Retrieved from www.hhs.gov/sites/default/files/ocr/privacy/hipaa/administrative/securityrule/securityrulepdf.pdf

United States Department of Public Health and Human Services and United States Department of Education (2008). *Joint guidance on the application of the Family Educational Rights and Privacy Act (FERPA) and the Health Insurance Portability and Accountability Act of 1996 (HIPAA) to student health records.* Retrieved from http://www2.ed.gov/policy/gen/guid/fpco/doc/ferpa-hipaa-guidance.pdf

ACKNOWLEDGMENTS

The authors wish to thank Laura A. Fisher for her research and writing assistance in the development of this Chapter.

ADDENDUM #1

School Nurse Strategies for Protecting Student Privacy

Martha Dewey Bergren, DNS, RN, NCSN, APHN-BC, FNASN, FASHA, FAAN

Meeting the privacy requirements for student's personally identifiable health information are an important responsibility for a school nurse. School nurses must balance the need to keep a student healthy against the unnecessary release of information. In addition to developing an understanding of Family Education Rights and Privacy Act (FERPA) and Health Insurance Portability and Accountability Act (HIPAA) requirements, three strategies will decrease anxiety when sharing information while protecting student privacy.

First, plan ahead. Before the school year begins, prepare the FERPA release or exchange of information authorizations for any student who has a care plan or receives medications or treatments during the school day. Standards of nursing practice demand that the nurse be able to communicate with a provider who has input into the student's plan of care or who has prescribed treatments or medication. If the exchange of information has been signed proactively, there will be no delay when a consultation is needed.

Second, partner with parents/guardians to assure that the plan of care is communicated with all who are charged with the students' safety or who must respond if a student's condition exacerbates. Parents/guardians should participate in the plan of care, including weighing in on who should receive the plan.

Third, when asked to aggregate health data, be sure to strip all identifiers from the report:

- Name
- Address
- Date and place of birth
- Telephone numbers
- Fax number
- Email address
- Social Security Number
- Medical record number
- Health plan beneficiary number

- Account number
- Student number
- Certificate or license number
- Any vehicle or other device serial number
- Web URL
- Internet Protocol (IP) Address
- Finger or voice print
- Photograph
- Any other characteristic that could uniquely identify the individual

The Department of Education Privacy Technical Assistance Center (PTAC) provides guidance on student privacy practices and steps for deidentification (PTAC, 2013).

School nurses have many resources to appropriately safeguard student privacy. In addition to the Department of Education PTAC, the National Association of School Nurses (NASN) provides student privacy webinars and other resources readily available on the NASN website (NASN, n.d.). If your state has a state school nurse consultant, they can provide assistance on meeting the federal and state specific privacy laws (National

Association of State School Nurse Consultants, n.d.). With preparation and prudence, school nurses are well equipped for the challenge of protecting their students' privacy.

REFERENCES

National Association of School Nurses. (n.d.). *HIPAA and FERPA*. Silver Spring, MD: NASN. Retrieved from https://www.nasn.org/nasn/nasn-resources/professional-topics/school-health-documentation/hipaa-ferpa

National Association of State School Nurse Consultants, (n.d.). *Welcome to the National Association of State School Nurse Consultants*. Retrieved from http://www.schoolnurseconsultants.org/

Privacy Technical Assistance. (2013). *Data deidenitfication: An overview of basic terms*. Washington, DC: U.S. Department of Education, Privacy Technical Center. Retrieved from http://ptac.ed.gov/sites/default/files/data_deidentification_terms.pdf

U.S. Department of Health and Human Services. (2015). *Guidance regarding methods for de-identification of protected health information in accordance with the Health Insurance Portability and Accountability Act (HIPAA) Privacy Rule*. Retrieved from https://www.hhs.gov/hipaa/for-professionals/privacy/special-topics/de-identification/

ADDENDUM #2

Exceptions to "Education Records" under FERPA

Erin D. Gilsbach, Esquire

A school may maintain some records that contain personally-identifiable information but are specifically exempted from the definition of "education records" under FERPA. Those records are:

1. **Sole-Possession Records.** To qualify as a sole-possession record, the record must be:
    a. Be used only as a personal memory aid
    b. Not be accessible or revealed to any person other than a temporary substitute

2. **Law Enforcement Records.** Some schools have law enforcement units, such as school resource officers (SROs), the officers of which have full law enforcement authority, including the authority to conduct a criminal investigation and arrest. Records from school law enforcement are exempt only if they are:
    a. Created by a law enforcement unit;
    b. Created for a law enforcement purpose; and
    c. Maintained by the law enforcement unit.

3. **Employment Records.** There are times when an employee's file may contain personally-identifiable information about a student, such as a worker's compensation claim that resulted after an employee intervened in a fight between two students. Employment records that contain PII are not "education records" subject to FERPA if they:
    a. Are made and maintained in the normal course of business;
    b. Relate exclusively to the individual in that individual's capacity as an employee; and
    c. Are not available for use for any other purpose.
    *Student employment records *are* "education records" subject to FERPA.

4. **Post-Attendance Records.** Any records that a school has received after a student graduates or transfers out of a school, if they are not directly related to the individual's attendance as a student, are not considered to be education records.

5. **Peer-Graded Scores.** Scores/grades on peer-graded papers are not education records until they have been recorded by the teacher.

6. **Treatment Records.** There is also an exception for what are commonly termed 'treatment records,' although this exception typically does not apply at the K-12 level. For the 'treatment records' exception to apply:
    *   the student must be 18 or older or attending a postsecondary school.
    *   Made or maintained by a physician, psychiatrist, psychologist, or other recognized professional or paraprofessional acting in his or her professional capacity or assisting in a paraprofessional capacity;

- Made, maintained, or used only in connection with treatment of the student; and
- Disclosed only to individuals providing the treatment.

It is important to note that, for the purpose of this definition, "treatment" does not include remedial educational activities or activities that are part of the program of instruction at the agency or institution, such as those that would be maintained as part of a student's records.

Chapter 12

EDUCATION LAW FOR CHILDREN WITH DISABILITIES: THE INDIVIDUALS WITH DISABILITIES EDUCATION ACT (IDEA) AND SECTION 504 OF THE REHABILITATION ACT OF 1973 (SECTION 504)

Attorney Alyce L. Alfano
Attorney Melika S. Forbes
Attorney Laura A. Fisher

DESCRIPTION OF ISSUE

Schools foster the development of society's next generation by providing environments where students have the opportunity to progress intellectually, socially, and emotionally. All students should be afforded an equal opportunity to progress. Just forty years ago, many students with disabilities were denied access to public education, placed in segregated classrooms, or otherwise not provided with adequate support for their needs. Since that time, two federal laws—Section 504 of the Rehabilitation Act of 1973 ("Section 504") and the Individuals with Disabilities Education Act ("IDEA")—have been enacted to remedy these practices. Both laws impose affirmative duties upon schools that receive federal funds, requiring them to promptly identify, evaluate, and address the individual needs of students with disabilities to ensure equal access to education.

Enacted in 1973, Section 504 was the first federal civil rights law prohibiting discrimination against individuals with disabilities. Section 504 applies generally to programs and entities receiving federal funds, including schools. Two years after the passage of Section 504, the IDEA was enacted to protect the rights of students with qualifying disabilities. The original acronym "IDEA" continues to be used colloquially and, for practical purposes, we refer to the legislation in its most recent form (as reauthorized by Congress in 2004) as the IDEA throughout this chapter. The IDEA provides federal financial assistance to states and school districts in exchange for compliance with certain mandates. The primary intent of the IDEA is to provide students with qualifying disabilities between the ages of three and twenty-one with educational services and supports so that they are able to benefit from public education at no expense to their parent/guardian(s).

School nurses play an important role in ensuring that children with disabilities receive appropriate IDEA or Section 504 services and supports. This chapter provides a summary of IDEA and Section 504. It also outlines legal obligations; discusses practical implications for school nurses working with students with disabilities; summarizes possible legal challenges that may arise under IDEA and Section 504; and offers insight in response to frequently asked questions.

BACKGROUND

IDEA—At a Glance

The IDEA applies to children with certain disabilities who, by reason of their disabilities, require special education and, in some cases, related services. The IDEA regulations define *special education* as specially designed instruction, at no cost to parent/guardian(s), to meet the unique needs of a student with a disability

(34 C.F.R. § 300.39). In order to qualify for services under the IDEA, a student must be identified under one of the following eligibility categories: autism; deaf-blindness; deafness; developmental delay (applicable to younger children only, as specifically delineated under state law); emotional disturbance; hearing impairment; intellectual disability; multiple disabilities; orthopedic impairment; other health impairment (which often includes ADD/ADHD); physical impairment; specific learning disability; speech or language impairment; traumatic brain injury; and visual impairment, including blindness (34 C.F.R. § 300.8).

Under the IDEA, school districts are obligated to offer a free and appropriate public education ("FAPE") to eligible students. The Supreme Court of the United States first analyzed this standard in *Board of Education v. Rowley* (1982). Under *Rowley,* the inquiry for determining whether a school district provided a student FAPE is two-fold. The first inquiry is whether the school district complied with the IDEA's procedural requirements. The second inquiry asks the substantive question of whether "the [Individualized Education Plan] developed... [is] reasonably calculated to enable the child to receive educational benefits" (Board of Education v. Rowley, 1982). More recently in *Endrew F. v. Douglas County School District* (2017), the Supreme Court refined the FAPE standard by ruling that school districts must provide an educational program reasonably calculated to enable a child to make progress appropriate in light of the child's circumstances—which is "markedly more demanding than the merely more than *de minimis* test...." Importantly, the *Endrew F.* Court did not overturn *Rowley.* Rather, *Endrew F.* sets forth a more general standard and underscores the necessarily fact specific nature of each case. Each student with a disability has unique needs and circumstances and therefore there can be no bright line rule governing precisely which educational supports or services satisfy the FAPE standard in every case. In reaching its conclusion, the Court reiterated that the IDEA does not "guarantee any particular level of education" and that it "cannot and does not promise any particular educational outcome." Moreover, the Court retained the "reasonably calculated" qualification, and explained that it "reflects a recognition that crafting an appropriate program of education requires a prospective judgment by school officials" based on the specific facts related to a student and informed by school officials' expertise and input from the parents or guardians. The Court went on to remind us that "[a]ny review of an IEP must appreciate that the question is whether the IEP is *reasonable,* not whether the court regards it as ideal." In its decision, the Court emphasized the deference owed to schools in the development of an appropriate IEP in explaining that such "deference is based on the application of expertise and the exercise of judgment by school authorities." The IDEA "vests these officials with responsibility for decisions of critical importance to the life of a disabled child" (Endrew F. v. Douglas County School District, 2017).

With the above standards in mind, the IDEA requires that a planning team ("IEP team") develop an eligible student's individualized educational plan ("IEP") to provide the student with FAPE. The IEP team by law is required to consist of certain individuals: the parent/guardian(s); a regular education teacher; a special education teacher; a representative of the school system able to make decisions on behalf of the system (such as an administrator); someone to interpret any relevant evaluation results (for example, a speech and language pathologist or an occupational therapist); and, at the discretion of the parent/guardian(s) or school district, other individuals who have knowledge or special expertise regarding the child (20 U.S.C. § 1414(d)(1) (B)). A school nurse will often be part of the IEP team when the student has health-related needs and/or takes medication. The child will also be included when appropriate (34 C.F.R. § 300.321).

The IEP team is responsible for discussing and planning evaluations as well as reviewing evaluation results and determining eligibility. When health issues are or may be implicated, the school nurse should assist in planning and determining what type of evaluation should occur. Additionally, the school nurse should analyze relevant documentation and help in designing the appropriate program for the student. The determination of whether a student qualifies for special education programming and services, or whether the student would be (more) appropriately served by a Section 504 Plan, will never be solely the school nurse's responsibility, however. The IEP meetings and IEP development are a team effort. Parts of the IEP include the student's present levels of academic and functional performance; parental input; recommendations and prior written notice; transition services, when appropriate and applicable; measurable goals and objectives; accommodations and modifications; special education and related services; a description of the student's educational placement (i.e., which school or specific program). The IEP also contains a service delivery grid for delivery of programming, including who will deliver the services, where and how frequently they will be delivered; and other considerations such as assistive technology needs; extended school year services; transportation needs; and nursing needs, if relevant (34 C.F.R. § 300.320).

In determining a student's educational placement, a primary and critical issue for the IEP team, the team must determine the least restrictive environment ("LRE") for that student. The IDEA regulations define LRE as the student being educated with non-disabled peers to the maximum extent appropriate (34 C.F.R. § 300.114). In other words, if and when possible, a student must be educated in regular education classrooms with supplemental aids and services. When this is not possible, the student may be educated in progressively more restrictive environments such as self-contained classrooms or private special education schools. There is no threshold amount of 'mainstreaming' required and courts will often defer to educational professionals about what constitutes LRE for a particular student.

Section 504—At a Glance

Section 504 is a federal civil rights law that prohibits discrimination against individuals with disabilities in programs or activities that receive federal funds and provides that "[n]o otherwise qualified handicapped individual …shall, solely by reason of…[a] disability, be excluded from participation in, be denied the benefits of, or be subjected to discrimination under any program or activity receiving federal financial assistance…" (29 U.S.C. § 794). Akin to the IDEA, Section 504 protects individuals with disabilities; however, individuals covered under Section 504 are significantly greater in number. In particular, Section 504 covers any individual—whether or not a student—who satisfies the legal definition of a person with a disability. An individual is protected by Section 504 if he or she has a physical or mental impairment that substantially limits one or more of his or her major life activities. Additionally, someone may also qualify as an individual with a disability under Section 504 if he or she has a record of such an impairment or is regarded as having such an impairment (34 C.F.R. § 104.3).

A non-exhaustive list of recognized impairments includes: orthopedic, visual, speech and hearing impairments; cerebral palsy; epilepsy; muscular dystrophy; multiple sclerosis; cancer; heart disease; diabetes; intellectual disabilities; emotional illnesses such as depression, bipolar, etc.; learning disabilities such as dyslexia; ADHD; HIV; tuberculosis; drug addiction; and alcoholism.

Section 504's protections are intended to be construed broadly in favor of expansive coverage and the regulations warn that determining whether an individual qualifies for protection under Section 504 does not require extensive analysis. Similarly, the term *major life activity* does not impose a strict standard and the activity need not be of central importance to daily life (*See* 28 C.F.R. § 35.108). Moreover, the regulations use broad language to define *physical impairment* and *mental impairment*. Under Section 504, *physical impairment* means "any physiological disorder or condition, cosmetic disfigurement, or anatomical loss affecting one or more … body systems;" while *mental impairment* means "any mental or psychological disorder" (34 C.F.R. § 104.3). Accordingly, the list of impairments that may satisfy these wide-ranging definitions is significant in scope. Section 504 coverage may apply to a large pool of individuals; however, this chapter will focus on Section 504's applicability in the education context.

Section 504 also requires schools to provide students with disabilities with FAPE (34 C.F.R. § 104.33). However, Section 504's definition of FAPE is different from the standard set forth under the IDEA. Section 504's regulations provide that FAPE requires schools to provide "regular or special education and related aids and services that (i) are designed to meet individual educational needs of handicapped persons as adequately as the needs of non-handicapped persons are met and (ii) are based upon adherence to procedures that satisfy the requirements of [the Section 504 regulations]" (34 C.F.R. § 104.33). Section 504 additionally requires that schools accommodate students with disabilities in programs and activities, including sports, extracurricular activities, and field trips (34 C.F.R. § 104.37). In effect, this regulation requires schools to level the playing field for students with disabilities so that they have educational opportunities equal to their non-disabled peers.

Schools have an affirmative duty to identify and evaluate students, and must provide eligible students equal access to education (34 C.F.R. § 104.35). Although this legal obligation does not rest on any singular school employee, a school nurse can be an essential member of the multidisciplinary team ("Section 504 team") charged with fulfilling the school's obligations under Section 504. Accordingly, it is necessary that school nurses understand their roles and responsibilities with regard to participation in Section 504 teams.

IMPLICATIONS FOR SCHOOL NURSE PRACTICE

School nurses are essential school personnel who, through assessment, observation, and implementation of treatment ensure that the health needs of all students are met while in the school environment. However, the IDEA and Section 504 place significant obligations on school nurses that many nursing preparation programs may not address. As noted above, the IDEA and Section 504 require school districts to promptly identify and evaluate students who may be eligible for protection under either law. Although school nurses may be called to serve as a member of a student's IEP and/or Section 504 team to assist in the evaluation of a student, a school nurse's obligation under both laws begins prior to a student's referral to an IEP or Section 504 team.

Role and Responsibilities

While the language of the IDEA and Section 504 places responsibility on the amorphous "school district" or "program," both laws require individual school employees to refer students believed to have a qualifying disability (in the case of the IDEA) or a disability (under Section 504) to the appropriate multidisciplinary evaluation team (*See, e.g.*, Rodiriecus L. v. Waukegan School District No. 60, 1996, and Board of Education of Fayette County, KY v. L.M., 2007). School nurses must be vigilant in identifying students who demonstrate health needs that could trigger the IDEA and/or Section 504. School nurses must immediately notify the school's Special Education or Section 504 Coordinator and, where appropriate, refer the student for evaluation to determine whether he or she is eligible for protection under the law. It is important to recognize that the information that forms the basis of the referral may come directly from a parent or an external healthcare provider or it may be based on the school nurse's observation of and/or interaction with the student. Regardless of the source of the information, the duty to identify students with disabilities promptly and refer such students for evaluation is primary.

In some cases, the student being evaluated will not have a health-related need or disability. In that event, it would be unlikely for a school nurse to serve as a member of the multidisciplinary team evaluating or planning for the student. However, where there is knowledge, a suspicion, a claim, or even the possibility that a student has a health-related need or disability the school nurse should participate as a member of the IEP or Section 504 team. As an IEP or Section 504 team member, the school nurse shares responsibility with the other team members to meet the requirements of the IDEA and Section 504.

To comply with the legal requirements, the team must first make an eligibility determination. Although eligibility determinations are team decisions, cases where health-related needs and/or disability are at issue may require significant contribution from the school nurse. The team members will rely on the school nurse's expertise to help them understand the student's health-related needs during the evaluation process. The school nurse will likely be called upon to assess the student's health-related needs and/or disability, interpret medical documentation, and communicate with external healthcare providers. Simply put, the school nurse will serve as a "translator" for the team members who lack medical expertise but need to understand medical information in order to make an informed eligibility determination and to understand how the health condition may affect the student's ability to benefit from or access his or her education. Thus, a school nurse's role, at the outset, is to come prepared with any data or documentation regarding the student's health needs and share such information prior to the meeting, if possible, to allow for a more productive and efficient discussion.

In the event that a student with health-related needs or disability is found eligible under the IDEA or Section 504, the team moves to the planning phase. As noted above, both the IDEA and Section 504 mandate that schools develop an appropriate plan—IEP or Section 504 Plan, respectively—to address the individual needs of an eligible student. Despite the shared goal, the substantive standard to satisfy the above requirement is different under each law. With respect to an IEP, the law requires an annual written plan that sets forth the detailed requirements described earlier in this Chapter. In contrast, Section 504 does not require a written plan; however, as a best practice, schools should and usually do provide a written plan as an accountability measure and to reduce misunderstandings. Written Section 504 Plans typically include descriptions of the qualifying disability, services and supports, (including setting, frequency and duration), as well as the accommodations to be received.

While the IEP team as a whole tackles the academic, developmental, social and emotional needs of the student, the responsibility of addressing the healthcare needs of the student falls squarely on the school nurse. The school nurse uses available data and documentation (or requests additional information) to accomplish the following: 1) determine the healthcare needs of the student; 2) recommend and/or conduct healthcare evaluations and/or assessments, as appropriate; 3) determine and recommend the appropriate healthcare services and supports required by the student to access his or her education; 4) provide input, based on nursing expertise, on the appropriateness of services and/or supports under consideration by the team; 5) determine whether, and to what extent, parent, student and/or non-nursing staff healthcare training is required; 6) draft individualized healthcare plans ("IHPs") and/or emergency care plans ("ECPs"), where appropriate; and 7) draft measurable and appropriate healthcare annual IEP goals and objectives, where appropriate. The school nurse may need to consult with the parent, student, and/or external healthcare providers such as treating physicians, mental health counselors, pediatricians, or psychiatrists. In instances where consultation with an external party is required, it is critical that the school nurse receive written parental consent. As detailed in *Chapter 10,* this consent should be obtained prior to any discussion and/or the release of student related information or records.

Following the development of an appropriate plan of services and supports summarized in a written IEP or Section 504 Plan, and assuming parental agreement the law requires the school to implement the plan with fidelity. As a first step, the written plan must be disseminated to each team member, including the parent(s) and school personnel who work with the student. While this dissemination is not usually the responsibility of the school nurse, a school nurse serving as a team member must obtain a copy of the finalized plan, which may include an attached IHP or ECP, and must review it to determine his/her responsibilities. The IEPs and Section 504 Plans may require school nurses to provide training to parent/guardian(s), students, and educators; to administer health services and supports; to supervise personnel administering health services and supports; to consult and collaborate with parent/guardian(s), school-based staff, or external healthcare providers at regular intervals; and/or to assist in planning and implementing a student's accommodations to allow for participation in sports, special events such as field trips, and extracurricular activities.

There is an implicit requirement that school nurses document their periodic monitoring and maintain detailed and accurate records of implementation of IDEA or Section 504 services, supports, and training. School nurses must monitor the progress of eligible students for the duration of the relevant plan. The laws also impose a duty to reconvene the IEP or Section 504 team if any of the following is applicable:

- Annual review of the student's progress towards his/her IEP goals and objectives and development of a new IEP based on the current evaluative information (IDEA only);
- Triennial review of the student's continued need for specialized instruction (IDEA only);
- Periodic review to ensure the student's Section 504 Plan is appropriate and determine whether any changes are necessary (Section 504 only);
- A change in the student's placement will occur; and/or
- A team member, including the parent(s), requests a meeting.

Thinking Ahead— Legal Peril under Special Education and Disability Laws

Parents who disagree with the identification, educational plan, or services being offered to their child through an IEP or Section 504 Plan may pursue legal remedies to address their concerns. Understanding the legal avenues available to parent/guardian(s) under both the IDEA and Section 504 will assist a school nurse in preparing to help and participate in a school district's defense. It is important to remember that under both IDEA and Section 504, a school nurse (or any other individual school employee) will not be named individually as a defendant. Rather, under both laws, parent/guardian(s) bring an action against a school district as a whole.

IDEA:

Due Process: Under the IDEA, parents may file for a due process hearing to pursue their disagreement with a school district over the identification, evaluation, educational placement, or provision of FAPE to their child

(34 CFR § 300.507). While school districts may also file due process hearing requests, it is much more common for parents to generate hearing requests. The due process hearing complaint must be in writing and contain certain components such as the student's name, the nature of the problem, related facts, and a proposed resolution (34 CFR § 300.508). Each state's educational agency has procedures for processing due process complaints and must ensure that the opposing party receives a copy of the complaint, that an impartial hearing officer is appointed, and that a hearing ensues in which both parties may be represented by attorneys (34 CFR § § 300.508-511).

Due process hearings are like trials. Both sides have the opportunity to present documents as exhibits to be reviewed by the hearing officer, who acts as the judge. Both sides also present witnesses who are questioned and provide direct testimony relevant to the issues and are also subject to cross examination.

The school nurse may be called upon to assist the district in gathering all the relevant health and medical documentation regarding the student in question for submission as evidence. Thus, if the school nurse's records are consistently clear, organized, and up to date, this will benefit both the district and the school nurse in preparing for a hearing. The school nurse may also be asked to consult with administrators and/or the school district's attorney to explain their interaction with a student or the parent/guardian(s), as well as his or her perspective on the health issues involved. Finally, the school nurse may be called as a witness by the school district's attorney or by the parents' attorney to testify under oath in response to questions about the student and situation at hand. Although this does not happen for school nurses frequently, it can be nerve wracking when it does. The school district's attorney should and probably will prepare the school nurse for questioning by reviewing both the content and the testimonial process in advance of testimony. The result of a due process hearing is a written decision by the hearing officer which must be followed by the parties if it is not appealed.

Prior to the hearing, the law requires the parties to try to resolve their differences through a Resolution Meeting or a mediation process (34 C.F.R. § 510). These meetings are negotiation sessions, sometimes facilitated by a neutral party, to assist the school district and the parent/guardian(s) in trying to reach an agreement on the outstanding issues. The school nurse may be asked to assist in gathering any relevant documentation to assist the administration and the school district's attorney in preparing for the negotiation session. Depending upon the nature of the dispute and the extent to which health issues are involved, the school nurse may also be asked to be present at the session to assist in understanding the facts and helping to craft workable solutions. The result of a successful mediation process is a written agreement guiding the parties' relationship going forward for a given period of time.

State Complaint: The IDEA provides that every state's primary educational agency establish a written procedure for the filing of complaints (34 C.F.R. § 300.151). Thus, each state has its own process for receiving, reviewing, and responding in writing to a parent's complaint regarding an alleged violation of their child's rights to special education identification, evaluation, or programming. Similar to due process complaints, these are most commonly filed by parents. However, organizations may also file complaints on behalf of a given student or group of students. School districts are notified of the complaint and given an opportunity to respond both verbally and in writing. The school nurse's assistance in helping to respond to a state complaint is similar to the role in responding to a due process complaint. Again, the school nurse will gather any relevant health and medical documentation regarding the student. Thus, once again, the importance of keeping clear and up-to-date records is critical. The school nurse may also be asked to explain to the school district's administration, attorney, or the state complaint investigator, his or her understanding of the facts and his or her perspective on the student's health needs. However, in the context of a state complaint, the school nurse will not have to testify under oath. At the conclusion of the state complaint investigation, the investigator issues a written report of findings. If it is found that certain corrective actions are required on the part of the school district, (such as new procedures for recordkeeping or additional staff training relating to student health or nursing issues), the school nurse will be informed of these actions and will participate in addressing them.

Section 504:

Office for Civil Rights Complaints: When a parent disagrees with a student's Section 504 Plan or its implementation, the most frequently filed complaint is with the federal Office for Civil Rights ("OCR"). OCR is the arm of the United States Department of Education responsible for protecting against discrimination on the basis of disability, among other things. Each area of the country has a regional OCR office which receives and processes complaints. Filing an OCR complaint is a relatively simple process for a parent and does not require the assistance of an attorney. In addition, there is no charge to the party filing the complaint. Once OCR receives a complaint, it decides whether the discrimination alleged fits under its domain. If so, OCR contacts the school district via written letter to explain that a complaint has been filed, provide an overview of the complaint, and request specific, detailed data and documentation from the school district. If the student has health issues, the school nurse will typically be an integral part of the school team responding to the OCR complaint. The nurse will be responsible for gathering and compiling all related documentation for the response. If the nurse has had regular interaction with the student and/or the parents, he or she will likely be asked to recount those interactions in response to OCR. Depending upon the extent to which OCR pursues its investigation of the complaint, OCR may request interviews with specific employees, including the school nurse. In the event this request is made, school administration and the school district's attorney will arrange the interview, which is usually telephonic, and help to prepare the school nurse for it. The result of an OCR investigation may be a determination or mutual agreement that certain training or other protocol must be put into place. In that event, the school nurse would be informed of the results of the investigation to know what steps to take.

Section 504 Hearing: Under Section 504, parents also have the right to request a hearing by an impartial hearing officer to address their concerns with a student's Section 504 Plan or its implementation. While this path is infrequently chosen by parents, school districts are required to inform parents that the process is available and to provide an impartial hearing officer if requested. In a Section 504 hearing, the role of the school nurse is similar to his or her role at a due process hearing under IDEA. The nurse would be responsible for assisting in gathering all health and medical records in the school's possession, acting as a consultant and advisor to the administration and the school district's attorney, and potentially testifying at the hearing.

Frequently Asked Questions

In preparing to write this resource and address the real concerns of school nurses, the editors and authors polled school nurses to solicit questions that arise related to school nurse participation in IDEA and Section 504 implementation. A few most frequently posed questions were chosen and responses are provided below.

Please note that these are examples not to be construed as specific legal advice applicable to any particular facts or case.

1. Should nurses be part of the Section 504 planning process?

   ANSWER: As expressed throughout this chapter, when a student has a health-related condition necessitating a Section 504 Plan, the school nurse will be an integral and necessary part of the planning team and will bear responsibility for educating necessary staff about the health-related components of the plan and assisting in its implementation.

2. If a Section 504 Plan states that a "Registered Nurse" will check a student's blood sugar, or perform another nursing task, does that bind the district to allow *only* the school nurse to complete that task?

   ANSWER: The short answer is yes. If a plan is so specific as to identify the qualifications of the individual implementing a component of the plan, it must be followed as written. Written IEPs or Section 504 Plans must be followed. Thus, it is best practice to broaden the language of the plan to say, for example, "registered nurse, or other qualified individual."

3. Should IHPs be attached to a student's IEP, if a student has both?

   ANSWER: While the IDEA does not require this, it is strongly recommended that the IHP be attached to the IEP. Then, any individual who is reading the IEP has full knowledge of the student's complete needs and plan. Please note that this does not mean that the IHP is actually incorporated as a part of the IEP itself; thus the IHP can be revised with parental and medical input without a formal IEP meeting.

4. Does a student need a Section 504 Plan if they have an existing IEP and IHP?

   ANSWER: A student eligible under the IDEA is not required to have a Section 504 Plan in addition to his or her IEP despite the fact that the student is still protected by Section 504. The sound development and implementation of an IEP satisfies the Section 504 FAPE standard (34 CFR 104.33(b)(2)).

5. Is it helpful/appropriate for Section 504 Plans to be specific as to medical order/protocol for a student?

   ANSWER: Typically, specific medical order/protocol is not contained in the Section 504 Plan, but rather, in the student's IHP, which can be included by reference for clarity. It is not usually appropriate or helpful to have specific medical protocol in a plan that would be disseminated to staff beyond the school health professionals. The law does not, however, prohibit this information from being included on a student's Section 504 Plan if it is helpful or appropriate in an individual circumstance.

6. Does a nurse potentially have individual legal liability for a plan if he or she has expressed his or her professional opinion and the team disagrees?

   ANSWER: Individual liability for school employees, including school nurses, does not accrue under either IDEA or Section 504. These laws allow parents to pursue legal remedies from a public school district as a whole, not from individual employees (*See, e.g.,* 20 U.S.C. § 1415; 34 C.F.R. § 104.36).

7. Is it possible that a student's IEP or Section 504 Plan may include specialized transportation and potentially require a nurse to ride that transportation with them?

    ANSWER: Yes. Under the IDEA, nursing services and/or specialized transportation are related services which may be incorporated into a student's IEP, if required (34 C.F.R. § 300.320(a)(4)). Similarly, it is possible that a student's medical needs require that his or her Section 504 Plan have these accommodations. For practical and logistical purposes, it would typically be a contracted nurse rather than a school nurse serving in this role.

8. What is the chain of command of administration regarding implementation of plans for students with healthcare needs?

    ANSWER: Each school district has its own internal structure that dictates who on a student's team is the "go-to" person, or case manager, for that student. Ultimately, the director of special education, Section 504 coordinator, or head of pupil personnel/student services is the individual responsible for the coordination of the student's IEP plan. Importantly, when there are healthcare needs involved, the school nurse will be a key voice in implementing and monitoring the implementation of the student's plan. In legal situations as described above, the school nurse may also be called upon to present, interpret, and answer questions regarding the healthcare plan documentation and implementation.

CONCLUSION

School nurses are the individuals within a school system with primary responsibility for the healthcare implications of an eligible student's IEP or Section 504 Plan. As key members of the team, school nurses bring their nursing training and knowledge to help shape and implement a student's needed plan. School nurses are key members of IDEA and Section 504 teams and, as such, they should be familiar with the legal aspects of both laws.

RESOURCES

See Addendum: The School Nurse's Role in the Identification Process for a 504 Plan

U.S. Department of Education Office for Civil Rights, *Parent and Educator Resource Guide to Section 504 in Public Elementary and Secondary Schools* (2016) available at https://www2.ed.gov/about/offices/list/ocr/docs/504-resource-guide-201612.pdf

Wright's Law. Special Education Caselaw. http://www.wrightslaw.com/caselaw.htm

REFERENCES

Board of Education v. Rowley, 458 U.S. 176 (1982)

Board of Education of Fayette County, KY v. L.M., 478 F.3d 307 (6th Cir. 2007)

Endrew F. v. Douglas County School District RE-1, 137 S. Ct. 988 (2017)

Rodiriecus L. v. Waukegan School District No. 60, 90 F.3d 249 (7th Cir. 1996)

Section 504 of the Rehabilitation Act of 1973, 29 U.S.C. § 794, 34 C.F.R. § 104.1 *et seq.*

The Individuals with Disabilities Education Act, 20 U.S.C. § 1400 *et seq.*, 34 C.F.R. § 300 *et seq.*

ADDENDUM

The School Nurse's Role in the Identification Process for a 504 Plan

Perry A. Zirkel, Esquire

© 2017

The school nurse is in a pivotal position at the student's intersection of physicians/healthcare providers, families, and school colleagues. Each of these other interested parties are likely not to be as familiar with Section 504 than the IDEA. In mediating among their perspectives, the school nurse needs to share and follow the following legal lessons with regard to the identification stage:

- "Child find" applies under Section 504 similar to its application under the IDEA. The key is triggering the requisite multi-disciplinary evaluation when the district has reason to suspect that the child may be eligible for a Section 504 Plan.

- Unlike the IDEA, eligibility does not require an adverse educational impact that necessitates special education. Instead, the three essential elements are: (a) a physical or mental impairment that limits; (b) one or more major life activities; and (c) to a substantial extent.

- For the first element, the school nurse plays a major continuing role particularly in helping to determine whether the child has a physical impairment based on available information, including diagnoses from medical and related personnel.

- The ADA Amendments of 2008 liberalized the eligibility standards for the second and third elements— "major life activity" and "substantial"—that increased the pivotal role of the school nurse. The ADA Title II regulations in 2016 added further reinforcement.

- For major life activities, the ADA Amendments added to the illustrative list various health-related items, such as bowel functions, bladder functions, and digestive functions. The recent ADA regulations specified additional examples, including immune system functions, circulatory system functions, and endocrine system functions. All of these additions obviously widen the scope of the interacting element of physical or mental impairments.

- For the ultimately critical "substantial" element, the ADA Amendments included various relevant interpretive standards, including that this determination be (a) without mitigating measures, such as medication, and (b) at the time that impairments that are episodic or in remission are active.

- Finally, the case law makes clear that "substantial" is a matter of duration as well as degree. Thus, for a temporary impairment, such as a concussion, the determination must be on an individual basis but may well be that the limitation is a matter of a few weeks rather than a few months, thus warranting a health plan rather than a 504 Plan.

Although the specific requirements and their application merits careful collaborative attention and assessment, including the school's administration and, in their discretion, the district's legal counsel, the school nurse plays a significant and central role in facilitating fulfillment of the district's the child find and eligibility obligations under Section 504 without under- or over-identification and with due regard for the safety of students and the integrity of the school's educational mission.

Chapter 13

HOMELESS/MCKINNEY-VENTO HOMELESS ASSISTANCE ACT

Julia Lechtenberg, MSN, RN, NCSN

DESCRIPTION OF ISSUE

Homelessness is a serious issue that can significantly affect a student's academic success. In 1987, in response to increasing and widespread homelessness, President Ronald Reagan signed into law the McKinney-Vento Homeless Assistance Act (the "Act"). The Act was the first piece of major federal legislation that addressed the needs of the homeless and the education of homeless children and youth thereby facilitating the removal of barriers to a homeless child's academic success (National Coalition for the Homeless, 2004). One of the Act's main goals is to ensure that homeless children and youth have equal access to the same free and appropriate public education as provided to other children and youth (Cory & Jovanovic, 2013).

The Act has been amended several times since its inception and was most recently reauthorized in December 2015 when President Obama signed into law Every Student Succeeds Act (ESSA, 2015). ESSA contains provisions to strengthen the Act, including:

- Provides increased emphasis on the identification of homeless children and youths including requirements that State Educational Agencies and Local Educational Agencies provide training and professional development opportunities for staff and to ensure that State coordinators and local liaisons are able to carry out their job responsibilities (U.S. Department of Education, 2016b).

- Provides increased funding to support the enforcement of the McKinney-Vento Act (National Alliance to End Homelessness, 2016; National Public Radio, 2016).

- Eligibility of homelessness must be determined based on the definition set forth by the U.S. Department of Housing and Urban Development (U.S. Department of Education, 2016b).

- Focuses on school stability by keeping homeless students in school of origin "for the duration of homelessness or until the end of the school year in which the child or youth becomes permanently housed" (U.S. Department of Education, 2016b, p. 2).

- Requires that local school districts track and report graduation rates for homeless students (National Public Radio, 2016).

- Removes barriers to accessing academic programs and extracurricular activities for qualifying homeless students such as charter and magnet school, summer school, vocational and technical education, advance placement courses and online learning programs (U.S. Department of Education, 2016b).

- Mandates that school districts reserve Title I, Part A funds to be used for the education or support of homeless students (i.e. academic tutoring or social work services due to domestic violence (National Center for Homeless Education, 2016a).

- Expands current transportation services from grades K – 12 to include district-run public preschools and Head Start programs (Blad, 2016).

- If a dispute arises between the school district and the parent / guardian of a homeless student the school district must immediately enroll the student and provide necessary transportation until the dispute is resolved, including through the appeal process (U.S. Department of Education, 2016a).

As most recently reauthorized, the Act defines homeless children and youth as:

(2) The term "homeless children and youths" –

(A) mean individuals who lack a fixed, regular, and adequate nighttime residence (within the meaning of [42 U.S.C. § 11302(a)(1)]); and

(B) includes -

(i) children and youths who are sharing the housing of other persons due to loss of housing, economic hardship, or a similar reason; are living in motels, hotels, trailer parks, or camping grounds due to the lack of alternative adequate accommodations; are living in emergency or transitional shelters; or are abandoned in hospitals;

(ii) children and youths who have a primary nighttime residence that is a public or private place not designed for or ordinarily used as a regular sleeping accommodation for human beings (within the meaning of [42 U.S.C. § 11302(a)(2)(C)]);

(iii) children and youths who are living in cars, parks, public spaces, abandoned buildings, substandard housing, bus or train stations, or similar settings; and

(iv) migratory children (as defined in [20 U.S.C. § 6399]), who qualify as homeless because they are living in the circumstances described in clauses (i) through (iii) (42 U.S.C. § 11434a (2).

It is worthy of note that, pursuant to Title IX, Part A of the Every Student Succeeds Act, "awaiting foster care placement" was removed from the definition of "homeless children and youths." The change, which was made on December 10, 2015, went into effect on December 10, 2016. "Covered states" have until December 10, 2017 to remove "awaiting foster care placement" from their definition of homeless.

BACKGROUND

Homelessness is a pervasive social issue that seriously influences a student's educational experience. Causes of homelessness are numerous and include poverty, unemployment, lack of affordable housing, illness and natural disasters (National Center for Homeless Education, 2014a). Homeless children may be bunking with family or friends, sleeping in shelters, staying in cars, parks, or public spaces (US Department of Education, 2015). Significant absenteeism has tangible impacts on a child's education. For example, children and youth that are not in school often have difficulty learning. In addition, chronic absenteeism negatively affects standardized test scores, grade-level retention rates and ultimately graduation rates (Institute for Children, Poverty & Homelessness, 2015).

There is a stigma associated with being homeless, making it difficult to identify homeless individuals and families. However, **current statistics indicate that the incidence of homelessness continues to increase with rates at their highest since homeless data has been collected** (National Center for Homeless Education, 2014a). Data compiled by the National Center for Homeless Education (2016b) revealed that the number of homeless students is on the rise with almost 1.3 million children and youth being homeless in 2013 – 2014 (Ingram, Bridgeland, Reed & Atwell, 2016).

Provisions in the McKinney-Vento Homeless Assistance Act require school districts to identify children and youth who are homeless and to provide appropriate transportation and education to homeless students. School districts are required to designate a district homeless coordinator, otherwise known as a local education agency liaison ("liaison") (42 U.S.C. § 11432(g)(1)(J)(ii)). The liaison is charged with enforcing the Act's requirements, including:

- identifying homeless children and youth within the school district;
- ensuring that homeless children and youths enroll in, and have a full and equal opportunity to succeed in, district schools;
- ensuring that homeless families, children, and youths receive educational services for which such families, children, and youths are eligible (e.g. Head Start and Early Head Start programs, Even Start programs, preschool programs administered by the district, and referrals to healthcare services, dental services, mental health services, and other appropriate services);
- informing the parents or guardians of homeless children and youths about the educational and related opportunities available to their children; and
- providing public notice of the educational rights of homeless children and youths (42 U.S.C. § 11432(g) (6)(A)).

An effective liaison should be empathetic to the needs of the homeless, have good communication skills, be familiar with community resources and have experience working with vulnerable children and youth (Washington Office of Superintendent of Public Instructions, 2014). The role of the liaison may be assigned to an existing school district employee to perform along with their other duties. School nurses possess many of the necessary traits making them potential candidates for the position. However, time constraints often interfere with the efforts that are needed for the school nurse to provide continual support to homeless children and youth at the district level. Nonetheless, there are several ways in which school nurses can assist a school district meet its responsibilities under the Act.

IMPLICATIONS FOR SCHOOL NURSE PRACTICE

Identification of Students

The identification of homeless students is the first step in providing necessary academic, medical and community resources that are needed to remove barriers to learning. District identification of homeless students can be challenging because students and parents may try to hide their homeless situation. However, school nurses can help identify homeless children and youth. Because school nurses provide a nurturing environment and the school nurse may be the student's only resource for health care, the school clinic is a safe-haven that homeless children and youth may frequent. Using keen assessment skills and open communication, the school nurse may be the first person to identify a homeless student. Warning signs to look for include:

- Poor hygiene;
- Food insecurity (hungry - may hoard food);
- Poor health;
- Transportation issues;
- High absenteeism and tardiness
- Falling asleep in class; and
- Emotional and behavioral issues (National Center for Homeless Education, 2014a).

School Entry

School districts are required to enroll homeless children immediately, even if they lack appropriate documentation such as immunization or medical records, proof of residency, guardianship documentation or special education paperwork (U.S. Department of Education, 2004). The school nurse is instrumental in securing immunization and medical records as quickly as possible. The school nurse may contact the students' previous school to obtain missing medical and immunization records. If a child or youth needs to obtain immunizations or other required health records, the enrolling school must immediately refer the parent, guardian, or unaccompanied you to the local liaison, who must assist in obtaining the immunizations, screening, or immunization or other health records (U.S. Department of Education, 2016a).

Access to Care

Homeless students may have unmet dental and medical needs due to limited access to care (National Center for Homeless Education, 2014a). In comparison to the general population, homeless children and youth nationally have a higher incidence of chronic diseases, wound infections, pneumonia and substance abuse (US National Library of Medicine, 2016). They often lack medical insurance and appropriate transportation thereby limiting access to much needed medical and psychiatric care.

The school nurse can coordinate with the district's liaison to utilize Title 1, Part A funds to pay for needed medical services such as immunizations, medical and dental services, vision exams and eyeglasses, hearing aids and social work services (National Center for Homeless Education, 2014b). The school nurse collaborates with the liaison and staff members to identify homeless students with chronic health diseases and unmet health needs and links these children and youth to necessary local resources. The school nurse may help parent/guardian(s) complete medical forms and health insurance applications.

Mental Health Concerns

Homeless children also have higher incidences of mental health problems (US National Library of Medicine, 2016), with homeless children of veterans often experiencing an even higher prevalence of mental health disorders including depression and post-traumatic stress disorder ("PTSD") (National Center for Homeless Education, 2015). Individuals suffering from PTSD can experience anxiety and irritability causing the child to take on the role of the parent. Title 1, Part A funds can also be used to pay for needed social work services for these individuals (National Center for Homeless Education, 2014b).

CONCLUSION

Homelessness is a serious issue that negatively influences a person's life and significantly impacts a student's academic success. The McKinney-Vento Homeless Assistance Act guarantees a free and appropriate education to homeless students. Homeless children and youth have the "right to enroll, attend, and succeed in school" (National Center for Homeless Education, 2014a, p. 4). When implementing the central features of the Act, school nurses in collaboration with the homeless liaison and the school community can identify and provide necessary resources needed to ease the detrimental effects of homelessness thereby promoting student academic success.

RESOURCES

Institute for Children, Poverty and Homelessness
http://www.icphusa.org/
(212) 358-8086

National Alliance to End Homelessness
www.endhomelessness.org
202-638-1526

National Association for the Education of Homeless Children and Youth
http://naehcy.org/
855-446-2673

National Call Center for Homeless Veterans Hotline
http://www.va.gov/homeless/nationalcallcenter.asp
1-877-4AIDVET

National Center for Homeless Education
http://center.serve.org/nche/
1-800-308-2145

National Center for Homeless Education
Homeless Liaison Toolkit
http://center.serve.org/nche/downloads/toolkit2/toolkit.pdf

Federal Register
McKinney-Vento Education for Homeless Children and Youths Program
https://www.federalregister.gov/articles/2016/03/17/2016-06073/mckinney-vento-education-for-homeless-children-and-youths-program

Legal References

ESSA – Legislation: Bill summaries, text, and U.S. Department of Education Guidance and Regulations
http://www.naehcy.org/essa-legislation-bill-summaries-text-and-us-department-education-guidance-and-regulations

McKinney-Vento Homeless Assistance Act (42 U.S.C. § 11431 et seq.)
http://www2.ed.gov/policy/elsec/leg/esea02/pg116.html

McKinney-Vento Homeless Assistance Act
Reauthorized December 10, 2015 by Title IX, Part A of the Every Student Succeeds Act
(Effective October 1, 2016)
http://www.naehcy.org/sites/default/files/dl/legis/NewMV2015clean.pdf

Publications

Bassuk, E.L., et al. (2014, November). *America's Youngest Outcasts: A Report Card on Child Homelessness*. The National Center on Family Homelessness. Retrieved from http://www.air.org/sites/default/files/downloads/report/Americas-Youngest-Outcasts-Child-Homelessness-Nov2014.pdf

Ingram, E., Bridgeland, J., Reed, B. & Atwell, M. (2016). *Hidden in plain sight: Homeless students in America's public schools*. Retrieved from http://civicenterprises.net/MediaLibrary/Docs/HiddeninPlainSightOfficial.pdf

REFERENCES

Blad, E. (2016, July 27). ESSA expands schools' obligations to homeless students, new guidance says. *Education Week.* Retrieved from http://blogs.edweek.org/edweek/rulesforengagement/2016/07/essa_expands_schools_obligations_to_homeless_students_new_guidance_says.html

Cory, A. & Jovanovic, J. (2013). The student's family. In J. Selekman (Ed.), *School nursing: A comprehensive text* (2nd ed.) (pp. 383-406). Philadelphia, PA: F.A. Davis Company.

Every Student Succeeds Act (ESSA). (2015). Every Student Succeeds Act of 2015, Pub. L. No. 114-95 § 114 Stat. 1177 (2015-2016).

Federal Register. (2016, March 17). *McKinney-Vento education for homeless children and youth programs.* Retrieved from https://www.federalregister.gov/articles/2016/03/17/2016-06073/mckinney-vento-education-for-homeless-children-and-youths-program

Ingram, E., Bridgeland, J., Reed, B. & Atwell, M. (2016). *Hidden in plain sight: Homeless students in America's public schools.* Retrieved from http://civicenterprises.net/MediaLibrary/Docs/HiddeninPlainSightOfficial.pdf

Institute for Children, Poverty and Homelessness. (2015). *Empty seats: The epidemic of absenteeism among homeless elementary students.* Retrieved from http://www.icphusa.org/PDF/reports/ICPH%20Policy%20Report_Empty%20Seats_Chronic%20Absenteeism.pdf

McKinney-Vento HOMELESS ASSISTANCE Act. (1987). H.R. 558 — 100th Congress: Stewart B. McKinney Homeless Assistance Act. P.L. 100-77. Retrieved from https://www.govtrack.us/congress/bills/100/hr558

McKinney-Vento Homeless Assistance Act. (2004). (Subtitle B – Section 725 [42 U.S.C. 11431 et seq.] as reauthorized by Title X, Part C of the Elementary and Secondary Education).

US National Library of Medicine. (2016). *Homeless health concerns.* Retrieved from https://medlineplus.gov/homelesshealthconcerns.html

National Alliance to End Homelessness. (2016*). FY 2016 budget rundown*. Retrieved from http://www.endhomelessness.org/page/-/files/FY%202016%20Budget%20Rundown.pdf

National Center for Homeless Education. (2014a). *Children and youth experiencing homelessness: An introduction to the issues.* Retrieved from http://center.serve.org/nche/downloads/briefs/introduction.pdf

National Center for Homeless Education. (2014b). *Serving students experiencing homelessness under Title I, Part A.* Retrieved from http://center.serve.org/nche/downloads/briefs/titlei.pdf

National Center for Homeless Education. (2015). *Supporting school success for homeless children of veterans and military service members.* Retrieved from http://center.serve.org/nche/downloads/briefs/vet.pdf

National Center for Homeless Education. (2016a). *Every student succeeds act of 2015.* Retrieved from http://center.serve.org/nche/legis/essa.php

National Center for Homeless Education. (2016b). *National overview.* Retrieved from http://profiles.nche.seiservices.com/ConsolidatedStateProfile.aspx

National Coalition for the Homeless. (2004). *McKinney – Vento act.* Retrieved from http://www.nationalhomeless.org/publications/facts/McKinney.pdf

National Coalition for the Homeless. (2009). *Education of homeless children and youth*. Retrieved from http://nationalhomeless.org/factsheets/education.html

National Public Radio. (2016). *As the number of homeless students soars, how schools can better serve them.* Retrieved from http://www.npr.org/sections/ed/2016/06/13/481279226/as-the-number-of-homeless-students-soars-how-schools-can-serve-them-better

U.S. Department of Education. (2015). *Education for homeless children and youths grants for state and local activitie*s. Retrieved from http://www2.ed.gov/programs/homeless/index.html

U.S. Department of Education. (2016a). *Education for homeless children and youths program non-regulatory guidance.* Retrieved from http://www2.ed.gov/policy/elsec/leg/essa/160240ehcyguidance072716.pdf

U.S. Department of Education. (2016b). *Key policy letters signed by the education secretary or deputy secretary.* Retrieved from http://www2.ed.gov/print/policy/elsec/guid/secletter/160726.html

U.S. Department of Education. (2004). *Laws and guidance / elementary & secondary education: Part c – homeless education.* Retrieved from http://www2.ed.gov/policy/elsec/leg/esea02/pg116.html

Washington Office of Superintendent of Public Instruction. (2014). *Designating a local homeless education liaison: A guide for school district administrators in Washington.* Retrieved from http://www.k12.wa.us/HomelessEd/pubdocs/Liaisonbrief.pdf

Chapter 14

MINORS' RIGHTS TO CONFIDENTIAL HEALTH SERVICES

Pamela Kahn, MPH, RN

DESCRIPTION OF ISSUE

The issues of minor confidentiality and consent are one of the most sensitive areas that a school nurse must handle in his/her work with children and adolescents. An understanding of both the federal and state laws that govern these issues is essential. The school nurse is charged with ensuring that a student receives the appropriate physical and mental health services that are needed. It is imperative that the nurse be knowledgeable about the laws and regulations guiding who has the ability to consent to certain services, and how to protect the confidentiality of health information.

There are numerous and complex laws and statutes that govern the privacy of healthcare information, and these laws and statues vary by state. This chapter offers a general overview of regulations that govern minor confidentiality and consent.

BACKGROUND

Over the past 30 years, the range of health services that minors may consent for has expanded significantly. These services include sexual and reproductive care, mental health services and substance abuse treatment (Guttmacher Institute, 2017) In most states, laws granting the ability to consent independently to specified health services apply to minors age 12 and older, (Guttmacher Institute, 2017) however some states describe certain cases in which minors may consent – only those who are married, pregnant or already parents. Nearly every state allows minor parents to make health care and other important decisions for their own children. The majority of states, at time of writing, require parental involvement in a minor's abortion, however many states allow minors to obtain contraceptive, prenatal and sexually transmitted infections services without parental consent (Guttmacher Institute, 2017).

The types of laws that are most pertinent to school nurses who work with students are: 1) the federal Health Insurance Portability and Accountability Act (HIPAA) medical privacy rules, (Rehabilitation Act of 1973 [§504], 2000); (2) the Family Educational Rights and Privacy Act (FERPA)(U.S. Department of Education, 2012); 3) Title X of the Public Health Services Act (Napili, 2014); 4) the Child Abuse Prevention and Treatment Act (CAPTA) (U.S. Department of Health & Human Services [USDHHS], n.d.); and 5) state privacy laws and minor consent laws. HIPPA and FERPA are both federal laws that limit the sharing of personal health information and protect the privacy of the records. In general, HIPAA pertains to disclosure of information maintained by healthcare providers, whereas FERPA addresses disclosure of information in education records that are maintained by schools.

The Health Insurance Portability and Accountability Act of 1996 (HIPAA) Privacy Rule

HIPAA was passed by Congress in 1996 to create standards that nationally protected the privacy of healthcare records. The HIPAA Privacy Rule took effect in 2003 establishing a standard federal floor of privacy protections for healthcare consumers. These rules limit how providers can use patients' medical information, and are designed to govern disclosure of protected health information. The Privacy Rule applies only to covered entities, it does not apply to all persons or institutions that collect individually identifiable health information. Covered entities are defined in the HIPAA Rule as 1) health plans, 2) healthcare clearinghouses, and 3) healthcare providers who electronically transmit any health information in connection with transactions for which USDHHS has adopted standards. Covered entities can be institutions, organizations, or persons (U.S. Department of Health and Human Services, National Institutes of Health [USDHHS/NIH], 2007).

The Family Educational Rights and Privacy Act (FERPA)

Congress passed FERPA in 1974, with intent to protect the privacy of educational records while at the same time assure parental access to these same records. A parent's right to access their child's health records is much broader under FERPA than under HIPAA. FERPA applies to educational agencies or institutions that receive federal funds from programs administered by the U.S. Department of Education. This includes public schools, school districts or local educational agencies, and postsecondary institutions such as colleges and universities. Generally elementary and secondary level private and parochial school if they do not receive federal funding, and as such are not subject to FERPA. FERPA also applies to agencies and organizations that consult or contract with an education agency (under certain circumstances) and to any person acting for such an agency, which would include school nurses, teacher, principals, etc. (USDHHS/NIH, 2007). For example, if a school nurse is hired by the local health department and assigned to a public school; the health records would remain part of the educational record and be subject to FERPA; not regulations pertaining to the health department, such as HIPAA.

FERPA protects educational documents that contain information on a student and are maintained by an educational agency or institution, or by a person acting for the agency/institution, for example school nurses who provide services but hired by hospitals or health department (US Department of Health and Human Services and US Department of Education [USDHHS & USDE], 2008). These documents may include immunization records, Individualized Education Program (IEP) documentation, and medical records that are part of a students' file. FERPA does not include oral communications or personal records that are kept in the sole possession of the maker, are used only as a personal memory aid, and are not accessible or revealed to any other person except a temporary substitute for the maker of the record (USDE, 2012).

FERPA requires that written permission is obtained before releasing any information in the educational record. Most often a parent or guardian would sign for the release of records, however once students reach the age of eighteen they may sign their own release forms.

There are exceptions to FERPA; some records may be released without written release. For example, directory information that includes student name, address, telephone listing, date/place of birth, major field of study, participation in officially recognized activities and sports, weight and height of members of athletic teams, dates of attendance, degrees and awards received, and the most recent previous educational agency or institution attended by the student may be shared with the general public (after the school district has followed certain procedures defined in FERPA (California School Health Centers Association, 2010). Another exception allows for the sharing of information with school officials in the same school who have a "legitimate educational interest" in the information, once the appropriate policies are in place at the district level. Exceptions to FERPA also exist during emergency situations and for school transfers. For example, a school official generally has a legitimate educational interest if the official needs to review an education record in order to fulfill his or her professional responsibility (USDE, 2015).

There are some situations in which student health information may not be considered an educational record, and is therefore not subject to FERPA:

Personal notes that a nurse has maintained regarding a student's health. These notes must be kept only as memory aids, must remain in the sole possession of the writer, are not used to replace or avoid normal documentation, and are shared with nobody except a temporary substitute registered nurse (RN) (Colorado Association of School-Based Health Care, n.d.)

A "treatment record" for a student who is at least eighteen years old. A treatment record is defined as a record made or maintained by a physician, psychiatrist, psychologist, or other recognized professional or paraprofessional acting in their professional capacity. These records must be made, maintained and used only in connection with treatment of the student, and disclosed only to individuals providing the treatment For example, treatment records would include health or medical records that a university psychologist maintains only in connection with the provision of treatment to an eligible student, and health or medical records that the campus health center or clinic maintains only in connection with the provision of treatment to an eligible student. Treatment records also would include health or medical records on an eligible student in high school if the records otherwise meet the above definition. (USDHHS & USDE, 2008).

Note that once such medical records are disclosed to someone other than "those persons providing treatment," then the records are no longer considered medical records excluded from FERPA (Catholic University of America, 2016). (*For more information on HIPAA and FERPA, please see Chapter 11*).

State Laws

There exists a variety of state laws that govern minor confidentiality and consent. These fall in the category of minor consent laws, medical records laws, professional licensing laws, funding program requirements and education laws.

Whether a minor can or cannot give consent for health care is dependent upon that state's particular law and regulations. Each state will have specific laws addressing the ability of a minor to obtain care without the consent of a parent or guardian. State laws take into consideration both the status of the minor (i.e. emancipated minors, those who live apart from parents, who are married, pregnant and/or parenting) as well as the type of care that is given (i.e. emergency, reproductive services, mental health or drug/alcohol) (American Academy of Pediatrics [AAP], n.d.) Often there are limitations associated with minor consent for mental health services (type of care, providers that are covered, number of visits, the age of the minor, number of visits, health professionals who are covered).

There are some states that have laws in place explicitly requiring that health information of a minor be disclosed to a parent. In these cases, the regulations allow the healthcare provider to disclose the information. Conversely, if state law prohibits disclosure of information to a parent, the regulations do not allow a healthcare provider to disclose. If state or other law either is silent on the question or permits disclosure (but does not require it), the provider is given the discretion to decide whether to grant parent access to the minor's health information (Colorado Association of School-Based Health Care, n.d.)

When HIPAA and state laws conflict, the provider must generally follow the law that provides the more rigorous confidentiality protection (Colorado Association for School-Based Health Care, n.d.). It is important to note that state laws may be more restrictive than HIPAA standard, in which case the state law would supersede the Federal standards.

Emancipation

Depending on the state and other considerations, emancipation usually occurs at the age of 18, the usual age of majority. An emancipated minor may be defined as a person who is not legally an adult, but is no longer dependent upon their parent(s). State requirements for emancipation prior to the age of majority differ, but in most cases a minor may become emancipated by getting married, joining the military, by having a child (whether married or not), by leaving home and becoming self-sufficient, or by court order. An emancipated minor may sign legally binding contracts, give medical consent and otherwise function as an adult in society.

The minimum age in most states at which a minor can petition a court for emancipation is at the age of 16, however, some states, such as California, allows those as young as 14 to file a court petition for emancipation (FindLaw, 2017). In most states, it is possible to become emancipated without filing a petition, but the options are limited and often require a parent or legal guardian's permission. It is important for the school nurse to become familiar with the laws regarding minor emancipation in the state in which they practice.

The HIPAA Privacy Rule and Adolescents

While HIPAA governs the sharing of information between healthcare providers, there are also provisions for minors who have legally consented to care. Under HIPAA, a minor has more power to control and limit release of their health records than under FERPA (Colorado Association for School-Based Health Care, n.d.) Generally, a parent is allowed, via HIPAA, access to their minor child's medical records when state or other law allows. However, there are three exceptions to the HIPAA Privacy Rule that may preclude parents from accessing records or granting access to others.

- o When parent consent is not required by state or other law and the minor has consented for their own care.
- o When a court directs that a minor receive care.
- o When, with parent agreement, a confidential relationship exists between the healthcare provider and the minor (AAP, n.d.).

HIPAA has special privacy protections that a minor may access. One of these allows minors to request that healthcare providers and healthcare plans communicate with the minor in a confidential manner by email, rather than by phone, or at a place other than their home. Minors may also request that the plan or provider limit disclosure related to treatment, payment or healthcare operations that normally would take place. Responses to these requests may vary by provider and plan, depending upon the type of request and of whom the request is made (English & Ford, 2016).

The HIPAA privacy rule allows a healthcare provider or plan to deny access to health records to parents who they suspect have subjected the minor to abuse, neglect or domestic violence or in situations when treating the parent as the personal representative could endanger the minor (English & Ford, 2004). The privacy rule also allows a provider or plan to disclose the health information of a minor to help prevent or diminish an imminent threat to the health and safety of a person or the public (English & Ford, 2004). It is recommended that providers consult with legal counsel when considering denying access to records under these privacy protections.

The HIPAA Privacy Rule allows a healthcare provider to disclose a student's protected health information (PHI) to a school nurse, physician or other healthcare provider for treatment purposes without the authorization of the student's parent or the student. A school nurse, for example, would be able to discuss healthcare needs, medication orders and other issues concerning the student's care while at school with the student's physician (USDHHS & USDE, 2008). A healthcare provider who is not employed by the school district and is subject to HIPAA may share confidential medical information with other healthcare providers for referral and treatment purposes without need of a signed release. However, if this information is shared with others who are not health professionals, including teachers and other school staff, a HIPAA compliant consent form is required before any information may be disclosed (California School Health Centers Association, 2010).

Federal Substance Abuse Confidentiality Requirements and HIPAA

Confidentiality requirements for federally assisted alcohol and drug abuse treatment programs are regulated by federal law and regulations that outline under what limited circumstances information about the client's treatment may be disclosed with and without the client's consent. These confidentiality requirements are often more restrictive than HIPAA regulations, and providers must follow the more stringent confidentiality protection. Generally, federally subsidized substance abuse treatment programs cannot disclose information without written consent. The minor's signed consent is required before health information can be released to anyone, including a parent or legal guardian. However, a program or individual may share information with a parent without obtaining prior written consent if:

- The minor's situation poses a substantial threat to the life or physical well-being of the minor or another;
- The threat may be reduced by communicating relevant facts to the minor's parents; **and**
- The minor lacks the capacity because of extreme youth or a mental or physical condition to make a rational decision on whether to disclose to the parents (Colorado Association of School-Based Health Care, n.d.).

Almost all states have implemented laws that allow minors to consent for treatment for substance abuse. School staff are encouraged to familiarize themselves with the laws pertaining to this consent for their specific states, and also with the confidentiality laws that apply for treatment programs that are not federally funded.

The Federal Title X Family Planning Program

The Federal Title X of the Public Health Service Act was created in 1970 with the goal of providing free or low-cost family planning and related health services available to eligible individuals, including adolescents.

Regulations require that Title X funded services are available to all adolescents, regardless of age. If services are wholly or partly funded by Title X, minors of any age or marital status may consent for these services, and provision of these services are not dependent upon parental consent or notification. The laws governing Title X funded programs guarantee the confidentiality of patient information, including that of minor patients. Covered entities are prohibited from making disclosures or granting access to parents without the minor's authorization (American Civil Liberties Union, 2003).

In cases where state law requires parental consent or notification for services, Title X providers must allow adolescents to obtain Title X services on their own consent. Family planning services that are funded through other federal programs, such as Medicaid, are governed by different confidentiality rules, but do provide protections for adolescents related to confidential contraceptive care.

IMPLICATIONS FOR SCHOOL NURSE PRACTICE

Privacy and Confidentiality Considerations

The complexity and variance of laws that surround minor confidentiality and consent create a necessity for the school nurse to be educated in applicable local, state and federal laws. School nurses will want to consider the rights of minors when developing school policies. Nurses must consider the age of a student, their emancipation status, the type of services that the student is seeking, etc. and determine how these various situations are governed by federal and/or state laws. School nurses must always keep in mind the goal of protecting the privacy of a student, while at the same time avoiding illegal or unethical disclosure of health information. It is important for the school nurse to consider the difference between observing laws regarding confidentiality and respecting the privacy of a student, and when it may be acceptable to violate said privacy. Privacy may be defined as the right of the student to keep information about themselves from being disclosed without their permission (Erickson & Millar, 2005). Confidentiality is how that information is handled by the nurse once information has been disclosed, and this disclosure has occurred in an atmosphere of trust (Erickson & Millar, 2005). Permission to disclose confidential information should always be obtained by asking the student; however, when the individual is incapacitated or in an emergency situation, healthcare providers may generally make disclosures if it is determined to be in the best interests of the individual (McGowan, 2012).

Support Systems

School nurses are obligated to provide the protections of confidentiality to students and their parent/guardian(s). At the same time, nurses face the challenge of encouraging communication between these students and their parent/guardian(s) in a way that is respectful of the student's need for privacy and recognizing the support that parent/guardian(s) can provide to their child in most situations. Where there are real and potentially dangerous consequences to talking with parent/guardian(s), (i.e. family violence, potential homelessness, etc.), school nurses can encourage students to look to other adults such as extended family members, social workers, clergy and others who may be able to offer support. When possible, school nurses should review with minors and parents the limits of confidentiality, and document all informed consent discussions. Publicizing information in their office and other public spots on campus on the rights of minor confidentiality may encourage students to seek health care even when they are unable to speak to family members or other adults. "After all, health care without adult involvement is preferable to no health care" (Feierman et al., n.d., p. 9).

While a school nurse may feel that confidentiality is in the best interest of a student, laws and regulations may prevent the nurse from guaranteeing this protection. In such situations, the nurse may want to consider referring the student to a Title X funded-clinic or other facility that can better meet the needs of the student. The critical point to remember is that if students are not assured access to confidential health care, they may simply stop seeking the services that they need. School nurses need to be aware of surrounding clinics and their policies around confidentiality.

HIPAA and FERPA

Additionally, a school nurse, whose records are subject to FERPA, cannot promise students that their education records that may contain health information will be kept confidential. In general, under FERPA, parents or guardians have access to the education records of their unemancipated minor children, including any health information contained in those records (English & Ford, 2004).

However, FERPA contains no obligation that schools notify parents about services that the minor has received without parent consent. As stated previously, if the nurse is holding information about the "minor consent" health information only in their personal notes (sole possession), these notes are not considered part of the education record and as such are not subject to the rules of FERPA. Health information in oral form or in personal notes is not covered by FERPA, and thus may be protected by HIPAA (California School-Based Health Association, 2010).

It is important to note that HIPAA states explicitly that its rules do not apply to health information held in an educational record; this information is subject to FERPA. Therefore, HIPAA and FERPA will never apply to the same information at the same time However, state medical confidentiality laws do not have this same exception. Therefore, state confidentiality law can apply to health information held in an education record subject to FERPA (California School Health Centers Association, 2010).

School Based Health Centers and Confidentiality

Schools that operate school based health centers (SBHC) must pay close attention to the interaction between HIPAA and FERPA regulations for services that the student may obtain at such centers. Depending upon whether the program or provider are considered an "educational agency "or the agent of the educational agency determines if the records of the school health program are subject to HIPAA or FERPA rules. The "Joint Guidance" issued by the U. S. Department of Education and the U.S. Department of Health and Human Services (USDHHS/USDE, 2008) provides some case examples that may be used to determine which federal law applies; unfortunately, there is no clear-cut checklist to determine where a program might fit. SBHC records are not subject to FERPA "if the center is funded, administered and operated by or on behalf of a public or private health, social services, or other non-educational agency or individual" (USDE/Family Compliance Center, 2004, para. 9). In such a case, the records would be subject to HIPAA, even if the services were being provided on school grounds since the SBHC would not be acting on behalf of the school. Conversely, if the SBHC is funded, administered and operated by or on behalf of a school or educational institution, the records are considered "education records" and are subject to FERPA (California School Health Centers Association, 2010). If in doubt, the provider is recommended to seek legal counsel as to which federal law governs school health records and school health staff.

(*Please see Chapter 40 for more information on school-based health centers*).

CONCLUSION

An important guiding principle in the school setting that should be considered is that confidential health information should be shared on a need-to-know basis only, and this sharing is in the interest of keeping a student safe and functioning to their highest capacity in the educational setting. Licensed staff (i.e. the school nurse) are responsible for educating all non-licensed staff on the appropriate sharing of health records, and informs non-licensed staff of the laws that govern the disclosure of such records.

Federal and state laws, as well as other rules and regulations govern the concepts of minor confidentiality and consent. School nurses need to be knowledgeable regarding their state's minor consent and privacy laws, as well as state health privacy laws in general. Additionally, the nurse needs to consider the culture of the institution in which they are employed, ensuring that school and district administrators are informed regarding the federal and state legal guidelines and support the important balance of parental and minor's rights.

When considering minor consent and confidentiality, the school nurse must honor both the legal and ethical obligations of a nurse to the patient.

RESOURCES

> Please see APPENDIX: "Minors May Consent to" and see Chapter 24 for more information on consent to healthcare.

American Academy of Pediatrics & Healthy Foster Care America. (n.d.) *Confidentiality Laws Tip Sheet* Retrieved from American Academy of Pediatrics: https://www.aap.org/en-us/advocacy-and-policy/aap-health-initiatives/healthy-foster-care-america/Documents/Confidentiality_Laws.pdf

Center for Adolescent Health & the Law: http://www.cahl.org/programs-and-activities/consent-confidentiality-protections/

Guttmacher Institute: https://www.guttmacher.org/

FindLaw. (2017). *Emancipation of minors basics.* http://family.findlaw.com/emancipation-of-minors/emancipation-of-minors-basics.html

National Center for Health Law: http://teenhealthlaw.org/

Gudeman, R., & Madg, S. (n.d.). *The Federal Title X Family Planning Program: Privacy and Access Rules for Adolescents*. Retrieved from National Center for Youth Law:: http://youthlaw.org/publication/the-federal-title-x-family-planning-program-privacy-and-access-rules-for-adolescents1/

Weiss, C. (2003). *Protecting Minors' Health Information under the Federal Medical Privacy Regulations*. Retrieved from American Civil Liberties Union: https://www.aclu.org/protecting-minors-health-information-under-federal-medical-privacy-regulations

REFERENCES

American Academy of Pediatrics. (n.d.). *Confidentiality laws tip sheet*. Retrieved from https://www.aap.org/en-us/advocacy-and-policy/aap-health-initiatives/healthy-foster-care-america/Documents/Confidentiality_Laws.pdf

American Civil Liberties Union. (2003). *Protecting minors' health information under the Federal Medical Privacy Regulations.* Retrieved from https://www.aclu.org/sites/default/files/field_document/med_privacy_guide.pdf

California School Health Centers Association. (2010). *HIPPA or FERPA? A primer on school health information sharing in California.* Retrieved from http://impact.sp2.upenn.edu/fieldctr/wp-content/uploads/2013/05/HIPAA%20or%20FERPA_A%20Primer%20on%20School%20Health%20Information%20Sharing%20in%20California.pdf

Catholic University of America. (2016). *FERPA.* Retrieved from http://counsel.cua.edu/ferpa/questions/

Colorado Association For School-Based Health Care. (n.d.). *Understanding minor consent and confidentiality in Colorado* . Retrieved from https://www.cde.state.co.us/sites/default/files/documents/healthandwellness/download/school%20nurse/understanding%20minor%20consent%20and%20confidentiality%20in%20colorado.pdf

English, A. & Ford, C.A. (2004). *The HIPPA privacy rule and adolescents: Legal questions and clinical challenges.* Retrieved from https://www.guttmacher.org/about/journals/psrh/2004/hipaa-privacy-rule-and-adolescents-legal-questions-and-clinical-challenges

English, A. & Ford, C.A. (2016). Privacy protection in billing and health insurance communications**.** *American Medical Association Journal of Ethics, 18*(3), 279-287. doi: 10.1001/journalofethics.2016.18.03.pfor4-1603

Erickson, J. & Millar, S. (2005.). Caring for patients while respecting their privacy: Renewing our commitment. *Online Journal of Issues in Nursing.* Retrieved from http://www.nursingworld.org/MainMenuCategories/ANAMarketplace/ANAPeriodicals/OJIN/TableofContents/Volume102005/No2May05/tpc27_116017.html

Feierman, J., Lieberman, D., Schissel, A., Diller, R., Kim, J. & Chu, Y. (n.d.). *Teenagers, health care & the law: A guide to minors' rights in New York State (2nd ed).* Retrieved from http://www.nyclu.org/files/thl.pdf

Guttmacher Institute. (2017). *An overview of minors' consent law.* Retrieved from https://www.guttmacher.org/state-policy/explore/overview-minors-consent-law

McGowan, C. (2012). *Patients' confidentiality. Critical Care Nurse, 32(*5), 61-64. doi: 10.4037/ccn2012135

Napili, A. (2014). *Title X (Public Health Service Act) Family Planning Program*. Retrieved from https://fas.org/sgp/crs/misc/RL33644.pdf

Rehabilitation Act of 1973, 29 U.S.C. § 504

U.S. Department of Education. (2012). *Family Educational Rights and Privacy Act regulations.* Retrieved from
https://www2.ed.gov/policy/gen/guid/fpco/pdf/2012-final-regs.pdf

U.S. Department of Education. (2015). *FERPA general guidance for students.* Retrieved from
https://www2.ed.gov/policy/gen/guid/fpco/ferpa/students.html

U.S. Department of Education, Family Compliance Office. (2004). *Letter to University of New Mexico re:
Applicability of FERPA to health and other state reporting requirements.* Retrieved from
http://familypolicy.ed.gov/content/letter-university-new-mexico-re-applicability-ferpa-health-and-other-
state-reporting

U.S. Department of Health and Human Services. (n.d.). *The Child Abuse and Prevention and Treatment Act.*
Retrieved from https://www.acf.hhs.gov/sites/default/files/cb/capta2010.pdf

U.S. Department of Health and Human Services & U.S. Department of Education. (2008). *Joint guidance
on the applicaion of the Family Educational Rights and Privacy Act (FERPA) and the Heath Insurance
Portability and Accountability Act of 1996 (HIPAA) to student health records.* Retrieved from
http://www2.ed.gov/policy/gen/guid/fpco/doc/ferpa-hipaa-guidance.pdf

U.S. Department of Health and Human Services, National Instittutes of Health. (2007). *HIPPA privacy rules.*
Retrieved from https://privacyruleandresearch.nih.gov/pr_06.asp

APPENDIX

MINORS MAY CONSENT TO:

STATE	CONTRACEPTIVE SERVICES	STI SERVICES	PRENATAL CARE	ADOPTION	MEDICAL CARE FOR MINOR'S CHILD	ABORTION SERVICES
Alabama	All[†]	All[*]	All	All	All	Parental Consent
Alaska	All	All	All		All	Parental Notice
Arizona	xAll	All		All		Parental Consent
Arkansas	All	All[*]	All		All	Parental Consent
California	All	All	All	All		▼ (Parental Consent)
Colorado	All	All	All	All	All	Parental Notice
Connecticut	Some	All		Legal counsel	All	All
Delaware	All[*]	All[*]	All[*]	All	All	Parental Notice[‡]
Dist. of Columbia	All	All	All	All	All	All
Florida	Some	All	All		All	Parental Notice
Georgia	All	All[*]	All	All	All	Parental Notice
Hawaii	All[*,†]	All[*,†]	All[*,†]	All		
Idaho	All	All[†]	All	All	All	Parental Consent
Illinois	Some	All[*]	All	All	All	Parental Notice
Indiana	Some	All		All		Parental Consent
Iowa	All	All				Parental Notice
Kansas	Some	All[*]	Some	All	All	Parental Consent
Kentucky	All[*]	All[*]	All[*]	Legal counsel	All	Parental Consent
Louisiana	Some	All[*]		Parental consent	All	Parental Consent
Maine	Some	All[*]				All
Maryland	All[*]	All[*]	All[*]	All	All	Parental Notice
Massachusetts	All	All	All		All	Parental Consent
Michigan	Some	All[*]	All[*]	Parental consent	All	Parental Consent
Minnesota	All[*]	All[*]	All[*]	Parental consent	All	Parental Notice
Mississippi	Some	All	All	All	All	Parental Consent
Missouri	Some	All[*]	All[*]	Legal counsel	All	Parental Consent
Montana	All[*]	All[*]	All[*]	Legal counsel	All	▼ (Parental Consent)
Nebraska	Some	All				Parental Consent
Nevada	Some	All	Some	All	All	▼ (Parental Notice)
New Hampshire	Some	All[†]	Some	All[Ω]		Parental Notice
New Jersey	Some	All[*]	All[*]	All	All	▼ (Parental Notice)
New Mexico	All	All	All	All		▼ (Parental Consent)
New York	All	All	All	All	All	
North Carolina	All	All	All			Parental Consent
North Dakota		All[*,†]	ξ[*]	All		Parental Consent
Ohio		All		All		Parental Consent

STATE	CONTRACEPTIVE SERVICES	STI SERVICES	PRENATAL CARE	ADOPTION	MEDICAL CARE FOR MINOR'S CHILD	ABORTION SERVICES
Oklahoma	Some	All*	All*	All†	All	Parental Consent and Notice
Oregon	All*	All	All*, ‡			
Pennsylvania	All†	All	All	Parental notice	All	Parental Consent
Rhode Island		All		Parental consent	All	Parental Consent
South Carolina	All◊	All◊	All◊	All	All	Parental Consent‡
South Dakota	Some	All				Parental Notice
Tennessee	All	All	All	All	All	Parental Consent
Texas	Some	All*	All*			Parental Consent and Notice
Utah	Some	All	All	All	All	Parental Consent and Notice
Vermont	Some	All		All		
Virginia	All	All	All	All	All	Parental Consent and Notice
Washington	All	All†	All	Legal counsel		
West Virginia	Some	All	Some	All		Parental Notice
Wisconsin		All				Parental Consent
Wyoming	All	All		All		Parental Consent and Notice
TOTAL	**26+DC**	**50+DC**	**32+DC**	**28+DC**	**30+DC**	**2+DC**

Notes: "All" applies to those 17 and younger or to minors of at least a specified age such as 12 or 14. "Some" applies to specified categories of minors (those who have a health issue, or are married, pregnant, mature, etc.) The totals include only those states that allow all minors to consent.

▼ Enforcement permanently or temporarily enjoined by a court order; policy not in effect.

* Physicians may, but are not required to, inform the minor's parents.

† Applies to minors 14 and older.

‡ Delaware's abortion law applies to women younger than 16. Oregon's prenatal care law applies to women at least 15 years old. South Carolina's abortion law applies to those younger than 17.

Ω A court may require parental consent.

ξ Minor may consent to prenatal care in the 1st trimester and the first visit after the 1st trimester. Parental consent required for all other visits.

◊ Applies to mature minors 15 and younger and to all minors 16 and older.

Source: Guttmacher Institute, An overview of minors' consent law, *State Laws and Policies (as of March 1, 2016),* 2016. Retrieved from https://www.guttmacher.org/state-policy/explore/overview-minors-consent-law. Reprinted with permission.

174

Chapter 15

LEGAL PROCEEDINGS-SUBPOENAS, LAWSUITS, AND INVESTIGATIONS

Erin D. Gilsbach, Esquire

DESCRIPTION OF ISSUE

While rare, there may be occasions where a school nurse will be called to testify in a legal proceeding, produce documents pursuant to a court order, participate in a criminal investigation, and even respond as a named party in a lawsuit. This chapter provides basic information describing each of these processes, highlighting best practices, and outlining a school nurse's options and legal obligations regarding each proceeding.

BACKGROUND

In order to better understand the implications of this topic for school nurse practice, the following basic information is important to know:

Subpoenas: A subpoena is a document used to summon witnesses or the submission of evidence before a court or other legal proceeding. There are generally three types of subpoenas:

- subpoenas that require testimony (sometimes referred to as "*subpoena ad* testificandum"); and
- subpoenas that require the production of documents for a legal proceeding (sometimes referred to as "*subpoena duces tecum*"); and
- subpoenas that require both testimony and the production of documents.

The legal process for the issuance of and compliance with subpoenas can vary depending upon the law applicable in the related court's jurisdiction. In most states, in order to be valid, a subpoena must be issued and signed by the court. Where a subpoena is not signed by a judge or court official, the school nurse may wish to seek legal counsel to verify that the document is a lawfully-issued subpoena.

Lawsuits – Lawsuits are generally commenced when one party files a formal written complaint with a court. Typically, a complaint must identify the accused party (the "defendant" in the case), allege facts establishing a cause of action, and identify the legal theory or cause of action that serves as the basis of the case being brought by the accuser (the "plaintiff" in the case).

Investigations – There are many different types of investigations that may occur within a school, but this chapter addresses investigations of students by law enforcement, child welfare officials, and U.S. Immigration and Customs Enforcement (ICE). Child abuse investigations are typically the most commonly-encountered investigations among school nurses, but other types of law enforcement investigations also occur in schools.

IMPLICATIONS FOR SCHOOL NURSE PRACTICE

Student Confidentiality and Subpoenas

The issuance of a lawful subpoena is one instance where a public school is permitted to disclose personally identifiable information from student records under the Family Educational Rights and Privacy Act (FERPA) (34 CFR §99.31(a)(9)(i)). In such cases, however, unless the court has specifically ordered that the information regarding the subpoena not be disclosed to the parents, the school is legally required to "make a reasonable effort to notify the parent" (or the student, if the student is at least eighteen years old) before complying with the subpoena in order to give the parent (or eligible student) time to seek protective action (FERPA at 34 CFR §99.31(a)(9)(ii)). As discussed in *Chapter 11* regarding confidentiality, a "parent," under FERPA, is defined as "a parent of a student and includes a natural parent, a guardian, or an individual acting as a parent in the absence of a parent or a guardian" (FERPA, 20 U.S.C. §1232g; 34 CFR §99.3).

Subpoenas Requiring the Production of Documents

Upon receipt of a subpoena to produce school-related documents, such as student records, school nurses should immediately notify their supervisor and/or building administrator. Because such a subpoena involves the potential release of education records, which is governed by FERPA, the school may need to take necessary action to notify parents (see the above discussion regarding "Student Confidentiality and Subpoenas") and/ or confirm the validity of the subpoena. Because nursing/health records are student records governed by FERPA's confidentiality and disclosure requirements, rather than medical records governed by HIPAA's privacy rule *(see Chapter 11; see also* U.S. Departments of Education and Health and Human Services, 2008), FERPA's notice provision, explained above, would apply.

Right to Counsel / Seeking the Advice of Counsel upon Receipt of Subpoena to Testify

While it may not always be necessary, individuals served with a subpoena to testify in a court proceeding may also have the right to have counsel present (typically at their own expense), depending upon the state and type of court (federal or state) in which the matter is brought. For example, the Federal Administrative Procedure Act, grants the right to representation by counsel where a subpoena to appear is issued. The federal rule states: "[a] person compelled to appear in person before an agency or representative thereof is entitled to be accompanied, represented, and advised by counsel or, if permitted by the agency, by other qualified representative. A party is entitled to appear in person or by, or with counsel in an agency hearing" (Federal Administrative Procedure Act, 5 U.S.C. §555(b), 1946).

Any time a school nurse is served with a subpoena related to either the school nurse's employment or a student in the school, the school nurse may wish to seek the advice of legal counsel (i.e., the school board attorney or a privately retained attorney – see commentary below) to ascertain whether the subpoena is valid, was properly served, and whether the testimony poses any potential personal liability for the school nurse. An attorney's involvement can often serve to eliminate the need for testimony by offering a written document or student records instead. If nothing else, the school nurse's attorney can contact the legal counsel representing the subpoenaing party and obtain more information about what that party expects to ask or elicit from the school nurse. This information can be extremely helpful both in the school nurse's preparation for testimony as well as to the school nurse's peace of mind knowing what will be expected of their testimony and what to anticipate in the legal proceeding. Legal counsel can also be beneficial when a school nurse is being called to testify in a court outside of their local area. Attorneys can often facilitate witness testimony via video conferencing or telephone conferencing.

The school nurse may not need to hire private counsel for these purposes. If the school nurse is a member of a collective bargaining unit ("union") or other representative organization, there may be a staff attorney responsible for providing this type of legal counsel. In some cases, where the subpoena is related to a custody or other matter that does not appear to present a conflict of interest, with the permission of the school administration, the school's legal counsel may be contacted to provide legal counsel to the school nurse and the school. Because school attorneys often represent the school in employment matters as well as general consulting matters, a school nurse may not wish to seek counsel from the school's attorney in cases that involve allegations of misconduct on the part of the school nurse, potential malpractice claims, or other potential liability that may have employment implications. (*Please see Chapter 2 for more information regarding malpractice*).

If the school nurse feels that he or she would be best served by hiring private counsel, or if the school nurse is unable to obtain access to an attorney through the union or school district, most general practice attorneys will agree to a limited consult on this type of matter for a set fee, if requested. Based upon that information, the school nurse can better determine whether to continue to retain private counsel or whether the risk of potential liability is small enough that the risk outweighs the expense of private attorney representation.

Technical Issues Regarding Issuance of Subpoena

Each state has its own rules regarding the requirements for serving someone with a subpoena, and rules regarding matters brought in state court may be different from the rules that apply to federal court proceedings. Consultation with an attorney who practices in the jurisdiction in question can verify that a subpoena, as well as its service, is valid. Unless the issue poses a significant threat of liability to the school nurse, seeking to have a subpoena quashed on a technicality, such as improper service, is usually not possible or cost-effective, since most courts allow parties to "cure" (a legal term meaning "correct" or "fix") procedural defects through proper re-service. In addition, minor spelling errors in a name or address, where the intended recipient is clear and/or where the subpoena reached the intended recipient despite such errors, are generally not enough to invalidate the subpoena.

Subpoenas Requiring an Individual to Testify in Child Custody Case

Many subpoenas issued to school nurses require the appearance of the school nurse as a witness in a child custody matter. In such cases, the parent who is calling the school nurse as a witness often believes that the school nurse has information that is helpful to their case (or harmful to the other parent's case) and will cause the judge to award custody in their favor. Custody cases in which school nurses are called to testify are generally cases involving custody of a child with medical needs. The parent may seek to have the school nurse testify as to which parent has been more engaged in addressing the student's health-related needs in the school setting, or which parent appears to be more knowledgeable about the student's health condition. In some cases, the parent calling the school nurse to testify may seek to have the school nurse testify about a conversation that the school nurse had with the student, or treatment provided by the school nurse in the school health office that may be significant to the custody issue at hand.

When providing testimony, the school nurse should focus on factual statements and should avoid hypothesizing or answering hypothetical questions to which the answer may change depending upon surrounding circumstances. For instance, a school nurse could comfortably consult nursing entries in the student health record to answer the question of which parent communicates with the school most often and/or addresses medical needs, such as changes in medication, most frequently. School nurses should avoid or be cautious about answering questions for which they do not have first-hand factual information, such as, "which parent is most concerned about the child's medical well-being?" While the school nurse may have an opinion on this question, he or she likely possesses no factual information regarding the quantification of either parent's concern.

Subpoena to Testify in Child Abuse Case

Another circumstance that frequently arises for school nurses is a subpoena to testify in a child abuse or child endangerment case. School nurses are often on the front lines of child abuse reporting and investigation in schools due to their medical/health expertise. School nurses are legally-mandated child abuse reporters in most states, and it is common for teachers, administrators, and other school employees to seek the opinion or advice of a school nurse in a case of suspected abuse. As a result, school nurses are usually called to testify in child abuse cases more often than their non-medical colleagues. Due to the highly protective immunity that is afforded to mandated reporters under most state laws, testimony in these types of criminal matters generally poses few legal issues and, unlike custody matters, where the student's health records are likely to be sufficient, a school nurse's testimony regarding the nature and extent of the injury to the child can be invaluable in the prosecution of a child abuse case.

It is a good idea for school nurses to be familiar with the immunity provisions in their state's law related to mandated child abuse reporting and participating in a legal proceeding regarding the abuse of a child, so that they can be fully informed as to whether they should seek legal counsel in cases where they are called as witnesses in child abuse cases. This information is often readily available through state department of health, state nursing organizations, and/or collective bargaining units. Due to the strong protections afforded to reporters and witnesses in most states, however, testifying in a child abuse case generally does not pose legal liability to the school nurse as a witness.

During testimony school nurses should limit their testimony to that of which they have factual knowledge and avoid making assumptions, suppositions, or hypotheses. For instance, in a child abuse case where a child suffers from chronic and untreated head lice, the school nurse could testify to the fact that the student has lice, when the school nurse became aware of the lice, what treatments the school nurse recommended, and what notifications and information were communicated to which parent on which date and by what means (phone call, meeting, email, note home, etc.). In most cases where both parents have partial custody, and the student lives with each parent for part of the week, it is unlikely that the school nurse would have sufficient information to be able to opine or hypothesize about in which household the lice problem exists, whether it is limited to only one household or is a problem in both, or which parent(s) may be at fault for the issue. While there may be other pertinent facts of which the school nurse has knowledge, such as if the condition clears up every time the mother is away on business and the child stays with the father for extended periods of time but then recurred when the mother returned and the child resumed the regular custodial arrangement, testimony should be based upon factual assertions, not generalizations or hypotheses. In the instance described above, a school nurse testifying that the head lice infestation "was probably the mother's fault" is an unnecessary statement. If there is a factual basis behind such a broad statement, it is the underlying set of facts upon which such an opinion could be made to which the school nurse should testify, not a conclusion for which no specific facts have been given.

Responding to a Lawsuit

Being served with a complaint as a named defendant in a legal action can be alarming, but, in most cases, there is little likelihood that the individually-named defendants in an action that is truly against the school, itself, will remain in the case for long. This is due to the heightened tort claims protections that are afforded to school employees in most states as well as the fact that most federal and state laws that are applicable to schools do not permit a cause of action against individual defendants. Upon a school nurse's receipt of a complaint in which he or she is a named defendant, the school nurse should immediately obtain legal counsel to determine what the next steps should be. Where the complaint involves the school or conduct that occurred when the school nurse was acting in their official capacity as school nurse, the school nurse should immediately notify the school administration. Depending upon the nature of the action and the school nurse's individual circumstances, the school nurse may be able to use counsel that might be available through a collective bargaining unit, if that is a service that is offered as part of membership, or the school nurse may need to secure private legal counsel. Either way, it is important to seek legal counsel as quickly as possible after being put on notice of direct involvement with a lawsuit, since the timeline for filing motions, responding to the complaint, and taking other necessary legal action has already begun. The school nurse's attorney can provide legal counsel regarding when and how to notify the school of the action, what information the attorney will need to defend the case or, ideally, have the school nurse removed from the case as a named defendant.

Litigation Hold

Any time there is pending litigation, litigation is threatened, or someone reasonably suspects that litigation is imminent, there may be an obligation to perform a "litigation hold," which means that all evidence potentially related to such litigation must be maintained and may not be destroyed. For instance, if a parent informs the school nurse that he is going to hire a lawyer to address a particular issue with legal action against the school or the school nurse individually, that may be sufficient to initiate a "litigation hold." Wherever a school nurse is aware of litigation or has reason to believe that there may be a lawsuit in the future, the school nurse should communicate that information directly to the school's administration and request guidance regarding the preservation of records.

Investigations

Schools are involved in numerous types of investigations of students by state and federal child welfare and law enforcement agencies, and some are more common than others. The nature of the investigation and investigator governs which laws are applicable in any given situation. Regardless of the nature or type of investigation, school nurses should immediately contact the school's administration any time an investigator is requesting or demanding personally identifiable student information.

Criminal Investigations

School nurses may be called upon to participate in a criminal investigation. Although there are some specific exceptions to FERPA's written parental consent requirement related to investigations by the U.S. Department of Homeland Security, personally identifiable information about students may only be shared with police in a criminal investigation if there is a valid judicial order, such as a search warrant or subpoena, and in most cases, parents must be notified prior to compliance. Prior to sharing any student information with police or participating in a criminal investigation, school nurses should notify school administration to ensure that all necessary protocols are followed.

Many schools have School Resource Officers, or "SROs", who assist with school safety. School resource officers have dual school and law enforcement roles. When asked by a school resource officer to share personally identifiable information about a student, the school nurse should discuss the request with a school administrator. Where an SRO is requesting the information in their law enforcement capacity, a valid warrant must be produced.

Child Abuse Investigations

School nurses are frequently asked to participate in child abuse investigations. Depending upon applicable state law, child abuse investigations may be conducted by local police, county child welfare agencies, or another entity. FERPA does not contain a specific exception to the written consent requirements for disclosures of student information in child abuse investigations. It does contain a "health or safety emergency" exception, which permits schools to disclose education records where there is an imminent threat to the health or safety of the child or others. In examining the issue, the Family Policy Compliance Office (FPCO), which is the federal office responsible for interpreting and enforcing FERPA, deemed that provision to not be applicable, as a matter of course, to mandated child abuse, due to the fact that a blanket release of information in cases where a school employee knows of or suspects that a child may be subject to abuse is overly broad for the "health or safety emergency" exception. The FPCO did conclude, however, that the Federal Child Abuse Prevention, Adoption and Family Services Act of 1988, which amended the Child Abuse Prevention and Treatment Act (CAPTA) supersedes FERPA (Letter to University of Mexico, FPCO, 2004, referencing 42 U.S.C. §§ 5106a(b)(1)(A) and 5106a(b)(4)(A) and 45 CFR 1340.14(c)) (Family Policy and Compliance Office, 2004). CAPTA requires the disclosure and redisclosure of information concerning child abuse and neglect to entities determined by the state to have a need for the information. Thus, federal guidance dictates that school employees may disclose personally identifiable information related to potential child abuse to the entities responsible for conducting child abuse investigations, which may include child protective services agencies and/or law enforcement.

Immigration and Customs Enforcement (ICE)/Immigration Investigations

The law does not prohibit the Immigration and Customs Enforcement (ICE) from conducting investigations and arresting or detaining undocumented students in schools, however, the Department of Homeland Security issued a policy statement in 1993 indicating that the Immigration and Naturalization Service (INS), which bore the responsibility of immigration enforcement prior to ICE, should "to attempt to avoid apprehension of persons and to tightly control investigative operations on the premises of schools..." (Policy Memorandum, U.S. Department of Homeland Security, 1993). That policy statement allows only specific INS employees to approve, in writing, operations at schools (Policy Memorandum, U.S. Department of Homeland Security, 1993).

Since, at time of publication, ICE has not publicized any updated policy concerning investigations in schools, this appears to still be the prevailing policy. However, federal policy may change at any time, and it is wise to seek legal counsel if confronted with such a situation.

Unlike child abuse investigations, no exception to FERPA's nondisclosure requirement exists for ICE investigations. Thus, any request for records by ICE would require a warrant or other judicial order. As with regular law enforcement investigations, school nurses should immediately involve their school administration regarding any requests for education records by ICE. Where no warrant or judicial order is produced, the school should seek legal counsel. Likewise, if a warrant is produced but its meaning is ambiguous, the school nurse may wish to consult with counsel.

CONCLUSION

School nurses may not be required to deal with subpoenas, lawsuits, or investigations by law enforcement or other agencies on a regular basis, but it is important for them to understand the legal issues involved and their rights and obligations under the law. In some instances, including situations where there is a question regarding what laws apply and/or what would constitute a legally defensible course of action, school nurses may need to seek legal counsel, either through the school, through their collective bargaining unit, if available/ applicable, or privately.

RESOURCES

> Please also see Chapter 2- Malpractice/Professional Liability.

FERPA – Full Text of Regulations can be found at the U.S. Department of Education's website: http://www2.ed.gov/policy/gen/reg/ferpa/index.html?exp=6

REFERENCES

Child Abuse Prevention, Adoption and Family Services Act of 1988, 42 U.S.C. §§ 5106a (b)(1)(A) and 5106a(b) (4)(A) and 45 CFR 1340.14(c)

Family Educational Rights and Privacy Act (FERPA), 20 U.S.C. §1232g, 34 CFR §§99.01, et seq. (1974)

Family Policy and Compliance Office. (2004, November 29). Letter to University of Mexico. Retrieved from http://www.ed.gov/policy/gen/guid/fpco/ferpa/library/baiseunmslc.html

Federal Administrative Procedure Act, 5 U.S.C. §555 (1946).

U.S. Department of Homeland Security, Bureau of Customs and Border Protection. (1993). *Memorandum from James A. Puleo, Acting Associate commissioner, on enforcement activities at schools, places of worship, or at funeral or other religious ceremonies, to district directors and chief patrol agents.* Retrieved from http://www.globallawcenters.com/pdfs/25357.pdf

U.S. Departments of Education and Health and Human Services. (2008*). Joint guidance on the application of the Family Educational Rights and Privacy Act (FERPA) and the Health Insurance Portability and Accountability Act of 1996(HIPAA) to student health records.* Washington, D.C.: Author. Retrieved from http://www2.ed.gov/policy/gen/guid/fpco/doc/ferpa-hipaa-guidance.pdf

Chapter 16

PARENTAL RIGHTS, CUSTODY AGREEMENTS AND PROTECTION FROM ABUSE ORDERS

Erin D. Gilsbach, Esquire

DESCRIPTION OF ISSUE

This chapter is designed to assist school nurses in identifying the legal parental authority rights in several different situations. It sets forth a process by which school nurses will be able to quickly recognize a legal issue in each scenario, identify the applicable law, and indicate who has parental and/or decision-making authority in that situation. The chapter also discusses the implications of custody agreements and protection from abuse orders (e.g., restraining orders) in the school setting.

BACKGROUND

School nurses encounter students from a wide array of backgrounds and families - students whose parents are divorced, students who live with individuals other than their parents, students who are in the foster care system, students whose parents are incarcerated, students who are living on their own, students who are homeless, etc. It is often difficult to know what rules apply in different situations. For example, can a step-parent view a child's school nursing records? Can a grandparent with whom a child is living (but without legal custody) agree to nursing related services in an Individualized Education Plan (IEP)? What happens when divorced parents disagree? What rights do foster parents have? Issues related to a child's family can be tricky, not only because of the many different types of families and living situations involved, but also because of the number of different state and federal laws that could potentially be implicated. This chapter provides a practical approach for school nurses in determining who has rights with regards to a child and what role non-parents may play in the child's education.

IMPLICATIONS FOR SCHOOL NURSE PRACTICE

Determining Who Has the Legal Authority

Different laws grant different rights to different people. What makes this issue truly tricky, though, is the fact that the term "parent" is used in a number of different school and state law contexts, including Family Education Rights and Privacy Act (FERPA), the Individuals with Disabilities Education Act (IDEA), state custody laws, and the definition is different for each. In order to reach a legally correct conclusion, school nurses must think critically about the issue at hand. There are three fundamental questions that must be asked whenever issues regarding parental rights and authority arise:

1	• **What is the legal issue?**
2	• **What law, if any, applies to this situation?**
3	• **How do laws identified in question 2 define "parent" or assign rights?**

As stated, above, the answers to the questions, while helpful at any given time, are not as important in the long-term as is the ability to identify and carefully frame, with precision, the questions to be answered. Applicable laws may change based on jurisdiction or time period, but mastering the analytical process of narrowing the scope of an issue from a generalized fact pattern that is presented in the course of a school nurse's duties to a narrowly-tailored query regarding applicable laws specific to a particular legal issue is the more relevant and important goal. It is also a skill that, once mastered, can be used over and over with successful results.

While this resource book was designed for the express purpose of providing school nurses, school administrators and school attorneys with a much-needed information on the law, there are limitations that apply to any legal resource, no matter how thorough and well-drafted. As the introductory materials of this book point out, the law is geographically specific and temporally specific. Different states have different laws, and laws are constantly changing. Thus, while this section provides helpful information regarding the substance of the laws, themselves, the more important purpose of this chapter, in general, and this section, specifically, is to assist school nurses in breaking down the issues and identifying the questions that need to be answered.

To better explain in more concrete terms, the analytical process required for make legally-defensible decisions regarding custody and other issues related to family law, the following scenario will be addressed throughout the remainder of this section:

Pursuant to the accommodations set forth in a student's Section 504 Plan, the school nurse communicates with the student's mother on a weekly basis by phone to let her know how the student is doing, communicate any concerns, and answer any questions the student's mother may have. Their phone calls occur regularly every week on the same date and at the same time. The parent calls the school nurse's direct line, which the nurse typically provides only in cases where direct communication is necessary, such as this. All other calls are transferred to the school nurse's office by the main office.

One week, the school nurse is surprised to find that, instead of mom, the student's grandmother has called. She called through to the school nurse's direct line at the correct time on the correct date, and she explained that the mother (her daughter) asked her to participate in this phone conference on her behalf while she was away on business. She tells the school nurse that the mother is away for an extended business trip and that she will be gone for the next three weeks. She explains that, since the child's father died a few years ago, she has been assisting her daughter with childcare whenever she is away. She also explains that the mother has left her with a copy of the student's Section 504 Plan, in the event that she would need to reference it. The grandmother is not able to provide contact information for the mother during her trip, since the mother is "overseas," and does not have cell phone access. She does, however, have a note scrawled in the mother's handwriting that states "I hereby give my mother, Ida Kenner, power of attorney over my children and full parental rights while I am gone."

Because she was not expecting to speak with the grandmother, and because she is uncertain about whether she can disclose the student's information to the student's grandmother, the school nurse kindly informs the grandmother that she will need to return her call, and they establish a suitable time later that day. The school nurse then checks her records and the records in the student's main office file. The mother has never provided the school with a consent form that would permit the student to disclose information from the student's records with the grandmother. The school nurse now needs guidance as to whether she can share this information or, if not, what would be legally required in order to allow her to do so.

In regular daily practice, the school nurse would likely consult with a member of the administration, who would probably be able to provide her with direction as to what she should do in this circumstance. We will use this scenario, however, to go through the 3-step-analysis process presented here in order to provide a concrete example of how to analyze parental authority and custody-related legal issues.

1 • **What is the legal issue?**

Because there are so many different laws that apply to schools, and because the school's obligations, as well as the law's definition of "parent," as described, above, varies significantly depending upon the law in question, the first thing that must be done is to clarify the legal issues that are posed by a given fact pattern. There are a number of legal issues regarding custody and parental authority that come up regularly in the context of school nursing practice. The graphic below identifies some of the most common legal issues addressed by schools and school nurses*, and the sections, below, provide an analysis of each issue identified.

*Note that this is certainly not an exhaustive list of family/custody-related legal issues that nurses will encounter, by any means. For instance, *Chapter 20* discusses do not attempt to resuscitate orders (DNARs), which generally require a combination of parental authority, state approval, and possibly other factors, such as the wearing of a state-issued wristband or other wearable DNAR notice.

The legal issue in the scenario presented, above, is one that schools face on a regular basis. It is a confidentiality of student records issue dealing with who has the right to access a student's records. In this case, the school nurse is aware that the mother, before she left, did not expressly sign a consent form to permit the grandmother to have the records. However, the mother did provide all of the necessary information to the grandmother to enable the grandmother to participate in the weekly phone conferences in her absence, and she provided the grandmother with a copy of the Section 504 Plan. This poses a number of questions. The school nurse is aware that FERPA applies not only to the student's records, themselves, but also to discussions involving information from those records. She is not certain; however, these facts can establish implied consent (it is clear that the mother wants the grandmother to have this information), but unclear whether written consent is required. If written consent is not required, can the mother's consent legally be implied by her actions of notifying the grandmother of the conference call standing appointment and providing her with the necessary information to participate in her absence? If not, is it possible that the grandmother could actually fall within FERPA's definition of "parent," at least while she is babysitting the student?

What does the school nurse specifically need to know in this context?

1. Is the "Power of Attorney" note a valid transfer of decision-making rights under the law?
2. What constitutes parental "consent" to have access to a student's records under FERPA?
   a. Is written consent required?
   b. If not, do the facts in this scenario effectively establish legal consent under FERPA?

3. Could grandmother qualify as a "parent" under FERPA for the purposes of being granted access to the student's records?

2 • What law, if any, applies to this situation?

Now that the legal issue at hand has been identified, the school nurse will determine what law applies. When making a determination as to what law applies in a particular situation, both state and federal laws must be considered. In addition, the type of school entity is important. For instance, a private school that does not receive any federal funding is not subject to many federal laws, such as the IDEA and FERPA. Private schools may receive different treatment with regards to state laws as well. Likewise, states may impose different requirements on public charter schools than they do on private schools and public school districts. Therefore, an understanding of the specific type of institution and the laws that apply to it is essential to answering these questions thoroughly and accurately.

School nurses do not need to become attorneys, however, in order to be able to effectively use this process. As with many aspects of the law, knowing the *questions* to ask is the most important part of the process. In the first step of the process, the issues were identified. Now, the appropriate applicable laws need to be identified. Knowing the issues allows the questions regarding applicable law to be far more exact. Adding the additional key components of federal vs. state and type of school (private, public, public charter, cyber charter, etc.) allows the questions to be framed with accurate precision. *What federal confidentiality laws apply to a charter school that receives federal funding? What state confidentiality laws apply to charter schools in my state? Is there a difference between the confidentiality standards set forth for charter schools in my state than those required of public school districts?* If the questions have been framed with this level of detail, obtaining the answers becomes a much simpler process, and there may be a number of readily-available resources that can help with the answers.

The next few paragraphs provide helpful information regarding applicable laws for each of the "Common Legal Issues in the School Setting" that were identified in the graphic, above.

The right/authority to view records and/or receive confidential information from records

The school nurse in the scenario knows that FERPA is the federal law that addresses student confidentiality and records access. (As stated in *Chapter 11* of this book, it is FERPA, not HIPAA, that governs confidentiality of student health records.) Thus, they are dealing with a disclosure of information issue under FERPA. The school nurse would also need to determine whether any state laws apply in this situation. Some states do not have state-specific laws addressing confidentiality, others have some, and still others may be heavily regulated and may have many additional requirements. In addition, even within a particular state's laws, there may be variation depending upon the type of school entity (school district, public charter, private school, etc.), as discussed, above, and those differentiations must be taken into consideration with any analysis. The school, in the scenario presented here, is in Pennsylvania, which, at the time of publication of this book, does not have any additional state confidentiality laws that would apply to this situation. Therefore, school nurses in Pennsylvania would be addressing the issue with regards to one primary law: FERPA.

Legal custody issues come into play, too, however. In the scenario, above, the mother assigns to the grandmother, in a handwritten note, "power of attorney" and the right to make decisions on behalf of her children. Is this a valid transfer of rights/authority? This issue will be explored in greater detail in the "Custody" section when answering Question #3.

Some of the other laws that might be implicated by the common legal issues that school nurses encounter, which are set forth in the graphic "Common Legal Issues in the School Setting" graphic, above. Remember that legal jurisdiction (geographical location), and type of entity will always factor into a legal analysis of applicable laws.

The right/authority to make medical decisions/consent to non-emergency medical treatment on behalf of a child

The issue of who can consent to medical treatment is a state-specific issue, so the answer will vary based upon specific state custody law requirements and/or state statutes regarding medical decision-making. Many states, however, include medical decision-making in legal custody rights (see the discussion regarding Question 3, below, for a discussion of the difference between legal and physical custody). While parental custody is a state law issue, most states differentiate among the different types of custody in the same manner.

The right/authority make general educational decisions on behalf of a child

In most states, educational decision-making goes hand-in-hand with medical decision-making, which generally accompanies legal custody, as discussed, above. As with medical decision-making, this is a state-specific issue, so it is possible that there may be additional state laws that apply. However, absent any other legal authority, the right to make general educational decisions about a child typically follows legal custody rights.

The right/authority to consent to special education services (including related services that may involve the school nurse) under the IDEA

The IDEA has a very specific provision that deals with this issue, which will be discussed in more detail, below. In short, however, the IDEA provides a hierarchical chain of authority in which the individual(s) that are highest on the chain has (have) the authority (34 C.F.R. § 300.30). A detailed explanation of the IDEA's chain of authority is provided, below.

The right/authority take physical possession of the child

State law may answer this question directly, however, parents are typically permitted to identify specific individuals who may pick up their child from school. In cases of divorced parents, however, the law varies from state to state. In some states, the non-custodial parent is not permitted to take possession of a child. In other states, custody agreements are legal documents that bind only the parties to the custody action, not the schools. Thus, as long as a school has no reason to believe that releasing the child will result in harm, the school may release a student to a non-custodial parent. In the event that the school is aware of an outstanding protection from abuse (PFA) order against a specific individual, however, that puts the school on notice that releasing the child to the individual against whom the PFA has been issued. In most states, the school will be prohibited, by law, from doing so. Even where there is no specific legal prohibition, however, there may be general liability if a school releases a child to an individual against who a PFA has been issued. In all such cases, schools should refrain from releasing the child to such individual or should contact their legal counsel.

The right to waive a child's right and release a 3rd party from liability on behalf of a child

Both the waiver of a child's rights and the ability to release a 3rd party from liability on behalf of a child are typically only permitted to be carried out by a parent or legal guardian, as is discussed, further, below. Where parents are divorced, these types of true legal authority generally fall within the scope of the parent(s) who has (have) *legal* custody, regardless of *physical* custody. State law governs these issues, however, so a legal opinion from a licensed attorney in the state in which the school is located may be necessary to obtain specific answers to these questions.

The right/authority to provide emergency care/services to a child

The provision of emergency care/services to a child extends to a number of individuals under a variety of legal theories. First and foremost, any individual providing or attempting to provide life-saving emergency care to a child is likely protected under a state's Good Samaritan laws. This would include emergency care provided by teachers, administrators, and other school employees. Although there are usually some limitations to the types of care a layperson could provide and still be protected under those laws, their protections are typically fairly expansive. It is important to note, however, that state law may carve out special exceptions for certain types of emergency care, such as specific requirements for the use of portable defibrillators (see the National Council of State Legislatures resource on "State Laws on Cardiac Arrest and Defibrillators" for a more expansive discussion of this topic), so it is crucial that school employees understand the parameters of their state Good Samaritan laws.

Additionally, schools, in most states, have *in loco parentis* authority over children while the children are in school. Some states have explicit *in loco parentis* statutes, while, in others, the *in loco parentis* authority has been established through common law (case law). While a school's *in loco parentis* authority is generally limited to the educational context and what is necessary for the school to receive during the school day, the provision of emergency care generally falls under that authority.

The provision of emergency care by school nurses, pursuant to responsibilities that are often set forth in statutes, is also generally permitted. While school nurses, as medical professionals, are held to a higher standard of care, and, thus, often are not protected by the typical Good Samaritan law, their background and licensure enable them to effectively and lawfully provide emergency care. Finally, first-responders, such as emergency medical technicians (EMTs) and emergency room medical personnel, have authority to provide life-saving care to students without parental permission. While there are, of course, some exceptions set forth under law for medical personnel, such as instances when a lawfully-issued DNAR order is in effect, the authority of a first-responder and/or emergency medical team to provide life-saving medical services/treatment is well-established.

3 • How do laws identified in question 2 define "parent" or assign rights?

Determining who is granted rights under each of the laws identified, above, as well as those granted under any applicable state laws, is the crux of this chapter. In most laws governing schools and school records, the rights are assigned to the parents of the student. However, as discussed, above, the term "parent" has become increasingly complex. This is complicated by the fact that different laws define "parent" differently, both on the state and federal levels, and the definitions are often quite technical and sometimes counterintuitive. For example, under some laws, a family friend who is watching a child during a parent's extended business trip can legally constitute a "parent", while others relying on strict legal assignations and court orders, limit the definition to mean only a natural parent or an individual who has obtained parental or guardian status through a court order.

As with the section above, while this resource provides information regarding the parameters of the term "parent" in some of the commonly-applicable federal school laws, it is the framing of the questions, themselves, as well as the more generalized understanding of the different contexts and circumstances in which the questions will arise, that is ultimately the most important part of the process. For instance, once the nurse decides that the specific issue at hand involves rights granted to parents under the IDEA, for example, determining who is a "parent" is under the IDEA is a fairly simple and straightforward process, as described, below. The hard part is framing the questions. Once that has been done, all the way through to this step in the process, the issues often seem far less complex, and the answers are far more readily available than they initially may have appeared to be.

FERPA

FERPA's definition of "parent" is directly at issue in the scenario presented regarding the school nurse providing confidential student information to the child's grandmother, with whom the child is temporarily living. In that scenario, the school nurse knows, from reading *Chapter 11* of this book, that FERPA has a very broad definition of parent. FERPA's definitions state that "parent means a parent of a student and includes a natural parent, a guardian, *or* an individual acting as a parent in the absence of a parent or a guardian." (34 CFR § 99.3). It is clear, in this situation, that the grandmother is a "parent" under FERPA, since she is watching the student in mom's absence. She is "acting as a parent in the absence of a parent," and, therefore, she falls within FERPA's definition of "parent." Because of that, she is able to have the same access to the student's educational records that the child's natural parent would have. The nurse may release the information and/or discuss the student's records without restriction, and no written consent is necessary. It is important to remember, however, that, in this scenario, the school nurse is dealing only with federal law, because no other state law applies. Applicable state laws should always be considered in addition to this federal law.

Under this liberal definition of "parent," there are many commonly-encountered individuals whose relationship with a child place them squarely within FERPA's definition of "parent." The U.S. Department of Education has determined that a parent is *absent* "if he or she is not present in the day-to-day home environment of the child" (FPCO 2004). Where an individual has day-to-day access to a child, such as a step-parent who is married to the parent with primary physical custody (FPCO 2004), an adult sibling who lives alone with a school-aged child, a neighbor with whom the child is living, and, as in this example, caregivers who are watching the children when the parent(s) are not available. In the scenario presented, it is the definition of "parent" under FERPA that gives the grandmother the authority to view and hear what is contained within the student's records, not the "power of attorney." There is no need for the school to prove that the parent *intended* for the grandmother to be able to have access to the information in the student's records. The mere fact that the grandmother is currently acting as the parent in the absence of the biological parent gives the grandmother the right to view the records, independent of the intention of the mother.

It is important to note that parents do not have the right to refuse or withhold consent from another individual. For instance, a child's mother cannot prohibit the school from releasing information to the father's girlfriend or wife from a subsequent marriage where the father has already provided valid consent or where such individual meets the definition of "parent" under FERPA (FPCO 2004). In the scenario provided here, even if she wanted to, the mother could not prohibit the grandmother from having rights under FERPA, due to the fact that the grandmother falls within the definition of "parent" under FERPA. The mother's intentions do not change the legal analysis regarding who is a parent. In cases involving divorced parents, however, particularly where there is significant animosity between the parents, it is often simpler for the school to obtain written consent for a new spouse or significant other to have access to the records than it is to explain that the new spouse or significant other may actually be a "parent," under FERPA.

Where this consent is obtained, however, schools still need to understand whether an individual falls within the definition of "parent" under FERPA, regardless of whether consent by a biological parent has been obtained. This is because those who meet the definition of "parent" are entitled to all of the parental *rights* afforded under FERPA. Those individuals for whom a parent has provided consent to have access to the records, but who do not meet FERPA's definition of "parent," do not have a *right* to such access (or any other parental right afforded under FERPA). That consent merely means that the school *may* lawfully disclose the information, but it is not *required* to do so. Thus, where a biological parent refuses to give consent, or where they are not present to do so, such refusal or inaccessibility does not alter the fact of who has parental rights under FERPA. In addition, individuals who meet the definition of "parent" under FERPA do not have the authority to challenge or prohibit access to a student's records by another individual where a "parent" has provided specific, FERPA-compliant written consent for another individual to have access to a student's records (FPCO 2004).

CUSTODY LAWS AND POWER OF ATTORNEY

Power of Attorney

Consider the mother's scrawled note, giving the grandmother power of attorney and authorizing the grandmother to make decisions, including educational decisions, on behalf of her children. Many states have some form of temporary Power of Attorney for Childcare, whereby a transfer of power of attorney would be permissible, if it were properly executed. For instance, Arizona Revised Statute 14-5104 states that a parent or a guardian of a minor or incapacitated person, through a properly-executed power of attorney, may delegate to another person, for a period not exceeding six months, any powers the parent may have regarding care, custody or property of the minor child or ward, except power to consent to marriage or adoption of the minor.

In Arizona's case, however, "properly-executed" means signed, witnessed, and notarized. Thus, mom's note falls short under this law.

In Ohio, however, the circumstances under which a grandparent can receive a Power of Attorney for childcare purposes are much more complicated, as there are a number of different laws that apply to grandparents. For instance, Ohio Revised Code §3109.65, provides a solution for the situation where a child is living with the grandparent and the parents of the child cannot be found. This is only a temporary solution and is not the same thing as legal custody, but it allows the grandparent to do necessary things for the child such as, enrolling the child in school and taking the child to the healthcare provider, etc. Pursuant to Ohio Revised Code §3109.67, Ohio's caretaker affidavit can also be utilized without attempting to locate the following parent, but only if: 1) If paternity has not been established with regard to the child's father; 2) If the child is currently under an existing custody order; 3) If the parent subject to the custody order is prohibited from receiving notice of relocation; or 4) If a parent's rights have been permanently terminated by a court of competent jurisdiction, pursuant to Chapter 2151 of the Ohio Revised Code.

In other states, such as Colorado, power of attorney for childcare petitions are not legally binding if they are signed only by the parties, witnesses and a notary. Instead, Colorado requires that all powers of attorney for childcare petitions be approved and signed by the Court (Colorado Revised Statutes 15-14-201 and 15-14-202). In these types of states, the mother's note would certainly not be sufficient to satisfy the legal requirements for a Power of Attorney.

In order to properly determine whether the mother's "Power of Attorney", in the scenario presented above, has any legal legitimacy, school nurses should be familiar with their state's laws regarding powers of attorney for childcare purposes. If the childcare provider, grandma, in this instance, has a legally-valid power of attorney, then the school nurse would need to ascertain the scope of that document. Does it provide educational decision-making rights? Does it fully transfer all parental rights for a limited period? What are the permissions and limitations of that document? If the school nurse has any questions, or if a parent or caregiver is asserting that the caregiver has more rights than it appears he or she legally possesses, the school nurse should discuss the situation with the building administrator and, if necessary, obtain a legal opinion from the school's legal counsel.

In the scenario provided here, however, the grandmother's "power of attorney" is not legally sufficient or binding. Since she meets the definition of "parent" under FERPA even without a valid power of attorney, though, the analysis remains the same. The grandmother is permitted to view the records, not due to a legally-recognized power of attorney status, but, rather, under FERPA's plain-language definition of "parent."

Custody

School nurses should always have a copy of the most recent custody order for a family in the student's nursing records. This will allow the school nurse to make fully-informed decisions regarding releasing a student during the school day, who has medical decision-making authority, and who is able to make educational decisions.

There are generally two different types of custody: *Legal custody* and *Physical custody*. Within those types, there can be shared/joint custody or sole custody.

Legal custody generally refers to the right to make major decisions on behalf of a child, including educational, medical, and religious decisions. In essence, it generally includes the basic parental rights *other than* physical custody.

Physical custody typically describes who has actual physical possession of the child.

In most states, **joint** legal custody is the default, even where one parent may be granted sole physical custody. **Joint legal custody**, both parents have legal custodial rights at all times. This is different from

joint physical custody, which divides the rights. With joint physical custody, one parent has physical custody on certain days of the week or week cycles, and the other has physical custody on the others.

Other terminology that is often used in describing custodial relationships includes **supervised custody**, where a non-custodial parent is permitted to have supervised visitations, and **primary physical custody**, where one parent has custody the majority of the time and the other parent has much more limited periods of custody, such as on weekends and/or holidays.

Different states have different specific laws and rules regarding custody, and custody definitions vary from state to state. For instance, Figure 1 below contains Pennsylvania's legal custody terms and definitions:

Figure 1

Custody and Grandparents Visitation Act – 23 Pa. C.S.A. 5301 et seq.
PA custody definitions, which can be found at 23 Pa. C.S.A. § 5322, are as follows:

- **"Legal custody."** The right to make major decisions on behalf of the child, including, but not limited to, medical, religious and educational decisions.
- **"Shared legal custody."** The right of more than one individual to legal custody of the child.
- **"Sole legal custody."** The right of one individual to exclusive legal custody of the child.
- **"Physical custody."** The actual physical possession and control of a child.
- **"Primary physical custody."** The right to assume physical custody of the child for the majority of the time.
- **"Partial physical custody."** The right to assume physical custody of the child for less than a majority of the time.
- **"Shared physical custody."** The right of more than one individual to assume physical custody of the child, each having significant periods of custodial time with the child.
- **"Supervised physical custody."** Custodial time during which an agency or an adult designated by the court or agreed upon by the parties monitors the interaction between the child and the individual with those rights.
- **"Sole physical custody."** The right of one individual to exclusive physical custody of the child.

From a practical perspective, the most important determination for a school nurse will be determining who has "legal custody." This is because, as stated above, it is the parents with "legal custody" that generally have the legal right to make legal, educational, and medical decisions on behalf of the child. Where the parents have provided documentation regarding custody arrangements and/or termination of custody orders, it is typically not difficult to identify where a parent's legal custody has been terminated. The termination of legal custody is a significant issue that courts do not take lightly. Courts are widely more in favor of leaving legal custody intact wherever possible.

Knowing who has "physical custody" is important when making decisions regarding the release of the child at the end of the school day and/or sending the child home early due to illness or other reasons. In some states, such as New Jersey, schools are legally required to abide by physical custody orders, where they are provided by parents.* In other states, such as Pennsylvania, while schools generally try to give deference to what is set forth within the physical custody agreement, schools are not parties to the agreements, themselves, and are, therefore, not bound by them (*23 Pa. CS 5406*). *PA law states that child custody determinations made by a PA court binds only those individuals who have been served proper notice as parties to the legal action or those who have "submitted to the jurisdiction of the court and who have been given an opportunity to be heard."* Because of the obligations of schools with regards to enforcement of custody agreements, it is essential that all school employees – including school nurses – understand their specific obligations under state law with regards to custody agreements.

> * See generally Somerville Board of Education v. Manville Board of Education, 167 N.J. 55 (2001); Roxbury Township Board of Education v. West Milford Board of Education, 283 N.J. Super. 505 (App. Div. 1995); F.C. v. Rockaway Township Board of Education, OAL Dkt. No. EDS 11128-04 (January 12, 2005) 2005 WL 327290 (N.J. Admin.); L.T. ex rel. C.T. v. Denville Township Board of Education, OAL Dkt. No. EDS 5899-03 (Oct. 27, 2004).

Custody and Decision-making: Consent to non-emergency medical treatment is generally reserved for parents who have legal custody. In Pennsylvania, parents who have legal custody have the right to make educational decisions on behalf of their child regardless of physical custody (23 Pa C.S.A. §5322. In Utah, the default rule is that parents with legal custody have the right (and obligation) to make medical decisions; however, in that state, divorced parents are legally required to develop a parenting plan, which may transfer the decision-making authority between the parents (Utah Code Ann §§30-3-10.7 to 10.9). For example, although both parents have legal custody, which generally grants medical decision-making rights, the parents could agree, in the parenting plan, that the mother will have the medical decision-making rights, and the father will have the educational decision-making rights. Thus, in that state, since the parental plan is mandatory for all parents as a condition of the granting of the divorce, schools should request that a copy of such plan be maintained on file, and school nurses should be familiar with the decision-making authority of each parent. Where no plan is provided, the school nurse should assume that both parents have medical decision-making authority.

IDEA

The IDEA federal regulations, at 34 CFR § 300.30, present a hierarchy of who can be considered a "parent" under that law. The individual on the highest level of the hierarchy is considered to be the lawful "parent" and is afforded the rights under the IDEA. It is only where there is no one that meets the first definition that the IEP team looks to the second tier, and so on. The hierarchy is as follows:

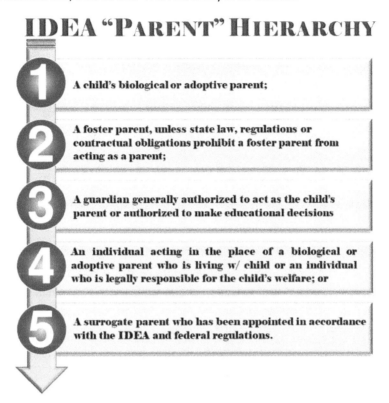

IDEA "PARENT" HIERARCHY

1 A child's biological or adoptive parent;

2 A foster parent, unless state law, regulations or contractual obligations prohibit a foster parent from acting as a parent;

3 A guardian generally authorized to act as the child's parent or authorized to make educational decisions

4 An individual acting in the place of a biological or adoptive parent who is living w/ child or an individual who is legally responsible for the child's welfare; or

5 A surrogate parent who has been appointed in accordance with the IDEA and federal regulations.

Where More Than One Person Qualifies Under This List:

The IDEA regulations, in 34 C.F.R. § 300.30, state that when a biological or adoptive parent attempts to assert rights under the law and more than one party qualifies as a parent, pursuant to this list, the biological or adoptive parent "trumps" and is presumed to be the parent unless the biological/adoptive parent does not have legal authority to make educational decisions for the child. If a judicial decree or order identifies a specific person(s) to act as the "parent" or to make educational decisions on behalf of the child (often an aspect of "Legal Custody") then that person is deemed the "parent." Unless legal custody involving educational decision-making has been revoked by the courts, both biological parents have rights under the IDEA.

Physical custody, or the lack thereof, has no bearing on a parent's rights under the IDEA. Even where a parent lives far from the student and has no physical custody rights, they are still a "parent" for the purposes of the IDEA unless his/her legal rights, or at least the educational decision-making component of them, have been terminated. Schools sometimes encounter this issue with regards to a parent who has been incarcerated. Such parents, unless their educational decision-making rights have been legally terminated, still retain the rights afforded to them under the IDEA.

Where a "Parent" Cannot be Found

Where no one qualifies as a "parent" under 1-4 of this list, the IDEA requires that a surrogate be judicially appointed to represent the interests of a child and act as a parent for the purposes of special education programming and IDEA decision-making. The court order must identify a specific person (20 U.S.C. 1415(b)(2); 34 CFR 300.30(b)(2)), and the judicially appointed surrogate may not be an employee of the district or any other agency involved in the education or care of the child (20 U.S.C. 1415(2)(A); 34 C.F.R. 300.519)). The IDEA regulations clarify, however, that being paid by the agency solely for the purpose of being a surrogate does not make the individual an "employee" for the purposes of the IDEA and, therefore, does not prohibit such an individual from serving as a surrogate (34 C.F.R. 300.519).

Handling Disagreements between Divorced and Separated Parents

Another very common issue that schools face is the issue of disagreements between divorced and separated parents. The above 3-step analysis can be useful in those types of cases, as well. Consider the following scenario:

> *A school nurse who regularly works with a medically-fragile student receives the following letter, signed by the student's mother:*
>
> > *I do not give permission for Wendy Smith to have any information related to my child, including any educationally or medically-related information. I further prohibit the school from meeting with Ms. Smith or contacting her regarding my child. Ms. Smith has no legal relationship with my child and does not have any legal right to my child's information or any legal authority to act in the capacity of a parent to my child. Please feel free to contact me if you have any questions.*
>
> *The school nurse is aware that the parents of the child have recently been through a very difficult divorce and custody battle. She also knows that the parents share custody, with the child living at her father's house every other week. Wendy Smith is her father's girlfriend, who lives with the father.*

Let's look at this issue and determine what obligations the school has and what parental authority the mother and the father's girlfriend have with regards to the student. Begin with the 3 steps outlined, above.

Step 1: What is the legal issue?

There are two legal issues in this scenario:

1. Does the mother have the authority to restrict the father's girlfriend's access to the student's information?

2. Does the father's girlfriend have the right to access the information as a "parent"?

Step 2: What laws apply?

Since this scenario deals exclusively with access to information from within the student's file, FERPA is the law that applies.

Step 3: How does the applicable law define "parent"?

FERPA's definitions state that "parent means a parent of a student and includes a natural parent, a guardian, *or* an individual acting as a parent in the absence of a parent or a guardian" (34 CFR § 99.3). In this case, the student lives with dad and Ms. Smith every other week. It could certainly be argued that Ms. Smith acts as the student's mother in the absence of her mother. However, if the school asks the father to sign a records release to permit Ms. Smith to have unlimited access to the student's records through written consent, the issue is clear, and the father has exercised his right under FERPA to grant written permission for Ms. Smith. While using the definition of "parent" to include Ms. Smith and using the written consent form signed by the father has the same result – indicating to the mother that Ms. Smith is able to access the educational records via the father's written consent is often less confrontational to explain than explaining to the mother that Ms. Smith is a "parent," under the law, for the purposes of FERPA. As discussed, above, one parent does not have the right or authority to override another parent under FERPA. Thus, the mother does not have the legal right to prohibit Ms. Smith from seeing the records if the father has expressly consented. As also discussed in the "FERPA" section, above, however, the school should be aware, however, of whether Ms. Smith's truly falls within the definition of "parent" under FERPA, since that would afford her all of the parental rights under FERPA, not simply to be able to have knowledge of the student's records.

Now, if the issue were one regarding decision-making authority under the IDEA or Section 504, there would be a different outcome. As set forth in the chart, above, the IDEA establishes specific requirements for who has the authority to make educational decisions on behalf of a child, and that authority *always* lies with the biological or adoptive parents. It is only where those individuals are not able to be contacted that the school would need to or be permitted to look further. Ms. Smith, while she may meet the definition of "parent" for the purposes of viewing education records under FERPA, does not have the authority to make decisions regarding the student's IEP. Likewise, Section 504 does not contain the same road definition of "parent" that FERPA does. Thus, the decision-making afforded to a "parent" under that law would be afforded to a biological parent or legal guardian.

Emancipated Students / Students over Age 18

The concept of "emancipation" is also a state law concept that varies significantly from state to state. With most school-related laws, however, the state law concept of emancipation plays little to no role in the parental rights question. Rather, each specific law sets forth its own requirements regarding what happens when a student becomes "emancipated." For instance, under FERPA, the parental rights transfer to the student once the student turns 18 or attends a post-secondary school (34 CFR §99.3(6)). Until then, all parental rights remain with the individual who falls within the definition of "parent" under FERPA, regardless of the student's emancipation status according to state law or any other applicable laws.

With regards to FERPA, however, it is important to note that there is an exception to the consent requirement that is applicable for students who are still in high school but have turned 18. That exception pertains to situations where "[t]he disclosure is to parents, as defined in §99.3, of a dependent student, as defined in section 152 of the Internal Revenue Code of 1986." In short, this generally means where the disclosure is to the parents of a student whom the parents can claim on their taxes. The full qualifications of IRC Section 152, however, are set forth, below:

(c) QUALIFYING CHILD For purposes of this section—

(1) IN GENERAL The term "qualifying child" means, with respect to any taxpayer for any taxable year, an individual—

> **(A)** who bears a relationship to the taxpayer described in paragraph (2),
>
> **(B)** who has the same principal place of abode as the taxpayer for more than one-half of such taxable year,
>
> **(C)** who meets the age requirements of paragraph (3),
>
> **(D)** who has not provided over one-half of such individual's own support for the calendar year in which the taxable year of the taxpayer begins, and
>
> **(E)** who has not filed a joint return (other than only for a claim of refund) with the individual's spouse under section 6013 for the taxable year beginning in the calendar year in which the taxable year of the taxpayer begins.

(2) RELATIONSHIP For purposes of paragraph (1)(A), an individual bears a relationship to the taxpayer described in this paragraph if such individual is—

> **(A)** a child of the taxpayer or a descendant of such a child, or
>
> **(B)** a brother, sister, stepbrother, or stepsister of the taxpayer or a descendant of any such relative.

(3) AGE REQUIREMENTS

(A)In general For purposes of paragraph (1)(C), an individual meets the requirements of this paragraph if such individual is younger than the taxpayer claiming such individual as a qualifying child and—

> **(i)** has not attained the age of 19 as of the close of the calendar year in which the taxable year of the taxpayer begins, or
>
> **(ii)** is a student who has not attained the age of 24 as of the close of such calendar year.

Under the IDEA, an "emancipated" student is contemplated in the hierarchical definition of "parent" discussed, above. If a student, regardless of age, did not have any of the described relationships in #s 1-4, below, the school would be required to seek an educational surrogate for the student. Since students are eligible for IDEA services through graduation or until age 21, whichever comes first, it is not uncommon for students to be considered "emancipated" under state law but still require an educational surrogate for the purposes of ensuring that the student's needs are being met through the IDEA programming. In most cases, both the student and the surrogate will be asked to sign off on the IDEA documentation.

For matters that do not involve the IDEA or FERPA, such as medical decision-making by an 18-year-old student, a state's legal age of consent will apply. Again, while this varies from state to state, most states establish the age of legal adulthood as age 18 for the purposes of being able to waive rights, assume liability, and make personal decisions. School nurses should check their state's specific laws, however, to determine what rights (if any) transfer to a student when they turn 18. Indeed, in some states, the age of legal adulthood can be 17 (or younger) in cases where the student is living on his/her own and caring for him/herself.

The "Invisible Ink" Doctrine

Waiving rights and releasing liability on behalf of a child can have significant consequences to the child that can last into adulthood. The waiver of liability may mean that if the child is severely injured in an accident on a school trip, the child may have no recourse to recover medical expenses for the injury. The waiver of due process rights may mean that a child has an expulsion or weapons offense on his/her permanent record, which could affect his/her ability to get into the college of his/her choice. These are important decisions. If an individual who does not have the right to make these types of waivers or releases does, indeed, sign them, from a legal perspective, the signatures have no effect. It is as if the signature had been written in invisible ink. Someone who does not have the authority to waive liability on behalf of a child cannot effectively do so, regardless of how many forms he or she signs. Likewise, if an individual does not fit the definition of a "parent" under FERPA, that individual has no legal right or authority to grant written consent for someone else to view the documents. If an individual does not meet the definition of "parent" under the IDEA, any permissions granted by that individual may be challenged by the 'real' IDEA-defined "parent." (Note: Any such challenge is likely to be successful, as it is the responsibility of the school to ensure that the appropriate parties are signing the documents.)

Protection from Abuse Orders (Restraining Orders)

Protection from Abuse orders (PFAs) are mandates issued by the court which prohibit an individual from abusing another individual. They are generally issued where there is a history or threat of abuse. Terminology varies from state to state regarding what constitutes "abuse," what the label is assigned to a specific state's version of a protective order (e.g., PFAs, restraining orders, protective orders, etc.). In addition, a state may have more than one type of protective order available. For instance, a state may offer a PFA for domestic violence and a restraining order for stalking/harassing behavior, etc. The American Bar Association's Commission on Domestic Violence has published a helpful state-by-state chart titled "Standards of Proof for Domestic Violence Civil Protection Orders (CPOs) By State." (*See" Resources*" section, below, for web address.) The chart sets forth the definition of domestic violence and evidentiary standard for each state's law.

For domestic-violence-related PFAs, state law often requires that there must be a special relationship between the parties, such as a family members, members of the same household, etc. In some states, this relationship can extend to in-laws and/or neighbors. PFAs/Restraining Orders are generally tailored by the court to serve the purpose necessary to protect the victim. A PFA/Restraining Order may contain all or some of the following provisions:

- Prohibit physical proximity, generally ordering abuser to stay a minimum number of feed/yards away from the victim and/or the victim's home, job, school, vehicle, etc.
- Prohibit communication, including calling, texting, emailing, etc.
- Permit only peaceful communication for very limited reasons, which may include child visitation or supervised visitation
- Require the surrender of any firearms and prohibit the purchase of firearms
- Require the abuse to attend counseling
- Grant possession of the household to the victim (temporary or long-term)
- Require the abuser to pay support to the victim
- Prohibit contact with minor children

Penalties for violation of a PFA/Restraining order can range from a contempt of court charge, which generally involves a fine; to a criminal misdemeanor; to a felony, for repeat violations or more serious threats. PFAs/ Restraining Orders are subject to the "Full Faith and Credit Clause" of the U.S. Constitution (U.S. Constitution, Article IV, Section 1), which means that, if a victim with a valid PFA/Restraining Order moves to a different state, the PFA/Restraining Order must be honored by the police of the new state. School nurses that are aware of situations involving domestic violence, particularly where protective orders have been issued by the court, be vigilant for potential signs of child abuse, as instances of domestic violence often bear strong correlations to situations where child abuse is prevalent (Anselmi, 2011).

CONCLUSION

It is important for school nurses to understand the legal issues at play in any given family-related scenario and to be able to systematically analyze those issues to determine who has parental authority and to make sure that all necessary protocols are being followed with regards to PFAs and custody orders.

RESOURCES

American Bar Association Commission on Domestic Violence, "Standards of Proof for Domestic Violence Civil Protection Orders (CPOs) By State." http://www.americanbar.org/content/dam/aba/migrated/domviol/pdfs/ Standards_of_Proof_by_State.authcheckdam.pdf

REFERENCES

Anselmi, K. (2011). Domestic violence and its implications on child abuse. *Nurse Practitioner,* 36 (11): 15–17.

Family Educational Rights and Privacy Act (FERPA), 20 U.S.C. § 1232g; 34 CFR Part 99. (1974).

Family Policy and Compliance Office (FPCO) (2004). *Letter to Parent re: Disclosure of Education Records to Stepparents.* Retrieved from U.S. Department of Education website at: *https://www2.ed.gov/policy/ gen/guid/fpco/ferpa/library/hastings082004.html.*

National Council of State Legislatures (2012). State Laws on Cardiac Arrest and Defibrillators. Retrieved from http://www.ncsl.org/research/health/laws-on-cardiac-arrest-and-defibrillators-aeds.aspx.

Individuals with Disability Education Improvement Act (2004), 20 U.S.C. 1400 et seq.

U.S. Constitution, Article IV, Section 1

Chapter 17

SCHOOLS' LEGAL RESPONSIBILITY FOR SCHOOL HEALTH SERVICES

Linda Davis-Alldritt, MA, BSN, RN, FNASN, FASHA

You can't educate a child who isn't healthy, and you can't keep a child healthy who isn't educated.
Former U.S. Surgeon General Dr. Joycelyn Elders

DESCRIPTION OF ISSUE

When parents send their children to school, they do so with the expectation that the school will provide education and keep their children safe and healthy during the process. Schools have legal, ethical, and moral responsibility for the provision of school health services. Overarching federal laws require that schools provide needed health services by qualified health professionals for children with disabilities. Corresponding state laws and United States Supreme Court rulings, as well as lower court decisions, reinforce this obligation. A large variety of other state laws require schools to provide a variety of school health services including physical health assessments, communicable disease surveillance and immunization compliance, chronic health conditions management, episodic care, and managing health emergencies.

BACKGROUND

Overview

Increasing numbers of students with a myriad of chronic conditions attend our public schools (Centers for Disease Control & Prevention [CDC], 2015a). It is conservatively estimated that over 30 percent of students have physical or mental health conditions (American Academy of Pediatrics (AAP), 2004/ 2009; AAP, 2016; U.S. Department of Health and Human Services [USDHHS], 2013; National Association of School Nurses (NASN), 2015a; USDHHS, 2016), all of which may affect/influence their ability to effectively benefit from their educational opportunities. Unaddressed health problems create major barriers to a student's ability to learn and achieve their full potential as students and as adults. There is no doubt that health and education are inextricably linked (Bradley, & Greene, 2013). It is also clear that investment in school health services and programs is time and money well spent both in terms of educational and health outcomes (Basch, 2010; 2011; Wang et al., 2014).

Federal and state laws, as well as several court decisions, guarantee the right of students with disabilities to have equal access to all school programs in the least restrictive environment. Schools also may face liability when unmet health problems interfere with student learning and safety. Additionally, as the number of students with chronic health conditions have increased, law makers have increasingly obligated schools with unfunded healthcare mandates. Too often, when education dollars are limited, school health services are viewed as expendable luxuries, unconnected to the general health and welfare of society, to be cut when school budgets must be reduced (Costante, 2001).

Despite federal, state, and case laws upholding the rights of students to school health services, there continue to be significant numbers, at least 20 percent, of students and their families who report not receiving needed physical and mental health services at school (AAP, 2004/2009; Aruda, Kelly, & Newinsky, 2011; Brener, Weist, Adelman, Taylor, & Vernon-Smiley, 2007). There is clearly the need for improved school health services (Brener, Wheeler, Wolfe, Vernon-Smiley, & Caldart-Olson, 2007).

Brief History

The century long history of school health services in the United States, has its roots in 19th century Europe, where school medical inspections were mandated by royal command in France in 1837, and soon adopted in most European countries, Egypt, and several countries in South America (Wold, 2001/2005). Following those examples many years later, American school medicine and health reformers in the 1890s began pushing for medical inspections of poor immigrant children who lived in the deplorable conditions of inner-city slums (Tyack, 1992). Medical inspections, the resulting exclusion of children with contagious conditions from school, and escalating school absenteeism led New York City School District to hire of the first U.S. school nurse, Lina Rogers, in 1902 (Maughan & Troup, 2011). After World War I, and the realization that many draftees had correctable physical defects, the National Education Association declared that health was among its seven primary principles of education (Kort, 2006). Between 1918 and 1921, most states had passed school laws requiring health and physical education (Kort, 2006). From the early 1920s, as health services were increasingly located in public schools, questions about priorities were increasingly debated with school health relegated to lower priority (Kort, 2006; Maughan & Troup, 2011).

Since funding for public schools came primarily from local property taxes, there were great disparities in all school services – both education and health – and many population sectors had no school services at all (Tyack, 1992). Some relief for school health services came in mid-1960s with the authorization of the *Elementary and Secondary Education Act of 1965*, which enabled school administrators to hire school nurses (Maughan & Troup, 2011). Still today, in spite of laws permitting school districts to receive Medicaid reimbursement for healthcare services to eligible students, at rates considerably lower than those permitted for private practitioners, the legal obligations that schools have to provide health services remain underfunded. The burden to provide school health services rests primarily with the education system and there is little acknowledgement that school health services, which serve approximately 97 percent of school-age children and youth, are part of the overall general healthcare system.

Historically, persons with physical or mental disabilities, in most cultures, have been subjected to discrimination of every sort for thousands of years, and only recently have they been moved into the mainstream (Martin, Martin, & Terman, 1996). Throughout most of the 20th century, schools in the United States provided minimal, if any, services to students with disabilities, and many of these children, particularly those with developmental disabilities, were institutionalized (Dang, 2010) or kept at home. In most states, state laws permitted school administrators to deny school enrollment to any student who was considered, by the administrator, to be uneducable (Martin et al., 1996). Some school districts admitted students with disabilities, but provided no special services, and other such students were put into special programs that were inadequate or inappropriate for the student's needs (Martin et al., 1996).

In the mid-1950s, the landmark United States Supreme Court case, *Brown v. Board of Education* (1954), that ended legal segregation in public schools and paved the way for integration, was a major civil rights victory. Following the authorization of the Civil Rights Act of 1964, in 1965, Congress authorized funding through the

Elementary and Secondary Education Act (ESEA) of 1965 to schools for educationally disadvantaged children from low income families (Gibbons, Lehr, & Selekman, 2013). In 1966, ESEA was amended to allow school districts to apply to the federal government for funding to educate handicapped children, and in 1970, ESEA was further amended to include Part B: The Education of the Handicapped Act (EHA) (Gibbons et al., 2013). *Brown v. Board of Education (1954)*, the Civil Rights Movement, and the subsequent versions of ESEA provided impetus for three important pieces of federal legislation which have significantly impacted the educational rights of persons with disabilities, and provide some of the basis for education's responsibility for school health services. These federal laws include the **Rehabilitation Act (1973), Section 504, Education for All Handicapped Children Act (1975)** which was reauthorized and renamed in 1990 as the Individuals with Disabilities Education Act (IDEA), then reauthorized in 2004 as the Individuals with Disabilities Education Improvement Act (IDEIA) of 2004, and **Americans with Disabilities Act (ADA) (1990)** which was reauthorized in 2008 as the ADA Amendments Act (ADAAA) of 2008.

Brief Literature Review

Reviewing the literature leaves no doubt as to the responsibility school districts, schools, and school personnel have for the provision of school health services. There are many references to the three overarching federal laws - Rehabilitation Act (1973); Section 504, Education for All Handicapped Children Act (1975); and Americans with Disabilities Act (ADA) (1990) - that obligate schools to provide services (Allensworth, Lawson, Nicholson, & Wyche, 1997; Bargeron, Contri, Gibbons, Ruch-Ross, & Sanabria, 2015; Brener et al., 2007; Caldart-Olson & Thronson, 2013; CDC, 2008; Galemore & Sheetz, 2015; Gibbons et al., 2013; Krin & Taliaferro, 2012; Maughan & Troup, 2011; NASN, 2013a; NASN, 2016; Sampson & Galemore, 2012; Zirkel, 2009; Zirkel, Granthom, & Lovato, 2012). The U.S. Department of Education's Office of Civil Rights (USDE/OCR) provides online compliance guidance related to federal statutory requirements under the ADAAA of 2008 and the Rehabilitation Act (1973), Section 504, for states and school districts (USDE/OCR, 2015; 2012).

Additionally, there are many more references to very specific health services covered by these the three main federal laws, as well as guidance on the meaning and impact of other federal and state statutes related to specific health conditions. Sicherer, Mahr, & AAP Section on Allergy and Immunology (2010), advise that federal laws protect the legal rights of students with severe life-threatening allergies. The Patient Protection and Affordable Care Act (ACA) of 2010 improves access to care for youth who have chronic physical health conditions (NASN, 2015c; USDHHS, 2016), as well as mental health concerns (National Conference of State Legislatures (NCSL), 2016). Students who have diabetes are entitled to health services at school, as well as an individualized health assessment (American Diabetes Association (ADA), 2012; Jackson et al., 2015; Kaufman, 2002), additionally Jackson et al. (2015) advise about state specific laws that protect school staff who assist students with diabetes care. In response to two federal laws related to reducing childhood obesity, the Healthy, Hunger-Free Kids Act of 2010, and the earlier Child Nutrition and WIC Reauthorization Act of 2004, states and school districts have turned to school nurses to assist with implementation of these laws (Hoxie-Setterstrom & Hoglund, 2011; Winterfeld, 2014). All states have enacted laws that include basic health requirements for school attendance (CDC, 2008; Dean et al., 2014; Maughan, 2009).

Some states have enacted laws specifically designating staffing, either school nurses or trained unlicensed assistive personnel (UAP), to accommodate student health needs. A Virginia law requires a specified number of UAPs, in addition to school medical or nursing personnel, who are trained to administer insulin and glucagon to students with diabetes (Hellems & Clarke, 2007). Michigan has developed a guidance document that delineates federal and Michigan specific school health services laws (Michigan Department of Education, Michigan Department of Community Health, 2013). A Nevada law directs all public schools to stock epinephrine and assigns coordination of the program to the school nurse (Vokits, Pumphrey, Baker, & Krametbauer, 2014). Federal laws requiring that youth with special healthcare needs who are transitioning to adult care be assisted in this process sparked Illinois to specify school nurses as key personnel to assist with transition planning (Bargeron et al., 2015).

In addition to information about federal and state laws requiring health services in schools, the literature review supports the link between health and education (Baisch, Lundeen, & Murphy, 2011; Basch, 2010; Bradley & Greene, 2013; Michael, Merlo, Basch, Wentzel, & Wechsler, 2015; NASN, 2016; Vinciullo & Bradley, 2009), as well as the social determinants of health, educationally relevant health disparities, student health, and academic performance (Basch, 2010, 2011; Viner et al., 2012).

Other related topics reviewed in the literature include:
- The incidence of chronic physical and mental health conditions in student populations.
- The history of school health services.
- Laws and support for addressing student mental health.
- Availability or lack of access to school health services.
- School health policy development.
- Fiscal support or funding problems related to delivery of school health services.
- The roles of the school nurse.

For the above topics, see references in the Table 1 below.

Table 1. Other related topics reviewed include:

Topic	Citations
The incidence of chronic physical and mental health conditions in student populations	(AAP, 2016; 2004;2009; CDC, 2015a; Dang, 2010; Dang, Warrington, Tung, Baker, & Pan, 2007; USDHHS, 2016; Martinez, 2016; NASN, 2013b; NASN, 2015b, 2015c)
The history of school health services	(Dang, 2010; Kort, 2006; Martin et al., 1996; Maughan & Troup, 2011; Tyack, 1992)
Laws and support for addressing student mental health	(AAP, 2016; 2004/2009; Bringewatt & Gershoff, 2010; Dang et al., 2007; Health Resources & Services Administration (HRSA), 2016; Langley, Nadeem, Kataoka, Stein, & Jaycox, 2010; Lohan, 2006; National Alliance on Mental Illness (NAMI), 2015; NASN, 2013b; NCSL, 2016; NCSL, 2009; Reinke, Stormont, Herman, Puri, & Goel, 2011; Shannon, Bergren, & Matthews, 2010; Silverman et al., 2016; USDHHS/enters for Medicare & Medicaid Services (CMS), 2013; Weist, Rubin, Moore, Adelsheim, & Wrobel, 2007)
Availability or lack of access to school health services	(AAP, 2016; Aruda et al., 2011; Basch, 2010; Brener et al., 2007; CDC, 2015b; Data Resource Center for Child and Adolescent Health, 2016; USDHHS, 2016; Langley et al., 2010; NASN, 2013b; NCSL, 2009)
School health policy development	(Brener et al., 2007; Jones, Brener, & Bergren, 2015; Krin & Taliaferro, 2012)
Fiscal support or funding problems related to delivery of school health services	(Allensworth et al., 1997; Basch, 2010; Briggs, Fleischhacker, & Mueller, 2010; CDC, 2008; Costante, 2001; Maughan, & Troup, 2011; NASN, 2013c)
The roles of the school nurse	(Allensworth & Kolbe, 1987; AAP, 2016; American Nurses Association (ANA) & NASN, 2011; Aruda et al., 2011; Bargeron et al., 2015; Caldart-Olson & Thronson, 2013; CDC, 2008; CDC, 2015b; Costante, 2001; Dang, 2010; Dang et al., 2007; Dean et al., 2014; Galemore & Sheetz, 2015; Gibbons et al., 2013; Hoxie-Setterstrom & Hoglund, 2011; Krin & Taliaferro, 2012; Lohan, 2006; NASN, 2013b; NASN, 2015b, 2015c; 2016; Sampson & Galemore, 2012; Shannon et al., 2010; Vinciullo & Bradley, 2009; Vokits et al., 2014; Wang et al., 2014; Zirkel, 2009; Zirkel et al., 2012)

Relevance to School Health/School Nursing

Chronic health issues are increasing in student populations. It is estimated that at least 34 percent of students in our schools have chronic health conditions (Martinez, 2016), including diabetes, epilepsy, severe food allergies, asthma, depression, attention deficit hyperactivity disorder (ADHD), and obesity. As the number of school-age children and youth with health problems increases, there is a corresponding increased need for school health services and school nurses (NASN, 2016). Despite overarching federal laws requiring schools to provide physical and mental health services for these students, in many states, communities, school districts, and schools within the same district, many students are not receiving the health services that they need and are entitled to (AAP, 2016; Aruda et al., 2011; Basch, 2010; Brener et al., 2007; Data Resource Center for Child and Adolescent Health, 2016; USDHHS, 2016; Langley et al., 2010; NCSL, 2009).

School nurses have the qualifications and skills to intervene with and coordinate care for acute, chronic, and potential health conditions. School nurses provide health education and promote wellness and prevention activities. They are liaisons between the education community and the healthcare community, and they connect students, staff, families and healthcare providers and advocate for a healthy and safe school environment. School nurses increase the ability of students and families to adapt to health and social stressors and help to mitigate educationally relevant health disparities (Basch, 2011) by collaborating with school and community support services to provide high quality school health services (CDC, 2015b).

As champions for student health and safety, school nurses must educate key stakeholders and decision-makers about student health issues (AAP, 2004/2009), and advocate for compliance with federal and state laws and regulations, which will ultimately lead to improved student health. In so doing, school nurses also help to reduce school liability by promoting and assisting with the implementation of adequate and appropriate school health services (NASN, 2015b).

IMPLICATIONS FOR SCHOOL NURSE PRACTICE

What School Health Services Are Schools Responsible to Provide?

Three overarching federal laws guarantee the rights of all students, including those with disabilities, to attend public school. These laws are:

- Education of the Handicapped Act (P.L. 91-230) of 1970, reauthorized as Education for All Handicapped Children Act of 1975, reauthorized and renamed the Individuals with Disabilities Education Act (IDEA in 1990 and reauthorized as the Individuals with Disabilities Education Improvement Act(IDEIA) of 2004,
- Rehabilitation Act of 1973, Section 504, and
- Americans with Disabilities Act (ADA) of 1990, which was reauthorized as the ADAAA of 2008.

The **Education for All Handicapped Children Act of 1975** was reauthorized and renamed the **Individuals with Disabilities Education Act (IDEA)** in 1990 and reauthorized as the **Individuals with Disabilities Education Improvement Act (IDEIA) of 2004.** – This law is the basis of how schools in all states provide special education and related services for eligible students from birth through their 21st year. The law requires public schools to evaluate children with disabilities, develop an education plan (now known as the individualized education program (IEP)), provide a free and appropriate public education (FAPE), in the least restrictive environment (LRE), and provide due process with an impartial hearing when there is a conflict between the school district and the parents of children with disabilities. In regard to children's health, the law requires that schools provide a broad range of services at school that enable eligible students to access educational opportunities just as non-disabled students have access.

The statute, 20 USC § 1401, defines child with a disability as a child "with intellectual disabilities, hearing impairments (including deafness), speech or language impairments, visual impairments (including blindness), serious emotional disturbance (referred to in this chapter as "emotional disturbance"), orthopedic impairments, autism, traumatic brain injury, other health impairments, or specific learning disabilities; and who, by reason thereof, needs special education and related services" (20 USC § 1401). This definition may also include children who have limited strength, vitality, or alertness due to chronic or acute health problems such as a heart condition, tuberculosis, rheumatic fever, nephritis, asthma, sickle cell anemia, hemophilia, epilepsy, lead poisoning, leukemia, or diabetes, multiple disabilities, or developmental delay (Galemore & Sheetz, 2015; Zirkel, 2009).

For younger children, aged three through nine years (or any subset of that age range, including ages three through five years), a child with a disability may, at the discretion of the state and the local educational agency, include a child experiencing developmental delays, as defined by the state and as measured by appropriate diagnostic instruments and procedures, in one or more of the following areas:

- physical development;
- cognitive development;
- communication development;
- social or emotional development; or
- adaptive development; and
- who therefore needs special education and related services (20 USC § 1401).

In the 2012-13 school year, there were over 6.4 million students – approximately 12.9 percent of the total public school enrollment – who qualified for special education and related services and 779,000 who were eligible as being "other health impaired" (U.S. Department of Education [USDE], 2016).

The school nurse is the only team member who is qualified to interpret medical records, evaluate the student's healthcare related service needs, develop individualized health plan (IHP) and emergency care (ECP) plans, and assist the team in developing the IEP to appropriately accommodate the student's health needs, and evaluate the effectiveness of the plans health-components, making revisions as necessary. Thus, with the help of the school nurse on the IEP, the student is enabled to participate in the educational program at school.

Under the IDEA, children with disabilities are identified by specified criteria and thorough assessment by a multidisciplinary team of professionals who are knowledgeable about the student (Dang, 2010). The team should include at least one regular education teacher, one special education teacher, a school representative, such as an administrator, the student's parent or guardian, and related specialists, including the school nurse, when the nurse's specialty will be discussed (Gibbons et al., 2013). The school nurse is the only team member who is qualified to interpret medical records, evaluate the student's healthcare related service needs, develop individualized health plan (IHP) and emergency care (ECP) plans, and assist the team in developing the IEP to appropriately accommodate the student's health needs, and evaluate the effectiveness of the plans health-components, making revisions as necessary. Thus, with the help of the school nurse on the IEP, the student is enabled to participate in the educational program at school (Galemore & Sheetz, 2015; Gibbons et al., 2013; Zimmerman, 2013; Zirkel, 2009). The development of the IHP cannot be delegated to UAP as the IHP documents the nursing process in accordance with the individual state nurse practice act (ANA & NASN, 2017; NASN, 2013d). The ECP is developed by the nurse from the information in the IHP (Zimmerman, 2013).

Depending on the student's needs, the school nurse may be identified on the IEP as a direct service or a related service. In these cases, the school nurse must supply information describing for the IEP the types of services to be provided, as well as the frequency and duration of the services. The student's IHP may be attached to the IEP, thereby providing the rationale for the health services the student will receive at school. When the IEP specifies needs for nursing services according to the IHP, and the student is Medicaid eligible, the direct care services provided by the nurse, may be reimbursable under the state's Medicaid program (Galemore & Sheetz, 2015; Gibbons et al., 2013; Hahn, & Sheingold, 2013; NASN, 2013c). IDEA (2004) requires that each student's IEP be updated each year (34 CFR 300.324(b)(1)(i)) and that a full-review of each student's eligibility and progress occur every three years, unless the student's parents and the school district agree that the reassessment is unnecessary (IDEA, 2004, 34 CFR § 300.303(b)(2)).

This law also requires school districts to identify, locate, and evaluate all previously unidentified children, ages birth through age 21, with disabilities, regardless of the severity of the disability, who may need special education services. This process is known as "child find". The requirement applies to all children who live within a state, including students attending private and public schools, children whose families are highly mobile, migrant children, homeless children, foster children, and state wards (IDEA, 2004, 20 U.S.C. 1412(a)(3)). Infants and children, from birth up to three years old with disabilities are served through Early Childhood Intervention programs where healthcare practitioners evaluate the infant or toddler for delays and deficits in social, emotional, physical, cognitive, communication, and adaptive development, and meet any needs through the development of an individualized family services plan (IFSP) which focuses on daily routines and family activities. At ages three to five years children with disabilities may be enrolled in public school early childhood education classes (Gibbons et al., 2013). As students with disabilities reach high school, transition planning for adulthood should begin and take into account the student's interests, strengths, and goals (Bargeron et al., 2015). While the student's IEP ends at age 22 (or younger if the state where the child resides specifies) and the student's Section 504 Plan lasts as long as the student is enrolled, the anti-discrimination protections of Section 504 last for life (Gibbons et al., 2013). The school nurse is in an ideal position to help students and families through all these phases.

The amendments in the 2004 reauthorization take into account disparities between schools that serve primarily white students and have mostly white teachers, mislabeling and higher dropout rates for minority students with disabilities, disproportionate rates of minority students in special education compared to the overall student population, and discrepancies in the numbers of minority students referred and actually receiving services in special education. The amendments also require that individual student's response to evidence-based interventions, otherwise known as Response to Intervention (RTI), be thoroughly assessed in determining if the student has a learning disability (NASN, 2013a).

The **Individuals with Disabilities Education Improvement Act (IDEIA) of 2004** also clarifies the role of the school nurse by stating "School health services and school nurse services means health services that are designed to enable a child with a disability to receive FAPE as described in the child's IEP. School nurse services are services provided by a qualified school nurse. School health services are services that may be provided by either a qualified school nurse or other qualified person" (IDEIA, 2004, 34 CFR § 300.34(c) (13)).

Rehabilitation Act of 1973, Section 504 – extends civil rights to all persons (including those covered under IDEA and adults) with mental or physical disabilities that substantially limit one or more major life activities, prohibits discrimination against persons with disabilities, requires the development of individualized accommodation plans (also known as Section 504 Plans), requires that any accommodations be 'reasonable', and requires access for individuals with disabilities to federally funded programs and activities, including schools and jobs, if the person is otherwise qualified (Gibbons et al., 2013; Sampson & Galemore, 2012). Because this law covers all individuals with disabilities, it is important for students with disabilities to understand what accommodations they need as they transition to adulthood (Gibbons et al., 2013).

As stated, Section 504 provides protections to all persons with disabilities. A student with one of the defined disabilities under IDEA and who needs an IEP is covered by Section 504, but rather than a Section 504 Plan, the student will have an IEP, as well as an IHP, as needed. A student with a disability other than one of those defined by IDEA, or who does not need special education services to achieve academically, may be eligible for a Section 504 Plan (Galemore & Sheetz, 2015). Determination of Section 504 eligibility must be made to the Section 504 team, which is comprised of parents and persons who are knowledgeable about the disability, the student and the student's eligibility for accommodations, and the appropriate accommodations to fit the student's needs (Gibbons et al., 2013). School nurses are vital members of the Section 504 team. The school nurse must be prepared to speak to how the student's disability impacts major life activities and to recommend accommodations that will support the student's school success (Galemore & Sheetz, 2015; Gibbons et al., 2013).

Americans with Disabilities Act of 1990 – This law expands the scope of the rights guaranteed by the Rehabilitation Act of 1973, in that it prohibits discrimination against persons with disabilities in all aspects of public life, including employment, education, transportation, and in all public and private venues that are generally accessible and open to the public.

This law has been reauthorized as the **ADAAA of 2008**. The ADAAA amendment to the definition of disability also amends the Section 504 definition. The changes include impairments that substantially limit one or more major life activities, including caring for oneself, performing manual tasks, seeing, hearing, eating, sleeping, walking, standing, lifting, bending, speaking, breathing, learning, reading, concentrating, thinking, communicating, working.

The amendments also include coverage of impairments that are episodic or in remission, that when active can substantially limit one or more major life activities. The ADAAA (2008), states that the listed activities are examples, and not a complete list of what may be included as major life activities (ADAAA, 2008). Additional changes resulting from the reauthorized ADAAA of 2008, are shown in Table 2.

Table 2. **Other changes in the amended ADAAA of 2008**

Other major bodily functions covered by the 2008 amendments include:	The amended law also states that mitigating measures have no bearing in determining whether a disability qualifies under the law. The mitigating measures include:
Functions of the immune system; Normal cell growth; and Digestive, bowel, bladder, neurological, brain, respiratory, circulatory, endocrine, and reproductive functions.	Medication, Medical supplies, Equipment, or appliances, Low vision devices (other than eyeglasses and contact lenses), Prosthetics, Hearing aids, Cochlear implants, or other implantable hearing devices, Mobility devices, Oxygen therapy equipment and supplies, Assistive technology, Reasonable accommodations, Auxiliary aids, Learned behavioral or adaptive neurological modifications.

Zirkel (2009), suggests that, for the school nurse, the expansion of impairments and major bodily functions, provides increased possibilities for conditions like sleep apnea, colitis, Crohn's disease, and irritable bowel syndrome to be covered by the ADAAA, 2008. The broadening of the definition of major life activities in the ADAAA, 2008, the addition of temporary or episodic impairments, and the requirement that mitigating factors may no longer considered, means that students who previously were ineligible now may qualify under Section 504, as a person with a disability (Sampson & Galemore, 2012; USDE, 2012; Zirkel, 2009). Zirkel (2009), also suggests that school nurses should be prepared for increasing requests to assist Section 504 teams determine if individual students meet the expanded eligibility standards under Section 504. Recognizing this, school nurses will also be contributing to "legally defensible and practically feasible answers" about the school's responsibility to provide health services for the increased numbers of eligible students under Section 504 (Zirkel, 2009, p. 260).

In response to the ADAAA, 2008, and parent complaints to the Office of Civil Rights (OCR), Zirkel et al. (2012) recommend that all students who currently have an individualized health plans (IHP) be screened in order to determine Section 504 eligibility under the school district's 'child find' obligations, and further evaluated if the screening results so indicate. School nurses clearly have a significant role in the screening and evaluation process (Zirkel et al., 2012). While it is recommended that every student with a disability should have an IHP (Gibbons et al., 2013), some children with disabilities may not have IHPs. School districts need to be aware that 'child find' obligations remain intact (Zirkel et al., 2012), and with the amendments of ADAAA, 2008, school districts may need to revise their Section 504 eligibility process and include the school nurse in that process to make "individualized but more expansive determinations" about Section 504 eligibility (Zirkel et al., 2012, p. 426).

In relationship to school health services in response to ADAAA, 2008 and Section 504, Zirkel et al., make the following recommendations for school nurses:

- Stay current with changes to Section 504 and student health conditions.

- Prioritize students with life-threatening conditions: regularly review emergency care plans, 504 Plans, and student safety measures.
- Screen all individual healthcare plans, student's attendance and health office visits.
- For student evaluation obtain parental consent and necessary medical information, complete evaluation process promptly, and give parents Section 504 procedural safeguards notice.
- Proactively discuss and determine as a team the student's need for accommodations and/or related aids and services according to Section 504's FAPE standards.
- Document and as needed, consult with other professionals.

[pp. 430-431.]

State Laws and School District Policies Mandating School Health Services

Special education legislation and court cases like *Irving Independent School Dist. V. Tatro* reinforce that schools in all states have a responsibility to provide nursing services (Maughan & Troup, 2011). In contrast with federal legislation related to school health services for students with disabilities, state laws, regulations, and school district policies, while varying widely, provide details and guidance for the provision of multiple services for all students. All states authorize some health services in school settings, and some states mandate the provision of specific health services. Determination of which health services are provided in schools and how they are delivered generally is left to local boards of education. Several states and many school boards mandate health services personnel to be in schools, typically school nurses and occasionally other qualified health professionals, such as school physicians. Most states do not require there to be a school nurse in every school. School health professionals must meet state professional licensure requirements to provide health services, but the requirements for school nurses vary from state to state. Lawmakers in at least 12 states have statutorily implemented nurse-to-student or nurse-to-school ratios (CDC, 2008). It is important that school nurses to be familiar with the laws that govern their practice, including their state nurse practice act and the particular state laws and school district policies that authorize or require school health services.

Most states mandate some type of school-wide monitoring and screenings by the school nurse, such as vision screenings and other types of or school entrance immunizations (Maughan & Troup, 2011). School testing and screening requirements typically cover five major areas:

- Communicable diseases, such as, tuberculosis;
- Chronic conditions, such as hearing loss, vision problems, developmental delays, and scoliosis;
- Injuries and unhealthy behaviors, such as tobacco use;
- Monitoring child abuse or neglect; and
- Height, weight, and body mass index (BMI) screening. (CDC, 2008)

In some states, testing and screening requirements are uniformly applied to all public schools in the state. Other states give discretion to local school districts in regard to certain conditions. The timing and process for health testing and screening vary widely across states and school districts. Some health conditions are screened periodically and others are screened only once in the student's career in the school district. Students are tested for other health conditions, especially communicable diseases such as tuberculosis, only when symptomatic indications warrant testing (CDC, 2008).

Many school districts require students to undergo a pre-participation physical examination sports or other extracurricular activities. Students not meeting the stated requirements may not be permitted to participate in these activities. Drug testing is a prerequisite for participating in sports in some states. While random drug testing for students is controversial, the requirement has been upheld by the courts (CDC, 2008).

Like their federal counterparts, corresponding state laws guarantee access to appropriate health services for students with special healthcare needs.

Medication administration to students is a standard component of school health services. Many states have laws that regulate self-administration of specified medications by students and many states permit delegation of medication administration to unlicensed assistive personnel (UAP). A variety of state laws regulate self-administration of medication. States and school districts may permit students to possess and self-administer medications. In 2004, Congress authorized preferential federal funding for states that permit students to possess and self-administer asthma inhalers, which resulted in most states authorizing these practices. Several states require schools to develop local policies that allow students to possess and administer asthma inhalers and epinephrine pens. Additionally, IDE-A (2004), Section 504, and ADAAA (2008), require schools to accommodate students whose asthma qualifies as a disability. Under these laws, students may be carry their inhalers for purposes of self-medication as provided in their asthma management plans (CDC, 2008).

When students require assistance medication administration, such as, epinephrine via auto-injector, oral medications, and other injectable medications that require handling of needles and blood, the school nurse or UAP, may be authorized to administer the medications. State law or regulation, such as the nursing practice act, may restrict this practice to specific licensed professionals. Some states have laws authorizing UAP to administer glucagon and provide other necessary services to diabetic students and to administer epinephrine to students experiencing anaphylaxis (CDC, 2008).

Figure 1. *In loco parentis* - When students come to school, schools assume custody of students and, simultaneously, students no longer enjoy the protection of their parents. Essentially, schools act instead of the parent or in place of the parent. The Latin term for this role is – *in loco parentis*. The term in modern usage has evolved from being a right of coercion or restraint used to discipline students to become an obligation or duty of school officials to provide protection to students. School officials hold authority over students due to *in loco parentis* and have a concurrent duty to protect the students. Several aspects of "in loco parentis" have been tested in the courts, for example *Tinker v. Des Moines Independent Community School District (1969), Hazelwood School District v. Kuhlmeier* (1987), *Vernonia School District v. Acton* (1995), and *Board of Education, Pottawatomie County v. Earls* (2002).

Some states' laws and school district policies control the process for obtaining consent for treatment in the school setting. Some states require parental consent for all or most school health services offered to minor students. Other states permit minor students to access some health services without prior parental consent (CDC, 2008). All states' consent provisions permit exceptions if a student's health is in immediate danger and parental consent cannot be obtained (CDC, 2008). In these situations, and similar situations, school personnel may cite *in loco parentis* to justify their actions (Figure 1).

Staffing: What is safe staffing for the school health office?

In the late 1970s, in response to federal legislation guaranteeing the rights of all students to attend public school, including those students with disabilities, NASN recommended, and the American Nurses Association, as well as other organizations endorsed, a school nurse-to-student ratio, which over the years evolved to a ratio of 1:750 (NASN, 2015b). However, given the increasing numbers of students with chronic health conditions and disabilities who now attend school and need specialized nursing care, utilizing a fixed workload ratio is no longer appropriate, adequate, or in compliance with federal and state laws, to meet today's students' highly complex healthcare needs (ANA, 2012; ANA & NASN, 2017; NASN, 2015b). Since 2015, the position of the NASN is that student health, safety, and learning ability will improve with daily access to a school nurse and to best meet student health and safety needs, school nurse workloads must be based on individual student and community health data (NASN, 2015b).

Evidence from recent studies demonstrates that appropriate school nurse staffing is associated with improved student attendance and academic performance (Cooper, 2005; Moricca et al., 2013; NASN, 2015b), improved vaccination rates, illness reduction, and improved management of chronic disease (Baisch et al., 2011; NASN, 2015b). Other studies have shown that when school nurses are on campus hundreds of hours each year are gained by administrators and teachers who are able to attend to student education rather than student health problems (Baisch et al., 2011; Hill & Hollis, 2012; NASN, 2015b). Additionally, adequate school nurse staffing is cost effective – for every dollar expended on school nursing, at least $2.20 is saved – and full-time school nurses reduce medical costs and contribute to the productivity of teachers and parents (Wang et al., 2014).

However, nationally, only 45 percent of schools have a full-time school nurse, 30 percent of schools have a part-time school nurse, and 25 percent of schools do not have a school nurse (NASN, 2015b). Inadequate school nurse staffing may contribute to negative outcomes for students and schools. For example, in two Philadelphia schools perhaps the lack of access to a school nurse contributed to the deaths of two students in 2014 (Boyle, 2014; NASN, 2015b; Superville & Blad, 2014). Inadequate staffing reduces the quality of care for students, raises stress for school nurses, and impacts school nurse job satisfaction, all of which may lead to nurse turnover and increased costs to school districts (American Association of Colleges of Nursing, 2014; NASN, 2015b). Inadequate staffing or no school nurse staffing at all, also raises questions about who is providing required school health services to students who need them, what are the qualifications of those individuals, and who is supervising them to ensure student safety. In districts with inadequate staffing, school nurses must help school decision-makers understand the critical importance of safe and adequate staffing to protect the students and to reduce liability for the district.

Determining adequate nurse staffing is a complex process (ANA, 2012; NASN, 2015b) that requires identifying the individual student's acuity level and healthcare needs, as well as assessing the social determinants of the community's health, that is, the social and economic conditions that impact the health outcomes of individuals within the community (CDC, 2014; USDHHS, 2014). In determining staffing, there must also be adherence to individual state nurse practice acts and other related state laws. School nurses are in key positions to educate school administrators regarding safe and adequate staffing for students with special healthcare needs (Dang, 2010). Sometimes, a school nurse will permit an unimmunized child in school or will not comply with nursing practice responsibilities because the school administrator said it was okay to not comply. This action would not be authorized, since school nurses have legal and ethical responsibilities to comply with their state nurse practice act, other applicable state laws, and standards of patient/client care. For adequate school nurse staffing to be in place, NASN (2015b) recommends:

- *Using a multifactorial health assessment approach that includes not only acuity and care but also social determinants of health to determine effective school nurse workloads for safe care of students.*

- *Developing evidence-based tools for evaluating factors that influence student health and safety and for developing staffing and workload models that support this evidence.*

- *Conducting research to determine the best models for school nurse leadership in school health, such as RN only, RN-led school health teams, and RNs certified in the specialty practice of school nursing.*

- *Increasing involvement of school nurses at national, state, and local levels in policy decisions that affect the health of students* (NASN, 2015b)

(Please see Chapter 7 for more information on safe school staffing and Chapter 12 for education laws for children with disabilities).

CONCLUSION

Federal laws require schools to provide the necessary health services for students with disabilities in order for these students to receive an appropriate education. Schools must also provide services for other students with acute or episodic health problems. Schools are mandated to provide health services, either by federal or state legislation or by risk and liability reduction. Other health services, including health screenings and immunizations are generally accepted as belonging in the schools, due more to access and efficiency, or if mandated by state law, rather than with liability. Because schools are where children are, schools are frequently viewed as the logical place for population-based health prevention (Allensworth et al., 1997).

School nurses who are knowledgeable of federal and state laws related to working with students with disabilities, chronic illnesses, or other difficulties will make important contributions to these students' health and academic achievement. School nurses are responsible for understanding the laws, referring students who may be eligible for accommodations or special education services, and participating on school teams that determine eligibility for services covered by Section 504 and IDEA (NASN, 2013a).

When providing health services for students, school nurses must be cognizant of their state nurse practice act, position and policy documents, and best practice guidelines, particularly the *School Nursing: Scope and Standards of Practice, 3rd Edition* (2017). These documents set the standard of practice for school nursing and school healthcare delivery.

The school nurse's role is to maintain or optimize the health of all students thus enabling them to fully participate in their educational program. For students with chronic or disabling conditions, the school nurse's individualized health assessment, planning, and interventions are important to service decisions and placement, and should be documented in the student's IHP (Gibbons et al., 2013; NASN, 2013d).

School nurses identify and address student health issues that impact school performance and are adept at navigating educational and medical systems (Baisch et al., 2011). School nurses have both opportunity and professional duty to advocate for compliance with federal and state laws related to school health services as well as district, state, and federal policies that support healthy school programs and environments (Hoxie-Setterstrom & Hoglund, 2011).

RESOURCES

Legal References

- o   Americans with Disabilities Act (ADA) 42 U.S.C. § 12101 (1990).
- o   ADA Amendments Act of 2008 (ADAAA) 42 USCA § 12101 (2008).
- o   Child Nutrition and WIC Reauthorization Act, Pub. L. No. 108-265, § 204, 729 (2004).
- o   Developmental Disabilities Assistance and Bill of Rights Act, Pub. L. No. 106-402, § 101 1680 (2000).
- o   Education for All Handicapped Children Act, Pub. L. No. 94-142, § 20 USC 1401. (1975).
- o   Elementary and Secondary Education Act, 20 U.S.C. 6301 et seq. (1965).
- o   Every Student Succeeds Act (ESSA), Public Law No: 114-95 (2015)
- o   Family Educational Rights and Privacy Act (FERPA), 20 U.S.C.S. § 1232g (1974).
- o   Health Insurance Portability and Accountability Act (HIPAA), Privacy Rule P.L. 104-191 (1996).
- o   Healthy, Hunger-Free Kids Act, Pub.L. 111–296. (2010).
- o   Individuals with Disabilities Education Improvement Act (IDEIA), 20 USC et seq., 64 (2004).
- o   McKinney-Vento Homeless Education Assistance Improvements Act, 42 U.S.C.S. 11431 et seq. (2001).
- o   Mental Health Parity and Addiction Equity Act (MHPAEA), (2008).
- o   Patient Protection and Affordable Care Act (ACA), P.L. 111-148 (2010).
- o   Protection of Pupil Rights Amendment (PPRA), 20 U.S.C.S. § 1232h (1978).
- o   School Access to Emergency Epinephrine Act, H.R. 2094 — 113th Congress (2013).
- o   Section 504 of the Rehabilitation Act, 29 U.S.C. § 701 et seq. (1973).

Case Law

Brown v. Board of Education of Topeka, 347 U.S. 483 (1954).

Tinker v. Des Moines Independent Community School District, 393 U.S. 503, 89 S. Ct. 733, 21L. Ed. 2d 731. (1969).

Pennsylvania Association for Retarded Children (Parc) v. Commonwealth of Pennsylvania, 334 F. Supp. 279 (E.D. PA 1972).

Mills v. Board of Education, 348 F. Supp. 866 (D.D.C. 1972) (1972).

Board of Education of the Hendrickson Central School District v. Amy Rowley, Supreme Court of the United States 458 US 176. (1982)

Irving Independent School Dist. V. Tatro, 468 US 883, 104 S. Ct. 3371, 82 L. Ed. 2d 664 - Supreme Court, (1984).

Hazelwood School District et al. v. Kuhlmeier et al., 484 U.S. 260 (1988).

Sacramento City Unified School District v. Rachel H., U.S. Court of Appeals for the Ninth circuit, 14 F.3d 1398 (1994).

W. B. v. Matula, 67 F.3d. 484, 3rd Cir. (1995).

Cedar Rapids Community School District V. Garret F., Supreme Court of the United States 526 U.S. 66 (1999).

Vernonia School District v. Acton, 515 U.S. 646, 115 S. Ct. 2386, 132 L. Ed. 2d 564 (1995).

Board of Education, Pottawatomie County v. Earls, 536 U. S. 822, 122 S. Ct. 2559, 153 L. Ed. 2d 735 (2002).

Position Papers, Clinical Guidelines

American Nurses Association. (2012). *ANA's principles for nurse staffing* (2nd ed.). Silver Spring, MD: Nursesbooks.org.

Fleming, R. (2011). Imperative issues affecting school nurse practice: Implications for the future of school nursing and child health in Washington State. A White Paper, Seattle: Washington State Nurses Association. Retrieved from https://www.wsna.org/assets/entry-assets/Nursing-Practice/Publications/school-nurse-white-paper-r2.pdf

Sarata, A.K. (2011). Mental health parity and the Patient Protection and Affordable Care Act of 2010. CRS Report for Congress. Retrieved from http://www.ncsl.org/documents/health/MHparity%26mandates.pdf

US Department of Education, Office of Elementary and Secondary Education. (2016). *Non-regulatory guidance: Student support and academic enrichment grants*. Washington, D.C: Author. Retrieved from http://www2.ed.gov/policy/elsec/leg/essa/essassaegrantguid10212016.pdf

Additional Resources

American Association for Pediatric Ophthalmology and Strabismus. (2016). *State-by-state vision screening requirements*. San Francisco, CA: Author. Retrieved from https://www.aapos.org/resources/state_by_state_vision_screening_requirements/

American Diabetes Association. (2012). Diabetes Care in the School and Day Care Setting. Diabetes Care 2012 Jan; 35(Supplement 1): S76-S80. http://dx.doi.org/10.2337/dc12-s076 Retrieved from: http://care.diabetesjournals.org/content/35/Supplement_1/S76.full

Mental Health/U.S. Department of Health and Human Services. https://www.mentalhealth.gov/index.html

National Technical Assistance Center for Children's Mental Health. http://gucchd.georgetown.edu/67211.html

Ruth Perou, R., Bitsko, R.H., Blumberg, S.J., Pastor, P., Ghandour, R.M.,. . Gfroerer, J.C. (2013). Mental Health Surveillance Among Children — United States, 2005–2011. *Morbidity and Mortality Weekly Report* (*MMWR*), *Supplements,* 62(02);1-35. Retrieved from http://www.cdc.gov/mmwr/preview/mmwrhtml/su6202a1.htm?s_cid=su6201a1_w

The Center for Health and Health Care in Schools. http://www.healthinschools.org/School-Health-Services.aspx Has links to *Laws, Rules, Regulations, and Guidelines for School Health* for all 50 states and information about *Medicaid and School Health Services.*

Substance Abuse and Mental Health Services Administration (SAMHSA). http://www.samhsa.gov/

REFERENCES

Allensworth, D.D. & Kolbe, L.J. (1987). The comprehensive school health program: Exploring an expanded concept. *Journal of School Health, 57*(10), 409–412. doi: 10.1111/j.1746-1561.1987.tb03183.x

Allensworth, D., Lawson, E., Nicholson, L., & Wyche, J., (Eds.). (1997). School health services. In *Schools and health: Our nation's investment* (Committee on Comprehensive School Health Programs in Grades K-12, Institute of Medicine, pp 153-236, Chapter 4). Washington, D.C.: National Academies Press Retrieved from https://www.nap.edu/read/5153/chapter/6

American Academy of Pediatrics, Committee on School Health. (2004, Reaffirmed 2009). School-based mental health services (Policy Statement). *Pediatrics*, 113(6): 1839-1845. Elk Grove Village, IL: Author Retrieved from http://pediatrics.aappublications.org/content/pediatrics/113/6/1839.full.pdf

American Academy of Pediatrics. (2016). Role of the school nurse in providing school health services (Policy Statement). *Pediatrics, 121*(5), 1052-1056. doi: 10.1542/peds.2016-0852.

American Association of Colleges of Nursing. (2014). *Nursing shortage*. Retrieved from http://www.aacn.nche.edu/media-relations/fact-sheets/nursing-shortage

American Diabetes Association. (2012). Diabetes care in the school and day care setting (Position Statement). *Diabetes Care, 35*(Supplement 1): S76-S80. doi: 10.2337/dc12-s076

American Nurses Association. (2012). *ANA's principles for nurse staffing (2nd ed.).* Silver Spring, MD: Nursesbooks.org.

American Nurses Association & National Association of School Nurses. (2017). *School nursing: Scope and standards of practice (3rd ed.).* Silver Spring, MD: Author.

ADA Amendments Act of 2008 (ADAAA), 42 USCA § 12101 (2008).

Aruda, M.M., Kelly, M., & Newinsky, K. (2011). Unmet needs of children with special health care needs in a specialized day school setting. *The Journal of School Nursing, 27*(3): 209-218. doi:10.1177/1059840510391670.

Baisch, M.J., Lundeen, S.P., & Murphy, M.K. (2011). Evidence-based research on the value of school nurses in an urban school system. *Journal of School Health, 81*(2), 74-80. doi: 10.1111/j.1746-1561.2010.00563.x

Bargeron, J., Contri, D., Gibbons, L.J., Ruch-Ross, H.S., & Sanabria, K. (2015). Transition planning for youth with special health care needs (YSHCN) in Illinois schools. *The Journal of School Nursing, 31*(4), 253-260. doi: 10.1177/1059840514542130

Basch, C.E. (2010). Healthier students are better learners: A missing link in school reforms to close the achievement gap. *EQUITY MATTERS: Research Review No. 6. A Research Initiative of the Campaign for Educational Equity* Teachers College, Columbia University. Retrieved from http://www.equitycampaign.org/i/a/document/12557_EquityMattersVol6_Web03082010.pdf

Basch, C. E. (2011). Healthier students are better learners: High-quality, strategically planned, and effectively coordinated school health programs must be a fundamental mission of schools to help close the achievement gap. *Journal of School Health*, Special Issue, *81*(10): 650–662. doi:10.1111/j.1746-1561.2011.00640.x

Boyle, J. (2014, September 3). Suit: Lack of school nurse contributed to 12-year-old asthmatic girl's death. *Pennsylvania Record*. Retrieved from http://pennrecord.com/news/14598-suit-lack-of-school-nurse-contributed-to-12-year-old-asthmatic-girls-death

Bradley, B.J. & Greene, A.C. (2013). Do health and education agencies in the united states share responsibility for academic achievement and health? A review of 25 years of evidence about the relationship of adolescents' academic achievement and health behaviors. *Journal of Adolescent Health*, *52*(5), 523–532. http://dx.doi.org/10.1016/j.jadohealth.2013.01.008

Brener, N.D., Weist, M., Adelman, H., Taylor, L., & Vernon-Smiley, M. (2007). Mental health and social services: Results from the school health policies and programs study 2006. *Journal of School Health*, *77*(8): 486–499. doi: 10.1111/j.1746-1561.2007.00231.x

Brener, N.D., Wheeler, L., Wolfe, L.C., Vernon-Smiley, M., & Caldart-Olson, L. (2007). Health services: Results from the school health policies and programs study 2006. *Journal of School Health*, *77*(8): 464–485. doi: 10.1111/j.1746-1561.2007.00230.xView/save citation

Briggs, M., Fleischhacker, S., & Mueller, C.G. (2010). Position of the American Dietetic Association, School Nutrition Association, and Society for Nutrition Education: Comprehensive School Nutrition Services. In *Journal of Nutrition Education and Behavior*, 42(6), 360–371. doi:10.1016/j.jneb.2010.08.007

Bringewatt, E.H. & Gershoff, E.T. (2010). Falling through the cracks: Gaps and barriers in the mental health system for America's disadvantaged children. *Children and Youth Services Review*,*32*, 1291–1299. doi:10.1016/j.childyouth.2010.04.021

Brown v. Board of Education of Topeka, 347 U.S. 483 (1954).

Caldart-Olson, L. & Thronson, G. (2013). Legislation affecting school nurses. In J. Selekman (Ed.), *School nursing: A comprehensive text* (2nd ed.) (pp. 225–256). Philadelphia, PA: F.A. Davis.

Centers for Disease Control and Prevention. (2008). A CDC review of school laws and policies concerning child and adolescent health. *Journal of School Health*, 78: 69–128. doi:10.1111/j.1746-1561.2007.00272_4.x

Centers for Disease Control and Prevention. (2015a). *Healthy schools: Chronic conditions*. Retrieved from http://www.cdc.gov/healthyschools/chronicconditions.htm

Centers for Disease Control and Prevention. (2015b). *Healthy schools: Components of the whole school, whole community, whole child (WSCC): Health services.* Retrieved from http://www.cdc.gov/healthyschools/wscc/components.htm

CFR, Title 34, Subtitle B, Chapter III, Part 300, Subpart D, § 300.303

CFR, Title 34, Subtitle B, Chapter III, Part 300, Subpart D, § 300.324

Cooper, P. (2005). Life before tests: A district's coordinated health approach for addressing children's full range of needs. *School Administrator, 62*(9), 25-34. Retrieved from http://www.aasa.org/ SchoolAdministratorArticle.aspx?id=7780

Costante, C.C. (2001). School health nursing: Framework for the future, Part I. *The Journal of School Nursing, 17*(1): 3-11. doi: 10.1177/105984050101700102

Dang, M.T. (2010). The history of legislation and regulations related to children with developmental disabilities: Implications for school nursing practice today. *The Journal of School Nursing, 26*(4): 252-259. doi: 10.1177/1059840510368162

Dang, M. T., Warrington, D., Tung, T., Baker, D., & Pan, R. J. (2007). A school-based framework from early identification and management of students with ADHD. *The Journal of School Nursing, 23*(1), 2–12. doi: 10.1177/10598405070230010201

Data Resource Center for Child and Adolescent Health. (2016, September 22). *Counsel or criminalize? Why students of color need support, not suspensions*. Retrieved from http://childhealthdata.org/about/news/ news-detail/2015/03/19/counsel-or-criminalize-support-for-students-of-color

Dean, B.B., Kindermann, S.L., Carson, T., Gavin, J., Frerking, M., & Bergren, M.D. (2014). Healthy kids: An assessment of program performance and participation. *The Journal of School Nursing, 30*(6): 430-439. doi: 10.1177/1059840514527622

Education for All Handicapped Children Act, Pub. L. No. 94-142, § 20 USC 1401. (1975).

Elementary and Secondary Education Act, 20 U.S.C. 6301 et seq. (1965).

Galemore, C.A. & Sheetz, A.H. (2015). IEP, IHP, and Section 504 primer for new school nurses. *NASN School Nurse, 30*(2): 85-88. doi: 10.1177/1942602X14565462

Gibbons, L. J., Lehr, K., & Selekman, J. (2013). Federal laws protecting children and youth with disabilities in the schools. In J. Selekman (Ed.), *School nursing: A comprehensive text* (2nd ed.) (pp. 257–283). Philadelphia, PA: F.A. Davis.

Hahn, J.A. & Sheingold, B.H. (2013). Medicaid expansion: The dynamic health care policy landscape. *Nursing Economic$, 31*(6), 267-272, 297. Retrieved from http://www.nursingeconomics.net/necfiles/13ND/ 267.pdf

Health Resources & Services Administration, Maternal & Child Health. (2016). *Early and periodic screening, diagnostic, and treatment*. Retrieved from http://mchb.hrsa.gov/maternal-child-health-initiatives/ mchb-programs/early-periodic-screening-diagnosis-and-treatment

Hellems, M.A. & Clarke, W.L. (2007). Safe at school: A Virginia experience. *Diabetes Care, 30*(6), 1396-1398. doi: 10.2337/dc07-0121

Hill, N.J. & Hollis, M. (2012). Teacher time spent on student health issues and school nurse presence. *The Journal of School Nursing, 28*(3), 181-186. doi: 10.1177/1059840511429684

Hoxie-Setterstrom, G. & Hoglund, B. (2011). School wellness policies: Opportunities for change. *The Journal of School Nursing, 27*(5): 330-339. doi: 10.1177/1059840511409755

Individuals with Disabilities Education Improvement Act (IDEIA), 20 USC § 1400 (2004).

Jackson, C.C., Albanese-O'Neill, A., Butler, K.L., Chiang, J.L., Deeb, L.C., Hathaway, K., . . . Siminerio, L.M. (2015). Diabetes care in the school setting: A position statement of the American Diabetes Association. *Diabetes Care*, *38*(10): 1958-1963. doi: 10.2337/dc15-1418

Jones, S.E., Brener, N.D., & Bergren, M.D. (2015). Association between school district policies that address chronic health conditions of students and professional development for school nurses on such policies. *The Journal of School Nursing*, 31(#): 163-166. doi: 10.1177/1059840514547275

Kaufman, F.R. (2002). Diabetes at School: What a Child's Health Care Team Needs to Know About Federal Disability Law. *Clinical Diabetes,* 20(2): 91-92. doi: 10.2337/diaclin.20.2.91

Kort, M. (2006). The delivery of primary health care in American public schools, 1890-1980. In J.G. Lear, S.L. Isaacs, & J.R. Knickman (Eds.), *School health services and programs,* (pp. 41-55). San Francisco, CA: Jossey-Bass.

Krin, P. & Taliaferro, V. (2012). Establishing policies and procedures: The core of school nursing practice. In C. Costante (Ed.), *School nurse administrators: Leadership and management,* (pp. 339-362). Silver Spring, MD: National Association of School Nurses.

Langley, A.K., Nadeem, E., Kataoka, S.H., Stein, B.D., & Jaycox, L.H. (2010). Evidence-Based Mental Health Programs in Schools: Barriers and Facilitators of Successful Implementation. *School Mental Health,* 2(3): 105–113. doi:10.1007/s12310-010-9038-1

Lohan, J.A. (2006). School nurses' support for bereaved students: A pilot study. *The Journal of School Nursing*, *22*(1): 48-52. doi: 10.1177/10598405060220010801

Martin, E.W., Martin, R., & Terman, D.L. (1996). The legislative and litigation history of special education. *The Future of Children*, *6*(1), 25-39. Retrieved from https://www.princeton.edu/futureofchildren/publications/docs/06_01_01.pdf

Martinez, A.K. (2016). *School attendance, chronic health conditions and leveraging data for improvement: Recommendations for state education and health departments to address student absenteeism.* Atlanta, GA: National Association of Chronic Disease Directors. Retrieved from http://c.ymcdn.com/sites/www.chronicdisease.org/resource/resmgr/school_health/NACDD_School_Attendance_and_.pdf

Martinez, M. E. & Cohen, R. A. (2015). Health insurance coverage: Early release of estimates from the National Health Interview Survey, January – March 2015. *National Center for Health Statistics*. Retrieved from http://www.cdc.gov/nchs/data/nhis/earlyrelease/insur201312.pdf

Maughan, E. (2009). Part 1—Factors associated with school nurse ratios: An analysis of state data. *The Journal of School Nursing*, *25*(3): 214-221. doi: 10.1177/1059840509336058

Maughan, E. & Troup, K.D. (2011). The integration of counseling and nursing services into schools: A comparative review. *The Journal of School Nursing, 27*(4): 293-303. doi: 10.1177/1059840511407778

Michael, S. L., Merlo, C. L., Basch, C. E., Wentzel, K. R. & Wechsler, H. (2015). Critical connections: Health and academics. *Journal of School Health*, *85*, 740–758. doi:10.1111/josh.12309

Michigan Department of Education, Michigan Department of Community Health. (2013). Laws that affect school health services programs in Michigan. Lansing, MI: Author. Retrieved from http://www.michigan.gov/documents/mde/Laws_That_Affect_School_Health_Services_Programs_in_Michigan_4-1-13_416788_7.pdf

Moricca, M.L., Grasska, M.A., BMarthaler, M., Morphew, T., Weismuller, P.C., & Galant, S.P. (2013). School asthma screening and case management: Attendance and learning outcomes. *The Journal of School Nursing, 29*(2), 104-12. doi: 10.1177/1059840512452668

National Alliance on Mental Illness. (2015). *State mental health legislation, 2015: Trends, themes and effective practices*. Arlington, VA: Author. Retrieved from http://www.nami.org/About-NAMI/Publications-Reports/Public-Policy-Reports/State-Mental-Health-Legislation-2015/NAMI-StateMentalHealthLegislation2015.pdf

National Association of School Nurses. (2013a). *Section 504 and Individuals with Disabilities Education Improvement Act – The role of the school nurse* (Position Statement). Silver Spring, MD: Author. Retrieved from http://www.nasn.org/PolicyAdvocacy/PositionPapersandReports/NASNPositionStatementsFullView/tabid/462/ArticleId/491/Section-504-and-Individuals-with-Disabilities-Education-Improvement-Act-The-Role-of-the-School-Nurse

National Association of School Nurses. (2013b). *Mental health of students* (Position Statement). Silver Spring, MD: Author. Retrieved from http://www.nasn.org/PolicyAdvocacy/PositionPapersandReports/NASNPositionStatementsFullView/tabid/462/ArticleId/36/Mental-Health-of-Students-Revised-June-2013

National Association of School Nurses. (2013c). *Reimbursement for school nursing health care services* (Position Statement). Retrieved from http://www.nasn.org/PolicyAdvocacy/PositionPapersandReports/NASNPositionStatementsFullView/tabid/462/ArticleId/569/Reimbursement-for-School-Nursing-Healthcare-Services-Adopted-June-2013

National Association of School Nurses. (2013d). *Individualized healthcare plans: The role of the school nurse* (Position Statement). Retrieved from http://www.nasn.org/PolicyAdvocacy/ PositionPapersandReports/ NASNPositionStatementsFullView/tabid/462/ ArticleId/32/Individualized-HealthcarePlans-The-Role-of-the-School-Nurse-RevisedJune-2013

National Association of School Nurses. (2015a). *Better health. Better learning.*™ **e-toolkit.** Silver Spring, MD: Author Retrieved from http://www.nasn.org/PolicyAdvocacy/BetterHealthBetterLearningeToolkit

National Association of School Nurses. (2015b). *School nurse workload: Staffing for safe care* (Position Statement). Silver Spring, MD: Author. Retrieved from http://www.nasn.org/PolicyAdvocacy/PositionPapersandReports/NASNPositionStatementsFullView/tabid/462/ArticleId/803/School-Nurse-Workload-Staffing-for-Safe-Care-Adopted-January-2015

National Association of School Nurses. (2015c). *The Patient Protection and Affordable Care Act: The role of the school nurse* (Position Statement). Silver Spring, MD: Author. Retrieved from http://www.nasn.org/PolicyAdvocacy/PositionPapersandReports/NASNPositionStatementsFullView/tabid/462/ArticleId/802/The-Patient-Protection-and-Affordable-Care-Act-The-Role-of-the-School-Nurse-Adopted-January-2015

National Association of School Nurses. (2016). *The role of the 21st century school nurse* (Position Statement). Silver Spring, MD: Author. Retrieved from https://www.nasn.org/PolicyAdvocacy/ PositionPapersandReports/NASNPositionStatementsFullView/tabid/462/ArticleId/87/The-Role-of-the-21st-Century-School-Nurse-Adopted-June-2016

National Conference of State Legislatures. (2009). Mental Health in Schools. *State Mental Health Lawmakers' Digest,* 6(2): 1-7. Washington, D.C.: Author. Retrieved from http://www.ncsl.org/print/health/forum/ DigestV6N2.pdf

National Conference of State Legislatures. (2016). Mental health benefits: State laws mandating or regulating. Washington, D.C.: Author. Retrieved from http://www.ncsl.org/research/health/mental-health-benefits-state-mandates.aspx

Patient Protection and Affordable Care Act (ACA), P.L. 111-148 (2010).

Reinke, W.M., Stormont, M., Herman, K.C., Puri, R., & Goel, N. (2011). Supporting children's mental health in schools: Teacher perceptions of needs, roles, and barriers. *School Psychology Quarterly*, 26(1), 1-13. http://dx.doi.org/10.1037/a0022714

Sampson, C. H., & Galemore, C. A. (2012). What every school nurse needs to know about Section 504 eligibility. *NASN School Nurse, 27*(2), 88-93. doi: 10.1177/1942602X12437879

Section 504 of the Rehabilitation Act, 29 U.S.C. § 701 et seq. (1973).

Shannon, R.A., Bergren, M.D., & Matthews, A. (2010). Frequent visitors: Somatization in school-age children and implications for school nurses. *The Journal of School Nursing, 26*(3), 169-182. doi:10.1177/105984050935677

Sicherer, S.H., Mahr, T., & American Academy of Pediatrics/The Section On Allergy and Immunology. (2010). Management of food allergy in the school setting (Clinical Report). *Pediatrics*, *126*(6), 1232-1239. doi:10.1542/peds.2010-2575

Silverman, B., Chen, B., Brener, N., Kruger, J., Krishna, N., Renard, P., . . . Avchen, R.N. (2016). School district crisis preparedness, response, and recovery plans — United States, 2012. *Morbidity and Mortality Weekly Report (MMWR)*, 65,949–953. doi: http://dx.doi.org/10.15585/mmwr.mm6536a2

Superville, D., & Blad, E. (2014). Philadelphia tragedy highlights role of school nurses. *Education Week, 33*, 7. Retrieved from http://www.edweek.org/ew/articles/2014/06/04/33philly_ep.h33. html?qs=Philadelphia+tragedy+highlights+role+of+school+nurse

Tyack, D. (1992). Health and social services in public schools: Historical perspectives. *The Future of Children, 2*(1): 19-31. doi: 10.2307/1602459 Princeton, NJ: Princeton University. Retrieved from https://www.jstor.org/stable/1602459?seq=1#page_scan_tab_contents

U.S. Code, Title 20, Chapter 33, Subchapter I § 1401(3)(A) (i-ii) & (B)(i-ii)

U.S. Department of Education, National Center for Educational Statistics. (2016). *Data & statistics: Fast facts: Special education: Numbers of students.* Retrieved from http://nces.ed.gov/fastfacts/display.asp?id=64

U.S. Department of Education, Office of Civil Rights (OCR). (2012). *Questions and answers on the ADA Amendments Act of 2008 for students with disabilities attending public elementary and secondary schools*. Retrieved from http://www2.ed.gov/about/offices/list/ocr/docs/dcl-504faq-201109.html

U.S. Department of Education, Office of Civil Rights (OCR). (2015). *Frequently asked questions about Section 504 and the education of children with disabilities*. Retrieved from http://www2.ed.gov/print/about/offices/list/ocr/504faq.html

U.S. Department of Health and Human Services, Health Resources and Services Administration, Maternal and Child Health Bureau. (2013a). *The national survey of children with special health care needs chartbook 2009–2010*. Rockville, Maryland: U.S. Department of Health and Human Services. Retrieved from http://mchb.hrsa.gov/cshcn0910/more/pdf/nscshcn0910.pdf

U.S. Department of Health & Human Services, Centers for Medicare & Medicaid Services. (2013b, January 16). *[Letter to State Health Official & State Medicaid Director] on application of the Mental Health Parity and Addiction Equity Act to Medicaid MCOs, CHIP, and Alternative Benefit (Benchmark) Plans]*. Retrieved from https://www.medicaid.gov/Federal-Policy-Guidance/downloads/SHO-13-001.pdf

U.S. Department of Health and Human Services. (2014). *Healthy People 2020, determinants of health*. Retrieved from http://www.healthypeople.gov/2020/about/DOHAbout.aspx

U.S. Department of Health & Human Services, Office of Adolescent Health, Physical Health & Nutrition. (2016). *Chronic conditions*. Retrieved from http://www.hhs.gov/ash/oah/adolescent-health-topics/physical-health-and-nutrition/chronic-conditions.html

Vinciullo, F.M. & Bradley, B.J. (2009). A correlational study of the relationship between a coordinated school health program and school achievement: A case for school health. *The Journal of School Nursing, 25*(6): 453-465. doi: 10.1177/1059840509351987

Viner, R.M., Ozer, E.M., Denny, S., Marmot, M., Resnick, M., Fatusi, A., & Currie, C. (2012). Adolescence and the social determinants of health. *The Lancet*, 379(9826), 1641–1652. doi: http://dx.doi.org/10.1016/S0140-6736(12)60149-4

Vokits, K., Pumphrey, I., Baker, D., & Krametbauer, K. (2014). Implementation of a stock epinephrine protocol. *NASN School Nurse, 29*(6), 287-291. doi: 10.1177/1942602X14546642

Wang, L.Y., Vernon-Smiley, M., Gapinski, M.A., DeSisto, M., Maughan, E., & Sheetz, A. (2014). Cost-benefit study of school nursing services. *Journal of the American Medical Association Pediatrics, 168*(7), 642-648. doi:10.1001/jamapediatrics.2013.5441

Weist, M.D., Rubin, M., Moore, E., Adelsheim, S., & Wrobel, G. (2007). Mental Health Screening in Schools. *Journal of School Health*, 77(2): 53–58. doi: 10.1111/j.1746-1561.2007.00167.x

Winterfeld, A. (2014). *State actions to reduce and prevent childhood obesity in schools and communities: Summary and analysis of trends in legislation*. Washington, D.C.: National Conference of State Legislatures. Retrieved from http://www.ncsl.org/documents/health/ChildhoodObesity52014.pdf

Wold, S. J. (2005). School health services: History and trends. In N.C. Schwab & M.H.B. Gelfman (Eds.), *Legal issues in school health services: A resource for school administrators, school attorneys, and school nurses,* (pp. 7-54). Lincoln, NE: Authors Choice Press.

Zimmerman, B. (2013). Student health and education plans. In J. Selekman (Ed.), *School nursing: A comprehensive text (2nd ed.)* (pp. 284–314). Philadelphia, PA: F.A. Davis.

Zirkel, P.A. (2009). History and expansion of Section 504 student eligibility: Implications for school nurses. *The Journal of School Nursing, 25*(4): 256-260. doi: 10.1177/1059840509336930

Zirkel, P.A., Granthom, M.R., & Lovato, L. (2012). Section 504 and student health problems: The pivotal position of the school nurse. *The Journal of School Nursing, 28*(6), 423-432. doi: 10.1177/1059840512449358

Chapter 18

CONSIDERATIONS WHEN DEVELOPING SCHOOL HEALTH SERVICES POLICIES

Lee-Ann Halbert, EdDc, JD, RN, MSN, CNM, NCSN

DESCRIPTION OF ISSUE

Nursing policies serve the purpose of giving structure to the practice of nursing in a particular setting. Without policies in place, nurses may not understand why they are to implement certain procedures, which can lead to questionable decision-making. Across a school district the lack of clear policies can lead to inconsistent practice among the members of the school health department. Such inconsistencies may lead to compromised outcomes and possible adverse events for students. This chapter will address how school health policies fit into and support evidence-based school health practice.

The terms "policy," "protocol," and "procedure" must be defined. A policy makes a general statement of "the deliberate course of action chosen by an individual or group to deal with a problem" (Mason, Leavitt, & Chaffee, 2014, p. 3). In the school setting, policies establish the guidelines for the nurse's actions, including, for example, the "administration of medications to schoolchildren" (Mason et al., 2014, p. 3). In the public school setting, board members of the local school districts develop and adopt the policies (Fowler, 2013). A protocol provides "an operational guideline for the implementation of a policy" (Proctor, 2013, p. 73). This is distinguished from a procedure, which is a written direction of how to carry out a particular intervention (Proctor, 2013).

It is important to know, that in adopting policies, there must be some authorization for department staff to do so. Whether by specific delegation of the state's board of education, public health department or by state law, either explicitly or implicitly, the validity of such policies may come under scrutiny or be questioned on the basis of lack of authority to create. Policies must be consistent with state law and other board/department policies. It would be prudent, prior to adopting policies, to seek the advice of board counsel to ensure that policies by the local board of education are in line with state laws and regulations.

BACKGROUND

Nursing policies are statements of what action will be taken in a specific situation (University of Wisconsin, 2016). Policies define, in general terms, how to respond to a situation or how to behave under certain conditions (Sudduth, 2016). These statements do not detail how the action will be implemented. Rather, the purpose is to provide a framework or goal to enable nurses to understand their roles and responsibilities in specific situations. While in the school health office, the nurse may encounter a multiplicity of clinical situations every day. Policies are specific to a particular clinical issue; they are not written to be generalizable to unrelated situations (Krin & Taliaferro, 2013).

The basis for policy creation in the school setting is the requirement that nurses keep patients/clients (i.e., students and staff) safe. The educational setting is a complex one, with both nursing and non-nursing professionals interacting daily. A system such as this may risk the patients' health (in this setting the patients

227

are the students, staff, visitors, and any other individuals to whom the nurse provides care) when these divergent specialties interact. The mere complexity of the system introduces risk to patient safety (Krin & Taliaferro, 2013). Added to this complicated setting is the fact that the primary goal of the setting is education, not healthcare.

Policies provide a "safety net" so nurses know what is expected of them during specific situations. The use of policies supports consistency across a healthcare setting (Patel, 2009). In a school district, the healthcare setting may encompass multiple buildings over a large geographical area. The policies assure that each nurse knows what is expected of him or her under certain conditions. As best as possible, each potential clinical concern should be addressed with the creation of a policy.

Policies are distinct from procedures in their detail. The word "protocol" is sometimes used interchangeably with "procedure," or it may refer to a specific outline of steps that may already be in place by a separate body of experts (Irving, 2016). **Procedures or protocols state exactly what the nurse should do under the conditions of the policy situation. When viewed this way, it is clear that procedures or protocols cannot be implemented without a policy in place to support the intervention of the procedure.**

IMPLICATIONS FOR SCHOOL NURSE PRACTICE

School nurses have a professional obligation to create and recommend policies for school nursing practice. Standard 14, "Quality of Practice," includes the responsibility to "provide critical review and/or evaluation of policies, procedures and/or guidelines to improve the quality of health care and the delivery of school health services" (ANA & NASN, 2017, p. 76).

School nurses should look to see what is done in comparable school settings when developing policies, e.g. substance abuse or zero tolerance policies). NASN and the National Association of State Boards of Education provide statements that apply to school nursing practice that can be used for writing policies. This helps develop what the "standard of care" is for school nurses in the same or similar circumstances. Standard of care is a concept not easily quantifiable; it is the perspective of what should happen if the circumstances were the same or similar to that being identified (Irving, 2016). For school nurses in a rural or remote area, the standard of care may be different from those in practice in an urban setting with emergency facilities just a few minutes away. Additional school policy information needs to be customized to their specific situation or state and specific information for individual states is easily located in a search online. When doing so, the school nurse should take steps to use reputable sites with accurate, evidence based health information.

Krin and Taliaferro (2013) provide a 12-step process for developing school health policies, as follows:

1. Identify the appropriate stakeholder members of a committee to develop the policy.
2. Assess the needs of the school setting for school health policies.
3. Determine what needs exist for a policy, based on the assessment of the setting.
4. Review available literature and data that pertain to the issue and policy.
5. Create a first draft of the policy.
6. Invite stakeholders to examine and comment on the draft of the policy.
7. Use the reviewers' comments to revise and finalize the policy.

8. Follow the procedure for the approval process of the document.
9. Distribute the new policy to all appropriate individuals.
10. Put the policy into place using supportive trainings and meetings as necessary.
11. Using a specific review schedule, re-evaluate the policy for efficacy of the policy.
12. If procedures are not already in place for the policy, develop them.

An additional issue when creating a policy is to consider what the potential consequences are for not working within the policy. Depending on the violation, the nurse who works outside the stated policies may face repercussions from the state Board of Nursing, civil suit, criminal charges, or a job action. The specific consequences will depend on the individual policy violation, and at what level it occurred. For example consider the following, if the nurse abided by the state Nurse Practice Act but did not follow the school policy, the nurse may be at risk for a personnel action from his/her school. If the violation is of a criminal nature, in addition to violating the state Nurse Practice Act, then the nurse may be also held criminally responsible.

CONCLUSION

It is tempting to assume that the school nurse is the one individual who should create policies without enlisting the support of non-nurse professionals. However, school nursing policies inform nurses regarding what to do in the educational environment. School nurses cannot separate the school setting from nursing practice when writing health policies. School health policies should support student health and academic achievement. Multiple individuals may be involved in this process.

When creating school health policies, it is essential to understand that these policies foster uniformity of response across the district for student safety. What is recommended to be done at one school should be consistent with recommendations for a different school within the same district for a similar population. This does not mean all policies will be exactly the same for all student populations; it is possible that some populations will require different policies, such as with self-carry policies of emergency medications that developmentally and age appropriate.

Finally, it is imperative to understand the distinction between policies and procedures. Policies must be in place to know what procedure is needed and under specific circumstances. The procedure (or protocol) will delineate how the intervention is completed.

RESOURCES

NASN (2016) has a substantial library of position statements, resolutions and consensus statements, and joint statements available online. These papers and statements can be used as resources for creating policies for school health. The full listing of these documents is found at this site: https://www.nasn.org/portals/0/binder_papers_reports.pdf

The Centers for Disease Control and Prevention (CDC) (2016) has a section on Adolescent and School Health. Within this section the CDC has literature on implementing policies on specific health issues, including HIV/STD Prevention. These can be located at https://www.cdc.gov/healthyyouth/about/policy.htm

The National Association of State Boards of Education (NASBE) (n.d.) maintains a State School Health Policy Database accessible at http://www.nasbe.org/healthy_schools/hs/index.php

The information is searchable by state enabling school nurses to determine what laws are in place regulating how care may be delivered in the school setting.

REFERENCES

American Nurses Association & National Association of School Nurses. (2017). *Scope and standards of practice: School nursing* (3rd ed). Silver Spring, MD: Author.

Fowler, F.C. (2013). *Policy studies for educational leaders: An introduction* (4th ed.). Boston, MA: Pearson.

Krin, P., & Taliaferro, V. (2013). Establishing policies and procedures: The core of school nursing practice. In C. Costante (Ed.), *School nurse administrators: Leadership and management.* Silver Spring, MD: National Association of School Nurses.

Irving, A. (2016). Policies and procedures for healthcare organizations: A risk management perspective. *Patient Safety and Quality Care* (e-newsletter). Retrieved from http://www.psqh.com/analysis/policies-and-procedures-for-healthcare-organizations-a-risk-management-perspective/

Mason, D.J., Leavitt, J.K., & Chaffee, M.W. (Eds.). (2014). *Policy and politics in nursing and health care* (6th ed.). St. Louis, MO: Elsevier.

Patel, C.S. (2009). Development of clinical policies and guidelines in acute settings. *Nursing Standard, 23*(27), 42-47. https://doi.org/10.7748/ns2009.03.23.27.42.c6837

Proctor, S. (2013). Standards of practice. In J. Selekman (Ed.), *School nursing: A comprehensive text* (2d ed.) (pp. 49-78). Philadelphia, PA: F.A. Davis Company.

Sudduth, A.L. (2016). Program evaluation. In J.A. Milstead (Ed.), *Health policy and politics: A nurse's guide* (5th ed.) (pp. 189-216). Burlington, MA: Jones and Bartlett Learning.

University of Wisconsin (2016). *Nursing resources: Standard, guideline, protocol, policy.* Retrieved from http://researchguides.ebling.library.wisc.edu/c.php?g=293229&p=1953402

Chapter 19

RESPONSIBILITIES IN THE SCHOOL SETTING FOR CHILD PROTECTION

Patricia K. Bednarz, RN, MN, FNASN

DESCRIPTION OF ISSUE

One of the most challenging roles for school nurses is protecting students from child maltreatment and at the same time supporting families to reduce the risk of further harm. Federal legislation, governmental agencies and the literature utilize the terms "child abuse and neglect" and "child maltreatment", therefore, this document will use the terms interchangeably, depending upon the source. Federal legislation lays the groundwork for state laws on child maltreatment by identifying a minimum set of acts or behaviors that define child abuse and neglect (Child Welfare Information Gateway, 2013). All states and U.S. territories have laws to protect children from child abuse, the criteria needed for outside intervention and identifying mandated reporters (Child Information Welfare Gateway, 2015a; Selekman, Pelt, Garnier, & Baker, 2013; Taliaferro & Resha, 2016; and National Association of School Nurses [NASN], 2013). School district policies and procedures should reflect state specific requirements and the defined roles of school personnel for recognizing and reporting child abuse and neglect (Laubin, Schwab & Doyle, 2012).

Kraft & Eriksson (2015) emphasized that child maltreatment is a global public health issue with major consequences for the individual child and society. In more recent years, there has been federal legislation to protect children from sex trafficking and female genital mutilation, also considered child maltreatment. The integration and coordination of social service, legal, health, mental health, domestic violence services, education, and substance abuse agencies and community-based organizations is imperative to prevent, identify and respond to the complex problem of child abuse (Child Abuse Prevention and Treatment Act [CAPTA], 2010).

BACKGROUND

Definitions

One of the key pieces of child maltreatment legislation is the Child Abuse Prevention and Treatment Act (CAPTA) that was most recently reauthorized in 2010 (CAPTA, 2010). CAPTA (2010) defined the term 'child abuse and neglect' as "any recent act or failure to act on the part of a parent or caretaker, which results in death, serious physical or emotional harm, sexual abuse or exploitation, or an act or failure to act which presents an imminent risk of serious harm" (p.6). The definition of child is a person under 18 years of age and not an emancipated minor (Child Welfare Information Gateway, 2016a). CAPTA does not provide specific definitions for physical abuse, neglect or emotional abuse although it does provide a definition of sexual abuse and cases of neglect related to withholding or failing to provide medical treatment (Child Welfare Information Gateway, 2016a).

It is critical to know that each state provides its own definitions of maltreatment within civil and criminal statutes generally including definitions of neglect, physical abuse, sexual abuse, and emotional abuse (Child

Welfare Information Gateway, 2016a) and to know the requirements of these statutes. School nurses can access individual state statutes at the Child Welfare Information Gateway (2016b).

The Centers for Disease Control and Prevention (CDC) (2016) defined child abuse and neglect as act or series of acts of commission or omission by a parent or other caregiver (e.g., clergy, coach, teacher) that results in harm, potential for harm, or threat of harm to a child. Acts of commission included physical abuse, sexual abuse and psychological abuse (CDC, 2016). Acts of omission included physical neglect, emotional neglect, medical and dental neglect, educational neglect, inadequate supervision, and exposure to violent environments (CDC, 2016). The CDC (2016) emphasized the need for a consistent definition to monitor the incidence of child abuse and neglect and to examine trends over time. The Child Information Welfare Gateway (2013) provides information about recognizing the signs and symptoms of child abuse and neglect.

Prevalence

The World Health Organization (WHO) (2016) stated that a quarter of all adults report having been physically abused as children and one in five women and one in 13 men report having been sexually abused as a child. The CDC (2014) reported that in 2012, U.S. state and local child protective services (CPS) received an estimated 3.4 million referrals of children being abused or neglected. The CDC (2014) further reported that of the child victims, 78% were victims of neglect; 18% of physical abuse; 9% of sexual abuse; and 11% were victims of other types of maltreatment, including emotional and threatened abuse, parent's drug/alcohol abuse, or lack of supervision. Other data reported by the CDC (2014) indicated that in 2012, an estimated 1,640 children died from child maltreatment (rate of 2.2 per 100,000 children). Age was shown to be an important factor for child abuse as 27% of victims were younger than 3 years, 20% of victims were age 3-5 years, with children younger than 1 year having the highest rate of victimization (21.9 per 1,000 children) (CDC, 2014). The perpetrators were found to be parents (80.3%), relatives other than parents (6.1%), and unmarried partners of the parents (4.2%) (CDC, 2014). The WHO (2016) identified characteristics of a child that may increase the likelihood of being maltreated, such as, being either under four years old or an adolescent; being unwanted, or failing to fulfil the expectations of parents; and having special needs, crying persistently or having abnormal physical features. Sabella (2016) identified indications of a history of sexual abuse, such as, inappropriate sexual knowledge, age-inappropriate sexual interest, and acting out sexually.

Victims of commercial sexual exploitation rarely self-identify but may have a history of running away from home, truancy, child maltreatment, involvement with CPS or the juvenile justice system, multiple sexually transmitted infections (STI), pregnancy, or substance use or abuse problems (Greenbaum, Crawford-Jakubiak, & Committee on Child Abuse and Neglect, 2015; Child Welfare Information Gateway, 2015b). Grace, Starck, Potenza, Kenney, & Sheetz (2012) specified that commercial sexual exploitation is sexual abuse. All children under the age of 18 who are induced to engage in commercial sex are victims of sex trafficking according to the Victims of Trafficking and Violence Protection Act of 2000 (U.S. Department of State, 2000). Examples of commercial sex trafficking that may involve minors include prostitution, pornography, and sex tourism (Child Welfare Information Gateway, 2015b). Many states have their own definitions of commercial sexual exploitation and sexually exploited children that will impact how children are treated (victims or delinquents) (Child Welfare Information Gateway, 2015b). Grace et al., (2012) indicated that school nurses cannot address this complex issue alone as it requires increased awareness by school personnel, as well as collaboration with child protective services, law enforcement, social services and a range of supportive agencies. The U.S.

Department of Education (USDE) (2015) indicated that to build healthy learning environments, educators must be knowledgeable about the signs of child trafficking, and the steps to take when behaviors at school are out of order.

Female genital mutilation and cutting (FMG/C) is child abuse and a reportable event (Novak, 2016). Most FGM/C cases are thought to take place between the ages of five and eight and therefore girls within that age bracket are at a higher risk (HM Government, 2014). Novak (2016) reported that FGM/C which has been prevalent in immigrant communities, was labeled a violation of human rights by the international community and emphasized the need for school nurses to understand the cultural, legal and social consequences. Currently, 24 states have laws addressing FGM/C that can be found at http:// www.equalitynow.org/sites/ default/files/ EN_FAQ_FGM_in_US.pdf (Equity Now, 2015).

Legal Framework for Child Protection

It is important for school nurses to understand that states specify what can be defined as child maltreatment in their particular jurisdiction and provide specific reporting standards. According to the USDHHS (2003) the law clearly specifies that reports must be made when the educator "suspects" or "has reasonable cause to believe" that there is abuse (p.30). The USDHHS (2003) explained that all states require an oral or written report (or both) be made to the agency or agencies responsible for child abuse and neglect, often within 24 – 48 hours.

The Child Welfare Information Gateway (2015a) provides a framework to help understand federal legislation that has affected child welfare. The U.S. Department of Health and Human Services (USDHHS) (2003) indicated that the involvement of educators in reporting child abuse and neglect is guided by federal standards and regulations and mandated by state and local laws, which identify what is required of the educator and how that obligation is to be fulfilled.

The three federal laws listed below pertain to child maltreatment.

Federal Law

Law	Brief Description
CAPTA Reauthorization Act of 2010 P.L. 111-320 Retrieved from https://www.childwelfare.gov/topics/systemwide/laws-policies/federal/search/?CWIGFunctionsaction=federallegislation:main.getFedLedgDetail&id=142	Enacted December 20, 2010 Purpose: To amend and reauthorize the Child Abuse Prevention and Treatment Act, the Family Violence Prevention and Services Act, the Child Abuse Prevention and Treatment and Adoption Reform Act of 1978, and the Abandoned Infants Assistance Act of 1988, and for other purposes.
Justice for Victims of Trafficking Act of 2015 P.L. 114-22 Retrieved from https://www.childwelfare.gov/topics/systemwide/laws-policies/federal/search/?CWIGFunctionsaction=federallegislation:main.getFedLedgDetail&id=162	Enacted May 29, 2015 Purpose: To provide justice for the victims of trafficking through grants to States for child abuse investigation and prosecution programs, services for victims of child pornography, and domestic child human trafficking deterrence programs. The act also authorized specialized training programs for law enforcement officers, first responders, health-care and child welfare officials, juvenile justice personnel, prosecutors, and judicial personnel to identify victims and acts of child human trafficking and to facilitate the rescue of child victims of human trafficking.
18 U.S. Code § 116 - Female genital mutilation Retrieved from https://www.law.cornell.edu/uscode/text/18/116	Purpose: The federal law addressing Female Genital Mutilation (FGM) in the U.S. makes it illegal to perform FGM in the U.S. or knowingly transport a girl out of the U.S. for purpose of inflicting FGM (Equity Now, 2016).

IMPLICATIONS FOR SCHOOL NURSE PRACTICE

School nurses play a key role in identifying and reporting child maltreatment as well as making sure that students receive the necessary counseling and support (Beard, 2014). Kraft & Eriksson (2015) found that both knowledge and experience were necessary for detecting and interpreting the signs of suspected child abuse but that lack of personal experience could be compensated through supervision, consultation, and networking with more experienced colleagues. Grace et al., (2012) suggested that because school nurses have open door policies and opportunities to observe students across grade levels, they are in a unique position to identify students at risk and intervene appropriately. Kraft, Rahm and Eriksson (2016) studied the ability of school nurses to detect and support child sexual abuse (CSA) and found school nurses avoided CSA due to arousal of strong emotions, ambivalence and a complicated disclosure process.

It is essential for school nurses to understand that they are among those legally required to report suspected child maltreatment (NASN, 2013). Although all states designate teachers as mandated reporters, other school employee mandated reporters vary by state (Child Welfare Information Gateway, 2012). If a mandated reporter does not report pertinent information within the legally required time, the reporter may be in violation of child protection and reporting laws. The Child Information Welfare Gateway (2015a) indicated that the circumstances under which a mandatory reporter must make a report vary from state to state but typically a report must be made when the reporter, in his or her official capacity, suspects or has reason to believe that a child has been abused or neglected. All jurisdictions have provisions in statute to maintain the confidentiality of abuse and neglect records (Child Information Welfare Gateway, 2015a). School nurses should verify their individual state requirements for reporting child maltreatment as they vary from state to state. Reporting child abuse and neglect can't be delegated to others (Laubin et al., 2012). School nurses can work collaboratively with other school personnel, such as, counselors, psychologists, teachers, administrators to support at-risk children, be a resource for child welfare agencies and refer families for additional services and support (Child Welfare Information Gateway, 2012).

School nurses can follow the NASN *Framework for the 21st Century School Nursing Practice* to prevent and protect students from child abuse and neglect (NASN, 2016). Public Health, leadership, care coordination, quality improvement and the *School Nursing: Scope and Standards Practice* (ANA & NASN, 2017) are the key principles of the framework that provide the foundation for the specialty practice of school nursing. The NASN's (2014) position statement, *Care of Victims of Child Maltreatment: The School Nurse's Role* indicates that school nurses serve a vital role in the recognition of early signs of child maltreatment, assessment, identification, intervention, reporting, referral and follow-up of children in need. *The Framework for 21st Century School Nursing Practice* and *School Nursing: Scope and Standards* and the NASN position statement together establish the basis for school nurses to intervene on behalf of students experiencing child maltreatment.

Scope and Standards of School Nursing Practice

- School nurses need to be current with the research, clinical practice, laws, and regulations regarding child maltreatment (NASN, 2013).
- School nurses need to be aware of their individual state law regarding reporting child maltreatment (Beard, 2014; NASN, 2013).
- School nurses need to know the law for exchange of information with those who have with services appropriate to investigation and treatment of Female Genital Mutilation/Cutting as well as an understanding of local immigration policies and practices to provide accurate counsel for students and families (Novak, 2016).
- School nurses need to understand that as a mandated reporter, they must make the decision to report regardless of what the supervisor or building administrator may say (Laubin et al., 2012; Selekman et al., 2013).
- School nurses need to understand that it is not their responsibility to conduct the investigation to determine whether abuse exists (Selekman et al., 2013).

Policy Development and Implementation

- Work with school administrators to ensure school district policies and procedures are in accord with state law and reflect the clearly defined roles and responsibilities of school personnel related to the recognition and reporting of suspected abuse and neglect (Laubin et al., 2012). The USDHHS (2003) provides guidance on developing school policies and procedures.

- Be aware that state agencies, such as department of child protection or a department of education may publish guidelines for schools that should be used in the training of staff and development of policies and procedures (Laubin et al., 2012).

- Know policies and procedures of the school or district for the process of reporting child maltreatment (NASN, 2013).

- Work with school administrators to develop policies about how to respond to a disclosure about sexual exploitation. The USDE (2015) identified the importance of developing and clearly articulating district- or school-wide policies on and protocols for identifying a suspected victim or responding to a disclosure from a suspected victim of child trafficking. Grace et al., (2012) suggested the child trafficking policy could be an addendum to the existing child abuse reporting protocol. The school policy should include assessment for safety concerns, immediate notification of school authorities, maintenance of confidentiality, documentation of the conversations, and filing of a report to the child protective services (Grace et al., 2012). The USDE (2015) provided a sample protocol for schools regarding child trafficking at https://safesupportivelearning.ed.gov/human-trafficking-americas-schools/sample-protocol-school-districts.

- Be knowledgeable about the problem of female genital mutilation and have a coordinated plan to protect and treat students who have been affected by this procedure (Novak, 2016).

Documentation

- Follow state law and school district policies and procedures for documenting and retaining records for suspected child maltreatment and sexual exploitation (Grace et al., 2012).

- Record the questions asked and answers given, as well as the sources for all of the information (Selekman et al., 2013).

- Document the child's and parent/guardian(s) response verbatim (Taliaferro & Resha, 2016).

- Use a body diagram noting all cutaneous lesions by size, location, and color (Glick, Lorand & Bilka, 2016).

- Include additional information, such as partial names, nicknames, addresses, last known contact, vehicle information when reporting sexual exploitation (Grace et al., 2012).

Surveillance

- Identify students who have been abused and neglected. Selekman et al., (2013) indicated that students seen in the health office can be assessed for malnutrition, body hygiene and suspicious injuries. Selekman et al. (2013) pointed out that one of the hallmarks of abuse is that stories don't match.

- Identify students with frequent somatic complaints that may be indicators of maltreatment (NASN, 2013).

- Know the signs of potential indicators of trafficking and exploitation described by the National Center for Missing and Exploited Children (2010) that include:
  1. History of emotional, sexual, or other physical abuse.
  2. Signs of current physical abuse and/or sexually transmitted diseases.
  3. History of running away or current status as a runaway.

4. Inexplicable appearance of expensive gifts, clothing or other costly items.

5. Presence of an older boyfriend/girlfriend.

6. Drug addiction.

7. Withdrawal or lack of interest in previous activities.

8. Gang involvement.

- Understand that male and female victims of sex trafficking and commercial exploitation of children may present for medical care for a variety of reasons related to trauma, infection, reproductive issues, and mental health problems (Greenbaum et al., 2015).

Prevention

- Educate and support staff regarding the signs and symptoms of child maltreatment (NASN, 2013; Selekman et al., 2013).

- Provide personal body safety education to students (NASN, 2013).

- Advocate and refer parent/guardian(s) to effective programs that support parent/guardian(s) and teach positive parenting skills, such as, home visiting programs by nurses to provide support, education and resources (Hodgkinson, Beers, Southammakosane, & Lewin, 2015; Pinzon, Jones, & Committee on Adolescence, and Committee on Early Childhood, 2012; WHO, 2016).

  o Understand that teen mothers may hold less realistic developmental expectations for their children (Pinzon et al., 2012). The Child Welfare Information gateway provides at tip sheet for teen parents at: https://www.childwelfare.gov/pubPDFs/teen.pdf

  o Provide resources for parents. The Child Welfare Information Gateway provides general resources and tips for parents at: https://www.childwelfare.gov/topics/preventing/promoting/parenting/general/

- Assist teen parents in accessing a primary care setting with a multidisciplinary treatment team (Hodgkinson et al., 2015).

Direct Care

- Understand that the immediate concern is to ensure that the student is safe and that any urgent or life-threatening medical conditions are addressed (Sabella, 2016).

- Support the victims of child maltreatment (NASN, 2013). Support is one of the protective factors that assist children in avoiding some of the negative health, emotional, and violent outcomes that can be associated with a history of child maltreatment (Beard, 2014). Listen to what the student is saying, be supportive and nonjudgmental, remain calm and assure the student they were right in telling the nurse (Sabella, 2016).

- Assess for any immediate safety concerns, understanding that this information cannot be kept in confidence (Grace et al., 2012).

- Explain to the student that information will not be discussed with other students but must be reported if there is anything that could bring harm to the student or others (Grace et al., 2012; Selekman et al., 2013). Consider that sexual exploitation carries additional stigma and should be handled with great care and discretion (Grace et al., 2012).

Collaborative Communication

- Follow state and school district mandatory guidelines for reporting child abuse/neglect (Taliaferro & Resha, 2016). Some State statutes will specify the type of information to submit in a report of suspected child maltreatment, such as, student's name, age, gender, and address; parent's name and address; nature and extent of the injury or condition observed; prior injuries and when observed; actions taken by the reporter (e.g., talking with the child); where the act occurred; reporter's name, location, and contact information (U.S. Department of Health and Human Services, 2003) (p 31).

- Link and refer victims and families to community resources (NASN, 2013; Beard, 2014). Refer children who have been abused to healthcare professionals who specialize in working with children who have been abused (Sabella, 2016).

- Collaborate with community organizations to raise awareness and reduce incidence (NASN, 2013).

- Work to establish/improve systematic collaboration and a trustful relationship with Children's Protective Services that can be accomplished by general repeated meetings, setting common guidelines, and consultations (Kraft & Eriksson, 2015).

Social Determinants of Health and Health Equity

- Work toward a comprehensive approach that includes recognizing the diversity of ethnic, cultural, and religious beliefs and traditions that may impact child rearing patterns, while not allowing the differences in those beliefs and traditions to enable abuse or neglect (CAPTA, 2010).

- Understand the student populations that may be at more risk for child maltreatment. "African-American children, American Indian children, Alaska native children, and children of multiple races and ethnicities experience the highest rates of child abuse or neglect" (CAPTA, 2010, p.5). The CDC (2014) reported the 2012 rates of victimization per 1,000 children were 14.2 for African Americans, 12.4 for American Indian/Alaska Natives, 10.3 for Multiracial, 8.7 for Pacific Islanders, 8.4 for Hispanics, 8.0 for non-Hispanic Whites, and 1.7 for Asians.

- Understand that recent research indicates that not all parents who experienced childhood maltreatment will perpetrate child abuse or neglect and that most parents who experienced maltreatment will not abuse or neglect their own children (The Child Welfare Information Gateway, 2016c)

- Understand that as with all sensitive and important meetings in the school, a family member, friend, or the student should not be used for interpretation (Novak, 2016).

WARNING

Red Flags

Detailed and lengthy questions used for screening child sexual abuse are best left to those with appropriate training and credentials (Sabella, 2016). A nurse may be well intentioned but may find that in a court of law, they could be accused of asking leading questions (Sabella, 2016).

CONCLUSION

Protecting students from child maltreatment requires knowledge about federal, state, and local law; school district policies and procedures; community resources; and current research that identifies emerging issues and strategies for intervention. School nurses can identify students at risk for child maltreatment and intervene on behalf of them to help them reach academic success and remain safe in their home and community environment.

RESOURCES

American Nurses Association and National Association of School Nurses. (2017). *School nursing: Scope and standards of practice* (3rd ed.). Silver Springs, MD: author.

Child Information Welfare Gateway (2013). *What is child abuse and neglect? Recognizing signs and symptoms.* Washington, DC: U.S. Department of Health and Human Services, Children's Bureau. Retrieved from https://www.childwelfare.gov/pubPDFs/whatiscan.pdf

Childhelp National Child Abuse Hotline is staffed 24 hours a day, 7 days a week, with professional crisis counselors who have access to a database of 55,000 emergency, social service, and support resources. All calls are anonymous. Contact them at 1.800.4.A.CHILD (1.800.422.4453).

National Child Traumatic Stress Network provides information in English and Spanish to parents whose children have been sexually abused. Information can be retrieved from www.nctsn.org/trauma-types/sexual-abuse

Polaris Project is a national resource for those who have been trafficked or forced into prostitution and need help getting out. Information can be retrieved from www.polarisproject.org

REFERENCES

American Nurses' Association and National Association of School Nurses. (2017). *School nursing: Scope and standards of practice.* (3rd ed.) Silver Spring, MD: Authors.

Beard, J.W. (2014). Adolescents and child maltreatment. *NASN School Nurse, 29*(2), 71-74. doi: 10.1177/1942602X13517721

Child Abuse and Prevention Treatment Act as Amended by P.L.111-320 the CAPTA reauthorization Act of 2010 (42 U.S.C. 5101 et seq; 42 U.S.C. 5116 et seq). Retrieved from https://www.acf.hhs.gov/sites/default/files/cb/capta2010.pdf

Centers for Disease Control and Prevention. (2016). *Child abuse and child neglect: Definitions.* Retrieved from http://www.cdc.gov/ViolencePrevention/childmaltreatment/definitions.html

Centers for Disease Control and Prevention. (2014). *Child maltreatment facts at a glance.* Retrieved from http://www.cdc.gov/violenceprevention/pdf/childmaltreatment-facts-at-a-glance.pdf

Child Welfare Information Gateway. (2012). *What is child welfare? A guide for educators.* Retrieved from https://www.childwelfare.gov/pubPDFs/cw_educators.pdf

Child Welfare Information Gateway. (2016a). *Definitions of child abuse and neglect in Federal law.* Washington, DC: U.S. Department of Health and Human Services, Children's Bureau. Retrieved from https://www.childwelfare.gov/topics/can/defining/federal/

Child Welfare Information Gateway. (2016b). *State statutes search.* Washington, DC: U.S. Department of Health and Human Services, Children's Bureau. Retrieved from https://www.childwelfare.gov/topics/systemwide/laws-policies/state/

Child Welfare Information Gateway. (2016c). *Intergenerational patterns of child maltreatment: What the evidence shows.* Washington, DC: U.S. Department of Health and Human Services, Children's Bureau. Retrieved from https://www.childwelfare.gov/pubs/issue-briefs/intergenerational/

Child Welfare Information Gateway. (2015a). *Mandatory reporters of child abuse and neglect. State Statutes.* Washington, DC: *U.S. Department of Health and Human Services, Children's Bureau.* Retrieved from https://www.childwelfare.gov/pubPDFs/manda.pdf#page=1&view=Introduction

Child Welfare Information Gateway. (2015b). *Child welfare and human trafficking* [Issue Brief 2015]. Washington, DC: U.S. Department of Health and Human Services, Children's Bureau. Retrieved from https://www.childwelfare.gov/pubPDFs/trafficking.pdf

Child Information Welfare Gateway. (2013). *What is child abuse and neglect? Recognizing signs and symptoms.* Washington, DC: *U.*S. Department of Health and Human Services, Children's Bureau. Retrieved from https://www.childwelfare.gov/pubPDFs/whatiscan.pdf

Equity Now. (2016). *Female genital mutilation in the United States.* Retrieved from http://www.equalitynow.org/sites/default/files/EN_FAQ_FGM_in_US.pdf

Glick, J.C., Lorand, M.A., & Bilka, K.R. (2016). Physical abuse of children. *Pediatrics in Review, 37*(4), 146-158. doi:10.1542/pir.2015-001

Grace, L.G., Starck, M., Potenza, J., Kenney, P.A., & Sheetz, A.H. (2012). Commercial sexual exploitation of children and the school nurse. *The Journal of School Nursing, 28*(6), 410-417. doi: 10.1177/1059840512448402

Greenbaum, J., Crawford-Jakubiak, J.E., & Committee on Child Abuse and Neglect (2015). Child sex trafficking and commercial sexual exploitation: Health care needs of victims. *Pediatrics, 135*(3), 566- 574. doi:10.1542/peds.2014-4138

HM Government. (2014). Multiagency practice guidelines: Female genital mutilation. Retrieved from https://www.gov.uk/government/ uploads/attachment_data/file/38125/ MultiAgencyPracticeGuidelinesNov14.pdf

Hodgkinson, S., Beers, L., Southammakosane, C., & Lewin, A. (2014). Addressing the mental health needs of pregnant and parenting adolescents. *Pediatrics, 113*(1), 114-122. doi: 10.1542/peds.2013-0927

Kraft, L.H. & Eriksson, U. (2015). The school nurse's ability to detect and support abused children: A trust creating process. *The Journal of School Nursing, 31*(5), 353-362. doi: 10.1177/1059840514550483

Kraft, L.H., Rahm, G., & Eriksson, U. (2016). School nurses avoid addressing child sexual abuse. *The Journal of School Nursing*, published online before print. doi: 10.1177/1059840516633729

Laubin, M., Schwab, N.C., & Doyle J. (2012). Understanding the legal landscape. In C. Costante, (Ed.) *School Nurse administrators: Leadership and management,* (pp.59-519). *Silver* Spring, Maryland: National Association of School Nurses.

National Association of School Nurses. (2013). *Child maltreatment: The role of the school nurse* [Issue Brief]. *NASN School Nurse, 28*(3), 167-168. doi: 10.1177/1942602X13478381

National Association of School Nurses. (2014). *Care of victims of child maltreatment: The school nurse's role* (Position Statement). Silver Spring, MD: Author. Retrieved from http://www.nasn.org/PolicyAdvocacy/ PositionPapersandReports/NASNPositionStatementsFullView/tabid/462/ArticleId/639/Child-Maltreatment-Care-of-Victims-of-The-School-Nurse-s-Role-Adopted-January-2014

National Association of School Nurses. (2016). Framework for the 21st century school nursing practice. *NASN School Nurse. 31*(1), 45-53. doi: 10.1177/194,602X15618644

National Center for Missing & Exploited Children. (2010). *Commercial sexual exploitation: A fact sheet*. Retrieved from http://www.missingkids.com/en_US/documents/CCSE_Fact_Sheet.pdf

Novak. B. (2016). The school nurse's role in addressing female genital mutilation. *NASN School Nurse*, published online before print. doi:10.1177/1942602X16648193

Pinzon, J.L., Jones, V.F., & Committee on Adolescence and Committee on Early Childhood, 2012. Care of adolescent parents and their children. *Pediatrics, 130*(6), e1743-e1756. doi: 10.1542/peds.2012-2879

Sabella, D. (2016). Revisiting child sexual abuse and survivor issues. *American Journal of Nursing, 116*(3), 48-54. doi: 10.1097/01.NAJ.0000481280.22557.45

Sabella, A. (2016, August 12). Most states allow religious exemptions from child abuse and neglect laws. *Pew Research Center*. Retrieved from http://www.pewresearch.org/fact-tank/2016/08/12/most-states-allow-religious-exemptions-from-child-abuse-and-neglect-laws/

Selekman, J., Pelt, P., Garnier, S., & Baker, D. (2013). Youth violence. In J. Selekman (Ed.), *School nursing: A comprehensive text* (2nd ed.) (pp. 1087-1117). Philadelphia, PA: F.A. Davis

Taliaferro, V., & Resha, C. (Eds.). (2016). Child maltreatment. *2016 School Nurse Resource Manual,* (pp.441 - 444). Nashville, TN: School Health Alert.

U.S. Department of Education, Office of Safe and Healthy Students. (2015). *Human trafficking in America's schools.* Washington, D.C., 2015. Retrieved from http://safesupportivelearning.ed.gov/human-trafficking-americas-school

U.S. Department of Health and Human Services. (2003). *The role of educators in preventing and responding to child abuse and neglect*. Retrieved from the Child Information Welfare Gateway at https://www.childwelfare.gov/pubPDFs/educator.pdf

U.S. Department of State. (2000). *Victims of Trafficking and Violence Protection Act of 2*000. Retrieved from http://www.state.gov/j/tip/laws/61124.htm

World Health Organization. (2016). *Child maltreatment*. Retrieved from http://www.who.int/mediacentre/factsheets/fs150/en/

Chapter 20

DO NOT ATTEMPT TO RESUSCITATE (DNAR) IN THE SCHOOL SETTING

Suzanne Putman, MEd, BSN, RN

DESCRIPTION OF ISSUE

There is a growing population of students who are routinely attending school with complex, chronic diseases and serious illnesses, including terminal and irreversible conditions. Medical advances in the diagnosis and treatment of chronic diseases, which were once considered fatal, are now being effectively treated, keeping school-aged children and adolescents living longer. While federal legislation supports school attendance by students with complex health needs, managing those needs can be a challenge. As the health needs of students who attend school with chronic diseases and serious illnesses continue to grow, the likelihood that a school district will be asked to honor a *Do Not Attempt to Resuscitate* (DNAR) order increases. The sensitivity of this issue, the variation of legal guidelines between states, and the interests of those involved make this a complex, challenging issue for school nurses. The paucity of information on this topic as it relates to school health and school nurse practice further makes this a difficult policy for school nurses to implement. Information needed to plan for the student with a DNAR order will be addressed in this chapter.

It is important to understand the terminology used when planning the care for end of life decisions. In the school setting, non-medical staff may view a DNAR order as "doing nothing" rather than providing supportive comfort care without prolonging the life-limiting condition. Allow Natural Death (AND) is another term that may be used. The shift toward palliative care brings about orders for comfort care referred to as Medical or Physician Orders for Life Sustaining Treatment (MOLST or POLST) (Zacharski et al., 2013).

BACKGROUND

Today's medical advancements have led to a growing population of school-aged students attending school who have survived, who are living with, or who are recovering from complex, serious health conditions. Rehm (2002) attributes this to increased survival rates in children with congenital or genetic conditions, as well as chronic conditions such as cystic fibrosis, cancer, human immunodeficiency virus and severe prematurity. Medical technological advances have transformed care from hospital settings to home and community, including schools. Other influences are related to increased activism by disability groups, and federal laws mandating access to education for students with disabilities (Rehm, 2002). Federal legislation guarantees all children, including those with chronic and serious health conditions a free and appropriate public education.

A comprehensive study by van Dyck, Kogan, McPherson, Weissman and Newacheck (2001) using a complex, multistage sample design found that 12.8% of children in the United States have a special health need. More recently, Bethell, et al. (2011) reported chronic health conditions in 19.2% of school-age children. Brenner, Wheeler, Wolfe, Vernon-Smiley, and Caldart-Olson (2007) states that 34.8% of U.S. schools have medically fragile students. Lastly, a policy statement issued by the American Academy of Pediatrics (AAP) reports that each day there are 3900 school-aged children within 6 months of dying from a chronic condition (2010).

In spite of this overwhelming evidence of the prevalence of students with chronic health conditions in the school setting, a frequently cited study reports that only a small percentage (20 percent) of school districts have a policy or procedure in place for honoring DNAR orders (Kimberly, Forte, Carroll, & Feudtner, 2005a). According to Weise (2010), this study was made available by the *American Journal of Bioethics* for commentary. This discussion sparked comments that underscore why a DNAR order for a student can be such a sensitive issue when presented to a school district. Concerns surfaced regarding legal liability, the nonmedical school staff's ability to make a critical medical judgment, and the potential traumatic impact on staff and students. The vulnerability, rights, and duty to protect students with life-limiting conditions from painful and ineffective interventions were also of concern. Others communicated agreement with honoring the DNAR order, that end of life decisions that had been made with thorough consideration by the parent/guardian(s) and their healthcare provider should not be taken lightly and are in the best interest of the child.

The AAP (2010) points out that laws regarding honoring DNAR requests in schools differ between states and that there are challenges in honoring a DNAR outside of the inpatient healthcare setting. In an article published by Zacharski et al. (2013) concerns related to fears of liability, lack of school nurses, and moral distress were factors of concern, stating that "school administrators, staff and school nurses feel uncomfortable and ill prepared when confronted by DNAR discussions" (p. 72). Yet, White (2005) points out that in the study by Kimberly et al. (2005b) "the authors overlook the pivotal role that the school nurses play with respect to DNAR orders as well as the delivery of school healthcare in general" (p. 83). Kimberly et al., (2005b), in a response to the selected commentaries, "emphasized a fundamental point of regret for not stressing in the article, namely the crucial role that school nurses play in caring for these children" (White 2005; Costante 1998).

The AAP (2010) identifies the school nurse as the pivotal person to facilitate the development of an Individualized Healthcare Plan (IHP) and Emergency Care Plan (ECP), which communicates the plans for end-of-life care for an individual student in the school setting. The Individuals with Disabilities Education Act (IDEA) (2004) is the federal law that gives students with chronic health conditions the right to attend school, although the challenge is whether the spirit of the law requires schools to make accommodations for the DNAR. Previous court decisions have consistently supported the "parent's right to make decisions on behalf of a minor child" (Deutch, 2015, p. 15). Additionally, competing interests (parent/guardian(s), medical community, school boards, school administrators, teachers' unions) can make this a particularly difficult policy to implement. Traditionally, in the medical setting, there is a multidisciplinary team approach to decisions pertaining to the implementation of a DNAR order, which is often lacking in the educational setting. It is important for the school nurse to understand these varied issues and keep the medical, developmental, social and spiritual needs of the student foremost when planning for care. Educating school staff on terminology and interventions, as outlined in the emergency care plan, can help ease apprehension.

IMPLICATIONS FOR SCHOOL NURSE PRACTICE

The role of the school nurse is multi-faceted. The purpose of this section is to provide standards and considerations for the school nurse caring for the student with a DNAR request for the school setting. Areas discussed include legal issues, standards of care, policy/procedure considerations, and psychosocial implications for the child and family.

Legal Issues

Engel, Favini, & Sindelar (2014) maintain that "laws cannot and do no attempt to address every special healthcare need or every school situation. They leave room for interpretation that...can frustrate and confuse education personnel, families and lawyers" (p. 37). Legal issues for the school nurse are complex when dealing with DNAR orders. Considerations include:

- Review of the state Nurse Practice Act, and any other state and federal laws or regulations pertaining to implementation of a DNAR in schools;
- Development of an ECP and an IHP, and/or Section 504 Plan if the student qualifies, for the student with a DNAR;
- Staff education and training on implementing the ECP, especially in the absence of the school nurse;
- Recognition of parental rights for DNAR for their child;
- Care of other students who may witness the death of the child; and
- Emotional support for school staff not familiar or comfortable with DNARs in school.

Key Considerations

Not only does the nurse working in the school setting have to be aware of the nurse practice act in the state the Registered Nurse (RN) is practicing in, state and federal regulations also need to be considered, including those related to education law. To responsibly implement care for a medically fragile student, the school nurse must be aware of legal obligations that may impact that care. Because the needs for the medically fragile students are complex, "there is ambiguity around professional and legal liability" in the delivery of care in the school setting (Rehm, 2002, p. 83). Rehm goes on to say that although much of the litigation related to medically fragile students in schools is access related, we must also consider liability related to quality-of-care standards and "issues of responsibility for care rendered by non-healthcare personnel in school settings" (p. 82). The AAP (2010) agrees, stating that the school nurse may not be available at the time of arrest, secondary to staffing needs, and that non-medical trained school staff may be the first to respond. As with any emergency care plan (ECP), it is vital that school staff be trained on the plan that outlines the implementation of the DNAR.

The IDEA (2004) guarantees students the right to receive their education in the least restrictive environment with appropriate accommodations and supplementary aids and services provided for support. Key points of IDEA are that the students' disability must interfere with their education, determining their eligibility for special education and related services. Related services include transportation and rehabilitative therapies such as speech, occupational and physical therapy, and counseling (Engel et al., 2014; Raymond, 2009). It was not until the 2004 reauthorization of IDEA that "school nurse services" was included in the list of related services (Mandlawitz & Brubaker, 2009). If the student does not qualify for special education services under IDEA, Section 504 of the Rehabilitation Act is another federal law that supports programming for students with a disability within the school.

- In a paper prepared for the National School Boards Association, Deutch et al. (2015) discussed legal authority related to DNAR orders.

- In *Lewiston, Maine Public Schools,* the Office for Civil Rights (OCR) became involved after a *parent submitted a DNAR request to the school district. Although there was not a court ruling in this case, an advisory letter was written by the OCR. Several notable recommendations can be gleaned from this case. A multidisciplinary team should address the DNAR request and develop the individualized ECP. Deciding whether to honor a DNAR should be made on a case by case decision by the multidisciplinary team after considering all aspects of the case. A multidisciplinary team consists of persons knowledgeable about the student including the student's parent, healthcare provider, and appropriate school personnel. In Lewiston, OCR determined that the manner in which this plan was developed comported generally with the approach approved by OCR in developing programs for students with disabilities. The plan was based on expert medical and other relevant information about the student, was appropriately documented, required a second medical opinion, and was of limited duration, ensuring that it would be reevaluated periodically.*

- In Massachusetts, the court ruled that the school must honor the DNAR order in *ABC and DEF School v. Mr. and Mrs. M* (Deutch et al., 2015). In this case, the court cited the constitutional right to privacy and the parents right to refuse medical treatment for their medically fragile minor child and the school was ordered to honor the DNAR.

- In 1994, the Maryland Attorney General J. Joseph Curran issued an opinion on whether a school must accept and honor a DNAR order:

  The opinion notes that "state courts, which generally decide matters concerning the family, give great deference to parental decisions involving minor children" (p. 4). The opinion states that schools must accept a DNAR order, concluding that "school officials have no legal basis for substituting their judgment for that of the parents and the physician" (p. 14). The Attorney General also offers opinions on other concerns that have been raised by schools. The esq and parent/guardian must clearly outline the medical treatment and support that are to be given, including comfort care. Staff must be notified of the DNAR and appropriately trained. It was opined that a school employee that does not honor the DNAR could be held liable for battery and other torts (p. 14). The Attorney General also addressed calling 911, stating that would be part of emergency procedure and doesn't constitute medical treatment or violate the DNAR order. Curran also commented on schools' concern regarding the effect on and potential liability to other students for emotional distress resulting from a student's death at school. The opinion was it was highly unlikely that a court would entertain a claim of emotion harm (p. 17). Including provisions for the other students in the classroom in the ECP, such as removing the students from the classroom is recommended.

- Lastly, the AAP advocates for the creation of legal standards that supports schools and school staff and protecting them from liability while honoring a DNAR order. Massachusetts is one state with clearly outlined regulations related to DNAR in schools.

Other Considerations

In addition to legal considerations, it important to take into account the developmental and social needs of the student. Selekman, Bochenek, & Lukens (2013) comments that children want to be with their peers, and even if their participation is limited it is "more preferable than waiting at home to die" (p. 714). Bioethicist and pediatrician Weise (2010) remarks that palliative care for children with life-limiting conditions has become an expected part of pediatric care. The shift toward palliative care brings about orders for comfort care (Zacharski et al., 2013). Further, there are positive effects for the child even at the end of life to attend school, eliminating isolation and offering social opportunities with peers.

Additionally, it is important to note the minimal effectiveness of CPR (less than 10% survival rate) away from the healthcare setting (AAP, 2010; Weise, 2010; Zacharski et al., 2013). The AAP and the National Education Association, in 1994, set guidelines about foregoing CPR for children and adolescents, stating, "It is ethically acceptable to forego CPR when it is unlikely to be effective or when the risks outweigh the benefits, including the parents' and child's assessment of the child's quality of life" (p. 1073). For many students with life-limiting conditions, the risk of CPR or other aggressive treatment could be ineffective or outweigh the benefits.

Key Strategies for the School Nurse

- It is important to identify laws related to DNAR directives in the educational setting (The State School Nurse Consultant or General Counsel at the state Department of Education is a good resource).
- The formation of a multidisciplinary team, including school and community members, is recommended when drafting a policy and creating a plan for response to honoring a DNAR.
- Using multidisciplinary teams aligns with regulations related to IDEA and Section 504 planning.
- The school support team may include school administrators, teachers, school social worker, school psychologist, school counselor, and others, along with the school nurse.
- Transportation staff should also be included on the team and accommodations for care that may be needed for the student during transport to school is essential to be included in the ECP.
- The parent/guardian is an important part of the support team, and the team can extend to include community members such as the healthcare provider, and palliative care and EMS staff.
- Recognize and identify the role of any siblings, if they are in the same building as the student.
- The school nurse should obtain a release of information and carefully review the DNAR to make sure it is complete.

DNAR Order

The DNAR order should provide clear and specific directives for school nurses to implement should the student experience cardiac or respiratory arrest. According to Zacharski et al. (2013), DNAR requirements differ between states. The AAP policy statement states "DNAR orders should be implemented in the context of palliative care, including plans for managing pain and other symptoms" (p. 1073).

Many states have a state Emergency Medical Services (EMS) Do Not Resuscitate form that is required to be completed. Some schools may have a specific order form for the school. That form may include the following information:

- School
- Student's Name and Date of Birth
- Physician's Name/Telephone/Address
- Specific instructions in regard to:

- ✓ Withholding cardiopulmonary resuscitation (CPR), artificial ventilation, or other related life sustaining procedures in the event of cardiac or respiratory arrest of the child
- ✓ Palliative care measures (control of bleeding, airway maintenance, appropriate nutrition, control of pain, positioning for comfort and other measures to ensure general comfort, and use of prescription medications)
- ✓ Other measures (suctioning and oxygen administration)
- Statement that EMS System (911) will be activated in response to a real or perceived emergency at school
- Who should be notified in the event of cardiopulmonary arrest
- Requirements for renewal of order
- Physician signature and state license number
- Parent/Guardian signature

Whenever possible, the use of the state form is advisable.

DNAR Guidelines

As stated previously, relatively few school districts have a policy in place that addressed DNAR orders. It is recommended that districts pro-actively create a policy so they are prepared when presented with a DNAR request. The literature encourages inclusion of comfort measures and other supportive care into the ECP (AAP, 2010; Deutch et al., 2015; National Association of School Nurses [NASN], 2014; Zacharski et al., 2013). Comfort measures include holding the student, keeping the student warm, positioning for comfort and other needed care, oxygen, suctioning, Heimlich maneuver for choking, and control of bleeding and pain. These palliative measures should be clearly outlined in the ECP (AAP, 2010; Selekman, Bochenek & Lukens, 2013). The ECP should be highly individualized and developed with input from the support team.

In addition to palliative measures, the plan should include a copy of the DNAR, clearly explain the role of staff members, and outline classroom management including privacy concerns. The ECP also should explain the plan for the other students should an emergency arise in the classroom (i.e., take the students to another location, outlining by whom and where, who to notify, etc.). The school nurse should work with the healthcare provider or palliative care team on a plan for transporting the student should an urgent situation come up. It needs to be clarified if 911 or another form of transportation previously arranged by the team should be called. It is recommended the EMS/transport company be notified of the DNAR and incorporate their input, particularly regarding communication in an emergency into the plan. All of these details must be clearly outlined in the plan in a step-by- step fashion. Emergency notification numbers of the parent/guardian also need to be included in the ECP. The plan should be reviewed by the support team and signed by the healthcare provider who wrote the DNAR order. If the student has an IEP or Section 504 Plan, make note of the ECP and DNAR in the document. As the school health professional, the school nurse has a unique role in coordinating the care of the student with a DNAR order with the parent/guardian, the school and the medical community.

DNAR Guidelines should include the following steps:

- Careful review of all required DNAR order forms
- Obtain release of information

- Organize multidisciplinary team meeting including transportation
- Review of state law and district policy
- Create a protocol for notification of EMS, family, healthcare provider, palliative care staff
- Note DNAR in IEP or Section 504 Plan
- Advise use of DNAR bracelet for out-of-hospital if indicated by state guidelines
- Conduct student assessment
- Assess staffing needs
- Identify staff training needs
- Develop an Emergency Care Plan (ECP)
- Documentation of training of identified school staff. Training should include a review of the DNAR, the ECP, and staff roles should clearly be communicated.

Components of Emergency Care Plan

- Original copy of DNAR order
- Disease directed interventions and symptom control
- Comfort measures
- Clearly explain staff roles, including transportation considerations
- Classroom management, including plan for other children in the room or nearby, should the student's health status change, including privacy considerations and a code that elicits quick response from staff members
- Emergency notification numbers for parent/guardian, healthcare provider, palliative care contact
- Plan should have an expiration date and be reviewed a minimum of annually by the multidisciplinary team
- Plan should be signed by the same healthcare provider that wrote the DNAR order and the parent/guardian

CONCLUSION

A question frequently asked by school nurses is how to handle a DNAR when schools and parents disagree on implementation. **Proactively developing a DNAR policy is highly recommended**. Creating a multi-disciplinary team, educating school staff and sharing information, both medical and from education-based resources (such as those noted from the National School Boards Association) may be helpful. Staff needs reassurance that care will not totally be withheld, and that comfort and other measures will be given as outlined in an individualized plan. Developing a list of supports and resources can also be beneficial.

RESOURCES

American Academy of Pediatrics. (2010). Policy Statement-Honoring Do-Not-Attempt Resuscitation Requests in Schools. This includes a helpful table outlining the components of a DNAR order.
http://pediatrics.aappublications.org/content/pediatrics/125/5/1073.full.pdf

Do Not Attempt Resuscitation (DNAR): Planning for the Child in School. Helpful checklist covering every aspect of planning for the care of a student with a DNAR order, including role of the crisis team. *NASN School Nurse, 28*(2), 71-75. doi: 10.177/1942602X12472540

Do Not Resuscitate (DNR) Orders: A Checklist for School Districts. http://www.nsba.org/sites/default/files/file/16_c_Do_Not_Resuscitate_DNR_Orders_A_Checklist_School_Districts.PDF

Massachusetts Children with "Do Not Resuscitate" or "Comfort Care" Orders in the School Setting. http://www.mass.gov/eohhs/docs/dph/regs/dnr-policy-107.pdf

National Association of School Nurses. 2014. Position Statement-Do Not Attempt Resuscitation (DNAR)-The Role of the School Nurse. https://www.nasn.org/PolicyAdvocacy/PositionPapersandReports/NASNPositionStatementsFullView/tabid/462/ArticleId/640/Do-Not-Attempt-Resuscitation-DNAR-The-Role-of-the-School-Nurse-Adopted-January-2014

Case Law

Lewiston, Maine, Pub. Sch., 21 IDELR 83 (OCR 1994)

ABC and DEF School v. Mr. and Mrs. M, 26 IDELR (LRP) 1103 (Super. Ct. Mass., 1997)

REFERENCES

American Academy of Pediatrics. (2010). Policy statement: Honoring do-not-attempt resuscitation requests in schools. *Pediatrics, 125*, 1073-1077. doi: 10.1542/peds.2010-0452

Bethell, C. D., Kogan, M.D., Strickland, B.B., Schor, E.L., Robertson, J., & Newacheck, P. (2011). A national and state profile of leading health problems and health care quality for US children: Key insurance disparities and across-state variations. *Academic Pediatrics, 11(3), 22-33.* doi: 10.1016/j.acap.2010.08.011

Brenner, N.D., Wheeler, L., Wolfe, L.C., Vernon-Smiley, M. & Caldart-Olson, L. (2007, October). Health services: Results from the school health policies and programs study 2006. *Journal of School Health, 77*(8), 464-485.

Carnevale, F.A., Rehm, R.S., Kirk, S. & McKeever, P. (2008). What we know (and do not know) about raising children with complex continuing care needs. *Journal of Child Health Care, 12*(4), 4-6. doi:10.1177/1367493508088552

Deutch, J.M., Martin, L.G., & Mueller, J. A. (2015). *Managing students with health issues: Section 504 plans, DNR orders and contagious diseases.* Retrieved from: https://www.nsba.org/sites/default/files/file/16_FINAL_Deutch_Martin_Managing_Students_with_Health_Issues_Paper.pdf

Engel, M., Favini, P.M., & Sindelar, T. (2014). Legal issues in the education of students with special health care needs. In S. Porter, M. Haynie, P. Branowickil & J.S. Palfrey (Eds.), *Supporting students with special health care needs: Guidelines and procedures for schools* (3rd ed.) (pp. 37-64). Baltimore, MD: Paul H. Brooks Publishing.

Heller, K.W., Fredrick, L.D., Best, S., Dykes, M.K., & Cohen, E.T. (2000, Winter). Specialized health care procedures in schools: Training and service delivery. *Exceptional Children, 66*(2), 173-186. doi: 10.1177/001440290006600203

Individuals with Disability Education Improvement Act (2004), 20 U.S.C. 1400 et seq.

Kimberly, M.B., Forte A.L., Carroll, J.M., Feudtner, C. (2005a, Winter). Pediatric do-not-attempt-resuscitation orders and public schools: A national assessment of policies and laws. *American Journal of Bioethics, 5*(1), 59-65. doi:10.1080/15265160590900605

Kimberly, M. B., Forte, A. L., Carroll, J. M., & Feudtner, C. (2005b). A response to selected commentaries on pediatric do-not-attempt-resuscitation orders and public schools: A national assessment of policies and laws. *American Journal of Bioethics*, 5(1), 19-W21. doi:10.1080/15265160590944102

Mandlawitz, M.R., & Brubaker, C.R. (2009). School nurses and the IDEA: Ensuring students are ready to learn. *NASN School Nurse, 24*(2), 71-74.

National Association of School Nurses. (2014). *Do not attempt resuscitation (DNAR)-The role of the school nurse* (Position Statement*). Retrieved from https://www.nasn.org/PolicyAdvocacy/ PositionPapersandReports/NASNPositionStatementsFullView/tabid/462/ArticleId/640/Do-Not-Attempt-Resuscitation-DNAR-The-Role-of-the-School-Nurse-Adopted-January-2014

Opinion on DNR. 79 Md. Op. Atty. Gen. 244 (Opinion No. 94-028, 1994).

Raymond, J.A. (2009). The integration of children dependent on medical technology into public schools. *The Journal of School Nursing, 25*(3), 186-193. doi: 10.1177/1059840509335407

Rehm, R.S. (2002, March). Creating a context of safety and achievement at school for children who are medically fragile/technology dependent. *Advances in Nursing Science,24*(3), 71-84. doi: 10.1097/00012272-200203000-00008

Selekman, J., Bochenek, J., & Lukens, M. (2013). Do not resuscitate orders. In J. Selekman (Ed.), *School nursing: A comprehensive text (2ⁿᵈ ed.)* (pp. 713-714). Philadelphia: F.A. Davis.

Taliaferro, V. & Resha, C. (Eds.). (2016). Do not attempt resuscitation. In V. Taliaferro & C. Resha (Eds.), *2016 School nurse resource manual* (pp. 421-423). Nashville, TN: School Health Alert.

van Dyck, P.C., Kogan, M.D., McPherson, M.G., Weissman, G.R. & Newacheck, P.W. (2004, September). Prevalence and characteristics of children with special health care needs. *Archives of Pediatrics & Adolescent Medicine, 158*(9),884-890. Retrieved from http://archpedi.amaassn.org/cgi/content/ abstract/158/9/884

Wang, K.-W.K. & Barnard, A. (2004). Technology-dependent children and their families: A review. *Journal of Advanced Nursing, 45*(1), 36-46. doi: 10.1046/j.1365-2648.2003.02858.x

Weise, K. L. (2010). Do-not-attempt-resuscitation orders in public schools. *American Medical Association Journal of Ethics*, 12(7), 569-572. Retrieved from http://virtualmentor.ama-assn.org/2010/07/pfor1-1007.html

White, G. (2005). Nurses at the helm: Implementing DNAR orders in the public school setting. *American Journal of Bioethics, 5*(1), 83-85. doi:10.1080/152651690928006

Zacharski, S., Minchella, L., Gomez, S., Grogan, S., Porter, S., & Robarge, D. (2013). Do not attempt resuscitation (DNAR) orders in school settings: Special needs nurses review current research and issues. *NASN School Nurse, 28*(2), 71-75. doi: 10.177/1942602X12472540

Chapter 21

PARENT REFUSAL, NON-COMPLIANCE, AND NON-RESPONSIVENESS

Erin D. Gilsbach, Esquire

DESCRIPTION OF ISSUE

School nurses often encounter parents who are non-responsive to requests for information or medical documentation for their child. In addition, some parents may refuse to permit particular nursing services. This chapter provides helpful information for school nurses when dealing with these challenging situations, as well as legally-defensible best practices regarding communication and documention related to this issue.

BACKGROUND

One of the most difficult things for a school nurse to encounter is seeing a child that needs or may need medical/health services and not being able to provide them due to lack of medical information from the healthcare provider or lack of permission from the parent. Such situations may have legal implications for both the school and the nurse. Should the school nurse report the situation to child services as potential child abuse? Does the school have an obligation to conduct a medical evaluation of the student? If so, what are the parameters of that obligation? Some of the solutions to these issues lie within the law, but most are simply a matter of good communication and documentation practices.

IMPLICATIONS FOR SCHOOL NURSE PRACTICE

Parent Non-Responsiveness

When a school nurse is aware of a medical or health-related issue that requires nursing services, parental cooperation is imperative. However, most school nurses have encountered situations where a parent simply does not respond to the school nurse's communications or fails to bring in medications or necessary medical devices. In these cases, where a parent is not refusing nursing treatment (which is discussed in a later section of this chapter) but, instead, is simply non-responsive to the school nurse's and/or school's attempts to obtain medication, medical orders, or other information, it is crucial that the school nurse determine the cause of the non-responsiveness. A parent's non-responsiveness may be the result of a number of very different situations. The section, below, serves as a guide in determining the cause of the non-responsiveness, beginning with the most basic. School nurses should attempt to rule out basic factors that may be causing the non-responsiveness, such as communication issues; comprehension or language barriers; misunderstandings; and family/home issues, such as homelessness, etc. The chart, below, identifies a process that is based on a series of investigative questions, which can be used to rule out these basic factors or, where necessary, identify and address them. The summary bullet points beside each investigative question are discussed in greater detail, below.

Investigative Questions

Is the parent receiving the communication from the school?	• Verify contact info. • Try different methods of communication • Consider potential residency/homelessness issues • Talk to the child (age-appropriate)
Does the parent understand what is being requested?	• Put it in writing (email, letter, etc.) • Make sure request is clear and fully explained • Investigate whether language barriers may exist (and if so, address them)
Does the parent understand the importance of the information and/or items to the school?	• Meet with and/or call parent to discuss • Put reasons in writing • Try having administrator contact parent
Does the school have a legal obligation to obtain a medical evaluation for the student?	• If necessary for 504/IDEA identifiation and/or provision of FAPE • Should be a team decision • Consider seeking a fact-specific legal opinion
Can/should the nurse communicate with the child's physician directly?	If school has the necessary signed FERPA consent More communication always better Consider requesting FERPA consent at start of each year
Can/should this parent's conduct be reported as potential neglect/child abuse?	• Possibly, if issuenot resolved through above process • Child abuse is a state-specific standard • Nurse may have mandatory reporting obligations

Communication logs, nursing notes, and other forms of documentation should be used to document the information that is obtained through these inquiries. This documentation may be important to show that the nurse and the school acted in accordance with best nursing standards and legal requirements if a lawsuit is filed.

Throughout this section, the following scenario will be used to discuss each of the questions that should be addressed:

> *A parent of a 2nd grader who has just transferred into the school indicates on her child's school enrollment forms that the child has asthma and is prescribed an emergency albuterol inhaler. The school nurse does not receive any additional information regarding the child's asthma, and the parent has not brought in the medication. The child has been sent to the school nurse's office on two different occasions due to shortness of breath and wheezing. The school nurse has called the home several times to speak with the parent, but no one answers. She has sent numerous letters and requests for medication home, but has received no response. She has advised the playground supervisors to limit the child's physical activity until they are able to obtain more information from the parent.*

INVESTIGATIVE QUESTION # 1: IS THE PARENT RECEIVING THE COMMUNICATION FROM THE SCHOOL NURSE/ SCHOOL?

In order to determine this, the school nurse will need to verify (and document) the contact information on file and the contact information being used to communicate with the parent. Sometimes the issue may be as simple as an inadvertent clerical or typographical error in the contact information being used. In the alternative, a parent may not be receiving communication due to a change in living arrangements or a change in telephone number or email address. If a parent is failing to respond to any nurse communications, consider whether one of these two issues may be present. First, check the information being used (the number being dialed, the email or physical address being used, etc.) against the student's records.

If that has been done, and there is no indication of a typo or a mis-dialed number, the school nurse should attempt to communicate with the parent using various other forms of communication.

Tips for Communicating with Parents

All communication with parents regarding the health needs of a child should be documented. Where a parent is non-responsive, the documentation should include information regarding the verification of the contact information being used. Sometimes the nurse may have reason to know, without a doubt, that there is no error in the method of communication or that the communication is reaching its intended recipient. Some instances of this would be where the nurse is calling and leaving messages on a voicemail that contains a pre-recorded message by the parent or where the nurse is simply hitting the "reply" button on an email that was sent by the parent. Nurses should carefully document the specifics of these situations in order to provide those important details. For instance, in addition to documenting in a nursing note "called parent at 2:15 pm and left message regarding need to bring in student's medication," the nurse should add: *"student's mother's voice was on voicemail recording."* This documents the additional crucial information that the nurse is making direct contact with the parents.

For instance, if prior communication has generally been attempted/conducted by phone, the school nurse should follow up with an email. If that is not successful, the school nurse should send written correspondence to the address on file stating the issue, asking the parent to contact the school nurse, and providing information at least two methods of possible communication (phone number and email address are preferable for ease of communication, but a fax number and mailing address could also be provided).

If that has been done, and there is still no indication as to whether the parent is receiving the information, either investigate or ask the appropriate office or individual at the school to investigate whether the parent's information needs to be updated due to a change in address, phone number, email, etc. The registration office may have updated information if the family moved or provided the school with a new phone number. The school's McKinney-Vento coordinator, who is responsible for ensuring compliance with the law protecting homeless students, may be aware of housing issues. Depending upon his/her age, the student may also be able to provide information regarding updated contact information, living arrangements, or even whether the parent has been receiving the communications from the school nurse. The child may also be able to provide insight into the potential reasons why the parent may not be responsive.

> **Scenario:** *In the scenario described, above, the school nurse does not know, for sure, whether her calls or letters are reaching the parent. There is no voicemail that picks up to tell her that it is the correct number, and she has received no response to her letters. She verifies the information with her own records. The number and address that she used are the same ones that she has in her files. She then verifies the information with the main office and checks to find out whether they have an alternative number and/or address in the student's main office file. There is no indication that either the number or the address are incorrect.*

INVESTIGATIVE QUESTION # 2: DOES THE PARENT UNDERSTAND WHAT IS BEING REQUESTED?

Another basic consideration is whether the parent understands what is being requested by the school. Putting the request in writing can help ensure that the request is clearly communicated. Written communication also provides –a documented record of the efforts made by the school to reach out to the parents. School nurses should take steps to ensure that the parent does not have any language issues or other barriers to understanding the request. Public schools have a legal obligation, under Title VI of the Civil Rights Act of 1964 (Title VI) and the Equal Educational Opportunities Act (EEOA), to ensure that they can communicate with parents whose first language is not English and who have limited English proficiency. All communications with the parent should encourage the parent to contact the school nurse directly if they have any questions or would like additional information. Most schools require parent/guardian(s) to fill out a "Home Language Survey" or otherwise provide information about home language at the time of registration, and this documentation is maintained in the student's permanent file.

In addition to assuring the parent is able to understand the language it which communications are written, it is also important that they understand the content and context of the message. Communications should be reviewed for the level of literacy with a goal of having communications at a 6th - 8th grade level. Even parents with good literacy skills may struggle with health-related terms. There are many resources for assessing and creating communications. The CDC, National Institutes for Health and US National Library of Medicine offer resources and online health literacy courses for health professionals. The Writing for the Public Online Training is part of Health Literacy training available. See the Resources section, below, for more information.

> **Scenario:** The school nurse *learns that both English and Spanish are spoken in the home. She then checks with the front office staff, who confirm to her that they often send forms home in Spanish, pursuant to the father's request. The school nurse does have Spanish language medication forms, so she completes one of those and sends it home. She decides that, for future communications, she will inquire as to whether it might be helpful for the parents to*

256

have an interpreter attend the meetings and/or provide translation services for phone calls. Unfortunately, despite these efforts, the parents continue to be non-responsive.

INVESTIGATIVE QUESTION # 3: DOES THE PARENT UNDERSTAND THE IMPORTANCE OF THE INFORMATION AND/OR ITEMS TO THE SCHOOL?

In some cases, a parent may understand the actual request being made but may not understand the importance of the information or items being requested. For instance, a mother may understand that the school is requesting that she bring in emergency epinephrine for her child, who has been diagnosed with a life-threatening food allergy, but she may not understand that it is critically important for her to provide it for her child. If the school has a written policy that requires each building and bus to be stocked with a dose of emergency epinephrine, she may be relying upon that medication if/when her child has an allergic reaction. Her reliance on the school's stock emergency epinephrine may be due, in part, to the fact that her insurance company does not cover a second dose of the medication for the student while he is at school. She may not have disclosed this information to the school nurse, and, because of that, the school nurse was unable to have a discussion with her about the importance of having designated emergency medication for this student. In this case, the school nurse and the parent each have important information that the other needs. The school nurse does not understand the parent's reasons for non-compliance with a simple medication request, and the parent does not understand importance of having a specifically-designated epinephrine auto-injector for her child.

For both questions 2 and 3, above, a meeting may be necessary to discuss the matter with the parent, make sure that the parent fully understands the request being made, and address any concerns or misconceptions that the parent may have. In the scenario, above, a meeting between the parent and the school nurse would be quite helpful, because it would give the school nurse the opportunity to discuss the parent's reasoning and allow the school nurse to understand what additional information needs to be communicated to the parent. If a parent is not responsive to requests for a meeting or phone conference or is not willing to participate in a conference, the school nurse should notify the school's administration. The parent may be more responsive to a building administrator's requests to meet.

> *Scenario: The school nurse decides to request that the parents come in for a meeting to discuss the matter. Once the school nurse understands the parents'' perspective, she can address the parents' concerns more directly and help the parent understand that, while the school does stock emergency doses of the medication, there is no guarantee that it will be available when the child needs it. The school nurse may also be able to provide parents with contacts and resources if the parent is unable to afford a second dose of the medication for school. This meeting may be very beneficial in addressing the parent's non-responsiveness.*
>
> *The school nurse makes several attempts to communicate with the parents by phone and email. She also sends out a handwritten note asking them to call her and set up a meeting. (She makes sure that the note is also translated into Spanish.) She does not receive a response. Concerned about the child's health, the school nurse requests a meeting with the building principal to discuss her concerns and determine what else can and should be done.*

INVESTIGATIVE QUESTION # 4: DOES THE SCHOOL HAVE A LEGAL OBLIGATION TO OBTAIN A MEDICAL EVALUATION FOR THE STUDENT?

If a school nurse knows that information regarding a child's medical condition is needed, and the parent does not have this information or has not provided it, the school may be required under Section 504 or the IDEA to obtain it. The Office of Civil Rights (OCR) has ruled that if the school suspects that a student has a disability that would qualify the student for Section 504 eligibility but needs more medical information, a medical assessment must be provided at no cost to the parent (OCR, 1993). If the medical information that the school is seeking is for a temporary condition, there is likely no Section 504 issue, and, thus, no obligation to obtain the information at school expense. Where the information is related to a non-temporary condition that satisfies the eligibility requirements under Section 504, however, the school needs to consider whether there is a requirement for the school to obtain the information.

A school may be obligated to obtain its own medical report where the parents prevent access to the student's medical providers and/or medical information. Schools cannot simply argue that the parents have restricted or thwarted their efforts to obtain medical information if the district has not sought to obtain its own medical information. In one case, a hearing officer concluded that both the parent *and* the district impeded the collaborative IEP process where the parent refused to provide access to her child's medical provider, and the district failed to seek an independent medical assessment. *Oconee County Sch. Dist.*, 8 GASLD 72 (SEA GA 2014). Thus, regardless of the parent's actions or inactions, the school may have a legal obligation to obtain a medical evaluation of the student.

Whether a medical evaluation is required at school expense is a question for the school's special education department and/or Section 504 team, which should include the school nurse in this such cases, or at least the school nurse's input. The special education department or Section 504 team (or Section 504 evaluators, if the student is not yet eligible) will need to determine whether the information is necessary for the school to be able to determine the child's eligibility and/or appropriate accommodations to enable the student to access the school and its programs. Medical assessments are only necessary if they are needed to determine eligibility or if FAPE cannot be provided without the additional information (OCR 1993). Due to the significance of the issue, it is prudent to seek a legal opinion from the school's legal counsel in such cases, prior to making a determination decision regarding eligibility, to determine whether a medical evaluation is necessary or legally advisable.

From the Case Files:

Courts are increasingly placing medical evaluation obligations on public schools. In one New Jersey case, the court held that a district's failure to facilitate a medical evaluation of a child after she began to exhibit noticeable signs of autism. *Millburn Twp. Bd. of Educ. v. J.S.O. and K.S.O.*, 63 IDELR 229 (D.N.J. 2014). Likewise, in a New Mexico case, it was determined that a charter school was in violation of the IDEA where it failed to seek its own medical assessment to confirm that a student had Tourette syndrome. In that case, the student had been erroneously classified as having an emotional disturbance.

Ralph J. Bunche Acad., 114 LRP 46982 (SEA NM 08/09/14)

> **Scenario:** *In the scenario, the school does not necessarily need medical information, it needs the student's prescribed medication. Even if the school were to do an evaluation for this student, school officials would not be able to obtain medication for the student. Thus, the school nurse needs to determine what else she can do to*

address the situation. She considers whether speaking to the healthcare provider may be of help. If the student no longer uses the medication, that would be valuable information to the school.

INVESTIGATIVE QUESTION # 5: CAN/SHOULD THE SCHOOL NURSE SPEAK TO THE CHILD'S HEALTHCARE PROVIDER DIRECTLY?

In some instances, a school nurse needs to communicate with a student's healthcare provider regarding a student's medication or diagnosis. For instance, a student may have a healthcare provider's note that requires clarification. The healthcare provider is able to provide such clarification under HIPAA, due to the fact that HIPAA permits such clarification between treating medical professionals without additional documentation/consent. Unfortunately, there is no similar exception to FERPA's consent requirement.

If the school nurse has a parent-signed FERPA consent on file for the student, the school nurse would be permitted to share information with the healthcare provider, as well. For this reason, it is an exemplary practice for school nurses to request FERPA consent at the beginning of each school year for all the students on their caseloads. The FERPA form should include consent to speak to the student's healthcare providers on an ongoing basis throughout the school year regarding issues related to the student's school-related medical needs, including medication administration/modifications, interpretation of medical orders, general health-related concerns.

From the Case Files:

Where a parent limits or prohibits access to a student's healthcare provider, a district may be able to obtain its own medical assessment. In a 2006 case in the 5th Circuit, the guardian of a student with dysautonomia restricted access to the student's physician, even modifying the physician's responses to the district's written questions. The student was medically fragile and prone to sudden, potentially fatal medical crises. The district took the parents to a hearing, arguing that, without more detailed medical information about the student, the district was unable to provide for the necessary accommodations. The court, in that case, ruled that the school district was entitled to its own independent medical evaluation, despite the fact that the student's guardian refused to give consent.

Shelby S. v. Conroe Independent School District, 45 IDELR 269 (5th Cir. 2006), *cert. denied*, 109 LRP 47876, 549 U.S. 1111 (2007).

Even if the school nurse does not have written parental consent to share information with the student's healthcare provider, the school nurse may still request clarification from the healthcare provider. In that conversation, however, the nurse would be precluded from sharing any information that the school nurse has about the student with the healthcare provider. Even so, although it would be a one-sided conversation, the healthcare provider may still be able to provide helpful and necessary information regarding the services that need to be provided to the student. If the school nurse is unable to make phone contact, the school nurse could send a written explanation of what is needed and why it is important to the school. Written communications sometimes get a better response, since the healthcare provider is able to quickly view and assess what is needed without engaging in a discussion where privacy concerns maybe at issue. Prior to sending such a written request/explanation, however, the nurse should ensure that there are no privacy concerns with doing so and that the nurse has permission, via valid FERPA consent, to release student information to the healthcare provider.

Scenario: *In this case, the school nurse, as a matter of procedure, has all parents sign FERPA consent forms at the beginning of the year that allow her to communicate with the students' healthcare* *providers. Therefore, when she contacts the student's healthcare providers to clarify a medical order or better understand a provider's description of a student's needs, she is able to share information with them, as well. The nurse confirms with this student's healthcare provider that the student does, indeed, need her medication and that the student has had several life-threatening asthma attacks in the last year where she was unable to breathe and needed to be taken to the emergency room.*

INVESTIGATIVE QUESTION # 6: CAN/SHOULD THIS PARENT'S CONDUCT BE REPORTED AS POTENTIAL NEGLECT/CHILD ABUSE?

If the school nurse has taken all the steps, above, and the parent is still non-responsive, the nurse should consider whether the non-responsiveness rises to the level of suspected child abuse. Each state's child abuse definitions and mandatory reporter requirements are different, so the nurse would need to assess the situation in light of applicable state child abuse laws. Because so many steps have been taken to rule out and address communication issues, misunderstandings, financial issues, family/home issues, etc., the nurse may likely come to the conclusion that the non-responsiveness rises to the level of child abuse. While the definition of abuse varies from state to state, a parent's failure to communicate with and/or provide necessary medical information to the school is likely to meet the definition of neglect. Some states also include failure to provide necessary medical services as a type of child abuse. If the parent's actions or inactions fall within the definition of child abuse, the school nurse, as a mandatory reporter, would be required to report them.

> **Scenario:** *Now that the school nurse is better aware of the student's medical condition and her need for the inhaler, she is extremely concerned. Since the parents needed to take her to the emergency room several times this year for breathing issues, they are certainly aware of her need for this life-saving medication. She has tried everything that she could to engage the parents and get them to provide the medication, to no avail. Their refusal to communicate with her or bring in the medication poses a serious risk to the child.*

Parents, generally, have the legal authority to make medical decisions on behalf of their child. *(For a more expansive discussion on the issue of parental authority, see Chapter 21.)* Under the IDEA, parents have the right to refuse to consent to special education services. However, where a parent is refusing to consent to school nurse services, and where the withholding of that service would result in harm to the child, the school nurse should, take all possible steps to speak to and/or meet with the parent to discuss the seriousness of the implications of the parent's refusal. Where the parent continues to refuse to consent to services, and where such services are necessary for the well-being of the child, document the refusal and contact the building administrator. The school nurse may be required to report the situation, pursuant to the school nurse's mandatory reporting obligations, as potential child abuse.

Where a student is non-compliant with requirements related to nursing services, the student's Section 504 or IEP team should be re-convened to determine whether the accommodations need to be modified. The team should review the reasons for non-compliance and identify possible behavior supports that may be necessary to ensure that the student receives the necessary medical services that they need. If the student does not have a Section 504 Plan or IEP, the school should consider whether they should have one. If the student requires nursing services for a non-temporary physical or mental impairment, the student likely qualifies under at least Section 504. *(See Chapter 12 regarding Section 504 eligibility).* The Section 504 or IEP Team, which would include the parent/guardian(s), would then be able to address the problem as a group, providing whatever modifications and/or supports are necessary to ensure that the student receives the appropriate medical services.

When the team is meeting to review the reasons for the student's refusal/non-compliance, the team should consider common issues that may cause refusal. These may include embarrassment to be singled out when needing to leave class to receive a medication; disappointment at having to miss a key social period, such as the beginning of lunch or recess; or even frustration at having to miss a portion of class and risk falling behind. All of these common issues can be readily addressed through the proper planning and adjustment of the student's schedule for nursing services. Where the basis for refusal is unclear, the team may wish to consider inviting the student into the meeting and discussing their concerns with him/her. Where it may be necessary or helpful, the student's healthcare provider can be contacted to provide insight and/or suggestions that may help alleviate the issue.

Tips for Documenting Communication with Parent/Guardian(s)

All communication with parents regarding the medical/health needs of a child should be documented. Where a parent/guardian is non-responsive, the documentation should include information regarding the verification of the contact information being used. Sometimes the school nurse may have reason to know, without a doubt, that there is no error in the method of communication or that the communication is reaching its intended recipient. Examples include where the school nurse is calling and leaving messages on a voicemail that contains a pre-recorded message by the parent or where the school nurse is simply hitting the "reply" button on an email that was sent by the parent. School nurses should carefully document the specifics of these situations to provide those important details. For instance, in addition to documenting the nursing note in the health record ("called parent at 2:15 pm and left message regarding need to bring in student's medication"), the school nurse should add: *"student's mother's voice was on voicemail recording."* This document the additional crucial information that the school nurse is making direct contact with the parents.

EMAIL TIPS

Strings of email conversations can often be lengthy and may include a number of different recipients at different points on the email chain's timeline, which can lead to accidental disclosure of information to an unintended recipient. Extended email chains that bounce around a school and possibly back and forth with the parents pose a heightened potential that the email will contain information that a future recipient may not be entitled to see, such as information regarding other students. Such email "conversations" also pose the risk that staff members will be too informal in their communications, forgetting that they are creating a record that may potentially be available for the parent's review pursuant to the Family Educational Rights and Privacy Act (FERPA). Such informality may lead to haphazard documentation and, at worst, communication that could be taken the wrong way by the parent and possibly be offensive.

These types of scenarios can be avoided if school employees simply engage the feature, if their systems support it, that simply removes the email chain from all reply or forwarded emails. In the alternative, where such feature is not available on the email program being used, a quick and reliable workaround is to simply make a point of beginning each email as a new email and refrain from using the "reply" and "forward" functions unless the communication necessitates doing so (and even then, only after thoroughly reviewing all the information being disclosed within the email chain).

261

Emails have the added benefit of providing their own documentation, if they are maintained. However, that documentation only lasts as long as the email is maintained. If the school nurse does not purposely save the email, and it simply exists in the school nurse's school email in or out-box, the school nurse has little control over how long and/or how that email is maintained is outside of the control of the school nurse. The email may be deleted from the server pursuant to a long-standing or new email destruction policy (many schools only maintain their non-saved emails for only 30-60 days). Thus, where an email can serve as documentation that the information was sent to the intended recipient, the school nurse should take specific steps to save that email in order to preserve it for documentation purposes.

In addition, certain email software/provider functions may not provide sufficient information to document that the email was sent using the "reply" feature, which would negate the documentation benefits discussed, above. For example, Microsoft Outlook has a function that disables the email chain feature on reply emails, so that when a sender replies to an email, the original email or email chain is not automatically included in the new email. Only the sender's current message is included in the new email, even though it is sent in response to one or more previous emails. While this feature has many legal-defensibility benefits (see text box), it would not achieve the purpose of documenting that the email was sent as a reply, because the original email would not be included. If such a feature is used, additional documentation would be required. The documentation could take a number of different forms, but a simple entry in the nursing notes is sufficient if it is done with specificity. For instance, instead of documenting "emailed parent" in the student health record, the school nurse should specify "emailed parent on [date] by replying to parent's email from [date]." In the alternative, a printout 0000or electronically-saved copy of the email that was sent, with an added note indicating that it was sent as a reply to the original email and giving the date and time of the original email, provides similar documentation.

Texting is not recommended as a method of communication with parent/guardian(s). It is difficult to document and/or save text messages in a manner that provides sufficiently comprehensive information, such as the date and time of the message; the context of the message, which may include a history of prior messages; texted responses to the specific message; and the actual text of the message. Collecting all this information regarding a text and documenting it properly is cumbersome and time-consuming, which increases the possibility that, in the fast-paced bustle of a school nurse's day, it will become overlooked. While methods such as screen capturing and/or preserving the texting log available through the cellular provider, may, and should, be employed to preserve this information if a parent does communicate via text messaging, email communication is a far superior method of written communication.

The content of text messages is also problematic. Typos, spelling errors, and unintended word choices abound in texting. Voice-to-text and auto-complete features often insert unintended word choices, which may go uncorrected and - or further confuse the meaning of the communication. Such errors may result in a plausible but unintended meaning, or they may result in a message that is undecipherable. In addition to errors, the nature and brevity of text messages makes the substance of a text message easy to misinterpret even if there are no typos or errors.

Another significant issue with texting is the fact that it requires that the parent/guardian have the school nurse's cell phone number. Unless the school nurse has a school-issued phone, this is generally not recommended. Providing a parent/guardian with access to a personal, private cell phone opens a host of issues, including parents having access to the school nurse after school hours. If the school nurse wishes to provide a cell phone number, a school-issued phone should be used. In such a case, the school nurse should establish clear parameters with the parents about the uses of the phone for communication purposes and should inform the parent that the phone is used only for school-related communication and that the school nurse does not have access to the phone after hours. Even with these precautions, however, texting poses practical and legal challenges, and school nurses should be cautious when considering using texting as a mode of communication with parent/guardian(s).

Many schools have policies regarding the use of texting by school employees as well as the use of personal cell phones for school-related communications. School nurses should always refer to their school's policy regarding texting prior to considering using text messages as a method of communicating with students or parents.

CONCLUSION

When a school nurse encounters a non-responsive parent, the school nurse should follow the investigative steps outlined in this chapter to eliminate any potential communication issues, language barriers, etc. Many of the issues may be resolved by determining if parent understands the request and how to comply. School nurses should remember that, pursuant to Section 504 and/or the IDEA, the school may have an obligation to obtain a medical evaluation of a child. With regards to student refusals, school nurses should re-convene the Section 504 and/or IEP team to discuss the reasons for the student refusal/non-compliance and develop a plan to address the issue. Where a parent is refusing a life-saving medication or acting in other ways that pose concern for the student's safety, the school nurse may have a legal obligation, as a mandated reporter, to report such conduct as potential child abuse.

RESOURCES

American Family Physician. *"Health Literacy: The Gap Between Physicians and Patients."*
Available at: http://www.aafp.org/afp/2005/0801/p463.html

Centers for Disease Control and Prevention, *"Health Literacy".*
Available at https://www.cdc.gov/healthliteracy/developmaterials/guidancestandards.html

Medline Plus. "How to Write Easy-to-Read Health Materials." Available at https://medlineplus.gov/etr.html

National Network of Libraries of Medicine. *"Professional Development: Health Literacy".*
Available at https://nnlm.gov/professional-development/topics/health-literacy

U.S. Department of Education. "FERPA: Full Text."
Available at: https://ed.gov/policy/gen/reg/ferpa/index.html.

REFERENCES

Equal Educational Opportunities Act, 20 U.S.C. §1701, et. seq. (1974)

Letter to Veir, 20 IDELR 864 (OCR 1993)

Oconee County Sch. Dist., 8 GASLD 72 (SEA GA 2014)

Ralph J. Bunche Acad., 114 LRP 46982 (SEA NM 08/09/14)

Shelby S. v. Conroe Independent School District, 45 IDELR 269 (5th Cir. 2006), cert. denied, 109 LRP 47876, 549 U.S. 1111 (2007).

NURSING CARE

Chapter 22

CHRONIC HEALTH CONDITIONS

Teresa DuChateau, DNP, RN, CPNP

DESCRIPTION OF ISSUE

Research indicates that 13% to 18% of children and adolescents have some sort of chronic health conditions and almost half could be considered disabled (Cohen et al., 2011; National Survey of Children's Health, 2011; Van Cleave, Gortmaker, & Perrin 2010). Because every student is different, schools are responsible for evaluating the health needs of students and, if needed, providing appropriate accommodations to ensure the educational success of students who have chronic illnesses. Regardless if accommodations are required, schools have a responsibility to ensure the safety of students with chronic conditions. This can include daily management of the student's health condition, establishing safety plans to respond to a student health emergency and providing education and training to the school staff and student on how to care for the student's health condition. Additionally, if a school nurse has delegated procedures and treatments to an unlicensed assistive personnel (UAP), the nurse retains accountability and must ensure adequate supervision and monitoring.

Students with chronic conditions may be eligible for services through the implementation of Section 504 of the Rehabilitation Act and the Individuals with Disabilities Education Improvement Act (IDEIA, formerly IDEA). The school nurse is a vital member of the team that identifies and assesses students with health concerns to determine if accommodations are needed.

BACKGROUND

There are a several federal laws that impact the care of students with chronic conditions in the school setting. These include:

- The Americans with Disabilities Act of 1990 (ADA),
- The Americans with Disabilities Act Amendment Act of 2008 (ADAAA) (*42 U.S.C. § 12102*),
- Section 504 of the Rehabilitation Act of 1973, (Rehabilitation Act of 1973 [§504], 2000),
- Individuals with Disabilities Education Act (IDEA) (Individuals with Disability Education Improvement Act [IDEIA], 2004),
- The Family Educational Rights and Privacy Act (FERPA) (20 U.S.C. § 1232g), and
- The Health Insurance Information Portability and Accountability Act (HIPAA).

The **ADA** was signed into law on July 26, 1990. The ADA "guarantees equal opportunity for individuals with disabilities in employment, public accommodations, transportation, State and local government services, and telecommunications" (U.S. Department of Education, 2006).

> *No individual shall be discriminated against on the basis of disability in the full and equal enjoyment of the goods, services, facilities, privileges, advantages, or accommodations of any*

place of public accommodation by any person who owns, leases (or leases to), or operates a place of public accommodation (sec 302a).

Public accommodation includes: places of lodging, places serving food or drink, places of entertainment, places of public gathering, retail businesses, service providers, public transportation depots, libraries and museums, parks, all schools, social service agencies, places of exercise or recreation (sec 301 7). Very little is not covered by this list, notable exceptions being private clubs and religious organizations (Bishop & Jones, 1993, p.4).

The **ADAAA** was enacted on September 25, 2008, and became effective on January 1, 2009. The ADAAA is the reinstatement of a "broad scope of protection" by expanding the definition of the term "disability." Congress found that persons with many types of impairments – including epilepsy, diabetes, multiple sclerosis, major depression, and bipolar disorder – had been unable to bring ADA claims because they were found not to meet the ADA's definition of "disability" (U.S. Equal Employment Opportunity Commission, n.d.); hence the need for the amendment.

The **IDEA**, formerly known as the Education for All Handicapped Children Act, P.L. 92-142, guarantees children with disabilities a "free, appropriate public education." This means that local school districts must develop and pay for an educational program that is tailored to the individual needs of the student with a disability. The following chart outlines the conditions that qualify as a disability under IDEA.

Autism	**Multiple disabilities**
Deaf-blindness	**Orthopedic impairment**
Deafness	**Other health impairment**
Developmental delay	**Specific learning disability**
Emotional disturbance	**Speech or language impairment**
Hearing impairment	**Traumatic brain injury**
Intellectual disability	**Visual impairment, including blindness**

(Center for Parent Information and Resources, 2016).

The **IDEA Child Find** requires that "all children with disabilities residing in the State, including children with disabilities who are homeless children or are wards of the State, and children with disabilities attending private schools, regardless of the severity of their disability, and who are in need of special education and related services, are identified, located, and evaluated" (34 C.F.R. 300.311(a)(1)). So not only must schools provide services under IDEA but they also must identify children if their condition is known to them.

Some students with chronic conditions may qualify for **Section 504** the Rehabilitation Act (Section 504). Section 504 prohibits schools that receive federal funding from discriminating against a student because of disability in academic and nonacademic activities, such as school field trips and extracurricular activities. "Section 504 requires recipients to provide to students with disabilities appropriate educational services designed to meet the individual needs of such students to the same extent as the needs of students without disabilities are met" (U.S. Department of Education, 2015, p.3).

The Section 504 regulatory provision at 34 C.F.R. 104.3(j)(2)(i) defines a physical or mental impairment as any physiological disorder or condition, cosmetic disfigurement, or anatomical loss affecting one or more of the following body systems: neurological; musculoskeletal; special sense organs; respiratory, including speech organs; cardiovascular; reproductive; digestive; genito-urinary; hemic and lymphatic; skin; and endocrine; or any mental or psychological disorder, such as mental retardation, organic brain syndrome, emotional or mental illness, and specific learning disabilities. The regulatory provision does not set forth an exhaustive list of specific diseases and conditions that may constitute physical or mental impairments because of the difficulty of ensuring the comprehensiveness of such a list.

A medical diagnosis of an illness does not automatically mean a student can receive services under Section 504, nor is Section 504 eligibility dependent upon a formal medical diagnosis. The illness/condition must cause a substantial limitation on the student's ability to learn or another major life activity. Other sources to be considered, along with the medical diagnosis, include aptitude and achievement tests, teacher recommendations, physical condition, social and cultural background, and adaptive behavior (U.S. Department of Education, 2015).

The **FERPA** (Family Education Rights and Privacy Act) is a federal law that protects the privacy of student's educational records. FERPA applies to educational agencies and institutions that receive funds under any program administered by the U.S. Department of Education. 'The term education records' is broadly defined to mean those records that are: directly related to a student, and maintained by an educational agency or institution or by a party acting for the agency or institution" (US. Department of Health and Human Services and U.S. Department of Education, 2008, p.1). These include health records, immunization records and nurse's notes.

The **HIPAA** (Health Insurance Portability and Accountability Act) was enacted to improve the efficiency and effectiveness of the healthcare system through the establishment of national standards and requirements for electronic healthcare transactions. The law was also developed to protect the privacy and security of individually identifiable health information. HIPAA excludes educational records covered by FERPA, including individually identifiable student health information (National Association of School Nurses [NASN], 2016). However, school nurses need to be familiar with HIPAA since many healthcare providers need to follow HIPAA requirements and this may impact the ability to obtain needed records without proper release of information forms.

(Please see Chapter 11 for more information on HIPAA/FERPA).

In addition to the aforementioned federal laws, states may also have laws that impact the care of students with chronic conditions, most commonly, the Nurse Practice Act (NPA). The NPA varies in each state but it typically outlines the state's standards of nursing, types of titles and licenses, requirements for licensure and grounds for disciplinary action, other violations and possible remedies. A state may also have administrative rules or regulations developed by the Board of Nursing (BON). These rules and regulations are developed to clarify or make the law more specific. The rules and regulations developed by the BON must be consistent with the NPA and cannot go beyond it. These rules and regulations undergo a process of public review before enactment. Once enacted, rules and regulations have the full force and effect of law (National Council of State Boards of Nursing, 2016).

A state's NPA may stipulate what tasks a nurse may delegate to an UAP. The NPA may also regulate which medications can be delegated to UAPs in the school setting. This can make it extremely challenging for school nurses since, in some states, nurses may be able to delegate the administration of glucagon but not the administration of insulin. At times the state's NPA is in direct conflict with state regulations and statutes. "State boards of nursing and individual state legislatures differ greatly in the intricate wording of statutes, rules, and regulations, creating difficulty establishing an understanding of the laws and whether they violate state NPAs" (Wilt & Foley, 2011, p.188). When discrepancies exist, school nurses should consult with their state BON and professional practice organization for guidance.

In addition to the federal laws that impact the care of students with chronic conditions, school nurses need to be aware of the state statutes and regulations that affect school district policy and practices related to student health and safety.

IMPLICATIONS FOR SCHOOL NURSE PRACTICE

Schools are responsible to ensure the safety of students when they are attending school and school sponsored events. One of the most significant challenges for school nurses is the increasing number of students with chronic health conditions and the lack of adequate school nurse services in many school districts. Although it is recommended that every school have a full-time school nurse (American Academy of Pediatrics, 2016; NASN, 2012) many school districts have inadequate school health services. The lack of school health staff does not mitigate the school's responsibility for ensuring they are providing a safe learning environment for students with health concerns.

One of the most vital roles of a school nurse is to assess students to determine their health status and health needs and to evaluate potential accommodation needs. The school nurse is needed to interpret medical diagnoses, orders and other healthcare information to develop plans of care that can be safely implemented in the school setting. These plans could include an Individualized Healthcare Plan (IHP), Section 504 Plan, or Emergency Care Plan (ECP) (Zirkel, 2009; NASN, 2012). Nursing assessment and planning are required for the development of these health plans (i.e., IHP and ECP) and, as such, the development of these plans cannot be delegated to others (NASN, 2012; National Council of State Boards of Nursing, 2016).

Students with disabilities or underlying health conditions, must be given an equal opportunity to participate in academic, nonacademic, and extracurricular activities. The challenge lies in ensuring that the appropriate health services are available for students who are wanting to participate in any school activity (U.S. Department of Health and Human Services and National Diabetes Education Program, 2010). School nurses can ensure the required health-related accommodations are being provided through the development of an IHP and ECP. The IHP outlines the nursing care plan for the students and can be used to demonstrate the application of the school nurse standards of care. The IHP "provides the health information and activities that can be incorporated into the health portion of other school-educational plans, such as the Individualized Education Plan or Section 504 Plan, to foster student academic success and to meet state and federal laws and regulations" (NASN, 2015, p. 1). The ECP should outline specific instructions on how school staff should respond to a particular health emergency. The ECP should include provisions for lockdown and shelter-in-place situations (NASN, 2014).

CONCLUSION

By nature of their position, school nurses are leaders within the school setting. School nurses are in a key position to educate school leaders about the needs of students with chronic health conditions. It is imperative that school nurses are educated on the federal and state laws that impact the care of students with chronic conditions so they can inform teachers, school leaders, and healthcare providers about the legal rights of students with chronic conditions. As healthcare leaders, school nurses must be aware of federal and state laws that affect their practice and the care of students in the school setting. School nurses must advocate for the rights and needs of students and speak up when the appropriate accommodations and safeguards are not in place.

RESOURCES

> **See ADDENDUM 1***:* **Differences Between Section 504 and IDEA**
> **and ADDENDUM 2: School Nurse's Role in Liability Prevention under Section 504 "Child Find" Provision.**

Helping the Student with Diabetes Succeed. A Guide for School Personnel. https://www.niddk.nih.gov/health-information/health-communication-programs/ndep/health-care-professionals/school-guide/Pages/publicationdetail.aspx

Legal Rights of Students with Diabetes. http://main.diabetes.org/dorg/PDFs/Advocacy/Discrimination/education-materials/legal-rights-of-students-with-diabetes/legal-rights-of-students-with-diabetes.pdf

Legal Rights of Children with Epilepsy in School and Child Care. An Advocate's Manual. http://epilepsy.prod.acquia-sites.com/sites/core/files/atoms/files/Legal-Rights-of-Children-with-Epilesy-in-School-and-Child-Care.pdf

Epilepsy Foundation of America. Questions and Answers on the Final Rule Implementing the ADA Amendments Act of 2008. http://www.epilepsy.com/sites/core/files/atoms/files/Q-A-on-final-Rule-Implementing-the-ADA-Amendments-Act-of-2008.pdf

CASE LAW:

San Francisco Unified School District, 5 ECLPR 377 (SEA CA 2002)	3 1/2-year-old M w/multiple disabilities.	P requested that SD address S's healthcare needs involving management of seizures. SD argued prolonged seizures were "medical emergencies" beyond the scope of their obligations	For P: SD must provide health services, and aides under the supervision of qualified nurse may evaluate seizures, administer and monitor medication, and administer ventilation intervention if needed.

Silsbee Independent School District, 25 IDELR 1023 (SEA TX 1997)	7-year-old M w/PD	SD argued that training staff in resuscitation technique and seizure was "medical training" not required under the IDEA. P argued that such training necessary to provide "related services", and that full-time nurse must be available at all times.	For P: Staff training in resuscitation and seizure management is related services to assist S in benefiting from special education instruction.
Gerber Union Elementary School District, 26 IDELR 199 (SEA CA 1997)	12-year-old M w/SED	P sought to compel the district to provide the 1:1 services of an aide specifically named in an interim IEP. SD argued aide was not adequate to provide the services the S needed, but would provide another trained adult with S at all times.	For P: The aide explicitly named on the IEP was an integral part of the IEP and continued services were necessary to ensure the stability of S's program.
Christian v. Clark County School District (Nevada State Review Officer Opinion, 2004). *	9-year-old w/ epilepsy	P requested that either she or a school nurse be on school grounds at all times in case the child needed Diastat; however, the school district stated that its emergency seizure management protocol (calling 911) was sufficient and that it was not required to provide the services of qualified personnel for this purpose. The district offered the option of reassigning the student to a school six miles away, where a registered nurse is present at all times.	For SD: school in issue was not required to provide a full-time nurse at the child's neighborhood school to administer Diastat. (Epilepsy Foundation, n.d.)
Hingham Public Schools, 33 IDELR 292 (SEA MA 2000)	5-year-old F w/Angelman Syndrome, a neurological disorder resulting in severe learning difficulties and seizure disorders.	P argued that S's IEP called for 1:1 aide with professional status and experience but assigned aide did not have those credentials. S's doctor recommended that due to S's severe learning problems, aide must have Master's degree and experience to maximize learning. SD stated that proposed aide is committed and relates well to S, thus meeting the professional status requirements. S is benefiting from current aide, so Master's and experience not necessary.	For P: Since IEP called for aide with professional credential, SD failed to comply and provide agreed-upon services. Although S would not require an aide with professional qualifications as long as supervising teacher is experienced, since IEP specified such credentials, the aide must meet those specifications.

Mobile County Board of Education, 34 IDELR 164 (SEA AL 2001)	16-year-old M w/MD	P alleged S suffered physical injuries due to inadequate protection by the SD. S was attacked and injured by three S's riding the bus. SD insisted that aide not furnished in order to foster greater independence of S by having him ride the bus without adult accompanying.	For P: Concomitant to responsibility to provide transportation to permit children to attend appropriate special education programs is the obligation to provide a safe environment for S's transported. An aide should have been assigned to accompany the S.
Board of Education of the City of New York, 28 IDELR (SEA NY 1998)	8-year-old M w/OHI, Tourette's Syndrome, and ADHD.	P contended IEP inadequate due to failure to train S's teacher, paraprofessional, classmates and other school personnel. SD argued IEP as proposed was appropriate.	For P: SD must provide training for S's teacher, paraprofessional, related service providers, & classmates. Initial and "update" training to be provided as necessary.

Note. M male; F female; P parent; SD school district; S student; MD mental disability; OHI other health impaired; PD physical disability; LPN licensed practical nursed; RN registered nurse.

Adapted from: Etscheidt, S. (2005). Paraprofessional services for students with disabilities: A legal analysis of issues. *Research & Practice for Persons with Severe Disabilities, 30*(2), 60–80. Retrieved from https://www.uvm.edu/~cdci/parasupport/reviews/Etscheidt.pdf. Reprinted with permission.

REFERENCES

American Academy of Pediatrics. (2016, June). Role of the school nurse in providing school health services (Policy Statement). *Pediatrics,137*(6), e20160852.Originally published online May 23, 2016. doi: 10.1542/peds.2016-0852

Americans with Disabilities Act Amendments. (2010). *42 U.S.C. § 12102.* Retrieved from http://www.ada.gov/pubs/adastatute08.htm

Bishop, P. C., & Jones, A.J. (1993). Implementing the Americans with disabilities act of 1990: A. Public Administration Review, 53(2), 121. Retrieved from *https://ezproxy.lib.uwm.edu/login?url=http://search. proquest.com.ezproxy.lib.uwm.edu/docview/197162844?accountid=15078*

Center for Parent Information and Resources. (2016). *Categories of disability under IDEA.* Retrieved from http://www.parentcenterhub.org/repository/categories/

Cohen, E., Kuo, D.Z., Agrawal, R., Berry, J.G., Bhagat, S.K.M., Simon, T.D. & Srivastava, R. (2011). Children with medical complexity: An emerging population for clinical and research initiatives, *Pediatrics, 127*, 529-538. doi:10.1542/peds.2010-0910

Epilepsy Foundation. (n.d.). *Diastat administration in school: Summary of relevant federal laws and selected cases.* Retrieved from http://www.epilepsyfoundation.org/epilepsylegal/upload/diastatschool.pdf

Etscheidt, S. (2005). Paraprofessional services for students with disabilities: A legal analysis of issues. *Research & Practice for Persons with Severe Disabilities, 30*(2), 60-80. Retrieved from https://www.uvm.edu/~cdci/parasupport/reviews/Etscheidt.pdf

Family Educational Rights and Privacy Act of 1974, 20 U.S.C. § 1232g (1974). Retrieved from https://www.law.cornell.edu/uscode/text/20/1232g

Health Insurance Portability and Accountability Act H.R. 3103 — 104th Congress: Health Insurance Portability and Accountability Act of 1996. Retrieved from https://www.govtrack.us/congress/bills/104/hr3103

Individuals with Disability Education Improvement Act (2004), 20 U.S.C. 1400 et seq. Retrieved from http://idea.ed.gov/download/statute.html

National Association of School Nurses. (2012). *Chronic health conditions managed by school nurses* (Position Statement). Retrieved from https://www.nasn.org/PolicyAdvocacy/PositionPapersandReports/NASNPositionStatementsFullView/tabid/462/ArticleId/17/Chronic-Health-Conditions-Managed-by-School-Nurses-Revised-January-2012

National Association of School Nurses. (2014). *Emergency preparedness and response in the school setting - the role of the school nurse* (Position Statement). Retrieved from http://www.nasn.org/PolicyAdvocacy/PositionPapersandReports/NASNPositionStatementsFullView/tabid/462/smid/824/ArticleID/117/Default.aspx

National Association of School Nurses. (2015). *Individualized Healthcare Plans: The role of the school nurse* (Position Statement). Retrieved from https://www.nasn.org/PolicyAdvocacy/PositionPapersandReports/NASNPositionStatementsFullView/tabid/462/ArticleId/32/Individualized-Healthcare-Plans-The-Role-of-the-School-Nurse-Revised-January-2015

National Association of School Nurses. (2016). *HIPAA and FERPA.* Retrieved from http://www.nasn.org/ToolsResources/DocumentationinSchoolHealth/HIPAAandFERPA

National Council of State Boards of Nursing. (2016). *Nurse practice act, rules & regulations.* Retrieved from https://www.ncsbn.org/nurse-practice-act.htm

National Survey of Children's Health. NSCH 2011/12. Data query from the Child and Adolescent Health Measurement Initiative, Data Resource Center for Child and Adolescent Health website. Retrieved from *http:/www.childhealthdata.org*

Rehabilitation Act of 1973, 29 U.S.C. § 504. Retrieved from https://www.dol.gov/oasam/regs/statutes/sec504.htm

Van Cleave, J., Gortmaker, S.L., & Perrin, J.M. (2010, Feb 17). Dynamics of obesity and chronic health conditions among children and youth. *JAMA,303*(7),623-30. doi: 10.1001/jama.2010.104

U.S. Department of Education. (2004). *Child find*. Part 300 / B / 300.111 / a / 1. Retrieved from
   http://idea.ed.gov/explore/view/p/,root,regs,300,B,300%252E111

U.S. Department of Education. (2006). *Americans with Disabilities Act* (ADA). Retrieved from
   https://ed.gov/about/offices/list/ocr/docs/hq9805.html

U.S. Department of Education. (2015). *Protecting students with disabilities*. Retrieved from
   http://www2.ed.gov/about/offices/list/ocr/504faq.html

U.S. Department of Health and Human Services & U. S. Department of Education. (2008). *Joint guidance
   on the application of the Family Educational Rights and Privacy Act (FERPA) and the Health Insurance
   Portability and Accountability Act of 1996 (HIPAA) to student health records*. Retrieved from
   http://www2.ed.gov/policy/gen/guid/fpco/doc/ferpa-hipaa-guidance.pdf

U.S. Equal Employment Opportunity Commission. (n.d.). *The Americans with Disabilities Act Amendments
   Act of 2008*. Retrieved from https://www.eeoc.gov/laws/statutes/adaaa_info.cfm

Wilt, L. & Foley, M. (2011). Delegation of Glucagon® in the school setting: A comparison of state legislation.
   The Journal of School Nursing, 27(3), 185-196. *doi:* 10.1177/1059840511398240

Zirkel, P.A. (2009). History and expansion of section 504 student eligibility: Implications for school nurses.
   The Journal of School Nursing, 25(4), 256-260. doi: 10.1177/1059840509336930

	IDEA (IEP)	Section 504	School Nursing Implication
ADDENDUM #1: Differences Between Section 504 and IDEA and School Nursing Implications **Kathleen Maguire, DNP, RN**			
Governance	Individuals with Disabilities in Education Act (IDEA) Education Law	Section 504 of the Rehabilitation Act of 1973 overseen by the Office of Civil Rights (OCR)	
Age	School-aged children	Covers individuals over a lifespan	
Eligibility Category	1. autism; 2. deaf-blindness; 3. deafness; 4. developmental delay (applicable to 3-5 year old children only); 5. emotional disturbance; hearing impairment; intellectual disability; multiple disabilities; orthopedic impairment; other health impairment (which often includes ADD/ADHD); 6. physical impairment; specific learning disability; speech or language impairment; 7. traumatic brain injury; and 8. visual impairment, including blindness	• Student who does not need special education or qualifies for special education and related services under IDEA • Physical or mental impairment substantially limiting a major life activity: walking, seeing, eating, breathing, learning Please note: the list of impairments substantially limiting a major life activity have been interpreted very expansively and that the "walking, seeing, etc...." listed are simply examples.	Examples: *Physical or Mental Impairment* • Neurological • Musculoskeletal • Respiratory • Digestive • Endocrine • Emotional • Specific learning disability • Immune disorder *Major life activity:* • Concentrating • Communicating • Bowel or bladder dysfunction • Thinking *Other:* • Temporary injuries caused by accidents • Asthma • Allergies • Diabetes • Communicable disease • *It is important to note that a "medical diagnosis does not automatically mean a student receives services under Section 504" (Martin, et al)
Requirement	Disability adversely affects education	Barriers to accessing education	
Identification	Child find: identify, evaluate, and determine eligibility for special education services	Identify and determine eligibility for Section 504 accommodations * See ADDENDUM #2	Refer children for IEP or Section 504 for evaluation if the school nurse suspects the need for services.

	IDEA (IEP)	**Section 504**	**School Nursing Implication**
Process	Full school team completes the comprehensive evaluation. Informed consent of the parent is required.	Impairment documentation from various sources: healthcare provider, parental input, evaluation data. Team decision does not require written consent of the parent.	Gathering information from multiple sources as appropriate to identify health history and potential health needs in school
Participation	• Multidisciplinary team of which school nurse is a member • Parent/Guardian	• Multidisciplinary team • Parent /Guardian • School nurse	Coordinate and collaborate with primary care providers and parents to gather appropriate mental or physical health documentation Assessment of student health status Development of: • Individualized Healthcare Plan • Individualized Emergency Care Plan
Plan	Individualized Education Plan • Specialized instruction by adapting content or delivery method of instruction	Section 504 • Accommodations • Equal access	*Examples of accommodations:* • Qualified interpreters • Adaptive writing tools • Assistive devices such as crutches, wheelchair, or walker • Medication administration or health procedure at school (such as blood glucose monitoring or G-tube feeding) • Other nursing services, such as monitoring and implementation of emergency plan for seizures • Assistance in note taking • Calculators or computers • Auditory support • Extra set of textbooks • Alternative test style • Modified workload • Untimed test • Breaks between classes • Adaptive gym • Adaptive desk • Elevator key
Evaluation	At least once every three years upon parental or teacher request.	Periodic May be temporary	Participation in reevaluation as appropriate

	IDEA (IEP)	Section 504	School Nursing Implication
Placement	May be a combination of special and regular education services Related services: speech, nursing hearing, physical or occupational therapy	Most commonly in a regular school classroom with related services or accommodations	Consult with appropriate school personnel to provide safe school environment.
Discipline	The disciplinary process for identified students involves the first step of a manifestation determination PPT Decision by special hearing if disability caused action Development of Functional Behavior Plan	The disciplinary process for identified students involves the first step of a manifestation determination Section 504 meeting. There is an exclusion for certain 504 students. No punishment or discrimination based on disability	Support ongoing interaction with the multi-disciplinary team, parent or guardian, and healthcare provider.

References:

Martin, Jose L., L.L.P. "Determining Eligibility Under Section 504: Fundamentals and New Challenge Areas." *The Council of Educators for Students with Disabilities*. Richards, Lindsay, & Martin, LLP, 2009. Web. June-July 2016.

http://www.504idea.org/Council_Of_Educators/Resources_files/Modern%20504%20Eligibility.pdf

ADDENDUM # 2

Lawrence J. Altman, Esquire

Do school nurses play a role in liability prevention under Section 504's "Child Find" provision?

YES! Under the Individual with Disabilities Education Act and Section 504 of the Rehabilitation Act, schools have an obligation under what is referred to as "Child Find" or identification and eligibility to locate and then assess any child that school staff believes might be disabled under the IDEA or Section 504. To illustrate, if the school nurse is made aware that a student uses an Inhaler to help when the child has an asthma attack, then the school has been made aware that this child might have a Section 504 disability. That student should undergo a Section 504 eligibility determination, and accommodations implemented by the school due to her asthma, such as the ability to carry her inhaler with her, the development of an emergency plan, and notification of her teachers and other relevant staff members of her disability-related day-to-day and emergency needs through dissemination of the student's Section 504 Plan.

Chapter 23

CONCUSSION MANAGEMENT

Cameron Traut, MS, BSN, RN, PEL-IL, NCSN
Nancy L. Dube, MPH, BSEd, RN

DESCRIPTION OF ISSUE

Definition

Concussion is defined as "a type of traumatic brain injury—or TBI—caused by a bump, blow, or jolt to the head or by a hit to the body that causes the head and brain to move rapidly back and forth. This sudden movement can cause the brain to bounce around or twist in the skull, stretching and damaging the brain cells and creating chemical changes in the brain" (Centers for Disease Control and Prevention [CDC], 2015a). The 4th International Conference on Concussion in Sport (McCrory et al., 2013) defines a concussion as "a complex pathophysiological process affecting the brain, induced by biomechanical forces...It may be caused by a direct blow to the head or elsewhere on the body with an 'impulsive' force transmitted to the head... It typically results in short-lived impairment of neurological function that resolves spontaneously... It is a functional not structural injury, which results in a 'graded set' of clinical symptoms - physical, cognitive, and emotional... "(p. 1-2).

Prevalence

Incidence has been increasing over time. It is difficult to determine exact statistics on the incidence and prevalence of concussions due to the lack of current descriptive research in this area, as well as the underreporting of concussions and the increase in sporting activities for children outside of school such as private sports organizations and clubs, as well as a variety of recreational activities (Institute of Medicine [IOM] and National Research Council [NRC], 2014). Data from the CDC shows a dramatic increase in the zero to four-year-old population and an increase in all other age groups. The increased incidence in five to 14-year-old students includes all ages, and all emergency department visits, not just sports-related events (CDC, 2015b).

A recent report collected information from three national databases and estimated between 1.1 and 1.9 million children equal to or under 18 years old sustained what they described as a *sports-and recreation - related concussion* annually (Bryan, Rowhani-Rahbar, Comstock & Rivara, 2016). According to a report by the Committee on Sports-Related Concussion in Youth (IOM & NRC, 2014), football is the sport with the highest reported incidence of concussion in both male and female sports. The highest reported incidence of concussion in men's sports occurred in football, ice hockey, lacrosse, wrestling, and soccer. The highest reported incidence of concussion in women's sports occurred in soccer, lacrosse, basketball, and at the collegiate level - ice hockey. There are other causes of concussions, non-sport related mechanisms of injury, such as falls, altercations, motor vehicle accidents, skate/long boarding, water/snow skiing, and other recreational activities (IOM & NRC, 2014).

BACKGROUND

As far back as the late 1800's through the early 20th century, concussions have been recognized as a serious medical condition. American football played a significant role in the evolution of concussion prevention and care due to the number of significant and sometimes life-threatening injuries (Stone, Patel, & Bailes, 2014). The first collegiate sports organization (predecessor to the NCAA) was formed in 1906 as a response to President Roosevelt's concerns about safety in collegiate sports. The NCAA followed in 1933 with directives for colleges stating players after sustaining a concussion/head injury must rest for 48 hours before returning to practice or play. In 1937, the American Football Coaches Association recommended that head-injured players be removed from play immediately (Waldron, 2013). An article appearing in the *New England Journal of Medicine* (Thorndike, 1952), advised players experiencing three concussions to leave the sport permanently for their own health and safety. Since then, there have been many articles, studies, controversies, and evolving research into the long-term effects of concussion including the effect on young students.

As research on the pathophysiology of a concussion continues to evolve, models of care and treatment continue to progress as well. For example, gone are the days that a coach and player would informally decide if the player felt well enough to return to competition after sustaining a hard hit. More recently, "cocoon therapy" was the approach to rest, which has evolved now into only 1-2 days of recommended total rest followed by gradually resuming some daily activities at a sub symptom, or below the current level of symptoms, threshold. Research is ongoing in the area of physical rest vs light physical activity sooner in recovery (Remaly, 2016). Management protocol has shifted over time from a three-day return to all activity to a gradual return to function, learn and play (McCrory et al., 2013).

Although most students recover from a concussion within an average of 1 to 3 weeks, how quickly they improve depends on many factors. These factors include duration of symptoms, age, pre-existing health conditions (both physical and mental), and compliance with recommended interventions for self-care after the injury. Most students who have had a concussion, experience symptoms which tend to impede the ability to perform daily activities, including work, academics, and interacting with family and friends during recovery (IOM & NRC, 2014).

Rest is very important after a concussion because it helps the brain to heal. Ignoring the symptoms and trying to "tough it out" often makes symptoms worse. Only when the symptoms have reduced significantly, in consultation with a healthcare professional, should the student slowly and gradually return to daily activities, such as work or school. If symptoms worsen, return, or new symptoms develop as activity increases, this may require the student to slow the return to activity and increase rest (Remaly, 2016).

For students, it is very important to remember recovery from a concussion is a process, a cyclical, not a linear, recovery. Students must be able to perform activities of daily living without symptoms before they can gradually return to academic work and athletic activities. This is described as returning to full function, learning, and play (McCrory et al., 2013).

Legal Issues

Glassman & Holt (2011) report new and evolving medical research on concussions, increased public awareness, and a general change in attitude on how to manage concussion injuries present a "significant risk management challenge for youth sports programs" (pg. 26). Now that there is increased awareness of the short-term and long-term health risks, as legally interpreted, an appropriate response is required (Glassman & Holt, 2011).

All 50 states and the District of Columbia currently have a sports concussion law. Most of the state laws have three items in common:

1) any athlete suspected of having sustained a concussion must immediately be removed from play;

2) the athlete may not be returned to action the same day; and

3) the athlete may be progressively returned to activity only after written clearance is provided by a licensed healthcare professional (the definition of which varies widely from state to state).

Some states have gone further to include all concussive incidents, not just those related to sports (National Conference of State Legislatures [NCSL], 2015).

Some state laws contain additional requirements, including mandates for specific athletic department personnel to complete an annual concussion education course, neurocognitive baseline testing implemented by schools, and student-athletes and parents/guardians be provided with concussion education materials along with signing a concussion information form. The full-text of each state law may be accessed through the National Conference of State Legislatures website (NCSL, 2015).

In recent years, there have been court decisions related to concussions in schools. In most cases, the courts looked at the "duty of reasonable care". Cases found against the school districts included lack of training or proper supervision during activities that led to injury. Many of the cases found in this review also included coaches independently returning students to activity without the student being cleared by a licensed healthcare professional (Anderson, 2014).

Situations of potential concern for the school nurse occur when the school policy is not implemented correctly or completely. Glassman & Holt (2011) share examples of "liability theories" which have been used in litigation:

1) "The school has no protocol, and should." Concussion protocols are part of the standard of care now, with most states having laws requiring some type of protocol or policy.

2) "School protocol is flawed." If the protocol is not aligned with commonly recommended protocol templates, this is a potential liability.

3) "School didn't follow protocol" which speaks for itself (p. 29).

Other liabilities noted in litigation examples have been:

1) issues with unsafe field of play/equipment conditions;

2) "failure to refer" to healthcare professionals;

3) "inadequate provision of information to other care providers"; and

4) "negligent supervision" of coaches or referees during the competition (Glassman & Holt, p. 30).

Some Examples of Recent Case Law

According to the 2014 Sports Law Year-in-Review by the National Federation of High Schools (Green, 2015), a Montana court approved a $300,000 settlement in Rouchleau v. Three Forks School District in 2009. This

281

case involved a traumatic brain injury suffered by a high school football player who allegedly was returned to action prematurely after suffering a concussion during a practice. The original filings in the suit claimed that shortly after being diagnosed with a concussion, the school's coaches allowed the player to return to action without written clearance by a licensed medical professional as mandated by the state's concussion protocol law and that the student-athlete then sustained a helmet-to-helmet hit, rendering him unconscious, resulting in permanent brain damage.

Another lawsuit (Green, 2015) was filed against a school district and soccer coach alleging premature return to action after a concussion in violation of the duty of reasonable care to evaluate student-athletes for incapacities, including return-to-action protocols after an injury. In M.U. v. Downingtown (PA) Area School District, the pleadings contended a 14-year-old female soccer player, while attempting to strike a header, suffered a concussion when the girl's face collided with the head of another player. The suit asserted that she was removed from the game for a few minutes, and despite exhibiting multiple indicia of a concussion, was allowed to return to action where she suffered another head-to-head hit resulting in a "second impact syndrome" traumatic brain injury. The suit invoked the state's concussion protocol law, which required that student-athletes who show signs of a concussion be immediately removed from play, cannot return to play the same day, and may return to action only after clearance from a licensed medical professional.

A 2012 lawsuit (Schoepfer-Bochicchio, & Dodds, 2015) addressed the school nurse's "duty of care." A football player at an Iowa high school, with a known neuro-vascular condition, sustained a concussion in October 2012. After the injury, the student athlete visited the nurse a few times with complaints of headache and double vision during class. The school nurse failed to report these complaints or the pre-existing condition to his coaches, and the student continued to participate in football. In November 2012, the student underwent brain surgery, was comatose post-operatively, and subsequently was permanently disabled, requiring assistive devices to walk. The school nurse and district were sued and found liable for being negligent in the school nurse's duty of care as she did not report the symptoms to a coach or the student's guardian, or refer the student to a healthcare provider.

IMPLICATIONS FOR SCHOOL NURSE PRACTICE

Conflicts can occur between school nurses and coaches, administrators, athletic directors, teaching staff, parent/guardian(s) and students. These conflicts are not new to school nurses. It is vital for the school nurse to ensure the "duty of safe care" through knowledge and implementation of the language of state laws, district policies, and the best practice guidelines provided by national organizations such as the CDC Heads Up Program, National Association of School Nurses (NASN), National Federation of High Schools (NFHS), and others. The school nurse has the knowledge to address and inform relevant staff members and caregivers about these issues.

The changing culture surrounding concussion management presents a challenge for school nurses. The school nurse assumes many roles within concussion care management in the school setting:

1) coordinator of individual student care,
2) concussion oversight committee member or leader,
3) prevention, advocacy, and

4) gatekeeper.

As with many other acute and chronic health conditions, the school nurse should coordinate the district's response to concussion management by advocating for prevention and care coordination (NASN, 2016a). The NASN *Framework for 21st Century School Nursing Practice* (2016b) can be used when describing the role of the school nurse in concussion management.

Care coordination: the school nurse coordinates care of the student returning to school with a concussion by working with the multidisciplinary team and advocating for the student's needs.

Leadership: the school nurse is a key leader in the formation of and participation in the school or district's concussion oversight committee as well as in development of the district concussion protocol.

Community/Public Health: the school nurse, as relevant to the unique practice settings in a school environment, is the gatekeeper in regards to adhering to state and local laws and policies, best practices, referrals to appropriate medical care, and identifying preventative measures in concussion car

Quality Improvement: the school nurse documents care, monitors prevalence, collects data, and continually evaluates protocols, care and management (NASN, 2016b).

The foundation for decision-making lies within each state's legal policy, starting with the Nurse Practice Act as well as the nurse's education and training as a clinician.

- The school nurse must be knowledgeable in his or her state's nurse practice laws as well as the most current research and evidence-based practices.
- Each state also has a set of rules enacted by their state boards of education which may affect the coordination of care in a school.
- The school nurse must be familiar with special education law at the federal and state level, as some students with prolonged symptoms will qualify for a Section 504 Plan or an individualized education plan (Zirkel & Eagan Brown, 2015).
- Sources for state legal mandates related to healthcare policy are the states/ boards of education and health departments (Shannon & Gerdes, 2016).
- All 50 states now have concussion laws which contribute to determining the course of care and management for all students (NCSL, 2015). These laws vary from state to state and school nurses must be well informed about the details of their own state's concussion laws.
- At the district level, the school nurse must be knowledgeable on the district board policies and how these policies relate to the district's concussion protocol (Shannon & Gerdes, 2016).

Along with the state nurse practice act and other state policies that elaborate on the care of specific health conditions, nursing education and training lay the foundation for any professional nursing decision made regarding patient care and management. The professional school nurse is expected to have competent clinical nursing skills, and be knowledgeable of the most current research and evidence-based practice related to school health and the specialty of school nursing (Selekman, 2013). In the ever-changing environment of concussion care and management, it is critical for the school nurse to have the current research and evidenced-based information readily accessible.

Protocols/Policies

School nurses have a complex set of laws, rules, and guidelines which must be acknowledged and constantly incorporated in their care (Selekman, 2013). This is well illustrated in the decision-making process when caring for a student with a concussion, which includes the development of protocols, procedures, and policies addressing concussion management in the school (Zirkel & Eagan Brown, 2015).

A protocol or policy for concussion care and management should be in place, either at the individual school or at district level. Some states dictate what should be in place and offer model policies. The school nurse plays a critical role in the development of this protocol or policy. It is also important to know the difference between policy and protocol. A policy is a formal written statement detailing the particular action to be taken in a particular situation that is contractually binding (University of Wisconsin-Madison [UWM], Health Sciences, 2016).

A protocol is an agreed framework outlining the care that will be provided to patients in a designated area of practice (UWM, 2016). Protocols are procedural statements written and used by nurses that outline the standard of practice for assessing and managing a specified clinical problem and authorize particular practice activities. Nursing protocols vary according to the level of education and licensure of the nurse who will implement the protocol (Shannon & Gerdes, 2016).

To elaborate, a protocol is a little more general, but still descriptive set of procedures, which is less binding than policy, and a little more interpretive or flexible as to how the procedures are implemented. Protocols, which can also be referenced to as clinical guidelines, are typically evidence-based and define the process of implementing policy and law. Since policies must always be school board-approved, they are typically less flexible and very binding (Selekman, 2013).

CONCLUSION

In summary, the role of a school nurse in concussion care has many facets, and is guided by following a decision-making checklist when developing policy and/or protocols, and when faced with challenging scenarios within concussion management and care in the school setting. Laws, board policies, protocols, and standards of care and best practice are the cornerstone of the decision-making process for a school nurse. Professional organizations provide position statements on a variety of issues and care, as well as access to current research, trends in practice, and expert practitioners.

> ### Decision-Making Checklist:
> 1. Federal Laws
> 2. State Laws
> 3. State Nurse Practice Act
> 4. State Board of Health policies/regulations
> 5. State Board of Education policies/regulations
> 6. Local School District Policy
> 7. Current nursing standards for best practice
>   a. School nursing: scope and standards of practice (NASN)
>   b. Nursing: scope and standards of practice (ANA)
> 8. Current evidence-based research
> 9. Professional organizations (i.e. NASN, state school nurse organizations, ASHA)
> 10. Examples of litigation/liability cases

The safety and health of the student remain the priority and focus of care as long as the school nurse reviews and incorporates these guiding principles and legal documents into all levels of their plan and practice.

RESOURCES

> **Please see ADDENDUM: Concussion Law Theories of Liability**

American Academy of Neurology (2016). Sports concussion resources. Minneapolis, MN. Retrieved from https://www.aan.com/contact-aan/

Centers for Disease Control and Prevention. (2015a). *HEADS UP to brain injury.* Atlanta, GA: National Center for Injury Prevention and Control; Division of Unintentional Injury Prevention. Retrieved from https://www.cdc.gov/headsup/

Children's Hospital of Philadelphia (2016). Concussion care for kids: Minds matter. Philadelphia, PA. Retrieved from http://www.chop.edu/centers-programs/concussion-care-minds-matter#.V-8m9_ArLIU

Colorado School Safety Resource Center (2016). *Concussion and traumatic brain injury.* Colorado Department of Public Safety, Denver, CO. Retrieved from https://www.colorado.gov/pacific/cssrc/concussion-traumatic-brain-injury

Lurie Children's Hospital, Institute of Sports Medicine (2015). *Return to learn after a concussion: A guide for teachers and school professionals.* Chicago, IL. Retrieved from http://luriechildrens.peachnewmedia.com/store/seminar/seminar.php?seminar=45893

Maine Department of Education (2015). Concussion management. Augusta, ME. Retrieved from http://www.maine.gov/doe/concussion/

National Federation of High Schools (2015). Sports medicine. Indianapolis, IN. Retrieved from
https://www.nfhs.org/resources/sports-medicine/

Nationwide Children's Hospital (2016). Concussion toolkit. Columbus, OH. Retrieved from:
http://www.nationwidechildrens.org/concussion-toolkit

Nebraska Sports Concussion Network (n.d.). *Return to learn and return to play guidelines*. Statewide
locations, NE. Retrieved from http://www.nebsportsconcussion.org/

New Jersey Department of Education (n.d.). *Model policy and guidance for prevention and treatment of
sports-related concussions and head injuries. Trenton, NJ. Retrieved from* http://nj.gov/education/aps/
cccs/chpe/concussions/policy.pdf

University of Pittsburgh Medical Center (2016). Sports medicine concussion program. Pittsburgh, PA.
Retrieved from: http://www.upmc.com/Services/sports-medicine/services/concussion/Pages/default.
aspx

REFERENCES

Anderson, P. (2014). *Legal issues surrounding concussions in youth and high school sport: Finding a
standard of care.* [PowerPoint slides]. Retrieved from https://law.marquette.edu/assets/sports-law/pdf/
Anderson.711.pdf

Bryan, M.A., Rowhani-Rahbar, A., Comstock, R.D., & Rivara, F. (2016). Sports- and recreation-related
concussions in US Youth. *Pediatrics, 138*(1), 1-8. doi: 10.1542/peds.2015-4635

Centers for Disease Control and Prevention. (2015a). *HEADS UP: Brain injury basics - What is a concussion?*
Atlanta, GA.: National Center for Injury Prevention and Control; Division of Unintentional Injury
Prevention. Retrieved from http://www.cdc.gov/headsup/basics/concussion_whatis.html

Centers for Disease Control and Prevention. (2015b). *Report to Congress on traumatic brain injury in the
United States: Epidemiology and rehabilitation.* Atlanta, GA: National Center for Injury Prevention
and Control; Division of Unintentional Injury Prevention. Retrieved from https://www.cdc.gov/
traumaticbraininjury/pdf/tbi_report_to_congress_epi_and_rehab-a.pdf

Glassman, S.J. & Holt, B.J. (2011). Concussions and student-athletes: Medical-legal issues in concussion care
and physician and school system risks. *New Hampshire Bar Journal, 52*(3), 26-35. Retrieved from
https://www.nhbar.org/uploads/pdf/BJ-Autumn2011-Vol52-No3-Pg26.pdf

Green, L. (2015). *2014 Sports law year-in-review*. Indianapolis, IN: National Federation of Sports. Retrieved
from http://www.nfhs.org/articles/2014-sports-law-year-in-review/

Institute of Medicine (IOM) and National Research Council. (2014). Sports-*related concussions in youth:
Improving the science, changing the culture.* Washington D.C.: National Academies Press. Retrieved from
http://www.ncbi.nlm.nih.gov/books/NBK169016/

McCrory, P., Meeuwisse, W.H., Aubry, M., Cantu, B., Dvorak, J., Echemendia, R.J., . . . Turner, M. (2013). Consensus statement on concussion in sport: The 4th international conference on concussion in sport held in Zurich, November 2012. *British Journal of Sports Medicine, 47*, 250-258. doi: 10.1136/bjsports-2013-092313

National Association of School Nurses. (2016a). *Concussions - the role of the school nurse* (Position Statement). Silver Spring, MD: Author. Retrieved from http://www.nasn.org/PolicyAdvocacy/PositionPapersandReports/NASNPositionStatementsFullView/tabid/462/ArticleId/218/Concussions-The-Role-of-the-School-Nurse-Revised-June-2016

National Association of School Nurses. (2016b). Framework for 21st century school nursing practice. *NASN School Nurse, 31*(1), 45-53. doi: 10.1177/1942602X15618644

National Conference of State Legislatures. (2015). *Traumatic brain injury legislation*. Washington D.C. Retrieved from http://www.ncsl.org/research/health/traumatic-brain-injury-legislation.aspx

Proctor, S. (2013). Standards of practice. In J. Selekman (Ed.), *School Nursing: A comprehensive text* (2nd ed.) (48-78). Philadelphia, PA: F.A. Davis Company

Remaly, J. (2016). Looking beyond rest to active and targeted treatments for concussion. *Neurology Review, 24*(6),1, 32-33. Retrieved from http://www.neurologyreviews.com/specialty-focus/traumatic-brain-injury-tbi/article/looking-beyond-rest-to-active-and-targeted-treatments-for-concussion/2fdc2b5d656e136eb42983a3a3a5dd37.html

Schoepfer-Bochicchio, K. & Dodds, M. (2015). *Concussion lawsuit examines school nurse's duty of care*. Retrieved from http://www.athleticbusiness.com/civil-actions/concussion-lawsuit-examines-school-nurse-s-duty-of-care.html

Shannon, R.A. & Gerdes, J.H. (2016). *Developing school health policies, protocols, and procedures? Help please!* [PowerPoint slides]. Presentation at the NASN 2015 Annual Conference, June 24, 2015.

Strough v. Bedford Community School District. (2012). http://www.iasd.uscourts.gov/sites/default/files/4-13-cv-147-HCA%20Strough%20v.%20Bedford%20Community%20School%20District%20et%20al.pdf

Stone, J.L., Patel, V., & Bailes, J. (2014). The history of neurosurgical treatments of sports concussion. *Neurosurgery, 75*, S3-S23. doi: 10.1227/NEU.0000000000000488

Thorndike, A. (1952). Serious recurrent injuries of athletes; contraindications to further competitive participation. *New England Journal of Medicine, 247*(15), 554-556. doi: 10.1056/NEJM195210092471504

University of Wisconsin-Madison, Health Sciences (2016). *Nursing resources: Standard, guideline, protocol, policy.* Madison, WI: Ebling Library. Retrieved from http://researchguides.ebling.library.wisc.edu/c.php?g=293229&p=1953402

Waldron, T. (2013, July). *The NCAA's history with concussions: A timeline*. Retrieved from https://thinkprogress.org/the-ncaas-history-with-concussions-a-timeline-530a8c5af0df#.i0qyx94ns

Zirkel, P.A. & Eagan Brown, B. (2015). K-12 students with concussions: A legal perspective. *The Journal of School Nursing, 31*(2), 99-109. doi: 10.1177/1059840514521465

ADDENDUM

Concussion Law Theories of Liability

Erin D. Gilsbach, Esquire

There are typically 4 different types of concussion-related legal actions that are brought by parents against school districts. They are:

- **Tort Claims** – most common in states with weak tort clais protections, but these cases can also be brought in states with strong tort claims protection if the parents are alleging that the harm was intentional.

- **Section 504** – While concussions are generally temporary in nature and, therefore, do not qualify under Section 504, each situation must be considered individually, since concussions can vary widely, Section 504 evaluation teams will consider the length, nature, and degree of a concussion.

- **Section 1983 / State-Created Danger** – Under this theory of law, parents have a very high burden, but some concussion cases have been successful. To prevail, parents need to prove:

  o the harm ultimately caused was foreseeable and fairly direct;

  o a state actor acted with a degree of culpability that shocks the conscience;

  o a relationship between the state and the plaintiff existed; and

  o a state actor affirmatively used his or her authority in a way that created a danger to the citizen or that rendered the citizen more vulnerable to danger than had the state not acted at all.

- **Concussion Law Compliance** – Many states now have laws setting forth specific obligations for schools with regards to concussion.

Chapter 24

CONSENT FOR HEALTHCARE SERVICES

Lorali Gray, MEd, BSN, RN, NCSN

DESCRIPTION OF ISSUE

School districts provide both educational and healthcare services to a diverse student population spanning the school-age years. In education, parental rights to consent and make decisions for their minor child generally goes without question. In school health however, school nurses often find themselves navigating challenging legal and ethical dilemmas of parental and minor consent. There are some complex situations that can put school nurses, administrators and other staff in the middle of sensitive adolescent and parental debate creating risk for liability over consent for services or treatment. Statutes and case law related to consent varies widely in any given state and have legal and ethical implications for policy and practice in a school setting. School nurses, school health staff and administrators must be knowledgeable or know where to find assistance in understanding relevant parental and minor consent laws in their state.

The provision of emergency care, conducting school health surveys, communicating with outside providers, administering medication, health care during a disaster and school health research are a few. Furthermore, statutes and minor case law in any given state have added to the legal implications for policy and practice in a school setting. Examples include referral for a myriad of healthcare services, release from school when ill, student photographs, random drug screening, privacy and confidentiality of counsel with students and the subsequent documentation and records management. Minors seeking counsel or care for reproductive health issues, sexually transmitted infections, mental health concerns, HIV/AIDs, drug and alcohol treatment and services can put school nurses, administrators and other staff in the middle of sensitive parental and minor debate creating risk for liability over consent for services or treatment. While a minor's legal ability to consent to a range of sensitive healthcare services has expanded greatly over the years, consent to healthcare services continues to be fraught with legal and ethical questions regarding minors and their rights to autonomy and capacity in decision making (Guttmacher Institute, 2016). Legally balancing minor autonomy and parental responsibility is a topic of continued debate and over time, one of the most controversial and challenging issues facing federal, state and local policy makers. Laws that govern minor's consent belongs to the states and can differ widely.

School nurses, school health staff and administrators must be knowledgeable or know where to find legal and risk management assistance in understanding relevant consent laws in their state regarding both parental consent and, for adolescents, minor consent (Cohn, Gelfman, & Schwab, 2001/2005). For minors, it is also necessary to understand any differences between general medical care and specific clinical services such as contraception, pregnancy, HIV/AIDS and abortion.

BACKGROUND

School nurses deliver health care and nursing services to students within the National Association of School Nurses (NASN) Framework for 21st Century School Nursing Practice (NASN, 2016). Within this framework, the key principal *Standards of Practice* has two components that directly relate to consent; code of ethics and standards of practice. Ethical care and practice protect parental rights as well as a minor's dignity, autonomy, rights, and confidentiality within the complex intersection of health, education, and nursing laws (NASN, 2016; American Nurses Association [ANA], 2015; ANA & NASN, 2017). Consent for care is further complicated by a diverse population of student needs and abilities such as developmental age, mental capacity, homelessness, poverty, foster placement, age of majority, emancipation, mature minor, or marital status.

Regardless of these complexities, school nurses are accountable and liable for ensuring proper consent whether from the parent, legal guardian or student for any medical or nursing care provided at school. They also have an obligation to fully inform the healthcare provider, parent or student of any unique clinical or environmental issues that could impact the outcome of said treatment in the school setting (Cohn et al., 2001/2005).

To better understand the complexities of parental and minor consent a literature review was conducted to explore scholarly work for history, definitions, legal and ethical relevance to school health and nursing.

History of Minor Consent

Early American law regarding minors was based on the viewpoint that children were property and had no rights. Additionally, with the emergence of the legal principal "age of majority" it was believed that anyone under the age of majority (age 16-18 in most states) was not capable to consent to matters about their health care (Cohn et al., 2001/2005). This was generally understood to mean that parent/guardian(s) were responsible for providing consent for health care for their child until either the age of majority or emancipation. While the law has traditionally considered minors to be incompetent to give consent, most states have implemented law that recognizes the ability of the adolescent to consent to medical care in specific situations. Examples include court ordered emancipation, situational emancipation, and very specific types of treatment the adolescent is seeking such as reproductive care and abortion (McNary, 2014).

The 1970s hallmarked the legality of abortion largely due to *Roe v. Wade*, 410 U.S. 113, and in 1977 the *Carey v. Populations Services International* decision, 413 U.S. 678, allowed the legal sale of contraceptives to minors and supported privacy of reproductive health services (Moon, 2012).

Nationally, over the past 30 years, the legal ability of a minor to consent to reproductive care, mental health services and alcohol and drug treatment has significantly expanded. See APPENDIX for an overview of minor consent laws across the United States.

The development over time of these laws recognizes that although parental involvement in critical healthcare services to minors is desirable, healthcare trends have shown that minors in need of confidential services will forgo important treatment if forced to involve their parents (Guttmacher Institute, 2016.) Therefore, the prevention of poor health outcomes and the reduction of unwanted pregnancy and disease became a big reason for this expansion. In addition, the associated support and protection of a minor's developing autonomy is a fundamental goal of pediatric health care (Moon, 2012).

Today, minor children are no longer legally considered property. Although, some policy makers, healthcare providers and school nurses do not agree on the level of minor decision-making capacity, the legal environment remains dynamic. There still remains a lack of consistency in both the definition and the laws surrounding the complexity of consent even though it has been more than 800 years after the first recorded age of consent laws (Robertson, 2016). Like all civil liberties, society continues to debate and adjust to changing societal norms. Attention remains to policy and practice when providing health care to minors, balancing parent's responsibility and the developing autonomy of minors to consent. *(See Chapter 14 for more information on minor consent).*

Definitions

To better understand the many types of consent and the complex nature of both their application and relevance to school health, nursing services, and decision-making they must first be defined.

Informed consent according to Chambliss & Schutt (2010), is given by persons who are competent, have consented voluntarily, are fully informed and have understood the risks and benefits of what they have been told. In a school setting, this is considered the approval given by a parent or guardian to a school official, based on full disclosure of relevant facts by the official (Schwab & Gelfman, 2001/2005). Written, informed consent from the parent/guardian is required for student participation in sports, after school extracurricular activities, the exchange or release of education records, specialized nursing services such as catheterization, physical assessment, physical examinations, other medical treatments, or non-routine services (Pohlman & Schwab, 2001). The provision of special education or Section 504 services for students with disabilities also requires informed, voluntary, and written parental consent that can be withdrawn at any time. Most districts have policy regarding parental informed consent to take and use photographs or video images of students at school. The states of Georgia and New Jersey passed legislation in 2010 and 2011 making it illegal for anyone other than the parent to videotape their child.

Implied consent on the other hand is assumed, rather than stated. According to Pohlman and Schwab (2001), when parents send their children to school they are giving "implied" consent to routine school health and nursing services provided to all students such as illness and injury care, vision and hearing screening and individualized healthcare plans (IHPs). Parents are usually informed of these services through published policies, handbooks, websites and programs and services that are available and provided to students during the school day. When a school nurse makes a home visit or conducts a health history assessment to gather relevant student health information, parental consent is implied (Schwab & Gelfman, 2001/2005). In addition, most states allow the treatment of minors in a life-threatening emergency when a parent or guardian is unavailable to provide consent. In these situations, consent is implied or presumed (Mc Nary, 2014).

Lastly, it is important to understand the distinction between passive and active consent. Passive consent occurs when a person has been informed and is considered to agree unless the parent specifically declines to allow a student to participate (they "opt out" of participation). This type of consent is used in schools related to sexual health education and for some student health surveys where all students participate unless the parent opt out their student.

The benefits of passive consent are less cost and labor for the district, an increase in response rates and a more representative sample of students participating. Active consent however, requires written permission and involves a person's willingness to participate by agreeing to a specific service or program such as student health questionnaires. For example, California Education Code sections 51513 and 51938(b) requires parent or guardian passive or active consent prior to administering the *California Healthy Kids Survey* to students. In addition, Chambliss & Schutt (2010) note active consent is common when a parent consents for their student to participate in school health research. Sometimes in school health research a parent may consent with the assent of the student. In this circumstance, assent means voluntary agreement. Conversely, dissent takes place if a parent makes a decision on behalf of the student and the student does not agree. (*Please see Chapter 8 for more information on research in school health*).

Relevance to School Health/School Nursing

School nurses uphold a protective relationship with the students they serve, acting "in loco parentis", in place of, or standing in for, the parent (Loschiavo, 2012). This is also a traditional legal concept describing the authority of a school official or other individual to act in the place of an absent parent (Schwab & Gelfman, 2001/2005). Given this responsibility, school nurses are time and again confronted with the question of who can legally provide consent for a student's healthcare treatment and services and under what circumstances. Is it the parent, guardian or the minor? To address this question, school nurses need to consider the student's age, the parental relationship, legal guardianship, the situation requiring consent and the federal, state and local laws regarding minors' consent. According to Pohlman and Schwab (2001), school nurses need to analyze each individual situation in light of their state nursing education statutes and district policy. Seeking legal and risk management counsel may be necessary to manage associated concerns of liability. (*Please see Chapter 16 for more information on parental rights*).

First, the student's age will be key in understanding who can legally provide consent. Students under the age of majority require parental consent to participate in various school activities and programs. For these children, consent is solely the responsibility of the parent/guardian. Although adolescents in the eyes of the law have limited decision-making capacity there are some exceptions for requiring parental consent. A few long- standing exceptions in some states are life-threatening medical emergencies, with no time to obtain parental consent, age of majority and the mature minor rule. The most common exception allows school nurses and administrators the authority to summon an ambulance in a life-threatening emergency for a child of any age.

In many states, adolescents can give consent for emergency medical care if waiting for parental consent increases the risk of harm (Moon, 2012). If the situation is medically urgent rather than life-threatening consent from the parent must be obtained (Laubin, Schwab, & Doyle, 2013). Child protective services or local law enforcement may have the authority in some states to consent for evaluation and treatment of any child or youth in cases of suspected abuse or neglect (AAP, 2011). Other exceptions occur at the age of majority when a student becomes a legal adult. This means the student can legally perform most tasks reserved for parents, which may include signing school related forms, absence notes, medication forms, permission slips to participate in school activities or releasing themselves from school. This includes the approval to disclose confidential health records. Additionally, students who have been granted legal emancipation from their parents or guardian at an earlier age have the same rights as a student who has reached the age of majority. An emancipated minor is usually under the age of 18, living financially independently from his or her parents, is married or serving in the military (Caldart-Olson & Thronson, 2013). State laws governing the emancipation of minors and age of majority can be found through Cornell University Law School's Legal Information Institute (n.d.).

The last exception related to student age is the mature minor rule. This rule is an ethically derived legal principal. It acknowledges the adolescent is developmentally capable of both understanding and has the capacity to consent to specific health services without permission from the parent (Lambelet, Coleman, & Rosoff, 2013). These laws describe an age when a minor can legally consent to very specific healthcare services such as contraception, abortion, mental health, drug and alcohol or HIV/AIDs treatment. However, parental consent in most states continues to be required for general medical care even though the minor is considered cognitively "mature" (Lambelet et al., 2013). There are instances however, noted by Chambliss & Schutt (2010), when a student may not be legally competent to consent due to mental illness, chronic disability or institutionalization. School nurses serving these students must be aware that in these circumstances the parent or guardian must give consent.

Parental relationships are also critical in determining who can provide consent. School nurses interact with many types of families and must be ready to apply legal and ethical practices to situations where parents are separated, divorced, have joint legal custody, or have limited authority per a state court order. In these situations, it must be determined which parent has legal authority to consent to treatment and how each parent is involved in the decision-making process (McNary, 2014). Because parents may hold differing opinions on the need for treatment or who is an appropriate provider, care is often sought without the knowledge of the other parent (Hecker & Sori, 2010; Shumaker & Medoff, 2013).

Likewise, parents who are deceased, deported, incarcerated or debilitated leave some students without any parental care. In other cases, the student's biological parent is no longer in the picture due to neglect, abuse or trauma (Briner, 2015). This is contributing to "unaccompanied youth" described as homeless, runaway, or sexually exploited and trafficking youth. In some states, this also includes a growing population of unaccompanied immigrant minors, the vast majority of whom are males escaping violence (Ciaccia & John, 2016). The federal McKinney-Vento Homeless Assistance Act of 1987 requires that homeless, unaccompanied children and youth be enrolled in school immediately, even without a parent/guardian. This however, creates concerns when a school nurse needs to refer these students for healthcare services. They face issues of consent for care, transportation and payment (Adams & Shineldecker, 2014). An example of legislation to address this concern was, in 2016, Washington State homeless students-educational outcomes legislation. A new section was added (section 7) to RWC 28A.320 to read as follows:

RCW 28A.320.147 "Homeless child or youth"—Informed consent for health care for patient under the age of majority—Exemption from liability.

> *(1) As allowed by RCW 7.70.065(2), a school nurse, school counselor, or homeless student liaison is authorized to provide informed consent for health care for a patient under the age of majority when: (a) Consent is necessary for nonemergency outpatient primary care services, including physical examinations, vision examinations and eye glasses, dental examinations, hearing examinations, and hearing aids, immunizations, treatments for illnesses and conditions and routine follow-up care customarily provided by a healthcare provider in an outpatient setting, excluding elective surgeries.*

Lastly, the involvement of grandparents, other caregivers, guardian ad litem, or foster parents can further complicate questions of consent. Depending upon the applicable state law, a natural or biological parent may still retain some or all consent rights/authority in cases where a child is placed within the foster system. Where a guardian ad litem is appointed, state law and/or judicial decree governs what consent and decision-making authority such guardian may have, if any, and such authority may be dramatically different from case to case. Consent for medical care within this system is often more complicated (Gudeman, 2014).

When considering the relevance of consent to school nursing practice, delivering respectful, equitable, age appropriate care and, reducing liability is based on an understanding of federal, state, and local law. While many of these laws do not specifically address consent in school settings, Laubin et al. (2013) states they are pertinent and must be considered in the development of district policy and practices.

IMPLICATIONS FOR SCHOOL NURSE PRACTICE

Challenges

 The specialty of school nursing has unique legal and ethical challenges related to parental consent, minor consent, and confidentiality of adolescent health care. School nurses interact with families, adolescent populations, and individual students in the delivery of multiple, complex, controversial healthcare services and counsel; interactions that also require communication and relationships with parents, school administrators and other healthcare professionals. It can be difficult for school nurses to understand and stay current on health and education law, nursing practice standards and scope of practice in a school setting, let alone communicate the intricacies and application of minor consent laws to parents and school administrators.

School nurses often find themselves in the middle of questions and concerns about consent for care. There are many examples: active versus passive consent, pregnancy testing and drug and toxicology screening at school, students refusing to take prescribed medication, do not attempt to resuscitate orders (DNAR), photographs of child abuse, rashes or injuries, parents refusing to sign consent for the nurse to communicate with a healthcare provider, school health research, care requested by a parent that does not meet standards of nursing practice, sexual health and alcohol and drug treatment referrals, mental health services, and releasing students from the health room. Other than general first aid, most health care is implemented per a healthcare provider order, parental input, and a nursing care plan.

Challenges of consent also go hand-in-hand with privacy, confidentiality, and the subsequent documentation of care. This includes the exchange or release of records to and from outside healthcare providers and their protection under state or federal law. In an effort to minimize these challenges, school nurses need to understand practice implications and potential unintended consequences of their decisions on students' health and wellbeing. (_Please see Chapter 21 for more information on parental refusal and non-compliance_).

Legal Implications

School nurses practice independently in a complex legal environment. This is due in part to the isolation from other healthcare professionals, the wide variety of job responsibilities, conflict between law and policy that guide school districts, and those that guide nursing practice (Cohn et al., 2001/2005). Many of the conflicts between federal, state, and local mandates result in differing school health policy standards and requirements (American Academy of Pediatrics (AAP), 2016).

Both law and legal principles impact care and counsel related to consent and nursing practice. According to Loschiavo (2012), there are three classifications of law that have legal implications for school nurses: criminal, civil, and administrative law.

- <u>Criminal law</u> provides evidence of a crime. Examples of criminal law related to school nursing include fraudulently tampering with records, practicing without a license, using illegal drugs and failing to report suspected child abuse.

- <u>Civil law</u> on the other hand effects the legal status of individuals or groups and addresses an alleged offense such as a breach of duty or confidentiality, negligence or violation of a minor's right to consent. The Family Educational Rights and Privacy Act (FERPA) that governs school records and the Health Insurance Portability and Accountability Act (HIPAA) that protects the confidentiality of health records are examples of civil law (Loschiavo, 2012).

- <u>Administrative laws</u> determine regulation, enforcement, and interpretation of the laws. State boards of nursing are responsible for regulating nursing practice and have the authority for enforcing nurse practice laws when there is a violation or failure to meet standards of nursing practice.

Three legal principles nurses must also be aware of related to consent are liability, negligence, and malpractice. (*Please see Chapter 2 for more information on malpractice*).

Day-to-day decisions school nurses make related to consent not only have legal and ethical consequences for school nurse practice, they may also result in poor health outcomes for the minor, for instance, delayed emergency medical care or treatment and counsel for a sexually transmitted infection, mental illness, substance abuse, or abortion.

> In a 1989 Alabama case *Arnold et al. v. Board of Education, 754 F. Supp. 853, a* civil rights action was brought against the school counselor, vice-principal, and school board alleging that the student involved had been coerced into having an abortion.

> While the final ruling was in favor of the school and that the student made her own decision regarding having an abortion, the case highlights the legal and ethical challenges that may rise related to consent.

Strategies and Solutions

School nurses must be aware of their liability. Solutions to avoid legal and ethical pitfalls surrounding consent are not always clear or direct. However, to minimize the risk there are a number of proactive strategies that can be implemented:

- <u>Be informed of federal, state and local law</u> - School nurses have an ethical responsibility to be aware of the federal, state, and local laws regarding parental consent, minor's consent and nursing standards in the state in which they practice and how they apply to either public or private school systems. Given the conflict that can often occur between the provisions of these laws, it is critical that school nurses communicate concerns in writing to their school administrators and proper legal authorities. This may include requesting legal interpretation by a state attorney general (Scott & Burbert, 2013).

- <u>Be knowledgeable of your district's policy and procedures</u> - Understanding district policy and procedures that guide school health services and first aid care are important risk management tools and assist in providing safe care (Laubin et al., 2013). Policy can cover many school practices that include or overlap with concerns of consent. For instance, student privacy and searches, confidentiality of health records, emergency treatment, photographing or videotaping students, sharing student information, students' rights and responsibilities, and pregnant and parenting teens to name a few. District policy and procedures should be reviewed regularly to stay current. They generally reflect legal mandates so compliance and alignment with nursing practice is imperative.

- <u>Practice within the scope of your nursing license and job description</u> - Another strategy is to practice within the scope of both a nursing license and district job description, keeping both current and reflective of the work and caseload. While a nursing license may encompass a broad range of professional responsibilities, a job description could be more restrictive within the school setting. Job descriptions are considered a local standard of care by courts of law to which a school nurse will be held accountable in a civil breach of duty case (Lechtenberg, 2009). Job descriptions may also include statements such as "other duties as assigned". This does not mean that nurses can take direction to provide services outside their scope of practice. Brent (2016) states that to avoid professional liability school nurses must adhere to state nursing practice laws regardless of guidance or "permission" from well-meaning healthcare providers or school administrators to do otherwise. Nurses who are contracted from an outside agency to provide services must comply with both their employer's policies and the district's policy all while functioning within their scope of nursing practice (Lechtenberg, 2009).

- <u>Seek guidance from leaders and experts in school nursing</u> - State departments of education often have a school health services and nursing consultant that can provide guidance, resources and support in resolving legal and ethical dilemmas. In addition, joining a professional state school nurse organization can provide opportunities for education, collegial support and guidance related to standards of care and the need for individual liability insurance coverage. (*Please see Chapter 1 for more information on professional licensure*).

- <u>Attend professional development opportunities</u> - State education and nursing law and regulations can be ever-changing. Minor consent laws can undergo ongoing scrutiny with likely, periodic revisions that are critical to school nursing practice. School nurses must stay up-to-date on these changes to ensure their practice is reflective of current law, practice, and knowledge. This can be accomplished by attending appropriate professional development opportunities, collaborating with local chapters of the American Academy of Pediatrics, and consulting with district legal counsel and risk management partners (Laubin et al., 2013).

- <u>Build relationships with students and families</u>- Other strategies include building relationships with students and families to gain trust and respect. Involve adolescents in the planning of their care, allowing autonomy and participation in decision-making within law, district policy, and developmental ability. Where language barriers exist, use a trained medical interpreter to obtain informed consent (AAP, 2011).

- <u>Obtain adequate consent </u> - Obtaining adequate consent from the appropriate person and the subsequent documentation of that consent is essential to support decisions made in the provision of nursing care. In the case of minor consent, each situation needs to be assessed individually and will likely need legal counsel and risk management guidance to determine the definition of a minor within the context of each state's laws and regulations. Lambelet, et al., (2013) also note it would behoove healthcare providers to ensure safekeeping of records pertaining to minor maturity and the consent process in case of litigation.

- Document appropriately and maintain confidentiality - Accurately and promptly document all care and services rendered along with the student's response. This demonstrates that standards of practice were followed. Documentation also includes all attempts and communications to contact parent/ guardian(s), school administrators and healthcare providers as well as unsafe practices. (Lechtenberg, 2009). Uphold confidentiality in both the provision of care and the subsequent documentation.

- Use ethical practices if conducting school health research - In regard to school research, ethicists consider students a vulnerable population (Cowell, 2011). If school health services research is conducted, using ethical protocols in accordance with standards and requirements of an Institutional Research Board (IRB) will safeguard participating students as well as the nurse's liability. Along with proper documentation of consent, overall risk will be decreased. (*Please see Chapter 8 for more information on research in school health*).

The best protection against liability according to Caldart-Olson & Thronson (2013) is to be knowledgeable about and adhere to relevant federal, state and local laws and regulations, have a systematic method to perform job functions and a system of documenting that reflects the work performed.

CONCLUSION

It is clear from the literature and case law that consent in the school setting is multifaceted and must be considered individually in light of federal and state law, nursing regulations, standards, and review of related district policy and procedures.

Due to the complexities of health and education law and the subsequent implications for liability, it is critical for school nurses and other district staff to be informed about federal, state, and local laws that impact parental and minor consent in the school setting. In these situations, the district and nurse should consult their legal counsel and risk management team for guidance as day-to-day practice may be ahead of law (Schwab & Gelfman, 2001/2005); however, many times there are no clear answers. A growing body of literature suggests that in an effort to make sound decisions, school districts should:

- promote school nurse professional development;
- use risk management strategies;
- implement appropriate policy;
- focus on student needs;
- promote good relationships with both students and parents;
- understand ethical and legal parameters; and
- know where to access assistance.

School nurses who are well-informed regarding parental and minor consent can provide leadership to safeguard student health. By doing so, they will also protect against district and nurse liability (Laubin et al., 2013). Minimizing risk also involves adhering to professional standards of practice and working with district administrators in the development of sound policy and procedures. Caldart-Olson and Thronson (2013) note the best protection for school nurses is information, communication, and documentation.

RESOURCES

Please see APPENDIX: Minors May Consent to...

American Bar Association Center on Children and the Law
ABA Center on Children and the Law
1050 Connecticut Ave NW, Suite 400
Washington, D.C. 20036
202-662-1740 Fax: 202-662-1755
ctrchildlaw@americanbar.org

Protects children's rights through advocacy, reform, policy, research, evaluation, training and legal practice.

National Center for Youth Law
405 14th St., 15th Floor
Oakland, CA 94612
tel: (510) 835-8098
fax: (510) 835-8099
email: info(at)youthlaw.org

Non-profit law firm that provides pro-bono support and resources to legal services programs, organizations, community groups and healthcare professionals representing low income children.

National Association of School Nurses (2011). *Pregnant and parenting students: The role of the school nurse* (Position Statement). Silver Spring, MD: Author.

National Association of School Nurses (2013). Drug testing in schools (Position Statement). Silver Spring, MD: Author.

National District Attorneys' Association (2013). *Minor Consent to Medical Treatment Laws.*
http://www.ndaa.org/pdf/Minor%20Consent%20to%20Medical%20Treatment%20(2).pdf

Office for Civil Rights
U.S. Department of Health and Human Services
200 Independence Avenue, SW
Room 509F, HHH Building
Washington, D.C. 20201
Toll-free: (800) 368-1019

TDD toll-free: (800) 537-7697

OCRPrivacy@hhs.gov

Protects fundamental non-discrimination and health information privacy rights by educating communities and investigating civil rights and patient health and safety complaints.

Case Law

Cales v. Howell Public Schools, 635 F. Supp. 454 (E.D. Mich. 1985)

Curtis v. School Committee of Falmouth, 652 N.E. 2d 580 (Mass. 1995)

Little v. Little 576 S.W. 2d 493 (1979)

Moule´ v. Paradise Valley Unified Sch. Dist. 863 F.Supp. 1098 (NO. 69 1994)

Odenheim v. Carlstadt-East Rutherford Reg. Sch. Dist. 510 A.2d 709 (Superior Ct.N.J. 1985)

Ohio v. Akron Center (88-805), 497 U.S. 502, 110 S. Ct. 2972, 111 L.Ed 2d 405 (1990)

Planned Parenthood v. Casey, 505 U.S. 833 (1992)

Veronia School District v. Acton, 515 U.S. 646

REFERENCES

Adams, P.M., & Shineldecker, S.C. (2014). Unaccompanied youth: School nurses caring for adolescent minors living without a parent or guardian. *NASN School Nurse, 29*(2), 90-95. doi:10.1177/1942602X13501202

American Academy of Pediatrics (2011). Consent for emergency medical services for children and

adolescents. Committee on Pediatric Emergency Medicine and Committee on Bioethics. *Pediatrics, 128*(2), 427-433. doi:10.1542/peds.2011-1166

American Academy of Pediatrics Council on School Health (2016). *School Health: Policy and Practice, (7th Ed.), p.3. Elk Grove Village, IL.*

American Nurses Association (ANA). (2015). *Code of ethics for nurses with interpretive statements* Retrieved from http://www.nursingworld.org/codeofethics

American Nurses Association (ANA) & National Association of School Nurses (NASN). (2011). *School Nursing: Scope and Standards of Practice* (2nd ed.), pp. 50-51. Silver Spring, MD.

Arnold et al. v. Board of Education, 754, F. Supp. 853 (S.D. Ala. 1990)

Brent, N. J. (2016). The state nurse practice act, nursing ethics and school nursing practice. *Avoiding Professional Liability Bulletin*. Retrieved from http://www.cphins.com/blog/post/the-state-nurse-practice-act-nursing-ethics-and-school-nursing-practice

Briner, L. (2015). *Responding to the sexual exploitation and trafficking of youth toolkit, first edition*. Center for Children and Youth Justice. Retrieved from https://www.google.com/url?sa=t&rct=j&q=&esrc=s&source=web&cd=1&cad=rja&uact=8&ved=0ahUKEwivkK_DptPPAhVD64MKHaMxCd4QFggiMAA&url=https%3A%2F%2Fsharepoint.washington.edu%2FACWE%2FIn-Service%2FIdentifying%2520and%2520Supporting%2520Commercially%2520Sexually%2520Exploited%2520Children%2520(for%2520CFWS%2520Workers)%2FCurriculum%2FAdditional%2520Information%2FToolkit%2520for%2520Sexual%2520Exploitation%2520and%2520Trafficking%2520of%2520Youth.docx&usg=AFQjCNFl77_56KbSITyn4fPUI3crgTZD_A&sig2=KVrInZ0wFVnQQaE_yQ5xJg

Caldart-Olson, L., & Thronson, G. (2013). Legislation affecting school nurses. In J. Selekman (Ed.), *School nursing: A comprehensive text* (2nd Ed.) (pp. 225-256). Philadelphia: F.A. Davis Company.

Carey v. Populations Services International 431 U.S. 678 (1977)

Chambliss, D.F., & Schutt, R. S. (2010). *Making sense of the social world: Methods of investigation* (3rd ed.). Thousand Oaks, CA: PineForge Press.

Ciaccia, K.A. & John, R.M. (2016). Unaccompanied immigrant minors: Where to begin. *Journal of Pediatric Health Care, 30*(3), 231-240. doi.org/10.1016/j.pedhc.2015.12.009

Cohn, S.D., Gelfman, M. H. B., & Schwab, N.C. (2005). Adolescent issues and rights of minors. In N.C. Schwab & M.H.B. Gelfman (Eds.), *Legal issues in school health services, pp.* 231-260. North Branch, MN: Sunrise River Press.

Cornell University Law School/ Legal Information Institute. (n.d.). *Emancipation of minors' laws*. Retrieved from http://www.law.cornell.edu/wex/table_emancipation

Cowell, J.M. (2011). Ethical treatment of school children in research: Assuring informed consent. *The Journal of School Nursing, 27*(4), 247-248. doi: 10.1177/1059840511414384

Gudeman, R. (2014). Consent to medical treatment for foster children: California Law. A guide for health care providers. *National Center for Youth Law*. Retrieved from http://youthlaw.org/wp-content/uploads/2015/11/Consent-to-Medical-Care-Foster-Care-2-5-14.pdf

Guttmacher Institute. (2016). *State policies in brief: An overview of minor's consent law.* Retrieved from https://www.guttmacher.org/state-policy/explore/overview-minors-consent-law

Hecker, L., & Sori, C. F. (2010). Ethics in therapy with children in families. In L. Hecker (Ed.), *Ethics and professional issues in couple and family therapy.* pp. 51–70. New York, NY: Routledge.

Lambelet Coleman, D. & Rosoff, P.M. (2013). The legal authority of mature minors to consent to general medical treatment. *Pediatrics, 131*(4), 786-793. doi:10.1542/peds.2012-2470

Laubin, M., Schwab, N.C., & Doyle, J. (2013). Understanding the legal landscape. In C. Costante (Ed.), *School nurse administrators: Leadership and management*, pp.459-519. Silver Spring, MD: National Association of School Nurses (NASN).

Lechtenberg, J. (2009). Legal aspects of school nursing. *School Health Alert Special Report*. Publisher: Robert Andrews. Nashville, TN.

Loschiavo, J. (2012). *Fast* facts for the school nurse, school nursing in a nutshell. New York, NY: Springer Publishing Company, LLC.

McKinney–Vento Homeless Assistance Act of 1987 (Pub. L. 100-77, July 22, 1987, 101 Stat. 482), 42 U.S. Code § 11301.

McNary, A. (2014). Consent to treatment of minors. *Clinical Neuroscience, 11*(3-4), 43-45. PMCID: PMC4008301

Moon, M. (2012). Adolescents' rights to consent to reproductive medical care: Balancing respect for families with public health goals. *American Medical Association Journal of Ethics, 14*(10), 805-808. doi: 10.1001/ virtualmentor.2012.14.10.msoc1-1210

National Association of School Nurses (NASN). (2016). Framework for 21st century school nursing practice. *NASN School Nurse, 30*(4), 218-231. doi:10.1177/1942602X15589559

Pohlman, K., & Schwab, N. (2001). Consent and release. *The Journal of School Nursing, 17*(3), 162-165. doi:1 0.1177/10598405010170030801

Roe v. Wade, 410 U.S. 113 (1973)

Robertson, S. (2016). Age of consent laws in children and youth in history. Retrieved from http://chnm.gmu.edu/cyh/teaching-modules/230

Scott, L. R., & Bubert, J.S. (2013). Legal issues related to school nursing practice: The foundation. In J. Selekman, (Ed.), *School nursing a comprehensive text* (2nd Ed.), pp. 196-224. Philadelphia: F.A. Davis Company.

Schwab, N.C., & Gelfman, M.H.B. (Eds.). (2005). Definitions. In N.C. Schwab & M.H.B. Gelfman (Eds.), *Legal issues in school health services, pp.* 614-615. North Branch, MN: Sunrise River Press.

Schwab, N.C., Gelfman, M.H.B., & Cohn, S.D. (2005). Fundamentals of U.S. law. In N.C. Schwab & M.H.B. Gelfman (Eds.), *Legal issues in school health services, pp.* 55-79. North Branch, MN: Sunrise River Press.

Shumaker, D., & Medoff, D. (2013). Ethical and legal considerations when obtaining informed consent for treating minors of high-conflict divorced or separated parents. *The Family Journal: Counseling and Therapy for Couples and Families, 21*(3),318-327. doi: 10.1177/1066480713478786

WA. STAT. RCW 28A.320.147."Homeless child or youth"—Informed consent for health care for patient under the age of majority—Exemption from liability. (2016, c 157 § 7.). Retrieved from https://app.leg.wa.gov/ rcw/default.aspx?cite=28A.320.147

APPENDIX

MINORS MAY CONSENT TO:

STATE	CONTRACEPTIVE SERVICES	STI SERVICES	PRENATAL CARE	ADOPTION	MEDICAL CARE FOR MINOR'S CHILD	ABORTION SERVICES
Alabama	All†	All*	All	All	All	Parental Consent
Alaska	All	All	All		All	Parental Notice
Arizona	xAll	All		All		Parental Consent
Arkansas	All	All*	All		All	Parental Consent
California	All	All	All	All		▼ (Parental Consent)
Colorado	All	All	All	All	All	Parental Notice
Connecticut	Some	All		Legal counsel	All	All
Delaware	All*	All*	All*	All	All	Parental Notice‡
Dist. of Columbia	All	All	All	All	All	All
Florida	Some	All	All		All	Parental Notice
Georgia	All	All*	All	All	All	Parental Notice
Hawaii	All*, †	All*, †	All*, †	All		
Idaho	All	All†	All	All	All	Parental Consent
Illinois	Some	All*	All	All	All	Parental Notice
Indiana	Some	All		All		Parental Consent
Iowa	All	All				Parental Notice
Kansas	Some	All*	Some	All	All	Parental Consent
Kentucky	All*	All*	All*	Legal counsel	All	Parental Consent
Louisiana	Some	All*		Parental consent	All	Parental Consent
Maine	Some	All*				All
Maryland	All*	All*	All*	All	All	Parental Notice
Massachusetts	All	All	All		All	Parental Consent
Michigan	Some	All*	All*	Parental consent	All	Parental Consent
Minnesota	All*	All*	All*	Parental consent	All	Parental Notice
Mississippi	Some	All	All	All	All	Parental Consent
Missouri	Some	All*	All*	Legal counsel	All	Parental Consent
Montana	All*	All*	All*	Legal counsel	All	▼ (Parental Consent)
Nebraska	Some	All				Parental Consent
Nevada	Some	All	Some	All	All	▼ (Parental Notice)
New Hampshire	Some	All†	Some	AllΩ		Parental Notice
New Jersey	Some	All*	All*	All	All	▼ (Parental Notice)
New Mexico	All	All	All	All		▼ (Parental Consent)
New York	All	All	All	All	All	
North Carolina	All	All	All			Parental Consent
North Dakota		All*, †	ξ*	All		Parental Consent
Ohio		All		All		Parental Consent

STATE	CONTRACEPTIVE SERVICES	STI SERVICES	PRENATAL CARE	ADOPTION	MEDICAL CARE FOR MINOR'S CHILD	ABORTION SERVICES
Oklahoma	Some	All*	All*	All†	All	Parental Consent and Notice
Oregon	All*	All	All*, ‡			
Pennsylvania	All†	All	All	Parental notice	All	Parental Consent
Rhode Island		All		Parental consent	All	Parental Consent
South Carolina	All◊	All◊	All◊	All	All	Parental Consent‡
South Dakota	Some	All				Parental Notice
Tennessee	All	All	All	All	All	Parental Consent
Texas	Some	All*	All*			Parental Consent and Notice
Utah	Some	All	All	All	All	Parental Consent and Notice
Vermont	Some	All		All		
Virginia	All	All	All	All	All	Parental Consent and Notice
Washington	All	All†	All	Legal counsel		
West Virginia	Some	All	Some	All		Parental Notice
Wisconsin		All				Parental Consent
Wyoming	All	All		All		Parental Consent and Notice
TOTAL	**26+DC**	**50+DC**	**32+DC**	**28+DC**	**30+DC**	**2+DC**

Notes: "All" applies to those 17 and younger or to minors of at least a specified age such as 12 or 14. "Some" applies to specified categories of minors (those who have a health issue, or are married, pregnant, mature, etc.) The totals include only those states that allow all minors to consent.

▼ Enforcement permanently or temporarily enjoined by a court order; policy not in effect.

* Physicians may, but are not required to, inform the minor's parents.

† Applies to minors 14 and older.

‡ Delaware's abortion law applies to women younger than 16. Oregon's prenatal care law applies to women at least 15 years old. South Carolina's abortion law applies to those younger than 17.

Ω A court may require parental consent.

ξ Minor may consent to prenatal care in the 1st trimester and the first visit after the 1st trimester. Parental consent required for all other visits.

◊ Applies to mature minors 15 and younger and to all minors 16 and older.

Source: Guttmacher Institute, An overview of minors' consent law, *State Laws and Policies (as of March 1, 2016)*, 2016. Retrieved from https://www.guttmacher.org/state-policy/explore/overview-minors-consent-law Reprinted with permission.

Chapter 25

MANAGEMENT OF DIABETES

Linda Davis-Alldritt, MA, BSN, RN, FNASN, FASHA

DESCRIPTION OF ISSUE

Diabetes management at school and during school-sponsored activities is full of complexities. Given the increasing incidence and prevalence of type 1 and type 2 diabetes in school-age children and youth, it is increasingly likely that most, if not all, school nurses will be caring for students who have diabetes at some point in their career. School nurses are key to coordinating care and helping students effectively and safely manage their diabetes at school (Breneman, Heidari, Butler, Porter, & Wang, 2015; Engelke, Swanson, Guttu, Warren, & Lovern, 2011). *The school nurse is the most appropriate person in the school setting to provide care for a student with diabetes* (National Diabetes Education Program [NDEP], 2016, p.11). The school nurse must use all available tools at their disposal and become familiar with the overarching federal, state, case laws, district policies, and nursing standards of care for students with diabetes.

Diabetes is one of the most common chronic childhood diseases and affects approximately 208,000 or 0.25 percent of all people under the age of 20 years (Centers for Disease Control and Prevention [CDC], 2014a). This means that about one of every 400 to 500 students in the United States has type 1 diabetes. While the precise number of school-age children who have type 2 diabetes is uncertain, the prevalence of type 2 in this age group is increasing (Rapp, Arent, Dimmick, Gordon, & Jackson, 2015). Globally, and in the United States, the incidence of both type 1 and type 2 diabetes in people under 20 years of age is increasing (American Diabetes Association [ADA], 2016; You & Henneberg, 2016).

In diabetes, blood glucose levels are above normal because the body cannot effectively use and store glucose. There are three main types of diabetes: type 1, formerly referred to as juvenile diabetes or insulin-dependent diabetes; type 2, which used to be called adult onset diabetes or non-insulin dependent diabetes; and gestational diabetes (Joslin Diabetes Center, 2016).

Effective management of diabetes requires maintaining blood glucose levels within the individual's target range. Consequently, diabetes must be managed continuously, 24 hours a day, 7 days a week. For school-age children and adolescents, the ongoing diabetes treatment regimen impacts the student's daily schedule and, if needed accommodations are not made, may affect the student's ability to have equal access to all school-related activities. Blood glucose levels outside the target range result from an imbalance between food, activity, medication and illness and may result in hypoglycemia or hyperglycemia. Hypoglycemia, low blood glucose level, must be treated immediately and if untreated will quickly progress, and can be fatal. Hyperglycemia, high blood glucose level, is associated with diabetic ketoacidosis (DKA), and if untreated, over time, can lead to long term complications, including death.

While both hyperglycemia and hypoglycemia can affect cognitive functioning and, as a result, school performance, even small fluctuations in blood glucose levels can impact the student's concentration, learning ability, ability to provide self-care and perform daily living tasks, including walking, talking, and eating. For students with diabetes to be safe at school and fully participate in all school activities, effective diabetes care at school is essential (National Diabetes Education Program (NDEP), 2016; Rapp et al., 2015). Unfortunately, despite federal and state laws guaranteeing protections for all students with disabilities, including diabetes, some students with diabetes continue to be denied services and support at school (Jackson et al., 2015; Schwartz, Denham, Heh, Wapner, & Shubrook, 2010).

BACKGROUND

Based on SEARCH for Diabetes in Youth data from 2008-2009, an estimated 18,436 people under 20 years are newly diagnosed with type 1 diabetes each year, and 5,089 people under 20 years of age are annually diagnosed with type 2 diabetes (CDC, 2014a). While the incidence of type 1 diabetes has been increasing by 2.8 percent to 4.0 percent annually worldwide in all age groups in the United States, the highest rate of new type 1 cases was in non-Hispanic white children and adolescents (CDC, 2014a; Dabelea et al., 2014). Several research studies have revealed that the greatest increase in the incidence of type 1 diabetes in the U.S. is occurring among children age five years and younger (Vehik & Dabelea, 2011). Although there are many theories as to why type 1 diabetes is increasing worldwide, to date none of the theories has been proven (Egro, 2013) and researchers have yet to determine what triggers the immune system to attack the beta cells in the pancreas. Researchers believe that the cause of type 1 diabetes is a combination of, as yet, unidentified environmental and genetic factors. It is believed that once the factors are identified, the autoimmune process that leads to type 1 diabetes can be halted (NDEP, 2016). At this time, there is no cure for type 1 diabetes. Treatment for type 1 diabetes includes taking insulin, monitoring blood glucose levels, eating foods that are healthy, counting carbohydrates, exercising regularly, and maintaining a healthy weight (NDEP, 2016).

With increasing obesity rates in children and adolescents, type 2 diabetes is becoming more common in people under 20 years old, particularly among minorities (Jacquez et al., 2008) and accounts for 20 to 50 percent of new cases. In the U.S., type 2 diabetes is most common among Native Americans, African Americans, Hispanic Americans and Asian Americans/Pacific Islanders (Joslin Diabetes Center, 2016). Incidence rates for type 2 diabetes are higher among individuals aged 10–19 years than in younger children. (CDC, 2014a; Dabelea et al., 2014). A progressive disease, type 2 diabetes usually begins with insulin resistance (NDEP, 2016). Overweight and obesity are risk factors for type 2 diabetes (Brown, 2015; Butler, Kaup, Swanson, & Hoffman, 2013; Dabelea et al., 2014).

Achieving and maintaining a healthy weight is essential to the management of type 2 diabetes. This includes lifestyle changes in eating habits and increasing physical activity levels. Making healthy food choices and getting regular exercise are critical to success. Children and teens with type 2 diabetes may also take medication (NDEP, 2016).

Older teens, as well as teens who are pregnant or parenting, should be aware that diabetes can develop during pregnancy. This type of diabetes is called gestational diabetes and is caused by hormones present during pregnancy. The pregnancy hormones can cause a shortage of insulin, called insulin resistance (NDEP, 2106). Generally, gestational diabetes is self-limiting, such that once the baby is born, this type of diabetes usually goes away. However, a woman who has had gestational diabetes has an increased risk of developing diabetes as she gets older. Additionally, the baby of this pregnancy is at increased risk for developing obesity and type 2 diabetes (NDEP, 2016), thus leading to increases in both the incidence and prevalence of that disease. Effective management of gestational diabetes includes monitoring blood glucose levels, eating a healthy diet, regular physical activity, and medication, if needed, to control blood glucose levels (Mayo Clinic, 2017).

Regardless of the type of diabetes the student has, thanks to federal and state laws guaranteeing the right of all students to attend school and participate fully and safely in all school sponsored activities, most of these young people are in school. To be most successful, maximize their school experience, and maintain blood glucose control, they need assistance from trained, knowledgeable staff and a safe school environment (American Association of Diabetes Educators [AADE], 2016; ADA, 2015). Each student with diabetes lives with the constant challenge of managing and adapting to this chronic disease that impacts many, if not all, parts of their being. Fortunately, many students with diabetes are treated fairly, with respect, and receive the care and accommodations to which they are rightfully entitled at school. Unfortunately, some students with diabetes experience discrimination due to their condition, violation of their rights to proper care and full inclusion, and their safety and health put at risk (Rapp et al., 2015).

Brief Literature Review

According to several authors, the incidence and prevalence of both type 1 and type 2 diabetes is increasing in the United States (ADA, 2016; CDC, 2014a; CDC, 2015; Chiang, Kirkman, Laffel, & Peters, 2016; Dabelea et al., 2014; Egro, 2013; Jackson et al., 2015; Jacquez et al., 2008; Miller, Coffield, Leroy, & Wallin, 2016; National Institute of Health (NIH), n.d.; Pettitt et al., 2014; Pohlman, 2005; Vihik, & Dabelea, 2011; Vihik et al., 2007) and globally (Chiang et al., 2016; Dabelea et al., 2014). Rates differ between the sexes, age, and race or ethnicity (Linder & Imperatore, 2013; Miller, Coffield, Leroy, & Wallin, 2016). At this time, while the rates of type 1 diabetes are increasing around the world, researchers have not yet identified the causative factors (Egro, 2013; Vihik & Dabelea, 2011).

Some studies have suggested that it is likely that maternal obesity and maternal diabetes will increase the prevalence of the type 2 diabetes in future generations (Godfrey et al., 2016; Hanson, Gluckman, & Bustreo, 2016). An article by Brown (2015) encourages school nurses to be aware of the risk factors for type 2 diabetes in attempts to reduce the prevalence of that disease for those children not born with type 2 diabetes resulting from maternal obesity and maternal diabetes (Brown, 2015).

Several articles review the broadening of federal protections for persons with disabilities, the specific inclusion of diabetes as a qualifying condition for services and accommodations under federal law, and conclude - without doubt - that schools have a legal requirement to provide services for children with diabetes (Gibbons, Lehr, & Selekman, 2013; Jackson et al., 2015; Jacquez et al., 2008; Kadohiro, 2012; Kaufman, 2002; National Association of School Nurses [NASN], 2013; Rapp et al., 2015; Schwartz et al., 2010; Zirkel, 2014). Zirkel, Granthom and Lovato (2012) advise in order to ensure that students' rights to appropriate health services at school are maintained, school nurses must understand the legal processes that govern these rights and school districts' responsibilities to provide services. Despite federal laws corresponding state laws, and subsequent case law, some students with diabetes, and their families, report challenges receiving services at school (Jackson & Albanese-O'Neill, 2016; Jacquez et al., 2008; Kadohiro, 2012; Pansier & Schulz, 2015; Schwartz et al., 2010).

Several articles address effective diabetes management at school and provide general recommendations for school nurses, school districts, and parents/guardians (Butler et al., 2013; Chiang et al., 2016; Jacquez et al.,

2008; NASN, 2012). Pansier & Schulz (2015) review literature addressing school-based diabetes management and outcomes between 2000 and 2013 (Pansier & Schulz, 2015). In an article about school nurses and care coordination, McClanahan, & Weismuller (2015) provide an integrative review of "six core essentials of nurse-provided care coordination" which include collaboration, communication, the nursing process in planning care, continuous coordination, clinical expertise, and complementary components (McClanahan, & Weismuller, 2015, p. 34). Bobo, Kaup, McCarty, & Carlson (2011) suggest the use of the "Healthy Learner Model" as an effective model program for diabetes management that has worked in several states (Bobo et al., 2011). Critical elements necessary for providing vital services that keep the student with diabetes safe at school are: planning and documentation, and the use of the student's diabetes medical management plan (DMMP) (NASN, 2012; NASN, 2015a, Jackson et al., 2015; NDEP, 2016); the development of individualized healthcare plans (Galemore & Sheetz, 2015; NASN, 2015a; NASN, 2016; Zimmerman, 2013, NDEP, 2016); and emergency plans for in school emergencies and away from school activities, such as field trips (Brown, 2016; Butler & Wyckoff, 2012; Doyle, 2013; NASN, 2014d; NDEP, 2016). Part of diabetes management requires supporting the student to independence (Jackson & Albanese-O'Neill, 2016; Siminerio, 2015) and assisting the student with transition from student to adulthood (ADA, 2016; Chiang et al., 2016; NASN, 2014e; Lotstein et al., 2013; Jackson & Albanese-O'Neill, 2016; Siminerio, 2015, NDEP, 2016). Malone & Bergren (2010) review the concept of *Failure to Rescue* as a measure of vigilance in healthcare settings, and how it relates to the ability of the school nurse to assess, plan, and anticipate the student's health needs, and be prepared to act appropriately in critical and potentially life-threatening health management situations.

Because fewer than half of all schools in the United States have a full-time school nurse, and because the numbers of children with chronic health conditions continues to increase, delegation to licensed practical or licensed vocational nurses (LPN/LVN) and unlicensed assistive personnel (UAP) is a reality in many schools. Several professional organizations and articles take an extensive look at the benefits, risks, and legalities, of delegation to LPN/LVNs and UAP (American Nurses Association [ANA] & NASN, 2017; ANA & the National Council of State Boards of Nursing (NCSBN), 2006; Gordon & Barry, 2009; Hootman, 2013; NASN, 2014d; NASN, 2015b; NASN, 2015c; Resha, 2010). Some authors discuss delegating specific medications for managing hypoglycemia (Wilt & Foley, 2011); and others provide recommendations on reducing the risks associated with delegation (Shannon, & Kubelka, 2013a; 2013b). The use of substitute school nurses raises other delegation questions (Vollinger, Bergren, & Belmonte-Mann, 2011) as does the increasing use of technological aids for students with diabetes (Brown, 2016).

For the health and safety of the student, and risk reduction for the school district and school nurse, delegation of nursing tasks to LPN/LVNs or UAP requires that the delegating nurse train the delegate in accordance with both the relevant state nurse practice act (NPA) and the standards established by the profession (ANA & NASN, 2017), as well as the medical community. Several training tools meet professional standards (Breneman, Heidari, Butler, Porter, & Wang, 2015; NASN, 2010; NASN, 2014c; NDEP, 2016).

IMPLICATIONS FOR SCHOOL NURSE PRACTICE

To optimize academic achievement, safety, and long-term health for students with diabetes, appropriate care at school is vital (Jackson et al., 2015). The results of the Diabetes Control and Complications Trial identified a significant link between blood glucose control and subsequent diabetes complications, with tight control reducing the complication risk. Achieving tight control requires frequent blood glucose checks, monitoring nutrition intake, adherence to medication regimen requiring multiple daily insulin injections or use of an infusion pump, and regular physical activity (Jackson et al., 2015). Failing to provide reasonable, as well as necessary, health and safety accommodations may have legal consequences for the school district, and possibly for the school nurse (Zirkel et al., 2012). When school staff are not adequately trained and supervised to safely and effectively respond to student health needs in both emergent and non-emergent situations, there is a risk of increased liability for the school district and school nurse, as well as increased morbidity, and possibly mortality (Shannon & Kubelka, 2013ab), for the student with diabetes.

Safe and effective care of students with diabetes, based on the nursing process, requires assessment, planning, coordination of interventions, and evaluation by the school nurse (ANA & NASN, 2017; Engelke et al., 2011). When the student with diabetes enters school, they will need an individualized healthcare plan (IHP) and an emergency care plan (ECP), developed by the school nurse in collaboration with the student and family, and based on the healthcare provider orders or diabetes medical management plan (DMMP). The IHP is both a clinical practice document and an administrative document grounded in the nursing process (NASN, 2015a). Depending on the student's needs, the school nurse may assist with an evaluation for either special education or Section 504 accommodations. As outlined in the IHP and DMMP, the school nurse helps the student to self-manage his/her diabetes and to eventually take on increasingly more responsibility for self-care (Jackson et al., 2015). At the same time, staff must be trained to provide the student with emergency care when needed, or even non-emergent care depending on school policies, state laws, and the school nurse staffing plan (NDEP, 2016).

Advocating for Compliance with Federal and State Laws, and District Policies

Three federal laws protect the rights of school-age children with disabilities, which includes diabetes, to have the care they need while at school. These laws include:

- Section 504 of the Rehabilitation Act (1973) (Section 504);
- The Education for All Handicapped Children Act (1975), reauthorized in 2004 as the Individuals with Disabilities Education Improvement Act (IDEIA) of 2004; and
- The Americans with Disabilities Act (ADA) (1990), reauthorized in 2008 as the ADA Amendments Act (ADAAA) of 2008.

These three laws work together to protect individuals with disabilities from exclusion and discriminatory treatment at school, at work, and in the community Disability Rights Education & Defense Fund [DREDF], 2016). Under these laws, schools are required to provide services and reasonably accommodate the special needs of students with diabetes and other disabilities, so that these students have the same access to educational opportunities as do all other children (Jackson et al., 2015; Jacquez et al., 2008). These laws also require that students with diabetes be individually assessed and that any identified needed accommodations should be documented in writing in either a Section 504 Plan or an Individualized Education Program (IEP) if the child has additional educational needs (Jackson et al., 2015). IDEA (2004) requires school districts to provide special education services to students suffering from episodes of hypoglycemia or hyperglycemia that could significantly interfere with their cognition and ability to learn (Jacquez et al., 2008). Under these federal and corresponding state laws, and based on evaluation results, it is intended that the needs of students with diabetes and other disabilities be provided at the student's usual school with as minimal disruption as possible to the school and the student, while permitting the student to have complete participation in all school activities (Jackson et al., 2015; Jackson, & Albanese-O'Neill, 2016).

While all states have laws that correspond to the three overarching federal laws, many states have passed diabetes-specific laws providing protections that enable unlicensed school personnel to provide care to students with diabetes. In these states, to ensure safe and effective care for children with diabetes, such personnel should be trained and clinically supervised by school nurses. Some state laws prevent unlicensed non-nursing school personnel from administering medications, particularly injectable medications, such as insulin and glucagon. Despite such state laws, school districts still must comply with federal requirements and provide students with diabetes appropriate and necessary health services in order for those students to be safe and to fully participate in the classroom and in all school-sponsored programs and activities, such as recess, sports, detention, school parties, school dances, and before-school and after-school programs and clubs (Jackson et al., 2015).

In addition to their requirement to adhere to federal and state laws, it is critical that school districts adopt policies and regulations for diabetes care at schools that align with the state's NPA and national diabetes management standards and guidelines. Often school administrators responsible for reviewing and developing district policies for board of education adoption are unfamiliar with laws and best practices relating to nursing practice, delegation of care tasks, and diabetes management. The standard of care is a significant factor, along with relevant laws including the state NPA, expert testimony, and professional organization position statements, used by the courts in professional liability cases (Pohlman, 2005). Consequently, it is imperative that school nurses be included as team members on district policy development committees when school healthcare decisions are being made (NASN, 2012a; Wilt & Foley, 2011).

Identifying and Serving Children with Diabetes

IDEA (2004) requires school districts to find and assess all previously unidentified students with disabilities, including diabetes, who may be eligible for special education services. This requirement is known as 'child find.' The requirement applies to all children and youth, through age 21, who live within a state (IDEIA, 2004, 20 U.S.C. 1412(a)(3)). In response to the broadening of ADA 2008, and subsequent Office of Civil Rights (OCR) complaints, Zirkel et al. (2012) recommends screening all students with IHPs for Section 504 eligibility in compliance with the school district's "child find" obligations. If the screening results so indicate, the school nurse should recommend further evaluation by the Section 504 team. School nurses have an important role in the identification, screening and evaluation process for "child find" (Zirkel et al., 2012).

Once students are identified as having diabetes, it is important to inform the family about their role in helping the school to help their child with diabetes remain safe and healthy at school. The 2016 NDEP guide, *Helping the Student with Diabetes Succeed: A Guide for School Personnel,* provides a list of actions families can follow to help ensure their child's successful school experience. Both the family and the student's healthcare team should work together to provide the school nurse, or the school administrator, if the school does not have a school nurse, with the information necessary to allow students with diabetes to fully and safely participate in all school activities (Jackson et al., 2015).

ACTIONS FOR PARENTS/GUARDIANS
From *Helping the Student with Diabetes Succeed: A Guide for School Personnel*
Permit the school and the child's healthcare providers to share medical information necessary for the child's safety at school.
Provide the school with accurate and current emergency contact information and keep the information updated.
Attend and participate in the initial and annual meetings of the school health team to discuss implementing the medical orders in the child's DMMP and review the services the child may need.
Participate in developing a Section 504 Plan, other education plan, or IEP
Provide specific information to the school health team about the child's diabetes and performance of diabetes care tasks at home.
Inform the school nurse or designated school staff about any changes in the child's health status or medical orders.
Notify the school nurse prior to the student attending school so proper staff training and communication can occur if the student is using an insulin pump.
Provide and maintain all supplies and equipment necessary for implementing the child's health care and education plans, including blood glucose monitoring equipment and Wi-Fi access for continuous glucose monitors (CGM), supplies for insulin administration and urine and blood ketone testing, snacks, quick-acting glucose products, and a glucagon emergency kit.
Consult with the school nurse to monitor supplies and replenish them, as needed, and refill or replace supplies that have expired.
Provide and maintain all supplies and equipment necessary to accommodate the child's long-term needs (72 hours) in case of a disaster or emergency.
Inform appropriate school staff (school nurse, principal, teachers, coaches, and others) when the child plans to participate in school-sponsored activities, including field trips.

Adapted from NDEP, 2016 & NDEP, 2012 with supplemental information from Brown, 2016; Butler & Wyckoff, 2012; Colorado Department of Education [CDE], 2016.

Annual Notification to Parents/Guardians

The families of children with diabetes should be informed, annually and in writing, of their rights and responsibilities related to medication administration at school. Typically, such information is included in required annual notices and activities that school districts send to the families of all students in districts. Four issues that should to be addressed in the annual notice and school district policy relate to medication administration, delegation of nursing tasks, provision of necessary supplies and equipment, and the use of service animals:

- Although parents/guardians may adjust medication doses at home in collaboration with their providers, in most states, school nurses can only accept medication-change orders from licensed providers who are authorized in the state to prescribe medication.

- In most states, unlicensed persons cannot delegate nursing tasks to school employees.
- Just as it is the responsibility of parents/guardians to provide the school with needed medication for students with diabetes, it is also the parents' responsibility to provide needed supplies for medication delivery, urine and ketone testing, and blood glucose monitoring, including Wi-Fi access for CGM (CDE, 2016), if such devices are used by the student.
- According to the United States Department of Justice and the ADA, schools, like other state and local government agencies must make "reasonable modifications" in policies to accommodate students with diabetes who rely on a service animal for assistance (U.S. Department of Justice, 2015). *(For more information on service animals, please see Chapter 41).*

In dealing with these issues, and in formulating responses to parents/guardians who desire to give medication change orders to school personnel, including school nurses, it is important to review the state NPA, the state Medical Practice Act, and other related state laws.

Planning Care and Services for Students with Diabetes

Each student with diabetes should have a DMMP from the healthcare provider and diabetes care team that provides medical orders addressing all facets of routine and emergency diabetes management for each child. The DMMP includes nutrition, medication, and physical activity needs; meal pattern; school schedule; social and cultural factors; acceptable range of blood glucose levels; other health issues; and action required for hypoglycemia or hyperglycemia episodes. Intrinsic to the DMMP is education for the student on diabetes self-management and consistent diabetes support (NDEP, 2016).

The school nurse is responsible for the development of an IHP and ECP for students with diabetes as this disease has the potential to impact school attendance and academic achievement. The school nurse uses the DMMP and additional assessment information to develop the IHP in collaboration with the student, family, and diabetes care team. While the DMMP and school nursing practice and judgement guide how the school nurse will care for student's health needs in schools, the IHP identifies the individualized health goals that the school nurse will help the student achieve each year with outcome of promoting self-management when appropriate. The IHP describes the student's daily health needs, outlines diabetes management strategies for school personnel, informs educational plans, such as Section 504 Plans and IEPs, identifies personnel obligations to effectively help the student achieve his or her goals; and promotes academic success. IHP development cannot be delegated to a LPN/LVN or UAP, because the IHP is based on the nursing process in accordance with the individual state NPA (ANA & NASN, 2017; NASN, 2013d). The needs of the student with diabetes will be outlined on the IHP and include blood glucose monitoring either via the finger stick method or with a Wi-Fi equipped continuous glucose monitor (CGM), unlimited access to bathrooms and water, administration of insulin or oral medication, and unrestricted access to food or snacks as needed (Jacquez et al., 2008). In addition to the IHP, the school nurse develops an individualized ECP, based on the IHP, for each student with diabetes, coordinates educating school staff about symptoms of hyperglycemia and hypoglycemia, and distributes copies of the ECP to all regular and substitute teachers who are responsible for the student at school and at school sponsored activities (Jacquez et al., 2008; NASN, 2012; NASN, 2015a; NDEP, 2016). The ECP is a confidential document that must be made accessible to personnel responsible for the student (NASN, 2015a).

If it is determined that the student is eligible for either a Section 504 Plan or an IEP, the school nurse is often the only member of the school team qualified to interpret medical records, assess the student's healthcare needs, develop the IHP and ECP, and assist the team in writing an education plan that appropriately accommodates the student's health needs. Dependent on the student's healthcare needs, the school nurse may be listed on the IEP or Section 504 Plan as a direct service or a related service. When this is the case, the school nurse needs to supply information about the types, frequency, and duration of the health services to be provided. Attaching the student's IHP to the IEP provides the rationale for the health services to be received at school. Necessary nursing services specified in the IEP as in accordance with the IHP, may be reimbursable under the state's Medicaid program, if the student is Medicaid eligible (Galemore & Sheetz, 2015; Gibbons et al., 2013; Hahn & Sheingold, 2013; NASN, 2013c). When the IEP or Section 504 Plan is due for review, the school nurse is the only team member qualified to evaluate the effectiveness of the plan's health-components and make necessary revisions (Galemore & Sheetz, 2015; Gibbons et al., 2013; Zimmerman, 2013; Zirkel, 2009).

Ensuring That Needed Services Are Delivered

While fewer than half of the nation's schools have a school nurse, and 25 percent have part-time school nurses, it is the position of NASN that students will be safer, healthier, and better able to learn with daily access to a school nurse (NASN, 2015d). Recent studies have found that adequate school nurse staffing supports improved attendance and academic performance (Cooper, 2005; Moricca et al., 2013; NASN, 2015b), and improved management of chronic diseases, like diabetes (Nguyen et al., 2008; Baisch, Lundeen, & Murphy, 2011; NASN, 2015d). Additional studies have demonstrated that by having a school nurse on campus, administrators and teachers gain hundreds of hours to focus on student education rather than address student health problems (Baisch et al., 2011; Hill & Hollis, 2012; NASN, 2015d) and parent lost productivity costs related to medication administration and student early dismissal (Wang et al., 2014). Adequate school nurse staffing is cost effective – for each dollar spent on school nursing, at least $2.20 is saved. Full-time school nurses add to teacher and parent/guardian productivity, and reduce medical costs (Wang et al., 2014To compensate for inadequate school nurse staffing, nurses must help administrators understand the significance of safe and adequate staffing to protect students with diabetes and reduce liability to the district.

Determining safe and adequate school nurse staffing is complex (ANA, 2012; NASN, 2015d) and requires a nursing assessment of the acuity level and healthcare needs of individual students and identification of the social determinants of the community's health, such as the social and economic conditions that impact community members' health outcomes (CDC, 2014b; USDHHS, 2014). This work must adhere to individual state NPAs and other related state laws (Dang, 2010). In districts with inadequate school nurse staffing, nurses must help administrators understand the significance of safe and adequate staffing in protecting students with diabetes and reducing liability for the district, accommodations must be made and may include hiring an additional school nurse for a particular building.

Delegating in Accordance with State NPA and Student Needs

The ANA defines delegation as "transferring the responsibility of performing a nursing activity to another person while retaining accountability for the outcome" (ANA, 2012, p. 5). The delegation of nursing tasks at school is valuable tool for the school nurse, when based on the ANA definition of delegation (ANA, 2012), and if allowed by the state NPA, other state laws and regulations, and professional nursing standards and guidelines. When allowed by law, delegation must be done only if it is safe for the student. Used appropriately, delegation can allow UAP to perform routine health services under the supervision of the school nurse, while simultaneously freeing the school nurse to provide for more complex student health needs, and perhaps reduce costs for the school district (ANA, 2012; ANA & NCSBN, 2006; Wilt & Foley, 2011). Before delegating a nursing task to a LPN/LVN or UAP, the school nurse must be competent in the performance of the task.

When delegating a nursing task, to ensure safe care for the student, school nurses should use the Five Rights of Delegation (ANA & NCSBN, 2006) to determine if the delegation is appropriate.

1. The Right task
2. The Right circumstances
3. The Right person
4. The Right directions and communication
5. The Right supervision and evaluation

Training and supervision are part of delegation. Delegating healthcare tasks to UAP creates professional, ethical, and legal questions for all nurses. The delegating school nurse must train, clinically supervise and evaluate the UAP to determine if the person is capable and competent to safely and effectively perform the delegated tasks. The school nurse determines the level and frequency of supervision unless state law dictates otherwise. The school nurse must document all delegation, and all training, supervision, and evaluation of delegates. Using procedure skills checklists is one strategy that may help to reduce delegation risks (Shannon, & Kubelka, 2013a; 2013b). Thorough documentation also reduces risks, and protects the student, the delegate, the school nurse, and the district.

If a school administrator assigns an individual who is not competent or capable to do a task, the school nurse must ask administration to assign a more qualified person. The school nurse may need to provide care for the student until a replacement delegate can found and trained. In situations where there is conflict with administration over delegation, the school nurse must adhere to the state NPA and standards of nursing practice (NASN, 2014d).

(Please see Chapter 4 for additional information on delegation and Chapter 47 for additional information on conflict with administration).

The provision of appropriate care of students with diabetes, requires the school nurse and other school staff to understand diabetes and be trained in diabetes management and in the treatment of diabetes emergencies. Trained, knowledgeable, and caring school personnel will help the student avoid dangerous hypoglycemic episodes and assist the student in achieving the tight control needed to reduce risks of diabetes complications (Jackson et al., 2015). The UAP need regular training programs and booster sessions to reinforce learning, particularly because sentinel events do not regularly occur in the school setting. Having written policies, protocols, and ECP in conjunction with training programs for UAP will ensure safe and appropriate care for students with diabetes (Wilt & Foley, 2011).

School staff training on diabetes care must convey sensitivity to the realities and frustrations for children and adolescents living with a disease requiring continuous balancing of a wide-range of self-care behaviors. Staff must avoid being judgmental about the blood glucose reading as being "good or bad" and instead approach it objectively as an opportunity for the student to help problem solve. The frustration for these students can be exacerbated by challenges at school in getting the help they need.

The 2016 NDEP Guide outlines three levels of training:

- Level 1. Diabetes Overview and Recognizing and Responding to Emergency Situations
  - o Train all school personnel in the following:
    - Overview of diabetes
    - Recognition and Response to hypoglycemia and hyperglycemia
    - Who to contact in a diabetic emergency
- Level 2. Diabetes Basics and Emergency Response
  - o Train teachers, and other school personnel who have responsibility for the student with diabetes during the school day in the following:
    - Level 1 content plus expanded overview of diabetes
    - Specific instruction on the ECPs for Hypoglycemia and Hyperglycemia
    - Activating Emergency Medical Services in a diabetes emergency
    - Roles and responsibilities of individual staff members
    - Impact of hypoglycemia or hyperglycemia on behavior and learning
    - Tips and planning needed for the classroom and for special events
    - The student's health care and education plans
    - Legal rights of students with diabetes
- Level 3. General and Student-Specific Diabetes Care Tasks
  - o Train designated diabetes personnel in the following:
    - Level 1 and Level 2 content and training
    - General training on diabetes care tasks specified in the student's DMMP
    - Student-specific training, using the student's equipment and supplies for each diabetes care task
    - Documentation of the performance of all care tasks
    - Plans for ongoing performance evaluation of trained diabetes personnel

Adapted from National Diabetes Education Program (NDEP). (2016). Helping the student with diabetes succeed: A guide for school personnel. Bethesda, MD: Author. Retrieved from https://www.niddk.nih.gov/health-information/health-communication-programs/ndep/health-care-professionals/school-guide/section3/Documents/NDEP-School-Guide-Full.pdf

Promoting Self-Management

From the time diabetes is diagnosed, self-management is a primary goal. Four additional type 1 general goals are: (1) normal growth and development; (2) tight control; (3) minimize short and long-term complications; and (4) positive psychosocial adjustment. Effective self-management, will accomplish all the goals. (Butler, Kaup, Swanson, & Hoffman, 2013). School nurses are uniquely positioned to encourage and reinforce self-management techniques and principles to students with diabetes because the school nurse sees these students on a regular, generally daily, basis (Ahmad & Grimes, 2011). To ensure student safety, the school district policies should include a requirement for the nurse to assess the student's capability and competence to perform self-administration (Laubin et al., 2012). Policies requiring authorization from the licensed healthcare provider and parent/guardian consent should mirror those governing all other medications.

Federal laws, IDEA (2004), Section 504, and ADAAA, along with corresponding state laws, protect the rights of students to carry glucagon, and to carry and self-administer insulin at school (Cicutto, 2009; Laubin et al., 2012). Glucagon may be self-carried but when it is needed – severe hypoglycemia emergency – the student will not be able to self-administer due to cognitive impairment and will need trained personnel to administer the medication. Educating students with diabetes on self-management and insulin self-administration are fundamental to the care coordination that school nurses provide. Self-administration of insulin and self-treatment of mild to moderate hypoglycemia is supported by healthcare experts because quick treatment of symptoms helps to reduce the effects of the disease and may prevent a hypoglycemia/hyperglycemia emergency episode. Additionally, self-administration leads to self-care competence, student independence, and improved self-esteem (Hootman, Schwab, & Gelfman, 2005).

Effective diabetes care depends on self-management. Ongoing diabetes self-management education and support is key to helping young people and their families learn about diabetes, sustain behavioral changes, and adjust to the reality of a chronic illness (Siminerio, 2015). Most individuals with diabetes eventually become responsible for all aspects of routine care, including blood glucose monitoring, insulin or other medication administration, recognition and prompt treatment of hypoglycemia and hyperglycemia, and carbohydrate counting. As the more basic aspects of self-care are mastered, the individual with diabetes learns how to balance food and medication intake with physical activity and other variables affecting blood glucose levels. For students, an age appropriate, competency-related level of responsibility for self-management must be allowed while the young person is in school (Jackson & Albanese-O'Neill, 2016). Diabetes self-management education and support is most effectively coordinated by a multidisciplinary team. School nurses are vital members of the student's diabetes healthcare team and in schools are the leaders of the school health team (Siminerio, 2015, NASN, 2017).

Anticipating Transition Planning

As young people with diabetes transition into emerging adulthood, the supportive infrastructure that is the family's care and supervision of diabetes management, frequently disappears. As a result, glycemic control tends to deteriorate; there are increased occurrences of acute complications; psychosocial, emotional, and behavioral challenges occur; and there is an emergence of chronic complications (ADA, 2016). During this challenging time, the ADA recommends a strong transition plan that anticipates upcoming changes (Chiang et al., 2016). What is most effective is comprehensive and coordinated planning beginning in early adolescence, or at the latest 1-year prior to the transition date, for the emerging adult to seamlessly move from pediatric to adult health care (ADA, 2016). During the adolescent years, the school nurse can help facilitate transition planning by providing online tools from NDEP and ADA and by writing into the student's IHP nursing interventions that promote "independent decision making related to healthy lifestyle choices and diabetes self-care" (Bobo & Butler, 2010, p. 115).

Arranging for Care/Medication Administration/Emergency Plans for Field Trips and Other Away from School Activities

Emergencies

School districts are responsible to their school communities to be prepared in the event of an emergency or disaster. Emergencies may happen at any time. All students with diabetes will require assistance during an emergency. The link between individual emergency readiness and disaster preparedness is fundamental. Schools that are well-prepared for individual emergencies involving a student or staff member are likely to be prepared for more involved events including community disasters (American Academy of Pediatrics [AAP], 2008a). When there is an emergency, the school nurse and other school personnel must to be prepared to provide care to students with diabetes at school and at all school-sponsored activities in which a student with diabetes participates (NDEP, 2016). As advocates for school safety, school nurses must take a leadership role before, during, and after an emergency, and address the needs of all school community members, that is, students, including students with diabetes, families, teachers, other school personnel, and administrators (NASN, 2014b).

In an emergency or disaster situation, to protect lives from the effects of the unexpected event, planned action is required (Doyle, 2011). Typically, disasters occur with little, or no, warning. The degree of disaster preparation directly affects the outcome. When disaster hits a school, local and regional emergency response resources may be overwhelmed or first responders' arrival may be delayed. However, minutes into a disaster a student with diabetes may need juice, glucose tablets, or a glucagon injection to reverse hypoglycemia. (Butler & Wyckoff, 2012).

School nurses need to participate in disaster planning and practice drills before a disaster occurs. School nurses can serve on community planning groups assessing resources and the school's ability to manage a disaster, developing disaster plans, and coordinating disaster drills to test these plans. School nurses are instrumental in identifying the individual disaster preparedness needs for students and school staff with diabetes (Butler & Wyckoff, 2012). The ECPs for students with special healthcare needs, including diabetes, must be a part of the school's broader disaster plan. Students with diabetes need additional disaster-preparedness planning, including the availability of medication, food, and water during a prolonged lockdown or shelter-in-place (AAP, 2008b).

(Please see Chapter 36 for additional information on disaster planning).

Emergency Medication

Many states have laws permitting UAP to be trained to respond to diabetes and other chronic disease emergencies. In these states, school districts that do not train UAP or stock authorized emergency medicine, may be liable and found negligent for not being prepared for emergencies.

Diabetes, along with several other chronic diseases, can rapidly cause life-threatening emergencies. Quick access to glucagon is linked to saving lives. Administration of glucagon, like all medication administration, is regulated by state law and school district policy. The school nurse should develop an IHP and ECP for all students with medical orders for glucagon or glucose tablets specifying the response needed for the student in case of an emergency (Allen, et al., 2012; NASN, 2012a; Sicherer, Mahr, and the Section on Allergy and Immunology,

2010). When a hypoglycemic episode occurs, it is critical that school district policies permit school staff to provide appropriate care for the student with diabetes, and that access to the student's emergency medication is immediate. School district policies and procedures must specify the location where the glucagon or glucose tablets are stored, the staff member(s) responsible for accessing and administering the medication, the staff member responsible for replacing outdated medication, and the staff member responsible for administering the medication on field trips. Additionally, the school nurse should train and supervise school staff as emergency UAP who should be assigned as "first responders" for students with diabetes who experience hypoglycemia (Allen et al., 2012; AAP, 2009).

Field Trips, Summer Programs, Before and After-School Programs, Science Camps

Students with diabetes are entitled by federal law and related state laws to have equal opportunity to participate fully in all school-sponsored programs and activities, including before- and after-school programs, field trips, special camps, and summer programs. Students with diabetes may not be excluded, even if providing for their full participation creates logistical or fiscal challenges. Without regard to venue or season of the year, relevant legal and clinical standards of safe medication administration apply (ANA & NASN, 2017; NASN, 2013). Students who require nursing or healthcare services at school will minimally require the same level of care during school-sponsored activities away from school (Hootman et al., 2005). To ensure the health and safety of all students with diabetes participating in extended day and away from campus activities, planning for these events should begin well-ahead of the intended date and include the school nurse in all the planning phases (NASN, 2013). The planning should start with an assessment by the school nurse of the activity (intensity, duration), location of activity, ability to self-manage and communicate with the parents/guardian and healthcare provider. For students with diabetes, to prevent hypoglycemia, target blood glucose ranges and insulin requirements may need to be changed depending on the activity.

State-to-state differences in laws pertaining to nursing practice create challenges for the care of students with diabetes on out-of-state field trips (Erwin, Clark, & Mercer, 2014). These challenges are somewhat reduced for school nurses who are licensed in one of the approximately 25 states in the Nurse Licensure Compact (NLC), as the NLC permits registered nurses (RN) and LPN/LVNs to practice across NLC state lines. Navigating practice licensure issues may be more cumbersome for school nurses licensed in non-Compact states. To further complicate matters, the NLC does not cover advanced practice RNs or UAP (USDHHS, 2010). Well before any away from school activity, and especially well ahead of out-of-state field trips involving students with diabetes, school nurses must review applicable state laws and regulations, including those pertaining to delegation in the states to be visited. The U.S. State Department provides guidance for out-of-country field trips (Erwin et al., 2014).

Field trips have become an increasingly important part of most schools' curricula. Student safety is high priority. The school nurse must facilitate communication involving pertinent school staff, parents/guardians, and the student, and oversee healthcare preparations for the trip. Planning for extended field trips should include the following actions:

Keeping Students with Diabetes Safe on School Field Trips

Travel with a copy of the student's IHP, ECP, and phone numbers
Train staff in the recognition and treatment of hypoglycemia and other diabetes care tasks (as permitted by state NPA and school policy)
Determine the level of assistance and supplies necessary, for blood glucose monitoring
Determine the level of assistance, and supplies necessary, for insulin administration
Establish a plan for proper insulin storage
Pack food/snack items (extra snacks may be needed for increased activity)
Pack fast acting carbohydrate, such as glucose gel or a glucagon kit, to be available in case of hypoglycemia
Investigate the state laws, regulations, and the scope of nursing practice in the state(s) to be visited, if the field trip is out of state.

Adapted from Erwin et al., 2014; Butler et al., 2013.

(Please see Chapter 51 for additional information on school-sponsored trips).

CONCLUSION

Ever increasing numbers of students with both type 1 and type 2 diabetes attend school each day. Students with diabetes require coordination of diabetes care tasks including insulin or oral medication administration, blood glucose monitoring, meal planning (including carbohydrate counting), and treatment of hypoglycemia and hyperglycemia. Schools are required by federal and state laws to accommodate the health services needs of students with diabetes safely and appropriately at school and during school-sponsored activities outside regular school hours. School nurses provide care coordination, support safe and effective diabetes management for students with diabetes at school and during school sponsored activates, and reduce liability risks for themselves, school staff, and the school district, by developing, implementing, and evaluating IHPs for all students with diabetes (McClanahan, & Weismuller, 2015). School nurses also document the delegation, training, supervision, and evaluation of UAP and LPN/LVN to provide care and comply with the state NPA and related state laws, standards of practice and care, and school district policy.

Students with diabetes are entitled to receive appropriate diabetes management in school, with minimal disruption to these routines. In accordance with federal and state laws, students should have the opportunity, when developmentally and cognitively appropriate, to self-manage all aspects of diabetes care at school, including, but not limited to performing blood glucose monitoring, administering insulin, having unrestricted access to meals/snacks/water/bathroom, managing hypoglycemia (with trained personnel prepared to provide glucagon treatment, if required) and hyperglycemia, and fully participating in all school-sponsored activities (Chiang, 2016).

RESOURCES

Please see APPENDIX: Brief History

Legal references

- Americans with Disabilities Act (ADA) 42 U.S.C. § 12101 et seq (1990).
- ADA Amendments Act of 2008 (ADAAA) 42 USCA § 12101 (2008).
- Child Nutrition and WIC Reauthorization Act, Pub. L. No. 108-265, § 204, 729 (2004).
- Developmental Disabilities Assistance and Bill of Rights Act, Pub. L. No. 106-402, § 101 1680 (2000).
- Education for All Handicapped Children Act, Pub. L. No. 94-142, § 20 USC 1401. (1975).
- Elementary and Secondary Education Act, 20 U.S.C. 6301 et seq. (1965).
- Every Student Succeeds Act (ESSA), Public Law No: 114-95 (2015)
- Family Educational Rights and Privacy Act (FERPA), 20 U.S.C.S. § 1232g (1974).
- Health Insurance Portability and Accountability Act (HIPAA), Privacy Rule P.L. 104-191 (1996).
- Healthy, Hunger-Free Kids Act, Pub.L. 111–296. (2010).
- Individuals with Disabilities Education Improvement Act (IDEIA), 20 USC et seq., 64 (2004).
- McKinney-Vento Homeless Education Assistance Improvements Act, 42 U.S.C.S. 11431 et seq. (2001).
- Mental Health Parity and Addiction Equity Act (MHPAEA), (2008).
- Patient Protection and Affordable Care Act (ACA), P.L. 111-148 (2010).
- Protection of Pupil Rights Amendment (PPRA), 20 U.S.C.S. § 1232h (1978).
- School Access to Emergency Epinephrine Act, H.R. 2094 — 113th Congress (2013).
- Section 504 of the Rehabilitation Act, 29 U.S.C. § 701 et seq. (1973).

Case law

- American Nurses Assn. v. Torlakson (2013), Cal.4th, No. S184583. (2013).
- Cedar Rapids Community School District V. Garret F., Supreme Court of the United States 526 U.S. 66 (1999).
- Mitts v. Hillsboro Union High School District, (1987).

OCR Agreements

The U.S. Department of Education's Office for Civil Rights is responsible for enforcing the rights of students with disabilities under Section 504 of the Rehabilitation act and the Americans with Disabilities Act. Below are several OCR decisions and settlements addressing students with diabetes.

- Irvine Unified School District (1995)
- Henderson County Public Schools (2000)
- Loudoun County Public Schools (1999)
- Onslow County Public Schools (2002)

Retrieved from: http://www.diabetes.org/living-with-diabetes/know-your-rights/for-lawyers/education-materials-for-lawyers/

Additional resources

American Diabetes Association. (2012). Sample Section 504 Plan. Retrieved from http://main.diabetes.org/dorg/PDFs/Advocacy/Discrimination/504-plan.pdf

National Diabetes Education Program. (2016). Diabetes Medical Management Plan (DMMP). Retrieved from https://www.niddk.nih.gov/health-information/health-communication-programs/ndep/health-care-professionals/school-guide/section3/Documents/NDEP-School-Guide-DMMP-508.pdf

National Diabetes Education Program (NDEP). (2016). *Helping the Student with Diabetes Succeed: A Guide for School Personnel*. Bethesda, MD: Author. Retrieved from https://www.niddk.nih.gov/health-information/health-communication-programs/ndep/health-care-professionals/school-guide/section3/Documents/NDEP-School-Guide-Full.pdf

National Diabetes Education Program (NDEP). (2013*). Resources for Diabetes in Children and Adolescents*. Bethesda, MD: Author. Retrieved from https://www.niddk.nih.gov/health-information/health-communication-programs/ndep/living-with-diabetes/youth-teens/Documents/youth_resdirectory_508.pdf

American Diabetes Association Website: http://www.diabetes.org/

Diabetes Pro, Professional Resources Online Website: http://professional.diabetes.org/content/fast-facts-data-and-statistics-about-diabetes/?loc=dorg_statistics

Joslin Diabetes Center: www.joslin.org

Juvenile Diabetes Research Foundation Website: http://jdrf.org/

National Association of School Nurses Diabetes in Children webpage http://www.nasn.org/ToolsResources/DiabetesinChildren

National Diabetes Educational Program: School Guide Promotional Tools Webpage: https://www.niddk.nih.gov/health-information/health-communication-programs/ndep/health-care-professionals/school-guide/promotional-tools/Pages/resourcedetail.aspx

REFERENCES

Ahmad, E., & Grimes, D.E. (2011). The effects of self-management education for school-age children on asthma morbidity: A systematic review. *The Journal of School Nursing, 27*(4), 282-292. doi: 10.1177/1059840511403003

Allen, K., Henselman, K., Laird, B., Quiñones, A., & Reutzel, T. (2012). Potential life-threatening events in schools involving rescue inhalers, epinephrine autoinjectors, and glucagon delivery devices: Reports from school nurses. *The Journal of School Nursing, 28*(1), 47-55. doi: 10.1177/1059840511420726

American Academy of Pediatrics. (2008a). Disaster planning for schools. *Pediatrics, 122*(4), 895-901. doi:10.1542/peds.2008-

American Academy of Pediatrics. (2009). Guidance for the administration of medication in school (Policy Statement). *Pediatrics,* 124(4), 1244-1251. doi: doi:10.1542/peds.2009-1953 Retrieved from http://pediatrics.aappublications.org/content/124/4/1244

American Academy of Pediatrics. (2008b). Medical emergencies occurring at School. *Pediatrics, 122*(4), 887–894 doi:10.1542/peds.2008-2171

American Association of Diabetes Educators. (2016*). Management of children with diabetes in the school setting* (Position Statement). Retrieved from https://www.diabeteseducator.org/docs/default-source/ practice/practice-resources/position-statements/diabetes-in-the-school-setting-position-statement_ final.pdf

American Diabetes Association. (2013). *History of diabetes*. Retrieved from http://www.diabetes. org/research-and-practice/student-resources/history-of-diabetes.html

American Diabetes Association. (2016). Children and adolescents. Sec. 11, standards of medical care in diabetes—2016. *Diabetes Care*, *39*(Supplement 1), S86-S93. Retrieved from http://care.diabetesjournals.org/content/39/Supplement_1/S86

ADA Amendments Act of 2008 (ADAAA), 42 USCA § 12101 (2008).

American Nurses Association. (2012). *Principles for delegation by registered nurses to unlicensed assistive personnel (UAP)*. Silver Spring, MD: Nursesbooks.org.

American Nurses Association & National Association of School Nurses. (2017). *Scope and standards of practice: School nursing* (3rd ed.) Silver Spring, MD: Authors.

American Nurses Association & National Council of State Boards of Nursing. (2006). *Joint statement on delegation*. Retrieved from https://www.ncsbn.org/Joint_statement.pdf

Baisch, M.J., Lundeen, S.P., & Murphy, M.K. (2011). Evidence-based research on the value of school nurses in an urban school system. *Journal of School Health, 81*(2), 74-80. doi: 10.1111/j.1746-1561.2010.00563.x

Bobo, N. & Butler, S. (2010). The transition from pediatric to adult diabetes health care. *NASN School Nurse,* 25(3): 114-115. doi: 10.1177/1942602X10363735

Bobo, N., Kaup, T., McCarty, P., & Carlson, J.P. (2011). Diabetes management at school: Application of the healthy learner model. *The Journal of School Nursing*, 27(3), 171-184. doi:10.1177/1059840510394190

Breneman, C.B., Heidari, K., Butler, S., Porter, R.R., & Wang, X. (2015). Evaluation of the effectiveness of the H.A.N.D.S. program: A school nurse diabetes management education program. *The Journal of School Nursing*, 31(6), 402-410. doi:10.1177/1059840514568895

Brown, C. (2016). 21st-century diabetes: Technology leads the way. *NASN School Nurse,* 31(5), 254-256. doi:10.1177/1942602X16661198

Brown, C. (2015). Recognizing diabetes in children: what does it look like? *NASN School Nurse, 30*(3), 150-152. doi:10.1177/1942602X15575354

Butler, S., Kaup, T., Swanson, M.A., & Hoffman, S. (2013). Diabetes management in the school setting. In J. Selekman (Ed.), *School nursing: A comprehensive text* (2nd ed). (pp. 872-898). Philadelphia, PA: F. A. Davis Company.

Butler, S. & Wyckoff, L. (2012). Addressing the emergency preparedness needs of students with diabetes. *NASN School Nurse. 27*(3), 160-162. doi: 10.1177/1942602X12442571

Canadian Diabetes Association. (2016). *History of diabetes.* Retrieved from http://www.diabetes.ca/about-diabetes/history-of-diabetes

Centers for Disease Control and Prevention. (2014a). *National diabetes statistics report: Estimates of diabetes and its burden in the United States*. Retrieved from http://www.cdc.gov/diabetes/pubs/statsreport14/national-diabetes-report-web.pdf

Centers for Disease Control and Prevention. (2014b). NCHHSTP social determinants of health: Frequently asked questions. Retrieved from http://www.cdc.gov/socialdeterminants/FAQ.html

Centers for Disease Control and Prevention. (2015). *Diabetes report card 2014*. Atlanta, GA: Author. Retrieved from http://www.cdc.gov/diabetes/pdfs/library/diabetesreportcard2014.pdf

Chiang, J.L., Kirkman, M.S., Laffel, L.M., & Peters, A.L. (2016). Type 1 diabetes through the life span: a position statement of the American Diabetes Association. *Diabetes Care, 37*,2034–2054. Retrieved from http://care.diabetesjournals.org/content/37/7/2034.long

Cicutto, L. (2009). Supporting successful asthma management in schools: The role of asthma care providers. *American Academy of Allergy, Asthma & Immunology, 124*(2), 390-393. doi:10.1016/j.jaci.2009.04.042

Colorado Department of Education. (2016). Standards of care for diabetes management in the school setting & licensed child care facilities – Colorado 2016. Retrieved from http://www.coloradokidswithdiabetes.org/wp-content/uploads/2016/08/Standards-of-Care-Diabetes-School-Management-Colorado-2016.pdf

Cooper, P. (2005). Life before tests: A district's coordinated health approach for addressing children's full range of needs. *School Administrator, 62*(9), 25-34. Retrieved from http://www.aasa.org/SchoolAdministratorArticle.aspx?id=7780

Dabelea, D., Mayer-Davis, E.J., Saydah, S., Imperatore, G., Linder, B., Jasmin Divers, J., . . . Hamman, R.F.; SEARCH for Diabetes in Youth Study. (2014). Prevalence of type 1 and type 2 diabetes among children and adolescents from 2001 to 2009. *Journal of the American Medical Association (JAMA), 311*(17),1778-1786. doi:10.1001/jama.2014.3201

Dang, M.T. (2010). The history of legislation and regulations related to children with developmental disabilities: Implications for school nursing practice today. *The Journal of School Nursing, 26*(4): 252-259. doi: 10.1177/1059840510368162

Diabetes Control and Complications Trials Research Group. (1993). The effect of intensive therapy of diabetes on the development and progression of long-term complications in insulin-dependent diabetes mellitus: The Diabetes Control and Complications Trial Research Group. *New England Journal of Medicine, 329*(14), 977-986. doi: 10.1056/nejm199309303291401

Doyle, J. (2013). Emergency management, crisis response, and the school nurse's role. In J. Selekman (Ed.). *School nursing: A comprehensive text* (2nd ed.) (pp.1216-1244). Philadelphia, PA: F.A. Davis Company.

Disability Rights Education & Defense Fund. (2016). *Laws.* Retrieved from https://dredf.org/legal-advocacy/laws/

Egro, F.M. (2013). Why is type 1 diabetes increasing? *Journal of Molecular Endocrinology, 51,* R1-R13. doi: 10.1530/JME-13-0067

Engelke, M.K., Swanson, M., Guttu, M., Warren, M.B., & Lovern, S. (2011). School nurses and children with diabetes: A descriptive study. *North Carolina Medical Journal, 72*(5):351-358. Retrieved from http://www.ncmedicaljournal.com/

Erwin, K., Clark, S., & Mercer, S.E. (2014). Providing health services for children with special health care needs on out-of-state field trips. *NASN School Nurse, 29*(2), 84-88. doi: 10.1177/1942602X13517005

Galemore, C.A., & Sheetz, A.H. (2015). IEP, IHP, and Section 504 primer for new school nurses. *NASN School Nurse, 30*(2), 85-88. doi:10.1177/1942602X14565462

Gibbons, L., Lehr, K., & Selekman, J. (2013). Federal laws protecting children and youth with disabilities in the schools. In J. Selekman (Ed.), *School nursing: A comprehensive text* (2nd ed.) (pp. 257–283). Philadelphia, PA: F. A. Davis Company.

Godfrey, K.M., Reynolds, R.M., Prescott, S.L., Nyirenda, M., Jaddoe, V.W.V., Eriksson, J.G., & Broekman, B.F.P. (2016). Influence of maternal obesity on the long-term health of offspring. *The Lancet: Diabetes & Endocrinology,* Published Online October 12, 2016. doi: http://dx.doi.org/10.1016/S2213-8587(16)30107-3

Hahn, J.A., & Sheingold, B.H. (2013). Medicaid expansion: The dynamic health care policy landscape. *Nursing Economic$, 31*(6), 267-272, 297. Retrieved from http://www.nursingeconomics.net/necfiles/13ND/267.pdf

Hanson, M., Gluckman, P., & Bustreo, F. (2016). Obesity and the health of future generations. *The Lancet: Diabetes & Endocrinology*, Published Online October 12, 2016, doi: http://dx.doi.org/10.1016/S2213-8587(16)30098-5

Hootman, J., Schwab, N.C., & Gelfman, M.H.B. (2005). School nursing practice: Clinical performance issues. In N.C. Schwab & M.H.B. Gelfman (Eds.), *Legal issues in school health services: A resource for school administrators, school attorneys, and school nurses,* (pp. 167-230). Lincoln, NE: Authors Choice Press.

Hootman, J. (2013). Staff management. In J. Selekman (Ed.), *School nursing: A comprehensive text* (2nd ed.) (pp. 1290–1321). Philadelphia, PA: F. A. Davis Company.

Individuals with Disabilities Education Improvement Act (IDEIA), 20 USC § 1400 (2004).

Jackson, C. C. & Albanese-O'Neill, A. (2016). Supporting the student's graduated independence in diabetes care. *NASN School Nurse, 31*(4): 202-204. First published on June 3, 2016. doi:10.1177/1942602X16651749

Jackson, C.C., Albanese-O'Neill, A., Butler, K.L., Chiang, J.L., Deeb, L.C., Hathaway, K., . . . Siminerio, L.M. (2015). Diabetes care in the school setting: A position statement of the American Diabetes Association. *Diabetes Care, 38*(10): 1958-1963. doi: 10.2337/dc15-1418

Jacquez, F., Stout, S., Alvarez-Salvat, R., Fernandez, M., Villa, M., Sanchez, J., . . . Delamater, A. (2008). Parent perspectives of diabetes management in schools. The Diabetes Educator, 34(6), 996-1003. doi: 10.1177/0145721708325155 Retrieved from http://tde.sagepub.com/content/34/6/996.short

Jörgens, V., & Grüsser, M. (2013). Happy birthday, Claude Bernard. Diabetes, 62(7), 2181–2182. doi: 10.2337/db13-0700

Joslin Diabetes Center. (2016). *General diabetes facts and information*. Retrieved from http://www.joslin.org/info/general_diabetes_facts_and_information.html

Kadohiro, J.K. (2012). What is it like to be a teen with diabetes? *NASN School Nurse, 27*(6), 301-303. doi:10.1177/1942602X12459963

Kaufman, F.R. (2002). Diabetes at school: What a child's health care team needs to know about federal disability law. *Clinical Diabetes, 20*(2): 91-92. doi: 10.2337/diaclin.20.2.91

Lakhtakia, R. (2013). The history of diabetes mellitus. *Sultan Qaboos University Medical Journal, 13*(3), 368–370. Retrieved from https://www.ncbi.nlm.nih.gov/pmc/articles/PMC3749019/

Laubin, M., Schwab, N.C., & Doyle, J. (2012). Understanding the legal landscape. In C. Costante (Ed.), *School nurse administrators: Leadership and management,* (pp. 459-519). Silver Spring, MD: National Association of School Nurses.

Linder, B., & Imperatore, G. (2013). Research updates on type 2 diabetes in children. *NASN School Nurse, 28*(3), 123-140. doi:10.1177/1942602X13479402

Lotstein, D.S., Seid, M., Klingensmith, G., Case, D., Lawrence, J.M., Pihoker, C., . . . Waitzfelder, B. (2013). Transition from pediatric to adult care for youth diagnosed with type 1 diabetes in adolescence. *Pediatrics*, *131*(4), e1062-70. doi: 10.1542/peds.2012-1450.

Malone, S.K., & Bergren, M.D. (2010). School nurses save lives: Can we provide the data? *The Journal of School Nursing, 26*(5), 344–351. doi:10.1177/1059840510376384

Martin, E.W., Martin, R., & Terman, D.L. (1996). The legislative and litigation history of special education. *The Future of Children*, *6*(1): 25-39. Retrieved from https://www.princeton.edu/futureofchildren/publications/docs/06_01_01.pdf

Mayo Clinic. (2017). Gestational diabetes: Treatments and drugs. Retrieved from http://www.mayoclinic.org/diseases-conditions/gestational-diabetes/basics/treatment/con-20014854

McClanahan, R. & Weismuller, P.C. (2015). School nurses and care coordination for children with complex needs: An integrative review. *The Journal of School Nursing, 31*(1), 34-43. doi:10.1177/1059840514550484

Miller, G.F., Coffield, E., Leroy, Z., & Wallin, R. (2016). Prevalence and costs of five chronic conditions in children. *The Journal of School Nursing, 32*(5), 357-364. doi: 10.1177/1059840516641190

Moricca, M.L., Grasska, M.A., B. Marthaler, M., Morphew, T., Weismuller, P.C., & Galant, S.P. (2013). School asthma screening and case management: Attendance and learning outcomes. *The Journal of School Nursing, 29*(2), 104-12. doi: 10.1177/1059840512452668

National Association of School Nurses. (2013). *Section 504 and individuals with disabilities education improvement act – the role of the school nurse* (Position Statement). Silver Spring, MD: Author. Retrieved from http://www.nasn.org/PolicyAdvocacy/PositionPapersandReports/NASNPositionStatementsFullView/tabid/462/ArticleId/491/Section-504-and-Individuals-with-Disabilities-Education-Improvement-Act-The-Role-of-the-School-Nurse

National Association of School Nurses. (2014a). *Emergency preparedness and response in the school setting - the role of the school nurse* (Position Statement). Silver Spring, MD: Author. Retrieved from http://www.nasn.org/PolicyAdvocacy/PositionPapersandReports/NASNPositionStatementsFullView/tabid/462/ArticleId/117/Emergency-Preparedness-and-Response-in-the-School-Setting-The-Role-of-the-School-Nurse-Revised-June

National Association of School Nurses. (2014b). *Helping administer to the needs of the student with diabetes in schools (H.A.N.D.S.): A program for school nurses*. Silver Spring, MD: Author.

National Association of School Nurses. (2014c). *Managing diabetes at school: Tools for the school nurse.* Silver Spring, MD: Author.

National Association of School Nurses. (2014d). *Nursing delegation to unlicensed assistive personnel in the school setting* (Position Statement). Silver Spring, MD: Author. http://www.nasn.org/PolicyAdvocacy/PositionPapersandReports/NASNPositionStatementsFullView/tabid/462/ArticleId/21/Delegation-Nursing-Delegation-to-Unlicensed-Assistive-Personnel-in-the-School-Setting-Revised-June-2

National Association of School Nurses. (2014e). *Transition planning for students with chronic health conditions* (Position Statement). Silver Spring, MD: Author. Retrieved from http://www.nasn.org/PolicyAdvocacy/PositionPapersandReports/NASNPositionStatementsFullView/tabid/462/ArticleId/644/Transition-Planning-for-Students-with-Chronic-Health-Conditions-Adopted-January-2014

National Association of School Nurses. (2015a). *Individualized healthcare plans: The role of the school nurse* (Position Statement). Silver Spring, MD: Author. Retrieved from http://www.nasn.org/PolicyAdvocacy/PositionPapersandReports/NASNPositionStatementsFullView/tabid/462/ArticleId/32/Individualized-Healthcare-Plans-The-Role-of-the-School-Nurse-Revised-January-2015

National Association of School Nurses. (2015b). *Role of the licensed practical nurse/licensed vocational nurse in the school setting* (Position Statement). Silver Spring, MD: Author. Retrieved from http://www.nasn.org/PolicyAdvocacy/PositionPapersandReports/NASNPositionStatementsFullView/tabid/462/ArticleId/864/Role-of-the-Licensed-Practical-Nurse-Licensed-Vocational-Nurse-in-the-School-Setting-Adopted-June-20

National Association of School Nurses. (2015c). *Unlicensed assistive personnel: Their role on the school health services team* (Position Statement). Silver Spring, MD: Author. Retrieved from http://www.nasn.org/PolicyAdvocacy/PositionPapersandReports/NASNPositionStatementsFullView/tabid/462/ArticleId/116/Unlicensed-Assistive-Personnel-Their-Role-on-the-School-Health-Services-Team-Adopted-January-2015

National Association of School Nurses. (2015d). *School nurse workload: Staffing for safe care* (Position Statement). Silver Spring, MD: Author. Retrieved from http://www.nasn.org/PolicyAdvocacy/PositionPapersandReports/NASNPositionStatementsFullView/tabid/462/ArticleId/803/School-Nurse-Workload-Staffing-for-Safe-Care-Adopted-January-2015

National Association of School Nurses. (2016). *The role of the 21st century school nurse* (Position Statement). Silver Spring, MD: Author. Retrieved from http://www.nasn.org/PolicyAdvocacy/PositionPapersandReports/NASNPositionStatementsFullView/tabid/462/ArticleId/87/The-Role-of-the-21st-Century-School-Nurse-Adopted-June-2016

National Association of School Nurses. (2017). *Diabetes management in the school setting* (Position Statement). Silver Spring, MD: Author. Retrieved from https://www.nasn.org/PolicyAdvocacy/PositionPapersandReports/NASNPositionStatementsFullView/tabid/462/ArticleId/22/Diabetes-Management-in-the-School-Setting-Revised-February-2017

National Diabetes Education Program (NDEP). (2016). *Helping the student with diabetes succeed: A guide for school personnel*. Bethesda, MD: Author. Retrieved from https://www.niddk.nih.gov/health-information/health-communication-programs/ndep/health-care-professionals/school-guide/section3/Documents/NDEP-School-Guide-Full.pdf

National Institute of Health: National Institute of Diabetes and Digestive and Kidney Diseases. (n.d.). *Diabetes in children and teens*. Retrieved from https://www.niddk.nih.gov/health-information/health-communication-programs/ndep/living-with-diabetes/youth-teens/Pages/index.aspx

Nguyen, T., Mason, K., Sanders, C., Yazdani, P., & Heptulla, R. (2008). Targeting blood glucose management in school improves glycemic control in children with poorly controlled type 1 diabetes mellitus. *Journal of Pediatrics, 153*(4), 575-578. *doi: 10.1016/j.jpeds.2008.04.066*

Pansier, B. & Schulz, P.J. (2015). School-based diabetes interventions and their outcomes: A systematic literature review. *Journal of Public Health Research*, *4*(1),467. doi: 10.4081/jphr.2015.467

Pettitt, D.J., Talton, J., Dabelea, D., Divers, J., Imperatore, G., Lawrence, J.M., . . . Hamman, R.F. (2014). Prevalence of diabetes in U.S. youth in 2009: The SEARCH for diabetes in youth study. *Diabetes Care, 37*(2), 402-408. Retrieved from http://dx.doi.org/10.2337/dc13-1838

Pohlman, K. J. (2005). Legal framework and financial accountability for school nursing practice. In N. C. Schwab, & M. H. B. Gelfman, (Eds.), *Legal issues in school health services,* (pp. 95-121). New York, NY: Authors Choice Press.

Polonsky, K.S. (2012). The past 200 years in diabetes. *The New England Journal of Medicine, 367,* 1332-1340. doi: 10.1056/NEJMra1110560

Rapp, J.A., Arent, S., Dimmick, B.L., Gordon, K., & Jackson, C. (2015). *Legal rights of students with diabetes.* Retrieved from http://www.diabetes.org/living-with-diabetes/know-your-rights/for-lawyers/education-materials-for-lawyers/legal-rights-of-students-with-diabetes.html

Resha, C. (2010). Delegation in the school setting: Is it a safe practice?" *OJIN: The Online Journal of Issues in Nursing, 15*(2), Manuscript 5. doi: *10.3912/OJIN.Vol15No02Man05*

Schwartz, F.L., Denham, S., Heh, V., Wapner, A., & Shubrook, J. (2010). Experiences of children and adolescents with type 1 diabetes in school: Survey of children, parents, and schools. *Diabetes Spectrum, 23*(1), 47-55. http://dx.doi.org/10.2337/diaspect.23.1.47

Section 504 of the Rehabilitation Act, 29 U.S.C. § 701 et seq. (1973)

Shannon, R.A., & Kubelka, S. (2013a). Reducing the risks of delegation: Use of procedure skills checklists for unlicensed assistive personnel in schools, part 1. *NASN School Nurse, 28*(4), 178-181. doi: 10.1177/1942602X13489886

Shannon, R.A., & Kubelka, S. (2013b). Reducing the risks of delegation: Use of procedure skills checklists for unlicensed assistive personnel in schools, part 2. *NASN School Nurse, 28*(5), 222-226. doi: 10.1177/1942602X13490030

Siminerio, L.M. (2015). Diabetes education and support: A must for students with diabetes. *NASN School Nurse. 30*(6), 320-321. doi:10.1177/1942602X15608685

U.S. Department of Health and Human Services. (2014). *Healthy People 2020, determinants of health.* Retrieved from http://www.healthypeople.gov/2020/about/DOHAbout.aspx

U. S. Department of Health and Human Services. (2010). *Telehealth licensure report: Special report to the Senate Appropriations Committee* (Senate Report No. 111-66). Retrieved from http://www.hrsa.gov/healthit/telehealth/licenserpt10.pdf

U.S. Department of Justice. (2015). Frequently asked questions about service animals and the ADA. Retrieved from https://www.ada.gov/regs2010/service_animal_qa.pdf

Vihik, K. & Dabelea, D. (2011). The changing epidemiology of type 1 diabetes: Why is it going through the roof? *Diabetes/Metabolism Research and Reviews, 27*(1),3-13. doi: 10.1002/dmrr.1141

Vehik, K., Hamman, R., Lezotte, D., Norris, J., Klingensmith, G., Bloch, C., . . . Debelea, D. (2007). Increasing incidence of type 1 diabetes in 0- to 17-year-old Colorado youth. *Diabetes Care, 30*(3), 503–509. doi: 10.2337/dc06-1837

Vollinger, L.J., Bergren, M.D., & Belmonte-Mann, F. (2011). Substitutes for school nurses in Illinois. *The Journal of School Nursing, 27*(2), 111-119. doi:10.1177/1059840510388517

Wang, L.Y., Vernon-Smiley, M., Gapinski, M.A., DeSisto, M., Maughan, E., Sheetz, A. (2014). Cost-benefit study of school nursing services. *Journal of the American Medical Association Pediatrics, 168*(7), 642-648. doi:10.1001/jamapediatrics.2013.5441

White, J.R. (2014). A brief history of the development of diabetes medications. *Diabetes Spectrum, 29*(3), 82-86. doi: http://dx.doi.org/10.2337/diaspect.27.2.82

Wilt, L., & Foley, M. (2011). Delegation of glucagon® in the school setting: A comparison of state legislation. *The Journal of School Nursing, 27*(3), 185-196. doi:10.1177/1059840511398240

You, W. & Henneberg, M. (2016). Type 1 diabetes prevalence increasing globally and regionally: the role of natural selection and life expectancy at birth. *BMJ Open Diabetes Research and Care, 4*(1). doi: 10.1136/bmjdrc-2015-000161

Zajac, J., Shrestha, A., Patel, P., & Poretsky, L. (2010). The main events in the history of diabetes mellitus. In L. Poretsky (Ed.), *Principles of Diabetes Mellitus* (pp. 3-16). Switzerland: Springer International Publishing. doi 10.1007/978-0-387-09841-8_1

Zimmerman, B. (2013). Student health and education plans. In J. Selekman (Ed.), *School nursing: A comprehensive text* (2nd ed.) (pp. 284–314). Philadelphia, PA: F. A. Davis Company.

Zirkel, P.A. (2009). History and expansion of Section 504 student eligibility: Implications for school nurses. *The Journal of School Nursing, 25*(4): 256-260. doi: 10.1177/1059840509336930

Zirkel, P.A. (2014). Unlicensed administration of medication The California Supreme Court decision. *NASN School Nurse*, *29*(5), 248-252. doi:10.1177/1942602X14540412

Zirkel, P. A., Granthom, M. F., & Lovato, L. (2012). Section 504 and student health problems: The pivotal position of the school nurse. *The Journal of School Nursing, 28*(6), 423–432. doi:10.1177

APPENDIX

Brief History

Diabetes, one of the earliest identified chronic diseases, was first documented around 1500 B.C.E. by the ancient Egyptians. Most sources agree that the term "diabetes," meaning "siphon," was used by the Greek physician Aretaeus, in the first century C.E., to describe the frequent urination and extreme thirst associated with the disease. In fifth century C.E. India, Sushruta, a physician, and the surgeon Charaka identified two types of diabetes, based on observations of age of onset, weight of the patient, and longevity after diagnosis, which were much later named type 1 and type 2. The famous Persian physician, Avicenna (980–1037 C.E.), observed and recorded in *The Canon of Medicine,* the progression and complications of diabetes. The word "mellitus," meaning "honey sweet," was added in 1675 by Thomas Wills in England when he rediscovered the sweetness of the urine and blood of patients with diabetes, that was first identified by Sushruta and Charaka over 1000 years earlier. One hundred years later, in 1776, Matthew Dobson in England was able to measure an excess concentration of glucose in the urine of patients with diabetes (Canadian Diabetes Association (CDA), 2016; Lakhtakia, 2013; Polonsky, 2012; Zajac, Shrestha, Patel, & Poretsky, 2010). In 1855, Claude Bernard, the French father of modern physiology, established the role of the liver in glycogenesis, and asserted that diabetes is due to excess glucose production (Jörgens & Grüsser, 2013; Zajac et al., 2010). Mering and Minkowski (Austria) discovered the role of the pancreas in the pathogenesis of diabetes in 1889. Later, this discovery was the basis of insulin isolation and clinical use by Dr. Frederick Banting and Charles Best at the University of Toronto, Canada in 1921 (CDA, 2016).

Throughout the history of diabetes, various remedies and diets were prescribed for patients. In 1916, Boston's Elliot Joslin complied a textbook The Treatment of Diabetes Mellitus reporting that mortality in patients with diabetes was lowered due to fasting and regular exercise. Over the next five decades, Joslin's continued research established him as a leading diabetes expert (ADA, 2013; CDA, 2016). Prior to the 1920s, there were no effective medications for diabetes management. As a consequence, diabetes was a fatal disease (White, 2014).

This changed dramatically in 1921, when Banting and Best, with the support of John J.R. Macleod, isolated and successfully injected a depancreatized dog with insulin (ADA, 2013; CDA, 2016; Zajac et al., 2010). After working with James Collip to purify insulin, in January 1922, Leonard Thompson, a 14-year-old charity patient in Toronto, Canada, was the first human to be injected with insulin. The insulin treatments were successful, allowing Thompson to live 13 more years until he died at age 27 from pneumonia. News of insulin spread to the United States, and In August 1922, the daughter of U.S. Secretary of State Charles Evans Hughes, Elizabeth Evans Hughes, age 13, barely able to walk and weighing 45 pounds, went to Toronto for insulin treatment. Elizabeth's response to insulin therapy was immediate, she had a productive life, and died at age 73 in 1981 (CDA, 2016; Zajac et al., 2010). In 1922, Eli Lilly and Company became the first company to commercially produce insulin. In October 1923, Banting and Macleod were awarded the Nobel Prize for the discovery of insulin – they shared their prize with Best and Collip (ADA, 2013; CDA, 2016; Zajac et al., 2010).

In 1940, the American Diabetes Association was founded and began to address the increasing incidence of diabetes and the complications associated with diabetes. Throughout the decades after the discovery of insulin advances were made in many areas of diabetes care and management that ultimately improved the quality and length of life for people with diabetes. These advancements include: medications to treat diabetes and hypoglycemia, meal planning based on calories, carbohydrate, protein, and fat in each serving of food, testing strips for urine and blood, standardized syringes, glucose meters and insulin pumps, pancreas transplant surgeries, advanced research on the pathophysiology of diabetes, implementation of tight control, and new classes of drugs for people with type 2 diabetes (ADA, 2013; CDA, 2016; Zajac et al., 2010).

While life was getting better medically for people with diabetes after the discovery of insulin and the many subsequent advancements in diabetes management, the passage of federal civil rights legislation after World War II, and particularly the authorization of three overarching federal laws in the second half of the twentieth century and in the first decade of the twenty-first century, protected the rights of all people with disabilities, including the right of all school-age children to have a free and appropriate public education (FAPE) in the least restrictive environment (LRE). These laws are the Rehabilitation Act (1973), Section 504; Education for All Handicapped Children Act (1975) which was reauthorized in 2004 as the Individuals with Disabilities Education Improvement Act (IDEIA) of 2004; and Americans with Disabilities Act (ADA) (1990) which was reauthorized in 2008 as the ADA Amendments Act (ADAAA) of 2008. All fifty states have subsequently passed corresponding state laws guaranteeing the rights of individuals with disabilities. Landmark court rulings, such *as Cedar Rapids Community Sch. Dist. v. Garret F., 119 S. Ct. 992* (U.S. 1999) reinforced the rights of students with disabilities to health services at school. Prior to these laws, persons with disabilities, including individuals with diabetes, were subjected to discrimination, frequently denied access to public education, and if they were granted access, were provided no supportive services to meet their special health or educational needs (Martin, Martin, & Terman, 1996). Unfortunately, not all school districts understand their obligations under these federal laws, and according to several reports, families and students with disabilities still report either not receiving needed health services, or receiving inadequate health services (Jackson et al., 2015; Jacquez et al., 2008; Schwartzet al., 2010).

Chapter 26

EXAMINING CHILDREN IN THE SCHOOL SETTING

Andrea Adimando, DNP, PMHNP-BC, BCIM

DESCRIPTION OF ISSUE

Examining children in a school-based setting is a task that many school nurses will be challenged with during their day-to-day operations. Understanding a few legal principles may enhance reducing liability related to exams in the school setting. The decision regarding the extent of the physical exam of a child requires careful consideration by the school nurse since legal ramifications for performing unnecessary or inappropriate physical exams, or for neglecting to perform an exam in an appropriate or timely manner in order to properly assess a child who may be in need of emergency or outside healthcare services can occur. Though very little has been written previously about this topic, case law may assist nurses in the decision-making process. This chapter provides a discussion of select cases, both state and federal, as well as general recommendations for best practice in providing safe, appropriate, and patient-centered care.

School nurses are faced daily with important decisions concerning the health and wellbeing of the students they serve. When children present with acute chief complaints, the school nurse must decide what assessment procedures he or she will utilize to best assess and manage the situation at hand. At times, the assessment may include a brief or comprehensive physical exam, in order to provide accurate assessment and treatment of the child in question. Given that physical exams involve the nurse inspecting, palpating, and auscultating certain areas of a child's body, this is a decision that the nurse must consider carefully. The school nurse should avoid not only potential legal ramifications that may result from performing unnecessary violations of the child's autonomy or privacy, but also charges of negligence related to not fully assessing the child. A school nurse can use clinical practice guidelines, his or her state's Nurse Practice Act (NPA), guidelines from the school nurse's certifying body (such as the National Board for Certification of School Nurses) and/or other clinical guidelines, clinical judgment, experience, and familiarity with relevant cases in order to make the clinical decision as to when to engage in physical examination of a child in a school-based setting.

BACKGROUND

Physical Examinations

The physical health of a student can undoubtedly contribute to the student's academic and social functioning within the school setting. Ideally, a school nurse should be aware of the medical history of each student – including immunization status, prior health issues/concerns, physical abilities, adversities or challenges, etc. - prior to engaging in any form of clinical assessment of the student, in order to perform safe, patient-centered care. This awareness of the child's medical history typically comes from school physicals, performed by the child's primary healthcare provider at regular, established intervals. In addition, parent/guardian(s) may provide information related to the student's previous medical history, current health status, and other issues the student may be having on a more transient basis. These forms of data can assist the school nurse in making accurate and patient-specific assessments of current health status.

In addition to the baseline school-focused physical exams that the majority of students receive from outside providers before or during the school year, students may present with acute complaints or concerns that warrant further investigation during the course of the school year. Depending on the nature of the complaint, the nurse may need to perform a problem-focused or a more global examination of the student when such episodic symptomatic needs arise. The main purpose of an exam of this type would be to: 1) assess the imminent health status of the student, 2) assess the level of contagiousness of the student's potential ailment, 3) assess the level of function of the student to determine whether the student can continue within the school setting at that particular time, and 4) to communicate to the student and parent/guardian any current health concerns and recommendations for follow up care.

Legal Considerations

All children are entitled to certain rights including patients' rights. It is the responsibility of the school nurse to be familiar with state and federal, laws and regulations including applicable professional practice standards prior to engaging in physically examining children in a school setting.

Consent

The school nurse has an ethical duty to ensure that the student who may be examined in the school setting has given informed consent prior to any form of treatment, including but not limited to physical examination (Cohn, Schwab, & Gelfman, 2001/2005; Coverdale, 2011; Hootman, Schwab, Gelfman, Gregory, & Pohlman, 2001/2005). Informed consent not only consists of the permission to treat the child, given by the parent/guardian and child (ideally and ethically by both), but also is given under the assumption that the care provided will be safe and appropriate according to the current clinical practice guidelines (Hootman et al., 2005). An exception to informed consent is only in a health or safety emergency when obtaining consent may delay treatment, which could cause harm to the child. When informed consent cannot be obtained due to an emergent situation, the school nurse should treat the child as indicated under the principal of *implied consent*. Some state statues allow persons to operate *"in loco parentis"* – in place of a parent – under certain circumstances. In such states this principle can be applied to the school setting should the student need care without having obtained prior parental consent (Maggiore, 2009).

Parental consent should be sought prior to evaluation of minors under the age of 12-14 (depending on the particular state's laws), except in an emergent case which may pose an imminent and significant health threat to the child (Cohn et al., 2001/2005). In many areas of nursing and medicine, however, an adolescent of 16 or 17 years of age is thought to be competent enough to give informed consent to examination and treatment. This is typically dictated by state laws and guidelines, and whether or not awaiting parental consent (vs. solely obtaining consent from the adolescent in question) would cause undue delay in medical assessment or care and potentially cause harm to said adolescent. However, in non-emergent situations it would be highly prudent of the school nurse to attain consent from the parent/guardian(s) of the adolescent concurrently wherever possible.

In the school setting, this is often established by passive consent, meaning that the parent is giving consent for the nurse to treat the child for routine matters unless otherwise specified or opted out. Schools often provide annual notification of some sort (whether it be an electronic communication, mailing, and/or school handbook) notifying parents of the services the school nurse provides, as well as the means for notifying the school should a family wish to opt out of these (or any specific) services. Regardless of the notion of passive and/or implied consent, asking for consent and receiving the student's permission is always considered best practice, even when the child is under the age of majority.

Constitutional and Legal Considerations

The Fourth Amendment of the U.S. Constitution protects individuals from unreasonable searches, calling such searches a violation of the individual's reasonable expectation of privacy (U.S. Const. amend. XIV). The school nurse must give extra consideration to this notion, as an examination – especially that of a strip-search type, such as in the case of suspected contraband or other similar safety concerns - that is perceived to be unnecessary may in fact constitute a violation of the Fourth Amendment. Further, the unpermitted "touching" of another person is a committal of the tort of battery.

Related Cases

> Hearring v. Sliwowski. *In the case of Hearring v. Sliwowski (2013), a student (B.H.) who complained of genital burning approached her school nurse with this complaint. The student's mother was called and reported a history of bladder infections in this student. The student was not examined at this time. However, when the student returned two days later with the same complaint, the school nurse brought the student (as well as the school secretary as a witness) to a private bathroom and visually inspected her genital area for any signs of irritation or infection. B.H.'s mother, who claimed that her child's 4th amendment right to be free from unnecessary searches was violated, brought suit against the school nurse shortly after this examination. Though she was initially found guilty of violating the student's 4th amendment rights by a district court, a higher court reversed the case, ruling that the nurse was entitled to qualified immunity, as no prior precedent of this type had been set. Qualified immunity is a legal term used to describe the protection of state or government employees from liability or civil lawsuits provided that their actions do not violate a clearly established law or constitutional rights of an individual, about which a reasonable person would have known (Schott, 2012). The court ruled that the school nurse's visual examination of B.H.'s genitals was not a strip-search type search with the intent of finding contraband, but was a realistic and appropriate attempt to assess and diagnose a medical condition based on her prior complaints ("Hearring v. Sliwowski," 2013).*

> Madden v. Hamilton County Department of Education. *In this particular case, the parent of a minor child (5 years old at the time) notified her child's school in writing of the presence of a latent congenital herpes simplex virus in her genital area. Three months later, the mother was contacted and asked to pick up her child from school, as well as to provide a letter stating that she was medically cleared to return to school despite an active lesion on her foot. When the mother inquired about how this lesion was found, it was brought to her attention that the school nurse had been conducting visual exams of the student's entire body on a daily basis for several weeks under the direction of her superiors. The student's mother filed suit against the school and the nurse, alleging that the school did not at any time ask for permission to examine the student from either of her parents despite contact numbers being readily available to them. National and state guidelines prohibited the school nurse from medically examining students' genitals without parental consent or the presence of a medical emergency. As it was determined that no emergency was present, the daily examinations were deemed to have been*

a violation of this student's Fourth amendment rights to be free from unnecessary searches and/or unwanted medical treatment. In a similar case, it was also determined that "a schoolchild's right to personal security and to bodily integrity manifestly embraces the right to be free from sexual abuse at the hands of a public school employee. The substantive component of the Due Process Clause protects students against abusive governmental power as exercised by a school."("Doe v. Claiborne Cnty., Tenn.," 1996; "Hearring v. Sliwowski," 2013). These exemplary cases demonstrate the caution that the school nurse must take when considering the purpose and the extent of an examination. Genital exams particularly, if conducted without parental knowledge or consent, must be contemplated circumspectly with the risks of liability weighed against the benefit to the student.

IMPLICATIONS FOR SCHOOL NURSE PRACTICE

Challenges and Considerations

Given the nature of the role of the school nurse, he or she may frequently be faced with the task of determining if and when a physical exam of any type is indicated at a given time, or whether this exam is better deferred to an outside provider. This can be challenging, as there may be legal implications for either course of action. A full physical assessment may be perceived as unnecessary and/or inappropriate in some cases, though not performing an adequate examination may be perceived as negligence in others. In one particular case, *Schluessler v. Independent School District* (1989), a nurse was charged with negligence after failing to appropriately assess a child having an asthma attack, leading to a delay in that child's receiving appropriate emergency care. The court determined that, "School nurses have a higher duty of care than hospital nurses to make an assessment of the need for emergency services" (Schluessler v. Independent School District 200, et al.., 1989). School nurses have the essential duty of recognizing emergency situations and providing appropriate follow up care and/or referral in these situations (Schwab & Gelfman, 2001/2005). This level of assessment and critical thinking may warrant a brief or comprehensive physical exam, especially in order to rule out trauma, significant injury, and/or need for emergency management of symptoms. Therefore, it is essential for the school nurse to use his or her best judgment, based on education, experience, and clinical guidelines to determine the level of examination that is necessary to appraise the clinical urgency of the situation at hand in order to rule out the need for further emergent evaluation or treatment.

Practice Recommendations

In considering the outcomes of the aforementioned cases involving either inappropriate physical examinations performed by the nurse or negligence at the hands of the school nurse, general recommendations for future school nurse practice can be made as follows:

1. Examination of a student's genitalia should generally be avoided when possible, due to potential legal and/or psychological consequences as described by the aforementioned cases. When it is within the school nurse's best judgment that this examination should in fact be performed within the school setting, and not deferred to an external/primary healthcare provider at a later date and time (such as in the case of blunt or acute trauma to the area or significant pain or discomfort that is prohibitive to the student's functioning), the examination should be done in the presence of another adult (preferably of the same gender as the child), and with verbal consent from one of the child's legal guardians.

2. Physical examinations should be as problem-focused and brief as possible within the school setting, without compromising adequate assessment of the complaint or concern of the student. The examination should be limited to the potentially affected body system(s) based on the student report and nurse's judgment.

3. Clothing removal should be kept to a minimum wherever possible, so as to protect the privacy and rights of the student in question. Gowns and proper drapery should be provided to the student, allowing him or her to cover the body areas that are not immediately being examined.

4. An adult witness should be present for physical examinations that require the student to disrobe wherever possible. This adult should preferably be the same gender as the student, unless the student specifically verbalizes otherwise.

5. Parental consent should be obtained wherever possible without compromising the immediate health of the student. This may be in the form of a global consent form sent to all parents at the beginning of the school year, indicating that students may be examined based on their acute complaints on a routine or emergent basis and/or verbal consent obtained from the parent immediately prior to an examination. If there is not adequate time or means to obtain verbal consent from a parent, a nurse should use his or her best judgment in physically examining students without this consent, and should be able to provide adequate rationale for performing this examination without said consent. For example, rationale may include risk for harm to the student or to other students should said examination not occur immediately.

6. Informed consent or assent for younger children should always be obtained from the student in question, regardless of the age of the student. In some states, a student aged 16 or above may be able to provide informed consent as an adult in certain situations, which would eliminate the need for parental consent. However, even in such states, it remains good practice to involve the parent when possible, so long as the student is comfortable and agreeable to parental involvement. If a student refuses an examination, the nurse should not proceed unless refraining from assessment/examination would cause imminent danger to the student.

7. Examination techniques should follow appropriate nursing guidelines related to the age, mental health status, physical health status, and acute health status of the child in question, to ensure that the exam is as pleasant and non-traumatic as possible (Hockenberry & Wilson, 2015). These will vary based on the age and developmental level of the child in question; however, school nurses should have a general knowledge of examination techniques and sequences that are appropriate to children of all ages and backgrounds.

8. If school staff and/or the school nurse suspect signs of sexual or physical abuse, the nurse should take measures to ensure the child's immediate safety as the primary priority. The school nurse should then, in conjunction with any other concerned staff members, file a report with the child protective service department in the particular state. The school nurse should take special care not to examine the child unless absolutely necessary for the child's immediate health and safety so as to avoid impeding any forensic investigation that may take place at the request of the child protective service agency. Should the agency(s) request a medical exam be performed as part of the investigation, the child should be

referred to his or her primary care provider, or to the local emergency room. Based on this author's experience, emergency room staff tends to be more efficient and experienced in performing such exams, and should be considered first line for referral purposes.

In addition to these generalized recommendations, school nurses should be aware of any state-specific guidelines, laws, or regulations that may warrant further consideration when making the decision to physically examine a child in the school setting, as well as any district or school related policies that may vary from one organization or location to another. It is ultimately the responsibility of the nurse to be aware of these factors in order to make safe and appropriate decisions in the best interest of the students he or she is tasked with assessing and treating.

CONCLUSION

In conclusion, a school nurse's decision as to whether or not to examine a child in a school-based health setting is one that should be carefully considered. Special consideration should be given to: 1) the particular complaint or concern of the student, including whether or not this complaint/concern can be deferred to an outpatient provider for assessment or requires more imminent follow up; 2) whether or not the school nurse has verbal or written consent to examine the child from the child's legal guardian and the child him/herself; 3) whether the situation is emergent in that the child may be placed in undue harm's way should the examination not take place by the school nurse in the school setting; and 4) any applicable state regulations or guidelines around this issue in the school nurse particular state of practice. The school nurse should also be familiar with previous cases surrounding this topic so as to mindfully physically examine a student. Conversely, the decision not to examine a patient may result in a claim of delay of treatment, such as in the case of an acute emergency that is not properly diagnosed or treated due to insufficient assessment of the child in question. With careful consideration, a school nurse can avoid litigation while providing safe, appropriate, and patient-centered care.

RESOURCES

> **Please see ADDENDUM #1: The Protection of Pupil Rights Act (PPRA)– Physical Exams /Screenings and ADDENDUM #2: Email Confirmation of Verbal Consent**

- *Hearring v. Sliwowski*

- *Madden v. Hamilton City Dept. of Education*

- *Poe v. Leonard*

- *Schluessler v. Independent School District 200, et al.*

- Schwab, N. C., & Gelfman, M. (Eds.). (2001/2005). *Legal Issues in School Health Services: A Resource for School Administrators, School Attorneys, School Nurses*. Lincoln, NE: Author's Choice Press.

- State Nurse Practice Acts

REFERENCES

Cohn, S. D., Schwab, N. C., & Gelfman, M. H. B. (2005). Adolescent issues and rights of minors . In N. C. Scwab & M. H. B. Gelfman (Eds.), *Legal Issues in school health services: A resource for school administrators, school attorneys, school nurses,* (pp. 231-261). Lincoln, NE: Author's Choice Press.

Coverdale, G. (2011). Promoting the health of school-aged children: An ethical perspective. In G. M. Brykczynska & J. Simons (Eds.), *Ethical and Philosophical Aspects of Nursing Children and Young People* (pp. 66-77). Oxford, United Kingdom: John Wiley & Sons.

Doe v. Claiborne Cnty., Tenn., 103 F.3d 495, 506 (6th Cir. 1996)

Hearring v. Sliwowski, No. 712 F.3d 275, 712 F.3d 275 (6th Cir 2013)

Hockenberry, M. J., & Wilson, D. (2015). *Wong's nursing care of infants and children* (10th ed.). St. Louis, Missouri: Elsevier Mosby. Entire book?

Hootman, J., Schwab, N. C., Gelfman, M. H. B., Gregory, E. K., & Pohlman, K. J. (2005). In N. C. Scwab & M. H. B. Gelfman (Eds.), *Legal Issues in school health services: A resource for school administrators, school attorneys, school nurses,* (pp. 175-178). Lincoln, NE: Author's Choice Press.

Maggiore, W. A., JD, NREMT-P. (2009). Providing EMS care for children when parents are absent. *Journal of Emergency Medical Services (JEMS)*, 1. Retrieved from http://www.jems.com/articles/2009/02/ providing-ems-care-children-wh-0.html

Schluessler v. Independent School District 200, et al., No. MM89-14V (105196) MM89-14V (105196) (Dakota District Court 1989)

Schott, R. G., J.D. (2012). Qualified immunity: How it protects law enforcement officers. *FBI Law Enforcement Bulletin.* Retrieved from https://leb.fbi.gov/2012/september/qualified-immunity-how-it-protects-law-enforcement-officers

Schwab, N. C., & Gelfman, M. (2005). *Legal issues in school health services: A resource for school administrators, school attorneys, school nurses*. Lincoln, NE: Author's Choice Press.

U.S. Constitution, Amendment XIV. Retrieved from http://www.usconstitution.net/xconst_Am14.html

ADDENDUM # 1

The Protection of Pupil Rights Act (PPRA)– Physical Exams /Screenings

Erin D. Gilsbach, Esquire

The PPRA states that schools are required to develop and adopt policies in consultation with parents, regarding the administration of physical examinations or screenings that the school may administer to a student, and that the PPRA requires prior parental notice for certain types of physical examinations or screenings. This law would not apply in instances where the physical examination is in response to a particular medical need of the child that requires prompt attention. The PPRA provision only applies to:

(iii) Any nonemergency, invasive physical examination or screening that is—

(I) required as a condition of attendance;

(II) administered by the school and scheduled by the school in advance; and

(III) not necessary to protect the immediate health and safety of the student, or of other students 20 U.S.C. § 1232h(c)(1)(D).

ADDENDUM # 2

Email Confirmation of Verbal Consent

Erin D. Gilsbach, Esquire

An excellent practice that can be used in MANY different contexts is the use of an email response to verbal consent from a parent. When a parent has authorized consent for a particular nursing service in a time-sensitive situation (written consent should be obtained in situations that are not time-sensitive), such as a physical exam, the parent's verbal consent should be followed up via email. The email should thank the parent for taking time to speak with the nurse, and confirm what was discussed, including the verbal consent. If the parent receives the email and does not respond, it can be inferred that they are in agreement with the substance. In a legal action, it would be very difficult for a parent to argue the facts, as stated in the email, in court at a later date if the parent did not raise the issue at the time the email was sent.

Chapter 27

MANAGEMENT OF HEAD LICE (PEDICULOSIS)

Shirley C. Gordon, PhD, RN, NCSN, AHN-BC

DESCRIPTION OF ISSUE

Head louse infestation (known as pediculosis) is a pandemic, communicable condition. Caused by the Pediculus Humanus Capitis (head louse), pediculosis is the most prevalent parasitic infestation among humans (Hodgdon, et al., 2010). In many countries, including the United States (U.S.), head louse infestations are highly stigmatized.

School nurses have the responsibility of protecting the community of children, educators, caregivers, support staff and others from exposure to communicable diseases/conditions. When head louse infestations occur in the community (schools, day care centers and camps), strong emotional reactions from parents, teachers, staff, and community members occur. The community expects school nurses and other healthcare providers to respond with evidenced-based approaches to diagnosis, treatment, and transmission prevention. This chapter provides an overview of head lice with a special focus on legal considerations in the management of head louse infestations in school settings.

BACKGROUND

Head lice have been around since antiquity and the relationship between humans and head lice is complex. Evidence of human and head lice cohabitation includes the discovery of desiccated lice and nits on Egyptian mummies and ivory nit combs dating back to the 12th and 13th centuries BC (Mumcuoglu & Zias, 1989). Attitudes toward louse infestations have changed overtime. For example, in the 18th century, louse infestations were common and thought to provide protection against childhood disease (Drisdelle, 2010).

Despite the long history between humans and head lice, infestations remain prevalent throughout the world (Hodgdon, et al., 2010). Reliable prevalence data on the number of head lice infestations occurring each year in the U.S. is unavailable. However, the Centers for Disease Control and Prevention (CDC) reports an estimated 6-12 million cases occur each year in children age 3-11 (CDC, 2013).

Despite low morbidity, head louse infestations impose significant social and financial costs on children and families. A recent cost analysis conducted in the United States indicates we spend an estimated $367 million dollars each year to combat head lice (West, 2004). This estimate takes into account consumer costs, lost wages, and school system expenses.

All ages and socio-economic groups experience head louse infestations. However, children ages 3-11 and their family members are predominantly affected (CDC, 2013). As a result, 3.45 million children enrolled in in pre-K through the 8th grade (National Center for Education Statistics, 2016) and their families are at increased risk for head louse infestations.

Factors influencing our understanding of which groups of people are largely affected include the negative impact of stigma on willingness to disclose the condition and seek help, vigilance of school personnel in identifying head lice, and the absence of a systematic, national prevalence data collection system.

Experts believe the number of head lice cases are increasing in England and the United States, despite efforts to effectively treat and control transmission. Emerging resistance to available pediculocides is a major contributing factor. In a recent study, researchers explored the prevalence of the kdr-type mutation (knockdown resistance allele frequencies) and permethrin resistance in head lice samples collected from around the country (Yoon et al., 2014). New York, Oregon, New Mexico, North Dakota, New Jersey, and Minnesota were the only states in which selected head lice samples did not demonstrate 100% resistance to permethrin. This new resistance evidence informs treatment recommendations. However, it is important to note resistance patterns vary across geographic and head lice samples in this study did not represent all regions in each state. Therefore, local resistance patterns are difficult to determine.

Biology

Our understanding of head louse biology directs school management policies and educational programs. Adult head lice are about 2-3 mm long or about the size of a sesame seed (Devore & Schutze, 2015). They are ectoparasites with a fused thoracic plate and six segmented legs (Meinking et al., 2011). The louse uses claws located at the end of each leg to hold onto hair strands and move quickly through hair. The shape of the claw varies and experts believe claw shape contributes to host selection. For example, head lice with a rounded claw shape prefer hair strands with a similar shape. The claws also limit the ability of the louse to crawl effectively on surfaces other than hair. Respiratory spiracles are located on each side of the thorax. The louse closes the spiracles when exposed to water and other liquids as a protective mechanism. Head lice do not have wings or hind legs at any time during their development. Therefore, they are not able to jump, hop or fly (CDC, 2015a).

Head lice have mouthparts designed to pierce the skin, inject saliva containing vasodilatory and anticoagulation properties, and suck capillary blood directly from the scalp of the host (Meinking et al., 2011). Head lice feed every 2-3 hours and "die of starvation and desiccation if feeding does not occur within the first hour after hatching" (p. 1545) and usually survive less than 24 hours away from the human host (Devore & Schutze, 2015).

Head lice are able to adapt to the hair and skin coloring of the human host. For example, it is common for head lice found on persons with blond hair to be lighter in color than lice found on persons with dark brown or black hair (Meinking et al., 2011). Color variation also occurs in response to feeding patterns. Lice that have recently fed will be darker in color. The ability to adapt to their surrounding makes lice more difficult to see and increases the likelihood of an inaccurate diagnosis.

In addition, most lice experts agree viable eggs are generally found within 6mm from the scalp. However, Meinking (1999) reported the presence of viable eggs several inches from the scalp in warm, humid climates.

Life Cycle

The life cycle of the head louse has implications for treatment recommendations and school management policies. Therefore, it is important that school nurses understand the life cycle stages and share this understanding with families. The APPENDIX provides a detailed description of the complex life cycle of the head louse presented by the CDC (Life Cycle Image, 2015). Please see appendix for additional information.

Transmission

Head lice are transmitted primarily through prolonged close head- to- head contact. They are prevalent in all age groups indicating transmission most likely occurs in community settings (Canyon & Speare, 2016). Adult lice are most likely to leave a healthy head in the presence of heavy infestations (Maunder, 1985). Indirect transmission through exposure to brushes, combs, and hats used or worn by persons with active infestations occur infrequently (Burkhart & Burkhart, 2007). Researchers have reported lice found on combs are often dead or injured making establishing an infestation on a new host unlikely (Chunge, Scott, Underwood & Zavarella, 1991).

Head lice live only on the human host and do not infest the environment such as carpets, furniture and mattresses. For example, Speare, Cahill & Thomas (2003) found live lice on only 4% of the pillowcases used by research volunteers with active head louse infestations. While the researchers suggested indirect transmission was possible, the transmission rate from pillowcases was not determined in this study. However, in a later descriptive study, Gordon (2007a) reported sleeping in bed with more than one person as a risk factor for children experiencing persistent head lice. The researcher reported head-to-head transmission during sleep as the most likely transmission mode. Some experts recommend persons who sleep in the same bed with persons diagnosed with active infestations should be treated prophylactically (CDC, 2016).

Environmental cleaning approaches (effective in controlling body lice) which include vacuuming car seats, upholstery, bed linens, and clothing that cannot be washed in hot settings over 130 degrees, etc. are often recommended to prevent transmission (CDC, 2016). However, there is no evidence to support environmental cleaning impacts head louse transmission and may contribute to the association between head lice, poor hygiene, and filthy environments.

Family caregivers are often concerned about transmission between family members and pets. Because head lice are species specific, they do not infest family pets (cats, dogs, birds, guinea pigs, etc.). Therefore, transmission of head lice does not occur between humans and pets (CDC, 2013).

Prevalence

The head louse is an equal opportunity parasite. They infest all socio-economic groups (Devore & Schutze, 2015) and most ethic groups (Meinking, 1999). In the United States, head lice are frequently found among Whites, Asians, Hispanics, and North, Central, and South American Indians (Meinking et al., 2011) In the past African-Americans were excluded from prevalence estimates because the infestation prevalence was only 0.3% of African-American children (Juranek, 1977). More recently, researchers suspect the American head louse has adapted to the host hair structure as a result of increased travel between countries. This adaptation has resulted in more African-American children being infested with head lice (Meinking et al., 2011).

Research studies exploring prevalence rates demonstrate mixed results regarding gender and hair length and type. Indicating gender, hair length and hair type are not significant risk factors in contracting head lice infestations (Canyon & Speare, 2016) but are factors in identification and treatment efficacy (Mumcuoglu, et.

al., 2006). Researchers report prevalence variations are most likely due to social norms and behaviors rather than physical characteristics of the host (Canyon & Speare, 2016).

For reasons that are not entirely clear, some students and families develop head louse infestations that persist for weeks, months or years. Gordon (1999, 2007a) defined persistent head lice as the diagnosis of an active infestation 3 times in 6 weeks that is not amenable to treatment. Factors contributing to persistent head lice include:

- Treatment failure from emerging resistance, improper use of treatment products, and/or treatments that target a specific life cycle phase.
- Failure to treat.
- Auto-re-infestation from eggs left on the hair.
- Re-infestation through contact with persons experiencing active infestations (often someone in the immediate family who is asymptomatic).

Effects on the Host

Itching is the hallmark symptom of head lice infestations. Researcher's estimate 50% of the population develops sensitivity to the saliva injected by the louse during feeding. Depending on host sensitivity, itching may be absent or manifest as mild to severe. In sensitive persons, it may take several weeks for itching to develop. "Small 2-3 mm erythematous macules, papules or acute hive-like reactions with typical flare and wheal formations" may occur at feeding sites." (Meinking et al., 2011, p. 1536).

Scratching in response to intense itching at feeding sites or in response to treatment products often results in skin excoriations on the scalp. Scalp excoriations can also occur as the result of the inappropriate, forceful use of plastic and metal nit combs, which are distinguishable by their linear appearance. Breaks in the skin from louse bites and excoriations serve as portals through which lice feces and bacteria can enter the host and cause secondary infection. Symptoms of secondary infection include low-grade fever, lymphadenopathy, itchy skin, and red sores with a yellow crust (impetigo). In rare, extreme cases anemia may occur.

In a study by Gordon (2007b), caregivers perceived scratching from head lice associated itching as a stigmatizing characteristic in school settings. Some participants reported keeping their children home until itching resolved to avoid having their children suffer targeting, bullying and social trauma. Parents may also confuse itching caused by scalp irritation from treatment products as a symptom of continuing infestation. As a result, parents continue the use treatment products in an attempt to eliminate head lice. A continuous itch-treatment cycle, illustrated in figure 1, can lead to parent frustration, misuse of treatment products and the use of unsafe treatment strategies.

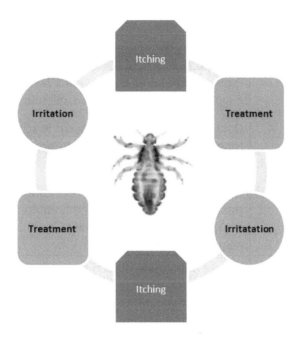

Figure 1: Itch-treatment Cycle. © 2015 Gordon. Reprinted with permission.

Individuals experiencing head lice infestations may also complain of fatigue and irritability referred to as "feeling lousy" (Meinking et al., 2011). Sleep disruption from nighttime louse activity may contribute to fatigue and irritability.

Misconceptions and Myths

There are many misconceptions and myths surrounding head lice transmission, treatment and prevention. Table 1 identifies common misconceptions and myths, corresponding truths and supporting references. School nurses should focus individual family and community education on dispelling common misconceptions and myths and promoting the safe treatment and prevention of head lice.

Table 1 **Misconceptions and Myths**

Misconception and Myths	Truths	Supporting Reference
Head lice spread easily in the classroom	Prolonged head-to-head contact is the major mode of head lice transmission. Only 1 in 10 transmissions occur in schools. Ninety percent of transmissions occur in the community. School nurses should encourage contact tracing of close family and community contacts to identify potential sources of head lice transmission.	CDC, 2015b Maunder, 1985
Head lice spread by sharing brushes, combs, hats, helmets and/or headphones with someone who has lice.	Fomite (inanimate object) transmission is RARE. Prevention efforts should focus on educating parents to identify head lice infestations early and initiate safe, effective treatment.	Devore & Schutze, 2015
Head lice spread by taking selfies.	Lice spread by prolonged, direct head-to-head contact. There is no evidence to suggest teens are acquiring head lice infestations through the act of taking selfie photographs or that there is an increase in the teen prevalence rate in the U.S.	Pollack, 2014
Lice can jump or fly from person to person.	Lice do not have wings or hind legs and therefore cannot jump, hop or fly.	CDC, 2015a Meinking et al., 2011
You can get head lice from pets.	Head lice are species specific. Animals including pets do not share head lice with humans. Do not treat pets for head lice.	Devore & Schutze, 2015 CDC, 2013
Extensive environmental cleaning of the classroom and/or home is necessary to eradicate head lice and prevent transmission.	Head lice live and lay eggs on the human host. They do not infest the environment. Environmental sprays are not effective and increase pesticide exposure unnecessarily. Clean hair care items and bedding used by persons who are infested	Speare, R., Thomas, G., & Cahill, C., 2002 Devore & Schutze, 2015
Poor personnel hygiene causes head lice.	Having head lice is not reflective of being dirty.	Devore & Schutze, 2015
Head lice is a sign of poor parenting and/or child neglect.	Anyone can get head lice.	Devore & Schutze, 2015

Misconception and Myths	Truths	Supporting Reference
If one member of the family has head lice, all members of a family must be treated at the same time.	Only persons with an active infestation (presence of at least one live louse) should be treated for head lice. All family members and close family contacts should be screened for head lice.	Devore & Schutze, 2015
Head lice spread diseases in schools.	The is no evidence to support head lice do not spread disease.	Devore & Schutze, 2015
African-Americans do not get head lice.	While the prevalence rate is significantly lower than other groups, head lice infestations occur among African-Americans.	Meinking et al., 2011 Juranek, 1977
Agricultural pesticides and veterinary flea and tick products can be safely used on humans.	Agricultural pesticides and veterinary flea and tick products are not formulated or tested on humans and may have impurities not found in pharmaceutical grade products designed to treat head lice. Agricultural and veterinary products are not safe for use on children or adults and should never be recommended or used.	Devore & Schutze, 2015
Head lice can spread in swimming pools.	Head lice do not spread in swimming pools. In an in vitro study, head lice on persons swimming in chlorinated pools survived immersion. However, there was no lice loss or person to person transmission observed.	Canyon & Speare, 2007
There are effective products to remove or loosen head louse nits/eggs from hair.	There is no evidence to suggest products designed to loosen head louse nits/eggs from hair are effective.	Burgess, 2010

IMPLICATIONS FOR SCHOOL NURSE PRACTICE

School nurses are often the first healthcare providers to identify a head lice infestation and assist families with treatment and prevention approaches. Devore & Schultze representing the American Academy of Pediatrics (AAP) (2015) and the National Association of School Nurses (NASN) (2016) both recommend head lice management policies and procedures based on the best available evidence. However, there are many challenges in caring for children diagnosed with head lice infestations in school settings.

Social Perceptions

In the U.S., the presence of head lice infestations creates strong emotional responses. Responses to head lice include disgust, horror, fear, frustration, anger, embarrassment, guilt, shock, shame, and dismay (Gordon, 2007a; Parison, Speare, & Canyon, 2013). The most common response is disgust (Parison et al., 2013). Feelings of disgust activate the human behavioral immune system (HBIS) which drives protective actions designed to prevent contact with potentially dangerous toxins, microbes, and/or parasites. Humans direct feelings of disgust outward towards those thought to be responsible and/or dangerous. Fear of head lice transmission elicits contamination-avoidance behaviors including identifying and avoiding persons with head lice.

Schools have historically used management policies and strategies such as school-based screening and forced exclusion from school for the presence of live head lice and nits (no-nit policy) to control the transmission of head lice. Anecdotally, there is considerable policy variation between states, school districts and even between schools within individual districts.

Parents have reported concern that once school personnel identify a child with a head lice infestation, they target their children and family resulting in mandatory school exclusions and retaliatory repeated screening procedures (Gordon, 2007a). Some parents change schools to avoid social stigma and/or to become disassociated with the derogatory labels *"licers"* or *"lice family"*.

School nurses should:

- Provide support and a caring environment in which a trusting relationship develops. Without trust, families may not disclose a diagnosis of head lice or be open to treatment recommendations and follow-up care.
- Design educational programs for parents and school personnel that focus specifically on transmission to allay fear of transmission and resulting negative social behavior.
- Avoid the use of derogatory labels when referring to children and families experiencing head lice infestations.
- Advocate for consistent non-exclusionary polices that follow authoritative, national recommendations.

Confidentiality

Because of social perceptions and stigma associated with head lice infestations and the possible negative social ramifications, it is especially important for school nurses to maintain strict confidentiality practices as described in the Health Insurance and Portability and Accountability Act, also known as HIPAA, (HIPAA, 1996) and the Family Educational Rights and Privacy Act, also known as FERPA (34 CFR § 99.2, FERPA 1974). While parents may feel they have a right to know if there is a child in the school with head lice, HIPAA and FERPA standards allow personal information to be shared only with persons who have a need to know. A head lice infestation is not considered a health hazard (CDC, 2013), therefore, school nurses do not have a duty to warn parents or school personnel (Shah, et. al., 2013). Parents may file a violation of privacy complaint if someone at the school discloses their child's head lice infestation to others. Letters sent home reporting a case of head lice in the classroom should be used with caution to avoid inadvertent discloses.

School nurses should:

- Maintain strict confidentiality practices.
- Train all school staff who have access to school health information on the importance of confidentiality practices.
- Report breaches of confidentiality.

348

Identification of Head Lice

Social stigma associated with head lice infestation contributes to parental hesitancy to disclose the condition inside or outside the family. As a result, parents do not share the presence of head lice with extended family members and treat children an average of 5 times before seeking assistance from a school nurse or other healthcare provider (Meinking et al., (2011); Gordon, 2007a). Hesitancy to disclose may delay diagnosis and contribute to transmission.

"The identification of eggs (nits), nymphs or adult lice with the naked eye establishes the diagnoses" of head lice (Devore & Schutze, 2015, p. 1356). However, school nurses should not recommend treatment unless the infestation is active (CDC, 2016; Devore & Schutze, 2015). Diagnostic confusion centers on distinguishing active infestation (presence of at least one live louse) from inactive infestation (presence of eggs, nits and pseudo nits such as dandruff, hair casts, hair debris, etc.). False negative diagnoses may delay treatment and increase the probability of transmission. False positive diagnoses often leads to unnecessary treatment, increased exposure to chemical pesticides and forced absences from school and work. In extreme cases, frustrated parents may resort to the use of unsafe treatment approaches such as agricultural and veterinarian treatment products, gasoline and kerosene (Gordon, 2007a). Unfortunately, given the size of newly hatched head lice, louse adaptive mechanisms, and lack of evidence-based screening techniques and training programs, diagnostic confusion is common (Pollack, Kiszewski, & Spielman, 2000).

The first step in identifying and treating head lice is to screen the head and hair of individuals for the presence of live lice. Therefore, effective, evidenced-based screening techniques are essential in determining treatment recommendations and treatment efficacy.

In a study by Gordon (2007a) exploring caring for children with persistent head lice, 100% of the primary caregiver participants reported never receiving instruction on when and/or how to screen family members for the presence of head lice. Without an effective screening technique, parents had no reliable way of knowing if their child had an active head lice infestation or if an infestation was successfully treated. Parental confidence in effectively screening family members for the presence of live lice may significantly influence caregiver strain and perceived shared vulnerability.

To date there are no research studies that describe effective screening techniques or educational programs for parents/family caregivers. Screening methods presented in the literature represent methods developed by researchers for products evaluation studies or for determining participant inclusion criteria. The lack of studies focusing on the development of parental screening programs presents a significant challenge to school nurses charged with educating family caregivers.

The school nurse should:

- Establish personal competency and confidence in identifying the presence of live lice (active infestation).
- Document assessment outcomes including integrity of the scalp and secondary infection if present.
- Request educational training if needed.
- Notify, educate and support family caregivers.
- Train family members to screen for the presence of live lice.

- Encourage family caregivers to check/screen all household members and other close contacts at the same time to identify transmission sources.
- Maintain strict confidentiality practices.

Treatment Recommendations

Treatment strategies should be safe, effective, readily accessible and affordable (CDC, 2016). The American Academy of Pediatrics (AAP) publishes a complete review of recommended treatment approaches periodically (Devore & Schutze, 2015). Common active ingredients in current over the counter products include permethrin 1% and pyrethrins plus piperonyl butoxide. Prescription products include malathion 0.5%, benzyl alcohol 5%, spinosad 0.9% and ivermectin 0.5%. "Lindane is no longer recommended by the American Academy of Pediatrics or the Medical Letter for use as treatment of pediculosis capitis" (Devore & Schutze, 2015, p. 1358).

No treatment product is 100% ovicidal (kills all eggs). Researchers report emerging pediculicide resistance around the world and anticipate increasing resistance in response to regional use of pediculicides over time (Devore & Schutze, 2015).

Care should be taken during all product applications to avoid contact with the eyes and to limit absorption through the skin by using warm water to rinse out products over the sink. Parents may confuse common topical reactions (itching and burning of the scalp) from pediculicides with ongoing infestation resulting in unnecessary, potentially harmful retreatment of their children (Gordon, 2007b; Devore & Schutze, 2015). Inflammatory responses can also cause flaking and scabbing on the scalp, which contributes to ongoing diagnostic confusion. Therefore, careful adherence to application instructions and limiting treatment to active infestations is essential.

Other treatment methods include manual removal (nit comb), natural products (essential oils), occlusive agents, and desiccation (high volume, warm air devise). Treatment strategies such the use of flammable agents (such as gasoline and kerosene), agricultural pesticides and products designed for use on animals are considered unsafe and should never be recommended for use on humans (Devore & Schutze, 2015). In addition, in most instances experts do not recommend prophylactic treatment with pediculicides (Mumcuoglu et al., 2007).

The school nurse should:

- Maintain up-to-date knowledge on available treatment approaches.
- Obtain and document a complete treatment history.
- Recommend treatment only if an active infestation is present.
- Respectfully review safe, effective, readily accessible and affordable treatment options and safety issues with family caregivers.
- Encourage family caregivers to follow manufactures guidelines when applying head lice treatment products.
- Document treatment recommendations and follow-up care.
- Report unsafe treatment approaches following appropriate state and/ or district requirements.
- Maintain strict confidentiality practices.

Screening and Mandatory Exclusion from School

The AAP (Devore & Schutze, 2015) and the NASN (2016) no longer support the use of school-wide screening programs and policies designed to exclude children from school for the presence of nits and/or live lice as methods for reducing transmission is schools. However, these organizations support **limited screening of children demonstrating symptoms conducted by trained personnel**.

Background for the recommendation: Researchers have challenged the effectiveness of school-wide screening programs and "no-nit" policies in reducing head lice transmission in school settings (Meinking et al., 2011). In one study, the number of nits in a child's hair and distance from the scalp were significant factors in predicting which children with "nits only" would convert to a live infestation (Hootman, 2002). Only 18% of children with "nits only" converted to live infestation. Children with 5 nits within ¼ inch from the scalp were most likely to develop a live infestation. Therefore, schools following a strict no-nit policy would send 82% of the children with nits-only home unnecessarily.

School nurses are required to protect the privacy of students during screening procedures. In school settings, consider screening a child for head lice may in itself be a stigmatizing event. School nurses should be familiar with the head lice policies in place at their school(s). Procedural safeguards include:

- Following the policy without discriminating against individual students or groups of students.
- Periodic policy review and update as needed.
- Availability of the policy to parents and/or family caregivers.
- Consideration of special protections that may apply for students who fall under the Americans with Disability Act.

School nurses should:

- Know their school and/or district head lice policies.
- Avoid school-wide and classroom-wide screening programs.
- Limit screening to children demonstrating symptoms.
- Support the use of trained personnel for screening.
- Maintain strict confidentiality practices.
- Follow procedural safeguards.
- Advocate for consistent, non-exclusionary policies that follow authoritative, national recommendations.

Storage of Pediculocides in School Settings

Chemicals in pediculocides (treatment products for head lice) can enter the body through absorption, inhalation and ingestion. In addition, some head lice treatment produces are flammable. As potentially hazardous chemicals, pediculoicdes fall under the Occupational Safety and Health Administration's (OSHA) Hazard Communication Standard (HCS) (OSHA, 2017). The intent of the HCS is to protect employees in the work setting. Employers are required to notify employees of the presence and potential exposure of all hazardous chemicals and train employees to handle products safely. Safety Data Sheets (SDS) have a standard 16 section format and are available for all potentially hazardous chemicals from the manufacturer. SDS include warnings for flammability, reactivity, health warnings and required personnel protection equipment. Many SDS can be located on the OSHA website or by searching the internet by product name or chemical name.

School nurses who store and distribute head lice treatment products within the school setting should:

- Maintain up to date SDS and advise personnel of the location of these documents.
- Train all personnel who come in contact with pediculocides to safely handle the products.
- Store all treatment products safely by following manufacturer recommendations.
- Keep products out of the reach of children to avoid accidental exposure and/or ingestion.

In addition, school nurses who treat children with pediculocides within the school setting should:

- Obtain parental consent for treatment.
- Be familiar with the specific product, its properties, potential side effects and potential interactions.
- Assess the child's health history, allergy and immune status prior to applying a pediculocide.
- Ensure that the application process is followed including appropriate follow-up.

Advocating for Change

School nurses play an important role in advocating for policy change. Long-standing policies based on fear of transmission are especially difficult to change. Pontius (2011) provides a successful exemplar depicting how one state moved from a no-nit exclusionary head lice policy to a non-exclusionary policy. Key elements of success were:

- Use of authoritative, evidence-based supporting materials.
- Documenting impact of the current policy.
- Enacting small policy changes and documenting impact of the change to allay fear.
- Ongoing communication with teachers, principals, school board members, and parents.

CONCLUSION

Head lice infestations are a highly stigmatized communicable condition. While most transmissions occur in family and community settings, school nurses are often the first to identify the presence of an active infestation. School nurses play an important role in decreasing stigma, promoting safe treatment strategies, allaying fear of transmission and advocating for non-exclusionary head lice management policies in school settings.

RESOURCES

American Nurses Association (ANA) & National Association of School Nurses (NASN). (2017). School nursing: Scope and standards of practice (3rd ed.). Silver Spring, MD: Author.

Centers for Disease Control and Prevention. (2015). Head lice information for schools. http://www.cdc.gov/parasites/lice/head/schools.html

Devore, C., Schutze, G., & The American Academy of Pediatrics' Council on School Health and Committee on Infectious Diseases. (2015). Head lice. *Pediatrics 135*(5), e1355-e1365. doi: 10.1542/eds.2015-0746

National Association of School Nurses (NASN). (2016). *Head lice management in the school settings* (Position Statement). Silver Spring, MD: Author. http://www.nasn.org/PolicyAdvocacy/PositionPapersandReports/ NASNPositionStatementsFullView/tabid/462/smid/824/ArticleID/934/Default.aspx

National Association of School Nurses (NASN). (2014). Lice Lessons. Silver Spring, MD: Author. https://www. nasn.org/ToolsResources/HeadLicePediculosisCapitis/LiceLessons

REFERENCES

Burgess, I.F. (2010). Do nit removal formulations and other treatments loosen head louse eggs and nits from hair? *Medical and Veterinary Entomology*, *24*(1), 55-61. doi: 10.1111/j.1365-2915.2009.00845.x

Burkhart, C.N., & Burkhart, C.G. (2007). Fomite transmission in head lice. *Journal of the American Academy of Dermatology, 56(6), 1044-1047.* doi:10.1016/j.jaad.2006.10.979

Canyon, D., & Speare, R. (2007). Do head lice spread in swimming pools? *The International Society of Dermatology*, *46*, 1211-1213. doi: 10.1111/j.1365-4632.2007.03011.x

Canyon, D., & Speare, R. (2016). Lice---head/body/public (Pediculosis, phthirus infestation, lousiness). *Clinical Advisor*. Retrieved from http://www.clinicaladvisor.com/dermatology/lice-headbodypubic- pediculosis-phthirus-infestation-lousiness/article/589056/

Centers for Disease Control and Prevention. (2013). *Parasites-lice- Index.* Retrieved from https://www.cdc.gov/parasites/lice/head/index.html

Centers for Disease Control and Prevention. (2015a). *Biology.* Retrieved from www.cdc.gov/parasites/lice/ head/biology.html

Centers for Disease Control and Prevention. (2015b). *Head lice information for schools*. Retrieved from http://www.cdc.gov/parasites/lice/head/schools.html

Centers for Disease Control and Prevention. (2016). *Parasites – lice – head lice - treatment*. Retrieved from http://www.cdc.gov/parasites/lice/head/treatment.html

Chunge, R.N., Scott, F.E., Underwood, J.E., & Zavarella, K.J. (1991). A review of the epidemiology, public health importance, treatment and control of head lice. *Canadian Journal of Public Health*, *82(3),* 196– 200. http://www.ncbi.nlm.nih.gov//pubmed/1884315

Devore, C., Schutze, G., & The American Academy of Pediatrics' Council on School Health and Committee on Infectious Diseases. (2015). Head lice. *Pediatrics, 135*(5), e1355-e1365. doi:10.1542/eds.2015-0746

Drisdelle, R. (2010). *Parasites: Tales of humanity's most unwelcome guests*. Berkeley, CA: University of California Press.

Family Educational Rights and Privacy Act (FERPA). U.S. Department of Education. (20 U.S.C. § 1232g; 34 CFR Part 99) Retrieved from https://ed.gov/policy/gen/guid/fpco/ferpa/index.html

Health Insurance Portability and Accountability Act of 1996, 45 C.F.R. § § 160, 162 and 164

Gordon, S.C. (2007a). Shared vulnerability: A theory of caring for children with persistent head lice. *The Journal of School Nursing*, *23*(5), 283-292. Retrieved from http://ezproxy.fau.edu/login?url=http://search. proquest.com/docview/213134889?accountid=10902

Gordon, S.C. (2007b). [Itching as a stigmatizing characteristic]. Unpublished raw data.

Gordon, S.C. (1999). Factors related to the overuse of chemical pesticides in children experiencing persistent head lice. *Journal of School Nursing*, *15*(5), 6-10. doi: 10.1177/105984059901500502

Hodgdon, H.E., Yoon, K.S., Previte, D.J., Kim, N.J., Aboelghar, G.E., Lee, S. H., & Clark, J.M. (2010). Determination of knock down resistance allele frequencies in global human head lice populations using the serial invasive amplification reaction. *Pest Management Science*, *66*,1031-1040. doi: 10.1002/ ps.1979

Hootman, J. (2002). Quality improvement projects related to pediculosis management. *The Journal of School Nursing*, *18*(2), 80-86. doi:10.1177/10598405020180020401

Juranek, D. D. (1977). Epidemiologic investigations of pediculosis capitis in schoolchildren. In M. Orkin, H.I. Maibach, I.C. Parish, et al.(Eds.). *Scabies and Pediculosis*, (p. 168 -173). Philadelphia, PA: Lippincott.

Life Cycle [Online Image]. Centers for Disease Control and Prevention. (2015). Retrieved from https://www.cdc.gov/parasites/lice/head/biology.html

Maunder, J.W. (1985). Human lice: Some basic facts and misconceptions. *Bulletin of the Pan American Health Organization*, 1985,*19(2)*,194–197. Retrieved from www.ncbi.nlm.nih.gov/ pubmed/4052692?tool=bestpractice.bmj.com

Meinking, T. L. (1999). Infestations. *Current Problems in Dermatology*, *11(3)*, 73-120. Retrieved from http://ac.els-cdn.com/S1040048699900054/1-s2.0-S1040048699900054-main.pdf?_tid=23e9b882-f872- 11e6-afc1-00000aacb35e&acdnat=1487708159_136a2f4ab1302eb81ac95e9a3686e04a

Meinking, T., Taplin, D., & Vicaria, V. (2011). Infestations. In L. A. Schachner & R.C. Hansen (Eds.). *Pediatric Dermatology*, 4th ed., pp 1535-1583. St. Louis, MO: Mosby Elsevier.

Mumcuoglu, K.Y., Barker, Burgess, I.F, Combescot-Lang, C. Dalgleish, R.C. Larsen, K.S. Miller, J. Roberts, R.J. & Taylan-Ozkan, A. (2007). International guidelines for effective control of head louse infestations. *Journal of Drugs in Dermatology*, 6(4), 409-414. Retrieved from http://www.lusfrinorge.no/documents/ Internasjonale%20retningslinjer,%20hodelus.pdf

Mumcuoglu, K.Y, Meinking, T.A., Burkhart, C.N., & Burkhardt, C. G. (2006). Head louse infestations: The "no nit" policy and its consequences. International Journal of Dermatology, 45(8), 891-896. doi:10.1111/ j.1365-4632.2006.02827.x

Mumcuoglu, K.Y., & Zias, J. (1989). How the ancients deloused themselves. *Biblical Archaeology Review, 15*, 66 – 69. Retrieved from http://phthiraptera.info/content/how-ancients-de-loused-themselves

National Association of School Nurses. (2016). *Head lice management in the school settings* (Position Statement). Silver Spring, MD: Author. Retrieved from http://www.nasn.org/PolicyAdvocacy/PositionPapersandReports/NASNPositionStatementsFullView/tabid/462/smid/824/ArticleID/934/Default.aspx

National Center for Education Statistics (NCES), (2016). Retrieved from http://nces.ed.gov/.

Occupational Safety and Health Administration (OSHA). (2017). *Hazard communication standard* (HCS). Retrieved from https://www.osha.gov/dsg/hazcom/

Parison, J., Speare, R. & Canyon, D. (2013). Head lice: The feelings people have. *International Journal of Dermatology, 52*(2), 169-171. doi: 10.1111/j.1365-4632.2011.05300.x

Pollack, R. (2014, February 24). *Re: Selfies (probably) not spreading lice among teens, expert says.* [Online comment]. Retrieved from http://www.nbcnews.com/science/weird-science/selfies-probably-not-spreading-lice-among-teens-expert-says-n37651

Pollack, R. J., Kiszewski, A.E. & Spielman, A. (2000). Overdiagnosis and consequent mismanagement of head louse infestations in North America. *Pediatric Infectious Disease Journal, 19*(8), 689-693. Retrieved from https://www.ncbi.nlm.nih.gov/pubmed/10959734

Pontius, D. (2011). Hats off to success. Changing head lice policy. *NASN School Nurse*, (November), 357-362. doi: https://doi.org/10.1177/1942602X11421349

Schaller, M., & Park, J. (2011). The Behavioral Immune System (and Why It Matters). Current Directions in Psychological Science, 20(2), 99-103. Retrieved from http://www.jstor.org/stable/23045760

Shah, S.K., Hull, S.C., Spinner, M.A., Berkman, B. E., Sanchez, L.A., Abdul-Karim, R., Hsu, A.P., Claypool, R. & Holland, S.M. (2013). What does duty to warn require? The American Journal of Bioethics, 13(10, 62-63, doi 10.1080/15265161.2013.828528

Speare, R., Thomas, G., & Cahill, C. (2002*).* Head lice are not found on floors in primary school classrooms. *Australian & New Zealand Journal of Public Health, 26*(3), 207-208. Retrieved from https://www.ncbi.nlm.nih.gov/pubmed/12141614

Speare, R., Cahill, C., & Thomas, G. (2003). Head lice on pillows, and strategies to make a small risk even less. *International Journal of Dermatology, 42*(8), 626-629. doi: 10.1046/j.1365-4362.2003.01927.x

West, D.P. (2004). Head lice treatment costs and the impact on managed care. *American Journal of Managed Care, 10*(9), 277-282). Retrieved from https://www.ncbi.nlm.nih.gov/pubmed/15515633

Yoon, K.S., Previte, D.J., Hodgdon, H.E., Poole, B.C, Kwon, D.H., El-Ghar, G.E., Lee, S.H. & Clark, J.M. (2014). Knockdown resistance allele frequencies in North American head louse populations. *Journal of Medical Entomology, 51*(2), 450-457. doi: 10. 1603/ME1313

APPENDIX: Life Cycle of Head Louse

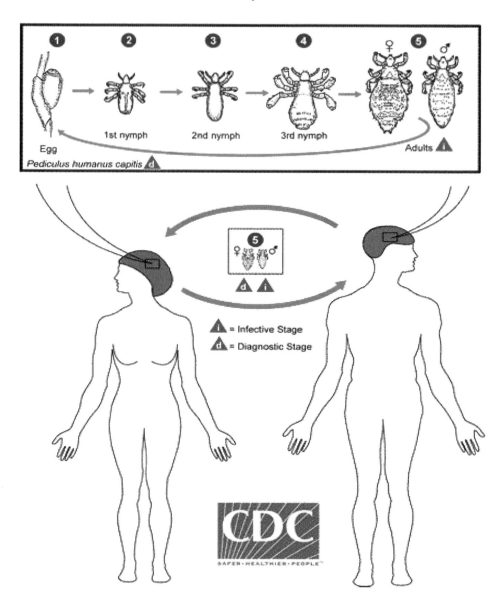

The life cycle of the head louse has three stages: egg, nymph, and adult.

Eggs: Nits are head lice eggs. They are hard to see and are often confused for dandruff or hair spray droplets. Nits are laid by the adult female and are cemented at the base of the hair shaft nearest the scalp ❶. They are 0.8 mm by 0.3 mm, oval and usually yellow to white. Nits take about 1 week to hatch (range 6 to 9 days). Viable eggs are usually located within 6 mm of the scalp.

Nymphs: The egg hatches to release a nymph ❷. The nit shell then becomes a more visible dull yellow and remains attached to the hair shaft. The nymph looks like an adult head louse, but is about the size of a pinhead. Nymphs mature after three molts (❸, ❹) and become adults about 7 days after hatching.

Adults: The adult louse is about the size of a sesame seed, has 6 legs (each with claws), and is tan to grayish-white ❺. In persons with dark hair, the adult louse will appear darker. Females are usually larger than males and can lay up to 8 nits per day. Adult lice can live up to 30 days on a person's head. To live, adult lice need to feed on blood several times daily. Without blood meals, the louse will die within 1 to 2 days off the host.

Life cycle image and information courtesy of DPDx.

Life Cycle [Online Image]. Centers for Disease Control (2015)

Chapter 28

LIFE-THREATENING EMERGENCIES:ANAPHYLAXIS, ASTHMA, AND ALLERGIES

Mariann F. Cosby, DNP, MPA, RN, PHN, CEN, NE-BC, LNCC, CLCP, CCM, MSCC

DESCRIPTION OF ISSUE

Anaphylaxis can occur without warning, can strike those with or without a previous history of an allergy, and may result in a fatal outcome (Sicherer, Simons, & American Academy of Pediatrics [AAP] Section on Allergy and Immunology, 2017). When symptoms of possible anaphylaxis are recognized, rapid administration of epinephrine can be life-saving (Sicherer et al., 2017). In 2013, federal legislation raised the awareness of the importance of the availability of non-student specific undesignated epinephrine in public schools (School Access to Emergency Epinephrine Act, 2013). This resulted in the passage of laws in 49 of the 50 states that allows for undesignated epinephrine to be on-hand for emergency administration in public schools (Asthma & Allergy Network, 2016).

Globally, the need to implement school-wide food allergy safety and undesignated epinephrine programs is apparent (Simons et al., 2011; Simons et al., 2013). However, at the local level there are challenges and barriers to operationalizing emergency preparedness plans that are vital to dealing with food allergies and the successful implementation of access to undesignated epinephrine (Tanner & Clarke, 2016). In an effort to facilitate a solution-mindedness orientation of these issues, the aim of the following discussion is to point out some of the potential legal implications for the school nurse and district to consider related to implementation delays and inadequate program planning, and other allergy and emergency medication related issues.

BACKGROUND

Anaphylaxis Overview

Anaphylaxis is life-threatening emergency defined as a serious generalized allergic or hypersensitivity reaction that is rapid in onset and can be fatal (Sicherer et al., 2017). Identified as a global health problem, the World Allergy Organization provides key anaphylaxis assessment and management information (Simons et al., 2011; Simons et al., 2013). Specifics include information on those who are vulnerable, risk factors for severe or fatal episodes, and cofactors that amplify anaphylaxis (Simons et al., 2013).

Infants and teenagers are segments of the population who are reported to have an increased vulnerability to anaphylaxis (Simons et al., 2013). Most episodes of anaphylaxis in infants and young children are triggered by food. The most common triggers of anaphylaxis in the pediatric population are six common foods: peanut, tree nuts, milk, eggs, crustacean shellfish, and finned fish (Sicherer et al., 2017). An individual's concomitant severe or uncontrolled asthma can increase hypersensitivity and risk of a fatal episode especially in adolescence (Bird & Burks, 2009; Sicherer et al., 2017; Simons et al., 2013). Occurrence after ingestion is typical, but can also occur after skin contact or inhalation of food particles (Simons et al., 2013). In addition to foods, other anaphylaxis triggers and mechanisms include venoms from bees and vespids (wasps), drugs and biologic agents, or reactivity to latex, chemicals, or other allergens and cofactors (Simmons et al., 2013; Sicherer et al., 2017).

Severity and clinical presentation of anaphylaxis can vary. Acute onset can occur within minutes or several hours of exposure or precipitating event. Presentation of anaphylaxis can mimic disorders such as acute asthma, acute generalized urticaria (rash), aspiration of foreign body, vasovagal episode, and anxiety or panic attacks (see APPENDIX for comparison of anaphylaxis and asthma symptoms and triggers) (Sicherer et al., 2017). Cofactors such as exercise, upper respiratory tract infections, fever, ingestion of nonsteroidal anti-inflammatory drugs or ethanol, emotional distress, and perimenstural status can lower the threshold at which the triggers can cause anaphylaxis (Sicherer et al., 2017).

Life-Saving Epinephrine

Epinephrine is the first-line medication of choice for the first-aid treatment of anaphylaxis (Russell & Schoessler, 2017; Sicherer et al., 2017; Simons et al., 2011). Once possible anaphylaxis is recognized, epinephrine can be life-saving due to its rapid onset of action that prevents and relieves airway obstruction, hypotension, and shock (Russell & Schoessler, 2017). Epinephrine is available in several forms, but in the school setting a pre-filled syringe of epinephrine known as an epinephrine autoinjector (EA), is appropriate for use by both school health professionals and lay responders as permitted by state law and school policy (Schoessler & White, 2013; Sicherer et al., 2017; Simons et al., 2011). It should be promptly administered via injection into the mid-outer thigh (vastus lateralis muscle) (Sicherer et al., 2017; Simons et al., 2011)

The importance of prompt response is essential as it is impossible to predict the student's response to an allergen. A student could recover spontaneously due to secretion of endogenous epinephrine or die within minutes without the life-saving treatment (Sicherer et al., 2017). Since there are no absolute contraindications to properly administered EA and serious side effects are rare in children, erring on the side of caution is advised (Sicherer et al., 2017; Simons et al., 2011; Simons et al., 2013). Prompt epinephrine injection can curtail the mild symptoms of anaphylaxis from rapidly progressing to a life-threatening systemic allergic reaction (Sicherer et al., 2017).

Antihistamines that may be part of an order set for a student with a known allergy are not life-saving (Russell & Schoessler, 2017; Simmons et al., 2011; Simmons et al., 2013). Antihistamines do not treat the symptoms of anaphylaxis but rather may relieve itching, flushing, urticaria (rash), and other allergy type symptoms (Russell & Schoessler, 2017). Antihistamines can take from one to two hours to provide relief and therefore should not be substituted for epinephrine when anaphylaxis is suspected (Simmons et al., 2011; Simmons et al., 2013). School nurses should advocate for students who may have healthcare provider orders that direct school staff to administer antihistamine before epinephrine (Russell & Schoessler, 2017). Antihistamines may be appropriate in treating mild allergies, but only epinephrine can treat anaphylaxis (Simons et al, 2011; Wang, Sicherer & AAP Section on Allergy and Immunology, 2017). Clear care plan instructions should accompany such orders to avert epinephrine administration delays (Wang, 2017; Wang et al., 2017).

Managing Anaphylaxis: Food Allergies and Asthma in Public School

Anaphylaxis and the associated life-threatening components of food allergies and asthma that can occur in children while attending school gained national attention and awareness with the passage of the School Access to Emergency Epinephrine Act (2013). This federal law encouraged states to adopt laws requiring schools to have on-hand stock or undesignated epinephrine to be used for any student who is reasonably believed to be having an anaphylactic reaction. Additionally, the law addressed the administration of the medication by trained unlicensed staff and offered a limited civil liability protection for those administering the medication.

Nearly simultaneously, in 2013, the Centers for Disease Control and Prevention (CDC) published the required national guidelines that were developed in response to the Food Allergy and Anaphylaxis Management Act (2010). The CDC developed the voluntary federal guidelines in collaboration with the National Association of School Nurses (NASN) and other groups to help schools manage the risk of food allergies, reduce allergic reactions, define roles of members of the school community, and improve responses to life-threatening reactions such as anaphylaxis.

Since 2013, all states with the exception of Hawaii have passed undesignated epinephrine laws permitting schools to stock emergency epinephrine and develop the corresponding emergency preparedness plans (Asthma & Allergy Network, 2016). This aligns with the importance for students to have access to life-saving epinephrine at school. Not only are children with food allergies at risk for having a reaction by accidentally eating a food allergen while at school, but 25% of anaphylaxis reactions that require treatment with epinephrine at school occur in students who have never been diagnosed with a severe allergy (Massachusetts Department of Public Health, 2012; McIntyre, Sheetz, Carroll, & Young, 2005). Schools need to be prepared to care for students with known allergies as well as those who experience their first allergic reaction while at school (Cosby, 2015; Sicherer, Mahr, & AAP Section on Allergy and Immunology, 2010).

IMPLICATIONS FOR SCHOOL NURSE PRACTICE

General Information

School nurses' involvement with food allergy management of students with known food allergies includes becoming cognizant of what is the comprehensive school and district-wide strategy to manage the risk of food allergy reactions in children (CDC, 2013). By becoming familiar with the accepted local methodology, the food allergy-related needs of a particular student with a food allergy can be addressed in a coordinated manner. Not only does this enhance student safety, but provides a means so that the legal requirements and considerations related to the applicable federal laws and regulation that address access and prohibit discrimination on the basis of disability are not violated.

Working with the school team, the school nurse can ensure that if the student's food allergy is a disability, the student's entitlements of Section 504 of the Rehabilitation Act of 1973 and the Americans Disability Act are protected (CDC, 2013). Similarly, if the student has an individualized education program (IEP) in place, which addresses special education and related services under part B of the Individuals With Disabilities Act (IDEA), the nurse, as part of the team, can more easily intervene to develop and integrate the individualized healthcare plan/food allergy action plan, and emergency care plan for the food allergy and epinephrine (CDC, 2013; Wang et al., 2017).

The school nurse is the appropriate professional to develop individualized healthcare plans and emergency care plans, as care planning is a standard of school nursing practice (American Nurses Association & NASN, 2017; Schoessler & White, 2013). Care plan creation is a nursing responsibility due to the assessment component of the process and cannot be delegated to unlicensed personnel (NASN, 2013). Although several anaphylaxis plans are available from various organizations, the American Academy of Pediatrics recognized that their use by health professionals varied (Wang et al., 2017). As a result, the American Academy of Pediatrics Allergy and Anaphylaxis Emergency Plan was developed to promote greater familiarly and standardization (Wang, 2017). The customizable plan is the first of its kind from the AAP and is available online (Wang, 2017).

Challenges Regarding Food Allergy

A challenge that the school nurse may encounter related to efforts to provide a student with an allergen free or reduced environment, is that other students in the school may need ready access to foods. School districts must provide a free and appropriate education (FAPE) for all students (Section 504 of the Rehabilitation Act of 1973; Individuals with Disabilities Act (IDEA) (1990). Therefore, it is important to keep in mind that for example, students with diabetes may require food snacks to be on their person (Section 504 of the Rehabilitation Act of 1973; Individuals with Disabilities Act (IDEA),1990). Hence, the rights of students who need immediate access to food in the classroom have to be balanced with those who want a food free/allergen classroom environment. Working with staff on strategies to educate and integrate solutions is part of the school nurse's role and challenges (AAP, 2008/2012).

There are legal implications for each of these situations. These challenges should be approached by making reasonable team efforts to accommodate both simultaneously, keeping in mind that a completely allergen free environment may be unreasonable (Russell & Huber, 2013). Depending on the nature of an allergy, food avoidance strategies can vary (Russell & Huber, 2013; Sicherer et al., 2010). Cases involving these types of situations include: *Liebau v. Romeo Comm. Schs.*, 2013 Mich. App. LEXIS 1322 (2013) (the court dismissed a lawsuit by a student disgruntled with the district's decision to adopt a "nut free" policy to protect the health and safety of students with peanut allergies); *T.F. v. Fox Chapel Area Sch. Dist.*, 589 Fed. Appx. 594 (3d Cir. 2014) (district did not violate a student's rights under Section 504 by refusing to adopt a nut free policy).

Working as a team through the inclusion of school staff, parents, the student, and legal counsel to work out an amenable solution that minimizes health related risks while preserving student rights, is desired (Russell & Huber, 2013). Obtaining guidance from the student's clinical team may also help by providing specific information on the nature of the allergy and other circumstances that may be unique to the school or student's age (Russell & Huber, 2013).

Challenges Related to Undesignated Epinephrine Program

Other challenges that carry legal implications include the implementation of the state-mandated or recommended undesignated epinephrine program (Schoessler, Albert, Levasseur, & Owens, 2014). Although the legislation that gave approval for such programs are in place in all but one state, the mechanics of how to operationalize and overcome implementation challenges has been lacking (Tanner & Clarke, 2016). Each school district must consider state laws and local setting circumstances when establishing which individuals are authorized to administer epinephrine (Tanner & Clarke, 2016). The case *Suing for Peanuts,* (Bridges, 2000) discusses the potential liability of negligently or failing to properly administer epinephrine.

Some of the challenges include addressing the utilization of unlicensed assistive personnel (UAP) in response to a possible anaphylaxis event in the absence of the school nurse (Tanner & Clarke, 2016). One example is developing and implementing the training for non-licensed staff on how to identify the signs and symptoms of anaphylaxis without requiring the assessment skills of the registered nurse. Another includes securing healthcare providers who are willing to write the standing orders for the undesignated or stock epinephrine so that the medication can be obtained (Schoessler et al., 2014). As typically the lead person for preparing for emergency response to anaphylaxis in schools, developing policies and protocols that provide the structure for the stock epinephrine program that addresses the legal risks and parameters was reported as the greatest struggle for school nurses (Tanner & Clarke, 2016).

When the stock epinephrine program is not in place or fully implemented, other legal implications and ethical dilemmas come into play. For example, school nurses should not be placed in a position of having to choose between the decision to save a life by using someone else's individually prescribed epinephrine that is on campus and the consequences of the decision (Morris, Baker, Belot & Edwards, 2011). As a licensed healthcare provider, should a school nurse administer the medication to a student for which there is no order, the nurse is at risk for practicing outside of the scope of practice (Buppert, 2013). License revocation and other disciplinary action against the professional license is at stake in this situation (Mathes & Reifsnyder, 2014). Additionally, by using another student's EA to rescue the student in need, the student to whom the EA is legally prescribed is then placed at risk as the EA is no longer available for that student should it be needed (Schoessler et al., 2014).

Addressing the Challenges

Administrative and operational obstacles that inadequately provide the necessary elements for or delay the implementation of a stock EA program create havoc and undue ethical dilemmas for staff. If this double jeopardy scenario cannot be averted, school nurses should document efforts to apprise key school district administration and legal counsel of the "what if" situation and come to a mutual understanding of what the nurse can or cannot legally do. The school nurse should consider asking for documentation of such a determination from school administration. As the school health expert, school nurses can also consider partnering and positioning themselves to advocate for efforts to remedy the obstacles so that mutually agreed upon solutions can be expeditiously reached (Schoessler et al., 2014; Tanner & Clarke, 2016).

Similar conversations should also occur to determine an agreed upon plan for communicating with parents who fail to provide the school with student specific epinephrine or other emergency medication (Sicherer et al., 2010). The school district's administration and legal counsel should be providing guidance and direction on how to best address those issues which pose life-threatening risks for the student without impacting a student's civil rights.

As an advocate for student safety and well-being, the school nurse can consider incorporating sense making strategies as part of the discussions (Caughron et al., 2011; Thiel, Bagdasorav, Harkrider, Johnson, & Mumford, 2012). The school nurse should be prepared to discuss the importance of balancing the legal and ethical elements in the decision-making process. Options that might be considered include 1) student's exclusion from school until medications are on site, 2) informing the parents that calling 911 may be the only option in the absence of them supplying the medication to the school, and 3) implications for notifying child protective services agencies if medical neglect is a consideration. In keeping with the team approach and legal implications, it is important that the school nurse is clear as to the strategies that are mutually agreed upon to be endorsed and upheld by district's legal counsel (Mathes & Reifsnyder, 2014).

CONCLUSION

It is important for school nurses and other school officials to be aware of the challenges and potential legal implications associated with anaphylaxis, food allergies, and students' access to the life-saving emergency medication epinephrine in schools. Due to these potentially life-threatening conditions, students' safety and well-being can be at risk. By raising awareness through the provided information, it is anticipated that the path will be paved for easier resolution. Reaching mutually agreeable interventions or strategies that can mitigate the legal/ethical issues and barriers that hinder a healthy and safe school environment for students needs to be the ultimate goal.

RESOURCES

Allergy & Asthma Network (in process for 2017). Allergy & Anaphylaxis: A Practical Guide for Schools and Families. www.allergyasthmanetwork.org/

American Academy of Allergy Asthma and Immunology (n.d.) Food Allergy. www.aaaai.org/conditions-and-treatments/allergies/food-allergies.aspx

AllergyHome.org (n.d.) Managing Food Allergies in Schools: Food Allergy Education for the School Community www.allergyhome.org/schools and https://community.kidswithfoodallergies.org/blog/free-online-food-allergy-training-for-school-staff

- This resource was developed in partnership with Kids with Food Allergies, the Asthma and Allergy Foundation of America New England Chapter, the Association of Camp Nurses, and the American Camping Association. It was modified for and approved by the Massachusetts Department of Public Health's School Health Services. It provides practical teaching tools, including presentations with audio to assist in nurse, staff, parent and student education. This resource provides school nurses with tools to assist in the training their school community, including students and parents without food allergies, and includes guidance for school nurses who will train staff on administration of epinephrine by auto-injector. It includes links to other allergy education sites, materials for families of children with food allergies, materials for others working in child care and camp programs.

American Academy of Allergy Asthma and Immunology (n.d.) Food Allergy. www.aaaai.org/conditions-and-treatments/allergies/food-allergies.aspx

- This site provides basic information about food allergy diagnosis, treatment, and management and helpful tips for people with food allergies. Resources include a sample Anaphylaxis Emergency Action Plan, guidance for schools, and *Guidelines for the Diagnosis and Management of Food Allergy in the United States: Report of the NIAID-Sponsored Expert Panel.*

American Nurses Association & National Council of State Boards of Nursing. (2006). Joint statement on delegation. https://www.ncsbn.org/Delegation_joint_statement_NCSBN-ANA.pdf

Dinakar C. (2012). Anaphylaxis in children: Current understanding and key issues in diagnosis and treatment. *Current Allergy and Asthma Reports*, 12, 641-649. doi:10.1007/s11882-012-0284-1

Food Allergy Research & Education (n.d.) http://www.foodallergy.org/home

- This site provides information to raise awareness and understanding of food allergies and to help those who support people with food allergies.

Food Allergy Research & Education (n.d.) How to CARE for Students with Food Allergies: What Every Educator Should Know http://allergyready.com

- This free online course, developed by Food Allergy Research & Education (F.A.R.E.), is designed to help teachers, administrators, and other school staff members prevent and manage potentially life-threatening allergic reactions. Educational materials include guidance for people who might be training staff how to use an epinephrine auto-injector.

Food Allergy Research & Education (n.d.). School Guidelines http://www.foodallergy.org/laws-and-regulations/statewide-guidelines-for-schools

- This site provides state guidelines for managing food allergies in schools.

Food Allergy Research & Education. (2015). School access to epinephrine map. http://www.foodallergy.org/advocacy/epinephrine/map

Gibbons, L. J., Lehr, K., & Selekman, J. (2013). Federal laws protecting children and youth with disabilities in the schools. In J. Selekman (Ed.), *School nursing: A comprehensive text* (2nd ed., pp. 257 - 283). Philadelphia, PA: F.A. Davis

Gupta, R. S., Springston, E. E., Warrier, M. R., Smith, B., Kumar, R., Pongracic, J., & Holl, J. L. (2011). The prevalence, severity, and distribution of childhood food allergy in the United States. *Pediatrics, 128*(1), e9-e17. doi:10.1542/peds.2011-0204

Kim H., & Fischer D. (2011). Practical guide for allergy and immunology in Canada. *Allergy, Asthma & Clinical Immunology, 7*(suppl. 1). http://www.aacijournal.com/content/7/S1/S6/table/T3

National Association of School Nurses (NASN). (2012). Allergy/anaphylaxis management in the school setting: Position statement. http://www.nasn.org/PolicyAdvocacy/PositionPatersandReports/NASNPostionStatementsFullView/tabid/462/ArticleId/9/Allergy-Anaphylaxis-Management-in-the-School-Setting-Revised-June-2012

National Association of School Nurses (NASN). (2014). Clinical conversations for the school nurse: Food allergy management in the school setting. https://www.nasn.org/nasn/programs/educational-initiatives/conversations-food-

National Association of School Nurses (NASN). (2014). Food allergy and anaphylaxis toolkit. https://www.nasn.org/ToolsResources/FoodAllergyandAnaphylaxis

- This site provides a variety of tools and templates to educate and help people who are responsible for managing students with food allergies as an integral part of the delivery of healthcare services in schools.

National Education Association (n.d.) Food Allergies: What School Employees Need to Know
http://neahin.org/foodallergies

- This booklet is designed to educate school employees about food allergies and how they can help to prevent and respond to allergic reactions in schools. Booklets are available in print and online in both English and Spanish.

National Institute of Allergy and Infectious Diseases. (2010). Guidelines for the diagnosis and management of food allergy in the United States: Report of the NIAID-sponsored expert panel. *Journal of Allergy and Clinical Immunology,* 126(suppl. 6), S1-S58.doi: http://dx.doi.org/10.1016/j.jaci.2010.10.007

National School Board Association. (2012). Safe at school and ready to learn: A comprehensive policy guide for protecting students with life-threatening food allergies (2nd ed.). https://www.nsba.org/sites/default/files/reports/Safe-at-School-and-Ready-to-Learn.pdf

- This guide is designed to help school leaders, especially school boards, make sure that policies at the district and school level support the safety, well-being, and success of students with life-threatening food allergies. It includes a checklist that school can use to assess the extent to which the guide's components are included in their food allergy policies and used in practice. It also has examples of state and local education policies.

World Allergy Organization http://www.worldallergy.org/anaphylaxis/

Legal Cases

Decisions focus on federal and/or state law, which can limit the usefulness in a general publication. Many cases are not published or are non-precedential; they can be referenced as secondary authority only, meaning that other courts are not bound by these decisions. Here are a few examples:

- In T.F. v. Fox Chapel Area School District, D.C. No. 2-12.cv-1066 (Sept. 12, 2014), the Third Circuit Court of Appeals ruled in a food allergy discrimination case finding that the school district was not "deliberately indifferent" to the child's rights.
http://www2.ca3.uscourts.gov/opinarch/134624np.pdf

- J.B. & T.B. v. Manalapan-Englishtown Regional Board of Education (SEA NJ 2007). Administrative Law Judge ordered the school to provide bus transportation to and from school and school-related activities with a trained aide who could monitor the child and administer an epi-pen.
http://www.wrightslaw.com/info/allergy.2007.manalapan.decision.pdf

- In Smith v. Tangipahoa Parish Sch. Bd., 2006 U.S. Dist. LEXIS 85377 (U.S. District Court for the Eastern District of Louisiana), the plaintiffs sued school for alleged discrimination under Section 504 of the Rehabilitation Act and Title II of the ADA. The court dismissed the claims finding that the school complied with healthcare providers' recommendations surrounding reported allergies and that the school did not discriminate by counting absences related to the student's impairment.

- In Liebau v. Romeo Cmty. Schs, 2013 Mich. App. LEXIS 1322 (Unpublished), school formulates 504 Plan for Student A who suffers from severe nut allergy and adopts a nut-free environment. Student B complains that she is not by the Section 504 Plan. The court dismisses various claims, including an equal protection claim, finding that the school has discretion to exercise its obligation to provide for the safety and welfare of other students and that the school-wide ban was arbitrary and irrational.

- *Mears v. Bethel School Dist. No. 403*, 332 P.3d 1077, 182 Wash. App. 919 (Ct. App. 2014). This appeal was from a defense verdict in a wrongful death case arising out of the death of Mercedes Mears. She had a history of persistent asthma and also had severe life-threatening allergies. Medications for her asthma (Albuterol inhaler) and allergies (Epinephrine) were available in the health office. When she began having difficulty breathing shortly after arriving at school on October 7, 2008, school staff believed she was having an asthma attack and not an allergic reaction. No attempt was made to administer the epinephrine for her allergic emergency or to start CPR and she died. Although the jury verdict found that the defendant was negligent, they found the negligence did not proximately cause the death. The issues with the bifurcation of negligence and the proximate cause of the death were not overturned in the appeal.

REFERENCES

American Academy of Pediatrics, Council on School Health. (2008). Medical emergencies occurring at school (Policy Statement). *Pediatrics, 122*(4), 887 - 894. doi: 10.1542/peds.2008-2171

American Academy of Pediatrics. (2012). Medical emergencies occurring at school (Policy Statement). American Academy of Pediatrics Publications reaffirmed. *Pediatrics, (129)*2:e561- doi/10.1542/peds.2011-3210. Retrieved from http://pediatrics.aappublications.org/content/122/4/887

American Nurses Association (ANA) and National Association of School Nurses (NASN). (2017). *Scope and standards of school nursing practice* (3rd ed.). Silver Spring, MD: Author.

Asthma and Allergy Network. (2016). *School stock epinephrine laws*. Retrieved from http://www.allergyasthmanetwork.org/advocacy/current-issues/stock-epinephrine/

Bird, J. A., & Burk, A. W. (2009). Food allergy and asthma. *Primary Care Respiratory Journal, 18*(4), 258-265. doi: 10.4104/pcrj.2009.00036.

Bridges, J. (2000, March). Suing for peanuts. *Notre Dame Law Review (75)* 1269. University of Notre Dame. Retrieved from https://litigation-essentials.lexisnexis.com/webcd/app?action=DocumentDisplay&crawlid=1&doctype=cite&docid=75+Notre+Dame+L.+Rev.+1269&srctype=smi&srcid=3B15&key=947a0c9188fb4039de0bea07d6583df7

Buppert, C. (2013). Can I use another student's epipen to save a child's life? *Medscape Nurses*. Retrieved from http://www.medscape.com/viewarticle/803235

Caughron, J. J., Antes, A. L., Stenmark, C. K., Thiel, C. E., Wang, X., & Mumford, M. D. (2011). Sensemaking strategies for ethical decision making. *Ethics & Behavior, 21*(5), 351-366. doi:10.1080/10508422.2011.604293

Centers for Disease Control and Prevention. (2013). *Voluntary guidelines for managing food allergies in schools and early care and education programs*. Washington, DC: US Department of Health and Human Services. Retrieved from www.cdc.gov/HealthyYouth/foodallergies/pdf/13_243135_A_Food_Allergy_Web_508.pdf

Cosby, M. F. (2015). *School nursing simulation: An evidence-based practice intervention for improved confidence in health-related school emergency first-responder role* (Doctoral dissertation, Capella University). Retrieved from https://www.nursinglibrary.org/vhl/bitstream/10755/581124/7/Simulation_DNP_Project_Cosby.pdf

Food Safety Modernization Act, Title 21, U.S. Code § 2205 (2010). Retrieved from http://www.fda.gov/food/foodsafety/fsma/default.htm

Liebau v. Romeo Cmty. Schs, 2013 Mich. App. LEXIS 1322 (Unpublished)

Massachusetts Department of Public Health. (2012). Data health brief: Epinephrine administration in schools 1-6. Retrieved from http://www.mass.gov/eohhs/docs/dph/com-health/school/epi-data-health-brief-12.pdf

Mathes, M., & Reifsnyder, J. (2014). *Nurse's law questions and answers for the practicing nurse*. Indianapolis, US: Sigma Theta Tau International. Retrieved from http://www.ebrary.com

McIntyre, C. L., Sheetz, A. H., Carroll, C. R., & Young, M. C. (2005). Administration of epinephrine for life-threatening allergic reactions in school settings. *Pediatrics, 116*(5), 1134-1140. doi:10.1542/peds.2004-1475

Morris, P., Baker, D., Belot, C., & Edwards, A. (2011). Preparedness for students and staff with anaphylaxis. *Journal of School Health, 81*(8), 471-476. doi:10.1111/j.1746-1561.2011.00616.x

National Association of School Nurses. (2013). *Individualized healthcare plans, the role of the school nurse* (Position Statement). Retrieved from http://www.nasn.org/Portals/0/positions/2013psihp.pdf

Russell A. F., & Huber, M. M. (2013). Food allergy management in elementary school: Collaborating to maximize student safety. *Journal of Asthma & Allergy Educators, 4*(6), 290-304. doi: 10.1177/2150129713486671

Russell, W. S. & Schoessler, S. (2017). To give or not to give epinephrine – That is (no longer) the question! *NASN School Nurse, 32*(3), 162- 164. doi/pdf/10.1177/1942602X17690402

Schoessler, S., Albert, L., Levasseur, S., & Owens, C. (2014). Saving lives at school: School nurses face the challenge of anaphylaxis in the school setting. *NASN School Nurse, 29*(2), 67-70. doi:10.1177/1942602X13516866

Schoessler, S., & White, M. (2013). Recognition and treatment of anaphylaxis in the school setting: The essential role of the school nurse. *The Journal of School Nursing, 29*, 407-415. doi:10.1177/1059840513506014

School Access to Emergency Epinephrine Act, Public Law 113-48, 113th Congress (2013). Retrieved from https://www.congress.gov/113/plaws/publ48/PLAW-113publ48.pdf

Sicherer, S. H., Mahr, T. & American Academy of Pediatrics Section on Allergy and Immunology. (2010). Clinical report: Management of food allergy in the school setting. *Pediatrics, 126*(6), 1232-1239. doi:10.1542/peds.2010-2575

Sicherer, S. H., Simons, F. E. R., & American Academy of Pediatrics Section on Allergy and Immunology. (2017). Epinephrine for first-aid management of anaphylaxis. *Pediatrics 139*(3) e1- e9. doi:10.1542/peds.2016-4006

Simons, F. E., Ardusso, L. R., Dimov, V., Ebisawa, M., El-Gamal, Y. M., Lockey, R.F., Worm, M. (2013). World allergy organization anaphylaxis guidelines: 2013 update of the evidence base. *International Archives of Allergy and Immunology 2013, 162*(3), 193-204. doi:10.1159/000354543

Simons, F. E., Ledit, R. F., Ardusso, L. R., Bilo, M. B. El-Gamal, Y. M., Ledford, D. K., … Thong, B. Y. (2011). World allergy organization guidelines for the assessment and management of anaphylaxis. *World Allergy Organization Journal, 4*(2), 13-37. doi:10.1097/WOX.0b013e318211496c

Tanner, A. & Clarke, C. (2016). Epinephrine policies and protocols guidance for schools. *NASN School Nurse 31*(1), 13-22. doi :10.1177/1942602X1560760

T. F. v. Fox Chapel Area School District, D.C. No. 2-12.cv-1066

Thiel, C. E., Bagdasorav, Z., Harkrider, L., Johnson, J. F., & Mumford, M.D. (2012). Leader ethical decision-making in organizations: Strategies for sensemaking. *Journal of Business Ethics, 107,* 49-64. doi: 101007/s10551-012-1299-1

Wang, J. (2017, February 13). Managing allergy, anaphylaxis: AAP releases customizable emergency plan. *American Academy of Pediatrics News*. Retrieved from http://www.aappublications.org/news/2017/02/13/Anaphylaxis021317

Wang, J., Sicherer, S. H., & American Academy of Pediatrics Section on Allergy and Immunology. (2017). Guidance on completing a written allergy and anaphylaxis emergency plan. *Pediatrics 139 (3)* e20164005. doi: 10.1542/peds.2016-4005

APPENDIX

Figure 1. Comparison of anaphylaxis and acute asthma symptoms.

Schoessler & White. (2013). Reprinted with permission.

Table 1. Comparison of Anaphylaxis and Acute Asthma Triggers.

Anaphylaxis	Asthma
Ingested foods	Respiratory infections
Insect stings	Allergens
	• Pet dander
	• Dust
	• Pollen
	• Mold
Medications	Irritants
	• Air pollution
	• Smoke
	• Chalk dust
	• Strong odors
	(eg, indelible markers, perfume)
Latex	Environmental
	• Dusty gym mats
	• Old books
	• Cleaning products
	• Fumes
Cleaning agents	Dry, cold air
Exercise	Exercise

Schoessler & White. (2013). Reprinted with permission.

Chapter 29

MARIJUANA USE IN SCHOOLS

Kathleen Patrick, MA, RN, NCSN
Kathy L. Reiner, MPH, BSN, RN

DESCRIPTION OF ISSUE

The National Council of State Legislatures (2016) reports that as of November 2016, twenty-eight (28) states and the District of Columbia have legalized medical marijuana or effectively decriminalized it. In addition, seventeen (17) states allow use of "low tetrahydrocannabinol (THC), high cannabidiol (CBD)" products to treat certain conditions including treatment of seizure disorders in children. The number of states that have legalized medical marijuana is likely to increase and laws vary from state to state. Each state that has legalized medical marijuana regulates the amount that the patient or caregiver can possess, the conditions that marijuana can treat, and requires registration. For a list of medical marijuana states along with the provision of each state, law see the National Council of State Legislatures website http://www.ncsl.org/research/health/state-medical-marijuana-laws.aspx. However, it is important to note that this continues to be illegal under federal law, although the current administration appears unlikely to enforce the federal ban if the person using the medical marijuana is doing so in compliance with state law (Liptak, 2017).

School nurses are the expert in medications and health conditions in the school setting (Holmes, Sheetz and American Academy of Pediatrics [AAP], 2016). Therefore, parents, school staff, and administrators will refer to the school nurse with questions about the use of medical marijuana in children and the administration of the drug in school. School nurses will need to be knowledgeable of state laws as well as consider policy implications related to their current medication administration policy. School nurses will also need to consider implications in states where marijuana use has been legalized for recreational use and potential considerations for youth.

BACKGROUND

Marijuana is derived from the plant *Cannabis sativa* (C. sativa) and refers to the dried leaves, seeds and flowers of the plant. The most common route of administration is inhalation, either by combustion and smoking the product or by vaporizing the active ingredients and inhaling the vapor. Marijuana can also be mixed into foods and ingested. A newly popular method is smoking or eating different forms of resins extracted from the marijuana plant. Smoking these resins is called "dabbing" and can deliver extremely large amounts of THC making this method more dangerous to the user. Approximately one hundred active compounds or cannabinoids have so far been identified in the plant (Hill, Williams, Whalley, & Stephens, 2012). The psychotropic effect which is generally desirable for recreational use of marijuana is from a specific cannabinoid, delta-9-tetrahydrocannabinol or THC. The amount of THC in any given plant can vary widely depending on strain or species used. Other cannabinoids such as cannabidiol (CBD) may have therapeutic effects and do not possess euphoric properties. CBD specifically has been used in the treatment of neurologic disorders such as epilepsy. There has been some research evaluating the use of marijuana in various neurologic disorders in adults but further research is necessary to understand the benefits and risks of products derived from C. sativa.

Reports of the use of marijuana for medical purposes date back several thousands of years. In the 1800's, a prominent English neurologist W. R. Gowers reported the use of a marijuana based product to treat seizures (Patel, 2016). Many of the products tested were high in THC. Recently products have been developed with low THC content and high CBD content.

There are anecdotal reports from providers and families on the successful treatment of children with neurologic disorders using products with high CBD content but limited research has been done in the use in children. Products with high CBD content can be obtained in various forms but are usually found in an oil or liquid form when administered to children. There is also a transdermal patch. CBD oil can contain varying amounts of THC and CBD and since it is manufactured in an unregulated situation, it may be difficult to determine the percentages of THC or CBD. The most recognized case for cannabinoid use in children involves a child, Charlotte, who was diagnosed with Dravet Syndrome and experienced 50 generalized seizures per day. After being unable to control the seizures with medications and diet, her mother began researching alternative methods. She connected with a grower of marijuana who was breeding a particularly rare, high CBD strain of cannabis (Maa, 2014). Charlotte's seizures were reportedly reduced after starting this high CBD extract and the drug was eventually named Charlotte's Web after her.

 A 2014 Cochrane Review of all published randomized controlled trials using marijuana indicated that no conclusions could be made regarding the efficacy of cannabinoids in the treatment of epilepsy (Gloss & Vickery, 2014). There have been reports that using THC may have long term effects on the pediatric brain and on brain volume (Battistella et al., 2014). For example, persistent use of cannabis is associated with neuropsychological decline and is more apparent in those who begin use during adolescence suggesting a neurotoxic effect on the developing brain (Meier et al., 2012).

Controlled Substance

All varieties of marijuana were classified as a Schedule 1 drug by the Drug Enforcement Agency (DEA) in 1970 when the U.S. Congress passed the Controlled Substance Act (CSA), (Department of Justice 2012). This Act classifies drugs based on potential for abuse and listed all forms of cannabis – including hemp – as a Schedule 1 drug. Schedule 1 status signifies that a drug has a high potential for abuse and no currently accepted medical use in either adults or the pediatric population. This list is updated annually by the DEA. In addition, the U.S. Food and Drug Administration (FDA) (2009) states that "marijuana has a high potential for abuse, has no currently accepted medical use in treatment in the United States, and has a lack of accepted safety for use under medical supervision" (p.§ 812, b, (1), c). This was reiterated in 2016 by the DEA so C. sativa continues to be a U.S. federally controlled substance, making possession and distribution illegal (Federal Register, 2016). This continued classification as a Schedule 1 drug hampers research since marijuana is not readily available for such purposes.

The FDA is responsible for conducting studies and clinical trials to determine benefits and risks of new medications. This drug approval process ensures that medications are safe and effective. Currently, there have not been sufficient clinical trials to support the benefits of marijuana (FDA, 2017).

Note that there are legal differences between marijuana at the state and federal levels. By the action of the Controlled Substances Act, marijuana is illegal at the federal level. In 2009, U.S. Attorney General Eric Holder stated, "It will not be a priority to use federal resources to prosecute patients with serious illnesses or their caregivers who are complying with state laws on medical marijuana, but we will not tolerate drug traffickers who hide behind claims of compliance with state law to mask activities that are clearly illegal." (U.S. Department of Justice, Drug Enforcement Administration, Diversion Control Division, 2012, para. 2). This approach appears to have been continued under the Trump Administration (Liptak, 2017).

In 2015 the American Academy of Pediatrics (AAP) updated their policy statement on legalization of marijuana for recreational or medical use. While the AAP reaffirmed its opposition to legalized marijuana, it did recognize "compassionate use" of marijuana for children with debilitating or life limiting diseases. The AAP strongly advocates for research on the use of medical marijuana in the pediatric population and the development of pharmaceutical cannabinoids (AAP, 2015).

Hemp

Hemp is a variety of the C. sativa plant and is grown specifically for industrial uses. It has been used for paper, textiles, food and rope for thousands of years. Both hemp and marijuana come from the same cannabis species, but are genetically distinct and are further distinguished by use and chemical makeup. President Obama signed the Agricultural Act of 2014, (P.L. 113-79) which defines industrial hemp (Cannabis plants containing 0.3% or less THC by weight) and authorizes institutions of higher education or state departments of agriculture in states that legalized hemp cultivation to conduct research and pilot programs (FDA, 2017).

IMPLICATIONS FOR SCHOOL NURSE PRACTICE

Medical Marijuana

It is important to understand the federal, state and municipal laws, as well as local school district policy as they apply to the school nurse. Registered nurses are required to abide by all state and federal laws under their Nurse Practice Act. Since medical marijuana is illegal under federal law, administration by a nurse would violate their Nurse Practice Act. School districts have questioned their liability under federal law which prohibits illegal drugs on school grounds or at school activities even if it is permitted under state law. Because use of medical marijuana in schools may cause school districts to violate federal drug-free workplace requirements, it may result in the loss of federal Title 1 funding, as well as U.S. Department of Agriculture funding that supports school nutrition programs. However, federal agencies have discretion in enforcing drug-free workplace requirements, so a loss of federal dollars is not guaranteed. In any case, loss of federal funding would likely only happen after a range of other options are utilized to compel compliance.

It is important to note that physicians are not writing a prescription for medical marijuana and are only recommending its use. In most cases, when used in children, parents are determining the therapeutic levels for their child. It also important to understand that because the FDA does not regulate medical marijuana, verification of purity and content cannot be determined.

As of July 2016, Washington joined New Jersey, Maine, and Colorado in allowing students to use medical marijuana at school (Education Commission of the States, 2017). States may differ in whether schools are required to allow medical marijuana use on school grounds or merely permit it if they choose. State nondiscrimination laws may also come into play when considering whether to allow the use of medical marijuana on school campuses. School nurses should refer to their state laws to determine the specific provisions in their state. Current policy in Colorado and New Jersey require that:

- Students using medical marijuana must have a valid medical recommendation;
- Only non-smokeable forms of marijuana may be administered on school grounds;
- Marijuana is administered by parents, legal guardians or primary caregiver; and
- Student cannot be punished for medical marijuana use.

In Colorado, two physicians must sign the registration request for a minor to obtain medical marijuana. The parent/guardian then submits the required paperwork to the state health department to obtain a "registry card". This card allows the parents to purchase a determined amount of medical marijuana at a dispensary for their child and the registry card must always be carried whenever medical marijuana is on their person. Under Colorado state law, the parent or caregiver is allowed to come onto school grounds to administer the medical marijuana but it must be removed from the school grounds with the parent/caregiver. The registry card must be renewed annually.

In New Jersey, Maine, and Colorado, the parent or primary caregiver, as defined in the state's law, is required to come to school to administer medical marijuana and may need to accompany the child if they require it on a field trip. This provision is in proposed 2017 Washington state legislation but is not currently required. If the field trip is out of state, schools and school nurses would need to abide by federal law. The federal government has jurisdiction over interstate commerce and since federal law still prohibits marijuana, possession would be illegal. Medical marijuana use in schools raises several key issues for policymakers. Most importantly, despite the differences in legal status of marijuana at the state level, it is still listed as a Schedule I drug under federal law.

FDA Approved Medications

It is important to note that two drugs have been approved by the FDA that contain synthetic cannabinoid compounds structurally related to the active components in marijuana. Dronabinal (Marinol) is a schedule III oral medication used for the treatment of AIDS related wasting and chemotherapy-induced nausea and vomiting. The other is nabilone (Cesamet), a schedule II oral medication prescribed for spasticity (Ammerman, Ryan & Alderman, 2015). Since these medications are not schedule I drugs and therefore not illegal under federal law, nurses could administer these drugs without violating their Nurse Practice Act.

A third drug, epidiolex (Sativex), is a plant derived oromucosal spray of a formulated extract of the Cannabis sativa plant that contains the principal cannabinoids THC and CBD as well as specific minor cannabinoids and other non-cannabinoid components. It is currently undergoing clinical trials under the Orphan Drug Act. The development of this drug is concentrating on severe, early-onset, treatment-resistant epilepsy syndromes including Dravet syndrome and Lennox-Gastaut syndrome (LGS). The Orphan Drug Act of 1983 is a law passed in the United States to facilitate development of orphan drugs for rare diseases which affect small numbers of individuals residing in the United States (FDA, 2013). There are no FDA-approved medications that are smoked.

FDA-approved drugs are carefully evaluated for safety, efficacy, and quality, and continue to be monitored by the FDA once they are on the market. The FDA supports sound, scientifically-based research into the medicinal uses of drug products that contain marijuana, and this agency continues to work with companies interested in bringing safe, effective, and quality products to the public.

Marijuana Use by Youth

In 2012 Colorado and Washington became the first states to legalize the sale and possession of marijuana for recreational use. Even if recreational marijuana is legal in the state, it is illegal for youth under 21 years of age to possess and use marijuana. According to the AAP, youth should not use marijuana because (AAP, 2015):

- It interferes with judgment, concentration, reaction time and coordination in ways that can make youth more likely to get into car accidents or otherwise injure themselves while using it.
- It interferes with brain functions such as memory, attention and problem-solving and can make it much harder for youth to learn and succeed in school.
- Contrary to what many people think, it can be addictive.
- Inhaling the smoke can cause lung problems and is a potential carcinogen.
- New research shows that marijuana use during adolescence and young adulthood, when the brain is going through many important changes, can lead to permanent problems with memory, learning and thinking.
- Youth who use marijuana regularly are less likely to finish high school or get other degrees, more likely to use other drugs, and more likely to try to commit suicide.

While causality has not been established, there may be an association with an increased risk of anxiety, depression, and early onset of schizophrenia depending on heavier marijuana use, increased potency and age of onset of use (Volker, Baler, Compton, & Weiss 2014).

The Center for Disease Control and Prevention reported from the 2015 Youth Risk Behavior Survey (MMWR) that nationwide 38% of students reported that they had ever used marijuana while 21.7% of students reported using marijuana one or more times during the 30 days prior to the survey. In Colorado where recreational marijuana has been legal since 2010, the 2015 Healthy Kids Colorado survey reported that marijuana use among youth has not increased since legalization and has remained relatively unchanged since the survey in 2009 (Colorado Department of Public Health and Environment, 2017).

Parents and other significant adults play a critical role in talking to their children about marijuana use but even parents need the right information. It is important to be honest and provide the facts on the health risks and legal consequences. A study conducted in Washington State on parent's attitudes and use showed while parents remained opposed to teen use of marijuana, there was an increase in approval of adult use and a decrease in the perceived harm of recreational marijuana. It also showed that parents needed facts and strategies when talking with their children about marijuana use (Kosterman et al., 2016). A toolkit for individuals working with youth was developed in Colorado to start the conversation with youth on their goals and how marijuana use can get in the way of achieving those goals (Colorado Department of Public Health and Environment, 2017).

Nursing Assessment of Student Impairment

As a health professional in the school building, the school nurse may be called upon to evaluate a student suspected of being under the influence of marijuana or other illicit drugs. District policy should define the role of the school nurse in these situations. The nurse is encouraged to develop the skills to recognize if there is impairment and whether the impairment is the result of a medical problem or is drug related. The Drug Impairment Training for Educational Professionals is a training offered from the National Drug Evaluation and Classification (DEC) Program and may be available in your community. A component of this training provides school nurses with a systematic approach to recognizing and evaluating individuals in the school setting who are abusing and impaired by drugs, both legal and illegal, in order to provide early recognition and intervention Information may be found at http://www.decp.org/community/ditep.htm. **In all cases, the nurse should avoid stating that a student is under the influence and only report on the signs and symptoms that are presented in as factual and objective manner as possible.**

Exposure to Marijuana in Children

There may be an occasion when a student comes to school with the odor of marijuana due to use by parents or a parent comes to school under the influence to pick up their child. It is important to consult with your local child welfare agency regarding the recommended response to these situations. School staff are mandatory reporters for child abuse and neglect according to your state's child welfare law. While marijuana use may be legal in your state, the child may be in a situation that places him/her in danger, in the same manner that a child could be in danger by a parent's use of legal alcoholic beverages. The safety of the child is paramount. Even if marijuana is legal in your state, conversation with your local child welfare agency should occur to determine how to handle individual situations.

Marijuana is usually smoked but with the legalization of the drug in some states, edibles have been developed for ease of administration. These edibles are infused in drinks, baked goods and even candy which mimic the look of popular types of store-bought candy. This increases the attractiveness to children and is the cause of an increase in accidental exposure. Some states have developed regulations requiring marijuana be stored in child-resistant containers. Colorado's regulation requires that a special symbol be added to packages of edible that would alert individuals that the product contains marijuana and to limit the amount of marijuana that can be in a serving.

A retrospective study of patients under 12 years of age evaluated for suspected ingestion of marijuana in a local Colorado hospital emergency department between January 2005 and December 2011 revealed a marked increase in children confirmed by toxicology screen of marijuana ingestion from October 2009 to December 2011. This was attributed to the 2009 decriminalization of medical marijuana in Colorado. Half of the accidental ingestion was attributed to food products laced with marijuana (Wang, Roosevelt, & Heard, 2013).

CONCLUSION

Every school nurse should review not only their state laws regarding medical marijuana, but also the Nurse Practice Act in their state and states in which they are licensed. As a requirement of their license, registered nurses must abide by all state and federal laws so it is important to understand that administering medical marijuana is currently illegal under federal law and would therefore violate their nurse practice act. As more states legalize medical marijuana, school nurses have a responsibility to stay informed about current research regarding medical marijuana and provide guidance to parents seeking treatments for children who do not respond to current therapies (Rollins, 2014).

Recreational marijuana use by students should be discouraged and is not legal in any case for those under 21. Schools are an important setting to provide prevention and reduction in illicit drug use including the use of marijuana.

RESOURCES

American Academy of Pediatrics Technical Report–The Impact of Marijuana Policies on Youth: Clinical, Research, and Legal Update. http://pediatrics.aappublications.org/cgi/doi/10.1542/peds.2014-4147

Colorado Department of Public Health and Environment. Connecting with Youth Groups. http://goodtoknowcolorado.com/bucket-list?utm_source=RMEP+Newsletter+List&utm_campaign= 3778cbb99c-EMAIL_CAMPAIGN_2016_10_30&utm_medium=email&utm_term= 0_cc70c5c1d3-3778cbb99c-225518657

Drug Impairment Training for Educational Professionals http://www.decp.org/coordinators/state/find.cfm

Education Commission of the States. http://www.ecs.org/medical-marijuana-in-schools-state-legislation-and-policy-considerations/

National Association of School Nurses. (2014). *Marijuana and children* (Position Statement). http://www.nasn.org/PolicyAdvocacy/PositionPapersandReports/NASNPositionStatementsFullView/ tabid/462/ArticleId/632/Marijuana-and-Children-Adopted-January-2014

NIDA (2016). Marijuana. https://www.drugabuse.gov/publications/drugfacts/marijuana

REFERENCES

American Academy of Pediatrics. (2015). *AAP reaffirms opposition to legalizing marijuana for recreational or medical use.* Retrieved from https://www.aap.org/en-us/about-the-aap/aap-press-room/pages/ american-academy-of-pediatrics-reaffirms-opposition-to-legalizing-marijuana-for-recreational-or-medical-use.aspx

Ammerman S., Ryan S., & Adelman, W. (2015). The impact of marijuana policies on youth: clinical, research, and legal update. *Pediatrics*, *135*(3). doi: 10.1542/peds.2014-4147

Battistella, G., Fornari, E., Annoni, J., Chtioui, H., Dao, K., Fabritius, M., Favrat, B., Mall, J., Maeder, P., & Giroud, C. (2014). Long term effects of cannabis on brain structure. Neuropsychopharmacology, *39*(9): 2041–2048. doi: 10.1038/npp.2014.67

Education Commission of the States. (2017). *Medical marijuana in schools: State legislation and policy considerations*. Retrieved from http://www.ecs.org/medical-marijuana-in-schools-state-legislation-and-policy-considerations/

Federal Register. (2016). *Establishment of a new drug code for marihuana extract*. Retrieved from https://www.federalregister.gov/documents/2016/12/14/2016-29941/establishment-of-a-new-drug-code-for-marihuana-extract

Gloss, D., & Vickery, B. (2014). Cannabinoids for epilepsy. *Cochrane Database of Systematic Reviews 2014, 3* Art. No. *CD009270*, doi: 10.1002/14651858.CD009270.pub3

Colorado Department of Public Health and Environment. (2017). *Healthy Kids Colorado Survey*. Retrieved from https://www.colorado.gov/pacific/cdphe/hkcs

Hill, A. J., Williams, C. M., Whalley, B. J., & Stephens, G. J. (2012). Phytocannabinoids as novel therapeutic agents in CNS disorders. *Pharmacology & Therapeutics,133*(1), 79-97. doi: 10.1016/j.pharmthera.2011.09.002

Holmes, B.W., Sheetz, A., & the American Academy of Pediatrics. (2016). Role of the school nurse in providing school health services (Policy Statement). *Pediatrics, 137* (6) e20160852. doi: 10.1542/peds.2016-0852

H.R.2642 - Agricultural Act of 2014. Retrieved from https://www.gpo.gov/fdsys/pkg/plaw-113publ79/html/plaw-113publ79.htm

Kosterman, R., Bailey, J.A., Gurrmannova, K., Jones, T.M., Eisenberg, N., Hill, K.G., & Hawkins, J.D. (2016). Marijuana legalization and parents' attitudes, use, and parenting in Washington State. *Journal of Adolescent Health, 59(*4),450-6. doi: 10.1016/j.jadohealth.2016.07.004

Liptak, Kevine. (2017). *White House: Feds will step up marijuana law enforcement*, Retrieved from http://www.cnn.com/2017/02/23/politics/white-house-marijuana-donald-trump-pot/index.html

Maa, E. (2014). The case for medical marijuana in epilepsy. *Epilepsia, 55*(6),783-786. doi: 10.1111/epi.12610

Meier, M.H., Caspi, A., Ambler, A., Harrington, H., Houts, R., Keefe, R.S., McDonald, K., Ward, A., Poulton, R., & Moffitt, T.E. (2012). Persistent cannabis users show neuropsychological decline from childhood to midlife. *Proceedings of the National Academy of Sciences of the United States of America,109*(40), E2657-E2664. doi:10.1073/pnas.1206820109

National Conference of State Legislatures. (2016). *State medical marijuana laws*. Retrieved from http://www.ncsl.org/research/health/state-medical-marijuana-laws.aspx

Patel, A. (2016). Medical marijuana in pediatric neurological disorders. *Journal of Child Neurology*, *31*(3), 388-391. doi: 10.1177/0883073815589761

Rollins, J.A. (2014). Pot for tots: Children and medical marijuana. *Pediatric Nursing*, *40*(2):59-60. Retrieved from http://www.medscape.com/viewarticle/824239

The Agricultural Act of 2014 (P.L. 113-79). (2014). Retrieved from https://www.fns.usda.gov/sites/default/files/agriculture%20act%20of%202014.pdf

U.S. Department of Justice, Drug Enforcement Administration, Diversion Control Division. (2012). *Controlled Substances Act*. Retrieved from https://www.deadiversion.usdoj.gov/21cfr/21usc/

U.S. Food and Drug Administration. (2009). *Controlled Substances Act*. Retrieved from https://www.fda.gov/regulatoryinformation/legislation/ucm148726.htm

U.S. Food and Drug Administration. (2013). *Orphan Drug Act*. Retrieved from https://www.fda.gov/RegulatoryInformation/Legislation/SignificantAmendmentstotheFDCAct/OrphanDrugAct/

U.S. Food and Drug Administration. (2017). *FDA and marijuana*. Retrieved from http://www.fda.gov/newsevents/publichealthfocus/ucm421163.htm

Volkow, N., Baler, R., Compton, W., & Weiss, S. (2014). Adverse health effects of marijuana use. *New England Journal of Medicine*, 370, 2219-27. doi:10,1056/NEJMra1402309

Wang, G.S., Roosevelt, G., & Heard, K. (2013). Pediatric marijuana exposure in a medical marijuana state. *JAMA Pediatrics*, *167*(7), 630-633 doi: 10.1001/jamapediatrics.2013.140

Chapter 30

MEDICATION ADMINISTRATION IN THE SCHOOL SETTING

Linda Davis-Alldritt, MA, BSN, RN, FNASN, FASHA
Bill Patterson, MPA, BSN, BA, RN

DESCRIPTION OF ISSUE

Increasing numbers of students with acute and chronic conditions, complex treatment regimens, and large arrays of daily medications have significantly altered the climate of our schools. Many students with chronic healthcare needs are only able to successfully participate at school due to effectiveness of their medication (Bergren, 2013). Schools are obligated to provide safe and appropriate care for students. Federal, and corresponding state laws, mandating the inclusion of children with special healthcare needs, require local educational agencies (LEA) to provide accommodations to meet the needs of these children. Such accommodations frequently include medication administration or supervision of those students who are authorized to self-administer their medication (Canham et al., 2007; Zirkel, Granthom & Lovato, 2012).

In today's schools, management and administration of medications is an unavoidable reality, and one of the most common health-related activities performed by school personnel (Hughes & Blegen, 2008). School officials must ensure student health by being prepared to effectively manage and administer many kinds of medicine. Most states have laws, and many LEAs have developed polices and guidelines, denoting medication management practices (Findlaw, 2016). For schools with a school nurse, the nurse has the expertise to safely administer medication and the skill to assess the effectiveness of the medication on the student (Southall, 2013). The school nurse also has the knowledge necessary to assist the LEA in the development and implementation of a district-wide medication management plan. Since not all schools have a school nurse, often school secretaries, health aides, teachers, and other school staff are recruited to assist with medication management and administration (Canham et al., 2007).

BACKGROUND

No one could have predicted thirty years ago the tremendous increase in the type and range of medications for children. This fact has made medication administration in school significantly more complex (McCarthy, Kelly, Johnson, Roman & Zimmerman, 2006). School-age children with a host of conditions from asthma to diabetes to Attention Deficit Hyperactivity Disorder (ADHD) must take medication during the school day to stay healthy and be ready to learn (Findlaw, 2016). Non-compliance with medication regimens has been associated with unsuccessful academic achievement, and poor behavioral and physical outcomes (Clay, Farris, McCarthy, Kelly & Howard, 2008). School policies related to medication compliance and management must be applied consistently throughout the school and LEA. As the school health professional, the school nurse should review all requests for medication administration, including self-administration requests, in accordance with the LEA's medication policies (National Association of School Nurses [NASN], 2017). Compounding medication management and daily medication administration challenges is the fact that fewer than half of the nation's 133,000 schools have a full-time school nurse (Fauteux, 2010). As a result, the task is often assigned by the school administrator to other school staff, who are typically unlicensed and have other full-time jobs at the school. If the school has a part-time school nurse, and state law permits, they may delegate medication administration to an unlicensed staff person, also known as unlicensed assistive personnel (UAP) (American Nurses Association [ANA] and National Council of State Boards of Nursing [NCSBN], 2006).

It is critical that LEAs adopt medication administration policies and guidelines that are in compliance with federal and state laws, including state nurse practice acts, and adhere to national school nurse standards of practice, school nursing protocols, and cover all district specific aspects of medication administration. Frequently legislators and other policymakers have no understanding of laws related specifically to nursing practice, yet are responsible for creating state laws on a wide variety of practices impacting nursing practice. Thus, school nurses should be engaged as members of policy development teams when decisions affecting school nursing practice are being made (NASN, 2017; Wilt & Foley, 2011). Unambiguous medication administration policies and guidelines will assist in keeping students safe at school by reducing confusion, misunderstanding, and medication error (American Academy of Pediatrics [AAP], 2010).

Medication administration for students is the most common component of school health services throughout the nation (Centers for Disease Control and Prevention [CDC], 2008; CDC, Adolescent and School Health, 2015a; CDC, Adolescent and School Health, 2015b). Between 2000 and 2016, at least 400 articles referencing various aspects of medication administration at school have been published in professional journals in the United States. Within that group of articles, federal and state laws related to the rights of eligible students to receive medication at school; school policies, procedures, and recommended guidelines on medication administration; medication management; emergency medication; delegation; medication error; medication administration at school sponsored events, particularly field trips; stock medication, such as, rescue inhalers, epinephrine auto-injectors, and over-the-counter (OTC) analgesics; and medical marijuana were the most frequently discussed topics. The concerns about and ramifications related to medication administration are many. A full history of medication administration in schools and a thorough literature review on the topic are provided in Appendices A and B at the end of this chapter.

IMPLICATIONS FOR SCHOOL NURSE PRACTICE

Medication administration is a primary duty for school nurses. Our schools have been significantly impacted by the increase in children with complex health conditions who require daily, and in some cases hourly, medication at school. School nurses are well-equipped to coordinate care and manage children's medication needs. However, frequently due to understaffing in the majority of schools, school nurses must delegate medication administration to unlicensed school staff. The tendency to use UAP in place of school nurses creates risk potential for the student, his/her parents, the LEA, and the delegating nurse. It is well documented that UAP make more medication errors than registered nurses (Canham et al., 2007; Celik, 2013; Richmond, 2011). It is incumbent on the school nurse to train and clinically supervise the UAP to reduce risk and ensure the health and safety of the student. To further reduce risk, school nurses must stay current and in compliance with federal and state laws, including the state nurse practice act, and LEA policies and procedures.

Challenges and Issues

Key challenges and issues facing the school nurse related to safe medication administration at school include:

- Compliance with applicable federal and state laws and regulations, state nurse practice act, and standards of school nurse practice
- Adherence to LEA policies and procedures, including
    o Relevant communication with the student, parent/guardian, healthcare provider, and school staff
    o Review of all medication orders
    o Appropriate storage and disposal of medication
    o Monitoring the medication's therapeutic benefits and other reactions
    o Consistent documentation
- Management of prescription, emergency, OTC, and stock medications
- Students carrying and self-administering medication
- Use of complementary and alternative remedies, and medical marijuana
- Acceptance and use of off-label and research medication
- Delegation to, and training and supervision of, UAP for medication administration when allowed
- Identifying and reporting factors that contribute to medication errors, such as:
    o Not enough time for training UAP
    o Even when trained, UAP lack the ability to problem solve issues due to a knowledge deficit of essential elements involved in the medication management process
    o Unsafe nurse to student ratio
    o Lack of priority for safe medication administration practices
    o Unclear, or no, requirements for reporting medication errors
- Maintenance of student rights to confidentiality
- Maintaining current knowledge and/or reliable information on medication including expected outcomes and possible adverse effects
- Staying current with, and providing nursing input on, proposed laws, regulations, LEA policies, and other actions potentially affecting school nursing practice

(Adapted from the following sources: AAP, 2009; AAP, 2016; American School Health Association (ASHA), 2003; CDE, 2005; NASN, 2017; New York State Center for School Health (NYSCSH), 2015; Texas School Nurses Organization (TSNO), 2010; USDHHS, 2016).

Public school medication administration policies and procedures should comply with federal and state laws and regulations. Medication administration in school is a required related service, under both Section 504 of the Rehabilitation Act of 1973 and Individuals with Disabilities Education Improvement Act (IDEIA), for protected students who need medication during the school day in order to safely access educational opportunities in the least restrictive environment. Under these federal laws, medication administration must be provided regularly, intermittently, or in emergency situations, unless a healthcare provider is required to administer the medication or it must be administered in a hospital or clinic. Section 504, IDEIA, and Americans with Disabilities Act Amendments Act of 2008 (ADAAA) provide protections for individuals with disabilities, but do not cover students who may need episodic medication for short-term illnesses (AAP, 2009).

All states have enacted laws, regulations, and guidance on medication administration for students that apply statewide. State laws vary, although in all states medication administration is a licensed function of healthcare providers and nurses. Some states' nurse practice acts authorize RNs to delegate nursing tasks, including medication administration, to licensed practical/vocational nurses (LPN/LVN) and UAP (NASN, 2017), other states only permit licensed professionals to administer medication (Laubin, Schwab, & Doyle, 2012). Many states limit the types of medication that may be delegated, particularly to UAP; however, in at least one state, California, trained UAP may administer any medication at school (*American Nurses Association v. Torlakson*, 2013).

The use of UAP to administer medication to students creates liability risks for the LEA and the school nurse, and health risks for the student, particularly related to medication errors (AAP, 2009). There is increased liability risk for unlicensed school staff in states that permit UAP to administer medication, particularly if the LEA does not require the UAP to be adequately trained, have on-going supervision by the school nurse, and work under the direction of the nurse, and in accordance with safe medication administration standards. LEAs that do not provide adequate staffing for safe medication administration practices and do not follow applicable healthcare standards may also be at higher liability risk for medication errors (Hootman, Schwab, & Gelfman, 2001/2005).

It is the responsibility of local boards of education to develop policies and procedures for the safe administration of medication to students who need medication at school and at school sponsored activities. LEA policies should be clear about the purpose of medication administration in district schools and the conditions and requirements under which the service will be provided. LEA policies and procedures should be grounded in applicable state health and education laws and regulations, and should not conflict with these laws or related professional standards in health fields, including dentistry, medicine, nursing, and pharmacology, or federal and state laws on controlled substances. Periodically, there are conflicts between state laws. When this occurs, LEAs are obligated to apply relevant safety standards for medication administration in district schools (Hootman et al., 2001/2005).

Strategies Addressing the Challenges and Issues with Medication Administration in Schools

Medication Policies & Procedures

While LEA policies and procedures need to correspond with state laws to ensure safe medication administration to students, they need to address the following:

- What medications may be administered at school and by whom.
- All allowed medication (prescription and non-prescription) be delivered to the school by the parent/guardian or other designated adult in the original container labeled with the student's name, medication name, dosage, route of administration, when the medication is to be given, the name of the licensed prescriber, the pharmacy contact information, and the medication expiration date.
- All allowed medication (prescription and non-prescription) requires written orders from an authorized prescriber and written/signed parent/guardian consent for medication administration and exchange of information between the school nurse and the healthcare provider to clarify questions and report outcomes – these written authorizations are filed in the student's health record.

- In emergency situations, school personnel are permitted to assume parent consent is given, although written and signed consent may not be available.

- Changes in medication orders, or new orders, are written and signed by the authorized prescriber. Changes that need to be implemented immediately may be taken verbally or via email if the LEA has policies regarding such actions that are in compliance with federal and state laws and regulations, and healthcare standards. School personnel, that is, school nurses, and other staff, if legally authorized (by state law or case law) to accept verbal orders, must be identified in the policy. A written and signed order should be obtained within 48 hours of receipt of the verbal or email order.

- Upon receipt, all medication is counted or measured with and signed off by the parent and the school nurse or other designated staff, and the amount received is documented.

- Controlled medication is counted and documented upon receipt as above, each time it is administered, and weekly or more often with another school staff member, preferably a school nurse or principal.

> *Can school nurses take medication orders from out of state providers who are not licensed in your state?*
>
> Under Article X of the U.S. Constitution, states are granted the authority to regulate practices that affect the health, welfare, and safety of their citizens including the practice of medicine, nursing, and pharmacology within their borders.
>
> Each state enacts their own licensing laws and regulations that are typically enforced by the appropriate state licensing agency. Generally, providers must be licensed in the state before they can prescribe medication, which would mean that school nurses would not be able to take medication orders from providers not licensed in their state; unless explicitly expressed in state laws or nurse practice act.
>
> School nurses must adhere to state nursing practice and licensing laws. Therefore, it is incumbent on school nurses to know what those laws are in their state. For more information, contact your state's board of nursing or your state school nurse consultant at either the state department of education or state health department.

- Medication never before administered to the student is not appropriate to be administered at school for the first time.

- Before administering any medication, the medication and the medication order are reviewed by the school nurse for the following: correct medication, correct/safe dosage, correct amount, administration directions, and expected outcomes and benefits. This information is incorporated into the student's medication plan that, as appropriate, may be inserted into the student's Individualized Healthcare Plan (IHP), Section 504 Plan as part of the student's accommodation plan, or individualized education program (IEP) for IDEA eligible students. All students with orders for emergency medications should have an Emergency Care Plan (ECP).

- Safe medication administration practices are followed by all responsible staff, which include checking the "six rights" of medication administration:
    1. Right individual
    2. Right medication
    3. Right dose
    4. Right time
    5. Right route
    6. Right documentation

- All medication is securely and appropriately stored in locked drawers, locked cabinets, or locked dedicated refrigerators, and in accordance with federal and state laws and regulations, and recommendations. A plan is developed for quick access and retrieval of emergency medications, such as glucagon, epinephrine, rescue inhalers, naloxone (for opioid overdose) and seizure control medication. (LEAs considering keeping emergency medications unlocked for quick retrieval should consult with their legal counsel).

- Access to medications is restricted and only available to the school nurse and trained staff, currently designated as being responsible for administering medications.

- All OTC and emergency stock medication require standing physician orders and parent/guardian permission in order to administer to students. If administered, the parent/guardian is notified. Who can administer medications given via standing physician orders varies from state to state. In many states, only an RN may administer such medication.

- Medication is not pre-poured for later administration or for someone else to administer.

- Documentation of medication administration is completed promptly, and includes notation of any medication errors made during the administration process.

- All medication errors, which include missed doses, failure to adhere to one or more of the six rights of medication administration, not being called to the office to receive medication, and lost, wasted, dropped, or stolen medication, are recorded on incident forms and reported to the parent/guardian, school nurse (if not the provider), school principal or designee, and the LEA's risk management department.

- Initial and on-going training and supervision by the school nurse is required and documented for UAP who are assigned to administer medications. Training includes all general standards of safe administration of medication, as well as student-specific medication and health needs. Training also includes legal and nursing practice standards, when to call the nurse, the importance of attention to detail and focus in all phases of the medication administration process, and the need to observe the student putting the medicine into his/her mouth and swallowing it. Additionally, training includes the

How should school nurses measure and track controlled liquid medication in bottles with no volume markings? Is it okay to pour the medication into a measuring container, note the volume, and return it to the prescription bottle?

Measuring and documenting controlled liquid medication, even in bottles with volume markings, is challenging. Pouring liquid medication into a measuring container is not good nursing practice, as it risks losing medication to spillage and more importantly it exposes the medication to contamination.

The label on the medication bottle should be marked with the total volume of the medication it contains. Additionally, the dosage and frequency should be marked on the prescription label. This information will enable the school nurse to estimate the number of doses in the bottle. All of this information should be recorded on the medication log, and each time the medication is given, the amount given should be recorded and the level of medication remaining in the bottle should be marked on the bottle with the date/time. Since controlled medication needs to be counted on a regular basis, by referring to the medication log and observing the level of medication remaining in the bottle, the count can be verified. It is important to note the literature reports that with liquid medication, there may be slightly more or less liquid than is indicated on the prescription label (Allnurses, 2017).

To avoid dosing errors, a recent study recommends that when dosing liquid medication, better accuracy can be obtained by using an oral syringe, rather than a medicine cup (Yin et al., 2016).

UAP signing an acknowledgement of training, the successful completion of a skill check list, which may include a self-assessment of the level of confidence in carrying out the assignment.

- Supervision of LPN/LVNs and UAPs assigned to medication administration is done by the school nurse. There is adequate school nurse staffing to support this safety function.

- LEA policy supports the registered school nurse's option to delegate or not to delegate medication administration for a specific student, in a specific situation, and/or to a specific UAP. While some state laws permit the school principal or other administrator to assign medication administration to UAP, the school nurse's decisions are based on professional assessment and clinical criteria, and are made in the interest of the student's health and safety.

- Self-administration procedures for students when allowed by state laws, and support by parents, providers and school nurse.

- All medication is returned to the parent/guardian at the end of the school year, when it is outdated, or at the end of the course of treatment. After appropriate notification to parents, any medication remaining at school is disposed of in accordance with state laws, regulations, and local ordinances. Medications, particularly controlled substances, are disposed of in the presence of another school employee, preferably the school principal or designee. The disposal is documented and signed by both parties.

- All student medication and health information is confidential, in accordance with FERPA requirements, and students are entitled to privacy when medication is being administered.

- Parents do not delegate nursing tasks to school personnel.

- Parents do not change medication dosage prescribed by a licensed provider or a manufacturer's printed dosage on medication container.

- Parents are informed annually in writing of their rights and responsibilities in regard to medication administration at school.

- The school nurse or other qualified staff conduct periodic reviews of all procedures associated with medication management.

(The above list of items identified as needing policies and procedures is adapted from the following sources: AAP, 2010; AAP, Council on School Health, 2009; Colorado Department of Education, 2015; Fobbs, 2015; Foley, 2013; Laubin, Schwab, & Doyle, 2012; NASN, 2017; NASN, 2014a; NYSCSH, 2015; Reutzel et al., 2008; TSNO, 2010; and Wisconsin Department of Public Instruction, 2009; Wilt & Foley, 2011).

Delegation of Medication Administration

School nurses must be familiar with state laws and regulations, related to medication administration and delegation. The ANA defines delegation as *transferring the responsibility of performing a nursing activity to another person while retaining accountability for the outcome* (ANA & NCSBN, 2006). Delegation of nursing tasks must be in compliance with the state's nurse practice act, other state laws and regulations, and professional nursing standards and guidelines.

When state law permits school nurses to delegate medication administration to UAP, it should only be done if it is safe for the student. The possible benefits and risks need to be considered in each instance. If an assessment needs to be done prior to medication administration, the task cannot be delegated because it would entail the

UAP making a nursing judgement. Before delegating medication administration, school nurses must consider the stability of the student's condition, the complexity of the administration process, the risk potential from a drug reaction or medication error, the competency, training and skills of the UAP, and the availability of the nurse to provide guidance and supervision. Even when state law provides liability immunity, school nurses should not delegate medication administration to UAP when there is a reasonable potential of harm for the student. Although the final decision to delegate to a UAP most often lies with the school nurse, decisions about delegation should be made in collaboration with the student, parent/guardian, healthcare provider, and rest of the school team. When UAPs are to provide medication administration, they must adhere to LEA policies and procedures, and the specific student's IHP, medication plan, or ECP (Resha, 2010; Washington State Department of Health, 2014). Use of procedure skills checklists and the development of an EAP as part of the student's IHP may help reduce risks associated with delegation (Shannon & Kubelka, 2013b).

Over-the-Counter (OTC) Medications

There are basically two categories of medication that are administered in schools: prescription and OTC medications. School nurses, in collaboration with school physicians, should develop safe practices for OTC use in schools, especially in states that do not have laws and regulations inclusive of or specific to OTC medications. Generally, the same policies and procedures for administering prescription medications should apply to OTC medications. Both prescription and OTC medications have potential for untoward side effects, and if over-used or abused, can increase risks of morbidity and mortality. In states where education laws permit schools to accept only parent consent for OTC administration to students, school nurses must verify that their practice act permits them to administer OTC medication without a licensed healthcare provider's order (AAP, 2009; AAP, 2010; Hootman et al., 2001/2005).

A primary function of school nursing is keeping students healthy, in school, and ready to learn. The appropriate use of OTC medication may enable students to feel better, stay in school, and more fully participate in the learning process. On the other hand, the use of OTC medication to manage complaints that are better managed with other self-care strategies, may be training students to rely on drugs rather than healthier alternatives. Also, OTC medications may mask underlying symptoms of more serious disorders, delay treatment, and have long-term consequences for the student (Hootman et al., 2001/2005).

When indicated and there is no student specific healthcare provider order for an OTC medication, in many cases, parents must leave work or otherwise arrange to bring their children OTC medications. Often, these children end up going home with their parent or other caregiver, and losing valuable class time (Foster & Keele, 2006). In an effort to keep students in school, some healthcare provider and school nurse teams have developed standing orders and protocols allowing the school to keep OTC medications in stock that school nurses administer to students "as needed." The protocols require a thorough assessment done by the school nurse prior to medication administration. Through these assessments, school nurses may identify other health conditions that require referral. UAP do not have the training, education, or license needed to do the pre-administration assessment. Strict adherence to the protocols helps ensure student safety and reduce risk for the school nurse. Typically, LEAs require annually renewed written permission from parents permitting the school nurse to administer the stock medication. Parents should be notified in writing each time the medication is given. (AAP, 2009; AAP, 2010; Wallace, 2016). Despite the interest in and perceived benefits of standing orders for OTC medications, the legal risk may outweigh the benefits of such orders. Hootman et al., (2001/2005), recommend that LEAs require students to have specific medical orders from their own healthcare provider for any medication, including OTC medicine, that is to be administered at school.

In schools, standing orders for emergency medications, such as epinephrine and glucagon, have saved lives of students and adults. Standing orders for emergency medications, like glucagon, epinephrine, anti-seizure medication, and naloxone, need to be renewed annually. School nurses who administer medications without an updated order may be at risk for practicing medicine without a license. School nurses should ensure that each school health office have a copy of current signed standing orders (Hootman, et al., 2001/2005).

Self-Administration of Medication

Federal laws, IDEA, Section 504, and ADAAA, along with corresponding laws in most states, protect the rights of students to carry and self-administer prescribed medications at school (Laubin et al., 2012). Self-management and self-administration education are fundamental in caring for children with chronic health conditions, such as asthma, severe food allergy, diabetes, and cystic fibrosis. Self-administration is supported by healthcare experts because quick treatment of symptoms helps to reduce the effects of the disease and may prevent an acute episode. Additionally, self-administration may lead to student independence, self-care competence, and improved self-esteem (Hootman et al., 2001/2005).

School nurses are in a unique position to reinforce self-management principles to students with chronic conditions because they have the opportunity to see such students on a regular, sometimes daily, basis (Ahmad & Grimes, 2011). LEA policies must be clearly written and define when and in what circumstances self-management and self-administration of medication is permitted (Hootman et al., 2001/2005). To ensure student safety, the policies should also include a requirement for a nursing assessment to determine that the student is capable and competent to perform self-administration (Laubin et al., 2012). Policies for authorization from the licensed healthcare provider and parent/guardian consent should be the same as those governing all other medications.

In accordance with federal and state laws, regulations, and standards, a responsible student should be allowed to carry and self-administer medication for urgent or emergent need if the medication does not require security or refrigeration. Controlled substances and medications with risk of abuse or sale to others are not candidates for self-administration (AAP, 2009). The school nurse should assist in determining when a student is proficient in medication management techniques used during school or, on the other hand, would benefit from supervised self-administration permitted (Hootman et al., 2001/2005). Medication carried by students must not be left unattended, and should always be on the student's person, or in the care of a supervising adult (AAP, 2009). However, the school nurse may need to train staff on helping the student in an emergency (Foley, 2013). If students forget to bring their medication to school, there should be plan to have backup medication in the school health office. Having this plan in place is especially important for emergency medication that is self-administered (Laubin et al., 2012).

Experimental and Off-Label Medications

Periodically medications approved for use by the United States Food and Drug Administration (FDA) in treating one type of health problem are prescribed for a different health condition. This practice is known as an off-label use of an FDA approved medication (AAP, 2014). Experimental medications are those drugs that are the subject of clinical trials to determine their effectiveness and safety; however, they are not currently approved by the FDA. Typically, only RNs or healthcare providers may administer experimental or research medications; however, when questions arise as to who may administer such medications, it is advisable to consult relevant state laws and regulations.

Since off-label medications are sometimes used for school-age children, or students may be participating in clinical trials for experimental drugs, LEA medication administration policies should include requirements for administering research medication at school. Typically, only RNs or healthcare providers may administer experimental or research medications; however, when questions arise as to who may administer such medications, it is advisable to consult relevant state laws and regulations. Schools should require that information on the medication be provided to the school, including the function of the medication, possible side effects, allergy potential, administration schedule and considerations, proper dosage, storage requirements and the intended benefit for the student (Johnson, Hayes, Reinstein, Simmons, & Benson, 2003). The school nurse should have product information to support safe administration at school (NASN, 2017). According to the American Academy of Pediatrics, Council on School Health (2012), school nurses do not have to honor requests to administer non-standard medications, such as doses that exceed manufacturer recommendations, alternative, homeopathic, off-label, experimental medications or nutritional supplements. However, the nurse should document the request and work to resolve the conflict with the parent, prescriber, and/or the school physician (AAP, 2009).

Complementary and Alternative Medicines

Complementary and alternative treatments are becoming increasingly popular for health problem management, and are often used without consultation with the healthcare provider. The National Center for Complementary and Integrative Health (NCCIH) defines complementary medicine as the use of a non-mainstream practice with conventional medicine and alternative medicine as the use of a non-mainstream practice instead of conventional medicine. Complementary and alternative medicine (CAM) practices include traditional Chinese medicine, naturopathy, homeopathy, dietary supplements, essential oils, and herbal remedies (USDHHS, 2016).

The popularity of CAM treatments and remedies has become an issue for schools as parent/guardian requests for the administration of these remedies at school is increasing. There are many information sources and websites; however, caution is advised as few of the claims have been scientifically validated. Alternative medications are not controlled by the FDA, and are not required to adhere to standards for accurate labelling, potency, or purity. Independent studies have shown that the potency level of some herbal remedies is very high and some contain traditional medicines, not listed on the package label. These medicines are typically added to further increase the potency of the remedy, and could cause harm (Johnson et al., 2003). Lack of data on their effectiveness and lack of safety information for these remedies limits their use at school (AAP, 2009). The school nurse is in an excellent position to provide students and their parents/guardians with current information about complementary and alternative therapies.

State laws and regulations typically specify whether school nurses can accept and implement orders from homeopathic and naturopathic practitioners. Consequently, school nurses must look to the state laws for guidance on the types of licensed providers from whom to take orders. In states that do not permit school nurses to take orders from alternative practitioners, school nurses can advise parents to suggest that the practitioner collaborate with healthcare provider who might be willing to provide the order, or that the practitioner order doses that do not need to be given during the school day. It is important to let the parents know that if school staff administer substances without adequate scientific data regarding safety, it may put both the student and the school at risk (Hootman et al., 2001/2005). As with experimental or research medications, requests to administer non-FDA sanctioned medications including alternative remedies often can not be honored by a LEA or a school nurse, especially if prescribed by unauthorized prescriber per state laws. The school nurse should document the decision and explain to the parent/guardian and as necessary, to the provider, that due to risks associated with alternative remedies, they should be administered outside of school (NYSCSH, 2015).

Problems exist even in states that permit school nurses to take orders from homeopathic and naturopathic practitioners. As healthcare professionals, for any medications the school nurse administers or delegates, they are accountable for knowing the therapeutic effects, potential side effects, contraindications, and safe dosage. For traditional medications that are researched and approved by the FDA, nurses can access the needed information in nursing and medical drug reference books. For alternative remedies, it is typically not possible to find scientific and research-based information to verify appropriate use, dosage, and potential therapeutic value or potential side effects (Hootman et al., 2001/2005; Wallace, 2016).

School nurses should stay current with the latest laws, research, and standards for alternative therapies and remedies, as well as with the cultural climate of the school community. Hootman et al. (2001/2005), suggest that a school health advisory council and an ethics committee can help the LEA to investigate the issues and develop policies and procedures to successfully address the issues.

Emergency Medication, Including Oxygen

Most states have laws that permit UAP to receive training in recognizing the signs and symptoms of anaphylaxis and the administration of epinephrine via auto-injector. Many states permit UAP to be trained to respond to diabetic and/or epileptic emergencies, most states have protocols for stock epinephrine for anaphylaxis emergencies, and some states require schools to stock albuterol inhalers in case of an asthma emergencies. In these states, LEAs that do not train UAP or stock authorized emergency medicine may be liable and found negligent for not being prepared for emergencies.

Several chronic diseases, including asthma, severe allergies leading to anaphylaxis, diabetes, and epilepsy and other seizure disorders can rapidly cause life-threatening emergencies. Immediate access to emergency medication is critical to successful outcomes. Emergency medication administration, like all medication administration, is governed by state laws and regulations and LEA policies, protocols, and procedures. Students with medical orders for emergency medications should have an ECP developed by the school nurse specifying the response needed for the student in case of an emergency (Allen, Henselman, Laird, Quinones, & Reutzel, 2012; NASN, 2017). When an emergency happens, it is crucial that school policies and school staff provide for the student's well-being, and that access to the student's emergency medication is immediate. To keep the medication safe and secure and administer the medication as quickly as possible, LEA policies and procedures must specify the location where the medication is stored, the staff member responsible for the medication, who replaces outdated medication and who is responsible for the medication for field trips. Additionally, school staff should to be trained and supervised by the school nurse as emergency UAP and assigned as "first responders" for students who experience medical emergencies (Allen et al., 2012; AAP, 2009).

Due to the increasing prevalence of asthma and anaphylaxis in school-age children and youth, there is a corresponding recognition about the advisability of adding oxygen to the list of medications and supplies that are included in the school emergency response plans (Goldman, 2015). Schools with school nurses should consult with their medical advisor about having a standing order for oxygen for students or staff with unanticipated medical problems. School nurses should work with school administrators and medical directors and state school nurse consultants, and review their nurse practice act to determine how to make oxygen part of their school and LEA's emergency response plan (Goldman, 2015).

Medical Marijuana

As of September 2016, four states: Colorado, Maine, New Jersey, and Washington, permit the administration of non-smokable prescribed medical marijuana in schools with the provision that the parent(s)/legal guardian or professional caregiver possesses and administers the medication when it is to be administered at school or during school-sponsored away from school activities (Augusta Public Schools Board of Education, 2016; Education Commission of the States, 2016; Regional School Unit 18 Board of Education, 2015). The FDA has noted "there is currently sound evidence that smoked marijuana is harmful" and "that no sound scientific studies support medical use of marijuana for treatment in the United States, and no animal or human data support the safety or efficacy of marijuana for general medical use" (NASN, 2014b, p. 2).

It is critical for school nurses to understand their state medical marijuana laws and regulations, and the implications of the laws for safe and appropriate practice. School nurses also need to know that under federal law, marijuana is illegal. Additionally, federal and many state laws make schools "drug-free zones," which means that it is illegal to have any drug, including marijuana, on or within a specified distance of the school campus (Safe and Drug-Free Schools and Communities Act, 1986). Consequently, LEAs that approve medical marijuana use in their schools, may put their federal education dollars at risk. LEAs, in the 25 states and the District of Columbia that permit medical marijuana generally, and that are considering permitting medical marijuana use in their schools, should review related state laws and consult with their legal counsel prior to implementation (Personal communication, Linda Davis-Alldritt, 2010).

School nurses should also be familiar with the pharmacology of medical marijuana, any clinical indications for its use, and potential side effects that may be observed in a student who possibly receives healthcare provider prescribed/administered marijuana before coming to school and/or prior to school-sponsored events (DeWitt-Parker, 2016).

As the school health expert, staff, administrators, students, and parents, may ask the nurse for help in understanding medical marijuana laws. If state law and district policy permit the use of medical marijuana at school, the school nurse should document the administration of medical marijuana and monitor the student's response to the treatment. In conjunction with the student, his/her parents, and the healthcare provider, the school nurse should develop an IHP that includes measures to take to ensure the student's safety as they return to the classroom, as well as contingency plans if the student has an untoward response to the treatment (DeWitt-Parker, 2016).

(*Please also see Chapter 29 for more information on medical marijuana*).

Field Trips, Summer Programs, Before and After-School Programs, Science Camps

Increasing numbers of children with special healthcare needs attend school and are entitled by federal law and corresponding state laws to have equal opportunity to participate fully in all school-sponsored activities, including enrichment activities like field trips, special camps, summer programs, and before- and after-school programs. Students with special healthcare needs, including those who need to take medication, may not be excluded, even when ensuring their full participation creates fiscal or logistical challenges. Without regard to the venue or the season of the year, safe medication administration legal and clinical standards apply (ANA & NASN, 2017; NASN, 2013). Students who require nursing or healthcare services at school will require, at least, the same level of care during school-sponsored activities away from school (Hootman et al., 2001/2005). To ensure the health and safety of all students participating in extended day and away from campus activities, planning for these events should begin well-ahead of the intended date and include the school nurse in all the planning phases (NASN, 2013).

Out-of-state field trips are particularly challenging due to state-to-state differences in laws pertaining to nursing practice (Erwin, Clark, & Mercer, 2014). For school nurses in one of the 25 states in the Nurse Licensure Compact (NLC), which permits registered nurses (RN) and LPN/LVNs to practice across state lines, these challenges are somewhat reduced. For school nurses working in non-Compact states, navigating practice licensure may be more cumbersome. Additionally, the NLC does not cover unlicensed school personnel or advanced practice RNs (USDHHS, 2010). Well before any off-campus activity, and especially well ahead of out-of-state field trips involving children who need health services, school nurses must review applicable state laws and regulations, including those pertaining to delegation in the states to be visited. The U.S. State Department can provide guidance for out-of-country field trips (Erwin et al., 2014).

State laws and regulations do not typically address many of the issues about medication administration that are related to school sponsored off-campus activities, including field trips, away camps, summer school programs, and worksite experiences. Even so, a thorough review of state laws, regulations, and standards of practice, as well as meticulous planning and creative problem solving, are required essentials for effective medication management for off-campus activities (Hootman et al., 2001/2005).

(*Please also see Chapter 51 for more information on school-sponsored trips*).

Students Who Fail to Come to Health Office for Medication/Students Who Refuse Medication

To maximize the therapeutic benefits of medication, medicine should be administered according per the schedule established by the healthcare provider's written order. For regularly scheduled medication (such as, a medication that is to be administered four times each day), it is not required to administer these medications within 30 minutes, either before or after, of a specific time. In 2011, the Institute of Safe Medical Practices determined that for hospital and clinical settings, it was not necessary to administer scheduled medications within 30 minutes of the ordered time, and hence medication administered outside of the "30-minute rule" no longer need generate a medication error report (Institute for Safe Medication Practices, 2011; USDHHS, 2011). That said, school nurses should interpret and establish a specific time to administer the medication at school to avoid daily re-interpretation of vague label instructions. The Institute of Safe Medication Practices (2011, p.2) provides the following guidance to hospitals: "time-critical scheduled medications at the exact time indicated when necessary or within 30 minutes before or 30 minutes after the scheduled time (or more exact timing when indicated, as with rapid-, short-, and ultra-short-acting insulins)" and for non-time critical medications, ". . .administered more frequently than daily but not more frequently than every 4 hours . . . Administer these medications within 1 hour before or after the scheduled time." An entirely missed medication dose does constitute an error and depending on the LEA's policy, would require an error report to be filed (Johnson et al., 2003).

When students do not come to the health office for their medication as scheduled, the school nurse and/or designated school staff remain responsible for administering the medication to the student. The school and LEA's acceptance of the written medical order from the healthcare provider and the written parent consent for the school nurse or designated school staff to administer the medication, create an obligation for the school/LEA to administer the medication as scheduled (Hootman et al., 2001/2005). If failure to administer the medication has negative or untoward outcomes for the student, litigation could result.

LEA medication administration policies and procedures should include guidance on what steps the school nurse and other designated school personnel must take when a student does not arrive in the health office to take a scheduled medication or when a student refuses to take a scheduled medication. LEA policy should specify that each student needing medication at school has a medication plan that includes each of the student's medications, as well as addressing any individually specific issues the student may have with medication, including problems with failing to come to the health office to take scheduled medication and/or refusing to take an ordered medication. The medication plan may include strategies to help the student remember to come to the health office to take medication or require the school nurse or other staff responsible for medication administration locate the student. Medication plans that are not achieving the anticipated results, may need to be revised. However, a punitive response to the student for forgetting to come to the health office, especially for students whose disability is manifested by poor organization or forgetfulness, may be considered discriminatory (Hootman et al., 2001/2005).

For students who refuse to take medication, school nurses and other designated staff should make every reasonable effort to administer the student's medication; however, physical restraint and force are not appropriate, safe, or legal, and could be judged as assault and battery. When students refuse to take medication at school, the school nurse should work with the parents/guardian; school administrator; other school staff, such as counselor, psychologist, or social worker; and the student's healthcare provider to develop other options. While alternate medication options are being explored, the student's educational needs must be served and the student cannot be excluded from school. If the student's behavior poses a serious risk of harm to self or others, then it may be appropriate for the student to be excluded, referred for a medical or psychiatric assessment, and information about available resources in the school and the community provided to the parents (Hootman et al., 2001/2005).

CONCLUSION

Every day in our schools, thousands of students with complex chronic and acute conditions need medication. Schools are required by federal and state laws to accommodate these students' medication administration requirements safely and appropriately at school and during school sponsored activities outside regular school hours. The safest and most appropriate school staff member to do and manage medication administration is the school nurse.

Proper management of medication administration is a safety issue for all concerned, and left undone, can potentially be the grounds for litigation. School nurses have the knowledge, skill, and experience to ensure safe medication use for all students. School nurses are the logical individuals to evaluate an LEA's medication administration process, ensuring that the LEA has proactive steps in place for student safety (Zirkel et al., 2012), and to assist in the development and implementation of any needed changes to the LEA's medication administration policies and procedures (NASN, 2017). Particularly, school nurse recommended policies and guidelines should clearly identify what comprises safe staffing, who is responsible for medication administration, when and to whom the administration of medication can be delegated, how medication must be stored, what is appropriate documentation, the amount and frequency of training UAP need, what are effective strategies to recognize current and avoid future medication errors, the necessary procedures for school sponsored activities, and what are the essential features of self-administration plans (Canham et al., 2007).

To keep students, school staff, and LEAs safe in regard to medication administration, there must be an adequate number of school nurses, other school health personnel, and resources housed within an infrastructure supportive of school health services (Knauer, Baker, Hebbeler, & Davis-Alldritt, 2015; Nadeau & Toronto, 2016). Additionally, school nurses must have reliable sources of medication information, and have the dedicated time to stay current with advanced clinical skills and knowledge, and to adequately train LPN/LVNs and UAP who may be delegated, in accordance with state laws, medication administration tasks (McCarthy et al., 2006; Rosenblum & Sprague-McRae, 2014).

RESOURCES

Legal references

- o   Americans with Disabilities Act, 42 U.S.C. § 12101 (1990).

- o   Americans with Disabilities Act Amendments Act, 42 USCA § 12101 (2008)

- o   Asthmatic Schoolchildren's Treatment and Health Management Act (PL 108-377) (2004). Retrieved from https://www.govtrack.us/congress/bills/108/hr2023

- o   Controlled Substances Act, 21 U.S.C. 13 § 801 et seq. (1970).

- o   Family Education Rights and Privacy Act (FERPA), 20 U.S.C. § 1232g, 34 C.F.R. (1974).

- o   Individuals with Disabilities Improvement Act (IDEIA), 20 USC et seq., 64 (2004).

- o   Safe and Drug-Free Schools and Communities Act (SDFSCA), Title IV--21st Century Schools Part A, 20 U.S.C. 7101 et seq. (1986).

- o   Secure and Responsible Drug Disposal Act, S. 3397 — 111th Congress (2010). Retrieved from https://www.govtrack.us/congress/bills/111/s3397

- o   School Access to Emergency Epinephrine Act, H.R. 2094 — 113th Congress (2013).

- Section 504 *of the* Rehabilitation Act, *29 U.S.C. § 701 et seq.* (1973).Title 21 (Food and Drugs) of the Code of Federal Regulations, Chapter II, Drug Enforcement Administration, 21 CFR *§* 1300.01 et seq. (2005).

- Uniform Controlled Substances Act, 21 U.S.C. 802 (1994).

- Good Samaritan Laws by State from Recreation Law. (2014). Retrieved from https://recreation-law.com/2014/05/28/good-samaritan-laws-by-state/

Applicable/Related Case Law

- *American Nurses Association v. Torlakson*, 57 Cal.4th 570 (2013)

- *Cedar Rapids Community School District v. Garret F.*, 526 U.S. 66 (1999)

- *Irving Independent School District v. Amber Tatro*, 468 U.S. 883 (1984)

Resources, such as position papers, clinical guidelines

- American Academy of Pediatrics, Committee on School Health. (2001). Guidelines for emergency care in school (Policy Statement). *Pediatrics*, 107, 435-436. Retrieved from http://pediatrics.aappublications.org/content/pediatrics/107/2/435.full.pdf

- American Academy of Pediatrics, Committee on School Health. (2003). Guidelines for the administration of medication in school (Policy Statement). *Pediatrics*, 107, 697-699. Retrieved from http://pediatrics.aappublications.org/content/pediatrics/107/2/435.full.pdf

- American Nurses Association and National Council of State Boards of Nursing [NCSBN] (2006). *Joint Statement on Delegation*. Retrieved from https://www.ncsbn.org/Delegation_joint_statement_ NCSBN-ANA.pdf

- Institute for Safe Medication Practices. (2011). ISMP acute care guidelines for timely administration of scheduled medications. Retrieved from http://www.ismp.org/tools/guidelines/acutecare/tasm. pdf

- Massachusetts Department of Public Health School Health Unit/Essential School Health Services. (2015). Field trip tool kit. Retrieved from https://neushi.org/student/programs /attachments/ FieldTrip.pdf

- Massachusetts Nurses Association Congress on Nursing Practice. (2011). Medication error (Position Statement). Canton, MA: Massachusetts Nurses Association. Retrieved from http://www.massnurses.org/nursing-resources/position-statements/med-errors

- National Association of School Nurses. (2013). Coordinated school health (Position Statement). Silver Spring, MD: Author. Retrieved from https://schoolnursenet.nasn.org/blogs/nasn-profile/2017/03/13/coordinated-school-health

o   National Association of School Nurses. (2014). Emergency preparedness and response in the school setting - The role of the school nurse (Position Statement). Silver Spring, MD: Author. Retrieved from https://schoolnursenet.nasn.org/blogs/nasn-profile/2017/03/13/emergency-preparedness-and-response-in-the-school-setting-the-role-of-the-school-nurse

o   National Association of School Nurses. (2017). Medication administration in the school setting (Position Statement). Silver Spring, MD: Author. Retrieved from https://schoolnursenet.nasn.org/blogs/nasn-profile/2017/03/13/medication-administration-in-schools

o   National Association of School Nurses. (2015). Naloxone use in the school setting: The role of the school nurse (Position Statement). Silver Spring, MD: Author. Retrieved from https://schoolnursenet.nasn.org/blogs/nasn-profile/2017/03/13/naloxone-use-in-the-school-setting-the-role-of-the-school-nurse

o   National Association of School Nurses. (2014). Nursing delegation to unlicensed assistive personnel in the school setting (Position Statement). Silver Spring, MD: Author. Retrieved from https://schoolnursenet.nasn.org/blogs/nasn-profile/2017/03/13/delegation-nursing-delegation-to-unlicensed-assistive-personnel-in-the-school-setting

o   National Association of School Nurses. (2015). Role of the licensed practical nurse/licensed vocational nurse in the school setting (Position Statement). Silver Spring, MD: Author. Retrieved from https://schoolnursenet.nasn.org/blogs/nasn-profile/2017/03/13/role-of-the-licensed-practical-nurselicensed-vocational-nurse-in-the-school-setting

o   National Association of School Nurses. (2013). School-located vaccination (Position Statement). Silver Spring, MD: Author. Retrieved from https://schoolnursenet.nasn.org/blogs/nasn-profile/2017/03/13/school-located-vaccination

o   National Association of School Nurses. (2014). School-sponsored before, after and extended school year programs: The role of the school nurse (Position Statement). Silver Spring, MD: Author. Retrieved from https://schoolnursenet.nasn.org/blogs/nasn-profile/2017/03/13/school-sponsored-before-after-and-extended-school-year-programs-the-role-of-the-school-nurse

o   National Association of School Nurses. (2013). School-sponsored trips, role of the school nurse (Position Statement). Silver Spring, MD: Author. Retrieved from https://schoolnursenet.nasn.org/blogs/nasn-profile/2017/03/13/school-sponsored-trips-role-of-the-school-nurse

o   National Association of School Nurses. (2015). Unlicensed assistive personnel: Their role on the school health service team (Position Statement). Silver Spring, MD: Author. Retrieved from https://schoolnursenet.nasn.org/blogs/nasn-profile/2017/03/13/unlicensed-assistive-personnel-their-role-on-the-school-health-services-team

o   National Diabetes Education Program (NDEP). (2010). *Helping the student with diabetes succeed: A guide for school personnel* (NIH Publication No. 03-5217). Washington, DC: U.S. Department of Health and Human Services. Retrieved from http://ndep.nih.gov/publications/PublicationDetail.aspx?PubId=97#main

o New York State Education Department. (2015). *Guidelines for medication management in schools*. Retrieved from http://www.p12.nysed.gov/sss/documents/MedicationManagement-final2015.pdf

o School Health Alert. (2016). *School nurse resource manual: A guide to practice* (9th ed.). Nashville, TN: Author.

o Schwab N.C. & Gelfman M.H.B. (Eds). (2005). *Legal issues in school health services: A resource for school administrators, school attorneys, school nurses.* Lincoln, NE: Authors Choice Press.

o Texas School Nurses Organization. (2010). Medication administration in the school setting (Position Statement). Retrieved from https://higherlogicdownload.s3.amazonaws.com/NASN/b385213b-35e8-49e3-97fe-d6627843f498/UploadedImages/Public%20Documents/tsno_medication_position.pdf

o United States Department of Education, Office for Civil Rights. (2012). *Questions and answers on the ADA Amendments Act of 2008 for students with disabilities attending public elementary and secondary schools.* Retrieved from http://www2.ed.gov/about/offices/list/ocr/docs/dcl-504faq-201109.html

o United States Department of Health and Human Services, Centers for Medicare and Medicaid Services. (2011). *Updated guidance on medication administration, hospital APPENDIX A of the State Operations Manual* (SOM). Baltimore, MD: Author. Retrieved from https://www.cms.gov/Medicare/Provider-Enrollment-and-Certification/SurveyCertificationGenInfo/downloads/SCLetter12_05.pdf

o United States Department of Health and Human Services, National Heart, Lung, and Blood Institute, NAEPP School Asthma Subcommittee. (2014). *Managing asthma: A guide for schools* (2014 Edition). Retrieved from http://www.nhlbi.nih.gov/health-pro/resources/lung/managing-asthma-guide-schools-2014-edition-html

o United States Department of Justice, Drug Enforcement Administration, Office of Diversion Control. (2016). *Title 21 United States Code (USC) Controlled Substances Act: Subchapter I — control and enforcement: Part B — Authority to control; standards and schedules: §812. Schedules of controlled substances.* Retrieved from http://www.deadiversion.usdoj.gov/21cfr/21usc/812.htm

Additional Resources, such as websites, journal articles

o American Academy of Allergy Asthma and Immunology. Anaphylaxis Emergency Action Plan http://www.aaaai.org/Aaaai/media/MediaLibrary/PDF%20Documents/Libraries/Anaphylaxis-Emergency-Action-Plan.pdf

o American Academy of Allergy Asthma and Immunology. Asthma Action Plan https://www.aaaai.org/Aaaai/media/MediaLibrary/PDF%20Documents/Libraries/NEW-WEBSITE-LOGO-asthma-action-plan_HI.pdf

o California Department of Education. (2013). *K.C. Settlement Agreement & Legal Advisory*. Retrieved from http://www.cde.ca.gov/LS/he/hn/legaladvisory.asp

REFERENCES

Ahmad, E., & Grimes, D.E. (2011). The effects of self-management education for school-age children on asthma morbidity: A systematic review. *The Journal of School Nursing, 27*(4), 282-292. doi: 10.1177/1059840511403003

Allen, K., Henselman, K., Laird, B., Quiñones, A., & Reutzel, T. (2012). Potential life-threatening events in schools involving rescue inhalers, epinephrine autoinjectors, and glucagon delivery devices: Reports from school nurses. *The Journal of School Nursing, 28(*1), 47-55. doi: 10.1177/1059840511420726

Allnurses. (2017). *How do you count liquid narcotics?* Retrieved from http://allnurses.com/general-nursing-discussion/how-do-you-445796.html

American Academy of Pediatrics. (2010). *Health and mental health services: Administering medications in school.* Elk Grove Village, IL: Author. Retrieved from http://www.nationalguidelines.org/guideline.cfm?guideNum=4-19

American Academy of Pediatrics, Committee on Drugs. (2014). Off-label use of drugs in children (Policy Statement). *Pediatrics, 133*(3), 563-567. doi:10.1542/peds.2013-4060

American Academy of Pediatrics, Council on School Health. (2009). Guidance for the administration of medication in school (Policy Statement). *Pediatrics, 124*(4), 1244-1251. doi:10.1542/peds.2009-1953

American Academy of Pediatrics, Council on School Health. (2016). Role of the school nurse in providing school health services (Policy Statement). *Pediatrics, 137*(6), e20160852. Retrieved from http://pediatrics.aappublications.org/content/pediatrics/early/2016/05/19/peds.2016-0852.full.pdf

American Health Information Management Association e-HIM Work Group on Maintaining the Legal EHR. (2005). Update: Maintaining a legally sound health record – paper and electronic. *Journal of AHIMA, 76*(10), 64A-L. Retrieved from http://library.ahima.org/doc?oid=57748

American Lung Association. (2014). Improving access to asthma medications in schools: Laws, policies, practices and recommendations (Issue Brief). Chicago, IL: Author. Retrieved from http://www.lung.org/assets/documents/asthma/improving-access-to-asthma.pdf

American Nurses Association, & National Association of School Nurses. (2017). *School nursing: Scope and standards of practice* (3rd ed.). Silver Spring, MD: Author.

American Nurses Association, & National Council of State Boards of Nursing. (2006). *Joint Statement on Delegation*. Retrieved from https://www.ncsbn.org/Delegation_joint_statement_NCSBN-ANA.pdf

American Nurses Association v. Torlakson, 57 Cal.4th 570. (2013). Retrieved from http://www.cde.ca.gov/LS/he/hn/documents/anavtorlakson2013.pdf

American School Health Association. (2003). Students with chronic illnesses: Guidance for families, schools, and students. *Journal of School Health, 73*(4), 131–132. doi: 10.1111/j.1746-1561.2003.tb03588.x

Americans with Disabilities Act, 42 U.S.C. § 12101 (1990).

Americans with Disabilities Act Amendments Act, 42 USCA § 12101 (2008).

Anderson, P., & Townsend, T. (2015). Preventing high alert medication errors in hospital patients. *American Nurse Today, 10*(5). Retrieved from https://americannursetoday.com/wp-content/uploads/2015/05/ant5-CE-421.pdf

Augusta Public Schools Board of Education. (2016). *JLCDA: Medical marijuana in schools* (Board Policy). Augusta, ME: Author. Retrieved from http://www.augustaschools.org/docs/JLCDA___Medical_Marijuana_in_Schools.pdf

Bergren, M.D. (2013). The case for school nursing: Review of the literature. *NASN School Nurse, 28*(1), 48-51. doi: 10.1177/1942602X12468418

Bergren, M.D. (2016). The feasibility of collecting school nurse data. *The Journal of School Nursing.* Published online before print June 5, 2016 doi: 10.1177/1059840516649233

Bobo, N., Kaup, T., McCarty, P., & Carlson, J.P. (2011). Diabetes management at school: Application of the healthy learner model. *The Journal of School Nursing, 27*(3), 3 171-184. doi: 10.1177/1059840510394190 Retrieved from http://jsn.sagepub.com/content/27/3/171.full

Canham, D.L., Bauer, L., Concepcion, M., Luong, J., Peters, J., & Wilde, C. (2007). An audit of medication administration: A glimpse into school health offices. *The Journal of School Nursing, 23*(1), 21-27. doi: 10.1177/10598405070230010401

Celik, L.A. (2013). Learning and applying new quality improvement methods to the school health setting. *NASN School Nurse, 28*(6), 306-311. doi: 10.1177/1942602X13496121

Centers for Disease Control and Prevention. (2008). A CDC review of school laws and policies concerning child and adolescent health. *Journal of School Health, 78,* 69–128. doi:10.1111/j.1746-1561.2007.00272_4.x

Centers for Disease Control and Prevention. (2014). *National diabetes fact sheet: National estimates and general information on diabetes and prediabetes in the united states, 2011.* Atlanta, GA: U.S. Department of Health and Human Services, Centers for Disease Control and Prevention. Retrieved from http://www.cdc.gov/diabetes/pubs/statsreport14/national-diabetes-report-web.pdf

Centers for Disease Control and Prevention, Adolescent and School Health. (2015a). *2014 national SHPPS fact sheets: Health services.* Retrieved from http://www.cdc.gov/healthyyouth/data/shpps/pdf/2014factsheets/health_services_shpps2014.pdf

Centers for Disease Control and Prevention, Adolescent and School Health. (2015b). Table 4.9: Percentage of schools with specific procedures for student medications, by school level—SHPPS 2014. *Results from the School Health Policies and Practices Study 2014.* Retrieved from http://www.cdc.gov/healthyyouth/data/shpps/pdf/shpps-508-final_101315.pdf

Clay, D., Farris, K., McCarthy, A.M., Kelly, M., & Howarth, R. (2008). Family perceptions of medication administration at school: Errors, risk factors, and consequences. *The Journal of School Nursing, 24*(2), 95-102. doi: 10.1177/10598405080240020801

Colorado Department of Education. (2015). *Guidance on delegation for Colorado school nurses & child care consultants*. Denver, CO: Author. Retrieved from https://www.cde.state.co.us/healthandwellness/guidance-on-delegation-for-colorado-school-nurses-child-care-consultants-2-2016

Dang, M. (2010). The history of legislation and regulations related to children with developmental disabilities: Implications for school nursing practice today. *The Journal of School Nursing, 26*(4), 252–259. doi:10.1177/1059840510368162

DeWitt-Parker, C. (2016). Medicinal use of marijuana: What school nurses need to know. *NASN School Nurse, 31*(3), 170-176. doi: 10.1177/1942602X16638815

Education Commission of the States. (2016). *Medical marijuana in schools: State legislation and policy considerations.* Denver, CO: Author. Retrieved from http://www.ecs.org/medical-marijuana-in-schools-state-legislation-and-policy-considerations/

Erwin, K., Clark, S., & Mercer, S.E. (2014). Providing health services for children with special health care needs on out-of-state field trips. *NASN School Nurse, 29*(2), 84-88. doi: 10.1177/1942602X13517005

Fauteux, N. (2010). Unlocking the potential of school nursing: Keeping children healthy, in school, and ready to learn. *Charting Nursing's Future: Reports on Policies That Can Transform Patient Care* (Issue 14). Princeton, NJ: Robert Wood Johnson Foundation. Retrieved from http://www.rwjf.org/content/dam/farm/reports/issue_briefs/2010/rwjf64263

Fobbs, E. (2015). Addiction trends require states to change school medication policies. *Policy Update, 22*(10). Alexandria, VA: National Association of State Boards of Education. Retrieved from http://www.nasbe.org/policy-update/addiction-trends-require-states-to-change-school-medication-policies/

Foley, M. (2013). Health services management. In J. Selekman (Ed.). *School nursing: a comprehensive text,* (2nd ed.), (pp. 1190-1215). Philadelphia, PA: FA Davis Company.

Foster, L.S., & Keele, R. (2006). Implementing an over-the-counter medication administration policy in an elementary school. *The Journal of School Nursing, 22*(2), 108-113. doi: 10.1177/105984050602200208

Goldman, P. (2015). Emergency first aid oxygen response in schools: O2 administration in schools by nurses and lay responders. *NASN School Nurse, 30*(2), 90-94. doi: 10.1177/1942602X14563802

Halfon, N., Houtrow, A., Larson, K., & Newacheck, P.W. (2012). The changing landscape of disability in childhood. *Future Child*. 2012;22(1):13-42. Retrieved from http://www.futureofchildren.org/publications/docs/22_01_02.pdf

Hootman, J., Schwab, N.C., & Gelfman, M.H.B. (2001). School nursing practice: Clinical performance issues. In N.C. Schwab, & M.H.B. Gelfman, (Eds.), *Legal issues in school health services: A resource for school administrators, school attorneys, and school nurses,* (pp. 167-230). North Branch, MN: Sunrise River Press.

Houtrow, A. J., Larson, K., Olson, L. M., Newacheck, P. W., & Halfon, N. (2014). Changing trends of childhood disability, 2001–2011. *Pediatrics, 134*(3), 530–538. Retrieved from http://doi.org/10.1542/peds.2014-0594

Hughes, R.G., & Blegen, M.A. (2008). Medication administration safety. In R.G. Hughes (Ed.), *Agency for Healthcare Research and Quality (US)*, 2-397 – 2-457. Rockville, MD: AHRQ. Retrieved from http://www.ncbi.nlm.nih.gov/books/NBK2656/

Individuals with Disabilities Education Improvement Act, 20 U.S.C. 1400 et seq. (2004).

Institute for Safe Medication Practices. (2011). *ISMP acute care guidelines for timely administration of scheduled medications.* Horsham, PA: Author. Retrieved from http://www.ismp.org/tools/guidelines/acutecare/tasm.pdf

Johnson, P.E., Hayes, J.M., Reinstein, V.F., Simmons, S.M., & Benson, J. (Eds.). (2003). *Medication use in schools*. Tallahassee, FL: Florida Society of Health-system Pharmacists.

Jones, S. E., & Wheeler, L. (2004). Asthma inhalers in schools: Rights of students with asthma to a free appropriate education. *American Journal of Public Health*, *94*(7), 1102–1108. Retrieved from http://www.ncbi.nlm.nih.gov/pmc/articles/PMC1448405/

Kleinschmidt, K.A. (2015). Procedure for the disposal of controlled medication in the school setting. *NASN School Nurse, 30*(5), 259-262. doi: 10.1177/1942602X14566467

Knauer, H., Baker, D.L., Hebbeler, K., & Davis-Alldritt, L. (2015). The mismatch between children's health needs and school resources. *The Journal of School Nursing, 31*(5), 326-333. doi: 10.1177/1059840515579083

Kohn, L.T., Corrigan, J.M., & Donaldson, M.S. (Eds.) & Committee on Quality of Health Care in America, Institute of Medicine. (1999). *To err is human: Building a safer health system*. Washington, DC: National Academy Press. doi: 10.17226/9728

Laubin, M., Schwab, N.C., & Doyle, J. (2012). Understanding the legal landscape. In C. Costante (Ed.), *School nurse administrators: Leadership and management,* (pp. 459-519). Silver Spring, MD: National Association of School Nurses.

Liberatos, P., Leone, J., Craig, A.M., Frei, E.M., Fuentes, N., & Harris, I.M. (2013). Challenges of asthma management for school nurses in districts with high asthma hospitalization rates. *Journal of School Health*, *83*(12), 867–875. doi: 10.1111/josh.12105

McCarthy, A.M., Kelly, M.W., Johnson, S., Roman, J., & Zimmerman, M.B., (2006). Changes in medications administered in schools. *The Journal of School Nursing, 22*(2), 102-107. doi: 10.1177/105984050602200207

McClanahan, R., & Weismuller, P.C. (2015). School nurses and care coordination for children with complex needs: An integrative review. *The Journal of School Nursing, 31*(1), 34-43. doi: 10.1177/1059840514550484

McIntyre C. L., Sheetz A. H., Carroll C. R., & Young M. C. (2005). Administration of epinephrine for life-threatening allergic reactions in school settings. *Pediatrics, 116*(5), 1134–1140. doi: 10.1542/peds.2004-1475

Nadeau, E.H., & Toronto, C.E. (2016). Barriers to asthma management for school nurses: An integrative review. *The Journal of School Nursing, 32*(2), 86-98. doi: 10.1177/1059840515621607

National Association of School Nurses. (2013). *School-sponsored trips, role of the school nurse* (Position Statement). Silver Spring, MD: Author. Retrieved from https://schoolnursenet.nasn.org/blogs/nasn-profile/2017/03/13/school-sponsored-trips-role-of-the-school-nurse

National Association of School Nurses. (2014a). *Emergency preparedness and response in the school setting - The role of the school nurse* (Position Statement). Silver Spring, MD: Author. Retrieved from https://schoolnursenet.nasn.org/blogs/nasn-profile/2017/03/13/emergency-preparedness-and-response-in-the-school-setting-the-role-of-the-school-nurse

National Association of School Nurses. (2014b). *Marijuana and children* (Position Statement). Silver Spring, MD: Author. Retrieved from https://schoolnursenet.nasn.org/blogs/nasn-profile/2017/03/13/marijuana-and-children

National Association of School Nurses. (2017). *Medication administration in the school setting* (Position Statement). Silver Spring, MD: Author. Retrieved from https://schoolnursenet.nasn.org/blogs/nasn-profile/2017/03/13/medication-administration-in-schools

New York State Center for School Health. (2015). *Medication FAQ's.* Retrieved from http://www.schoolhealthservicesny.com/faq.cfm?subpage=45

Peery, A.I., Engelke, M.K., & Melvin S. Swanson, M.S. (2012). Parent and teacher perceptions of the impact of school nurse interventions on children's self-management of diabetes. *The Journal of School Nursing, 28*(4), 268-274. doi: 10.1177/1059840511433860

Pettitt, D. J., Talton, J., Dabelea, D., Divers, J., Imperatore, G., & Lawrence, J. M., (2014). Prevalence of diabetes in U.S. youth in 2009: The SEARCH for diabetes in youth study. *Diabetes Care, 37*(2), 402–408. http://doi.org/10.2337/dc13-1838

Quaranta, J.E., & Spencer, G.A. (2016). Barriers to asthma management as identified by school nurses. *The Journal of School Nursing*. Prepublished April 4, 2016 as doi: 10.1177/1059840516641189

Regional School Unit 18, Board of Education. (2015). *JLCDA: Medical marijuana in schools* (Board Policy). Oakland, ME: Author. Retrieved from http://www.rsu18.org/index.php?id=2&sub_id=9299

Resha, C. (2010). Delegation in the school setting: Is it a safe practice? *Online Journal of Issues in Nursing, 15*(2), Manuscript 5. doi: 10.3912/OJIN.Vol15No02Man05

Reutzel, T.J., Desai, A., Workman, G., Atkin, J.A., Grady, S., Todd, T., & Dang, T. (2008). Medication management in primary and secondary schools: Evaluation of mental health related in-service education in local schools. *The Journal of School Nursing, 24*(4), 239-248. doi: 10.1177/1059840508319629

Reutzel, T., & Watkins, M. (2006). Medication management in primary and secondary schools. *American Journal of Pharmaceutical Education, 70*(1). PMCID: PMC1636904. Retrieved from http://www.ncbi.nlm.nih.gov/pmc/articles/PMC1636904/

Richmond, S.L. (2011). Medication error prevention in the school setting: A closer look. *NASN School Nurse, 26*(5), 304-308. doi: 10.1177/1942602X11416369

Rosenblum, R.K., & Sprague-McRae, J. (2014). Using principles of quality and safety education for nurses in school nurse continuing education. *The Journal of School Nursing, 30*(2), 97-102. doi: 10.1177/1059840513489710

Safe and Drug-Free Schools and Communities Act (SDFSCA), Title IV--21st Century Schools Part A, 20 U.S.C. 7101 et seq. (1986).

Schaffer, M.A., Anderson, L.J.W., & Rising, S. (2016). Public health interventions for school nursing practice. *The Journal of School Nursing, 32*(3), 195-208. doi: 10.1177/1059840515605361

Schoessler, S., & White, M.V. (2013). Recognition and treatment of anaphylaxis in the school setting: The essential role of the school nurse. *The Journal of School Nursing, 29*(6), 407-415. doi: 10.1177/1059840513506014

Schwab, N.C., Hootman, J., & Gelfman, M.H.B. (2001). School nursing practice: Professional performance issues. In N.C. Schwab, & M.H.B. Gelfman (Eds.), *Legal issues in school health services: A resource for school administrators, school attorneys, and school nurses*, (pp. 123-165). North Branch, MN: Sunrise River Press.

Section 504 of the Rehabilitation Act, 29 U.S. Code § 701 (1973).

Shannon, R.A., & Kubelka, S. (2013a). Reducing the risks of delegation: Use of procedure skills checklists for unlicensed assistive personnel in schools, part 1. *NASN School Nurse, 28*(4), 178-181. doi: 10.1177/1942602X13489886

Shannon, R.A., & Kubelka, S. (2013b). Reducing the risks of delegation: Use of procedure skills checklists for unlicensed assistive personnel in schools, part 2. *NASN School Nurse, 28*(5), 222-226. doi: 10.1177/1942602X13490030

Slomski, A. (2012). Chronic mental health issues in children now loom larger than physical problems. *Journal of the American Medical Association*, *308*(3), 223-225. Retrieved from https://www.communitycarenc.org/media/files/jama-july-2012-chronic-mental-health-issues-children-now-loom-larger-p.pdf

Southall, V.H. (2013). Promoting the value and image of school nursing. In C. Costante (Ed.), *School nurse administrators: Leadership and management,* (pp.575-602). Silver Spring, MD: National Association of School Nurses.

Tanner, A., & Clarke, C. (2016). Epinephrine policies and protocols guidance for schools: Equipping school nurses to save lives. *NASN School Nurse*, *31*(1),13-22. doi: 10.1177/1942602X15607604

Taras, H., Haste, N.M., Berry, A.T., Tran, J., & Singh, R.F. (2014). Medications at school: Disposing of pharmaceutical waste. *The Journal of School Health*, 84(3), 160–167. doi: 10.1111/josh.12132

Texas School Nurses Organization. (2010). *Medication administration in the school setting* (Position Statement). Author. Retrieved from https://higherlogicdownload.s3.amazonaws.com/NASN/b385213b-35e8-49e3-97fe-d6627843f498/UploadedImages/Public%20Documents/tsno_medication_position.pdf

United States Department of Education, Office for Civil Rights. (2012). *Questions and answers on the ADA Amendments Act of 2008 for students with disabilities attending public elementary and secondary schools.* Retrieved from http://www2.ed.gov/about/offices/list/ocr/docs/dcl-504faq-201109.html

United States Department of Health and Human Services, Centers for Medicare and Medicaid Services, Office of Clinical Standards and Quality /Survey & Certification Group. (2011/11/18, Revised 2011/12/02). *Updated guidance on medication administration, Hospital Appendix A of the State Operations Manual* (SOM) [Letter to State Agency Directors]. Baltimore, MD: Author. Retrieved from https://www.cms.gov/Medicare/Provider-Enrollment-and-Certification/SurveyCertificationGenInfo/downloads/SCLetter12_05.pdf

United States Department of Health and Human Services, Health Resources and Services Administration. (2010). *Telehealth licensure report: Special report to the Senate Appropriations Committee* (Senate Report No. 111-66). Retrieved from http://www.hrsa.gov/healthit/telehealth/licenserpt10.pdf

United States Department of Health & Human Services, National Institutes of Health, National Center for Complementary and Integrative Health. (2016). *Complementary, alternative, or integrative health: What's in a name?* (NCCIH Pub No.: D347). Retrieved from https://nccih.nih.gov/sites/nccam.nih.gov/files/Whats_In_A_Name_06-16-2016.pdf

United States Department of Justice, Drug Enforcement Administration, Office of Diversion Control. (2016). *Title 21 United States Code (USC) Controlled Substances Act: Subchapter I — control and enforcement: Part B — Authority to control; standards and schedules: §812. Schedules of controlled substances.* Retrieved from http://www.deadiversion.usdoj.gov/21cfr/21usc/812.htm

Van Cleave, J., Gortmaker, S., & Perrin, J. (2010). Dynamics of obesity and chronic health conditions among children and youth. *Journal of the American Medical Association*, *303*(7), 623–630. doi: 10.1001/jama.2010.104

Wallace, A.C. (2016). *Managing use of over-the-counter medications in the school setting: Keeping kids in school and ready to learn. NASN School Nurse*, 31(4), 210-213. doi: 10.1177/1942602X16636123

Wang, L.Y., Vernon-Smiley, M., Gapinski, M.A., Desisto, M., Maughan, E., & Sheetz, A. (2014). Cost-benefit study of school nursing services. *Journal of the American Medical Association, Pediatrics, 168*(7), 642-648. doi:10.1001/jamapediatrics.2013.5441

Washington State Department of Health, Nursing Care Quality Assurance Commission. (2014). *Registered nurse delegation in school settings* (Advisory Opinion No. 4.0). Retrieved from http://www.doh.wa.gov/portals/1/documents/6000/registerednursedelegationinschoolsettings.pdf

Wilt, L., & Foley, M. (2011). Delegation of glucagon® in the school setting: A comparison of state legislation. *The Journal of School Nursing*, 27(3), 185-196. doi: 10.1177/1059840511398240

Wisconsin Department of Public Instruction. (2009). *Delegation, the nurse practice act, and school nursing in Wisconsin*. Madison, WI: Author. Retrieved from http://dpi.wi.gov/sites/default/files/imce/sspw/pdf/snpracticeact.pdf

Yin, H.S., Parker, R.M., Sanders, L.M., Dreyer, B.P., Mendelsohn, A.L., Bailey, S., . . . Wolf, M.S. (2016). Liquid medication errors and dosing tools: A randomized controlled experiment. *Pediatrics, 138*(4): 1-11. doi: 10.1542/peds.2016-0357

Zadikoff, E.H., Whyte, S.A., DeSantiago-Cardenas, L., Harvey-Gintoft, B., & Gupta, R.S. (2014). The development and implementation of the Chicago public schools emergency Epi-Pen® policy. *Journal of School Health,* 84(5), 342–347. doi: 10.1111/josh.12147View/save citation

Zirkel, P.A. (2012). Liability for student deaths from asthma. *NASN School Nurse*, 27(5), 242-244. doi: 10.1177/1942602X12449058

Zirkel, P.A., Granthom, M.F., & Lovato, L. (2012). Section 504 and student health problems: The pivotal position of the school nurse. *The Journal of School Nursing*, 28(6), 423-432. doi: 10.1177/1059840512449358

Other REFERENCES Consulted

Awbrey, L.M., & Juarez, S.M. (2003). Developing a nursing protocol for over-the-counter medications in high school. The Journal of School Nursing, 19(1), 12-15. doi: 10.1177/10598405030190010301

California Department of Education. (2005). Program advisory on medication administration. Sacramento, CA: Author. Retrieved from http://www.cde.ca.gov/ls/he/hn/documents/medadvisory.pdf

Cicutto, L. (2009). Supporting successful asthma management in schools: The role of asthma care providers. American Academy of Allergy, Asthma & Immunology, 124(2), 390-393. doi:10.1016/j.jaci.2009.04.042.

Farris, K.B., McCarthy, A.M., Kelly, M.W., Clay, D., & Gross, J.N. (2003). Issues of medication administration and control in Iowa schools. Journal of School Health, 73(9), 331-337. doi: 10.1111/j.1746-1561.2003.tb04188.x

Ficca, M. and Welk, D. (2006). Medication administration practices in Pennsylvania schools. Journal of School Nursing, 22(3), 148-155. doi: 10.1177/10598405060220030501

Gordon, S.C., & Barry, C.D. (2009). Delegation guided by school nursing values: Comprehensive knowledge, trust, and empowerment. The Journal of School Nursing, 25(5), 352-360. doi: 10.1177/1059840509337724

Kelly, M.W., McCarthy, A.M., & Mordhorst, M.J. (2003). School nurses' experiences with medication administration. The Journal of School Nursing, 19(5), 281-287. doi: 10.1177/10598405030190050601

McCarthy, A.M., Kelly, M.W., & Reed, D. (2000). Medication administration practices of school nurses. Journal of School Health, 70(9), 371–376. doi: 10.1111/j.1746-1561.2000.tb07277.x

Reutzel, T.J., & Patel, R. (2001). Medication management problems reported by subscribers to a school nurse listserv. The Journal of School Nursing, 17(3), 131-139. doi: 10.1177/10598405010170030401

Sicherer, S.H., Mahr, T., & the Section on Allergy and Immunology. (2010). Clinical report: Management of food allergy in the school setting. Pediatrics, 126(6), 1232-1239. doi: 10.1542/peds.2010-2575.

APPENDIX A - History of Medication Administration

Historically, medication administration in all healthcare settings, and in schools, has been a nursing duty (Hughes & Blegen, 2008; NASN, 2017). However, as increasing numbers of students with disabilities, chronic conditions, and complex healthcare needs enter school, the school community has researched ways to support and promote their academic success, including how to cost-effectively provide medication assistance to keep these students healthy and in school. With fewer than half of the nation's schools having a full-time school nurse, when state laws permit, school administrators frequently assign medication administration tasks to UAP (AAP, Council on School Health, 2016; Fauteux, 2010; McClanahan & Weismuller, 2015; NASN, 2017).

While medication administration to students is now a common activity for school staff, until the passage of the Education for All Handicapped Children Act (Public Law 94-142) in 1975, children with chronic health conditions and disabilities were typically institutionalized or kept at home (Dang, 2010; Hughes & Blegen, 2008; McClanahan & Weismuller, 2015). Prior to the enactment of Public Law 94-142, which has evolved into the Individuals with Disabilities Education and Improvement Act (IDEIA) of 2004, some states did have provisions in their education statutes that provided for episodic oral medication, particularly antibiotics, to be administered at school by the school nurse or other school personnel. California, for instance, passed such a law in the mid-1960s.

Overarching federal laws, including Section 504 of the Rehabilitation Act of 1973 (Section 504), the Americans with Disabilities Act of 1990 (ADA), and the Individuals with Disabilities Education and Improvement Act of 2004 (IDEIA), require that children with health needs receive health services at school. The passage of the Americans with Disabilities Amendments Act of 2008 (ADAAA), broadens the scope of both the ADA and Section 504, and overturns earlier case law interpretations that had denied Section 504 eligibility to individuals with impairments that caused substantial limitations at work or at school, such as diabetes, life-threatening allergies, and ADHD (United States Department of Education, Office for Civil Rights, 2012). However, federal law leaves the detail of medication administration at school to the states and school districts (Laubin, Schwab & Doyle, 2012; Zirkel, et al., 2012). States have the authority via the Tenth Amendment to the United States Constitution to regulate activities affecting the health, safety, and welfare of their citizens (U.S. Department of Health and Human Services [USDHHS], 2010). Consequently, most states have passed laws that authorize LEAs to adopt local policies and regulations on medication management and administration in schools (Canham, et al., 2007).

Other federal laws and regulations, including the Controlled Substances (CSA) and Uniform Controlled Substances (UCSA) Acts, and Title 21, Section 1300 of the Code of Federal Regulations (CFR), which deal with controlled substances, may also impact medication administration in schools, particularly for medications that are classified as controlled substances (DeWitt-Parker, 2016; Findlaw, 2016; Laubin, et al., 2012). As a key part of federal drug abuse prevention efforts, in 1970 Congress passed the CSA and Title 21 CFR-Part 1300, and thus instituted scheduling substances based on their potential for abuse and consequent dependence. Marijuana is included in Schedule 1, along with other substances that are classified as having a high potential for abuse and no currently accepted medical treatment use in the United States (United States Department of Justice, Drug Enforcement Administration, Office of Diversion Control, 2016).

Recently, with the passage of *Asthmatic Schoolchildren's Treatment and Health Management Act* (PL 108-377) of 2004 and federal level encouragement (American Lung Association, 2014), all states have passed laws permitting students with asthma to carry and use rescue inhalers, as necessary. With the passage of *School Access to Emergency Epinephrine Act* of 2013, many states have passed laws permitting students with severe allergies to carry epinephrine auto-injectors and self-administer epinephrine, when needed (Findlaw, 2016).

APPENDIX B – Literature Review

Federal and State Laws

LEAs are required by federal and corresponding state laws to ensure that all students have equal opportunity and access to all academic, nonacademic, and other school sponsored activities. Students with disabilities and those requiring health services cannot be excluded or have their access to these activities denied (Erwin et al., 2014; Jones & Wheeler, 2004; Van Cleave, Gortmaker & Perrin, 2010). **All LEAs should have policies and procedures for safe and effective medication administration** (AAP, Council on School Health, 2016). Approximately, ninety-seven percent of schools report having procedures for medication administration to students (CDC, Adolescent and School Health, 2015a; CDC, Adolescent and School Health, 2015b). While all states have laws related self-management of some chronic conditions (Findlaw, 2016), not all LEAs have adopted policies related to student self-management. For example, eighty-two percent of schools have policies permitting students to carry and self-administer asthma inhalers; sixty-one percent of schools' policies permit students to carry and self-administer epinephrine via auto-injector; fifty-one percent of schools have policies permitting students to carry and self-administer insulin and other injected medications; and fewer than twenty percent of schools' policies permit student to carry and self-administer any prescription or over-the-counter medication (CDC, Adolescent and School Health, 2015b).

Policies, Procedures, and Protocols

Policies, procedures, and protocols provide school nurses and other school employees with reliable guidance and when adhered to, reduce the risk of performance errors that could cause harm or even litigation (Allen et al., 2012; AAP, Council on School Health, 2016; ANA & NASN, 2017; Kleinschmidt, 2015; Nadeau &Toronto, 2016; Richmond, 2011; Shannon & Kubelka, 2013b; Tanner & Clarke, 2016; Taras, Haste, Berry, Tran & Singh, 2014; Wallace, 2016; Wilt & Foley, 2011). LEA policies and procedures define the scope and standards of nursing practice and outline an expected standard of behavior for school employees (ANA & NASN, 2017; Schwab et al., 2001/2005) and may limit employee and LEA liability (Zadikoff, Whyte, DeSantiago-Cardenas, Harvey-Gintoft & Gupta, 2014; Zirkel, 2012). School nurses must know and follow their district's policies and procedures (Schwab et al., 2001; Shannon & Kubelka, 2013a).

Children with Special Healthcare Needs

There has been a dramatic increase in the number of children entering school with special healthcare needs, including the need for medication each school day (Bergren, 2013; Knauer et al., 2015; McCarthy et al., 2006). The prevalence of students with diabetes, both type 1 and type 2, has increased significantly according to the Centers for Disease Control and Prevention (CDC) and other researchers (Bobo et al., 2011; CDC, 2014; Pettitt, et al., 2014). A recent study estimated that 30 to 50 percent of school-age children experience at least one chronic condition, requiring medication, each year (Halfon, Houtrow, Larson & Newacheck, 2012). Another study found that in the last 50 years, along with an increase in childhood disabilities generally, the number of children with mental health and neurodevelopmental conditions has increased (Houtrow, Larson, Olson, Newacheck & Halfon, 2014), so that for the first time, the most prevalent disabilities in U.S. children are mental health conditions. Still another study revealed that the number of psychotropic medications administered at school validates the assertion that mental health and behavioral issues have exceeded physical health conditions for school-age children (Slomski, 2012). Asthma, which until a few years ago was the most common disabling condition for children is in 6th place (Slomski, 2012).

Medications

Increased numbers of children with chronic conditions who need medication during the school day, translates into increased amounts and types of medications for school personnel to administer. Additionally, many of the medications administered in school are controlled substances, which require special handling (Bergren, 2016; Canham et al., 2007; Clay et al., 2008; McCarthy et al., 2006; Taras et al., 2014; Texas School Nurses Organization, 2010). In one study, at the end of the school year in a large school district of 133,000 students, researchers identified 926 separate packages, that were left in the school health offices, consisting of medications for asthma, pain (analgesics), allergy, behavioral issues (controlled substances), psychiatric conditions, gastrointestinal conditions, cold and cough, diabetes, epilepsy, cardiovascular conditions, and corticosteroids (Taras et al., 2014). In a 2006 study, researchers found that 191 "unique pharmaceutical agents" were administered during the regular school day (McCarthy, et al., 2006, p. 105). In another study of 10 schools, researchers collected data on 154 medications prescribed for students (Canham et al., 2007). Students with potentially life-threatening conditions, such as asthma, severe allergies, or diabetes, may need emergency medications during the school day, or at school-sponsored activities (Allen, et al., 2012; Erwin et al., 2014; Peery, Engelke & Swanson, 2012; Schoessler & White, 2013; Tanner & Clarke, 2016; Wilt & Foley, 2011; Zadikoff et al., 2014), and in some cases, these students may need emergency oxygen (Goldman, 2015).

Medication Management

Medication management is an important school nursing function (Foster & Keele, 2006). Effective medication management at school enables students who need medication during the school day to optimize their academic achievement (Bobo et al., 2011). Medication management in schools has many components, all of which need to be consistently documented, including: obtaining needed medication and/or supplies from parents (Liberatos et al., 2013; Quaranta & Spencer, 2016), medication transport to school; medication acceptance by school staff; secure and appropriate medication storage; administration to students in accordance with the six rights of medication administration; observation of the effectiveness of the medication; appropriate delegation to licensed practical/vocational nurses (LPN/LVN) and UAP, if permitted; appropriate disposal of medication at the school year's end or when expired (Kleinschmidt, 2015; Reutzel & Watkins, 2006; Taras et al., 2014); appropriate authorizations, including faxed orders and electronic signatures (American Health Information Management Association e-HIM Work Group on Maintaining the Legal HER, 2005); and reporting and tracking medication errors (Canham et al, 2007). Medication management also involves developing protocols for administering stock medications and OTC medications (Allen et al., 2012; Foster & Keele, 2006; Goldman, 2015; Tanner & Clarke, 2016; Wallace, 2016). Medication management further includes provision of student medication for school sponsored events, such as field trips (Erwin et al., 2014; McIntyre, Sheetz, Carroll, & Young, 2005).

Delegation

For a variety of reasons, including several years of reductions in education budgets, fewer than half of all schools in the United States have a full-time school nurse (CDC, Adolescent and School Health, 2015a; Fauteux, 2010; Wang et al., 2014). To meet the need to accommodate students requiring health services at schools,

411

LEAs are increasingly using UAP, typically school office staff, to administer medication, if allowed by state law (Schaffer, Anderson, & Rising, 2016). As a consequence, many school nurses must now train and supervise school secretaries and clerks, who already have full-time duties in the school office, to administer student medication (Canham et al., 2007; Nadeau & Toronto, 2016). Prior to delegating medication administration to UAP, the school nurse assesses the student to determine if the task can be delegated and what level of supervision and training the UAP needs to safely perform the task (NASN, 2012a). Competing priorities for these UAP, coupled with their lack of medical background, increase the possibility for medication errors (Canham et al., 2007). The incidence of medication errors is higher when medication is administered by UAP than when school nurses administer medication. One study found that documentation errors made by a UAP correlated with the potential for missed or double dosing errors and medication theft (Celik, 2013). The risks of delegation can be reduced through the use of procedure skills checklists, development of individual healthcare plans (IHP) and emergency action plans (EAP), and adoption of federal and state agency guidelines, and professional organization guidelines (Shannon & Kubelka, 2013b). When permitted by law and appropriately applied, delegation to UAPs is an effective tool for the school nurse (ANA & NCSBN, 2006). However, the American Academy of Pediatrics recommends that when a registered nurse is not available to administer any medication at school, the task should be delegated to an LPN/LVN (AAP, Council on School Health, 2009; AAP, Council on School Health, 2016).

Medication Errors

Medication errors occur in all clinical settings, and in school health offices. In hospitals, mistakes involving medications are among the most common healthcare errors (Anderson & Townsend, 2015). The 1999 Institute of Medicine (IOM) report, *To Err is Human*, reviewed medication errors by licensed healthcare staff working in clinical settings, and found at the time that medication errors caused 7,000 deaths annually (Kohn, Korrigan, & Donaldson, 1999). The literature revealed that common medication errors, often linked to UAP in schools, include incorrect medication dose, missed medication doses, expired medication, inconsistent documentation and poor record keeping, over- and under-dosing, inappropriate and unsafe medicine storage, lack of healthcare provider authorization, transcription inaccuracies, and medication administered to the wrong student (Canham et al., 2007; Celik, 2013; Richmond, 2011). Periodically errors in timing have been an issue for schools. However, based on survey results reported by the Institute for Safe Medication Practices in 2011, the "30- minute rule" – which required that scheduled medication in hospital and clinical settings be given within 30 minutes of the provider specified time of administration – was rescinded by the federal Office of Clinical Standards and Quality (Institute for Safe Medication Practices, 2011; USDHHS, 2011). **Consequently, LEA policies that reference the "30-minute rule" may need to be revised.**

Chapter 31

SUPPORTING STUDENTS WITH MENTAL/BEHAVORIAL HEALTH CHALLENGES

Antoinette Towle, EdD, APRN

DESCRIPTION OF ISSUE

One in five children live with a mental health illness, but only 20% of these children actually receive the needed services and supports in schools (National Alliance on Mental Illness [NAMI], 2016). An undiagnosed, untreated, or inadequately treated mental health illness impacts a student's ability to learn. Half of individuals living with mental illness experience the onset of their illness by the age of 14, and approximately 50% of these students will drop out of school (NAMI, 2016). Mental health encompasses behavioral, emotional, neuro-developmental, psychiatric, psychological and substance abuse issues. Family and community stressors and issues can contribute to mental health conditions as well as to its somatic manifestations (American Academy of Pediatrics [AAP], 2009). Imbalance between any or against these factors can interfere with the child's ability to learn, grow, and become a productive adult. While many students may experience mental health concerns during their school years and may need intermittent interventions, this chapter focuses on students with significant mental health concerns requiring more intensive interventions.

BACKGROUND

Because children spend the majority of their day in school, schools provide a unique opportunity in helping to identify the early warning signs of a mental health illness, Schools can link students and families to appropriate, effective services. According to the National Association of School Nurses (NASN) in the *Case for School Nursing* (2012), school nurses spend 32% of their time providing mental health services. Therefore, school nurses have firsthand experience with the prevalence of depression, self-harm, and suicidality among students (Zupp, 2013). School nurses are very often the first person to assess and identify the subtle signs of a mental health problem.

School nurses play a key role in providing early identification and intervention for these students and their families. They help educate staff and administration recognize signs and symptoms of potential mental health issues and help build upon their ability to address barriers to learning. Presently there are no specific federal laws and few state laws mandating that schools provide preventative mental health services, such as *Screening, Brief Intervention, Referral and Treatment* (SBIRT) in Massachusetts. School nurses are uniquely positioned between policymakers and the student body as caregiver, advocate, and expert (Cooper, Clements, & Holt, 2012). This unique position provides the school nurse with the ability to identify and intervene with at risk adolescents, as well as lead in developing prevention policy (Cooper et al., 2012).

IMPLICATIONS FOR SCHOOL NURSE PRACTICE

Rights and Protection

A student's emotional, behavioral and/or mental health illness very often affects their ability to learn and be successful in school. Many of these students require extra support and/or special education services to be successful. Some students suffering with mental health illness are considered "disabled" as defined by the law. There are several federal, state, and local laws and policies enacted to protect the rights of students with disabilities, which include students disabled due to mental illness. Although these policies and laws are very important, the two with the greatest impact in working with students with mental health disabilities are the Individual with Disabilities Education Act (IDEA) and accommodations through Section 504 of the Rehabilitation Act (1973) (U.S. Department of Education [USDE], 2010).

The Individuals with Disabilities Education Improvement Act (IDEIA) (2004) mandates that all students with disabilities receive a free appropriate public education to meet their unique needs and prepare them for further education, employment, and independent living (USDE, 2010). Prior to IDEIA, over 4 million students with disabilities were denied appropriate access to public education. Many students were denied entry into public school altogether, while others were placed in segregated classrooms, or in regular classrooms without adequate support for their special needs (USDE, 2010). IDEIA has four parts: A, B, C, and D. Part A of IDEIA outlines the basic foundation of the Act, defines the terms used within the Act, and explains the purpose and responsibilities of the Office of Special Education Programs as it relates to the ACT. Part B of IDEIA outlines the educational guidelines for school children 3-21 years of age. IDEIA provides financial support to states and local school districts. In order to receive IDEIA funding, IDEA requires school districts to comply with these six main principles:

1. Zero Rejection which means that schools must educate all children with disabilities regardless of the nature or severity of the disability.
2. Provide a *Free Appropriate Public Education* (FAPE) to students who qualify as a student in need of special education services.
3. Evaluate a child to consider if s/he is a child in need of special education services, upon request of parent or suspicion of the district.
4. Provide a FAPE to students in the *Least Restrictive Environment*, such that students are presumed able to be educated with their nondisabled peers.
5. Include parents in educational decision making.
6. Provide information to parents regarding parents' rights to challenge actions taken by the district regarding their child's FAPE.

Part C of IDEA refers to early identification of and interventions for children with disabilities with children from birth to 2 years of age. This portion of IDEA provides guidelines concerning the funding and services families may be entitled to base on their child's needs. Families receive an Individualized Family Service Plan (IFSP). This plan lays out the priorities, resources, and concerns of the family. It also describes the goals for the child, the services to be provided, and steps for eventual transitioning of the child into formal education. The final section of IDEIA, part D, describes national activities, such as grants, projects, additional resources, to be undertaken to improve the education of children with disabilities.

414

The IDEIA and accommodations though Section 504 of the Rehabilitation Act (1973), require all public schools and private schools who receive federal funding to provide special services for students with disabilities (USDE, 1995). For students with mental health needs to be considered eligible for these special services, a student is eligible under Section 504 if they have a physical or mental impairment that substantially limits one or more of the student's major life activities. Under the IDEA, a student needs to fall within one of the set disability categories and must be in need of special-designed instruction in order to qualify. If the student's mental health problem meets this criterion, the student may be considered disabled under the categories of emotional impairment or other health impairment. The student's parent(s), the legally responsible caregiver of the child, or the school system (e.g. classroom teacher or school social worker) can request the student be evaluated for special education services. Once the school system receives this request in writing, the school has 30 days to complete the assessment to determine eligibility for services.

The assessment is usually completed by a team which may include the school or school district's social worker, psychologist, teachers, school nurses and others depending on the student's individual needs. The assessment usually consists of a series of psychological tests that help the team learn more about the student's abilities, behavior, and day-to-day functioning at school. The assessment may also include pertinent information about the student's educational and medical history, social and emotional development, and how they function at school in all settings. IDEIA requires that a Functional Behavioral Assessment (FBA) be completed when: (1) a child with a disability is removed or absent for more than ten school days, (2) for any misconduct that may or may not be a manifestation of the child's disability or involves weapons, drugs, or serious bodily injury, regardless of the outcome of the manifestation determination review, or (3) for behavior that interferes with the learning environment (IDEIA, 2004).

After completion of the assessment, and if the student is deemed eligible for services, the Individualized Education Plan (IEP) is created. The team, which includes the student (age 13 or older) and his/her parents, put together the most appropriate educational plan including any special services for the student. Specific goals, along with objective outcome measures are determined. In addition to outlining educational goals and expectations, the FBA is carefully reviewed and a Behavioral Intervention Plan (BIP), also called a Positive Behavioral Support Plan (PBSP) is developed. The BIP/PBSP specifically targets the student's undesirable behaviors with interventions that are linked to the functions of the behavior; each intervention specifically addresses a measurable, clearly-stated targeted behavior (Special Education Guide, 2016). The BIP includes prevention strategies geared toward stopping undesirable behavior before it begins, as well as appropriate behaviors and strategies to teach the student appropriate ways to deal with the situation. Environmental concerns are key to the student's success. After considering all information, such as the IEP, FBA and BIP/PBSP, the IEP team may determine that a change in a student's schedule or in the arrangement of his or her classroom is necessary and should be part of the BIP. Because the BIP is a legal document and part of the student's IEP, it must be adhered to completely, and it cannot be modified without a formal IEP team meeting. If a student experiences disciplinary removals resulting in a change of placement for more than ten days, the law requires that the IEP team meet to determine manifestation of the child's disability, which may require a change in the IEP and/or BIP (Special Education Guide, 2016). At the IEP team meeting, the team reviews whether or not the student's disruptive behavior which caused him/her to be removed from their class is a manifestation of their disability and whether or not the student can safely return back to their former classroom. Only after the team has reviewed the students current IEP, FBA and BIP/PBSP and discussed all possible modifications and changes that may need to be implemented, the student may return back to their former classroom. If the team rules that the students present learning environment if not safe, and or meeting the student's needs, a change in placement may be required.

A Section 504 Plan is a legal document that provides services and accommodations to regular education students. Section 504 of the Rehabilitation Act of 1973, defines a disability as a "physical or mental impairment that substantially limits a person's ability to participate in a major life activity, such as learning" (U.S. Department of Labor, 1973). Section 504 has a much broader definition of "disability" than is stated in the specific disabilities listed in IDEA. To be eligible for a Section 504 Plan the only requirement that must be met is that the student has a disability and that the disability must interfere with the student's ability to learn in a general education classroom. Therefore, students who may not be eligible for an IEP might be eligible for a Section 504 Plan.

A Section 504 Plan's intent is to help meet a student's physical or emotional need, enabling them to achieve academic success in school, within in a regular classroom setting. The students' parents or care giver may request a Section 504 Plan for their child. The rules regarding who must participate on the Section 504 team are less specific than they are for an IEP. The team usually consists of people who are familiar with the student, understand the evaluation data, and the special services options. Unlike an IEP, there is no standard a Section 504 Plan and it doesn't have to be a written document. The plan usually includes:

- list of specific accommodations
- supports or services for the student
- names of who will provide each service
- name of the person responsible for ensuring the plan is implemented

Some examples of accommodations requested may include: adjustment to test taking (more time, questions given orally), seating near the blackboard or near the teacher, and/or be excused from class to get medications. Legally schools are required to notify parents / care givers if any accommodations are not able to be met or need to be changed, however unlike the IEP, a formal meeting is not required. Also unlike IEP's that are required to be reviewed at least once a year, each individual state determines when Section 504 Plans are reviewed and reevaluated. In addition, States do not receive extra funding for Section 504 Plan students as they do for students with IEP's, however the federal government can take funding away from schools / programs who do not comply with Section 504 Plans and guidelines.

Privacy and Confidentiality

The Family Educational Rights and Privacy Act (FERPA) (20 U.S.C. § 1232g; 34 CFR Part 99) is a federal law that protects the privacy of student education records (USDE, 2015). The law applies to all schools that receive funds under an applicable program of the USDE. Under FERPA, parents have access to their child's education record until the child turns 18 years old and is deemed an "eligible student". At 18 these rights transfer to the student, unless the student is declared legally incompetent to handle their own affairs.

Schools must have written permission from the parent or eligible student to release any information from a student's education record, except in certain circumstances as noted below. It is important to note what is considered part of the education record. According to FERPA (34 CFR § 99.2) education records are records that are directly related to a student and are maintained by an educational agency or institution, or by a party acting for or on behalf of the agency or institution. These records include but are not limited to grades, transcripts, class lists, student course schedules, health records (at the K-12 level), student financial information (at the postsecondary level), and student discipline files. FERPA allows schools to disclose those records, without consent, to the following parties or under the following conditions (34 CFR § 99.31):

- School officials with legitimate educational interest
- Other schools to which a student is transferring
- Specified officials for audit or evaluation purposes
- Appropriate parties about financial aid to a student
- Organizations conducting certain studies for or on behalf of the school
- Accrediting organizations
- To comply with a judicial order or lawfully issued subpoena
- Appropriate officials in cases of health and safety emergencies
- State and local authorities, within a juvenile justice system, pursuant to specific State law

It is important to note that in cases of health and safety emergencies, such as a student potentially harming themselves or others, schools have the right to release confidential information to the proper authorities to ensure safety. Any information so shared during the emergency must be relevant to the situation and appropriately limited to the safety concern at the time. Adherence to confidentiality and privacy should otherwise be maintained.

The Health Insurance Portability and Accountability Act (HIPAA); Pub.L. 104–191, 110 Stat. 1936, enacted August 21, 1996) is a law created to protect the confidentiality and security of healthcare information (U.S. Department of Health & Human Services [USDHHS], 2017). However, in most cases, the HIPAA Privacy Rule does not apply to schools because the school is either not a HIPAA covered entity or is a HIPAA covered entity but maintains health information only in the student's education records which is protected by FERPA, therefore, is not subject to the HIPAA Privacy Rule (USDHSS, 2017).

Psychotropic Medication

Psychotropic medications, which include anticonvulsants, antidepressants, antihypertensive, antipsychotics (neuroleptics), anxiolytics (antianxiety), mood stabilizers, selective norepinephrine reuptake inhibitors, selective serotonin reuptake inhibitors, and stimulants, are often used to treat psychiatric disorders or illnesses in students. There are few laws that specifically address the administration of psychotropic medications to students (Asher, 2013), thus mandating that schools treat psychotropic medication in the same way as other medications. Under the federal law, IDEIA (2004) and Section 504, schools that receive federal funding are mandated to provide "required related services", including medication administration. Depending on state law, some states only permit licensed personnel to administer medication to students, while other states allow school personnel to administer medication and consult with parents regarding the efficacy of medications in connection with academic, functional, or behavioral performance in school.

The NASN encourages school districts to develop written medication administration policies and procedures that focus on safe and efficient medication administration, which includes all medication types including psychotropic (NASN, 2017). It is important that these policies are consistent with federal and state laws, nursing practice standards and established safe practices in accordance with evidence based information. The administration of emergency psychotropic medications or as needed medications (PRN's), should adhere to the same state laws, regulations, guidelines, and local school district policies and protocols. The school nurse should have a detailed emergency care plan in place based upon the student's prescribing provider's orders regarding the use of the medication.

Psychotropic medications can be very useful medications in treating the student's mental illness but the student may experience negative side effects. As students begin to feel the positive effects of the medication, they may discontinue them due to the negative side effects (e.g. weight gain), or their belief that they no longer need the medication because they feel so much better. In accordance with IDEIA (2004) the *Prohibition on Mandatory Medication Amendment*, schools are prohibited from requiring a child to take a psychiatric drug as a requisite for attending school. Through building positive relationships with students, school nurses can encourage, educate, and counsel students to continue their medication. School nurses, through ongoing assessment and careful monitoring, must communicate and collaborate closely with the underage student's parents, and primary healthcare provider. They must be alert to any behavior changes as well as medication refusal. Most psychotropic medications maintain a therapeutic blood level for a period of time, therefore it can take time before the medication is no longer effective. Intervention is indicated if a student, without a healthcare provider's order, discontinues necessary medication. However, schools cannot force students to take medication as a condition to attend school. Schools are required by federal and state laws, and school district, policies, to provide a safe school environment for all students. If a student is disruptive and this results in an unsafe environment or the student demonstrates unsafe behavior that can result in harm to themselves or others, school administration is, in many cases, required to remove the student from the school environment. It is not uncommon in the case of a student with a mental health illness, for a symptomatic student, to be transported to a local emergency room for assessment and evaluation.

Students who are re-entering the school after a hospitalization often need a great deal of support, which requires team communication, collaboration, and flexibility. The team needs to meet prior to the re-entry back into the school to create an action plan for re-entry. The team must review all current and relevant documents and findings that may impact the student's academic success, as well as safety. The students current IEP and BIP need to be reviewed and modified if need be. Prior to changing or modifying the BIP, a FBA may need to be completed. The FBA will review and update any strategies to incorporate in the BIP in the areas of:

- Prevention
- Replacement behavior instruction
- Positive reinforcement
- Planned consequences
- Emergency interventions, if appropriate
- Home/School collaboration (Resa, 2008)

Safety and Emergencies

Suicide is the third leading cause of death for youth under age 18 (NAMI, 2014). Students with disabilities, which include mental health disabilities, are at increased risk of self-harming behaviors whether intentional and unintentional, including suicide. Prevention is the number one goal. Over the past decade, a great deal of legislative focus has centered on policy concerning prevention, early intervention, and crisis preparedness regarding psychiatric emergencies (NAMI, 2014). According to NAMI, Congress has mandated that states allocate 5 percent of their 2015 federal mental health block grant funds to early intervention with youth experiencing symptoms of psychosis (2014). School districts must have detailed policies and procedures to assess safety in schools. During IEP team meetings and BIP development, school personnel, the student, and family must discuss safety concerns and develop a plan to deal with a psychiatric emergency safely and effectively. This plan needs to be shared with all school personnel working with the student in the event the plan needs to be implemented. School districts seeking to avoid liability issues are those that have developed and implemented effective policies and procedures regarding the handling of psychiatric emergencies that could arise (Knoll, 2015).

CONCLUSION

At the present time, there are no universal standards for mental health screening for children. There are no specific federal laws, other than IDEA and Section 504 of the Rehabilitation Act, mandating mental health services for children or adolescents. Individual states have started to implement policies and regulations regarding such services; however, they vary from state to state and dependent upon funding. Because children/adolescents spend the majority of their day in school, schools play a significant role in early identification and intervention. School nurses are stepping up to take a leading role in educating personnel, families, students and policy makers on mental illness and its impact on students, families, and communities.

RESOURCES

Family Educational Rights and Privacy Act (FERPA).
http://www2.ed.gov/policy/gen/guid/fpco/ferpa/index.html

The Health Insurance Portability and Accountability Act (HIPPA)
https://www.hhs.gov/hipaa/

Individuals with Disabilities Education Improvement Act. (2004). 20 U.S.C. 1400, § 602 (26) [Definitions]. Code Federal Regulations (CFR), part 300.
http://uscode.house.gov/view.xhtml?path=/prelim@title20/chapter33&edition=prelim

Section 504 of the Rehabilitation Act of 1973 (P.L. 102-569. 199229 U.S.C.A – 794; 34 C.F. R., Part 104). U.S. Department of Labor.
https://www.dol.gov/oasam/regs/statutes/sec504.htm

REFERENCES

American Academy of Pediatrics, Committee on Psychosocial Aspects of Child and Family Health and Task Force on Mental Health. (2009). The future of pediatrics: Mental health competencies for pediatric primary care. *Pediatrics, 124*(1), 410-421. Retrieved from http://pediatrics.aappublications.org/content/124/1/410

Asher, A. (2013). *Teachers are partners in the treatment of special education students prescribed psychotropic medications.* National Center for Youth Law. Retrieved from https://youthlaw.org/publication/teachers-as-partners-in-the-treatment-of-special-education-students-prescribed-psychotropic-medications/

Cooper, G.D., Clements, P.T., & Holt, K.E. (2012). Examining childhood bullying and adolescent suicide: Implications for school nurses. *The Journal of School Nursing, 28*, 275-283. doi: 10.1177/1059840512438617

Knoll, J. (2015). Lessons from litigation. *Psychiatric Times*. Retrieved from http://www.psychiatrictimes.com/career/lessons-litigation

National Association of School Nurses. (2012). *The case for school nursing.* Retrieved from http://www.nasn.org/portals/0/about/2012_The_Case_for_School_Nursing.pdf

National Association of School Nurses. (2017). Medication administration in the school setting. *Position Statement*. Retrieved from https://schoolnursenet.nasn.org/blogs/nasn-profile/2017/03/13/medication-administration-in-schools

National Alliance on Mental Illness. (2014). *State mental health legislation 2014 trends, themes & effective practices.* Retrieved from http://www.nami.org/legreport2014

Resa, W. (2008). *Guidelines for behavior intervention.* Retrieved from http://www.lcisd.k12.mi.us/UserFiles/Servers/Server_78652/File/specialed/Behavior/WAYNE%20RESA%20Behavior%20Document.pdf

Special Education Guide. (2016). *Functional: Behavioral assessment and behavior intervention plans*. Retrieved from http://www.specialeducationguide.com/pre-k-12/behavior-and-classroom-management/functional-behavior-assessment-and-behavior-intervention-plans/

U.S. Department of Education. (1995). *The civil rights of students with hidden disabilities under section 504 of the rehabilitation act of 1973. Office for civil rights.* Retrieved from http://www2.ed.gov/about/offices/list/ocr/docs/hq5269.html

U.S. Department of Education. (2004). *Individuals with Disabilities Education Improvement Act.* 20 U.S.C. 1400, § 602 (26) [Definitions]. Code Federal Regulations (CFR), part 300. Retrieved from: http://uscode.house.gov/view.xhtml?path=/prelim@title20/chapter33&edition=prelim

U.S. Department of Education. (2010*). Thirty-five years of progress in educating children with disabilities through IDEA.* Retrieved from http://www2.ed.gov/about/offices/list/osers/idea35/history/idea-35-history.pdf

U.S. Department of Education. (2015). *Family educational rights and privacy Act (FERPA). Family Policy Compliance Office.* Retrieved from http://www2.ed.gov/policy/gen/guid/fpco/ferpa/index.html

U.S. Department of Health & Human Services. (2017). *Health information privacy.* Retrieved from https://www.hhs.gov/hipaa/

U.S. Department of Health & Human Services. (2017). *The Health Insurance Portability and Accountability Act* (HIPAA). Pub.L. 104–191, 110 Stat. 1936. Retrieved from: https://www.hhs.gov/hipaa/

U.S. Department of Labor (1973). *Section 504 of the Rehabilitation Act.* (P.L. 102-569. 199229 U.S.C.A – 794; 34 C.F.R., Part 104). Retrieved from https://www.dol.gov/oasam/regs/statutes/sec504.htm

Zupp, A. (2013). School nurses as gatekeepers to plan, prepare, and prevent child and youth suicide. *NASN School Nurse*, *28*(1), 24-26. Retrieved from http://journals.sagepub.com/doi/pdf/10.1177/1942602X12468331

Chapter 32

NALOXONE USE IN THE SCHOOL SETTING

Rebecca King, MSN, RN, NCSN

DESCRIPTION OF ISSUE

The United States is in the midst of an epidemic of opioid drug overdose (poisoning) deaths. Since 2000, the rate of deaths from drug overdoses has increased 137%, including a 200% increase in the rate of overdose deaths involving opioids (opioid pain relievers and heroin) (Rudd, Aleshire, Zibbell, & Gladden, 2016). Together, heroin and prescription pain medications take the lives of more than 28,000 Americans per year — over 75 people per day. They also cause hundreds of thousands of non-fatal overdoses and an incalculable amount of emotional suffering and preventable healthcare expenses (Davis, 2016).

Efforts are needed in school communities to protect youth prone to experimentation and persons already dependent on opioids from overdose and other harms. This includes expanding access to and use of naloxone, a safe and effective antidote for all opioid-related overdoses (Volkow, Aleshire, Zibbell, & Gladden, 2014).

The safe and effective management of opioid pain reliever (OPR)-related overdose in schools should be incorporated into the school emergency preparedness and response plan. The registered professional school nurse (hereinafter referred to as school nurse) can provide leadership in all phases of emergency preparedness and response. When emergencies happen, including drug-related emergencies, managing incidents at school is vital to positive outcomes. The school nurse is an essential part of the school team responsible for developing emergency response procedures. School nurses in this role should facilitate access to naloxone for the management of OPR-related overdose in the school setting (National Association of School Nurses [NASN], 2015a).

BACKGROUND

The opioid epidemic is one of unintended consequences. Dr. Nora Volkow, Director of the National Institute on Drug Abuse with the National Institutes of Health, presented at the Senate Caucus on International Narcotics Control on May 14, 2014 and stated several factors are likely to have contributed to the severity of the current prescription drug abuse problem we are facing today. They include drastic increases in the number of prescriptions written and dispensed, greater social acceptability for using medications for different purposes, and aggressive marketing by pharmaceutical companies (Volkow, 2014). The abuse of and addiction to opioids such as heroin, morphine, and prescription pain relievers is a serious global problem that affects the health, social, and economic welfare of all societies. The number of prescriptions written for opioid pain relievers escalated from around 76 million in 1991 to nearly 207 million in 2013, with the United States their biggest consumer globally, accounting for almost 100 percent of the world total for hydrocodone (*e.g.,* Vicodin) and 81 percent for oxycodone (*e.g.,* Percocet) (Volkow et al., 2014).

Drug overdose deaths involving heroin continue to sharply rise, with heroin overdoses more than tripling in four years. This increase mirrors large increases in heroin use across the country and has been demonstrated to be closely tied to opioid pain reliever misuse and dependence. Past misuse of prescription opioids is the strongest risk factor for heroin initiation and use, specifically among persons who report past-year dependence or abuse (Jones, Logan, Gladden, & Bohm, 2015). The increased availability of heroin, combined with its relatively low price (compared with diverted prescription opioids) and high purity appear to be major drivers of the upward trend in heroin use and overdose (Cicero, Ellis, Surratt, & Kurtz, 2014).

Implications for Youth

This epidemic has placed our students and school communities at serious risk. Studies indicate that one in four teens have taken a prescription drug for reasons other than for what it was intended and 16.8% of 12th grade students report taking a prescription drug (e.g., Oxycontin, Percocet, Vicodin, codeine, Adderall, Ritalin, or Xanax) without a prescription one or more times during their life (Feliz, 2014; Kann et al., 2016). Recent data indicates that opioid related deaths in youth between the ages of 12-25 has either doubled, tripled or quadrupled in 35 states (Trust for America's Health, 2015). Additionally, more than 90% of adults who develop a substance use disorder began using before they were 18 years old (Healthday, 2015).

When asked how prescription opioids were obtained for nonmedical use, more than half of the 12th graders surveyed said they were given the drugs or bought them from a friend or relative. Youth who abuse prescription medications are also more likely to report use of other drugs. Multiple studies have revealed associations between prescription drug abuse and higher rates of cigarette smoking; heavy episodic drinking; and marijuana, cocaine, and other illicit drug use among adolescents, young adults, and college students in the United States (Substance Abuse and Mental Health Services Administration [SAMSHA], 2011).

Schools additionally need to be attuned to an unlikely subset of students who have the potential to misuse opioid painkillers- the student athlete. The number of participants in high school sports increased for the 27th consecutive year in 2015-16 according to the annual High School Athletics Participation Survey conducted by the National Federation of State High School Associations (NFHS). Based on figures from the 51 NFHS member state high school associations, which includes the District of Columbia, the number of participants in high school sports reached an all-time high of 7,868,900 (NFHS, 2016). Every 25 seconds, or 1.35 million times a year, a young athlete suffers a sports injury severe enough to go to the emergency room (Safe Kids Worldwide, 2013). These injuries place young adolescents at risk for substance use disorder because of increased access to opioid medications through prescriptions or handouts from injured teammates. By the time high school athletes become seniors, approximately 11% will have used a narcotic pain reliever such as OxyContin or Vicodin—for nonmedical purposes (Veliz, Boyd, & McCabe, 2013).

An overdose of opioids (either from prescribed opioid painkillers or heroin) decreases respirations and if not reversed, will cause death. While education and prevention is necessary to curb this epidemic, every effort must be made to prevent death from an overdose. School nurses are first responders in the school setting and should have as many available tools as they can to save lives. Naloxone is an opioid antagonist, and immediately reverses the life-threatening effect of an overdose. Naloxone has been available for use in the U.S. since 1971 and directly targets opioid receptor sites reversing the cause of opioid related deaths, respiratory depression. It has no other action if opioids are not in the system (Wermeling, 2015). Naloxone is available for administration via two routes, intra-nasally and in an auto-injector to be given intramuscularly.

Legal Response to the Epidemic

New Mexico became the first state to recognize the lifesaving ability of naloxone and enact legislation to increase access in 2001. Forty-six states and D.C. now have laws providing immunity to medical professionals, including school nurses, who prescribe or dispense naloxone or persons who administer naloxone. The majority of these laws were passed within the last five years and promote the use of naloxone in addition to training and education on recognizing and preventing overdoses (National Conference of State Legislators [NCSL], 2016).

School Nurses as Change Agents

"This can't happen to me", "not my kid", or "not in our school" are very scary words anyone, any parent or any school or district administrator can say. Addiction can happen to anyone, anywhere...it does not discriminate. School nurses are first responders in the school setting and are leaders in planning for and managing emergencies in the school setting. School nurses practicing primary prevention also work to prevent potential emergencies by raising awareness, and educating students and families on healthy behaviors and reducing risks. School nurses now possess a naloxone position document from the National Association of School Nurses (NASN) (2015a) endorsing school nurses have access to naloxone just like they do with other lifesaving medications such as epinephrine for life threatening peanut allergies. Early access to naloxone in the event of an opioid overdose can prevent loss of life and often is the first step in recovery in opioid abuse (NASN, 2015a).

IMPLICATIONS FOR SCHOOL NURSE PRACTICE

Administration of Naloxone

Opioid overdose kills thousands of Americans every year. Many of these deaths are preventable through the timely provision of the inexpensive, safe, and effective drug naloxone and the summoning of emergency responders (Davis, Webb & Burris, 2013). In response to this public health crisis, many state laws are being enacted or amended to increase access to naloxone and encourage bystanders to summon medical assistance in the event of overdose. There are laws aimed at increasing lay access to naloxone by reducing barriers to prescription and administration and laws that address criminal concerns for Good Samaritans who summon aid in overdose situations.

Once only given in the inpatient hospital setting, naloxone use has expanded to communities in an effort to save lives in the midst of the opioid overdose epidemic. Community access to naloxone was historically limited by laws and regulations that pre-date the overdose epidemic. In an attempt to reverse the unprecedented increase in preventable overdose deaths, the majority of states have recently amended those laws to increase access to emergency care and treatment for opiate overdose (Davis, 2016). By June 22, 2016, all but three states (KS, MT, and WY) had passed legislation designed to improve layperson naloxone access. These states have made it easier for people who might be in a position to assist in an overdose to access the medication, encouraged those individuals to summon emergency responders, or both (Davis, 2016).

Although naloxone is a prescription drug, it is not a controlled substance and has no potential for abuse (Davis, 2016). It is regularly carried by medical first responders (professional responders such as police, firefighters, and EMS personnel) but can also be administered by ordinary citizens with little or no formal training, making it ideal for use in a school setting. School nurses act as first responders in the school setting and can train staff, school resource officers or unlicensed assistive personnel (UAP) on its use.

Concerns have been similarly voiced around the use in schools of the lifesaving drug epinephrine, a rescue medication for anaphylaxis. On November 13, 2013, 113 P.L. 48, *School Access to Emergency Epinephrine Act*, made a certification concerning the adequacy of the state's civil liability protection law to protect trained school personnel who may administer epinephrine to a student reasonably believed to be having an anaphylactic reaction. This act requires elementary and secondary schools in such a state to:

1) permit trained personnel to administer epinephrine to a student reasonably believed to be having such a reaction,

2) maintain a supply of epinephrine in a secure location that is easily accessible to trained personnel for such treatment, and

3) have in place a plan for having on the school premises during operating hours one or more designated personnel trained in administration of epinephrine (H.R. 2094, 2016).

In 2015 the American Heart Association (AHA) stated in their CPR and ECC (Emergency Cardiovascular Care) Guidelines that unresponsive persons with known or suspected opioid overdose can be administered naloxone with apparent safety and effectiveness in the first aid and BLS (Basic Life Support) setting. They are now recommending naloxone administration by lay rescuers and HCPs (healthcare providers), and they are offering simplified training (AHA, 2015).

Support for Naloxone Access in Schools

Increased naloxone access is supported by a large number and variety of organizations, including the World Health Organization, the American Medical Association, the American Public Health Association, and the National Association of Boards of Pharmacy. It is a key component of the federal government's response to the overdose epidemic, and is supported by agencies including the Centers for Disease Control and Prevention (CDC), the Substance Abuse and Mental Health Services Administration (SAMHSA), and the Office of National Drug Control Policy (Davis, 2015).

In an effort to save more lives from opioid overdose, SAMSHA published the *Opioid Overdose Prevention Toolkit – 2014*. The toolkit equips communities and local governments with material to develop policies and practices to help prevent opioid-related overdoses and deaths. It also serves as a foundation for educating and training (SAMHSA, 2016).

Massachusetts demonstrated that opioid overdose death rates were reduced in communities where state supported overdose education and nasal naloxone distribution (OEND) programs were implemented. They equipped people at risk for overdose and bystanders with nasal naloxone rescue kits and trained them how to prevent, recognize, and respond to an overdose by engaging emergency medical services, providing rescue breathing, and delivering naloxone. This study provides observational evidence that by training potential bystanders to prevent, recognize and respond to opioid overdoses, OEND is an effective intervention (Walley et al., 2013).

Implementation of a Naloxone Administration Program in School

Schools should be responsible for anticipating and preparing to respond to a variety of emergencies (Doyle, 2013). The school nurse is often the first health professional who responds to an emergency in the school setting. The school nurse possesses the education and knowledge to identify emergent situations, manage the emergency until relieved by emergency medical services (EMS) personnel, communicate the assessment and interventions to EMS personnel, and follow up with the healthcare provider. This harm reduction approach can prevent overdose deaths by reversing life-threatening respiratory depression. When administered quickly and effectively, naloxone has the potential to immediately restore breathing to a victim experiencing an opioid overdose (Hardesty, 2014).

In September 2016, the NASN introduced the *Naloxone in Schools Toolkit* as part of the association's proactive efforts to educate school communities about the country's ongoing opioid epidemic, following the release of their position document in June 2015 about use of naloxone in the school setting. The toolkit includes training presentations and resources to help school nurses, leaders, and community members take the appropriate steps to identify and react to a possible opioid overdose in a school setting.

The toolkit provides a list of essential questions to consider in the development of a Naloxone in School Program and can serve as a needs assessment and guide to begin program implementation. The questions can help guide schools in assessing state laws, district policies, state school nurse practice, education, medication storage, and community need.

Where laws permit, the school nurse is also capable of training unlicensed assistive personnel (UAP) or other lay staff in the use and administration of naloxone. It is the professional responsibility of the school nurse to identify UAP in the school setting and to train, evaluate for competency, monitor and supervise the selected individuals (NASN, 2015b).

According to NASN's *Naloxone in Schools Toolkit* (2016), training of UAP's should entail:

- Asking whether delegation of naloxone administration to UAPs is a safe decision based on the structure of the school environment, school nurse: pupil ratio, and other roles and responsibilities of the school nurse.

- Deciding if there are enough UAPs willing and competent, in each school building, to administer naloxone to ensure a safe and timely response to a potential overdose.

- Educating the UAP to determine when naloxone should be administered, what potential side effects look like, and what supportive care should follow.

- Determining how often education and training will be provided.

- Determining if the UAPs trained to administer naloxone should also be required to be certified in CPR.

CONCLUSION

According to Davis (2016), it is reasonable to believe that laws that encourage the prescription and use of naloxone and the timely seeking of emergency medical assistance will have the intended effect of reducing opioid overdose deaths. Such laws have few if any foreseeable negative effects, can be implemented at little or no cost, and will likely save both lives and resources.

It is undisputed that, if administered in time, naloxone reverses opioid overdose in the vast majority of cases (Davis, 2016). Medical risks regarding naloxone administration are low, and in most if not all cases are much lower than failing to administer the medication in the event of opioid overdose. The sooner naloxone is administered and respiratory depression is reversed, the better outcomes are likely to be. It therefore makes sense to increase access to the medication, and to fund robust evaluations to ensure that increased access has the intended effect, that any negative consequences are addressed, and that best practices are identified and publicized (Davis, 2015).

RESOURCES

Centers for Disease Control and Prevention. (2016). Injury Prevention & Control: Opioid Overdose. http://www.cdc.gov/drugoverdose/pubs/index.html

Centers for Disease Control and Prevention (CDC). (2015a). Injury prevention and control: Prescription drug abuse. Retrieved from http://www.cdc.gov/drugoverdose/

Centers for Disease Control and Prevention (CDC). (2015b). *Data overview*. Retrieved from http://www.cdc.gov/drugoverdose/data/index.html

Centers for Disease Control and Prevention (CDC). (2016). *High school youth risk behavior survey, 2015*. Retrieved from www.cdc.gov/healthyyouth/data/yrbs/pdf/2015/ss6506_updated.pdf

Davis, C. (June 2015). Naloxone for Community Opioid Overdose Reversal. Policy Brief. Public Health Law Research: Making the Case for Laws that Improve Health. http://publichealthlawresearch.org

Davis, C. (June 2016). Legal Interventions to Reduce Overdose Mortality: Naloxone Access and Overdose Good Samaritan Laws, The Network for Public Health Law. Retrieved from: https://networkforphl.org/_asset/qz5pvn/network-naloxone-10-4.pdf

National Association of School Nurses. (2015a). *Naloxone use in the school setting: The role of the school nurse* (Position Statement). Silver Spring, MD: Author.

National Association of School Nurses. (2015b). *Unlicensed assistive personnel: Their role on the school health services team* (Position Statement). Silver Spring, MD: Author.

National Association of School Nurses. (2016). Naloxone in Schools Toolkit. https://www.pathlms.com/nasn/courses/3353. The toolkit includes training presentations and resources to help school nurses, leaders, and community members take the appropriate steps to identify and react to a possible opioid overdose in a school setting.

National Association of School Nurses. Drugs of Abuse. https://www.nasn.org/ToolsResources/DrugsofAbuse

National Conference of State Legislators. (4/12/2016). Drug Overdose Immunity and Good Samaritan Laws. http://www.ncsl.org/research/civil-and-criminal-justice/drug-overdose-immunity-good-samaritan-laws.aspx

National Institute on Drug Abuse (NIDA). https://www.drugabuse.gov/related-topics/trends-statistics

Network for Public Health Law. (2016). *Legal interventions to reduce overdose mortality: naloxone access and overdose good samaritan laws.* https://www.networkforphl.org/_asset/qz5pvn/network-naloxone-10-4.pdf

Substance Abuse and Mental Health Services Administration (SAMHSA). *Opioid overdose prevention toolkit - updated 2016.* http://store.samhsa.gov/product/opioid-overdose-prevention-toolkit-updated-2016/sma16-4742

REFERENCES

American Heart Association. (2015). *2015 American Heart Association (AHA) guidelines update for CPR and emergency cardiovascular care (ECC).* Dallas, TX: American Heart Association.

Cicero, T.J., Ellis, M.S., Surratt, H.L., & Kurtz, S.P. (2014). The changing face of heroin use in the United States: A retrospective analysis of the past fifty years. *JAMA Psychiatry* 2014,*71*, 821–6. doi: 1001/jamapsychiatry.2014.366

Davis, C., Webb, D., & Burris, S. (2013). Changing law from barrier to facilitator of opioid overdose prevention. Symposium conducted at the Public Health Law Conference: Practical Approaches to Critical Challenges, Spring 2013. *Journal of Law and Medical Ethics, 41*(1), 33-36. doi: 10.1111/jlme.12035

Davis, C. (2015, June). *Naloxone for community opioid overdose reversal* (Policy Brief). Public Health Law Research: Making the Case for Laws that Improve Health. http://publichealthlawresearch.org

Davis, C. (2016, June). *Legal Interventions to reduce overdose mortality: Naloxone access and overdose Good Samaritan laws.* The Network for Public Health Law. Retrieved from https://networkforphl.org/_asset/qz5pvn/network-naloxone-10-4.pdf

Doyle, J. (2013). Emergency management, crisis response, and the school nurse's role. In J. Selekman (Ed.) *School nursing: A comprehensive text* (2nd ed.) (pp. 1216-1244). Philadelphia, PA: F.A. Davis Company.

Feliz, R. (2014). *National study: Teens report higher use of performance enhancing substances.* Partnership for DrugFree Kids. Retrieved from http://www.drugfree.org/newsroom/pats-2013-teens-report-higher-use-of-performance-enhancing-substances

Hardesty, C. (2014). Five things to know about *opioid overdose*. Office of Drug Control Policy. Retrieved from http://whitehouse.gov/blog/2014/02/10/5-things-know-about-opioid-overdoses

Healthday. (2011, July 29). *Addiction starts early in American society, report finds.* U.S. News and World Report. Retrieved from http://health.usnews.com/health-news/family-health/childrens-health/articles/2011/06/29/ addiction-starts-early-in-american-society-re-port-finds

H.R. 2094. (2013). *School access to Emergency Epinephrine Act*. Retrieved from https://www.congress.gov/bill/113th-congress/senate-bill/1503

Jones, C.M., Logan, J., Gladden, R.M., & Bohm, M.K. (2015). Vital signs: demographic and substance use trends among heroin users—United States, 2002–2013. *MMWR Morbidity Mortality Weekly Report 2015, 64,* 719–25. Retrieved from http://www.physiciansforlife.org/cdc-vital-signs-demographic-and-substance-use-trends-among-heroin-users-united-states-2002-2013/

Kann, L., McManus, T., Harris, W.A., Shanklin, S.L., Flint, K.H., Hawkins, J., ... & Zaza, S. (2016). Youth Risk Behavior Surveillance — United States, 2015. *MMWR Surveillance Summary 2016, 65*(No. SS-6),1–174. Retrieved from http://www.cdc.gov/healthyyouth/data/yrbs/pdf/2015/ss6506_updated.pdf

National Association of School Nurses. (2015a). *Naloxone use in the school setting: The role of the school nurse* (Position Statement). Silver Spring, MD: Author.

National Association of School Nurses. (2015b). *Unlicensed assistive personnel: Their role on the school health services team* (Position Statement). Silver Spring, MD: Author.

National Conference of State Legislators. (2016, April 12). *Drug overdose immunity and Good Samaritan laws*. Retrieved from http://www.ncsl.org/research/civil-and-criminal-justice/drug-overdose-immunity-good-samaritan-laws.aspx

National Federation of State High School Associations. (2016). *High school sports participation increases for 27th consecutive year*. Retrieved from https://www.nfhs.org/articles/high-school-sports-participation-increases-for-27th-consecutive-year/

Rudd, R.A., Aleshire, N. Zibbell, J.E., & Gladden, M. (2016, January 1). Increases in drug and opioid overdose deaths-United States, 2000–2014. *MMWR Morbidity Mortality Weekly Report, 64*(50), pp. 1378-82. Retrieved from https://www.cdc.gov/mmwr/preview/mmwrhtml/mm6450a3.htm

Safe Kids Worldwide. (2013). *1.35 million children seen in emergency rooms for sports-related injuries.* Retrieved from http://www.safekids.org/press-release/135-million-children-seen-emergency-rooms-sports-related-injuries

Substance Abuse and Mental Health Services Administration. (2016). *SAMHSA opioid overdose prevention toolkit*. HHS Publication No. (SMA) 14-4742. Rockville, MD: Substance Abuse and Mental Health Services Administration. Retrieved from http://store.samhsa.gov/shin/content//SMA16-4742/SMA16-4742.pdf

Substance Abuse and Mental Health Services Administration. (2011). *Results from the 2010 National Survey on Drug Use and Health: Summary of National Findings,* NSDUH Series H-41, HHS Publication No. (SMA) 11-4658. Rockville, MD: Substance Abuse and Mental Health Services Administration.

Trust for America's Health. (2015). *Reducing teen substance misuse: What really works.* Retrieved from http://www.healthyamericans.org/reports/youthsubstancemisuse2015

Veliz, P.T., Boyd, C., & McCabe, S.E. (2013). Playing through pain: sports participation and nonmedical use of opioid medications among adolescents. *American Journal of Public Health, 103*(5), e28-e30. doi:10.2105/AJPH.2013.301242

Volkow, N.D., Frieden, T.R., Hyde, P.S., & Cha, S.S. (2014). Medication-assisted therapies—tackling the opioid-overdose epidemic. *New England Journal of Medicine, 370,* 2063–6. doi: 10.1056/nejmp1402780

Volkow, N.D. (2014, May 14). America's addiction to opioids: Heroin and prescription drug abuse. *Presentation to the United States Senate Caucus on International Narcotics Control*, Hart Senate Office Building, Washington, DC.

Walley, A. Y., Xuan, Z., Hackman, H.H., Quinn, E., Doe-Simkins, M., Sorensen-Alawad, A., Ruiz, S., & Ozonoff, A. (2013). Opioid overdose rates and implementation of overdose education and nasal naloxone distribution in Massachusetts: Interrupted time series analysis. *BMJ* 2013, *346*, f174. doi: http://dx.doi.org/10.1136/bmj.f174

Wermeling, D. P. (2015). Review of naloxone safety for opioid overdose: practical considerations for new technology and expanded public access. *Therapeutic Advances in Drug Safety*, *6*(1), 20–31. http://doi.org/10.1177/2042098614564776

Chapter 33

SCHOOL SCREENINGS

Lee-Ann Halbert, EdDc, JD, RN, MSN, CNM, NCSN

DESCRIPTION OF ISSUE

School health screenings enable the school nurse to uncover potential health issues in students. When conducted at regularly scheduled periods in the students' educational careers, screenings provide the opportunity to support students' health through education and, as necessary, referrals to appropriate health providers. These health inspections are not substitutes for regular health care nor are they intended to diagnose medical problems. They are to be used for early detection of potential health needs through appropriate referrals, and prevention of more serious health issues. The American Academy of Pediatrics (AAP) (2008) supports the school nurse's role in conducting school health screens to identify students with heath needs at an early phase.

Currently no national school health screening laws or regulations exist; however, these requirements are controlled at the local level, either by state requirements, or within each school district and vary from state to state (Bobo, Kimel, & Bleza, 2013). School health screenings date back to the end of the 19th century (Allensworth, Lawson, Nicholson, & Wyche, 1997). Health care was initially introduced into schools for the purposes of identifying students with communicable diseases and preventing further transmission of these illnesses. Screenings soon expanded to include all students in an effort to identify children with vision problems (Allensworth et al., 1997). Over time, although state specific, these screenings have broadened to include checking hearing, height, weight, blood pressure, dentition, posture and back (scoliosis), in addition to vision. The connection between student health and improved academic achievement is well established (Basch, 2011). Because of this connection to increased academic performance and improved student health, screenings should be used to identify health concerns before they escalate into more serious health problems.

The potential for legal issues regarding screenings is based on multiple concerns including knowing individual state requirements for screenings, who may perform them, and what to do with the results. This chapter will provide the resources to address these questions. As a general guideline, school nurses need to be aware of the screening requirements in their states and districts. Failure to screen students as indicated can have a negative impact on their educational development (Bobo et al., 2013).

BACKGROUND

Although health screenings conducted by school nurses fall under the general umbrella of "screenings," each type has its own history, value, recommended schedule, and manner in which the screenings are completed. Not all health screenings will be required in every state or school district. For these reasons, the background of the individual screenings will be discussed within each screening section. Failure to screen properly or follow up as indicated raises the possibility of a legal challenge. Compliance with the screening laws, regulations, and policies, and performing these examinations with the clinical knowledge of why they were introduced into the school setting can reduce the risk of legal challenges. A separate regulatory issue concerns consent for school health care, including screenings. School nurses are directed to consult their individual state laws and regulations, and district policies, to determine if minor school students may consent to or decline health screens, or if parent or guardian consent is required. A state or individual school district, if permitted under state laws and regulations, may require parents/guardians and/or students to opt out of school health care, including screening. Otherwise, it may be assumed the student and parent/guardian has consented to the screening.

While the laws vary on the state level, on the federal level the Individuals with Disability Education Improvement Act 2004 (IDEIA, 2004) includes the "Child Find" component (20 U.S.C. 1412(a)(3)). This section requires that a school system locate and identify students eligible for special education services. School health screenings are one way of meeting this requirement.

Vision Screenings

Among the identified variables that affect student performance is vision ability, an area of clinical need that can be identified by the school nurse. Addressing student vision needs has been identified as one method to improve academic achievement across all student demographic groups (Basch, 2011). According the National Association of School Nurses (NASN), as many as 25% of children in schools have vision problems (NASN, 2016). Identifying these children can lead to higher academic success when this is coupled with appropriate referrals and follow up care, as indicated. Research demonstrates the direct relationship between vision problems and compromised academic success (Maples, 2003). Vision screening by the school nurse or trained volunteer is one component of eye care, in addition to that provided by professional eye specialists. The American Association for Pediatric Ophthalmology and Strabismus (AAOPS) recommends screening children's vision every 1-2 years starting at age 6 (AAOPS, 2016a). The multiple components of vision screens can include checking visual acuity as well as an inspection of the eye area (AAPOS, 2016a). While no cases were located, this raises the possibility of a legal challenge if a school nurse fails to perform a scheduled vision screen and/ or referral, and any effect this failure may have had on academic achievement.

Hearing Screenings

Auditory acuity is another area of need for students to achieve academically at optimal levels. Gottardis, Nunes, and Lunt (2011) point to the delay in mathematical achievement among students with hearing impairment. Easterbrooks and Beal-Alvarez (2012) point to similar findings in their study related to hearing loss and reading ability of students. These authors also point to the historical data correlating students with even less significant hearing loss achieve at a lower academic level (Easterbrooks & Beal-Alvarez, 2012). Like vision screens, missing a hearing screen and the potential of lower academic achievement of a student may be a cause for concern, although no such cases were located.

Scoliosis Screening

Scoliosis screening in schools dates back to the 1960's (Grivas et al., 2007). Although typically performed to screen for scoliosis, examinations of the student's back were previously done for a posture check for issues related to diseases (Jakubowski, & Alexy, 2014). Screening for scoliosis remains an unsettled topic among healthcare professionals (Hresko, Talwalkar, & Schwend, 2015). Even the manner of completing a scoliosis screening varies among practitioners (Hresko et al., 2015). Although many states presently have laws or regulations for screenings by a school nurse, many do not (Jakubowski & Alexy, 2014). Concerns about the screenings relate primarily to false positives and resulting interventions (Jakubowski & Alexy, 2014).

Blood Pressure

According to the Centers for Disease Control and Prevention (CDC), obesity among our youth has increased more than two-fold since the last century (CDC, 2015). Statistics point that an alarming one-third of our youth are overweight or obese (CDC, 2015). The relationship between overweight and hypertension has been made, pointing to the value of school nurses screening for blood pressure (King, Meadows, Engelke, & Swanson, 2006). Armed with information about the family trends regarding obesity and hypertension, school nurses can make appropriate recommendations for their students.

Weight and/or Body Mass Index (BMI)

As noted, the youth population is experiencing an unprecedented level of overweight and obesity (CDC, 2015). Screenings by school nurses can support the efforts to improve the overall health and nutrition of the students through implementations that fit in their own school communities (Schroeder, Travers, & Smaldone, 2016).

BMI screenings are a more controversial screening topic than weight screenings. Current AAP guidelines support that BMI be calculated and discussed through the student's medical home (CDC, n.d.). The NASN recommends that school nurses participate in BMI screening as part of weight screening (NASN, 2013). Although many schools have a nurse available to conduct BMI screening, there is no assurance that a nurse is available for all BMI screenings. Among the concerns about conducting BMI screening in schools is the proper use of the data, ongoing evaluation of the BMI screening program, and assuring privacy of students who are screened for BMI (CDC, n.d.). Other risks from BMI screening include proper education for parents so the BMI result is used appropriately and effectively, and that students not be labeled because of any particular BMI result (Ikeda, Crawford, & Woodward-Lopez, 2006). The CDC offers additional recommendations that include assuring detailed explanations for their use be provided to parents, and that follow up with the student who receives a referral for high BMI be implemented (CDC, 2015).

Dental Screenings

According to the World Health Organization (WHO), as many as 90% of school students worldwide have dental caries (WHO, 2012). Dental problems and the related pain can lead to tooth loss, dental and other diseases, and emotional issues (WHO, 2012). Both across the world and in the United States, a lower socioeconomic status is correlated with higher dental problems (CDC, 2014; WHO, 2012). In the United States, as many as 20% of our youth have a cavity in need of treatment (CDC, 2014). Almost 900,000 school days are lost each year to dental disease (Tetuan, McGlasson, & Meyer, 2005). These missed days can lead to lower academic achievement (Jackson, Vann, Kotch, Pahel, & Lee, 2011). As with other types of screenings, knowledge of the student population can aid the school nurse in developing appropriate interventions (Tetuan et al., 2005).

IMPLICATIONS FOR SCHOOL NURSE PRACTICE

As noted, multiple types of screenings may be required in the school setting. Each of these screenings may be controlled by state or laws or regulations, or school district policies requiring the screens, or they may be silent on the topic. With so many types of screens, it is necessary for the school nurse to become familiar with the state and local school district requirements, as well as the method for performing each screen. Specialty healthcare providers who address each issue have their own training manuals and protocols available to school nurses, or these may be available through a state department or agency. Additionally, NASN offers a variety of resources for many of the screens. The key issue here is to be properly trained in performing the screening correctly. An incorrectly done screen can lead to false findings. A primary point to remember is if the school nurse performs a screen, the nurse should implement an appropriate intervention with the information gained from the screening, including referral where indicated or required by the law or regulations, or applicable policy. It is useless or potentially harmful to ignore findings from a screen. A nurse who ignores positive results may lead a parent or guardian to assume the findings are negative.

At the same time, the nurse must also respect the autonomy of the students. It is possible that not every student – or student's parent or guardian – will want the school nurse to complete a screen. Individual school systems will have their own instructions regarding how permission must be obtained for the screens, whether requiring affirmative permission by the parent or guardian, or an "opt out" requirement for parents or guardians. The student's desires must also be considered when evaluating whether to complete a screen.

When conducting the screens proper personnel should be used for the screening process. In addition to having the necessary education and training to perform the screenings accurately, issues of confidentiality must also be noted. For some screens, such as scoliosis, a screening protocol in the district may designate physical education teachers as acceptable for screening the students, *as long as they have been properly trained for the role and are permitted under the state laws or regulations.* Bear in mind, however, that these non-nursing personnel, and any other volunteers who assist the nurse, may not understand issues of confidentiality when conducting screens. The school nurse should be certain to abide by the school policies and protocols when allowing non-nursing personnel to participate in the screening process. This should include instruction regarding maintaining confidentiality of the students. The Family Educational Rights and Privacy Act (FERPA), a federal law, prohibits the disclosure of information obtained in the screenings by the nurse or any individual assisting in the screenings to anyone without an educational need to know the information (FERPA, 2013).

CONCLUSION

With the overwhelming research pointing to the academic benefits of a healthier student population, screenings are of benefit to the students and a valuable use of a school nurse's time. Although the students are a "captive audience" for the school nurse's screening efforts, we must also look to the students and families for permission to complete the screenings. Finally, compliance with local district policies, state laws and regulations, and federal confidentiality laws should guide the school nurse's practice for performing screens and providing appropriate follow up. Lack of completing screens as directed, performing them improperly, or failure to notify parents when required may have legal implications for the school nurse and the school.

RESOURCES

Requirements for screenings will be specific to the individual states and, possibly, each individual school district. In addition to the information provided here, the school nurse should do a search for support information specific to the state and school district, especially to ensure information is the most current and up to date.

NASN has materials available on the individual types of screens available at www.nasn.org

AAPOS has summarized **vision screenings** for all states in a table available at https://www.aapos.org/ resources/state_by_state_vision_screening_requirements/ (AAPOS, State by state vision screening requirements, 2016b). It should be noted that individual states may have updated their vision screening requirements since the table was compiled. **School nurses are directed to review the information for alignment with current laws and regulations.**

See APPENDIX for a table that summarizes where school nurses can locate information regarding school health services including requirements for school health screens in their state.

Case Law

A recent New Jersey case, Parsons v. Mullica Township Board of Education (2016), applied the Tort Claims Act (TCA) of that state in dismissing a claim against the school nurse for failure to inform parents of the results of a vision screen on their child. This case was not decided on its merits; rather, the case was dismissed based on the immunity of the school district for which the nurse worked.

REFERENCES

Allensworth, D., Lawson, E., Nicholson, L., & Wyche, J. (Eds). (1997). *Schools and health: Our nation's investment.* Washington, DC: National Academy Press.

American Academy of Pediatrics. (2008). Policy statement: Role of the school nurse in providing school health services. *Pediatrics, 121,* 1052-1056. doi: 10.1542/peds.2008-0382

American Association for Pediatric Ophthalmology and Strabismus (AAOPS). (2016a). *Vision screening recommendations.* Retrieved from https://www.aapos.org/terms/conditions/131

American Association for Pediatric Ophthalmology and Strabismus (AAOPS). (2016b). *State-by-state vision screening requirements.* Retrieved from https://www.aapos.org/resources/state_by_state_vision_ screening_requirements/

Basch, C. (2011). Healthier students are better learners: A missing link in school reforms to close the achievement gap. *The Journal of School Health, 81*(10), 593 – 598. Retrieved from http://www.equitycampaign.org/i/a/document/12557_EquityMattersVol6_Web03082010.pdf

Bobo, N., Kimel, L., & Bleza, S. (2013). Promoting health at school. In J. Selekman (Ed.), *School nursing: A comprehensive text* (2nd ed.) (pp. 440-472). Philadelphia, PA: F.A. Davis Company.

Centers for Disease Control and Prevention (CDC). (n.d.). *Body mass index measurement in school: BMI executive summary.* Retrieved from http://www.cdc.gov/healthyschools/obesity/bmi/pdf/bmi_execsumm.pdf

Centers for Disease Control and Prevention (CDC). (2015). *Children's BMI tool for schools.* Retrieved from http://www.cdc.gov/healthyweight/assessing/bmi/childrens_bmi/tool_for_schools.html

Centers for Disease Control and Prevention (CDC). (2015). *Childhood obesity facts*. Retrieved from https://www.cdc.gov/healthyschools/obesity/facts.htm

Centers for Disease Control and Prevention (CDC). (2014). *Children's oral health*. Retrieved from http://www.cdc.gov/oralhealth/children_adults/child.htm

FERPA (2013). *Family Educational Rights and Privacy Act.* 20 U.S.C. § 1232g (b) (1) (A)

Gottardis, L., Nunes, T., & Lunt, I. (2011). A synthesis of research on deaf and hearing children's mathematical achievement. *Deafness and Education International, 13* (3), 131-150. doi:http://dx.doi.org/10.1179/1557069X11Y.0000000006

Grivas, T.B., Wade, M.H., Negrini, S., O'Brien, J.P., Maruyama, T., Hawes, M.C., Rigo, M., ..., & Neuhous, T. (2007). SOSORT consensus paper: School screening for scoliosis. Where are we today? *Scoliosis, 2*(17). doi:10.1186/1748-7161-2-17

Hresko, M.T., Talwalkar, V.R., & Schwend, R.M. (2015). *Screening for the early detection for idiopathic scoliosis in adolescents* (Position statement). *SRS/POSNA/AAOS/AAP Position Statement.* Retrieved from https://www.srs.org/about-srs/news-and-announcements/position-statement---screening-for-the-early-detection-for-idiopathic-scoliosis-in-adolescents

Ikeda, J.P., Crawford, P.B., & Woodward-Lopez, G. (2006). BMI screening in schools: Helpful or harmful. *Health Education Research, 21*(6), 761-769 doi: 10.1093/her/cy1144

Individuals with Disability Education Improvement Act (2004), Child Find, 20 U.S.C. 1412(a) (3)

Individuals with Disability Education Improvement Act (2004), Child Find, 20 U.S.C. 1412(a) (3) Easterbrooks, S.R., & Beal-Alvarez, J.S. (2012). States' reading outcomes of students who are d/Deaf and hard of hearing. *American Annals of the Deaf, 157*, 27-40. doi:10.1353/aad.2012.161

Jackson, S., Vann, W.F., Kotch, J.B., Pahel, B.T., & Lee, J. Y. (2011). Impact of poor oral health on children's school attendance and performance. *American Journal of Public Health, 101*(10), 1900 – 1906. doi: 10.2105/AJPH.2010.200915

Jakubowski, T.L., & Alexy, E.M. (2014). Does scoliosis screening make the grade? *NASN School Nurse, 29*(5), 258-265. doi: 10.1177/1942602X14542131

King, C.A., Meadows, B.B., Engelke, M.K., & Swanson, M. (2006). Prevalence of elevated body mass index and blood pressure in a rural school-aged population: Implications for school nurses. *The Journal of School Health, 76*(4), 145-149. doi:10.1111/j.1746-1561.2006.00083.x

Maples, W.C. (2003). Visual factors that significantly impact academic performance. *Optometry, 74*(1), 35-49. Retrieved from http://www.add-adhd.org/pdfs/08_visual_factors_Maples.pdf

National Association of School Nurses (NASN). (2016). *Vision and eye health*. Retrieved from https://www.nasn.org/ToolsResources/VisionandEyeHealth

National Association of School Nurses. (2013). *Overweight and obesity in youth in schools: The role of the school nurse* (Position Statement). Retrieved from https://www.nasn.org/PolicyAdvocacy/PositionPapersandReports/NASNPositionStatementsFullView/tabid/462/smid/824/ArticleID/39/Default.aspx

Schroeder, K., Travers, J., & Smaldone, A. (2016). Are school nurses an overlooked resource in reducing childhood obesity? A systematic review and meta-analysis. *The Journal of School Health, 86*(5), 309-321. doi: 10.1111/josh.12386

Tetuan, T.T., McGlasson, D., & Meyer, I. (2005). Oral health screening using a caries detection device. *The Journal of School Nursing, 21*(5), 299 – 306. doi: 10.1622/1059-8405(2005)21[299:ohsuac]2.0.co;2

World Health Organization (WHO). (2012). *Oral health.* Retrieved from http://www.who.int/mediacentre/factsheets/fs318/en/

APPENDIX

State (and Washington DC)	State School Health Services Website
Alabama	https://www.alsde.edu/sec/pss/Pages/home.aspx
Alaska	http://dhss.alaska.gov/dph/wcfh/pages/school/default.aspx
Arizona	http://www.azed.gov/health-nutrition/
Arkansas	http://www.arkansascsh.org/support-the-program/screenings-in-schools.php
California	http://www.cde.ca.gov/ls/he/hn/
Colorado	https://www.cde.state.co.us/healthandwellness/snh_healthservices
Connecticut	http://www.sde.ct.gov/sde/cwp/view.asp?a=2678&q=320768
Delaware	http://www.doe.k12.de.us/domain/150
Florida	http://www.floridahealth.gov/programs-and-services/childrens-health/school-health/
Georgia	https://dph.georgia.gov/school-health
Hawaii	http://health.hawaii.gov/school-health/
Idaho	http://sde.idaho.gov/student-engagement/school-health/index.html
Illinois	https://www.isbe.net/pages/school-health-issues.aspx
Indiana	http://www.doe.in.gov/student-services/health
Iowa	https://www.educateiowa.gov/pk-12/learner-supports/school-nurse
Kansas	http://www.kdheks.gov/c-f/school.html
Kentucky	http://education.ky.gov/districts/SHS/Pages/default.aspx
Louisiana	https://www.louisianabelieves.com/schools/public-schools/health-services
Maine	http://www.maine.gov/education/sh/
Maryland	http://archives.marylandpublicschools.org/MSDE/divisions/studentschoolsvcs/student_services_alt/school_health_services/
Massachusetts	http://www.mass.gov/eohhs/gov/departments/dph/programs/community-health/primarycare-healthaccess/school-health/
Michigan	http://www.michigan.gov/mde/0,4615,7-140-74638_74640---,00.html
Minnesota	http://education.state.mn.us/MDE/dse/health/svcs/index.htm
Mississippi	http://msdh.ms.gov/msdhsite/_static/43,0,343.html
Missouri**	http://health.mo.gov/living/families/schoolhealth/ And http://health.mo.gov/living/families/schoolhealth/pdf/ManualForSchoolHealth.pdf
Montana	http://dphhs.mt.gov/schoolhealth
Nebraska	http://dhhs.ne.gov/publichealth/Pages/schoolhealth.aspx
Nevada	http://dpbh.nv.gov/Programs/SH/School_Health_-_Home/
New Hampshire	http://education.nh.gov/instruction/school_health/health.htm

New Jersey	http://www.state.nj.us/education/students/safety/health/services/
New Mexico	https://nmhealth.org/about/phd/hsb/osah/
New York	http://www.schoolhealthservicesny.com
North Carolina	http://www.nchealthyschools.org
North Dakota	http://www.ndhealth.gov/csh/
Ohio	https://www.odh.ohio.gov/odhprograms/chss/schh/School%20Health.aspx
Oklahoma	https://www.ok.gov/health/Community_&_Family_Health/Maternal_and_Child_Health_Service/Child_and_Adolescent_Health/School_Health/
Oregon	https://public.health.oregon.gov/HealthyPeopleFamilies/Youth/HealthSchool/SchoolBasedHealthCenters/Documents/SBHC__Pubs/SHS_flyer_FINAL.pdf
Pennsylvania	http://www.health.pa.gov/My%20Health/School%20Health/Pages/Mandated-School-Health-Program.aspx#.V6jorGV0000
Rhode Island**	http://sos.ri.gov/documents/archives/regdocs/released/pdf/DOH/5471.pdf And http://www.thriveri.org/about.html
South Carolina	http://www.scdhec.gov/Health/FHPF/SchoolNursesChildcareCenters/
South Dakota	https://doh.sd.gov/schoolhealth/
Tennessee	http://www.tennessee.gov/education/topic/coordinated-school-health
Texas	https://www.dshs.texas.gov/schoolhealth/
Utah	http://www.tobaccofreeutah.org/pdfs/school_resource_guide_2012-2013.pdf
Vermont	http://healthvermont.gov/local/school/SchoolHealth-Standards_of_Practice.aspx
Virginia	http://www.doe.virginia.gov/support/health_medical/
Washington	http://www.k12.wa.us/HealthServices/
Washington, DC	http://doh.dc.gov/service/child-adolescent-and-school-health-services
West Virginia	https://wvde.state.wv.us/healthyschools/
Wisconsin	http://dpi.wi.gov/sspw/pupil-services/school-nurse
Wyoming**	https://edu.wyoming.gov/in-the-classroom/health-safety/ And https://wsna.nursingnetwork.com

**Note: A second resource website was added to these states because of the need for additional information.

NURSING COORDINATION

Chapter 34

MANAGEMENT OF CHRONIC ABSENTEEISM

Suzanne Levasseur, MSN, APRN, CPNP, NCSN

DESCRIPTION OF ISSUE

School attendance affects academic success and frequent absences, whether excused or unexcused, greatly increases the student's risk of poor academic achievement as well as incidences of dropping out of high school, (Jacobsen, Meeder & Voskuil, 2016). Chronic medical conditions can contribute to chronic absenteeism and the school nurse can have a positive effect on helping students with a chronic health condition improve attendance.

While absenteeism refers to the number of excused and unexcused absences as well as suspensions, an unexcused absences from school, as determined by state law or policy is considered truancy (Truancy Prevention, n.d.) Compulsory education laws are determined by state legislation and often district policy. Each state determines school attendance laws which determine the age at which a child must begin attending school, the age at which a child may legally drop out of school and at what number of unexcused absences in a month or year makes a student truant.

BACKGROUND

The first compulsory education law was in enacted the state of Massachusetts in 1642. While other states followed, it was not until the 1930's that states were successful in enforcement (Katz, 1976).

Even as early as kindergarten, students who are chronically absent have lower math and reading skills as well as declines in social adjustment (Jacobsen, Meeder & Voskuil, 2016). Schools have the responsibility to provide notices to families which explain the truancy laws, district policy and consequences for nonattendance. If a child is considered truant, at some point judicial intervention may be warranted. Parents are responsible for ensuring that their child attends school regularly and if that responsibility is not met the parent may be faced with statutory penalties. Educational neglect is often in a state's definition of child abuse or neglect. Often times, although parents want their children to attend school, they have run out of strategies to use at home in attempting to get their student to attend school.

Truancy cases are complicated and require the school team to determine a cause or underlying reason for the truancy. School teams should consider that the student may have a disability that may require special education services or services under Section 504. Although absences alone do not determine eligibility, repeated absences may be enough to suspect a disability and districts personnel should consider undertaking a special education evaluation prior to initiating a judicial referral. This would be warranted under the district's child find obligation which requires districts to identify and evaluate students who may be in need of special education (Martin, 2013). A student with poor attendance due to a chronic or frequent episodic illness may also be eligible for eligibility under Section 504.

On December 10th, 2015, President Obama signed an education bill into law that required states to report chronic absenteeism rates for schools. This *Every Student Achieves Act*, a reauthorization of *No Child Left Behind*, is the first education law that mentions attendance.

IMPLICATIONS FOR SCHOOL NURSE PRACTICE

School nurses have an important role in the management of a student with poor school attendance, whether there is chronic absenteeism or the student meets the legal definition of truancy in the state. Many health conditions may lead to frequent absences and it may be the school nurse that first notes the condition and effect on school attendance. The importance of documenting excused and unexcused absences should be communicated to the school nurse in order to allow better data collection. It may also be the school nurse who determines if the absences are truly illness related. The nurse will be part of the school team to determine which accommodations may be necessary. In some cases, homebound instruction may be warranted. Each case should be evaluated individually.

As chronic disease may be a barrier to school attendance so may be other issues, such as the need to care for siblings or other family members or lack of basic needs such as transportation, food or clothes. A student may have an aversion to school due to academic or social struggles or feel unsafe at school. Anxiety-based or other mental health disorders may also contribute to school refusal behavior. Homebound instruction as part of possible educational placements may be requested for students with mental health issues or school refusal. Homebound instruction does not allow students to interact with their peers during the school day and has implications related to the least restrictive environment (LRE) laws. Often an extended homebound period makes it more difficult for the student to return to school and does not provide the student with the full experience of coming to school.

In the case of *Bradley v. Arkansas Department of Education, 45 IDELR 149, 443 F.3d 965 (8th Cir. 2006)* the courts found in favor of the district after the parent requested homebound-based education on a diagnosis of school phobia and the district determined that home was not the appropriate placement and that in filing truancy the principal did what state law required (Martin, 2013).

Improving attendance requires the active participation of school administrators, school counselors, social workers, school nurses and community agencies as needed. Juvenile Review Boards, child protection services and other social service agencies may also be utilized. It is also important for the school nurse to engage local healthcare providers to collaborate with schools to address chronic absenteeism or truancy. Healthcare providers are often unaware of a patient's lack of attendance at school. Starting this dialogue can be helpful especially when there are frequent "doctor's notes" excusing the absences.

Strategies to Address Chronic Absenteeism

Attendance Monitoring

Although Average Daily Attendance (ADA) of a school or district can provide valuable data, a system should be put in place to monitor individual student attendance. It may be the school nurse that brings excessive absenteeism or truancy to the attention of the administrator or the administrator may bring this to the attention of the school nurse.

Formation of District and School Attendance Teams

Active engagement of school administrators and school staff, with clear responsibilities and roles to adopt a comprehensive, tiered approach is needed to improve attendance.

Tiered Supports

Tiered supports can begin with Tier 1 interventions that start with prevention and focus on all students to clearly articulate and communicate attendance policies while supporting an engaging school climate:

- Engage students and parents.
- Provide engaging curriculum.
- Recognize good and improved attendance.
- Provide a breakfast program.
- Organize health interventions and a schoolwide approach to wellness through flu clinics and a healthy indoor air quality program.
- Provide parent/guardian and student education for better management of health issues.

Tier 2 interventions would provide personalized early intervention for students who are frequently absent:

- Conduct a home visit or parent conference.
- Provide outreach by the school nurse especially related to health issues.
- Engage the healthcare provider for students with health concerns such as asthma that are impacting attendance.
- Offer counseling or family –based services as a related service through the Individualized Education Plan (IEP) process.
- Identify barriers such as transportation or housing and partner with community agencies to obtain needed resources.
- Develop a student attendance success plan to develop strategies to support improved attendance.

Tier 3 interventions are for students who need intensive case management or coordination with local agencies or law enforcement:

- Refer to a community agency capable of supporting family needs that may be affecting attendance.
- Refer to a community-court based program or resource addressing truancy and/or schools should assign a mentor in the school community.
- Consider an alternative educational setting.

CONCLUSION

Chronic absenteeism influences educational success, as well as incidences of early delinquency and school drop- out. Academic consequences of lost instructional time can be great. School districts need to develop a comprehensive approach, beginning with preventive, universal programming and attendance monitoring for all students. Although students may miss school for understandable reasons such as chronic illness or social issues such as homelessness, determining the reason for the chronic absences is essential to determine targeted strategies for the individual student.

Prior to chronic absenteeism or when truancy has reached thresholds for state laws requiring judicial intervention, a meeting with the parent/guardian should be held and interventions put in place. Districts and school nurses in particular should have policies, procedures and tiered interventions in place to help prevent and mitigate truancy. Families should also be notified that nonattendance of school mandates districts to file truancy.

In addition, poor school attendance may prompt districts to suspect a disability and a special education or Section 504 eligibility hearing may be warranted. School nurses will be essential in identifying health and other barriers and leading their school teams in addressing the issue.

RESOURCES

See ADDENDUM: Attendance and the School Nurse

Attendance Works
www.attendanceworks.org

Connecticut State Department of Education: *Utilizing Local Support Resources Prior to Referral of Students for Family with Service Needs Series 2009-10 Circular Letter C-2*
http://www.sde.ct.gov/sde/lib/sde/pdf/circ/circ09-10/c2.pdf

Strategies for Youth
http://strategiesforyouth.org/

Pfrommer, J. (2013). *Serving students with medical needs: Achieving legal compliance with 504.* (p.34). Palm Beach Gardens, FL: LRP Publications.

Legal Cases

Bradley v. Arkansas Department of Education, 45 IDELR 149, 443 F.3d 965 (8th Cir. 2006)

REFERENCES

Every Student Succeeds Act (ESSA). (2015). Every Student Succeeds Act of 2015, Pub. L. No. 114-95 § 114 Stat. 1177 (2015-2016).

Jacobsen, K., Meeder, L. & Voskuil, V. (2016). Chronic student absenteeism: The critical role of the school nurses. *NASN School Nurse, 31*(3), 179-186. doi: 10.1177/1942602X16638855

Katz, M. S. (1976). *A history of compulsory education laws*. Retrieved from http://files.eric.ed.gov/fulltext/ED119389.pdf

Martin, J. L. (2013). *Truancy, work refusal and home problems: When are schools responsible? (pp.19-28).* Palm Beach Gardens, FL: LRP Publications.

Truancy Prevention. (n.d.). *Truancy definition, facts and laws.* Retrieved from http://www.truancyprevention.org/

ADDENDUM

Attendance and the School Nurse

Lawrence J. Altman, Esquire

Q: Is it important for a nurse to identify and follow up on truancy issues that are or may be disability-related?

A: Failure to provide accommodations for a student who is experiencing absenteeism due to a Section 504 or IDEA-eligible disability can result in liability for a public school, and nurses are often on the front lines of the school's defense. If the nurse learns that a child is missing a significant amount of school due to the disability, then the school nurse should promptly report this situation to the Special Education Director and/or the Section 504 Director. Taking this step and moving forward on an assessment for the child and/or reconvening the IEP or Section 504 Team to consider the absenteeism issue lessen the chance of a successful complaint against the school and help defend the school against a claim that it violated the child's right to a Free Appropriate Public Education by failing to spot and/or properly accommodate a student's disability. If a school does not have in place proper policies, protocols, and procedures for evaluating and/or accommodating a child under Section 504, the nurse should bring the issue to the attention of building and/or district-level administration and should take steps to assist in the creation of such. Some communities have laws that involve criminal action against parents who do not see that their child is coming to school unless there is a valid reason for the child not being present. For example, Kansas City Missouri has a compulsory student attendance law. If a child is absent for more than a designated percentage of the time during the school year, the parents of the child are reported to the prosecuting attorney, who will then issue a show cause order for the parents to appear before a judge to explain the absences. If medical reasons are provided by the parents for their child's absences, the school nurse may need to provide documentation as to whether or not the nurse received any medical documentation to support the defense and, if so, what the district did to try to accommodate the student's medical needs.

Q: How are student attendance issues and Section 504 related?

A: Section 504 is an anti-discrimination law that requires schools receiving federal funding not to dis-criminate against a child because of the child's disability. So, if a child's Section 504 Plan requires the nurse to administer insulin to a diabetic child but fails to do so, and, for this reason, the child 's parents elect not to send the child to school, this would indicate that the child's failure to attend school may have been

caused by the nurse's failure to follow the child's Section 504 Plan. Accordingly, the school would have violated Section 504. Another example is when a school nurse discovers that the reason for the child's failure to attend school may have been caused when informed that the child was hospitalized after attempting self-harm. If the school has in place proper policies, protocols, and procedures the nurse must report this to the school's IDEA Coordinator and/or Section 504 Coordinator, because the IDEA and Section 504 would require action be taken by the school to take steps to allow the child to attend school and receive a FAPE, even if the child, prior to the incident, had not received IDEA services or Section 504 accommodations. Further, assuming that the school has policies, protocols, and procedures in place in this case, best practice would be for the school to require the child's healthcare provider to send to the school a proposed child safety plan before the child returns to the school. This may include medical information or administration of medication. Accordingly, the nurse would be a vital component in the child's receipt of a FAPE.

Chapter 35

ACCIDENT AND INJURY REPORTING

Timothy E. Gilsbach, Esquire

DESCRIPTION OF ISSUE

When an accident or injury occurs on school grounds, a school nurse has two roles to play. First, a school nurse is generally expected to take the lead in determining if anyone was injured and, if so, to take steps to treat them and, if needed, get them additional help (NASN, 2014a). Second, sometimes overlooked, the nurse also serves in the role of historian with the unique perspective of often being the only person present with a medical background to provide a record of what happened and what was done (Mississippi Nursing Foundation, 2013).

BACKGROUND

When litigation involving schools occurs, one of the first things that likely will occur is that records and documents regarding the incident in question are requested (Calisi, 2016). In addition, documentation of events created at or about the time of an events' occurrence, and prior to any litigation that may come, are typically viewed as far more reliable accounts of what occurred than accounts that are given months or even years later or after litigation is commenced (Calisi, 2016). Lastly, from a healthcare perspective, it is important to make sure that information is accurately recorded so that it may be shared with any future healthcare providers as they work with the student or staff member (Morales, 2012). As a result, it is critical that nurses are accurate and factual in their accident reports.

IMPLICATIONS FOR SCHOOL NURSE PRACTICE

When Does an Accident Report Need To Be Completed?

An accident or injury should be considered school related, in that the school nurse may need to be involved and complete an accident or injury report, when the incidence occurs at school during normal school hours, at any school related activity, or while the student is being transported to or from school (Utah Board of Health [UBOH], 2016). While nurses should review the policy and procedures of his or her school entity to determine when an accident report should or must be completed, an accident or injury report should, at a minimum be completed in any of the following three (3) circumstances (UBOH, 2016; Ohio Board of Health [OBOH], 2015):

1. The student misses one half day (1/2) or more of school due to the injury or, if the injured party is an employee they miss one half day (1/2) or more of work.
2. The student or employee seeks medical attention from their healthcare provider, emergency room or urgent care center due to the injury.
3. EMS or 911 is called due to the injuries or for any reason.

It is important to note that in addition to an accident or injury report, if the school nurse assessed or treated the student, documentation of care should also be recorded in the student health record in accordance with standard documentation procedures. For vents that do not require an accident or injury report, information should be documented in the student's health record or other appropriate form (Mississippi Nursing Foundation, 2013).

What Needs to And Should Be Included In The Report?

As with all nursing records, accident and injury reports should be objective, legible, free of spelling and grammatical errors, free of errors and erasures, completed in blue or black ink, and accurate (Morales, 2012). If available the accident and injury forms should be filled out electronically (UBOH, 2016; NASN, 2014b). The following information should be included in the report (OBOH, 2015).

- Name of the injured person and the person's date of birth, grade, (if a student), and gender.

- For students, the name of the parent or guardian and whether that person was contacted about the incident and, if so, how, what information was provided and the response from parent or guardian.

- It should be documented if the nurse provided information about the injury to any other parties, including school principal or other administrator and, in the case of a non-student, if someone else outside of the school was notified.

- The name of the school building that the employee or student is assigned. In the event of a visitor to the school building, as noted below, the location where the injury occurred should be noted and, if known, the reason for why this person was in the school building should be noted.

- The location of the accident or injury including where in the school building the accident or injury occurred, any equipment involved and a description of any unusual circumstances, such as the type of flooring or surface where the incident occurred.

- The time and date of the accident or injury including, where appropriate, if the time is an estimated or exact time.

- An explanation of the incident, including a listing of any witnesses, any contributing factors and a brief description of the incident. To the extent that the nurse is relying upon what others individuals reported regarding the incident, the report should clearly identity what was reported and by whom and if they observed the reported information so as to be clear what was observed directly by the nurse and what was reported to the nurse and by whom. In addition, to the extent other staff members were involved in the initial treatment of the student or injured party should also be noted. In describing the incident, care should be taken to avoid assigning blame or fault to any person or item and instead it should be an objective and factual accounting of what happened.

- The nature of the injuries, including where on the injured party's body the injury is located and the type of injury, for example was it a scrape, puncture, cut or burn. In addition, any special circumstances should be noted, including if there was a vehicle involved, if it involved any specific substance such as chemicals or if there was drugs or alcohol involved, if known. Descriptions of special circumstances should be as factual as possible. For example, if the nurse observes the presence of drugs or alcohol that should be described, but if the individual in question appears to be under the influence of drugs or alcohol it should be noted what symptoms appear and, only if professionally appropriate, that this could be a sign of intoxication.

- What medical assistance was provided to the injured party, including any medications provided including dose, time, and route should be noted.

- What future medical assistance was recommended, if any, and how this information was provided to the injured party or, if a student, to student's parent or guardian.

- Was the student or injured party's care transferred to someone else, including parent or guardian or EMS. What was the condition of the student or injured party when this transfer occurred? What instructions, if any, were provided to the person to whom the injured party's care was transferred?

Who May See the Information in the Report?

For students, any educational entity that receives federal funds is subject to the Family Educational Rights and Privacy Act (FERPA) and any state law or regulations that relate to the handling and sharing of student records. FERPA requires that records to which it applies be kept confidential and not disclosed unless permitted under FERPA (U.S. Department of Education [USDE], 2010). FERPA applies to student records handled by school nurses irrespective of whether they are employed directly by the school or employed by an agency with which the school contracts. In addition, to FERPA school nurses must be aware of and comply with school district policy regarding the confidentiality of the information they obtain in their role as a school nurse.

FERPA applies to all records maintained by the school district and are directly related to a student (USDE, 2010). Such records include all health records maintained by the school district, including treatment records and immunization records (USDE, 2010). This would include accident and injury reports about students.

Generally speaking, *maintained* includes any records kept by the school district, although some courts have suggested there must be an intent to keep it (*Owasso Independent School District v. Falvo*, 2002; *Bryner v. Canyons School. District,* 2015). **However, when unsure if FERPA applies, school staff are well advised to presume it does apply and keep the records confidential**. With respect to *directly related to a student*, this is requirement is met if it includes the student's name, initials, identification number, provides information from which someone could identify the student (*Letter to Doe*, 2011) and has even been found to include information if it permits identity of the student by "face, body shape, clothing or otherwise" (*Bryner v. Canyons School District.*, 2015).

Disclosure of FERPA records or the information contained in those records is limited to those circumstances provided for under FERPA and its implementing regulations (USDE, 2010). There are several provisions that permit disclosure that are applicable to accident and injury records (USDE, 2010):

- The records or information may be disclosed to the parent and student.

- The information or records can be disclosed if the parent or guardian or student over the age of 18 gives consent in writing to release the information. This consent must state what information can be disclosed and to whom it may be disclosed.

- The information may be disclosed if it qualifies as directory information, which should be defined with specificity in the District's Policy and Annual Notification to Parents. In addition, a school nurse should be aware that a parent or guardian may opt out of the directory information disclosure and, if the parent or guardian does, the disclosure under this provision is not permissible.

- The school district may disclose the information in response to a lawful subpoena or court order, but typically must notify the parent or guardian or student over the age of 18 of the same prior to the release unless the subpoena or court order provides that parent or guardian are not to be notified.

- The information may be disclosed if there is "an articulable and significant threat to the health or safety or other individual" that such information is necessary to protect. However, it is expected that when applying this provision for disclosure that it is necessary that the information be disclosed so quickly that there is not time to get a subpoena or court order. Typically, under these circumstances it is expected that such information is for law enforcement, public health officials or trained medical personnel.

- The information may be released to other school officials if the information is educationally relevant to that person and typically it is a staff member who does or will be working with the student.

Lastly, it is important to note that under FERPA, the district is required to maintain a record of any such disclosures with the student's records (USDE, 2010).

For non-student, such as staff and school visitors, school nurses need to protect the confidentiality of the information that they obtain consistent with their ethical obligations as a nurse and with the requirements of state law regarding the confidentiality of employment records. As a result, school nurses should generally take steps to keep information in such records confidential and only disclose the same if permissible. Typically, disclosure of this information is only permitted if the person whom it is about consents, a provision of law or the rules of ethics would permit disclosure, or if ordered to do so by court order or subpoena. **When in doubt, school nurses should not disclose the information and seek guidance from legal counsel or your professional organization about confidentiality requirements.**

CONCLUSION

Given that the record of accidents or injuries at school may become evidence in litigation and such information is needed to provide further care to the student or school employee, it is essential that school nurses make sure such reports are accurate and comprehensive. In addition, school nurses need to be aware of the limits on who this information can be disclosed to as such records qualify as educational records under FERPA and state law. Lastly, it is essential that school nurses become aware of any addition guidelines or regulations under state law or under district policy and comply with the same.

RESOURCES

National Association of School Nurses Website – http://www.nasn.org/

Your state School Nurses Association or Organization Website

Ohio Department of Health Student Injury Report – available at https://www.odh.ohio.gov/-/media/ODH/ASSETS/Files/chss/school-nursing/studentinjuryreport.pdf?la=en

Student Injury Report Form Utah Department of Health – available at https://sir.health.utah.gov/pdf/Student_Injury_Report_Form.pdf

Michigan School Injury Report Form – available at http://www.vbisd.org/cms/lib6/MI01000711/Centricity/Domain/10/Student%20Incident%20Form%208-25-10.pdf

REFERENCES

Bryner v. Canyons School District, 351 P.3d 852 (UT Ct. App. 2015).

Calisi, A. (2016). Liability and injury compensation for accidents at school. *Injury Claims Coach*. Retrieved from www.injuryclaimcoach.com/accident-at-school.html.

Letter to Doe, 111 LRP 64583 (FPCO 2011).

Mississippi Nurses Foundation. (2013). *Mississippi school nurse procedures and standards of care*. Retrieved from http://www.mde.k12.ms.us/docs/healthy-schools/procedures-manual-.pdf?sfvrsn=0

Morales, K. (2012). *17 Tips to improve your nursing documentation*. Retrieved from www.nursetogether.com/nurse-documentation-helpful-tips-every-nurs.

National Association of School Nurses. (2014a). *Emergency preparedness and response in the school setting – The role of the school nurse* (Position Statement). Retrieved from https://www.nasn.org/PolicyAdvocacy/PositionPapersandReports/NASNPositionStatementsFullView/tabid/462/ArticleId/117/Emergency-Preparedness-and-Response-in-the-School-Setting-The-Role-of-the-School-Nurse-Revised-June

National Association of School Nurses. (2014b). *School nurse role in electronic school health records* (Position Statement). Retrieved from https://www.nasn.org/PolicyAdvocacy/PositionPapersandReports/NASNPositionStatementsFullView/tabid/462/ArticleId/641/Electronic-School-Health-Records-School-Nurse-Role-in-Adopted-January-2014

Ohio Department of Health. (2015). *Student injury report form guidelines*. Retrieved from https://www.odh.ohio.gov/odhprograms/chss/schnurs/nurseforms.aspx.

Owasso Independent School District v. Falvo, 534 U.S. 426 (2002)

U.S. Department of Education. (2010). *Family Educational Rights and Privacy Act (FERPA) and the disclosure of student information related to emergencies and disasters*. Retrieved from http://www2.ed.gov/policy/gen/guid/fpco/pdf/ferpa-disaster-guidance.pdf

Utah Board of Health. (2016). *Student injury report*. Retrieved from https://sir.health.utah.gov/

Chapter 36

DISASTER PREPAREDNESS FOR SCHOOL HEALTH SERVICES

Linda S. Kalekas, MSN, RN, NCSN, TNCC

DESCRIPTION OF ISSUE

Key Components of Disaster Preparedness for School Health Services includes:

1. Understanding of overarching federal, state, territorial, tribal, county and local laws or policies that influence disaster preparedness requirements for schools;

2. Knowledge of the National Incident Management System (NIMS) and Incident Command System (ICS) and how it impacts the disaster preparedness cycle for schools;

3. Knowledge of emergency and disaster preparedness planning and the physical plans for schools using an all-hazards approach;

4. Participation of school health services personnel in emergency operations planning, training and exercises to include prevention, planning, response, recovery, and mitigation phases of emergency management;

5. Knowledge of the school nurse's role in emergency and disaster preparedness and response in the school setting, including potential Incident Command System (ICS) roles;

6. Ability to demonstrate competency in performing emergency and disaster response duties such as communications, chain of command, integration into the incident command system on-scene, and coordination of casualty care with other first responder agencies on-scene;

7. Ability to ensure first responder safety, appropriate use of personal protective equipment, and safe use of all emergency equipment and supplies as provided by school health services or schools for use during events; and

8. Awareness of the school nurse's professional liability related to education, training, and skills competency for disaster preparedness.

The Federal Emergency Management Agency (FEMA) defines a disaster as "an occurrence of a natural catastrophe, technological accident, or human-caused event that has resulted in severe property damage, deaths, and/or multiple injuries" (FEMA, 2008. p. 278). A disaster will usually occur with little or no forewarning. The size of a disaster is measured relative to the onset, duration, magnitude and geographical scope of its impact. There is usually significant loss of human life, extensive damage to physical property and critical infrastructure, as well as large economic or environmental losses resulting from a disaster. Ability to manage the disaster sequelae is dependent upon the extent to which essential personnel and resources are capable of responding to the type of disaster that has occurred.

The U.S. National Preparedness Goal is to ensure for the American public, "a secure and resilient Nation with the capabilities required across the whole community to prevent, protect against, mitigate, respond to, and recover from the threats and hazards that pose the greatest risk" (Department of Homeland Security [DHS], 2015, para. 2). Existing legal precepts for federal emergency authority and immunity are based upon laws and policies which provide an overarching framework for disaster preparedness in all state, territorial, tribal, county and local jurisdictions. Schools are an integral part of the communities where they reside and school districts may overlap with multiple government and non-government entities. Schools are an essential partner in the ability of the local community to effectively engage in all phases of emergency management including "prevention, preparedness, response, recovery and mitigation" as defined by the Federal Emergency Management Agency (FEMA, 2013, p.2). Successful outcomes during and after a disaster are often the product of excellent collaboration among all stakeholders prior to a real-world event.

School crisis and emergency preparedness plans are developed in accordance with state statutes derived from federal laws and policies. It is essential for school nurses to become familiar with legal directives and school plans governing emergency preparedness, school safety and school health in the state where they are licensed. The Council of State Governments Justice Center (2014) recently conducted state-by-state research and compiled a list of statutes which address core elements of school safety plans across the nation. Nurses must become familiar with the residential state, county and local statutes which define the difference between crisis, emergency or disaster conditions. State laws will govern the authorized acts of a licensed nurse under emergency or special conditions, such as disasters, occurring within the state.

School nurses have a unique role to protect and serve the nation's children whenever disaster strikes during the school day. According to the National Association of School Nurses (NASN), "school nurses are a vital part of the school team responsible for developing emergency response procedures for the school setting using an all-hazards approach" (NASN, 2014, para. 2). Once a disaster has occurred, school nurses will have either a direct or supportive role in conducting medical and psychological triage, implementing life-saving interventions, providing pre-hospital emergency care, coordinating the transfer of care of victims to emergency medical services and providing support for on-scene fatality management. It is important to know if local, county or state laws would compel a public or private school nurse to serve in a disaster relief or disaster service worker status. Once an emergency or disaster declaration has been issued, public healthcare employees in many states may be legally mandated to work in response to a disaster. For example, in California, "as a city, county, or state agency or public district employee, you may be called upon as a disaster service worker in the event of an emergency" (California Government Code, Section 3101, 2016).

Disaster planning for at-risk school populations includes identifying students who are medically fragile and those students who require specialized nursing procedures or emergency medications. Furthermore, the school nurse assists in identifying students who have access or functional needs to ensure safety accommodations are in place and appropriate adult assistance is available during emergencies. In a policy statement provided by the American Academy of Pediatrics (AAP), part of being prepared for a disaster means, "Children with special healthcare needs must be identified and have valid emergency care plans in place, including plans for managing both individual emergencies related to the child's illness and plans to manage the complex medical needs of the student in the event of a larger community emergency" (AAP, 2008/2012, para. 18).

Due to the unique nature of the school nurse's role in disasters, education and training as part of disaster preparedness is needed to ensure competency as a first responder in extreme medical casualty or public health disaster situations. While specific training or certification in these aspects of care may not be legally mandated or employer-required, there are educational programs available that could enhance the school nurses' competence in disaster response. Additionally, many school districts will mandate annual education, training, practice drills or exercises for all of its employees who might respond to acts of violence, terrorism, and man-made or natural disasters.

BACKGROUND

Historical Perspective

Disasters have been occurring throughout time and are memorialized in some of the earliest recordings of American history. The execution of young females identified as "witches" in Salem, Massachusetts in 1692 is one of the earliest mass killings ever recorded. Subsequent U.S. disasters have included tragedies such as shipwrecks, railroad accidents, bridge and dam failures, flooding, fires, droughts, airplane crashes, explosions, tornados, hurricanes, blizzards, coal mine accidents, earthquakes, volcanic eruptions, avalanches, bombings, stampedes, military strikes, hazardous material spills, terrorism and much more. Any of these events may adversely impact schools located in a community affected by disaster.

Schools are sometimes targets for manmade disasters and each of the disasters described here are situations that a school nurse may be confronted with at any time. On May 18, 1927, a series of attacks by a disgruntled community member occurred in Bath Township, Michigan killing 38 elementary school children and 6 adults and injuring at least 58 other people in what has become known as the Bath School Massacre. There have been hundreds of school shootings or school bombings since the Bath School incident. Several of these school disasters resulted in deaths of 10 or more along with significant numbers of injured victims. One such mass casualty incident occurred during a shooting at the University of Texas in Austin on August 1, 1966 where 15 people died and 32 were injured. Another well-known school shooting occurred at Columbine High School in Columbine, CO on April 20, 1999 resulting in 13 dead and 21 injured when two teenage boys went on a shooting spree at their school. The Virginia Tech shooting on April 16, 2007 resulted in 32 dead and 17 injured at the University in Blacksburg, VA. On December 14, 2012 at Sandy Hook Elementary School in Newtown, Connecticut, 20 students and 6 adults lost their lives in one of the deadliest school shootings to date.

School disasters occur overseas as well and may represent acts of terrorism. The Beslan No. 1 School siege in the Russian Federation of North Ossetia began on September 1, 2004. The horrific events lasted three days and involved the capture of over 1,100 students, parents and staff taken as hostages on the first day of the school year. The siege ended with the death of at least 385 people on September 4, 2004. With the tragedy at Beslan No.1 School, an alarm was sounded for American communities to recognize that schools in the U.S. might also become a target for terrorism. On December 2, 2015, 14 people were killed and 22 were seriously injured in a terrorist attack at the Inland Regional Center in San Bernardino, California. The Inland Regional Center, while not a school, provided care for children and adults with severe disabilities.

Federal Emergency Authority and Immunity

Following the terrorism events of September 11, 2001, the United States government issued a series of new or revised federal laws and policies (Figure 1) designed to direct national emergency preparedness and response activities. Presidential directives set overarching policy for homeland security in the wake of the horrific events and loss of life that occurred in New York, Virginia, and Pennsylvania, that fateful day. Among all of the Homeland Security Policy Directives (HSPDs) and Presidential Policy Directives (PPDs) issued, the tenets of

HSPD-5 (management of domestic incidents), HSPD-21 (public health and medical preparedness) and PPD-8 (national preparedness) have the greatest influence upon disaster preparedness for school districts and school nurses.

The National Emergencies Act (NEA) (Pub. L. 94–412, 50 U.S.C. § 1601-1651) authorizes the president to declare a national emergency and subsequent federal and state authorizations provided by other federal legislation are activated upon that declaration. The Robert T. Stafford Disaster and Emergency Assistance Act (Public Law 93-288, as amended, 42 U.S.C. 5121 et seq.), widely known as the Stafford Act, authorizes the federal government to provide financial, technical and logistical disaster relief to states and other U.S. localities during disasters. Each state has legislation authorizing the Governor to declare a "major disaster" or "state of emergency" whenever state resources become overwhelmed in response to a disaster scenario. Once a Governor makes such a declaration, the Federal Emergency Management Agency (FEMA) will begin providing disaster relief and assistance to the state or locality in distress.

If federal buildings are involved, or if multiple states are impacted, the Stafford Act may authorize federal assistance even without a formal Governor request. Additionally, there are federal laws in place to enhance inter-state cooperation during disasters. States have adopted language in their emergency management statutes to conform to federal guidelines so that they may benefit from state-to-state assistance under the Emergency Management Assistance Compact (EMAC) (Pub. L. No. 104-321, 1996). EMAC provides a framework for one state providing assistance to another state to be reimbursed and also ensures liability, compensation, and licensure protections when personnel or other resources cross state lines to help.

Following the terrorist attacks on 9/11, the President called for all government and non-government entities to develop a model for emergency preparedness planning that aligned with a national template. In accordance with the guidelines provided by the DHS, the template used by all entities is the CPG 101 document. According to the DHS, the "CPG 101 is the foundation for state, territorial, tribal, and local emergency planning in the United States. Planners in other disciplines, organizations, and the private sector, as well as other levels of government, may find this Guide useful in the development of their EOPs" (FEMA, 2010, Introduction).

Tenets of emergency management are derived from the National Response Framework (NRF) and the National Incident Management System (NIMS). On-scene emergency and disaster first responders (including school nurses and other school staff) utilize the Incident Command System (ICS) to operationalize the planning, operations, logistics, finance and administration, as well as intelligence functions of NIMS. State legislation drives the development of inter-connected emergency operation plans (EOP) across all jurisdictions, including both government and non-government organizations (NGOs), within a state. Regional trauma systems further direct and influence the management of medical surge victims to acute-care facilities and the delivery of emergency medical services out in the field and across a large disaster impact area.

Figure 1: Federal Emergency Authority and Immunity Laws & Policies

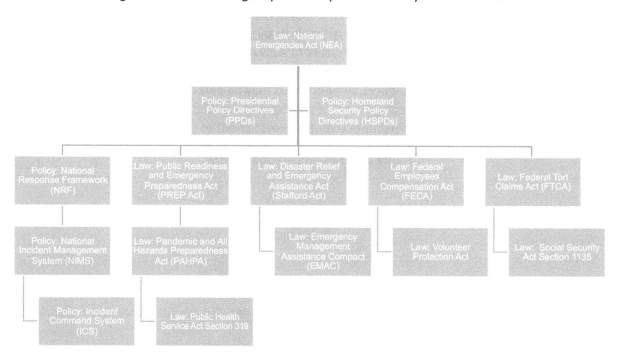

IMPLICATIONS FOR SCHOOL NURSE PRACTICE

While educational leadership focuses primarily on academic goals and objectives for student learning, a host of potential natural and man-made or technological hazards may adversely affect school, student and staff safety at any moment. Acts of school violence, severe weather and hazards, and global terrorism may contribute to the risks and liability for students and school staff. The public's traditional perception that schools are safe havens for children is challenged whenever disaster strikes.

Following a disaster, a school district may be on its own for some time before assistance becomes available through traditional means from the Emergency Medical System (EMS) and law enforcement (LE) agencies. Thus, each school district will benefit from development of an EOP and school-based emergency response plans which encompass long-term mass care capability. Mass care within a school district often involves a memorandum of understanding (MOU) with the American Red Cross or other NGO's for the use of school facilities, busses, and staff. School district EOPs and school-based plans might also plan for mass casualty incident (MCI) response capability. MCI management may be the duty of a school nurse (by virtue of nursing licensure and training) until help arrives, so the school district/school should have a plan for this function that involves the school's emergency response team helping with triage at the direction of the school nurse. School nurses trained to initiate triage, provide pre-hospital care, and ready victims for transport during an MCI may be the weakest link in the school nurse's level of preparedness! In order for schools to build an effective disaster preparedness coalition with other jurisdictions, EOPs must be developed based upon collaboration with all appropriate stakeholders. It is critical that school administrators and faculty are fully informed about and trained on the school's emergency plans and be able to understand their role during all phases of the FEMA Preparedness Cycle (Figure 2) as a result of any emergency or disaster.

Area hospitals, health and medical facilities, and emergency medical services may not be able to sustain full operational capacity during a disaster due to adverse impacts on personnel, facilities or critical infrastructure. Additionally, EMS and local acute care facilities may simply be overwhelmed dealing with the excessive volume of medical surge. School districts may find it necessary to activate the district emergency operations centers (DOC/EOC) or municipal EOC in order to facilitate the high demand for personnel, equipment and supplies to deal with the disaster impact. Health services administrators may be part of the team responding to the EOC to assist the school district with planning, operations, and logistics demands throughout the disaster. The EOC will collaborate with on-scene school personnel and other jurisdictions to provide support.

Figure 2: FEMA Preparedness Cycle

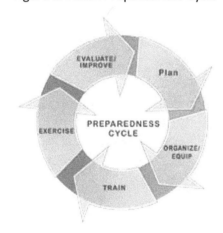

Schools will implement emergency plans using Incident Command System (FEMA, Emergency Management Institute, 2017) principles. An initial communication to staff will alert them to implement appropriate protective measures based upon the emergency plan guidelines. Use of an all-hazards approach to planning and implementation of emergency plans enables schools to set guidelines for four or five specific response capabilities that are well-defined and easy to learn. With practice, staff and students will know how to implement evacuation, reverse evacuation, shelter-in-place, lockdown and reunification procedures in response to an emergency or disaster event at their schools.

School districts generally have many resources in the areas of communications, transportation, facilities, food services, maintenance personnel, emergency managers, police or security monitors, school nurses, health aides, counselors, and psychologists. Mutual aid agreements and pacts established prior to a real-world event are essential to ensuring strong, reliable response and recovery capabilities in an actual disaster. School districts and their respective health services personnel are further challenged to develop and implement continuity of operations plans (COOP) for staff and students that provide a framework for resuming the school district's primary goal of educating students as soon as possible.

School Nurse Role as First Responder

By Governor's Order or state law or policy, many states may require public school nurses to serve as disaster service workers during a state of emergency or disaster declaration. Their nursing expertise may be required to help restore essential health and medical services for a disaster impact area within or overlapping the school district. Any school nurse who performs medical triage, life-saving interventions and emergency treatment

within their scope of practice and when performed in good faith during a disaster will likely have
from civil liability but laws vary from state-to-state. Therefore, it is very important to know the laws in the
jurisdiction where the nurse practices.

According to Brent (2001), "The area of school nursing which holds the most potential for professional liability
is that of acute and emergency care" (p. 410). School nurses must be capable of coordinating health and
medical services on school district property to reduce the risk of death and injury during emergency situations.
Case law illustrates that school nurses must exercise professional judgement to demonstrate competency in
injury assessment, to provide appropriate emergency care, and to determine which injuries require medical
referral. "Even though nurses who are employees of public school districts are granted certain immunities
from lawsuits based upon ordinary professional negligence, school nurses must be certain to provide nursing
care to students consistent with established standards of school nursing practice" (Brent, 2001, p. 412).

School-based emergency operations planning must address the need for multiple methods of communications
so that school nurses can access school administration, staff, nursing supervisors, police, fire and emergency
medical services during emergencies. School nurses must be capable of implementing and responding to
evacuation, reverse evacuation, shelter-in-place, lockdown, and reunification procedures at their schools.
Knowledge of how and when to implement these response actions is paramount to self-survival, especially
during active assailant or active shooter situations.

Due to the risk of being exposed to chemical, biological, radiological, nuclear and high-yield explosives
(CBRNE) materials, school nurses should receive hazardous materials awareness level training to minimize
risk of exposure. School nurses must be knowledgeable about first responder safety and appropriate levels of
personal protective equipment (PPE) needed to safely care for disaster victims. Available PPE might include
gowns, gloves, and masks including N95 masks, goggles and shields. Decontamination of victims requires
specialized training and should not be attempted unless the school nurse is knowledgeable and trained in the
performance of dry doff and wet doff procedures.

During mass casualty incidents (MCIs), school nurses are first responders on their school campuses providing
disaster triage and life-saving care. Conducting triage during a disaster requires a transition from everyday
health office triage when the nurse would give her attention to the most seriously injured or ill students
first. In an MCI, the school nurse will be forced to consider which victims are viable based upon the number
of personnel, equipment and resources on hand to treat. Those victims with the most serious injuries or
illness may not receive immediate care in a disaster with mass casualties. For example, cardio-pulmonary
resuscitative measures may not be initiated for anyone who arrests during the incident as the focus may be
upon using resources for those who can be saved.

School nurses may want to seek additional training to learn field triage protocols which explain how to categorize
victims based upon severity of injury. A variety of tagging systems are available and nurses are advised to
contact their local EMS facilities to see which type of tag system is being used in their local community. The
ability of school nurses to make death pronouncements differs state-to-state so school nurses should seek
guidance from their State Board of Nursing. A local source of information regarding fatality management could
be obtained your local coroner's office. If the mass casualty incident is a potential crime scene, preservation of
evidence would take precedence over school nurses moving deceased victims.

School Nurse Role in a Public Health Disaster

School nurses routinely monitor student populations for signs and symptoms of communicable disease and serve as sentinels for actual or potential public health outbreaks. Public health emergency operation plans for infectious diseases will include mobilization and demobilization of pre-determined points-of-dispensing (PODs) which are often located at public schools. PODs are used to provide mass vaccine prophylaxis and medication treatment to the public as a result of biological terrorism or widespread communicable disease outbreaks such as influenza. Schools may also be identified as locations for isolation and quarantine during an epidemic or pandemic.

School Nurse Competency for Disaster Preparedness

School nurses must be able to demonstrate competency in their emergency response role during drills, exercises, and actual emergencies. Opportunities to practice and demonstrate understanding of the chain of command and communication responsibilities is essential to ensure rapid reporting and response during emergency situations. Awareness of school nurses' limitations in skills, knowledge, and authority in response to disasters is essential to minimize legal risks when performing disaster response actions. School nurses have a responsibility to help schools plan, organize, equip, train, exercise, evaluate and improve upon response and recovery capabilities for the continued provision of school health services during disasters. Further, the preparedness cycle can be utilized to ensure school nurses can make the shift necessary from everyday crisis or emergency operations to a disaster level response capability when necessary.

Education and training of school nurses should emphasize:

- NIMS and ICS,
- Knowledge of the school EOP and the nurse's role(s),
- Use of emergency communication systems,
- Donning and doffing of personnel protective equipment,
- Disaster triage,
- Life-saving interventions, and
- Pre-hospital treatment of both children and adults.

Mental health triage and first aid training is essential and should be provided to all school staff who volunteer to assist. School nurses need the ability to identify immediate personnel, equipment and supply needs, and must know how to utilize available resources wisely recognizing that management of resources may shift from those whose death is imminent to those who have a viable chance of survival.

Conducting drills and exercises for a shelter-in-place due to a chemical, biological, radiological, nuclear, or explosive incendiary device (CBRNE) event response would result in the ability to minimize potential exposure to hazardous materials for everyone involved should an actual CBRNE event occur. School nurses require education and training about mass sheltering and medical surge procedures established for their local communities. Schools may serve as alternative collection sites during mass migration events, or as mass shelters for victims displaced from their homes during a disaster. Knowledge of preservation of crime scene evidence, provision of post-mortem care, and transfer of bodies to mortuary personnel is also warranted.

Development of a certification program specifically designed for school nurses in disaster preparedness is appropriate. The National Association of School Nurses (NASN) developed the School Emergency Triage Training (SETT) Program™ to assist school nurses with basic disaster triage knowledge and training. School nurses may also benefit from a program that provides education and training for pre-hospital trauma and treatment skills. Most of the existing nursing certifications address the needs of patients in the acute care hospital or emergency room setting. School nurses may function as first responders in the field similar to emergency medical services personnel such as emergency medical technicians (EMTs) or paramedics. Restrictions on nursing scope of practice and licensure may prohibit do not permit school nurses from performing many of the life-saving functions that are entrusted to paraprofessionals in the field setting.

EMTs and paramedics have field guidelines for triage and follow medically approved standing orders for initiation of intravenous therapy and administration of emergency drugs. Most school nurses are not performing these duties in schools and probably do not have standing orders for these actions. School nurses may seek additional certifications such as Basic Disaster Life Support (BDLS) or Pre-Hospital Trauma Life Support (PHTLS) to gain the knowledge and skills needed for mass casualty care. These, along with other certification programs, will teach triage, intubation, intravenous therapy, emergency medication administration and other life-saving interventions; however, individual State laws and the Nurse Practice Act may not permit the school nurse to perform some duties in the school setting. Additionally, the school or district that a nurse is employed with may not be willing to support the liability associated with performing some of these procedures in the school health setting. Nurses need to be assured they have medical-legal support for advanced practice roles.

Funding is needed to support planning, operations, equipping, education, training and exercising of school nursing personnel. Prior to a real-world event, school districts need to assert their value to the local community and ensure they are participants during local, county and statewide planning and exercises. School nurses are beneficial to their school staff and students in any potential disaster and are able to perform better if allowed to participate in tactical and operational disaster tabletops exercises as well as basic drills and functional or full-scale exercises involving multi-jurisdictional entities prior to a real-world event.

CONCLUSION

School nurses have an ethical and professional duty to respond to public and mental health emergencies, to protect the public during public health disasters and to be prepared to respond to mass casualty incidents involving school campuses during disasters. Minimizing loss of life and limb is the number one priority for school nurses as they actively engage in disaster response. School nurses must be educated, trained and practiced; and, they must have an appropriate level of equipment and supplies to safely respond during natural and man-made or technological disasters.

RESOURCES

Center for Disease Control and Prevention, National Center for Injury Prevention and Control, Division of Violence Prevention. (2016). *Understanding school violence, fact sheet 2016*. https://www.cdc.gov/violenceprevention/pdf/school_violence_fact_sheet-a.pdf

Federal Emergency Management Agency (FEMA), Emergency Management Institute). (2017). Courses for Independent Study. This includes courses for National Incident Management System (NIMS) and Incident Command System (ICS). https://training.fema.gov/is/

Myre, G. (2015). *A Tally of Mass Shootings in the U.S.* Nevada Public Radio, NPR Now: Reported on December 3, 2015.

National Association of School Nurses. School Emergency Triage Training (Sett) https://www.nasn.org/ContinuingEducation/LiveContinuingEducationPrograms/ SchoolEmergencyTriageTraining

REFERENCES

American Academy of Pediatrics, Council on School Health. (2008, Reaffirmed in 2012). Disaster planning for schools. *Pediatrics, 122*(4). Retrieved from http://pediatrics.aappublications.org/content/122/4/895

Brent, N.J. (2001). *Nurses and the law: A guide to principles and applications* (2nd ed.). Philadelphia, PA: W.B. Saunders Company. ISBN 0-7216-9195-1.

California Government Code. (2016). *California public employee disaster service workers.* California Government Code 3100-3109. Retrieved from http://www.leginfo.ca.gov/cgi-bin/displaycode?section=g ov&group=03001-04000&file=3100-3109

Council of State Governments Justice Center, New York. (2014, February). School safety plans: A snapshot of legislative action. Retrieved from https://csgjusticecenter.org/wp-content/uploads/2014/03/NCSL-School-Safety-Plans-Brief.pdf

Department of Homeland Security. (2015). *National preparedness goal* (2nd ed). Retrieved from https://www.fema.gov/media-library-data/1443799615171-2aae90be55041740f97e8532fc680d40/ National_Preparedness_Goal_2nd_Edition.pdf

Emergency Management Assistance Compact. (1996), PUBLIC LAW 104–321. Retrieved from https://www.congress.gov/104/plaws/publ321/PLAW-104publ321.pdf

Federal Emergency Management Agency. (2008). *Guide for all-hazard emergency operations planning* (SLG 101), 1996, p. GLO-1. Retrieved from http://www.training.fema.gov/hiedu/docs/terms%20and%20 definitions/terms%20and%20definitions.pdf

Federal Emergency Management Agency. (2010). D*eveloping and maintaining emergency operations plans: comprehensive preparedness guide (CPC) 101, version 2.0.* Retrieved from *https://www.fema.gov/media-library-data/20130726-1828-25045-0014/cpg_101_comprehensive_preparedness_guide_developing_ and_maintaining_emergency_operations_plans_2010.pdf*

Federal Emergency Management Agency. (2013). *Guide for developing high-quality school emergency operations plans*. Retrieved from *https://www.fema.gov/media-library-data/20130726-1922-25045-3850/rems_k_12_guide.pdf*

Federal Emergency Management Agency. (2016). *Preparedness cycle.* Retrieved from
https://www.fema.gov/media-library/assets/images/114295

National Association of School Nurses. (2014). *Emergency preparedness and response in the school setting -
the role of the school nurse* (Position Statement). *Silver Spring, MD: Author.* Retrieved from
http://www.nasn.org/PolicyAdvocacy/PositionPapersandReports/NASNPositionStatementsFullView/
tabid/462/ArticleId/117/Emergency-Preparedness-and-Response-in-the-School-Setting-The-Role-of-the-
School-Nurse-Revised-June

National Emergencies Act. (1976). Pub. L. 94–412, 90 Stat. 1255, codified at 50 U.S.C. § 1601-1651

Robert T. Stafford Disaster and Emergency Assistance Act. (2013). Public Law 93-288, as amended, 42 U.S.C.
5121 et seq.

Chapter 37

IMMUNIZATION COMPLIANCE

Linda Davis-Alldritt, MA, BSN, RN, FNASN, FASHA

DESCRIPTION OF ISSUE

School immunization laws have a long history in the United States and have substantially reduced the incidence of communicable and vaccine preventable diseases throughout the country (Orenstein & Hinman, 1999). In 1855, to prevent the spread of smallpox, Massachusetts passed the first compulsory school immunization law (Hodge & Gostin, 2002; The College of Physicians of Philadelphia, 2016e) and in 1860, a New York State law authorized local boards of education to exclude unvaccinated children (Escobar, 2014). By the latter half of the 20th Century, all 50 states had passed school immunization laws (Orenstein & Yang, 2015). School immunization requirements have helped reduce or eliminate the incidence of many vaccine preventable diseases, including smallpox, polio, measles, rubella, mumps, diphtheria, pertussis, and varicella (Boyer-Chu, 2013; Salmon et al., 2005). While vaccines have significantly contributed to many worldwide public health achievements, and have been acclaimed as one of the ten great public health achievements of the 20th century (Centers for Disease Control and Prevention [CDC], 1999; CDC, 2011), they have also been the basis of legal and ethical controversy (The College of Physicians of Philadelphia, 2016a).

Challenges related to state and local vaccination requirements for schools are particularly complex. For example, questions regarding individual civil liberties versus public health and welfare, parent and staff misperceptions of vaccine safety and disease risk, access disparities to vaccine, and an organized anti-vaccine movement (The College of Physicians of Philadelphia, 2016a) have contributed to declining vaccination rates in many areas in the country. Serious outbreaks of vaccine preventable diseases have been fueled by decreased uptake vaccines, misinformation, and falsified research data, resulting in increased absenteeism and subsequent loss of school revenue (Poland & Jacobson, 2011). Additional challenges to compliance with school immunization laws include missing or incomplete vaccination records, parent and healthcare provider buy-in, school nurse staffing issues, and due to competing priorities, school administration adherence to school vaccination laws (Mazyck, 2010). Typically, the threat of exclusion for non-compliance helps to enforce school law (Orenstein & Hinman, 1999).

BACKGROUND

Every child, in every school in this country, is entitled to safety (Association of Supervision and Curriculum Development [ASCD] & CDC, 2014). School immunization assist in ensuring school age children healthy and safe learning environments. Further, by reducing the threat of communicable illnesses overall, school absenteeism is reduced, and families and communities incur less risk of morbidity and mortality (Orenstein & Hinman, 1999).

Schools play an important role in community transmission of vaccine preventable diseases. The concept of "herd immunity," implies that the risk of disease is lowered in susceptible individuals if a large percentage of a general population is immune to specific diseases, and supports school immunization efforts (Fine, Eames,

& Heymann, 2011). However, vaccines, while proven to be successful in protecting the publics' health, remain controversial for some individuals and groups.

In the United States, there is no national vaccination requirement for school entry or attendance. The framers of the Constitution seemed to favor the rights of individuals as set forth in the Bill of Rights. The Tenth Amendment states that those powers not specifically delegated to the federal government are reserved for the states, including the development and enforcement of school immunization mandates. All 50 states and the District of Columbia (DC) have school immunization laws and regulations that generally reflect the Advisory Committee on Immunization Practices (ACIP) recommendations (National Conference of State Legislatures [NCSL], 2017), and all states and DC allow medical exemptions from mandated school immunizations (NCSL, 2016). Medical exemptions may be permanent or temporary. As of 2016, forty-seven states and DC allow religious exemptions and eighteen allow philosophic or personal belief exemptions. California, Mississippi, and West Virginia only allow medical exemptions (NCSL, 2016). All 50 states, DC, and all U.S. territories have some type of immunization registry, either statewide, regional, or local, and as of 2013, according to the CDC, 90 percent of children age 6 and under were part of a registry (NCSL, 2017).

For the purposes of this chapter, the terms "vaccination and immunization" are used interchangeably. While all vaccinations can lead to immunization, immunizations are not the same as vaccines. Vaccines are a type of artificial immunization.

LITERATURE REVIEW

There is no doubt that vaccines have dramatically improved global public health (CDC, 1999; CDC, 2011; Hinman et al., 2011; Katz, Capua, & Bocchini, 2012; The College of Physicians of Philadelphia, 2016c). Data supports that school immunization requirements improve attendance and overall community health (ASCD & CDC, 2014; Findlaw, n.d.; Fine et al.,2011; Lott & Johnson, 2012a/b; Orenstein & Hinman, 1999). Vaccine delivery through school-based immunization programs is a viable and cost effective option to improve coverage for vaccine preventable diseases (Federico, Abrams, Everhart, Melinkovich, & Hambidge, 2010; Fiala et al., 2013; Jacob et al., 2016; Paul & Fabio, 2013).

Mandatory Vaccination

In response to mandatory vaccination and exclusion for unvaccinated or incompletely vaccinated students, some populations resist complying with immunization laws (The College of Physicians of Philadelphia, 2016b; Wolfe & Sharp, 2002). The issues of concern for those opposed to mandatory vaccination center around individual rights, fear about vaccine safety, false information, mistrust of government, and religious or philosophical objections (Buchanan, 2008; Luthy, Beckstrand, Callister, & Cahoon, 2012; Poland & Jacobson, 2011; The College of Physicians of Philadelphia, 2016b). In recent years, the development of hepatitis B and HPV vaccines against diseases that are different from other vaccine-preventable diseases, and subsequent legislative attempts to mandate these vaccines, have prompted new anti-vaccine protests from parents who oppose just these two vaccines (Harvard Law Review Association, 2008). Of prime concern for public health advocates is finding and using effective strategies to address the threat of vaccine hesitancy and refusal (Sadaf, Richards, Glanz, Salmon, & Omar, 2013; Salmon & Omer, 2006; Siddiqui, Salmon, & Omer, 2013).

Exemptions to School Immunizations

All states have adopted exemptions to school immunization laws (NCSL, 2016). There are three types of exemptions:

- Medical, which all states permit;
- Religious, which all states except California, Mississippi, and West Virginia, permit; and
- Philosophical (due to personal, moral, or other beliefs), which eighteen states permit (Cole & Swendiman, 2014; Findlaw, n.d.; The College of Physicians of Philadelphia, 2016d).

While allowing for medical need or individual preference, there are risks associated with the exemptions to school immunization laws including geographical clustering of unimmunized individuals and the weakening of herd immunity, which contribute to disease outbreaks in schools and communities (Blank, Caplan, & Constable, 2013; Buttenheim, Jones, & Baras, 2012; Feikin et al., 2000; Gaudino & Robison, 2012; Lieu, Ray, Klein, Chung, & Kulldorff, 2015; Lobo, 2016; Salmon et al., 2005; Wang, Clymer, Davis-Hayes, & Buttenheim, 2014). In response to serious concerns about the risk that exemptions present, alternative strategies to reduce the negative impact of exemptions have been suggested (Constable, Blank, & Caplan, 2014; Harvard Law Review Association, 2008; Hendrix, Sturm, Zimet, & Meslin, 2016; Jones & Buttenheim, 2014). Suggested alternatives include raising financial liability for parents who refuse to vaccinate their children through reforms in tax law, increased health insurance costs, and reducing public funding (i.e., vouchers and tax credits) for private and charter schools that permit intentionally unvaccinated students to attend those schools (Constable et al., 2014; Harvard Law Review Association, 2008; Hendrix et al., 2016; Jones & Buttenheim, 2014). Many parents who seek exemptions rely on herd immunity to protect their child from disease. It is argued that these parents should share some of the substantial financial burden resulting from their decisions (Constable et al., 2014). Recently, the American Academy of Pediatrics (AAP) has issued a policy statement that encourages all states to only permit medical exemptions from school immunization requirements (AAP, 2016).

School Nurse's Role

Since the inception of school nursing in New York City in 1902, school nurses have played vital roles in keeping children healthy and safe while they are at school. School nurses provide both individual and population based services in the schools; they are on the front lines against infectious disease and are part of the public health infrastructure of the United States; they remove barriers and positively impact immunization compliance; and they are key players in immunization surveillance and reporting, and in planning and coordinating school-located immunization programs (American Nurses Association [ANA] & National Association of School Nurses [NASN], 2017; Holmes, Sheetz, & AAP Council on School Health, 2016; Lineberry & Ickes, 2014; Maughan, Bobo, Butler, & Schantz, 2016; Selekman & Coates, 2013; Wold & Selekman, 2013).

IMPLICATIONS FOR SCHOOL NURSE PRACTICE

Since 1902, when Lina Rogers was hired by the New York City Board of Education as the nation's first school nurse to reduce absenteeism related to infectious diseases, school nurses have been at the forefront of disease surveillance, prevention, and management. School nurses have repeatedly demonstrated their worth in keeping children healthy, safe, in school, and ready to learn. For instance, during the 2009 H1N1 influenza pandemic, it was a school nurse, Mary Pappas, in New York City who recognized and alerted the CDC to an outbreak of flu-like symptoms at her school (Fauteux, 2010). School nurses provide important public health services including health education, immunization surveillance by maintaining student health records and reporting immunization compliance to state departments of public health, and organizing and staffing immunization clinics (Luthy, Thorpe, Dymock, & Connely, 2011; Schaffer, Anderson, & Rising, 2016; Savage & Kub, 2009).

School nurses are often referred to as "gatekeepers" in regard to communicable disease prevention. Parents, healthcare providers, and communities rely on school nurses to keep children safe and healthy while at school. School administrators rely on school nurses to provide guidance to staff, parents, and students about school immunization requirements, compliance, and enforcement. School nurses are a trusted source of health information for students and families. They are well positioned to educate students, families, and school staff about the importance of immunizations, including addressing safety concerns (NASN, 2015).

Every school day in the United States, approximately 55 million students and 7.0 million teachers, administrators, and other school personnel gather in the nation's 133,000 schools (CDC, 2010), placing the nation's approximately 66,000 school nurses on the frontlines of disease surveillance (Fauteux, 2010). School nurses promote healthy habits, address students' episodic and chronic health conditions, and play an important role in preventing, managing and containing communicable disease outbreaks in the school and community (Fauteux, 2010). Schools with school nurses tend to have better vaccine coverage and fewer non-medical exemptions than schools without school nurses (Baisch, Lundeen, & Murphy, 2011). School nurses correctly identify students who are out of compliance with state immunization laws and effectively communicate with administrators and parents what is needed to bring students into compliance. School nurses communicate with parents, school staff and students, addressing concerns and providing information about immunizations that may improve compliance. Charles Basch makes the case that disparities experienced by low income and urban minority youth can be reduced when student health issues are prioritized and partnerships are developed between education and health (Basch, 2010). School nurses build partnerships with healthcare providers and local health departments to improve vaccine access and overall health for all students (Holmes, et al, 2016; NASN, 2016).

Immunization Compliance Review

As communicable disease "gatekeepers," an important part of the school nurse's role is to review, or train other school staff to correctly review, student immunization records for school entry and school attendance. Notifying parents early and often, in writing and via various media sources, of school entry and attendance requirements, well ahead of the start of school, enables families to collect needed immunization records and reduces the possibility of attendance denial or exclusion (Sadaf et al., 2013). To be most effective, notifications should be distributed in the language and reading level of the target population. Similar suggestions apply to notifying parents and older students about the passage and implementation of new school immunization laws (Boyer-Chu, 2013). Boyer-Chu (2013) found success in achieving compliance with a new immunization law through a partnership between the school district and the local health department, buy-in from school district administration, a well-publicized and implemented exclusion policy, electronic data monitoring, low cost and free immunization clinics, and use of media to publicize the new law.

Deciphering immunization records, especially those of immigrant or foreign exchange students, may be challenging. APPENDIX B of the CDC's Epidemiology and Prevention of Vaccine-Preventable Diseases (13th ed.), also known as the "Pink Book," referenced in the resource section of this chapter, includes translations of foreign language terms and vaccines.

Most states have a statewide Immunization Information System (IIS) (CDC, 2016b), formerly known as "immunization registries." State IISs are available for clinicians to enter and retrieve immunization data from the IIS. Depending on the state and the school district, school nurses or other school staff may have full or partial access to their state's IIS. Bobo et al., (2013) reported that only 15 percent of school nurses surveyed had full IIS access, in other words, they were able to both read and enter data. In that same study, approximately half of the school nurses had read-only access, and over 20 percent reported not being able to use their state's IIS. School nurses can access information about their state's IIS on the CDC Webpage at http://www.cdc.gov/vaccines/programs/iis/contacts-registry-staff.html.

Increasing access to state IISs will ultimately improve immunization record keeping, guide public health activities that improve immunization rates, and reduce the incidence of vaccine-preventable disease (Bobo et al., 2013). Other benefits of IIS access and use, for all school-related users – school and public health nurses, other school staff, parents, students, healthcare providers, and school located vaccination clinic (SLVC) staff – include standardized vaccination records, enhanced continuity of care, reduced costs for immunization management (Bobo et al., 2013; Davis, Varni, Barry, Frankowski, & Harder, 2016), and prevention of convenience non-medical exemptions due to unavailable vaccination records (Luthy et al., 2012).

Since all states require immunizations for school entry and attendance, parents need to be encouraged to keep personal copies of their children's immunization records. School nurses and other school staff can use opportunities presented at kindergarten round-ups, back to-school nights, parent-teacher meetings, and similar school events to educate parents about the value of vaccination and the importance of keeping copies of immunization records available at home (Hootman, Schwab, & Gelfman, 2001/2005). In a few states, parents are able to directly access the state IIS to retrieve their children's immunization records; however, this access is not yet available in all states (CDC, 2016b).

Some parents may not know that school health records, including immunization records, are part of the student's educational record, and as such are confidential. School nurses can reassure parents that the Family Educational Rights and Privacy Act (FERPA), ensures the privacy of educational records and requires written parental consent prior to sharing student information. School nurses, and other school staff, need parental consent prior to sharing school immunization information with the state and local public health agencies and healthcare providers, and prior to inputting student specific data into a state or regional electronic iIIS (Bobo, Etkind, Martin, Chi, & Coyle, 2013). Federal laws, such as FERPA, preempt state laws that would allow information sharing of immunization status.

Non-Compliance

For parents who do not comply with immunization laws, the school nurse needs to determine if non-compliance is due to missing or lost vaccination records, lack of access to healthcare, not having time for preventive care due to work schedule(s), being uninsured or underinsured, being illiterate or lacking English language skills, or holding religious or philosophical beliefs against vaccinations (Boyer-Chu & Wooley, 2008). When there are language barriers, it may be possible to bring in an interpreter from the school district office or a local hospital – it is not generally advisable to use children to translate (Boyer-Chu & Wooley, 2008). If the parent expresses concern or beliefs against immunization, it may be an opportunity to clarify their misperceptions and dispel false information about vaccines (Luthy et al., 2012). Once the cause(s) of non-compliance is identified, the school nurse can begin to address the barriers.

If the parent is unable to locate the student's vaccination record, and unless the record can be found or retrieved from the student's healthcare provider(s) or other sources, the student may need to be revaccinated. Some healthcare providers have been and may be reluctant to release the student's immunization record directly to the school nurse, citing the Health Insurance Portability & Accountability Act (HIPAA) Privacy Rule as the rationale for their position. In 2013, HIPAA, Section 164.512(b), was modified to permit providers to release student immunization records to school personnel with the oral consent of the parent or guardian.

All 50 states, D.C., and all U.S. territories have laws identifying mandated reporters, that is, persons who are required to report suspected child abuse and neglect to local child protective services and/or law enforcement. If a school nurse has a reasonable suspicion that the reason a child is out of compliance with school immunization requirements is due to neglect, then child abuse and neglect reporting law requires the nurse to report suspected medical neglect to the appropriate agency in that state. There is precedent *In The Matter of Spencer Stratton* (2002) that non-compliance with state immunization law could be judged to be medical neglect.

Access

Access for many children and teens to vaccination services is a challenge, and access is particularly problematic for the nearly six million children under age eighteen, who have no healthcare insurance (United States Census, 2014). Since about 95 percent of our nation's children and teens attend school, there is no doubt that schools, in partnership with public health agencies, are logical places to provide this population with required school immunizations and annual vaccination against influenza (ASCD & CDC, 2014; Mazyck, 2010). School-based health centers (SBHC) and SLVC, many of which are able to deliver vaccines at no cost through the federal Vaccines for Children program, reduce barriers for uninsured and under-insured students, deliver vaccinations in a familiar setting, and make it possible for parents to not miss work (Federico et al., 2010; Jacob et al., 2016). SLVCs offer opportunities to provide access for children and teens who, without these clinics, may remain unvaccinated (Kansagra et al., 2014). SLVCs can also be effectively used during communicable disease outbreaks to target students and their families in mass community immunization programs (Fiala, et al., 2013).

Most parents believe that schools are particularly convenient and safe venues for teen vaccination, and that parents who are single, who have uninsured children, and whose children attend schools in low income areas are highly supportive of school-based immunization programs (Kelminson et al., 2012). Allowing parents to accompany their child for vaccinations given at school may increase access, as does providing subsidized immunizations through programs like Vaccines for Children. Both strategies increase vaccine uptake at SLVCs (Kelminson et al., 2012).

Physicians are generally supportive of SLVCs as venues for vaccination programs during disease outbreaks, but less supportive of SLVCs as sites to deliver routine immunizations. Strategies to overcome healthcare provider hesitation may include developing partnerships between healthcare providers and SLVCs, and providing information to providers about the availability and complementary role of SVLCs can have to providers' practices (Fiala et al., 2013). For instance, in 2008, when the Advisory Committee on Immunization Practices (ACIP) recommended annual influenza immunization for all children aged six months to 18 years, about 30 million additional people were added to the yearly vaccination cohort – a staggering number for individual providers, but a manageable one for SLVCs (Mazyck, 2010).

Provision of Vaccines at School

In order to provide immunizations at school, pre-planning and preparation are critical. The CDC's (2011) Webpage on Influenza School-located Vaccination (SLV): Information for Planners, as referenced in the resource section of this chapter, has links to information and materials needed to run a successful SLVC. To provide immunizations at school there needs to be a supportive district policy; partnership with the local health department and/or local healthcare providers; access to, and proper storage for, vaccines; a funding source to pay for supplies and clinic staffing; medical orders and protocols authorizing nurses to administer immunizations; written informed parent consent or informed student consent for those over eighteen years; and appropriate vaccine information statements (VIS), in multiple languages, from the CDC (Boyer-Chu & Wooley, 2008; Lott & Johnson, 2012a/b).

As of 2013, the National Vaccine Childhood Injury Act (1986), requires vaccine providers to give patients or their parents the appropriate VISs prior to each dose of the following vaccines: Diphtheria, tetanus and pertussis containing vaccines (DTaP, DT, Td, and Tdap), Haemophilus influenzae type b (Hib), Hepatitis A, Hepatitis B, Human Papillomavirus (HPV), Influenza (both Inactivated and Live, Intranasal vaccines), MMR, MMRV, Meningococcal, Pneumococcal Conjugate (PCV13), Polio, Rotavirus, Varicella (CDC, 2013). It is important to document that the VIS information was given and discussed. If parents are illiterate the VIS information must be read to, or summarized for, the parent(s).

Failure to follow medical and nursing protocols and standards of practice while administering immunizations, as well as failure to obtain written informed consent either from the parent(s), guardian, or students over eighteen years, could be grounds for disciplinary action against the school nurse and legal action against the school district (Hootman et al., 2001;2005). The National Vaccine Injury Compensation Program (VICP), as referenced in the resource section of this chapter, provides compensation for persons who have adverse reactions to covered vaccines. Qualified healthcare providers who administer vaccines included in the National Childhood Vaccine Injury Act (NCVIA) are afforded liability coverage through that Act. The NCVIA may not protect providers who are negligent when administering immunizations, and a negligence claim could be filed if a provider fails to follow the standard of practice and an injury results. Individual states and some municipalities may have laws or ordinances that provide immunity for government officials. Local school districts generally have liability insurance for administrators and employees that may provide protection, as long as negligence is not involved. It is generally advised that school nurses carry their own malpractice insurance, regardless of what liability protection their school district has for employees. Caution should be used if district policy permits taking parent consent to treat or administer any medication via telephone. If telephone consent must be taken, it is advisable to have two school employees listen and clearly document the parent's oral consent or refusal (Hootman et al., 2001;2005).

Unvaccinated Children or Vaccine Refusal

National childhood vaccination programs and state school immunization laws have been successful in reducing the incidence of vaccine-preventable diseases that in the past caused major morbidity and mortality in children (Buttenheim et al., 2012). As an example, endemic measles, which prior to the introduction of the measles vaccine in 1963 (The College of Physicians of Philadelphia, 2016c), sickened millions and killed thousands of children each year, was eliminated in the U.S. by 2000 (Buttenheim et al., 2012). However, the risk of disease remains as some children remain unimmunized due to medical contraindications, religious beliefs, or philosophical beliefs. An example of ongoing risk for unvaccinated individuals was the 2015 measles outbreak linked to a California amusement park that sickened 173 people from 24 states and Washington D.C. (Yox, Scudder, & Stokowski, 2015). Each state has its own laws and rules for accepting or denying exemption requests.

Some parents are vaccine hesitant. Recent studies have identified several concerns that parents have with required vaccinations, including vaccine efficacy versus vaccine risk, adverse reactions, mistrust of traditional healthcare providers and/or involvement with alternative medicine practitioners, distrust of government, and privacy concerns (Federico et al. 2010; Gaudino & Robison, 2012; Luthy et al., 2012; Siddiqui et al., 2013; Wang et al., 2014). Additionally, some vaccine hesitant parents, who have never experienced or observed a vaccine preventable disease, believe that there is low susceptibility and low risk to vaccine preventable diseases, and that otherwise healthy children and teens do not need any, or more, immunizations. These parents may believe that there is more risk to receiving the vaccine than not being vaccinated (Feikin et al., 2000) Other parents erroneously believe that giving multiple vaccines simultaneously to infants and toddlers will overwhelm or weaken the child's immune system. These parents may request alternate immunizations, which are not evidence-based and leave children at risk for disease long periods of time (Yox, Scudder, & Stokowski, 2015). Some parents have the misconception that natural immunity derived from having the disease is more effective and safer than vaccination, hence the interest in some communities in exposing young children to disease at "chickenpox parties" (CDC, 2016a).

School nurses have a vital role in protecting the health of all students by dispelling the many myths about immunizations and in helping parents overcome vaccine hesitancy by providing evidence-based information about vaccine safety and effectiveness. The controversy over the safety of childhood immunizations, particularly the MMR, in light of the fraudulent data linking the vaccine to autism that Andrew Wakefield published in 1998, which was retracted by The Lancet in 2010, has caused many parents to be hesitant about immunizations, and in some cases to refuse to have their children vaccinated (Buttenheim et al., 2012). Even though Wakefield's fraudulent study was retracted, and studies have repeatedly shown that licensed vaccines have very high safety ratings, many parents continue to have vaccine safety concerns that they try to deal with in a variety of ways, including delaying vaccinations or relying on herd immunity, to protect their individual child (Constable et al., 2014).

The whole population absorbs the risk that intentionally unvaccinated individuals pose for the community (Constable et al., 2014). Intentionally unvaccinated children, with nonmedical exemptions, not only are at high risk for vaccine-preventable diseases themselves, but also may infect others who are not old enough to be vaccinated, have medical exemptions, or have unknowingly experienced a vaccine failure (Salmon et al., 2005). It is critical that the school nurse track these students, be vigilant in the surveillance of potential disease outbreaks, and in following exclusion procedures when outbreaks occur. For intentionally unimmunized American children, those with personal belief exemptions (PBE), a recent study revealed that the average risk of infection with measles was between 22 and 35 times more than for children vaccinated against the disease. In that same study, for day care, pre-school, and primary school age children with PBEs, who are more susceptible than older children, the risk of measles infection was 62 times greater (Feikinet al., 2000).

Availability of School Nurses

When schools have adequate school nurse staffing (NASN, 2015), school nurses can provide accurate, scientifically-based information in language that parents can understand in order to help parents make informed decisions about immunizing their children. By familiarizing themselves with common and more challenging questions that parents may ask about vaccinations, school nurses can readily discuss vaccine issues with parents, individually and in groups (CDC, 2017; Luthy et al., 2012), and via school newsletters and social media sites.

Even though school nurses are considered by many as communicable disease gatekeepers, because there are no federal requirements for school health services, other than those in place to protect children with special healthcare needs, support for school nurses and school health services depends, for a large part, on the interests and budgets of local boards of education or, in some cases, on the needs and budgets of local health departments (Lear, 2007). Some states mandate school nurses in every school; however, most states do not. Consequently, the availability of school nurses to review immunization records, conduct health surveillance, and report, prevent, and manage communicable disease varies widely between the states and within most states (NASN, 2016), all of which could pose legal issues for school nurses and school districts. In a recent study in California, only 43 percent of the school districts reported having a school nurse, and in those districts with nurses, the nurse to student ratio varied from "1 nurse to 829 students to 1 nurse to 13,383 students" (Baker, Hebbeler, Davis-Alldritt, Anderson, & Knauer, 2015, p. 320).

In schools and districts without adequate school nurse staffing, questions arise and procedures need to be in place regarding who is responsible for monitoring compliance to immunization requirements, who trains school staff on how to review student immunization records, who answers parent and student questions about vaccine preventable disease, and who educates hesitant parents on the safety and efficacy of modern vaccines.

Exemptions

For children who are exempted medically, the exemption is either permanent or temporary. Permanent exemptions are typically granted because the healthcare provider has determined that it would be unsafe for the child to receive a specific vaccine. Reasons for temporary exemptions include chemotherapy and other temporary medical conditions – most states require that such exemptions be renewed yearly. Typically, state laws also require that the healthcare provider specify in writing the reason for the medical exemption, and in the case of temporary exemptions, that the estimated duration of the exemption be stated. With regard to religious and philosophical exemptions, it is important for school districts and school personnel, including school nurses, to know the criteria used in their state for granting or denying such exemptions. Forty-seven states that permit religious exemption, and eighteen permit philosophical or personal belief exemptions (NCSL, 2016). Some parents request convenience immunization exemptions because over time, their child's vaccination record has been misplaced or lost or is incomplete for some reason. Luthy et al. (2012) found that more than 25 percent of the parents felt that filling out an exemption request was easier than retrieving their child's vaccination record.

As rates of non-medical exemptions rise in specific schools or communities, clusters of intentionally unvaccinated individuals grow, and herd immunity, which remains intact as long as most group members are vaccinated or immune, is threatened (Buttenheim et al., 2012; Salmon et al., 2005). States with fewer requirements for nonmedical immunization exemptions have significantly higher rates of exemptions than states with more requirements and there is a corresponding increase of vaccine-preventable diseases in states with higher rates of non-medical exemptions (Blank et al., 2013). There is no doubt of the need for social and policy change to stem this trend (Blank et al., 2013; Lobo, 2016). State laws for non-medical exemptions need to balance between restricting the numbers of such exemptions in order to maintain adequately high vaccination rates and making certain that adopted exemptions are fair (Salmon et al., 2005). Some states have legislatively mandated annual vaccine discussions with healthcare providers or school nurses for parents seeking non-medical exemptions (Blank et al., 2013; Hendrix et al., 2016; Wang et al., 2014), as one way to ensure that exemptions are not requested just for convenience (Constable et al., 2014). These education efforts should include print and online information about vaccine safety, as well as information that dispels anti-vaccination misinformation (Poland & Jacobson, 2011). Additionally, messaging should be tailored to address specific concerns of individual parents in order to enhance parent discussions and improve vaccine acceptance (Siddiqui et al., 2013).

Whenever exemptions are granted, school nurses must keep track of unimmunized students and provide surveillance in anticipation of disease outbreaks. Additionally, parents or guardians and older students, need to be notified, preferably by the school nurse and in writing, of the health risks associated with vaccine refusal, and of the school or district procedures which exclude and permit the re-entry of unvaccinated students when a disease outbreak occurs. It is reasonable to ask the parent(s) to sign the notice acknowledging that they received the information – the signed notice can then be filed with the exemption request. Many districts also send immunization and exclusion information, along with other annual notifications, in writing to all parents at the beginning of each school year, and require that parents return a signed acknowledgement of the notifications.

State laws vary regarding exclusion of unvaccinated exempted students when there is a disease outbreak. In 2015, twenty-seven states allowed for exclusion of exempted students during a disease outbreak (CDC, 2015). While there have been legal challenges to exclusion practices, in Phillips v. City of New York (2015), the court upheld the right of school districts to temporarily exclude unvaccinated students during disease outbreaks. When exempted students are excluded from school during a disease outbreak, the length of the exclusion may vary depending on the disease incubation period, state law, and school district policy (Hootman et al., 2001; 2005).

CONCLUSION

Overall, school immunization laws have improved compliance rates and dramatically reduced the incidence of vaccine-preventable diseases and associated morbidity and mortality. In spite of these successes, there is still resistance and hesitancy on the part of some individual parents and within some population groups. Improved school nurse staffing, parent education about the risks and benefits of vaccine, overcoming access barriers with free vaccine and school-located vaccination clinics, better record keeping through use of immunization information systems, and reducing the use of immunization exemptions should eventually overcome vaccine-hesitancy and resistance.

It is well established that schools with school nurses generally have higher immunization compliance rates than those schools without school nurses (Baisch et al., 2011). When there are school nurses in the school, they bridge the gap between education and health and promote vaccinations as one means of keeping students safe, healthy, in school, and ready to learn. School nurses are trusted professionals and are able to effectively remove barriers to immunization uptake and compliance.

Health is typically not integrated into the core mission of education at any level, local, state, or federal (Basch, 2007). Competing priorities, particularly in tight budget times, frequently challenge school and district administration support for school health services (Lear, 2007) and immunization enforcement. Even in those states with school nurse mandates, funding streams are periodically unreliable, and reduced resources can lead to "under-filling" school nursing positions with unlicensed personnel. Unlike the professional school nurse, unlicensed personnel may be unable or reluctant to articulate the value of vaccination, the effectiveness of school immunization clinics, and/or the need to enforce school immunization laws, including exclusion, to the school administrator (Robert Wood Johnson Foundation, 2013), in terms that resonate with the administrator, such as the increased likelihood of disease outbreak, school absences, and ultimately lost school revenue. Additionally, when schools do not have qualified health personnel or under-fill school nurse positions with unlicensed personnel, there may be no one at the school to legally administer vaccines and/or document that vaccinations were given. Further, without a school nurse, students who are out of compliance may not be excluded, leaving them, and others who cannot be immunized for medical reasons, at risk for vaccine preventable diseases and prolonged school absences (Baisch et al., 2011).

RESOURCES

- Legal references

    o Family Educational Rights and Privacy Act. Pub L No. 93-380 (1974)

    o Health Insurance Portability and Accountability Act of 1996 (HIPAA). Pub.L. 104–191, 110 Stat. 1936.

    o Individuals with Disabilities Improvement Act (IDEIA), 20 USC et seq., 64 (2004)

    o National Vaccine Childhood Injury Act (NCVIA) - 42 U.S.C. § 300aa-26 (1986)

    o Rehabilitation Act of 1973, 29 USC ch. 16; 34 CFR sec. 104.4(a) (1994)

    o Vaccination Assistance Act of 1962

- Case law

    o In the matter of Stratton, No. 563P02. 573 S.E.2d 512 (2002) 356 N.C. 436 – [Upheld a trial court order to immunize children who had been adjudicated dependent and neglected by their parents, appellants, and their legal custody resided with the Mecklenburg County Department of Social Services]

- o Jacobson v. Massachusetts, 197 US 11, 25 S. Ct. 358, 49 L. Ed. 643 - Supreme Court, 1905

- o Lynch v. Clarkstown Central School District, 155 Misc.2d 846 (1992). [Upheld district decision denies a medical exemption due to lack of credible medical evidence for the exemption]

- o Phillips v. City of New York, 775 F. 3d 538 - Court of Appeals, 2nd Circuit (2015). [Upheld school immunization law and right of schools to temporarily exclude unvaccinated students during disease outbreaks]

- o Prince v. Massachusetts, 321 U.S. at 166–7, 64 S.Ct. at 442 – U.S. Supreme Court, 1944. [Neither rights of religion nor rights of parenthood are beyond limitation. Acting to guard the general interest in youth's well-being, the state as *parens patriae* may restrict the parent's control by requiring school attendance, regulating or prohibiting the child's labor, and in many other ways. Its authority is not nullified merely because the parent grounds his claim to control the child's course of conduct on religion or conscience. Thus, he cannot claim freedom from compulsory vaccination for the child more than for himself on religious grounds. The right to practice religion freely does not include liberty to expose the community or the child to communicable disease or the latter to ill health or death.]

- o Seubold v. Fort Smith Special Sch. Dist., 237 S.W.2d 884, 887 (Ark. 1951) [mandatory school vaccination does not deprive individuals of liberty and property interests without due process of law]

- o Zucht v. King, 260 U.S. 174, 176 (1922) [the Supreme Court upheld a local ordinance requiring vaccinations for schoolchildren. The Court invoked Jacobson for the principle that states may use their police power to require vaccinations, and noted that the ordinance did not bestow "arbitrary power, but only that broad discretion required for the protection of the public health."

- Resources, such as position papers, clinical guidelines

  - o Centers for Disease Control and Prevention. (2015). *Epidemiology and Prevention of Vaccine-Preventable Diseases* (13th ed.). (Hamborsky, Kroger, & Wolfe, Eds.) Washington D.C.: Public Health Foundation. This reference is also known as the "Pink Book."

  - o Centers for Disease Control and Prevention. Talking with Parents about Vaccines for Infants: Strategies for Healthcare Professionals. https://www.cdc.gov/vaccines/hcp/conversations/downloads/talk-infants-color-office.pdf

  - o Committee on Practice and Ambulatory Medicine, Committee on Infectious Diseases, Committee on State Government Affairs, Council on School Health, Section on Administration and Practice Management; American Academy of Pediatrics. (2016). Medical versus nonmedical immunization exemptions for child care and school attendance (Policy

Statement). Elk Grove Village, IL: American Academy of Pediatrics.
http://pediatrics.aappublications.org/content/early/2016/08/25/peds.2016-2145

- Committee on Infectious Diseases; American Academy of Pediatrics. (2015). *Red Book 2015: Report of the Committee on Infectious Diseases* (30th ed.). Elk Grove Village, IL: American Academy of Pediatrics

- Immunization Action Coalition. Influenza School-Located Vaccination: Information for Planners, CDC overview about how to conduct school-located vaccination clinics. http://www.immunize.org/school-vaccination/

- Myers, M.G. & Pineda, D. (2008). *Do vaccines cause that?! A guide for evaluating vaccine safety concerns*. Galveston, TX: Immunizations for Public Health (I4PH) Press.

- National Association of School Nurses. (2015). Immunizations (Position Statement). Silver Spring, MD: Author. https://schoolnursenet.nasn.org/blogs/nasn-profile/2017/03/13/immunizations-ps

- National Association of School Nurses. (2013). Public health as the foundation of school nursing practice (Resolution). Silver Spring, MD: Author. https://higherlogicdownload.s3.amazonaws.com/NASN/3870c72d-fff9-4ed7-833f-215de278d256/UploadedImages/PDFs/Position%20Statements/Other%20Professional%20Practice%20Documents/resolutionph.pdf

- National Association of School Nurses. (2013). School-located vaccination (Position Statement). Silver Spring, MD: Author. https://schoolnursenet.nasn.org/blogs/nasn-profile/2017/03/13/school-located-vaccination

- National Association of School Nurses. (2015). School nurse workload: Staffing for safe care (Position Statement). Silver Spring, MD: Author. https://schoolnursenet.nasn.org/blogs/nasn-profile/2017/03/13/school-nurse-workload-staffing-for-safe-care

- National Association of School Nurses. (2016). The role of the 21st century school nurse (Position Statement). Silver Spring, MD: Author. https://schoolnursenet.nasn.org/blogs/nasn-profile/2017/03/13/the-role-of-the-21st-century-school-nurse

- Offit, P.A. and Moser, C.A. (2011). *Vaccines and your child: Separating fact from fiction.* Columbia University Press. New York, New York.

- School Health Alert. (2016). *School nurse resource manual: A guide to practice* (9th ed.). Nashville, TN: Author.

- Schwab N.C. & Gelfman M.H.B. (Eds.). (2001/2005). *Legal issues in school health services: A resource for School Administrators, School Attorneys, School Nurses*. Lincoln, NE: Authors Choice Press.

- Additional Resources

  - American Immunization Registry Association. http://www.immregistries.org/

  - Centers for Disease Control and Prevention. (2016). For Immunization Managers: Requirements and Laws. Retrieved from http://www.cdc.gov/vaccines/imz-managers/laws/

  - Centers for Disease Control and Prevention. (2011). Influenza (Flu): Influenza School-located Vaccination (SLV): Information for Planners. http://www.cdc.gov/flu/school/slv/index.htm

  - Centers for Disease Control and Prevention. (2015). Parents' Guide to Childhood Immunizations. http://www.cdc.gov/vaccines/parents/tools/parents-guide/index.html

  - Centers for Disease Control and Prevention. (2015). Print Materials for Preteens and Teens. Retrieved from http://www.cdc.gov/vaccines/who/teens/products/print-materials.html

  - Centers for Disease Control and Prevention. (2016). Recommended Immunization Schedules for Persons Aged 0 Through 18 Years. http://www.cdc.gov/vaccines/schedules/downloads/child/0-18yrs-child-combined-schedule.pdf

  - Centers for Disease Control and Prevention. (2015). Vaccines & Immunizations. http://www.cdc.gov/vaccines/index.html

  - Centers for Disease Control and Prevention. (2015). Vaccines and Preventable Diseases. http://www.cdc.gov/vaccines/vpd-vac/default.htm

  - Centers for Disease Control and Prevention. (2016). Vaccine Information Statements (VIS). http://www.cdc.gov/vaccines/hcp/vis/

  - Child Trends Data Bank. (2016). http://www.childtrends.org/?indicators=health-care-coverage

  - Every Child by Two. (2017). 2017 State of the immunion: A report on vaccine-preventable diseases in the U.S. Washington, DC: Author.

  - History of Anti-vaccination Movements. http://www.historyofvaccines.org/content/articles/history-anti-vaccination-movements

  - Immunization Action Coalition/School-Located Vaccination. Retrieved from http://www.immunize.org/school-vaccination/

  - National Center for Education Statistics. http://nces.ed.gov/fastfacts/display.asp?id=372

  - National Conference of State Legislatures. States with Religious and Philosophical Exemptions from School Immunization Requirements. http://www.ncsl.org/research/health/school-immunization-exemption-state-laws.aspx

  - U.S. Department of Health and Human Services, Health Resources and Services Administration. (2016). National Vaccine Injury Compensation Program (VICP). http://www.hrsa.gov/vaccinecompensation/

REFERENCES

American Academy of Pediatrics, Committees on Practice and Ambulatory Medicine, Infectious Diseases, and State Government Affairs, Council on School Health, and Section on Administration and Practice Management. (2016). Medical versus nonmedical immunization exemptions for child care and school attendance (Policy Statement). *Pediatrics, 138*(3), 1-5. doi: 10.1542/peds.2016-2145

American Nurses Association & National Association of School Nurses. (2017). *Scope and standards of practice: School nursing* (3rd ed.). Silver Spring, MD: ANA & NASN.

Association for Supervision and Curriculum Development & Centers for Disease Control and Prevention. (2014). *Whole school, whole community, whole child: A collaborative approach to learning and health.* Retrieved from http://www.cdc.gov/healthyschools/wscc/wsccmodel_update_508tagged.pdf

Baisch, M.J., Lundeen, S.P., & Murphy, M.K. (2011). Evidence-based research on the value of school nurses in an urban school system. *The Journal of School Health, 81*(2), 74–80. doi: 10.1111/j.1746-1561.2010.00563.x

Basch, C.E. (2010). Healthier students are better learners: A missing link in school reforms to close the achievement gap [Research Review No. 6]. *Equity Matters.* New York, New York: Columbia University. Retrieved from http://www.equitycampaign.org/i/a/document/12557_EquityMattersVol6_Web03082010.pdf

Baker, D.L., Hebbeler, K., Davis-Alldritt, L., Anderson, L.S., & Knauer, H. (2015). School health services for children with special health care needs in California. *Journal of School Nursing*, 31(5), 318-325. doi: 10.1177/1059840515578753

Blank, N.R., Caplan, A.L., & Constable, C. (2013). Exempting schoolchildren from immunizations: states with few barriers had highest rates of nonmedical exemptions. *Health Affairs, 32*(7), 1282-1290. doi: 10.1377/hlthaff.2013.0239

Bobo, N., Etkind, P., Martin, K., Chi, A., & Coyle, R. (2013). How school nurses can benefit from immunization information systems: Information exchange to keep students in school and ready to learn. *NASN School Nurse, 28*(2), 100-109. doi:10.1177/1942602X12467651

Boyer-Chu, L. & Wooley, S.F. (2008*). Give It a shot! Toolkit for nurses and other immunization champions working with secondary schools* (2nd ed.). Kent, OH: American School Health Association.

Boyer-Chu, L. (2013). Tips for Tdap triumph implementing a statewide law in an urban school district. *NASN School Nurse*, 28(3), 134-137. doi: 10.1177/1942602X12471200

Buchanan, D. R. (2008). Autonomy, paternalism, and justice: Ethical priorities in public health. *American Journal of Public Health*, 98(1), 15–21. doi: 10.2105/AJPH.2007.110361

Buttenheim, A., Jones, M., & Baras, Y. (2012). Exposure of California kindergartners to students with personal belief exemptions from mandated school entry vaccinations. *American Journal of Public Health, 102*(8), e59-e67. doi: 10.2105/AJPH.2012.300821

Centers for Disease Control and Prevention. (1999). Impact of vaccines universally recommended for children—United States, 1900-1998. *Morbidity and Mortality Weekly Report*, 48(12), 243-248. Retrieved from https://www.cdc.gov/mmwr/preview/mmwrhtml/00056803.htm

Centers for Disease Control and Prevention. (2011). *Ten great public health achievements*—United States, 2001-2010. *Journal of the American Medical Association*, 306(1), 36-38. Retrieved from http://jama.jamanetwork.com/article.aspx?articleid=1104063

Centers for Disease Control and Prevention. (2013). *Vaccine information statements* (VIS). Retrieved from http://www.cdc.gov/vaccines/hcp/vis/about/facts-vis.html#law

Centers for Disease Control and Prevention. (2015). Public health law: State school immunization requirements and vaccine exemption laws. Retrieved from https://www.cdc.gov/phlp/docs/school-vaccinations.pdf

Centers for Disease Control and Prevention. (2016a). *Chickenpox* (Varicella). Retrieved from http://www.cdc.gov/chickenpox/about/transmission.html

Centers for Disease Control and Prevention. (2016b). *Immunization information systems (IIS): Contacts for IIS immunization records.* Retrieved from http://www.cdc.gov/vaccines/programs/iis/contacts-locate-records.html

Centers for Disease Control and Prevention. (2017). *Provider resources for vaccine conversations with parents.* Retrieved from https://www.cdc.gov/vaccines/hcp/conversations/index.html

Cole, J.P., & Swendiman, K.S. (2014). *Mandatory vaccinations: Precedent and current laws* (Congressional Research Service Report). Retrieved from https://www.fas.org/sgp/crs/misc/RS21414.pdf

Constable, C., Blank, N.R., & Caplan, A.L. (2014). Rising rates of vaccine exemptions: Problems with current policy and more promising remedies. *Vaccine*, 32(16), 1793–1797. doi:10.1016/j.vaccine.2014.01.085

Davis, W.S., Varni, S.E., Barry, S.E., Frankowski, B.L., & Harder, V.S. (2016). Increasing immunization compliance by reducing provisional admittance. *The Journal of School Nursing*, 32(4), 246-257. doi: 10.1177/1059840515622528

Escobar, N.A. (2014). Leaving the herd: Rethinking New York's approach to compulsory vaccination. *Brooklyn Law Review, 80*(1), 255-283. Retrieved from http://brooklynworks.brooklaw.edu/cgi/viewcontent.cgi?article=1005&context=blr

Fauteux, N. (2010). Unlocking the potential of school nursing: Keeping children healthy, in school, and ready to learn. *Charting Nursing's Future: Reports on Policies That Can Transform Patient Care* (Issue 14). Princeton, NJ: Robert Wood Johnson Foundation. Retrieved from http://www.rwjf.org/content/dam/farm/reports/issue_briefs/2010/rwjf64263

Federico, S.G., Abrams, L., Everhart, R.M., Melinkovich, P., & Hambidge, S.J. (2010). Addressing adolescent immunization disparities: A retrospective analysis of school-based health center immunization delivery. *American Journal of Public Health*, 100(9), 1630-1634. doi: 10.2105/AJPH.2009.176628

Feikin, D.R., Lezotte, D.C., Hamman, R.F., Salmon, D.A., Chen, R.T., & Hoffman, R.E. (2000). Individual and community risks of measles and pertussis associated with personal exemptions to immunization. *Journal of the American Medical Association, 284*(24), 3145-3150. doi:10.1001/jama.284.24.3145

Fiala, S.C., Cieslak, P.R., DeBess, E.E., Young, C.M., Winthrop, K.L., & Stevenson, E.B. (2013). Physician attitudes regarding school-located vaccination clinics. *Journal of School Health*, *83*(5), 299–305. doi: 10.1111/josh.12031

Findlaw. (n.d.). *School vaccinations*. Retrieved from http://education.findlaw.com/school-safety/school-vaccinations.html

Fine, P., Eames, K., & Heymann, D.L. (2011). "Herd immunity": A rough guide. *Clinical Infectious Diseases*, *52*(7), 911-916. doi: 10.1093/cid/cir007

Gaudino, J.A., & Robison, S. (2012). Risk factors associated with parents claiming personal-belief exemptions to school immunization requirements: Community and other influences on more skeptical parents in Oregon, 2006. *Vaccine*, *30*(6), 1132–1142. doi:10.1016/j.vaccine.2011.12.006

Harvard Law Review Association. (2008). Toward a twenty-first-century Jacobson v. Massachusetts. *Harvard Law Review*, *121*(7). Retrieved from http://www.harvardlawreview.org/wp-content/uploads/pdfs/a_twenty-first-century_jacobson_v_massachusetts.pdf

Hendrix, K.S., Sturm, L.A., Zimet, G.D., & Meslin, E.M. (2016). Ethics and childhood vaccination policy in the United States. *American Journal of Public Health*, *106*(2), 273-278. doi: 10.2105/AJPH.2015.302952

Hinman, A.R., Orenstein, W.A., & Schuchat, A. (2011). Vaccine-preventable diseases, immunizations, and MMWR --- 1961—2011. [Supplements]. *Morbidity and Mortality Weekly Report*, *60*(04), 49-57. Retrieved from http://www.cdc.gov/mmwr/preview/mmwrhtml/su6004a9.htm

Hodge, J.G. & Gostin, L.O. (2002). School vaccination requirements: Historical, social, and legal perspectives: A state of the art assessment of law and policy. *Center for Law and the Public's Health*, Retrieved from http://www.publichealthlaw.net/Research/PDF/vaccine.pdf

Holmes, B.W., Sheetz, A., & AAP Council on School Health (2016). Role of the school nurse in providing school health services [Policy statement]. *Pediatrics*, *137*(6). doi: 10.1542/peds.2016-0852

Hootman, J., Schwab, N.C., Gelfman, M.H.B. (with Gregory, E.K. & Pohlman, K.J.) (2001; 2005). School nursing practice: Clinical performance issues. In N.C. Schwab N.C. & M.H.B. Gelfman (Eds.), *Legal issues in school health services: A resource for school administrators, school attorneys, school nurses* (pp. 167-230). Lincoln, NE: Authors Choice Press.

Jacob, V., Chattopadhyay, S.K., Hopkins, D.P., Morgan, J.M., Pitan, A.A., Clymer, J.M., & the Community Preventive Services Task Force. (2016). Increasing coverage of appropriate vaccinations, a community guide systematic economic review. *American Journal of Preventive Medicine*, *50*(6), 797–808. Retrieved from http://www.thecommunityguide.org/vaccines/vpd-ajpm-econ-increasing-coverage.pdf

Stratton, No. 563P02. 573 S.E.2d 512 (2002) 356 N.C. 436.

Jones, M., & Buttenheim, A. (2014). Potential effects of California's new vaccine exemption law on the prevalence and clustering of exemptions. *American Journal of Public Health*, *104*(9), e3-e6. doi: 10.2105/AJPH.2014.302065

Kansagra, S.M., Papadouka, V., Geevarughese, A., Hansen, M.A., Konty, K.J., & Jane R. Zucker, J.R. (2014). Reaching children never previously vaccinated for influenza through a school-located vaccination program. *American Journal of Public Health*, *104*(1), e45-e49. doi: 10.2105/AJPH.2013.301671

Katz, J.A., Capua, T., & Bocchini, J.A. (2012). Update on child and adolescent immunizations: selected review of US recommendations and literature. In H.H. Bernstein (Ed.), *Current Opinion in pediatrics*: *Office pediatrics*, *24*(3)407–421. doi: 10.1097/MOP.0b013e3283534d11

Kelminson, K., Saville, A., Seewald, L., Stokley, S., Dickinson, L.M., Daley, M.F., . . . Kempe, A. (2012). Parental views of school-located delivery of adolescent vaccines. *Journal of Adolescent Health*, *51*(2), 190–196. doi:10.1016/j.jadohealth.2011.11.016

Lear, J.G. (2007). Health at school: A hidden health care system emerges from the shadows. *Health Affairs*, 26(2), 409-419. doi: 10.1377/hlthaff.26.2.409

Lieu, T.A., Ray, G.T., Klein, N.P., Chung, C., & Kulldorff, M. (2015). Geographic clusters in under immunization and vaccine refusal. *Pediatrics, 135*(2), 280-289. doi:10.1542/peds.2014-2715

Lineberry, M.J., & Ickes, M.J. (2014). The role and impact of nurses in American elementary schools: A systematic review of the research. *The Journal of School Nursing*, *31*(1), 22-33. doi: 10.1177/1059840514540940

Lobo, J. (2016). Vindicating the vaccine: Injecting strength into mandatory school vaccination requirements to safeguard the public health. *Boston College Law Review*, *57*(1), 261-296. Retrieved from http://bclawreview.org/files/2016/02/06_lobo.pdf

Lott, J., & Johnson, J. (2012a). Promising practices for school-located vaccination clinics—Part I: Preparation. *Pediatrics*, 129, S75-S80. doi: 10.1542/peds.2011-0737F

Lott, J., & Johnson, J. (2012b). Promising practices for school-located vaccination clinics––: Part II: Clinic operations and program sustainability. *Pediatrics*, *129*, S81-S87. doi: 10.1542/peds.2011-0737

Luthy, K.E., Beckstrand, R.L., Callister, L.C., & Cahoon, S. (2012). Reasons parents exempt children from receiving immunizations. *Journal of School Nursing*, *28*(2), 153-160. doi: 10.1177/1059840511426578

Luthy K.E., Thorpe A., Dymock L. C., & Connely, S. (2011). Evaluation of an intervention program to increase immunization compliance among school children. *The Journal of School Nursing*, 27(4), 252–257. doi: 10.1177/1059840510393963

Maughan, E.D., Bobo, N., Butler, S., & Schantz, S. (2016). Framework for 21st century school nursing practice. *NASN School Nurse, 31*(1), 45-53. doi: 10.1177/1942602X15618644

Mazyck, D. (2010). School-located vaccination clinics: Then and now [Supplement]. *The Journal of School Nursing*, *26.* Retrieved from http://journals.sagepub.com/toc/jsnb/26/4_suppl

National Association of School Nurses. (2015a). *Immunizations* (Position Statement). Retrieved from http://www.nasn.org/portals/0/positions/2015psimmunizations.pdf

National Association of School Nurses. (2015b). *School nurse workload: Staffing for safe care* (Position Statement). Silver Spring, MD: Author. Retrieved from https://schoolnursenet.nasn.org/blogs/nasn-profile/2017/03/13/school-nurse-workload-staffing-for-safe-care

National Association of School Nurses. (2016). *Public health and school nursing: Collaborating to promote health* (Position Statement). Retrieved from https://higherlogicdownload.s3.amazonaws.com/NASN/3870c72d-fff9-4ed7-833f-215de278d256/UploadedImages/PDFs/Position%20Statements/Other%20Professional%20Practice%20Documents/resolutionph.pdf

National Conference of State Legislatures. (2017). *Immunizations policy issues overview*. Retrieved from http://www.ncsl.org/research/health/immunizations-policy-issues-overview.aspx

National Conference of State Legislatures. (2016). States with religious and philosophical exemptions from school immunization requirements. Retrieved from http://www.ncsl.org/research/health/school-immunization-exemption-state-laws.aspx National Vaccine Childhood Injury Act, 42 U.S. Code § 300aa–26 (1986)

Orenstein, D.O. & Yang, Y.T. (2015). From beginning to end: The importance of evidence-based policymaking in vaccination mandates. *The Journal of Law, Medicine & Ethics, 43*(s1), 99-102. doi: 10.1111/jlme.12228

Orenstein, W.A., & Hinman, A.R. (1999). The immunization system in the United States - the role of school immunization laws [Supplement]. *Vaccine, 17*(3), S19-24. Retrieved from https://www.researchgate.net/publication/12740712_The_Immunization_System_in_the_United_States-the_Role_of_School_Immunization_Laws

Paul, P., & Fabio, A. (2013). Literature review of HPV vaccine delivery strategies: Considerations for school- and non-school based immunization program. *Vaccine*, 32(3), 320–326. doi:10.1016/j.vaccine.2013.11.070

Poland, G.A., & Jacobson, R.M. (2011). The age-old struggle against the antivaccinationists. *New England Journal of Medicine, 364*(2), 97-99. doi: 10.1056/NEJMp1010594

Robert Wood Johnson Foundation. (2013). *School nurse shortage may imperil some children, RWJF scholars warn: Cuts to state and local education budgets weaken school health services, despite increased need for school nurses.* Retrieved from http://www.rwjf.org/en/library/articles-and-news/2013/12/School-Nurse-Shortage-May-Imperil-Some-Children.html

Sadaf, A., Richards, J.L., Glanz, J., Salmon, D.A., & Omer, S.B. (2013). A systematic review of interventions for reducing parental vaccine refusal and vaccine hesitancy. *Vaccine, 31*(40), 4293–4304. doi:10.1016/j.vaccine.2013.07.013

Salmon, D.A., & Omer, S.B. (2006). Individual freedoms versus collective responsibility: immunization decision-making in the face of occasionally competing values. *Emerging Themes in Epidemiology, 3*(13). doi: 10.1186/1742-7622-3-13

Salmon, D.A., Sapsin, J.W., Teret, S., Jacobs, R.F., Thompson, J.W., Ryan, K., & Halsey, N.A. (2005). Public health and the politics of school immunization requirements. *American Journal of Public Health*, *95*(5), 778–783. doi: 10.2105/AJPH.2004.046193

Savage, C., & Kub, J. (2009). Public health and nursing: A natural partnership. *International Journal of Environmental Research and Public Health*, *6*(11), 2843–2848. doi:10.3390/ijerph6112843

Schaffer, M.A., Anderson, L.J.W., & Rising, S. (2016). Public health interventions for school nursing practice. *The Journal of School Nursing*, 32(3), 195-208. doi: 10.1177/1059840515605361

Selekman, J., & Coates, J. (2013). Disease prevention. In J. Selekman (Ed.), *School nursing: a comprehensive text* (2nd ed.) (pp. 473-515). Philadelphia, PA: FA Davis Company.

Siddiqui, M., Salmon, D.A., & Omer, S.B. (2013). Epidemiology of vaccine hesitancy in the United States. *Human Vaccines & Immunotherapeutics*, *9*(12), 2643-2648. doi:10.4161/hv.27243

The College of Physicians of Philadelphia. (2016a). *The history of vaccines: Ethical issues and vaccines*. Retrieved from http://www.historyofvaccines.org/content/articles/ethical-issues-and-vaccines

The College of Physicians of Philadelphia. (2016b). *The history of vaccines: History of anti-vaccination movements*. Retrieved from http://www.historyofvaccines.org/content/articles/history-anti-vaccination-movements

The College of Physicians of Philadelphia. (2016c). *The history of vaccines: Timelines*. Retrieved from http://www.historyofvaccines.org/content/timelines/smallpox#EVT_000019

The College of Physicians of Philadelphia. (2016d). *The history of vaccines: Vaccination exemptions*. Retrieved from http://www.historyofvaccines.org/content/articles/vaccination-exemptions

The College of Physicians of Philadelphia. (2016e). *The history of vaccines: Timelines.* Retrieved from http://www.historyofvaccines.org/timeline#EVT_69

United States Census. (2014). *Number of children without health insurance declines, while it rises for working-age adults.* Retrieved from http://www.census.gov/newsroom/press-releases/2014/cb14-42.html

Wang, E., Clymer, J., Davis-Hayes, C., & Buttenheim, A., (2014). Nonmedical exemptions from school immunization requirements: A systematic review. *American Journal of Public Health*, *104*(11), e62-e84. doi: 10.2105/AJPH.2014.302190

Wold, S. & Selekman, J. (2013). Frameworks and models for school nursing practice. In J. Selekman (Ed.), *School nursing: A comprehensive text* (2nd ed.) (pp. 79-108). Philadelphia, PA: F.A. Davis Company.

Wolfe, R. M., & Sharp, L. K. (2002). Anti-vaccinationists past and present. *British Medical Journal*, *325*(7361), 430–432. doi: http://dx.doi.org/10.1136/bmj.325.7361.430

Yox, S.B., Scudder, L., & Stokowski, L.A. (2015). *Medscape vaccine acceptance report: Where do we stand?* Retrieved from http://www.medscape.com/features/slideshow/public/vaccine-acceptance-report#page=1

APPENDIX - History of Immunizations

The history of human vaccination against infectious disease goes back centuries. The Chinese, as early as 1000 C.E., began inoculating matter from small pox pustules to prevent the spread of infection. In 1721, during a smallpox epidemic in Boston, a local healthcare provider, at the urging of the influential Puritan minister, Cotton Mather, inoculated 248 people against smallpox. The fatality rate for those who were inoculated was about three percent. For those who caught the disease and were not inoculated was fourteen percent. Even with the lifesaving success of inoculation, Cotton Mather was strongly criticized and received death threats from people opposed to vaccination (The College of Physicians of Philadelphia, 2016c).

In 1796, the news about Edward Jenner's landmark work, using cowpox to create a vaccine to prevent smallpox, spread quickly and resulted in widespread endorsement and adoption of vaccination. In 1813, Congress established the National Vaccine Agency, and in 1855, Massachusetts passed the first school immunization law. Despite the success of vaccination in reducing the incidence of smallpox in the 1800s, some groups continued to be wary of vaccination. Severe epidemics of smallpox, such as the one in Montreal, Canada, in 1885, where over 3,000 people died within nine months, resulted from vaccine refusal in the anti-vaccination population (The College of Physicians of Philadelphia, 2016c).

When Britain passed a mandatory vaccination law for all babies in 1853, and another law in 1867, requiring vaccination for all children to up to age 14 years, with fines or imprisonment for parents who did not comply, organized resistance began almost immediately (Wolfe & Sharp, 2002). In response to the anti-vaccine movement, Parliament passed a new law in 1898, with a "conscience clause" which permitted the parents to request a vaccine exemption and introduced the term "conscientious objector" (Wolfe & Sharp, 2002, p. 2).

The anti-vaccine movement gained momentum in other countries in Europe and in the United States. As a result, in the late 1800s, anti-vaccinationists were successful in abolishing mandatory vaccination laws in several states (Wolfe & Sharp, 2002). In 1905, when Massachusetts' mandatory smallpox vaccination law was challenged in the U.S. Supreme Court in the case of Jacobson v. Massachusetts, the Court ruled that states, to preserve public health have the authority to enforce mandatory vaccination laws (Cole & Swendiman, 2014; Harvard Law Review Association, 2008; The College of Physicians of Philadelphia, 2016c).

As more states adopted mandatory school immunization requirements in the early 20th century and required that unvaccinated children be excluded from school attendance, anti-vaccination proponents began to challenge school smallpox vaccination requirements. For example, in 1922, in the case of Zucht v. King, which alleged that local school immunization requirements violated student Rosalyn Zucht's Fourteenth Amendment rights. The U.S. Supreme Court dismissed the case by stating that local ordinances are state laws and states have the authority to mandate vaccination (Cole & Swendiman, 2014; Harvard Law Review Association, 2008; The College of Physicians of Philadelphia, 2016c). Routine vaccination in the U.S. against smallpox ended in 1972, and in 1980, the World Health Organization (WHO) declared that smallpox had been eradicated throughout the world (The College of Physicians of Philadelphia, 2016c).

Despite anti-vaccination sentiment in some populations, between Jenner's early work and 1900, four other vaccines for cholera, plague, rabies, and typhoid fever were developed. From 1900 to 1999, 21 additional vaccines against infectious diseases were developed and/or licensed, (CDC, 1999) and since then, many more have been developed and licensed. Currently, vaccination against sixteen communicable diseases/conditions are recommended for all children under the age of eighteen years (Hinman, Orenstein, & Schuchat, 2011).

By the early 1950s, repeated outbreaks of infectious diseases and the success of disease prevention though vaccination, lead to increased pressure to support a national immunization program. In 1955, with the introduction of the new polio vaccine, federal funds supported a national campaign to encourage childhood vaccination against this disease (CDC, 1999). Since 1962, the federal Vaccination Assistance Act has provided financial and direct support for local and state vaccination programs that have boosted immunization levels for the country's children. In 1977, the Childhood Immunization Initiative established a comprehensive immunization program that includes vaccinations for needy children, regular review of school-age children's immunization records, and annual reports to local health departments. The Childhood Immunization Initiative of 1993, established the Vaccines for Children (VFC) program, which supports vaccination for both uninsured and underinsured children, and funds vaccinations recommended by the Advisory Committee on Immunization Practices (ACIP) records (Hinman et al., 2011).

Chapter 38

SUPPORTING LGBTQ STUDENTS IN THE SCHOOL SETTING

Suzanne Levasseur, MSN, APRN

DESCRIPTION OF ISSUE

Discrimination in education refers to the disfavorable treatment of students based on their membership in a protected class. Federal and state civil rights laws exist to prohibit discrimination by local educational agencies and to guarantee equal educational opportunities among students. Local educational agencies, however, are constantly challenged by developing social norms that impact the application of these civil rights laws. This chapter will focus on the newly emerging discrimination of lesbian, gay, bisexual, transgender, queer or questioning (LGBTQ) students.

BACKGROUND

Discrimination of students often manifests in bullying behavior toward the student. In general, bullying is defined as unwanted, aggressive behavior among *school*-age children that involves a real or perceived power imbalance. Bullying behavior is repeated, or has the potential to be repeated, over time (U.S. Department of Health and Human Services, n.d.). Bullying remains a problem among teens in the United States. In 2014, the U.S Department of Education's Office of Civil Rights noticed an increasing number of complaints regarding bullying of students with disabilities (Pfrommer, 2015). Every state has legislation related to bullying, but the laws are far from uniform.

The United States Department of Education's Office for Civil Rights (OCR) is responsible for the enforcement of federal laws that prohibit discrimination on the basis of sex, race, color, national origin, disability and age. These laws apply to all local educational agencies that receive federal funding. These laws include:

- Title VI of the Civil Rights Act of 1964, which prohibits discrimination on the basis of race, color and national origin;
- Title IX of the Education Amendments of 1972, which prohibits sex discrimination;
- Section 504 of the Rehabilitation Act of 1973, which prohibits discrimination on the basis of disability;
- Title II of the Americans with Disabilities Act of 1990, which applies to all public entities and also prohibits discrimination on the basis of a disability; and
- The Individuals with Disabilities in Education Improvement Act (IDEIA) (2004), which provides for special education and related services to children with qualifying disabilities.

The U.S. Department of Education has clarified that inadequate administrative responses to allegations of bullying, especially involving disabled or LGBTQ students, can be a violation of federal civil rights law (Blad, 2016). In a "Dear Colleague" issued on October 26, 2010, (USDE/OCR, 2015) the OCR explained that harassment based on a student's disability can result in the denial of a free and appropriate public education (FAPE).

LGBTQ Students

Attending a school with a safe and supportive environment is especially important for LGBTQ students, however, some LGBTQ youth are more likely than their heterosexual peers to experience difficulties in their lives and school environments, such as violence. A national study of middle and high school students shows that LGBT students (61.1%) were more likely than their non-LGBT peers to feel unsafe or uncomfortable as a result of their sexual orientation (CDC, 2015).

The U.S. Departments of Justice and Education clarified the rights of transgender students and the corresponding responsibilities of local educational agencies in a *"Dear Colleague" letter* issued on May 13, 2016. The Departments explained that the prohibition against sex discrimination under Title IX of the Education Amendments of 1972 encompasses discrimination based on a student's gender identity. As such, discrimination based on a student's transgender status may be a Title IX violation. Importantly, schools are obligated to acknowledge transgender students' identities by granting them access to facilities (i.e. locker rooms and restrooms) that correspond with their gender identities (U.S. Department of Justice [USDOJ]/U.S. Department of Education (USDE), 2016). On February 22nd, 2017 under the Trump administration the federal Title IX protections were rescinded and guidance provided indicated that student's rights should be determined state by state. Many states have continued to follow the guidance provided in the *"Dear Colleague"* letter of May 13, 2016.

The 2016 Departments' interpretation of transgender student rights and local educational agency responsibilities is aligned with several cases upholding the right of transgender students to use school facilities corresponding to their gender identities. Over twenty states, however, have reacted to the Departments' 2016 guidance by filing lawsuits objecting to the recommendation that transgender students be allowed to use restrooms and locker rooms matching their gender identities (Ring, 2016). With the new administration (2017), other states may continue to challenge the 2016 guidance from the Departments.

The Departments' letter also includes guidance for local educational agencies regarding:

- The use of names and pronouns consistent with the student's gender identity in student records and academic settings;
- Transgender student participation in single-sex classes consistent with their gender identity; and
- The need for local educational agencies to maintain confidentiality in student records regarding birth names and sexes assigned at birth.

IMPLICATIONS FOR SCHOOL NURSE PRACTICE

As a member of the school team, the school nurse is in a key position to advocate for all students, and especially for LGBTQ and disabled students. School nurses understand physical and psychological development and also have knowledge of the educational system, family systems and community resources. They are often in the position to bridge the gap between schools and families, and healthcare providers. The school nurse can be a leader in drafting policies and guidelines that support a safe and inclusive school environment. The school health office is often a place where students feel safe and welcomed. School nurse thus have the opportunity to provide a confidential, culturally sensitive and supportive environment where the needs of the student can be assessed and addressed as needed.

Health risks are disproportionately high among students who are victims of bullying (CDC, 2015.). Researchers from the CDC employed the 2013 National Youth Risk Behavior Survey to examine the association between bullying and missing school. They determined that about 25% of high school students experienced bullying, and 15.5% of these students missed one or more days of school because as a result (Steiner & Rasberry, 2015). The school nurse can be instrumental in making the connection between school attendance and possible cases of bullying.

In addition, school nurses can:

- Provide resources to families to aid students with unique needs;
- Encourage reporting of any acts of bullying;
- Assess students with somatic complaints for bullying and stress;
- Refer students and families as needed to outside agencies or healthcare providers;
- Support policies that address bullying;
- Collaborate with school teams and administrators to implement appropriate interventions to address bullying concerns;
- Educate school staff regarding the rights of LGBTQ youth and students with disabilities;
- Help school staff learn and utilize proper terminology in addressing LGBTQ youth; and
- Promote clubs or organizations such as Best Buddies or the Gay and Straight Alliance that encourage the physical and psychological health of students.

Lawrence Altman, Esquire

Q: What is the role of the school nurse in Title IX issues?

A: Title IX makes all staff mandatory reporters of sexual harassment or sexual violence. It is not uncommon for a school nurse to be the first to learn that a child he or she is seeing informs the nurse that the child has been subjected to sexual harassment or sexual violence. The school nurse may also learn that the child is staying away from school because of fear or the trauma caused by the attacks. Upon learning of this from the child, the school nurse is legally required to promptly in form the Title IX Coordinator of the District of the alleged incident. Hopefully, the school will have in place proper Title IX policies, protocols, and procedures. If not, the nurse should bring the policy issue to the attention of school and/or district administration.

CONCLUSION

Federal civil rights laws exist to protect students from discrimination based on their membership in certain groups. These laws are increasingly being interpreted to protect historically marginalized students, including those in the LGBTQ community and the disabled. School nurses are positioned to be leaders within their school communities, promoting respect for diversity and helping to identify those students who may be victims of bullying or other discrimination. Preventive strategies should be put in place through a comprehensive model that protects all students from bullying.

RESOURCES

> *Please see Chapter 44 for more information on bullying.*

National Association of School Nurses. (Revised 2016). *LGBTQ Students: The Role of the School Nurse* (Position Statement). Silver Spring, MD. Retrieved from www.NASN.org/policy/advocacy/positionpapers.

Gay, Lesbian, Straight Education Network (GLSEN). (Revised 2016). GLSEN Model District Policy for Transgender and Gender Nonconforming Students. New York, NY. Retrieved from https://www.glsen.org/sites/default/files/GLSEN%20Trans%20Model%20Policy%202016_0.pdf.

U.S. Department of Education, Office for Civil Rights *Know Your Rights*. Retrieved from http://www2.ed.gov/about/offices/list/ocr/know.html.

Legal References: Doe v. Regional School Unit 26, 2014 ME 11, 86 A.3d 600 (ME 2014)

REFERENCES

Americans with Disabilities Act of 1990, 42 U.S.C. §§ 12101-12213.

Blad, E. (2016, May 31). School civil rights took spotlight under Obama. *Education Week, 35* (32), 1, 14-15. Retrieved from www.edweek.org/ew/articles/2016/06/01/school-civil-rights-took-spotlight

Centers for Disease Control and Prevention. (2015). *Bullying and absenteeism: Information for state and local education agencies.* Retrieved from http://www.cdc.gov/healthyyouth/health_and_academics/pdf/fs_bullying_absenteeism.pdf

Lambda Legal. (2015). *Equal access to public restrooms (frequently asked questions).* Retrieved from http://www.lambdalegal.org/know-your-rights/transgender/restroom-faq

Individuals with Disability Education Improvement Act of 2004, 20 U.S.C. §§ 1400 *et seq.*

Pfrommer, J. (2015). *Disability-based bullying and harassment in the schools: Legal requirements for identifying, investigating and responding.* Palm Beach Gardens FL:LRP publications.

Rehabilitation Act of 1973, 29 U.S.C. §§ 701 et seq.

Ring. T. (2016, July 8). 10 More states sue Obama administration over trans student guidance. *Advocate.com.* Retrieved from http://www.advocate.com/transgender/2016/7/08/10-more-states-sue-obama-administration-over-trans-student-guidance

Steiner, R.J., & Rasberry, C.N. (2015). Associations between in-person and electronic bullying victimizations of missing school because of safety concerns among U.S. high school students. *Journal of Adolescence, 43,* *1-4.* Retrieved from http://www.jahonline.org/article/S1054-139X(14)00594-1/pdf

U.S. Department of Health and Human Services. (n.d.) *What is bullying?* Retrieved from https://www.stopbullying.gov/what-is-bullying/

Title VI of the Civil Rights Act of 1964. 42 U.S.C. §§ 2000d *et seq.*

Title IX of the Education Amendments of 1972. 20 U.S.C. §§ 1681 *et seq.*

U.S. Department of Education, Office for Civil Rights. (2010). *Dear colleague letter: Harassment and bullying.* Retrieved from http://www2.ed.gov/about/offices/list/ocr/letters/colleague-201010.html

U.S. Department of Justice/U.S. Department of Education. (2016). *Dear colleague letter: Transgender students.* Retrieved from http://www2.ed.gov/about/offices/list/ocr/letters/colleague-201605-title-ix-transgender.pdf

Chapter 39

PRIVATE DUTY NURSE CARE

Bill Patterson, MPA, BSN, BA, RN

DESCRIPTION OF ISSUE

There has been an unprecedented increase in the number of children in the United States that are surviving and thriving despite complex health conditions and complications associated with prematurity, birth complications, severe congenital anomalies and acquired health conditions. Advances in healthcare technology, pharmaceuticals and medical science has spurred the increase in the population of children with special healthcare needs requiring continuous or one-to-one nursing care in schools (Allen, Cristofalo, & Kim, 2011; Burns et al., 2010, Elam & Irwin, 2015). School districts are not only faced with the dilemma of how to meet the educational needs of children with complex health conditions, they are also challenged with how to provide and pay for necessary healthcare services while the child is at school.

Under Cedar Rapids v. Garrett F. (1999) and Irving v. Tatro (1984), the U.S. Supreme Court determined that under the Individuals with Disabilities Education Act (IDEA) of 2004 "related services" provision, school districts are required to provide "school health services," including one to one care or continuous nursing services, if those services are "related" to enabling a disabled child to remain in school and "make such access meaningful." School districts were tasked with providing what is primarily known as private duty nursing, typically provided in home and community settings via health insurance or private pay. School health services are required to be provided under Federal law under related services when required to assist a child with a disability to benefit from his/her special education, as outlined in the child's individual education program (IEP), which is required under IDEA (IDEA, 2004). Private duty nurses could also be utilized under the related services provision under Section 504 of the Rehabilitation Act of 1973 if lacking the sufficient school nursing personnel to meet the needs of complex chronic condition(s) of students. Shannon and Minchella (2015) believe personal nurse is the most appropriate term as it denotes this nurse is assigned to care for a specific student or students, as opposed to a school nurse who is the nurse for the whole school community or the school's population-focused nurse. For clarity and consistency, private duty nurse will be the term utilized throughout this chapter.

Understanding the role of the school nurse, if available, is essential to ensure that private duty nurses are not operating separately and out of alignment with respective state and federal laws, rules and regulations pertaining to education. The extent of medical treatments required by some students in schools, as prescribed by community-based healthcare providers, leaves schools to question the difference between educationally necessary and rehabilitation-related services (Elam & Irwin, 2015). Collaboration and understanding of roles and relationships between school nurses, school level personnel and private duty nurses is key to ensuring student's health and safety while attending school.

BACKGROUND

It may be generally assumed that private duty nursing is a more recent job sector creation, but actually it is not novel, rather we are witnessing nursing's return to its origins. Schools of nursing began appearing in the United

States towards the latter half of the 19th century, but most hospitals did not hire or hired limited numbers of graduate nurses. This was due in part because of a nurse's training, which required a student nurse to provide the majority of patient care in hospitals affiliated with schools of nursing (Whelan, 2012). As a result, most nurse graduates sought employment in the private duty arena. Regardless of setting, the patient assumed full responsibility for payment of the nursing services and private duty nurse assumed the entire care of the patient (Whelan, 2000).

A change in payment structure for private duty nursing services has evolved over time, shifting to primarily private and public health insurance plans. Granted, there are still some private pay arrangements. Fee-for-service payment systems have shifted over to managed care plans involving case managers to mitigate increasing healthcare related costs. For children with disabilities receiving services under the IDEA with an Individualized Education Program (IEP) or Individualized Family Service Plan (IFSP) [legal plan of services under Part C of IDEA], Medicaid is the primary payer to the Department of Education (Centers for Medicare and Medicaid Services [CMS], 1997).

Respective states' Medicaid programs have generated policies, rules and requirements for Medicaid reimbursement programs for the school-based health related services provision in the school setting. Collaboration and mutual understanding with respective states' Department of Health, Human Services and Education is essential. Many states such as Arkansas, New York, Minnesota, Texas, Kentucky, Maryland, Missouri and Indiana have gone to great lengths to define private duty nursing or personal nursing services and delineate roles and responsibilities not only in the nursing services provision but also in the areas of financing, payment and liability.

Delivery of Services Using Private Duty Nurses

School teams, under the IDEA are comprised of those who know the student's needs best (34 C.F.R. §300.321, 2006). The school conducts an evaluation to determine eligibility of special education and related services to be provided for the student to access a free appropriate public education (FAPE) (34 C.F.R. §300.34, 2006). The school nurse is an invaluable resource in providing a nursing assessment of students' healthcare needs and determining the type of personnel necessary to provide nursing services (Wisconsin Department of Public Instruction [DPI], 2011). The school nurse can provide a holistic view of the student's needs in the context of health-related services provision in school and associated settings.

Service Delivery Models

States and school districts utilize various models of service delivery to meet the school health and related services needs mandated under IDEA. As with most things in life, there are pros and cons of each. To further complicate understanding of the mandate, there are also related services and accommodations under the mandates of Section 504 of the Rehabilitation Act of 1973 and the Americans with Disabilities Act Amendments Act of 2008 that must also be considered. The most common service delivery models of nursing services delivery are: 1) employee-based and 2) third party or contracted private duty nurses (Shannon & Minchella, 2015). School districts must consider the benefits and risks associated with both models in relation to their constituency.

<u>Employee Based</u>

The benefits of employee-based service provision are that the school district has more control over:

1) job description;
2) supervision;
3) nursing and educational duties (may include nursing delegation);
4) accountability of nursing care;
5) flexibility of scheduling; and
6) communication protocols between the special needs nurse and school nurse, parents, school personnel and medical provider(s).

The disadvantages are:

1) the school district must hire and supervise the nurse (i.e., including liability); and
2) there may be limited availability of nurses to provide backup coverage when that private duty or personal nurse is out sick or otherwise absent from work.

<u>Third Party or Contracted Private Duty Nurse</u>

Advantages of utilizing third party or contracted private duty nurses are:

1) either the family or agency hires the nurse;
2) the agency provides backup nursing coverage, if provisions built into the contract;
3) decreased or shared liability between the private duty nurse/agency and the school district;
4) family's comfort with a nurse who is often already familiar with and knows their child; and
5) continuity of nursing care between home and school.

The negatives of the third party or contracted private duty nurse model are:

1) the private duty nurse's inability to provide care to other students (including delegation);
2) federal funding limitations;
3) lack of involvement of the nurse in student's educational needs; and
4) the lack of direct accountability to school personnel for nursing care.

(The above list of items identified as pros and cons of nursing service delivery models are adapted from Independent School District 196, 1997; Maez, 2014; Maryland State School Health Services, 2003; Portage Township School Corporation, 2010; Shannon & Minchella, 2015; Wisconsin DPI, 2011).

IMPLICATIONS FOR SCHOOL NURSE PRACTICE

Staffing Determination

The level of nursing care determination for students is the responsibility of the Individual Education Plan (IEP) team. The most qualified member of the IEP team to assess the student's health condition(s) and recommend whether continuous nursing care is required at school is the professional school nurse (Gibbons, Lehr, & Selekman, 2013). Licensed primary medical care provider (e.g., healthcare provider) orders are required for nursing services as an IEP Team cannot prescribe health services for a nurse to follow. Most of the healthcare procedures required to be done in public schools must be supervised or performed by state-licensed health personnel such as a registered nurse (American Federation of Teachers [AFT], 2009). One nurse to one student may be necessary when the student requires continuous nursing judgment and care (National Association of School Nurses [NASN], 2012). There may be situations where several students in a classroom may require continuous monitoring with multiple treatments and/or procedures and one nurse may still be able to meet their needs (Shannon & Minchella, 2015). The licensed Registered Nurse (RN) or school nurse is the most qualified member of the IEP team to address these needs and to help the team to make the most informed decision on appropriate staffing meeting the health and safety needs of the student(s).

Consideration of the qualifications of the provider required to meet the student(s) needs are also within the realm of the school nurse. Determination of whether another RN (e.g., private duty nurse or school/district employed nurse), a licensed practical/vocational nurse, or an unlicensed assistive aide (UAP) who is delegated simple, straightforward nursing task(s) can be made by the school nurse, if permitted by school nurse's respective state nurse practice acts. School nurses must know their respective, and potentially neighboring, state's laws regarding delegation. The school nurse would be factoring in safety and fiscal accountability measures into the decision-making as they relate to the school and family. School nurses may want to educate other school team members that insurance companies have life-time maximums, putting a family at risk for surpassing those limits when increasing services to cover school needs under the family's health insurance plan.

Bear in mind that as the most qualified member of the IEP team to address the health and nursing needs of students, a higher level of accountability and responsibility falls upon the school nurse. The school nurse should consult with his or her state nursing organization and/or school nursing organization, on insurance or liability protection coverage as purchasing of a personal malpractice insurance plan may be warranted.

Liability and Private Duty/Personal Nurses

With the ever-increasing litigious nature of our country, it is understandable (and wise) that school districts, administrators, and school nurses be aware of potential liabilities in decision-making and provision of school health services for students. With the ever-increasing litigious nature of our country, it is understandable (and wise) that school districts, administrators, and school nurses be aware of potential liabilities in decision-making and provision of school health services for students. To ensure the school district is covered, it is critical that contracts and/or memoranda of understanding with agency nurses is specifically detailed as to all services rendered and responsibilities of all parties involved. This includes, but not limited to: common clauses, provisions, provider obligations, compliance with utilization review standards, protocols, quality assurance program, complaints, maintenance and retention of records and confidentiality, payment, use of name, relationship of the parties, notification, hold harmless, no balance billing clauses, insurance and indemnification, term, suspension and termination, declarations, closing and due diligence (Schwab & Gelfman, 2001/2005).

These concepts may quite possibly be new to a school nurse, having not been taught in nursing school, so it is best to approach this need much like the IEP process - as a team. It is important to work with the district procurement and contracts specialist, school attorney and other legal and financial professionals in the school district to ensure that the educational, fiscal and medicolegal liabilities are considered and mitigated to best meet the needs of the students and the school district. If issues arise, it is more than likely that they will be decided on a case by case basis, making it extremely important that they are carefully considered and included in the documents.

As the school nurse with the specialized health expertise, know thy practice (i.e., respective state Nursing Practice Act[s]). The school nurse will be depended upon to provide particular expertise in meeting the healthcare needs of students (Elam & Irwin, 2015). If in doubt or uncertain on areas in the nursing field, consult your nursing organization and national and state school nursing organization, along with respected colleagues and mentors in school nursing. Research and become familiar with all school health and school nursing related statutes, administrative policies and procedures and local (if any) and state laws, regulations, and guidelines. This will not only help in the development of strong contracts or memoranda, but it will also protect the school nurse in all facets of providing school health and school nursing services in the school and community setting.

Roles/Relationships

As school nurses are nurses for the health of all students and whole school communities, it can become confusing when private duty or personal nurses enter as service providers within a school community. Clear delineation and understanding of roles, as well as responsibilities, must take place. It may be too late to ask questions after a student with the private duty/personal nurse has entered a school campus. It is important for the school nurse to work with the school administrators, in addition to fiscal and legal professionals, to address any and all ambiguities to ensure that the student(s), school nurse, school personnel, and school district are covered when the student(s) are in school.

Communication protocols, policy and procedures, training, orientation, health procedures or protocols, emergency procedures, creation and implementation of Individualized Health Plans (IHPs), documentation, schedules, chain of command, personnel rules, etc. are some of the items that should be covered in a checklist when working with contracted private duty/personal nurses in school (Maryland State School Health Services, 2003; Shannon & Minchella, 2015). When working with a contracted LPN, it is imperative to clarify the role between the school nurse and the contract LPN. When developing the IEP, clarification on whose roles and responsibility is it to develop the IHP for the LPN to implement and is the contract agency responsible for the nursing clinical supervision and delegation, if permitted by respective school nurse's state, of nursing tasks to the LPN employee.

A proactive approach by school nurses to issues, including collaborating with the school's administrator, in addition to district legal and fiscal professionals, prior to the entry into any situation such as this is strongly recommended. It may also be necessary to seek clarification from the respective state Board of Nursing or State Department(s) of Education and Health on any ambiguities when it comes to nursing delegation and supervision.

CONCLUSION

Private duty or personal nurses are not a nouveau creation but rather a three-hundred sixty degree turn to the roots of nursing care. The inclusion of private duty or personal nurses into the school setting is a more modern nursing delivery care model. As school districts have come to understand, based upon case law and U.S. Supreme Court decisions, the provision of FAPE to some IDEA and Section 504 eligible students may include continuous nursing care delivered to one or more students. One such delivery model of these services is the use of private duty or personal nurses, either contracted or employee-based. Regardless of nursing services delivery model, **creation of clear and delineated policies, contracts, memoranda of understanding, guidelines, job descriptions and protocols/procedures is necessary**. In absence of anything written, anything goes and mitigating potential litigation is nearly impossible.

With the increase in the population of children with special healthcare needs due to advances in medical science and technology, resultant increases in fiscal and legal costs will logically correlate. It behooves school districts to include school nurses in strategically planning and coordinating how to mitigate these areas of concern to ensure the health and safety of IDEA and Section 504 eligible students.

RESOURCES

American Nurses Association & National Council of State Boards of Nursing [NCSBN] (2006). *Joint Statement on Delegation*. Retrieved from https://www.ncsbn.org/Delegation_joint_statement_NCSBN-ANA.pdf

American School Health Association. (2008). Special Legal Issue: A CDC review of school laws and policies concerning child and adolescent health. *Journal of School Health, 78*(2).

Arkansas Department of Health and Human Services. (2009). *Provider manual update: Section II – Private duty nursing services*. Retrieved from https://www.medicaid.state.ar.us/download/provider/provdocs/manuals/.../pdn_ii.doc

Centers for Medicare and Medicaid Services. (1997). *Medicaid and school health: A technical assistance guide*. Retrieved from https://www.medicaid.gov/medicaid-chip-program-information/by-topics/financing-and-reimbursement/downloads/school_based_user_guide.pdf

Kentucky Board of Nursing. (2016). *Advisory opinion statement: Roles of nurses who provide "private duty" nursing* (AOS #22). Retrieved from http://kbn.ky.gov/practice/Documents/aos22.pdf

Lechtenberg. J. (2009). Special report: Legal aspects of school nursing. *School Health Alert.* Retrieved from http://www.schoolnurse.com/public/images/Legal%20Aspects%20of%20School%20Nursing%2004-2009.pdf

Missouri Department of Social Services. (2010). *Provider bulletin: Private duty nursing school based services* (Vol. 33, No. 13). Retrieved from https://dss.mo.gov/mhd/providers/pdf/bulletin33-13_2010nov30.pdf

National Association of School Nurses. (2013). *Coordinated School Health* (Position Statement). Retrieved from http://www.nasn.org/Portals/0/positions/2013pscoordinated.pdf

New York State Department of Health & New York State Education Department. (2015). *Clarification on Medicaid reimbursement for nursing services* (Issue #15-02). Retrieved from http://www.oms.nysed.gov/ medicaid/medicaid_alerts/alerts_2015/15_02_clarification_medicaid_reimbursement_nursing_ services_3_4_15.pdf

Selekman, J. (Ed.). (2013). *School nursing: A comprehensive text*. Philadelphia, PA: F.A. Davis.

Shenkman, E. (2001). *An analysis of Medicaid private duty nursing for children with special health care needs*. Retrieved from University of Florida Center for Medicaid and the Uninsured website: http://fcmu.phhp.ufl.edu/research/focus/pdf/Report00-2001-MedicaidPrivateDutyNursingForChildrenWith SpecialNeeds.pdf

Taliaferro, V. & Resha, C. (Eds.). (2016). School nurse resource manual (9th edition). Nashville, TN: SchoolNurse.com.

Texas Department of Aging and Disability Services. (2013). *Medically dependent children program provider manual*. Retrieved from http://www.dads.state.tx.us/handbooks/appendix/21.htm

Washington State Health Care Authority. (2016*). Private duty nursing for children: Provider guide*. Retrieved from http://www.hca.wa.gov/assets/billers-and-providers/private_duty_nursing_bi.pdf

REFERENCES

Allen, M.C., Cristofalo, E.A., & Kim, C. (2011). Outcomes of preterm infants: Morbidity replaces mortality. *Clinics in Perinatology, 38*, 441-454. Retrieved from https://www.researchgate.net/profile/Elizabeth_ Cristofalo/publication/51617304_Outcomes_of_preterm_infants_morbidity_replaces_mortality/ links/00b7d51897e6c837ae000000.pdf

American Federation of Teachers. (2009). *The medically fragile child: Caring for children with special healthcare needs in the school setting*. Retrieved from https://www.aft.org/sites/default/files/ medicallyfragilechild_2009.pdf

Assistance to States for the Education of Children with Disabilities, 34 C.F.R. Part 300 (2006). Retrieved from http://idea.ed.gov/explore/view/p/,root,regs,300,D,300%252E304

Burns, K.H., Casey, P.H., Lyle, R.E., Mac Bird, T.M., Fussell, J.J., & Robbins, J.M. (2010). Increasing prevalence of medically complex children in US hospitals. *Pediatrics, 126*, 638-646. Retrieved from https://www.researchgate.net/profile/James_Robbins2/publication/46380901_Increasing_Prevalence_ of_Medically_Complex_Children_in_US_Hospitals/links/544153430cf2a6a049a57317.pdf

Cedar Rapids Community School District v. Garret F., 526 U.S., 66. (1999). Retrieved from http://www.wrightslaw.com/law/caselaw/case_Cedar_Rapids_SupCt_990303.htm

Centers for Medicare and Medicaid Services. (1997). *Medicaid and school health: A technical assistance guide*. Retrieved from https://www.medicaid.gov/medicaid-chip-program-information/by-topics/ financing-and-reimbursement/downloads/school_based_user_guide.pdf

Elam, M., & Irwin, M.K. (2015). Meeting the health care needs of students with severe disabilities in the school setting: Collaboration between school nurses and special education teachers. *Psychology in the Schools, 52*(7), 683-701. doi: 10.1002/pits.21849

Gibbons, L., Lehr, K., & Selekman, J. (2013). Federal laws protecting children and youth with disabilities in the schools. In J. Selekman (Ed.), *School nursing: A comprehensive text* (2nd ed.) (pp. 257-283). Philadelphia, PA: F.A. Davis.

Independent School District 196. (1997). *Private duty nurses* (506.3.2AR). Retrieved from http://www.district196.org/district/schoolboard/policies/500/506.3.2ar.pdf

Individuals with Disability Education Improvement Act (2004), 20 U.S.C. 1400 et seq.

Irving Independent School District v. Tatro, 468 U.S. 883. (1984) Retrieved from http://usedulaw.com/350-irving-independent-school-district-v-tatro.html

Maez, G. (2014). *Health services, nursing services, and private duty nurses*. Paper presented at 2014 Texas Council of Administrators of Special Education, Austin, TX. Retrieved from http://c.ymcdn.com/sites/www.tcase.org/resource/resmgr/interactive14_handouts/health_services,_nursing_ser.pdf

Maryland State School Health Services. (2003). *Maryland state school health services guidelines: Model policy for the management of students requiring a private duty nurse in schools*. Retrieved from http://www.marylandpublicschools.org/NR/rdonlyres/6561B955-9B4A-4924-90AE-F95662804D90/3294/PDN2004.pdf

National Association of School Nurses (NASN). (2012). *Chronic health conditions managed by school nurses* (Position Statement). Retrieved from https://www.nasn.org/PolicyAdvocacy/PositionPapersandReports/NASNPositionStatementsFullView/tabid/462/ArticleId/17/Chronic-Health-Conditions-Managed-by-School-Nurses-Revised-January-2012

Portage Township School Corporation. (2010). Administrative guidelines: Private duty nurses (5310.01). Retrieved from http://www.neola.com/portagetwp-in/search/ag/ag5310.01.htm

Rehabilitation Act of 1973, 29 U.S.C. § 504

Schwab, N.C. & Gelfman, M.H.B. (Eds.). (2005). *Legal issues in school health services: A resource for school administrators, school attorneys and school nurses,* (pp. 465-471). Lincoln, NE: Authors Choice Press.

Shannon, R.A. & Minchella, L. (2015). Students requiring personal nursing care in school. *NASN School Nurse, 30*(2), 76-80. doi: 1177/1742602x155569781

Whelan, J.C. (2000). Too many too few: The supply, demand, and distribution of private duty nurses, 1910-1965. *Dissertation Abstract,* AAI9965594. Retrieved from http://repository.upenn.edu/dissertations/AAI9965594/

Whelan, J.C. (2012). When the business of nursing was the nursing business: The private duty registry system, 1900-1940. *The Online Journal of Issues in Nursing, 17*(2). Retrieved from http://nursingworld.org/MainMenuCategories/ANAMarketplace/ANAPeriodicals/OJIN/TableofContents/Vol-17-2012/No2-May-2012/Private-Duty-Registry-System-1900-1940.html

Wisconsin Department of Public Instruction. (2011). *1:1 Nursing services for students with special health care needs*. Madison, WI. Retrieved from http://dpi.wi.gov/sites/default/files/imce/sspw/pdf/snnursingservices.pdf

Chapter 40

SCHOOL BASED HEALTH CENTERS AND THE SCHOOL NURSE

Sara Rigel, MPH, CHES
Mary Newell, PhD, RN, NCSN

DESCRIPTION OF ISSUE

School Based Health Centers (SBHC) providers and school nurses collaborate to enhance students' health, overall well-being and academic success. Privacy, confidentiality and a sense of well-being for students play a key role in both sets of services. Schools and healthcare providers operate under different privacy guidelines, and some local school districts and states have different policies and interpretation of these guidelines. It is practical for both the school nurse and the SBHC to understand the various laws protecting student and health information in order to work more effectively together. In addition to the laws protecting student health information, the challenge also exists to define and delineate the roles and responsibilities of the school nurse and members of the SBHC team. This is necessary in order to provide a seamless and comprehensive care protocol for students and their families.

BACKGROUND

School nursing in the United States (U.S.) has been in existence for many decades, but has become increasingly more complex as student health needs have escalated and the role itself has expanded in scope of practice and care delivery. The primary purpose of school nursing has been prevention of disease and elimination of medical barriers to student learning and academic success (National Association of School Nurses [NASN], 2016a). The school nurse is responsible for the day-to-day management of the health of all the students (NASN, 2016c).

School based health centers (SBHC) were developed to support student success and even further remove barriers to medical and mental health needs. They provide easy access for student use and services such as well-child care and illness prevention, counseling, immunizations, dental, adolescent reproductive healthcare, including pregnancy testing, STI testing and treatment, social services, health education and individualized mental health therapy. Collaboration between healthcare providers in the SBHC and the school nurse may enhance student well-being, academic outcomes and improve attendance (Robert Wood Johnson Foundation [RWJF], 2010). Therefore, SBHCs can successfully exist in all schools no matter the level of school nursing services, they do not take the place of the school nurse but rather serve student healthcare needs which are not being met by local community healthcare providers (Keeton, Soleimanpour, & Brindis 2012).

SBHCs were developed in public schools to help remove barriers so students could access healthcare services. They are primary healthcare centers staffed by advanced registered nurse practitioners or physician assistants. They are able to diagnose and treat common students' acute health problems. They can also help in the management of chronic health conditions such as diabetes or asthma. School nurses and SBHCs share an important mission – protecting and advancing the health and well-being of school–age children. Collaboration between healthcare providers in the SBHC and the school nurse enhances the students' health thereby positively impacting academic achievement (Walker, Kerns, Lyon, Bruns, & Cosgrove, 2010).

SBHCs can enhance an existing school nurse program and the way the two programs interface is essential for their success. Please see APPENDIX for more background and information on how the programs can co-exist successfully to effectively advance student well-being and academic achievement.

IMPLICATIONS FOR SCHOOL NURSE PRACTICE IN CO-LOCATED OFFICES WITH SBHCS

Sharing of Information

Schools and healthcare providers are important partners in protecting children and adolescents from health threats. Sharing data between schools and healthcare agencies (including SBHCs), in some instances, is the only realistic and reliable method for getting the information necessary to conduct public health activities, such as tracking student immunization out-of-compliance rates in order for the SBHC to provide vaccinations so the student can remain in school.

The Health Insurance Portability and Accountability Act (HIPAA Pub.L. 104–191, 110 Stat. 1936, [1996]) prohibits covered entities from disclosing protected health information (PHI) to any third parties, unless the individual, in this care the student who is the subject of the information (or the individual's personal representative), authorizes it in writing or the rule otherwise permits the disclosure (ASTHO, 2016). Protected health information includes any information in the healthcare record including treatment plans and patient information. For example, a student over the age of 13 has the right to have the SBHC not disclose mental health information and treatment plans to the school or his/ her parents (HIPAA, 1996). Medical providers in SBHCs must usually abide by the policies and rules spelled out by HIPAA guidelines

HIPPA does allow for sharing of medical information for the purposes of coordinating patient care, for example monitoring for influenza outbreaks and administering flu shots. School nurses, however, as employees of a public school district or contracted to provide services in a public school system, are bound by The Family Educational Rights and Privacy Act (FERPA) (20 U.S.C. § 1232g; 34 CFR Part 99) which prevents disclosure of personally identifiable information (PII) in a student's education record without the consent of a parent or eligible student (aged 18 or older) unless an exception to the law's general consent requirement applies, such as health emergency or safety (ASTHO, 2016). This restriction on disclosure may include school immunization records, Individualized Education Plan (IEP), Individualized Healthcare Plans (IHPs), medication administration records, incident/ accident reports, educational needs records and other specialized medical records such as sport physicals and documentation of specialty care visits held by the school nurse. The U.S. Department of Health and Human Services and the U.S. Department of Education (2008) have offered joint guidance on the application of HIPAA and FERPA specifically to student health records. Though this guidance helps provide examples where disclosure of health and education records may be appropriate; interpretations by states and school districts still vary widely (ASTHO, 2016). Except where allowed by law, disclosure of personally identifiable health information between the SBHC and the school nurse should occur after obtaining an appropriate release of information.

Federal privacy protections for student education records, (i.e., Family Educational Rights and Privacy Act [FERPA]) have created confusion and difficulties for public health efforts to conduct ongoing and emergency public health activities in schools such as monitoring for infectious disease or influenza outbreaks (Association of State and Territorial Health Officials [ASTHO], 2016). Therefore, this inability to disclose information may interfere with monitoring efforts.

Under FERPA guidelines a school may disclose directory information about a student such as name, address, telephone number, date of birth without parental permission, but does not allow disclosure of vaccination status, if it is part of the academic record. Additionally, schools must give parents and eligible students a reasonable period of time to request that this information cannot be disclosed (ASTHO, 2016) For example, to support vaccination compliance for school entry, it could useful to share vaccination status with the SBHC healthcare provider so that the provider could conduct outreach and complete vaccines for those students who are in need of certain immunizations. Even though the purpose of sharing would be care coordination followed by (and allowed) HIPPA; many district do not allow this information to be shared and consider it protected by FERPA. (*Please see Chapter 11 for more information on FERPA and HIPAA*).

Consent to Treat

Where possible, in parallel to the consent to treat process, both school nurses and SBHCs should encourage the use of appropriate release of information forms and consents to facilitate referrals and coordinate care of students. Consent refers to permission for care to be given to a student or student's representative. There should be coordination between the SBHC and school nurse including delineation of roles and responsibilities. This should include development of protocols defining permission to share medical information. SBHCs should ensure confidentiality regarding the sharing of medical information under state and federal laws. In addition, the SBHC should annually obtain written consent from enrolled students and parents of their rights and responsibilities confidentiality, informed consent, release of information and financial responsibilities.

Unlike school nursing services, a student must enroll in the SBHC with required permission and consent from parent. The healthcare provider in a SBHC must obtain the student's or student's representative informed consent prior to performing any test, procedure or treatment. For health care of a minor (under 18 years of age) the law requires parental consent. The law also recognizes that some minors are competent to understand potential implications of medical procedures. Some states permit certain minors to give consent to their own medical care. This may include emancipated minors, mature minors, married minors, minor parents, pregnant minors, minors in the military, runaway minors, homeless youth, high school graduates and minors or an age specified by law (ASTHO, 2016). In some states, minors can self-consent and present unaccompanied for certain services, outlines by state laws.

There are additional situations where minors can consent to medical treatment without parental consent. It is believed that if minors had to seek parental consent for medical care or treatment for these conditions, they might not follow through due to fear of parental reactions. These situational conditions, although vary from state to state, may include the right to contraceptive care, testing and treatment for STDs, HIV/AIDs, treatment for substance abuse and outpatient mental healthcare services (ASTHO, 2016).

(Please see Chapter 24 for more information on consent for treatment).

Confidentiality

Confidentiality refers to the student's right to not have health records disclosed to others without consent. Health and educational records housed in the school are protected by FERPA laws. Federal laws stipulate who has the right to access records. FERPA provides more access for parents to their student's school health and educational records. Whereas, the medical records of a SBHC, in some instances are held to stricter standards of confidentiality for example, if the student received medical care for a sexually transmitted infection, the minor can give consent and the SBHC cannot share the information with the parent. Health records maintained by the SBHC are governed by HIPAA laws (ASTHO, 2016).

When the SBHC is not run by school staff, there must be clear distinction made to determine which records are to be maintained by the school or the SBHC. Policies and procedures must be developed to distinguish between records that can and cannot be accessible to parents or guardians. Record keeping and information disclosure procedures for a SBHC and the school nurse must be formalized preferably with legal counsel to ensure student confidentiality is protected (ASTHO, 2016).

Collaboration

Role of the school nurse in relation to the SBHC staff:

It is recommended that school nurses:

- Function as part of the team developing rationale for and the design plan for the SBHC
- Facilitate access to the full array of services to the SBHC for students
- Facilitate *Release of Information* and FERPA consents where necessary and beneficial to continuity of care between school nurse and medical provider
- Refer and coordinate care for students who are enrolled for care in the SBHC

Role of the SBHC staff in relation to the school nurse:

It is recommended that the staff of the SBHC:

- Include the school nurse as part of the design team, and in all phases of planning, implementing and evaluating a SBHC
- Include the school nurse as a member of a team that provides health services for shared clients utilizing a holistic health approach
- Facilitate *Release of Information* and FERPA consents where necessary and beneficial to continuity of care between school nurse and medical provider

In partnership:

It is recommended that the school nurse and SBHC staff:

- Coordinate nursing and treatment compliance care plans for clients who require follow-up care
- Work together to document services that will allow data collection to study outcomes of care, cost-effectiveness of care and other identified outcomes using an evidence-based system of care

- Develop policies and systems that insure the quality and confidentiality of care received by students
- Jointly plan and implement health promotion and disease prevention programs to improve health outcomes for all members of the school and community
- Within parameters of confidentiality, notify school staff of students who have health needs which may require accommodations during the school day
- Jointly monitor student grades and attendance patterns

This integration of school nursing services and the services of the SBHC ensures that students will have access to the health and mental health services they may require.

CONCLUSION

Societal changes have resulted in more healthcare services being delivered in the school. This change is related to advances in medical practice, changes in disease patterns, growth in medical technology, and an increase in the number of working parents. With more complex healthcare services being provided during the school day, the school health room or SBHC may become the student's only medical home during the school year. Students who use SBHC have been shown to have better grades and attendance (Walker et al., 2010) and can be viewed as an integral strategy to help students succeed in school.

School nurses are the leaders in the school providing oversight for the health and safety of students. Licensed Registered Nurses need to be present in the schools in order to advocate for school nursing services for every child. SBHCs contribute to academic achievement by addressing physical, mental and behavioral health problems by qualified medical and mental health professionals and link students to health services and resources available in the community. Through collaboration between the school nurse and the SBHC with community providers, primary care, mental health, health education and dental care services can be provided to students and their families. Ultimately this collaboration will improve student outcomes, attendance patterns, academic achievement and success.

RESOURCES

> **See Appendix: Interface between SBHCs and School Nurses and ADDENDUM:**
> **Parental Understanding of School-Based Health Center Records.**

National Association of School Nurses: https://www.nasn.org

National Clearinghouse for Educational Facilities: http://www.ncef.org/healthcenters.cfm

School-Based Health Alliance: www.sbh4all.org

REFERENCES

American Academy of Pediatrics, Council on School Health. (2016). *Role of the school nurse in providing school health services.* Retrieved from http://pediatrics.aappublications.org/content/early/2016/05/19/peds.2016-0852

Association of State and Territorial Health Officials. (2016). *Comparison of FERPA and HIPAA privacy rule for accessing student health data.* Retrieved from http//www.astho.org/Programs/Preparedness/Public-Health-Emergency-Law/Public-Health-and-Schools-Toolkkit/Comparison-of-FERPA-and-HIPAA-Privacy-Rule/

Baisch, M.J., Lundeen, S.P. & Murphy, M. K. (2011). Evidence-based research on the value of school nurses in an urban school system. *Journal of School Health, 81*(2), 74-80. doi: 10,0000/j.1746-1561.2010.00563.x.

Centers for Disease Control and Prevention. (2016). *Health and academics.* Retrieved from www.cdc.gov/healthyyouth/health_and_academics/index.htm

Dilley, J. (2009). *Research review: School-based health interventions and academic achievement.* Washington State Board of Health, Washington State Office of Superintendent of Public Instruction, Washington State Department of Health. Retrieved from http://here.doh.wa.gov/materials/research-review-school-based-health-interventions-and-academic-achievement/12_HealthAcademic_E09L.pdf

Family Educational Rights and Privacy Act of 1974, 20 U.S.C. § 1232g (1974).

Health Insurance Portability and Accountability Act of 1996, Pub. L. No. 104-191 (1996).

Institute of Medicine. (2011). *The future of nursing leading change, advancing health.* Washington D.C.: The National Academies Press.

Keeton, V., Soleimanpour, S., & Brindis, C. D. (2012). School-based health centers. in an era of health care reform: Building on history. *Current Problems Pediatric Adolescent Health Care, 42*(6), 132-158. doi:10,1016/j.cppeds.2012.03.002

Knopf, J. A., Finnie, R. K. C., Peng, Y., Hahn, R. A., Truman, B. I., Vernon-Smiley, M., & Fullilove, M. T. (2016). School-based health centers to advance health equity. *American Journal of Preventive Medicine, 51*(1), 114–126. doi:10.1016/j.amepre.2016.01.009

National Assembly of School Based-Health Centers. (2010). *About school-based health care.* Retrieved from http://www.nasbhc.org/site/c.jsJPKWPFJrH/b.2561553/k.843D/about_sbhcs.htm

National Association of School Nurses. (2015). *The complementary roles of the school nurse and school based health centers* (Position Statement). Silver Spring, MD: Author. Retrieved from https://schoolnursenet.nasn.org/blogs/nasn-profile/2017/03/13/school-based-health-centers-the-complementary-roles-of-the-school-nurse-and

National Association of School Nurses. (2016a). *The role of the 21ˢᵗ century school nurse* (Position Statement). Retrieved from https://www.nasn.org/Policy/Advocay/PositionPapersandReports/ NASNPositionStatementsFullView/tabid/462/smid/824/ArticleD/87/Default.aspx

National Association of School Nurses. (2016b). *School nursing and school based health centers: Working together for student success.* Retrieved from https://www.nasn.org/portals/0/resources/21stCentury/ SchoolNurseFramework2015.pdf

National Association of School Nurses. (2016c). *Definition of school nursing.* Retrieved from http://www.nasn.org/rolecareer

National Center for Education Statistics. (2016*). Fast facts.* Retrieved from http://nces.ed.gov/fastfacts/#

Robert Wood Johnson Foundation. (2010). Unlocking the potential of school nursing: Keeping children healthy, in school and ready to learn. *Charting Nursing's Future*. Retrieved from http://www.rwjf.org/ en/research-publications/find-rwjf-research/2009/01/charting-nursing-future-archives/unlocking-the- potential-of-school-nursing.html

U.S. Department of Education & U.S. Department of Health ND Human Services. (2008). *Joint guidance on the application of the Family Educational Rights and Privacy Act (FERPA) and the Health Insurance Portability and Accountability Act of 1996 (HIPAA) to student health records.* Retrieved from http://www2.ed.gov/policy/gen/guid/fpco/doc/ferpa-hipaa-guidance.pdf

Walker, S. C., Kerns, S. E. U., Lyon, A. R., Bruns, E. J., & Cosgrove, T. J. (2010). Impact of school-based health center use on academic outcomes. *Journal of Adolescent Health*, *46*(3), 251–257. doi:10.1016/j. jadohealth.2009.07.002

APPENDIX: Interface between SBHCs and School Nurses

What is a School Based Health Center?

SBHCs began in the early 1970s due to the increasing number of children and adolescents who lacked access to health care. This need included cultural and age-sensitive healthcare delivery suited to their developmental needs. SBHCs may provide comprehensive medical and mental health care to students. This may include services such as well-child exams, immunizations, family planning and individualized mental health therapy (National Assembly of School-Based Health Centers, 2010).

A broad array of research and a recent systematic review has found that SBHCs are effective in improving a variety of education and health related outcomes. Substantial educational benefits associated with SBHCs include reductions in rates of school suspension or high school non-completion, and increases in grade point averages and grade promotion (Knopf et al., 2016). A 2009 study of Seattle SBHC users showed improved attendance and GPA as compared to non-users. Healthcare utilization also improved, including substantial increases in recommended immunizations and other preventive services (Walker et al., 2010). Access to SBHCs where students spend their time reduces out of school time for students, out of work time for families, and enables integration of school success goals into the medical and mental health treatment of students.

SBHCs can help students address a variety of unhealthy behaviors that can create long term health risks. In addition, SBHCs work collaboratively to complement the care provided by school nurses. This collaboration enhances students' health, overall well-being and academic success.

Multiple health professionals in a school setting may have distinctive and complementary roles their student based objectives are met effectively through open communication and professional collaboration. Working as partners, school nurses and staff of the SBHC are able to increase compliance with treatment plans, facilitate access to needed health and mental health care, monitor outcomes of care, uniformly document care, collect data about health needs and outcomes of care, and provide case management – all necessary for improving the quality of health care and academic outcomes for our students (Dilley, 2009). Services are available to eligible students who enroll to receive care in the SBHC. While SBHCs do exist in schools that have limited nursing services, they do not take the place of the role of the school nurse (NASN, 2016b). School nurses and SBHC staff work in collaboration to develop polices, collect data, and evaluate health outcomes for students (NASN, 2015).

Collaboration between healthcare providers in the SBHC and the school nurse will enhance students' health, academic outcomes, life-long achievement and overall student well-being. The challenge is to define and delineate the roles and responsibilities of school nurses and members of the SBHC team in order to provide seamless and comprehensive care for students and their families in an evidence-based system of care without duplication of services.

Role of the School Nurse

As the role of school nurses have expanded they have continued to have a positive impact in the schools they serve. In a study conducted by the Milwaukee Public School System identified that principals and clerical staff reported spending less time addressing student health issues when a nurse was present in the school (Baisch, Lundeen, & Murphy, 2011).

After the child's home, the school represents the second most influential environment in a child's life. Teachers, school administrators and parents know that a student who arrives at school fed, rested, healthy and engaged is ready to learn. The Centers for Disease Control and Prevention (CDC, 2016) identified that academic success of youth is strongly linked with their health. In turn, academic success is a primary indicator of the overall well-being of youth, and is a primary predictor and determinant of adult health outcomes (American Academy of Pediatrics, Council on School Health, 2016). The role of the school nurse encompasses both health and educational goals. School nurses must be prepared to provide care for increasingly complex health needs in a school setting where academic success is considered a top priority (Institute of Medicine, 2011).

Today's professional school nurse has a diverse and challenging role. Under the requirements of federal law, more disabled students are attending public school (NASN, 2016b). The school nurse must assess each student's health status, identify problems that may create a barrier to educational progress, and develop a healthcare plan for management of the problems in the school setting. The nurse is a vital part of the educational team, identifying the health issues that may impact the student's learning.

Advanced technology has impacted the practice of school nursing. Information on diseases and care measures can be quickly accessed now on the internet. The student health record has become electronic along with the daily health room log of visits. Health data on a specific student can easily be retrieved and reviewed and shared with the student's health provider as part of telemedicine. Parents appreciate the ease of nurse – healthcare provider communication as it keeps their student in the school and not in a waiting room. Advances in patient care technology have also improved disease management and quality of life, examples include insulin pumps, vagal nerve stimulators and cardiac monitoring devices. School nurses provide effective evidence based case management for chronic diseases such as asthma, diabetes, and anaphylactic food allergies (NASN, 2016c).

School nurses will continue to see an increase in acute and chronic health conditions impacting students. Consistent nursing interventions implemented early will decrease health complications. Through support and education by the nurse and medical management from the SBHC more students will be able to stay in the classroom and stay healthy. Teachers and administrators are not health professionals and have other important duties to fulfill during the school day. They identify the nurse as the healthcare expert in the school setting.

REFERENCES

American Academy of Pediatrics, Council on School Health. (2016). *Role of the school nurse in providing school health services*. Retrieved from http://pediatrics.aappublications.org/content/early/2016/05/19/peds.2016-0852

Baisch, M.J., Lundeen, S.P. & Murphy, M. K. (2011). Evidence-based research on the value of school nurses in an urban school system. *Journal of School Health*, *81*(2), 74-80. doi: 10,0000/j.1746-1561.2010.00563.x.

Centers for Disease Control and Prevention. (2016). *Health and academics*. Retrieved from www.cdc.gov/healthyyouth/health_and_academics/index.htm

Dilley, J. (2009). *Research review: School-based health interventions and academic achievement.* Washington State Board of Health, Washington State Office of Superintendent of Public Instruction, Washington State Department of Health. Retrieved from http://here.doh.wa.gov/materials/research-review-school-based-health-interventions-and-academic-achievement/12_HealthAcademic_E09L.pdf

Institute of Medicine. (2011). *The future of nursing leading change, advancing health. Washington D.C.*: The National Academies Press.

Knopf, J. A., Finnie, R. K. C., Peng, Y., Hahn, R. A., Truman, B. I., Vernon-Smiley, M., & Fullilove, M. T. (2016). School-based health centers to advance health equity. *American Journal of Preventive Medicine, 51*(1), 114–126. doi:10.1016/j.amepre.2016.01.009

National Assembly of School Based-Health Centers. (2010). *About school-based health care.* Retrieved from http://www.nasbhc.org/site/c.jsJPKWPFJrH/b.2561553/k.843D/about_sbhcs.htm

National Association of School Nurses. (2015). *The complementary roles of the school nurse and school based health centers* (Position Statement). Silver Spring, MD: Author. Retrieved from https://schoolnursenet.nasn.org/blogs/nasn-profile/2017/03/13/school-based-health-centers-the-complementary-roles-of-the-school-nurse-and

National Association of School Nurses. (2016b). *School nursing and school based health centers: Working together for student success.* Retrieved from https://www.nasn.org/portals/0/resources/21stCentury/SchoolNurseFramework2015.pdf

National Association of School Nurses. (2016c). *Definition of school nursing.* Retrieved from http://www.nasn.org/rolecareer

Walker, S. C., Kerns, S. E. U., Lyon, A. R., Bruns, E. J., & Cosgrove, T. J. (2010). Impact of school-based health center use on academic outcomes. *Journal of Adolescent Health, 46*(3), 251–257. doi:10.1016/j.jadohealth.2009.07.002

ADDENDUM

Parental Understanding of School-Based Health Center Records

Erin D. Gilsbach, Esquire

School-based health centers can be confusing to both parents and faculty/staff, due to the potential for confusion over who has access to what medical information. Generally, in order to be most legally protected, the school-based health center will maintain its own records, and the school will not have significant engagement in their processes. This will ensure that the records remain "health records" with the medical entity and will not cross over the line into "education records." Maintaining the records as education records may cause the medical partners concern, due to the fact that the privacy standards are so different. Thus, it is a good idea to keep them separate from the school in all ways. Whatever the arrangement is, schools and school nurses should take great care to inform the parents as to how much access the school does or does not have to the school-based health center records. This is imperative, since a parent may believe that they do not need to inform the school about a particular condition or medical need that a child has due to the fact that the school-based health center is already aware of it. In that case, the parent's reasonable misunderstanding about the handling of school-based health center records, and their lack awareness of what the school has access to may result in serious harm to the child. In addition, clarifying the access issue with parents in writing will help in the event that a child find case is brought against the district for failure to spot and issue that the parents and/or student had previously brought to the attention of the school-based health center. It is possible that parents might reasonably rely on the district to ensure that if there is a need for accommodations, the District will already be aware and will provide them. Thus, it is important that the district be very clear about the nature of the records and the school's access to them, so that no issues arise that may increase the district's risk of liability and/or result in harm to the student.

Chapter 41

ADDRESSING SERVICE ANIMALS IN THE SCHOOL SETTING

Antoinette Towle, EdD, APRN

DESCRIPTION OF ISSUE

Case 1: *Hunter, an 11-year-old 6th grade boy, who was once a healthy, energetic and athletic, suddenly has a stroke. The stroke damaged the left temporal lobe of his brain causing him to have speech, memory, and learning delays. The damage also caused him to start having seizures. His seizures are frequent, come without warning, and very difficult to control even while on medication. Hunter is always at risk of hurting myself. He had to quit sports because the seizures were too frequent. He requires someone to be with him at all times even at night just in case a seizure occurs and he suffers an injury or needs emergency medication. Classmates were afraid to be around him after witnessing his seizure activity. Hunter went from living a "normal" active life to a life with no privacy, no independence, and no friends.*

At age 13, Hunter was introduced to Argos, a Yellow Labrador service dog. The service that Argos provides is to alert Hunter about 5 minutes before each seizure giving him time to sit down safely. Argos will rub his entire face on Hunter's thigh and will not stop until Hunter sits down. Once the seizure occurs, Argos will lick Hunter's face attempting to wake him up. If Hunter does not wake up, Argos is trained to find help. The school nurse was the designated person for Argos to go too. Thanks to the services provided by Argos, Hunter has regained his independence and privacy. Argos has not only been a safety net for Hunter but also for his classmates, who are no longer afraid to be around him, but to the school nurse as well.

Case 2: *Andrew, a typical six-year old, first grade student, enjoys riding his bike and playing with his toy construction vehicles or video games. But Andrew also lives with the life-threatening challenges of Type 1 Diabetes. Diagnosed at just three years of age, Andrew only knows daily life with a dozen or more finger-poke blood glucose checks, counting carbohydrate intake, and night-time blood glucose checks. Blood glucose levels that are too high or too low are life-threatening events for children with Type 1 diabetes. Molly, a diabetic alert service animal, provides Andrew with another tool to monitor his diabetes anytime and anywhere he is, especially during his busy school day.*

The service that Molly provides is to continually monitor specific smells or scents on Andrew's breath that indicate rapidly dropping or low blood sugar levels. She is trained to "alert" Andrew, usually by pawing or nudging him. Molly is taught to alert and be persistent to the point where she will go get help if Andrew does not respond. Additionally, Molly is trained to retrieve essentials needed such as Glucose tablets, Glucagon, insulin, juice boxes, testing meters or retrieve medication from a designated spot in the classroom or students home. Molly has also been trained to go to the school nurses office to summon emergency medical help if needed. Molly is an extremely valuable tool in keeping Andrew safe and healthy not only at home but also in school. A four-legged helper to the school nurse as well!

A request to bring a service animal into the school setting can cause a great deal of apprehension for school administrators, staff and students. School administrators must comply with complex disability discrimination laws enacted by local and federal agencies. They must also ensure the health, safety, and wellbeing of all students and staff in their schools. Protecting students and staff with severe allergies to animal dander and/or a fear of animals and at the same time accommodating a service animal for a disabled individual requires a great deal of teamwork and planning. Nurses can be leaders in this area because of the unique role they play in the school setting. In addition to their skill and expertise at assessing, planning, and implementing care for all students, especially those with special healthcare needs. It is the position of the National Association of School Nurses (NASN) that school nurses play an integral role in helping to facilitate the team planning process necessary to successfully integrate "service animals" into schools (Garrett, Teskey, Duncan, & Strasser, 2014).

Over the past five years, evidence-based research has demonstrated the positive impact that service animals have in working with individuals with disabilities (Winkle, Crowe & Hendrix, 2012). These service animals are individually trained to perform specific work or tasks for the disabled individual. Such work or tasks may include:

- guiding a student who is legally or completely blind
- alerting a hearing impaired or deaf student
- pulling a wheelchair
- alerting about and protecting a student who is having a seizure
- reminding a student to take a medication
- stop or interrupt sudden, impulse, out of control running episode or self-harm behaviors of a student with autism.
- calming a student who might be suffering from Post-Traumatic Stress Disorder (PTSD) during an anxiety attack

The American Disability Act (ADA) generally requires that local buildings, including schools, must accommodate service animals, including a trained dog or, in specific circumstances, a miniature horse (U.S. Department of Justice [USDJ], 2011). On the other hand, "emotional support" or "therapy" animals are treated differently under the ADA, because these emotional support and therapy animals do not receive the same level of training as a service animal.

BACKGROUND

In 2010, The U.S. Department of Justice (DOJ) issued revised regulations under the ADA because, in part, of uncertainty regarding what types of animals qualified as a "service animal" under the ADA. The revisions clarified that, generally speaking, the service animal must be a dog or, in specific circumstances, a miniature horse (USDJ, 2011). Note that, a school is not automatically required to allow a miniature horse in the building. Instead, the school must determine whether it can reasonably modify its policies, practices or procedures to allow a miniature horse into the building. 28 C.F.R. § 35.136. Therefore, no other animal, wild or domestic, is permitted to be a service animal under the ADA. School nurses should consult with their local attorney to determine if state law allows other types of animals as "service animals."

School nurses should consult with their local attorney to determine if state law allows other types of animals as "service animals". The DOJ's regulatory revisions further explained and clarified that a service animal must be required for the disabled individual and specifically trained to do work or a task for such individual. As a general rule, service animals must be allowed in: government agencies, businesses, profit and nonprofit organizations, and schools (USDJ, 2011). As such, schools are generally required to permit service animals to accompany students with disabilities in all areas that students have access. Other federal laws such as Section 504 of the Rehabilitation Act of 1973 (29 U.S.C. §794), and the Individuals with Disabilities in Education Act (20 U.S.C. §1400 et seq) further reinforce the use of service animals in the school setting (Minchella, 2011). In addition to federal mandates, many states require additional rules and regulations regarding the use of service animals within that state (Service Dog Central, 2014). Therefore, it is important to research state laws when dealing with a request for a service animal.

In accordance with the ADA, service animals must be harnessed, leashed, or tethered, unless those devices interfere with the service animal's work or the individual's disability prevents using those devices (USDJ, 2011). If a device is not used, the individual must have the ability to control the animal at all times, such as by voice, or signal command or by an electronic remote. School administrators and staff must be careful about inquiring into a service animal: as a general rule, school staff may only ask about the work or task the animal been trained to perform (USDJ, 2011). The law prohibits school staff from requiring medical documentation regarding the student's disability and documentation regarding the service animal's identification card or training. It is also prohibited to ask that the animal demonstrate its ability to perform the work or task. School districts that tend to be aggressive in the enforcement of service animals could be subject to a lawsuit. *See, e.g., K.D. v. Villa Grove Cmty. Unit Sch. Dist. No. 302 Bd. of Educ.,* 403 Ill. App. 3d 1062 (Ill. App. Ct. 4th Dist. 2010) (district wrongly removed a student with autism's service dog); *Kalbfleisch v. Columbia Cmty. Unit Sch. Dist. Unit No. 4,* 396 Ill. App. 3d 1105 (Ill. App. Ct. 5th Dist. 2009).

IMPLICATIONS FOR SCHOOL NURSE PRACTICE

School nurses are leaders in the development and evaluation of school health policies and programs that address the health and safety needs of students in the school environment (ANA & NASN, 2017). School nurses work in inter-professional teams to help identify student health issues and special needs that are pertinent to especially student's academic success. As health leader of the team, the school nurses role is to ensure that students are healthy and safe, enhancing their ability to learn and achieve academic success. A student with a service animal especially requires an interdisciplinary team approach with open communication, planning, and ongoing coordination to be successful in the school environment. This team needs to collaboratively assess, plan, implement, and evaluate how the service animal can be successfully integrated into the school setting. They also need to provide education to school staff and students, as well as demonstrate advocacy and support to the student and the service animal.

School nurses can take the lead in completing the initial health and safety assessment for a request for a service animal to accompany a child in school. Some initial questions to ask upon receiving a request may include:

- Is the service animal required because of a defined disability?
- How will the animal impact the student's academic and behavioral functions to support his or her education?
- Does the student need the service animal for equal access to educational services and programs?

- What work or task has the service animal been trained to perform?
- How will the service animal alert its handler/student to an impending incident, such as an oncoming seizure or low blood glucose?

(Minchella, 2011)

In addition to these question, the school nurse must assess the following:

- How will having a service animal in a building affect students/staff that may have an allergy to the service animal or a distinct fear of the animal?
- Federal and state laws mandate that a disabled student (with or without a service animal) be granted the same educational opportunities as their non-disabled peer, how does the school provide care to the student allergic to animal dander/fur or who is afraid of animals?

(Minchella, 2011)

Following school district policy and procedure is essential when it is determined that a "service animal" should be incorporated into a student's educational plan. Staff should also contact the district's attorney to ensure the district complies with all applicable local, state and federal requirements. School districts are required to make "reasonable accommodations" in their policies and procedures to confirm with the DOJ's ADA regulations. (Jacobs, 2011). A district's policies may include the following:

- Stated compliance with current federal, state and local laws.
- Required written documentation from a licensed veterinarian that the service animal is in good health and appropriately vaccinated.
- Guidelines regarding education and training of staff and students about: the role of the service animal, the laws permitting them access to public places, and interactions with the service animal.
- Guidelines about how the service animal will be controlled in the educational setting, according to the USDJ: "Service animals must be harnessed, leashed, or tethered unless these devices interfere with the service animal's work or the individual's disability prevents using these devices. In that case, the individual must maintain control of the animal through voice, signal, or other effective controls" (USDJ, 2011, para. 6).
- Regulations state that the service animal is not be permitted to stay at school if the animal is out of control; the animal's handler does not take effective action to control it; or the animal is not housebroken (USDJ, 2011).
- Regulations state that the school district is not responsible for the care, including elimination needs, food or a special location for service animals (USDJ, 2011). The animal's owner/family is responsible for the "care and supervision of the service animal" (USDJ, 2011).
- Regulations state that the disabled student is unable to provide care for their service animal at school, a documented plan needs to be in place stating who is responsible to care for the animal while the student is in school (Minchella, 2011).
- Regulations state that if there is more than one service animal in a school building at one time, appropriate arrangements to socialize the animal's needs to be made in a controlled environment prior to or after school hours.

- Regulations state that if the service animal is a miniature horse, the school district needs to evaluate the type, size, and weight of the miniature horse and determine whether the school can safely accommodate the service animal (USDJ, 2011).

- Federal requirements do not require a service animal to wear a vest or harness identifying them as a service animal. Some states may require identification, thus review your individual state's requirements to determine specific regulations.

CONCLUSION

In today's economic and legally sensitive environment, School nurses are being required to care for not only larger numbers of students but also more medically and mentally complex students. They also must ensure the health, safety, and wellbeing of all students and staff in their schools. Service animals in the school setting need to be thought of as a positive tool, a second set of eyes that helps the school nurse care for that particular student. School nurses must be leaders in helping school staff and students understand and value the purpose and functions of a service animal. As leaders, school nurses must facilitate interprofessional collaboration between the school, the student's family, and student to ensure that the maximum benefits are being obtained from the service animal.

As research continues to discover and uncover new strategies to help enhance and enrich the lives of students, especially students with disabilities, school nurses will continue to be challenged about how to implement these strategies. With the advancement in the work and tasks that service animals can provide to students with disabilities, the use of a service animal has opened a whole new world of challenges for schools. School nurses need to embrace this new four legged "tool" and utilizes his/her services to the fullest to positively impact the lives of our students and their families.

RESOURCES

- Frequently Asked Questions about Service Animals and the ADA: U.S. Department of Justice Civil Rights Division Disability Rights Section https://www.ada.gov/regs2010/service_animal_qa.html

- Service Dogs in the School Setting. OSBA. https://www.ohiobar.org/ForPublic/Resources/LawYouCanUse/Pages/LawYouCanUse-683.aspx

- Service Animals and Emotional Support Animals. ADA National Network. https://adata.org/publication/service-animals-booklet

- Service Dog Central http://servicedogcentral.org/content/node/59

REFERENCES

American Nurses Association & National Association of School Nurses. (2017). *School nursing: Scope and standards of practice (3rd ed.).* Silver Spring, MD: Author.

Individuals with Disabilities Educational Act (IDEA) of 2004, 20 U.S.C. Sec. 1400 et seq.; 34 C.F.R. Parts 300 et seq. Retrieved from http://www.copyright.gov/legislation/pl108-446.pdf

Jacobs, M. (2011). *Service animals in the schools: What every district needs to know about the ADA rules*. Tallahassee, FL:LRP Publications, Inc.

Minchella, L. (2011). Hot topics in special needs school nursing: Service animals in schools. *NASN School Nurse, 26*(2), 78-81. doi: 10.1177/1942602X11399385

National Association of School Nurses. (2014). *Service animals in school*. (Position Statement). Retrieved from: https://www.nasn.org/PolicyAdvocacy/PositionPapersandReports/ NASNPositionStatementsFullView/tabid/462/ArticleId/726/Service-Animals-in-School-Adopted-June-2014

Rehabilitation Act (Section 504): 29. U.S.C, 794; 20 U.S.C. 1405; 34 C.F.R. Part 104. Retrieved from http://www.dol.gov/oasam/regs/statutes/sec504.htm

Service Dog Central. (2014). *Service dog (assistance dog) laws*. Retrieved from http://servicedogcentral.org/ content/node/59

U.S. Department of Justice. (2011). *The 2010 revised ADA requirements: Service animals*. Retrieved from: https://www.ada.gov/service_animals_2010.pdf

Winkle, M., Crowe, T.K., & Hendrix, I. (2012). Service dogs and people with physical disability partnerships: A systematic review. *Occupational Therapy Interventions, 19*, 54-66. doi: 10.1002/oti.323

Chapter 42

THE SCHOOL NURSE AND SEXUAL HEALTH EDUCATION

Wendy L. Sellers, MA, RN, CPC
Patricia K. Bednarz, RN, MN, FNASN

DESCRIPTION OF ISSUE

Sexual health education is a vital topic for schools to include in the curriculum due to the impact that sexual behaviors of youth can have on their school success. Students who are bullied, sexually harassed, pregnant, parenting, or infected with sexually transmitted infections/diseases are not able to reach their goals compared to students who do not experience these challenges. Comprehensive sexual health education and HIV prevention programs can reduce these negative outcomes (Centers for Disease Control and Prevention [CDC], 2010; Advocates for Youth, 2009; Future of Sex Education [FOSE], 2010).

For these reasons and more, schools are intent on providing quality sexual health education that equips students with the knowledge, skills, and attitudes that will allow them to enjoy academic success and develop into sexually healthy adults. At the same time, many schools are hesitant to teach sexual health education because of the sensitivity of the subject matter and the potential for controversy. Some schools fear negative parental responses to sex education. Debate over teaching abstinence-only versus comprehensive sex education may erupt. Disagreements about which topics to include and what, if any, values to include in sex education can result in schools implementing sex education that is ineffective and irrelevant to students.

School nurses may be called upon to deliver sexual health education directly or may be advocates and supports for sexual health education delivered by health education classroom teachers. School nurse participation in school sexual health education can add to the efficacy of instruction (Borawski et al., 2015).

BACKGROUND

Students of all ages are influenced by sexual messages and modeling from adults, peers, and media, originating in their homes, schools, and communities. Sexual messages can be misleading and misunderstood, and some modeling can be negative. As a result, students may act out sexually in ways that are harmful, illegal, and/or developmentally inappropriate. Puberty affects students as young as eight years of age and continues through age 17 or later (WebMD, 2007). Although students may become reproductively mature at young ages, their emotional, social, and mental development takes much longer. The influence of hormones and a highly sexualized society can result in students who are confused, scared, precociously sexual, and at heightened risk of negative outcomes related to sexual activity (Maron, 2015; Mendle, 2007).

CDC (2016a) reports that forty-one percent of U.S. high school students have ever had sex. Four percent had sex before age 13. Of the 30% of currently active high school students, only 57% reported use of a condom; 18% reported use of birth control pills; 5% reported use of the shot, patch or ring; and 3% reported use of an IUD or implant during most recent sexual intercourse. Only 9% of currently sexually active high school students reported use of both a condom and another contraceptive method during most recent sexual intercourse (CDC, 2016a).

Because of the sensitive nature of sexual health education and the potential for controversy, schools may not teach sexual health education in the most effective and comprehensive manner. Yet, surveys of parents across the U.S. reveal that the majority of parents support sexual health education in schools and want more sexual health education taught in schools. While half of polled parents responded that their child's school spent the right amount of time on sexual health education, one third said their child's school spent too little time on sexual health education. Ninety percent of polled adults think it is "somewhat important" or "very important" to have sexual health education as part of the school curriculum. The largest group of parents (46%) want schools to teach students about both abstinence and condoms and contraception use. Only seven percent of Americans state that sexual health education should not be taught in schools (National Public Radio/Kaiser Family Foundation/Kennedy School of Government, 2004).

Federal law does not require that sexual health education be taught in schools. Laws in 24 states and the District of Columbia require sexual health education in public schools (National Conference of State Legislatures, 2016); however, very little guidance or enforcement is provided, even when required. In this void, local school districts are left to make their own decisions regarding what, if any, sexual health education is taught. School nurses are often called upon to lead or support local efforts to implement sex education in schools.

IMPLICATIONS FOR SCHOOL NURSING PRACTICE

The National Association of School Nurses (NASN) (2012) believes the school nurse plays a vital role in the development and implementation of instructional programs that utilize evidence-based strategies to prevent unintended pregnancies and sexually transmitted infections including HIV. School nurses need to be fully aware of their state laws and school district policies concerning sexual health education, as well as current research about effective strategies to implement sexual health education programming. By doing so, school nurses can ensure that their schools are in compliance with their state guidelines and school policies. *Public Health, Care Coordination* and *Leadership* are three of the five key principals of the NASN *Framework for the 21st Century* (NASN, 2016) that provide the foundation for school nursing practice and can guide school nurses to advocate for sexual health education and reduce risk for school populations. The NASN position statement, *School Health Education about Human Sexuality* (2012) and the *School Nursing: Scope and Standards of Practice* (American Nurses Association [ANA] & NASN, 2017) also provide foundational guidance for the nursing role in enabling school districts to provide sexual health education to students.

Leadership

School nurses must understand the laws within their state for providing sexual health education as they vary across the country. School nurses need to determine the following to ensure sexual health education programming is functioning within state law:

- General requirements for sexual health education: Some state laws delineate specific requirements for sexual health education, such as stating that sexual health education must be medically, factually or technically accurate (Guttmacher Institute, 2016; National Conference of State Legislatures, 2016). Other general state requirements may include prohibition of including religion, or that sexual health education must not be biased against any race, sex, or ethnicity (Guttmacher Institute, 2016).
- Parental rights: Some states allow or mandate parental involvement in sexual health education programming. At this time, four states require parental consent for sexual health education instruction

(active consent) and 35 states and the District of Columbia allow parents to opt-out on behalf of their children (passive consent) (Guttmacher Institute, 2016; National Conference of State Legislatures, 2016).

- Content requirements for sexual health education: content requirements can differ across the country; however, may include requirements for contraception information, abstinence information, importance of engaging in sexual activity only within marriage, discussion of sexual orientation, inclusion of information on the negative outcomes of teen sex and pregnancy, provision of information about skills for healthy sexuality, healthy decision making and family communication (Guttmacher Institute, 2016).

- Content requirements for HIV education: At this time, 20 states require information on condoms or contraception (Guttmacher Institute, 2016), and 39 states require that abstinence be included when HIV education is taught (Guttmacher Institute, 2016).

School health policies support and provide guidance to school nurses as they address children's health issues. School nurses may be in the position to collaboratively develop or revise sexual health education program policies. The *National Sexuality Education Standards* (Future of Sex Education, 2011) provide guidance on the essential minimum core content for sexuality education that is developmentally and age-appropriate for students in grades K–12. School nurses can utilize the national standards to identify any gaps in education or services to students. Some states provide model policies for sexual health education that can also provide direction for sexual health education programming. States may also define who can teach sexual health education and the required professional development. NASN (2012) recommends that sexual health education programming include a plan for professional development and training to enhance instruction and student learning. The U.S. Department of Education Office for Civil Rights (2015) provides information about Title IX and single-sex education for schools. Title IX protects people from discrimination based on sex in education programs or activities that receive federal financial assistance. School districts need to comply with Title IX obligations when planning for sexual health education policies and programming.

The Whole School, Whole Community, Whole Child model (CDC, 2016b) may assist school districts as they develop policies and practices for sexual health education programming. By utilizing this model, school nurses can engage additional advocacy partners and stakeholders from the school and community to ensure research-based policies are in place for students to receive a comprehensive sexual health education program. Key partners may include parents, educators, students, community health professionals and faith leaders to advocate for adoption and implementation of effective programs of instruction. The CDC (2015a) provides rationale for exemplary sexual health education that can assist school nurses in their advocacy role of helping students make healthy decisions now and in their future.

Sex Education Advisory Boards (SEABs), may be required by some states' laws, but even without a requirement, are also an effective tool to implement sexual health education programming in a school district. The role of the SEAB could include the following:

- Review and recommend curriculum and other materials for classroom teaching
- Ensure sexual health education programming is adhering to state law and school policy
- Evaluate, measure and report on program goals

- Ensure individuals teaching the curriculum have the appropriate credentials, certifications and professional development
- Ensure there is diversity within the decision-makers for sexual health education programming (parents, students, teachers, cultural and ethnicity, community)
- Provide oversight to parent communication and notification about sexual health education programming
- Recommend resources for parents, teachers and students

Public Health

Surveillance

School nurses should utilize state and local data to plan, implement, and evaluate sexual health education programming. The Youth Risk Behavior Survey (YRBS) (CDC, 2016a) reports on trend data that show youth risk behaviors and is available at the state and national level. State and local public health data can identify sexually transmitted disease (STD) rates as well as teen pregnancy rates that may support the need for sexual health education programming. The CDC (2016c) provides national data that describes the risk behaviors and current strategies to reduce teen pregnancy rates and STDs. School nurses can also review the *School Health Profiles* (CDC, 2015b) that provide information about school health policies and practices from individual states and territories.

Surveys that assess the parent's view about sexual health education in their child's school, specific topics to be taught, and when they should be introduced can also inform school policy. Surveys of students' sexual behavior and attitudes may be implemented, but they require parental consent prior to administration (U.S. Department of Education, 2014).

Access to Care

One of the most important roles for school nurses in HIV/STD and pregnancy prevention is facilitating student access to sexual health services within the boundaries of school district policies as well as state and federal law. School nurses need to assess their state's minor consent laws, state laws for sexual health education, school policy, and federal confidentiality laws, including the Family Educational Rights and Privacy Act (FERPA) (U.S. Department of Education, 2012) and the Health Insurance Portability and Accountability Act (HIPAA) (U.S. Department of Health and Human Services, 1996). Establishing partnerships with adolescent-friendly providers of sexual health services (e.g., testing for HIV, other STDs and pregnancy; contraception; HPV vaccinations) in the community to facilitate access for students is an important prevention strategy. Collaboration with the local health department and community-based organizations can help identify providers and resources in the community. The Healthy Teen Network (2013) provides a free sample lesson on linking students to sexual health care.

Outreach

Transparency and open communication with all stakeholders is fundamental to successful sexual health education programming. School nurses need to follow state law and school district policy for matters concerning parental notification. Parent communication about the sexual health education program is especially important to help parents understand the following:

- Mission, goals and objectives
- Curriculum objectives and topics of discussion
- Sexual health education school policy
- State law regarding sexual health education
- Methods of parent notification about when curriculum is being taught
- Parental rights related to sexual health education, including passive or active consent
- Qualifications of individuals teaching sexual health education
- Where to go in the school district with questions/concerns
- Resources for parents on how to talk to their child about their expectations for sexual behavior
- Resources in the community that serve adolescents

Certain states require public hearings to gain input from stakeholders regarding the sexual health education curriculum. Public hearings are an excellent venue to connect with parent groups, school groups, and community agencies and provide an opportunity to share the goals and objectives of the sexual health education program.

Health Education

When school nurses provide sexual health education in the classroom setting, they need to follow state law regarding any credentialing, certifications or professional development that is required. Sexual health education is most often taught within health education courses. Therefore, any sexual health education instruction should be aligned to the National Health Education Standards (CDC, 2016d) and/or the state health education standards.

Many topics related to sexual behavior might best be treated as safety issues rather than being included in sexual health education. These would include sexting, sexual harassment, human trafficking for sex, and child sexual abuse. Some states' laws may allow parents to opt-out or remove their children from sexual health education. If safety issues related to sexual behavior are included as part of sex education instruction, the children who need this instruction the most are likely to be removed from the lessons that would equip them to protect themselves. By teaching these vital topics outside the sexual health education curriculum, the opt-out option is not required. Also, sexual health education messaging should be positive, not fear-based. If sexual health education instruction is filled with legal issues and frightening messages, time is taken away from positive sex messaging and skill development, such as healthy relationship skills, that young people need to develop into sexually healthy adults. Wherever instruction about sexting and other legal topics is included, school nurses should know their state laws and school policies in order to comply with reporting requirements and access available resources to seek help for young people who are effected.

In addition to following state laws and district policy, school nurses need to advocate for use of evidence-informed, age-appropriate and theory-driven sexual health education curricula that have been developed and evaluated by experts in that field, rather than creating lessons. The Future of Sex Education (2011) recommends a planned and sequential K-12 curriculum that is part of a comprehensive school health education program.

Tools are available to assess the effectiveness of an existing curriculum (Kirby, Rolleri & Wilson, 2007), and databases can guide selection of new curricula (National Campaign to Prevent Teen and Unplanned Pregnancy, n.d.; U.S. Department of Health and Human Services, Office of Adolescent Health, 2015). The required content for sexual health education and identification of topics that are prohibited from being discussed in sexual health education may be delineated in the state law.

Measuring, evaluating, and reporting on program goals is a necessary component to monitor the success of the sexual health education program, as well as provide feedback to key stakeholders. Use of student pre- and post-tests can be used to assess gains in student knowledge and skills. Curriculum pacing guides help ensure that sufficient time is allocated to teaching the sexual health education curriculum and that all sex educators are implementing the lessons at the same time across multiple buildings. Teacher implementation logs are also helpful to determine if the lessons are being taught with fidelity and what, if any, modifications have occurred. Utilizing student risk behavior surveys such as the YRBS, can provide insight to changes in student behavior regarding sexual risk taking (Kirby et al., 2007; CDC, 2016e; U.S. Department of Health and Human Services, Child and Family Bureau, n.d.).

Direct Care

School nurses may be charged with responding to questions from students and/or parents individually about sexual behavior, growth and development, and/or reproductive health. For this reason, school nurses need to be aware of their state law requirements about topics that can be discussed or topics that are prohibited. Brewen, Koren, Morgan, Shipley & Hardy (2014) point out that that laws governing confidentially rules and consent for care vary by state. School nurses need to be aware of their state's minor consent laws, as well as state laws concerning reportable incidents.

School nurses are mandated reporters. Therefore, it is important not to promise students that you will keep your conversations confidential. Instead, assure them that you will not share your conversations with anyone unless it becomes apparent that the student is in danger of harming themselves or someone else or if someone is harming them. In that case, the school nurse would need to talk to someone who can provide the needed help.

Providing a private space for students to share questions and concerns is essential. School nurses address a broad scope of health concerns from students. Similar to other health concerns, questions about sexual behavior or reproductive health need to be documented to meet the standard of practice and comply with the NASN standards of school nursing practice. Documentation is the legal requirement for nursing care in any practice environment.

At times, students who are younger than the age of legal consent may disclose that they are having sexual intercourse. School nurses and teachers often wonder if this is a reportable incident. If the sexual behavior is between students of similar age and is consensual, this is not a reportable incident. For example, the case of People v Beardsley (People v. Beardsley 263 Mich.App 148), found this based on the Statutory language in that state. However, school nurses need to be aware of state laws regarding criminal sexual contact, sexual assault, and age discrepancies. It is important to access authoritative sources of information, rather than relying on commonly held beliefs regarding adolescent sexual behaviors.

Developing a guideline for answering student questions may help the individuals implementing the curriculum to stay within the limits of the state law and school district policy. At a minimum, answers to student questions should be accurate, affirming, positive, and age and developmentally appropriate. For any questions that cannot be answered at school, students should be pointed to another source to find the answer.

If asked to initiate STD testing of students at school, school nurses will need to work with their state and local health departments to adhere to state laws related to parent notification, partner notification, and students' confidentiality, as well as the clinical protocols required.

Social Determinants of Health and Health Equity

The CDC (2014b) defines health equity as "everyone having an equal chance to be healthy regardless of their background that includes a person's race, ethnicity, income, gender, religion, sexual identity, and disability" (p.1). The CDC (2014b) continues to emphasize that research shows there is a higher rate of STDs among some racial or ethnic minority groups compared to whites but that these higher rates are not caused by color or heritage, but by social conditions that are more likely to affect minorities, such as, poverty, gaps between the rich and the poor, few jobs, and low education levels. Other school populations that can be at disproportionate risk include sexual minority youth (CDC, 2014a) and students with intellectual disabilities (Sweeney, 2008).

School nurses can advocate for health equity within their student population by:

- Utilizing risk behavior trend data,
- Collaborating with community stakeholders,
- Engaging parents and students from diverse backgrounds,
- Communicating effectively to school boards, school administrators and school staff, and
- Ensuring parent materials are easy to understand and translated when appropriate.

WARNING

As highly respected members of the school community, school nurses are positioned to develop trust and support for sexual health education in schools. In order to do so, school nurses need to be aware of potential red flags for sexual health education programming, including the following:

- Use of inappropriate terms and language;
- Lack of transparency with parents, students, teachers, school administrators, and the community;
- Not honoring parents' roles;
- Lack of diversity on the sexual health education advisory committee or other decision-making bodies; and
- Lack of support from the school district administration and/or school board.

531

CONCLUSION

School nurses are in an ideal position to advocate for all students to receive sexual health education. Research supports the need for comprehensive, research-based or evidence-based curriculum that provides the skills and support needed for students to make healthy decisions that impact their current and future health. State laws regarding sexual health education vary across the country and may impact the role for school nurses in providing sexual health education. School nurses need to understand and follow school district policies and state laws when they advocate and implement sexual health education programming. Utilizing local, state, and national data and following best practice is imperative to develop effective policies and interventions for school populations.

> **See ADDENDUM: Q & A - Protection of Pupil Rights Act**

RESOURCES

"Keep It Simple: A Lesson in Linking Teens to Sexual Health Care Lesson Plan": This free lesson teaches teens how to access sexual health care. Healthy Teen Network. http://www.healthyteennetwork.org/keep-it-simple-lesson-linking-teens-sexual-health-care-lesson-plan

"Model PPRA Model Notice and Consent/Opt-Out for Specific Activities": This sample parent notification form meets the federal requirements. https://www2.ed.gov/.../ppra-gen-not-cons.doc

National Campaign to Prevent Teen Pregnancy: This website offers many resources to support sexual health education. http://thenationalcampaign.org/

National Health Education Standards: These standards guide health education nationally. Each standard is explained by the Centers for Disease Control and Prevention. http://www.cdc.gov/healthyschools/sher/standards/index.htm

"National Sexuality Education Standards: Core Content and Skills, K–12": These are the minimum recommended standards for sex education, developed by national experts and published by Future of Sex Education. http://www.futureofsexed.org/documents/josh-fose-standards-web.pdf

School Nursing: Scope & Standards of Practice (3rd ed.). American Nurses Association & National Association of School Nurses. (2017). Silver Spring, MD: Authors.

Sex, Etc.: This monthly newsletter is written by and for adolescents and is published by Answer, a national organization that provides and promotes unfettered access to comprehensive sexuality education for young people and the adults who teach them. http://sexetc.org/

"State Policies in Brief: An Overview of Minors' Consent Law" (2016): This fact sheet provides state laws on minors' consent. Guttmacher Institute. https://www.guttmacher.org/state-policy/explore/overview-minors-consent-law

"State Policies in Brief: Sex and HIV Education": This fact sheet outlines state policies related to sex education. Guttmacher Institute. https://www.guttmacher.org/sites/default/files/pdfs/spibs/spib_SE.pdf

"State Policies on Sex Education in Schools": This fact sheet outlines state policies related to sex education. National Conference of State Legislatures. http://www.ncsl.org/research/health/state-policies-on-sex-education-in-schools.aspx

"Trends in the Prevalence of Sexual Behaviors and HIV Testing, National YRBS: 1991-2015": This fact sheet provides trend data from the national YRBS. Centers for Disease Control and Prevention. https://www.cdc.gov/healthyyouth/data/yrbs/pdf/trends/2015_us_sexual_trend_yrbs.pdf

REFERENCES

Advocates for Youth. (2009). *Comprehensive sex education: Research and results*. Retrieved from http://www.advocatesforyouth.org/publications/1487

American Nurses Association & National Association of School Nurses. (2017). *School nursing: Scope & standards of practice* (3rd ed.). Silver Spring, MD: Authors.

Borawski, E. A., Tufts, K. A., Trapl, E. S., Hayman, L., Yoder, L. & Lovegreen, L. (2015). Effectiveness of health education teachers and school nurses teaching sexually transmitted infections/human immunodeficiency virus prevention knowledge and skills in high school. *The Journal of School Health,85*(3), 189-196. doi: 10.1111/josh.12234 .Retrieved from http://www.ncbi.nlm.nih.gov/pmc/articles/PMC4703031/

Brewen, D., Koren, A., Morgan, B., Shipley, S., & Hardy, R.L. (2014). Behind closed doors: School nurses and sexual education. *The Journal of School Nursing, 31*(1), 31-41. doi: 10.1177/1059840513484363

Centers for Disease Control and Prevention (2010). *Effective HIV and STD prevention programs for youth: A summary of scientific evidence*. Retrieved from https://www.cdc.gov/healthyyouth/sexualbehaviors/pdf/effective_hiv.pdf

Centers for Disease Control and Prevention. (2014a). *LGBTQ programs at-a-glance*. Retrieved from http://www.cdc.gov/lgbthealth/youth-programs.htm

Centers for Disease Control and Prevention. (2014b). *STD health equity*. Retrieved from http://www.cdc.gov/std/health-disparities/default.htm

Centers for Disease Control and Prevention. (2015a). *Adolescent and school health. Strategy summaries*. Retrieved from http://www.cdc.gov/healthyyouth/fundedpartners/1308/strategies/index.htm

Centers for Disease Control and Prevention. (2015b). *School health profiles*. Retrieved from http://www.cdc.gov/healthyyouth/data/profiles/index.htm

Centers for Disease Control and Prevention. (2016a). *Youth risk behavior surveillance system (YRBS)*. Retrieved from http://www.cdc.gov/healthyyouth/data/yrbs/index.htm?s_cid=hy-homepage-002

Centers for Disease Control and Prevention. (2016b). *Whole school, whole community, whole child*. Retrieved from http://www.cdc.gov/healthyyouth/wscc/index.htm

Centers for Disease Control and Prevention. (2016c). *Reproductive health: Teen pregnancy*. Retrieved from http://www.cdc.gov/teenpregnancy/

Centers for Disease Control and Prevention. (2016d). *National health education standards*. Retrieved from http://www.cdc.gov/healthyschools/sher/standards/index.htm

Centers for Disease Control and Prevention. (2016e). *A framework for program evaluation*. Retrieved from http://www.cdc.gov/eval/framework/

Future of Sex Education. (2010). *Comprehensive sex education and academic success*. Retrieved from http://futureofsexed.org/compacademic.html

Future of Sex Education (2011). *National sexuality education standards core content and skills, K–12*. Retrieved from http://www.futureofsexed.org/documents/josh-fose-standards-web.pdf

Guttmacher Institute. (2016). *State policies in brief. Sex and HIV education*. Retrieved from https://www.guttmacher.org/sites/default/files/pdfs/spibs/spib_SE.pdf

Healthy Teen Network. (2013). *Keep it simple: A lesson in linking teens to sexual health care lesson plan*. Retrieved from http://www.healthyteennetwork.org/keep-it-simple-lesson-linking-teens-sexual-health-care-lesson-plan

Kirby, D., Rolleri, L. A., & Wilson, M. M. (2007). *Tool to assess the characteristics of effective sex and STD/HIV programs.* Retrieved from http://recapp.etr.org/recapp/documents/programs/tac.pdf

Maron, D. F. (2015). Early puberty; Causes and effects. *Scientific American.* Retrieved from http://www.scientificamerican.com/article/early-puberty-causes-and-effects/

Mendle, J., Turkheimer, E., & Emery, R. E. (2007). Detrimental psychological outcomes associated with early pubertal timing in adolescent girls. *Dev Rev.* 2007 Jun; 27(2): 151–171. doi: 10.1016/j.dr.2006.11.001

National Association of School Nurses. (2012). *School health education about human sexuality* (Position Statement). Retrieved from https://www.nasn.org/PolicyAdvocacy/PositionPapersandReports/NASNPositionStatementsFullView/tabid/462/ArticleId/43/School-Health-Education-about-Human-Sexuality-Revised-2012

National Association of School Nurses. (2016). Framework for the 21st century school nursing practice. *NASN School Nurse, 31*(1), 45-53. doi: 10.1177/194,602X15618644

National Campaign to Prevent Teen and Unplanned Pregnancy. (n.d.). *Effective programs database: Interventions with evidence of success.* Retrieved from http://thenationalcampaign.org/effective-programs

National Conference of State Legislatures. (2016). *State policies on sex education in schools*. Retrieved from http://www.ncsl.org/research/health/state-policies-on-sex-education-in-schools.aspx

National Public Radio/Kaiser Family Foundation/Kennedy School of Government. (2004) *Sex education in America: General public/parents survey.* Retrieved from https://kaiserfamilyfoundation.files.wordpress.com/2013/01/sex-education-in-america-general-public-parents-survey-toplines.pdf

People v. Beardsley, 688 N.W.2d 304 (Mich. Ct. App.) (2004). Retrieved from https://www.courtlistener.com/opinion/2206051/people-v-beardsley/

Sweeney, L. (2008). Human sexuality education for students with special needs. *NASN Newsletter, 23*(2), 21-22. doi: 10.1177/104747570802300210

U.S. Department of Education (2012). *Family Educational Rights and Privacy Act Regulations (34 CFR Part 99.31).* Retrieved from http://www2.ed.gov/policy/gen/reg/ferpa/index.html

U.S. Department of Education. (2014). *Model notification of rights under the protection of pupil rights amendment (PPRA).* Retrieved from http://www2.ed.gov/policy/gen/guid/fpco/ppra/modelnotification.html

U.S. Department of Education Office for Civil Rights. (2015). *Title IX and sex discrimination.* Retrieved from http://www2.ed.gov/about/offices/list/ocr/docs/tix_dis.html

U. S. Department of Health and Human Services, Family and Youth Services Bureau. (n.d.). *Fidelity monitoring tip sheet.* Retrieved from http://www.acf.hhs.gov/sites/default/files/fysb/prep-fidelity-monitoring-ts.pdf

U.S. Department of Health and Human Services, Office of the Assistant Secretary for Planning and Evaluation (1996). *Health insurance portability and accountability act of 1996.* Retrieved from https://aspe.hhs.gov/report/health-insurance-portability-and-accountability-act-1996

U.S. Department of *Health* and Human Services, Office of Adolescent Health. (2015). *Evidence-based programs.* Retrieved from http://www.hhs.gov/ash/oah/oah-initiatives/teen_pregnancy/db/tpp-searchable.html

WebMD. (2007). *The facts about puberty (for guys).* Retrieved from http://teens.webmd.com/boys/features/the-facts-about-puberty-for-guys

ADDENDUM

Q & A - Protection of Pupil Rights Act

Carol Marchant, Esquire with Erin D. Gilsbach, Esquire

Q: Are there any laws that might impact educational programs provided by school nurses?

The Protection of Pupil Rights Act, or the PPRA, is a federal law that may impact a school nurse's practice. Atty. Carol Marchant, Assistant Division Counsel with the Fairfax County Public Schools in Fairfax, VA, highlights the importance of this law.

"It is very important that nurses have a good understanding of the requirements of the PPRA, particularly if they are going to be teaching a class or addressing groups of students. Like FERPA, the PPRA applies to all schools that receive federal funding, and it establishes specific parental rights regarding the use of surveys in public schools."

So what types of surveys are covered under the PPRA?

Atty Marchant explains.

"The PPRA governs surveys, analyses, or evaluations given to students under the age of 18 that involve any of eight specific topics. The eight topics identified under the PPRA are:

1. political affiliations or beliefs of students or their parents;
2. mental or psychological problems of students or their families;
3. sexual behavior or attitudes;
4. illegal, anti-social, self-incriminating, or demeaning behavior;
5. critical appraisals of other individuals with whom the students have close family relationships;
6. legally-recognized privileged relationships (lawyers, healthcare providers, ministers, etc.);
7. religious practices, affiliations, or beliefs of students or their parents; and
8. income (other than questions required by law related to financial assistance for a program)."

Atty. Marchant emphasizes that nurses need to be aware not only of the topics identified by the PPRA, but also of the parental rights afforded under the law. "Because there are a number of topics in this list that might be addressed by a school nurse in a class or when speaking with a group of students, nurses need to be aware of the parameters of the law. Under the PPRA, schools are legally required to provide notice to parents before surveying students on one or more of the topics. That notice has to inform parents that they have the right to see the survey before it is given and/or to opt their child out of the survey.

The law is enforced by the U.S. Department of Education's Family Policy and Compliance Office (FPCO), which is the same office designated by law to address FERPA violations."

As with FERPA, there is no private cause of action for PPRA violations, which means that it can't be enforced through individual lawsuits, but the FPCO does have the authority to withhold federal funding for schools that violate its provisions. "Because of this," Atty. Marchant adds, "it is imperative that schools, including school nurses, understand their obligations and responsibilities under the PPRA."

For more information about the PPRA, go to: http://familypolicy.ed.gov/ppra

Chapter 43

SOCIAL MEDIA AND TECHNOLOGY: IMPLICATIONS FOR SCHOOL HEALTH

Jessica R. Porter, BSN, RN, NCSN

DESCRIPTION OF ISSUE

While social media and digital communication technologies offer many opportunities for school nurses to communicate quickly and effectively, school nurses must exercise caution and follow professional guidelines to minimize the risk of breaching patient privacy and confidentiality. It is the responsibility of the professional school nurse to understand the potential benefits of engaging with others on social media platforms as well as the possible risks, and steps that can be taken to reduce those risks.

Because the widespread use of social media has evolved so quickly, there are currently few specific regulations on the appropriate use of social media and other digital communication technologies such as text messaging and email communication by the school nurse. Without specific regulation from employers and state regulators, school nurses may make decisions based on misconceptions or misunderstandings about social media. School nurses need to know that resources are available to guide them in utilizing social media professionally and appropriately by thinking critically before they act and always considering nursing's professional filters (Fraser, 2011).

BACKGROUND

Definition

Social media has been defined by Kaplan and Haenlein (2010, p. 61) as "a group of Internet-based applications that build on ideological and technological foundations of Web 2.0, and that allow the creation and exchange of user-generated content". Social media overlaps with but is not limited to social networking applications. The number and variety of social media applications and platforms continue to increase but the most common formats utilized by nurses are Facebook®, Twitter®, Instagram®, LinkedIn®, YouTube®, and blog platforms. A survey conducted by the Pew Research center in 2013 revealed that 73% of online adults reported using a social networking platform of some kind and 42% reported using multiple social networking platforms (Duggan & Smith, 2014).

Appropriate professional use of social media as a school nurse is based on maintaining privacy and confidentiality. These two terms are related but not synonymous. Privacy is defined by the Centers for Disease Control and Prevention (CDC) as "right of an individual to keep his or her health information private" (2016) while confidentiality is defined as "the duty of anyone entrusted with health information to keep that information private" (CDC, 2016, p. 1).

Discussion of nurses and social media is complex because nurses interface with social media as both individuals and as professionals, and sometimes on behalf of their institutions. The intended audience is varied as well, ranging from family and friends, to nurse colleagues, to patients and their families (Jackson, Fraser, & Ash, 2014).

Other Communication Technologies

Separate from social media but related are the digital communication technologies of email and texting. Like social media, these modes of communication seem to offer faster and more efficient methods of contact with parents and students but pose unforeseen risks to patient privacy and confidentiality. Emailing of health information has its own set of risks related to privacy and patient confidentiality which can be overcome with strict Information technology (IT)oversight. Texting is also a promising communication technology but its risks include unauthorized individuals gaining access to health information stored on a mobile device and the converse risk of important health information being unavailable to other healthcare providers caring for the patient (Greene, 2012).

Benefits

There are many benefits to nurses being active on social media. As individuals, school nurses utilize a variety of social media platforms to connect and communicate with friends and family. As members of their school team, school nurses frequently connect with teachers and other school staff on social media supporting one another and building community. As health professionals, school nurses are increasingly using social media to share strategies and best practices with other school nurses from across the country. Some school nurses utilize social media platforms such as Twitter® to share health promotion messaging campaigns with parents. Some school nurses also represent their professional organizations on social media platforms and communicate with other health organizations. Additionally, because many school nurses live and work in the same community, there is frequently overlap between friends, family, neighbors, parents, and even work colleagues. This presents an additional challenge to maintaining privacy and confidentiality of student health information.

Through social media nurses can connect and communicate with their school nurse colleagues and share information about best practices but the nurse should be aware of the possible risks of inappropriate use of social media and consequences of such inappropriate use. **The greatest risk of inappropriate use of social media and the most commonly violations reported to state boards of nursing involve breach of patient privacy** (Spector & Kappel, 2012).

Lack of Case Law

Because the emergence social media is a relatively recent phenomenon, case law and specific statutory regulations regarding inappropriate use of social media are still minimal at this time (Lambert, Barry & Stokes, 2012). Data is starting to emerge from state boards of nursing (BONs) on the numbers and nature of complaints of inappropriate social media use by nurses from employers as well as patients and families. If a complaint is filed, the BON may conduct an investigation of the grounds of unprofessional conduct, moral turpitude, mismanagement of patient records, revealing privileged nurse-patient communication, or breach of confidentiality (National Council of State Boards of Nursing [NCSBN], 2011).

What are the Standards?

Use of social media is subject to the same professional standards that guide all aspects of nursing practice. Part of those standards is the application of *professional filters* when considering the implications of social media. These professional filters include (Fraser, 2011):

- **State and federal laws including the Health Insurance Portability and Accountability Act (HIPAA) and the Family Educational Rights and Privacy Act (FERPA).** While most information gathered and maintained by the school nurse is regulated by FERPA (U.S. Dept. of Education & U.S. Dept. of Health and Human Services, 2008) rather than HIPAA, both laws protect privacy and confidentiality of student records (Association of State and Territorial Health Officials, 2016). Parents who feel that the school nurse has divulged confidential student health records could lodge a FERPA complaint with the U.S. Department of Education.

- **Nurse regulators.** state and regional bodies including BONs that set standards for nursing practice. If a school nurse uses social media inappropriately, a parent/ guardian or even the school nurse's employer may file a complaint with the state BON. These complaints may result in investigation by the BON and possible disciplinary action (Cronquist & Spector, 2011).

- **Employers.** Employers put policies in place regarding how a nurse functions at work but also how an employee's actions outside the workplace can affect the institution. School nurses should know that employers monitor not only social media activity carried out on employer-owned computers from work but also can monitor an employee's personal social media postings. Inappropriate social media posting, even if posted outside of the workplace, can result in employer sanctions and even termination of employment (Sanchez, Levin, & Del Riego, 2012).

- **Professional standards.** The school nurse's education, licensure, and nursing standards set the expectations of professional practice. For school nurses, their nursing standards are

  o ANA's *Nursing Scope and Standards of Practice* (2015)

  o ANA's *Code of Ethics for Nurses With Interpretive Statements* (2015)

  o ANA & NASN's *School Nursing: Scope and Standards of Practice* (2017)

These professional organizations do not play a regulatory role but their nursing standards make up part of the broader definition of standard of care against which possible cases of negligence or nursing malpractice are compared.

Misconceptions and Misunderstandings about Social Media

Although there are rare cases of intentional breaches of patient confidentiality on social media, the majority of breaches of patient privacy and confidentiality by nurses on social media have been unintentional, often due to myths and mistaken beliefs about the nature of social media. NCSBN (2011) has summarized these common myths and factors that may lead a nurse to commit an inadvertent breach of privacy and confidentiality on social media in a 2011 white paper:

- A mistaken belief that the communication or posting is private and accessible only by the intended recipients.

- A mistaken belief that the content deleted from a site is no longer accessible.

- A mistaken belief that disclosing private or confidential information about patients is harmless if the communication is accessed only by the intended recipient.

- A mistaken belief that discussing or referring to patients is acceptable if they are not identified by name, but by a nickname, room number, diagnosis, or condition.

- Confusion regarding a patient's right to disclose personal information (or a healthcare organization's right to disclose otherwise protected information with a patient's consent) and the need for healthcare providers to refrain from disclosing patient information without a care-related need for the disclosure.
- The ease of posting and the commonplace nature of sharing information via social media. (NCSBN, 2011)

IMPLICATIONS FOR SCHOOL NURSE PRACTICE

The ANA (2015) and the NCSBN (2011) have developed guidelines to assist nurses in utilizing social media while minimizing the risks.

- Nurses must not share individually identifiable patient health information online.
- Nurses must not transmit via electronic media any patient-related image.
- Nurses must not take photos or videos on personal cell phones. Any treatment-related photos or videos should be taken following employer guidelines and on employer equipment.
- Nurses must maintain professional boundaries with patients on social media.
- Nurses should report any breaches of patient privacy or confidentiality that they observe to their nursing supervisor.
- **Remove all patient identifiers**. The same guidelines that a nurse would employ when speaking of his/her practice with friends of family apply to discussions on social media (Fraser, 2011).
- Never mention a patient's name – neither first nor last, to someone who is not part of the care team (In the school setting, under FERPA guidelines, the care team includes teachers and other school officials that have "legitimate educational interests") (U.S. Department of Education & U.S. Dept. of Health and Human Services, 2008).
- Avoid indirect identifiers by removing any reference to the dates care was provided or the location where care was provided. For example, a prudent school nurse might talk about "students with diabetes I've cared for over the years" instead of "a third grader we have in my school this year with diabetes."

Other Digital Communications

As with social media, the courts have yet to weigh in on how digital communications such as email and text communications between parents and school staff are to be handled (Wernz & Radelet, 2013). In some jurisdictions, the courts have said that the FERPA regulations never intended every parent-teacher email to be made part of the student's educational record. School nurses need again to keep in mind they should exercise even greater caution than teaching staff because FERPA regulations do spell out that communication including student health information is part of the educational record and as such is subject to guidelines on privacy, security and archiving. School nurses need to be aware of their school district's record retention policy and any specific district or state guidelines on the retention of medical records and parent communications related to student health.

Concerns about the privacy, confidentiality, and archiving of student health records all underscore the importance of carrying out work-related digital communication only on work computers, on work email accounts as opposed to private email accounts, and on work phones rather than personal cell phones.

Texting

Text messaging, also known as short message service (SMS) is a medium of digital communication that offers the potential benefits of speed of communication and greater access to clients. School nurses and parents have expressed eagerness to utilize texting since many parents are able to respond quickly to text in situations like meetings or waiting rooms where phone communication might not be possible. Many health organizations are exploring SMS texting as a medium to reach specific audiences with targeted health messages. While the medium does have great potential, healthcare providers need to be aware that client-provider texting presents risks to patient privacy and the security of confidential health information that is exchanged (Green, 2012).

CONCLUSION

Social media and other digital communication technology offer many potential benefits to school nurse practice. To safely incorporate these platforms into their practice professional school nurses must educate themselves about the benefits and the risks of these modes of communication. Even if specific social media regulations are not yet in place in some work settings, school nurses can utilize critical thinking skills and their professional filters as well as guidance from professional nursing organizations regarding how to mitigate any risk to student privacy and confidentiality.

Social media platforms and applications will continue to evolve and expand. The platforms as well as the risks will evolve, however the school nurse's commitment to protecting the privacy and confidentiality remains paramount. School nurses have a pressing responsibility to work with regulatory agencies and their employers to develop policies and guidelines for safe and appropriate utilization of social media and other digital communication technology.

RESOURCES

American Nurses Association. (2015). *Social Networking Principles Toolkit*. Retrieved from http://www.nursingworld.org/socialnetworkingtoolkit.aspx
    Includes Factsheet – Navigating the World of Social Media
    Tip Card for Nurses Using Social Media
    6 Tips for Nurses Using Social Media Poster
    Social Networking Principles for Nurses

National Council of State Boards of Nursing. (2011). *Social media guidelines for nurses*. [Media clip]. Retrieved from https://www.ncsbn.org/3493.htm

National Council of State Boards of Nursing. (2011). *A nurse's guide to the use of social media*. [Brochure]. Retrieved from https://www.ncsbn.org/NCSBN_SocialMedia.pdf

REFERENCES

American Nurses Association. (2015). *Nursing scope and standards of practice.* Washington, DC: Author.

American Nurses Association. (2015). *Code of ethics for nurses with interpretive statements.* Washington, DC: Author.

American Nurses Association. (2015). *Social networking principles toolkit.* Retrieved from http://www.nursingworld.org/socialnetworkingtoolkit.aspx

American Nurses Association & National Association of School Nurses. (2017). *School nursing: Scope and standards of practice* (3rd ed.). Washington DC: Authors.

Association of State and Territorial Health Officials. (2016). *Comparison of FERPA and HIPAA Privacy Rule for accessing student health data.* Retrieved from http://www.astho.org/programs/preparedness/public-health-emergency-law/public-health-and-schools-toolkit/comparison-of-ferpa-and-hipaa-privacy-rule/

Centers for Disease Control and Prevention. (2016). *HIPAA, privacy, and confidentiality.* Retrieved from http://www.cdc.gov/aging/emergency/legal/privacy.htm

Cronquist, R., & Spector, N. (2011). Nurses and social media: Regulatory concerns and guidelines. *Journal of Nursing Regulation, 2*(30), 37-40. doi: http://dx.doi.org/10.1016/S2155-8256(15)30265-9

Duggan, M., & Smith, A. (2014). *Social media update 2013.* Washington, DC: Pew Research Centre. Retrieved from http://pewinternet.org/Reports/2013/Social-Media-Update.aspx

Fraser, R. D. (2011). *The nurse's social media advantage: How making connections and sharing ideas can enhance your nursing practice.* Indianapolis, IN: Sigma Theta Tau International.

Greene, A. H. (2012). HIPAA compliance for clinician texting. *Journal of AHIMA, 83*(4), 34-36. Retrieved from http://library.ahima.org/doc?oid=105342#.V9AAYq3koWc

Jackson, J., Fraser, R., & Ash, P. (2014). Social media and nurses: Insights for promoting health for individual and professional use. *The Online Journal of Issues in Nursing, 19*(3), Manuscript 2. *doi*: 10.3912/OJIN. Vol19No03Man02

Kaplan, A.M., & Haenlein, M. (2010). Users of the world, unite! The challenges and opportunities of social media. *Business Horizons, 53*(1), 59-68. doi: 10.1016/j.bushor.2009.09.003

Lambert, K.M., Barry, P., & Stokes, G. (2012). Risk management and legal issues with the use of social media in the health care setting. *Journal of Healthcare Risk Management, 31*(4), 41-7. doi: 10.1002/jhrm.20103

National Council of State Boards of Nursing. (2011). *A nurse's guide to the use of social media* (White Paper). Retrieved from https://www.ncsbn.org/2930.htm

Sánchez Abril, P., Levin, A., & Del Riego, A. (2012). Blurred boundaries: Social media privacy and the twenty-first-century employee. *American Business Law Journal, 49*(1), 63-124. doi: 10.1111/j.1744-1714.2011.01127.x

Spector, N., & Kappel, D. (2012). Guidelines for using electronic and social media: The regulatory perspective. *OJIN: The online Journal of Issues in Nursing. 17(3),* Manuscript1. Retrieved from http://www.nursingworld.org/MainMenuCategories/ANAMarketplace/ANAPeriodicals/OJIN/TableofContents/Vol-17-2012/No3-Sept-2012/Guidelines-for-Electronic-and-Social-Media.htm

U.S. Department of Education & U.S. Department of Health and Human Services. (2008). *Joint guidance on the application of the Family Educational Rights and Privacy Act and the Health Insurance Portability and Accountability Act of 1996 to student health records.* Retrieved from http://www2.ed.gov/policy/gen/guid/fpco/doc/ferpa-hipaa-guidance.pdf

Wernz, J., & Radelet, F. (2013). *Are emails, texts, tweets, and other digital communications student records under FERPA and state law?* Retrieved from http://www.jdsupra.com/legalnews/are-emails-texts-tweets-and-other-dig-60950/

Chapter 44

VIOLENCE IN SCHOOLS/RESTRAINTS OF STUDENTS

Kathleen A. Hassey, MEd, BSN, BA, RN
Jenny M. Gormley, MSN, RN, NCSN

DESCRIPTION OF ISSUE

The topic of violence in schools in the United States can generate great concern for adults who seek to provide safe and effective learning environments for students. School nurses, educators, and administrators focus on student growth and achievement. The concept of intentional harm challenges the school community. Nonetheless, school staff must understand the issue of violence in schools to help prevent harm and provide appropriate response based on the best evidence available. This chapter is organized to:

- Define violence in schools
- Share the incidence/prevalence of school violence
- Identify school violence as a public health issue
- Describe school violence prevention efforts
- Share the role of the school nurse in identifying, preventing and responding to violence in schools

BACKGROUND

Definitions: How Does Violence Present in Schools?

As with other phenomena involving student behaviors and attitudes, school violence must be defined clearly to facilitate discussion of the issue, to track the problem, and to measure impacts of efforts to prevent and improve response to violence. According to the World Health Organization (WHO), violence is the "intentional use of physical force or power, threatened or actual, against oneself, another person, or against a group or community, which either results in or has a high likelihood of resulting in injury, death, psychological harm, mal-development, or deprivation" (WHO, 2017, para. 2). For the purposes of this chapter, the more specific definition from the Centers for Disease Control and Prevention (CDC) is used: "School violence is youth violence that occurs on school property, on the way to or from school or school-sponsored events, or during a school-sponsored event. A young person can be a victim, a perpetrator or witness of school violence. School violence may also impact adults." (CDC, 2016a, p. 1) Examples of school violence include: bullying, physical fighting, use of weapons, electronic aggression and gang violence (CDC, 2016b). Interactions involving violent behavior occur between individuals/groups such as: student on student, student on staff, staff on student, staff on staff, outside perpetrator on students and staff. Depending on the situation, the school district may face liability for violence that occurs on school grounds. *See Doe v. Claiborne County, Tenn.,* 103 F.3d 495 (6th Cir. 1996) generally holding that "a school system has an unmistakable duty to create and maintain a safe environment for its students" (Doe v Claiborne County, 1996, para. 74).

The use of restraints, seclusion, and corporal punishment in school is controversial. While there are no federal laws specifically prohibiting use of these techniques by staff to control student behavior, many states have statues, policies and guidelines regarding their use (see next section). School nurses may witness and be asked to assess students during and after use of these techniques; a discussion of restraint, seclusion and corporal punishment is warranted in this chapter. As with violence in schools, definitions are provided.

Physical restraint refers to:

"A personal restriction that immobilizes or reduces the ability of a student to move his or her torso, arms, legs, or head freely. The term physical restraint does not include a physical escort. Physical escort means a temporary touching or holding of the hand, wrist, arm, shoulder, or back for the purpose of inducing a student who is acting out to walk to a safe location." (U.S. Department of Education [USDE], 2012, p.10).

Mechanical restraint refers to:

"The use of any device or equipment to restrict a student's freedom of movement. This term does not include devices implemented by trained school personnel, or utilized by a student that have been prescribed by an appropriate medical or related services professional and are used for the specific and approved purposes for which such devices were designed" (USDE, 2012, p.10).

Seclusion refers to:

"The involuntary confinement of a student alone in a room or area from which the student is physically prevented from leaving. It does not include a timeout, which is a behavior management technique that is part of an approved program, involves the monitored separation of the student in a non-locked setting, and is implemented for the purpose of calming." (USDE, 2012, p.10).

Corporal punishment refers to:

"a discipline method in which a supervising adult deliberately inflicts pain upon a child in response to a child's unacceptable behavior and/or inappropriate language. The immediate aims of such punishment are usually to halt the offense, prevent its recurrence and set an example for others. The purported long-term goal is to change the child's behavior and to make it more consistent with the adult's expectations. In corporal punishment, the adult usually hits various parts of the child's body with a hand, or with canes, paddles, yardsticks, belts, or other objects expected to cause pain and fear." (American Academy of Child & Adolescent Psychiatry, 2014, para 1).

While support for use of these techniques varies in U.S. schools, it is important to note the similarities in definitions of violence in that the intent of the adult initiating physical interaction with the student is to cause emotional and behavior changes in that student.

Incidence, Prevalence, Impact: How Serious Is the Issue of Violence In Schools?

The CDC, United States Justice Department and USDE have collaborated on the collection and analysis of data about violence in schools, including violent deaths, since the early 1990's. According to the CDC, a violent death in school is "a fatal injury (e.g., homicide, suicide or legal intervention) that occurs on school property, or during or on the way to/from school-sponsored event" (CDC, 2016c, para. 2). Regarding school homicides, the CDC's School Associated Violent Death Study (CDC, 2016b) shows **between 14 and 34 school-age children are victims of homicide on school grounds on their way to and from school—each and every year.** The following facts provide more detail about school violent deaths:

- Most school-associated violent deaths occur during transition times – immediately before and after the school day and during lunch.
- Violent deaths are more likely to occur at the start of each semester.
- Nearly 50 percent of homicide perpetrators gave some type of warning signal, such as making a threat or leaving a note, prior to the event.
- Firearms used in school-associated homicides and suicides came primarily from the perpetrator's home or from friends or relatives.
- Homicide is the second leading cause of death among youth aged 5-18. Data from the CDC study (2016c) indicate that between 1% and 2% of these deaths happen on school grounds or on the way to or from school. These findings underscore the importance of preventing violence at school as well as in communities (CDC, 2016c).

   Aside from the practical aspect of not wanting students to be harmed, school officials may also have a legal duty to ensure that the school environment is reasonably free from risk of harm. See William G., 40 Cal. 3d 550, 221 Cal. Rptr. 118 (1985) for the school role in maintaining a safe environment for all students. Several court cases have addressed a school district's liability after a student's death. For instance, in Maness v. City of New York, 607 N.Y.S.2d 325, 325 (N.Y. App. Div. 1st Dep't 1994), a 13-year old student was shot to death near the junior high school during the lunch hour. The school allowed students to leave the building during the lunch hour. On the day in question, the student left the building, waited near a parked car, and was shot after an argument erupted. The student's mother filed a negligence action against the student, alleging that the district was negligent in not providing adequate supervision over the students outside of the school building during the lunch hour. The court held that there was no evidence to establish a sufficient causal connection between the student's actions outside of the school building and the resulting gunshot wound. Other court cases have addressed similar issues and arrived at opposite conclusions. See Mirand v. City of New York, 84 N.Y.2d 44, 46 (N.Y. 1994) (sufficient evidence existed to hold school district liable for negligent supervision when student fight occurred after district knew of prior altercation and death threat to students). As a result, district staff should be careful to ensure appropriate supervision in the school building to prevent violence.

The CDC has also collected data on non-fatal violence in schools over the previous 25 years. Students were asked to report incidences of violence in the previous 12 months for the CDC study (2016d). The following statistics for high school students in the 2015 study indicate that:

- 7.8% reported being in a physical fight on school property,
- 5.6% reported that they did not go to school on one or more days in the last 30 days because they felt unsafe at school or on their way to school,

- 4.1% reported carrying a weapon (gun, knife or club) on school property on one or more days,
- 6.0% reported being threatened or injured with a weapon on school property,
- 20.2% reported being bullied on school property, and
- 15.5% reported being bullied electronically (CDC, 2016d, p. 1).

Even though these numbers are concerning, the CDC has published the *Trends of the Youth Risk Behavior Survey* (YRBS) from 1991-2015 and many of the factors remain stable or decreased as can be seen in Table 1 (CDC, 2015a, p. 1).

Table 1.

Trends in the Prevalence of Behaviors that Contribute to Violence on School Property
National YRBS: 1991—2015

The national Youth Risk Behavior Survey (YRBS) monitors priority health risk behaviors that contribute to the leading causes of death, disability, and social problems among youth and adults in the United States. The national YRBS is conducted every two years during the spring semester and provides data representative of 9th through 12th grade students in public and private schools throughout the United States.

					Percentages								Change from 1991–2015[1]	Change from 2013–2015[2]
1991	1993	1995	1997	1999	2001	2003	2005	2007	2009	2011	2013	2015		
Carried a weapon on school property (such as, a gun, knife, or club, on at least 1 day during the 30 days before the survey)														
—[3]	11.8	9.8	8.5	6.9	6.4	6.1	6.5	5.9	5.6	5.4	5.2	4.1	Decreased 1993—2015 Decreased 1993—1997 Decreased 1997—2015	Decreased
Were threatened or injured with a weapon on school property (such as, a gun, knife, or club, one or more times during the 12 months before the survey)														
—	7.3	8.4	7.4	7.7	8.9	9.2	7.9	7.8	7.7	7.4	6.9	6.0	Decreased 1993—2015 No change 1993—2003 Decreased 2003—2015	No change
Were in a physical fight on school property (one or more times during the 12 months before the survey)														
—	16.2	15.5	14.8	14.2	12.5	12.8	13.6	12.4	11.1	12.0	8.1	7.8	Decreased 1993—2015 Decreased 1993—2011 Decreased 2011—2015	No change
Did not go to school because they felt unsafe at school or on their way to or from school (on at least 1 day during the 30 days before the survey)														
—	4.4	4.5	4.0	5.2	6.6	5.4	6.0	5.5	5.0	5.9	7.1	5.6	Increased 1993—2015	Decreased
Were bullied on school property (during the 12 months before the survey)														
—	—	—	—	—	—	—	—	—	19.9	20.1	19.6	20.2	No change 2009—2015	No change

[1] Based on linear and quadratic trend analyses using logistic regression models controlling for sex, race/ethnicity, and grade, p < 0.05. Significant linear trends (if present) across all available years are described first followed by linear changes in each segment of significant quadratic trends (if present).
[2] Based on t-test analysis, p < 0.05.
[3] Not available.

Where can I get more information? Visit www.cdc.gov/yrbss or call 800–CDC–INFO (800–232–4636).

National Center for HIV/AIDS, Viral Hepatitis, STD, and TB Prevention
Division of Adolescent and School Health

In terms of restraint and seclusion, the USDE Office of Civil Rights (OCR) announced in 2009 that the annual *Civil Rights Data Collection* (CRDC) would include questions on the use of these controversial behavior techniques in public schools. The latest data publicly available from the 2013-2014 school year includes every public school and district in the nation with 99.5% of schools and 50 million students represented (*USDE*, CRDC, 2016). This shows that more than 100,000 students were reported to be physically restrained or secluded, including more than 69,000 students with disabilities in special education served by the Individual Disabilities Education Act (IDEA).

Corporal punishment is legal in 19 states (Alabama, Arizona Arkansas, Colorado, Florida, Georgia, Idaho, Indiana, Kansas, Kentucky, Louisiana, Mississippi, Missouri, North Carolina, Oklahoma, South Carolina, Tennessee, Texas and Wyoming). The map below illustrates the percentage of public schools reporting corporal punishment by state based on data reported for the CRDC (Gershoff & Font, 2016, p. 5).

Figure 1. Legality of corporal punishment and percentage of public schools reporting any corporal punishment by state

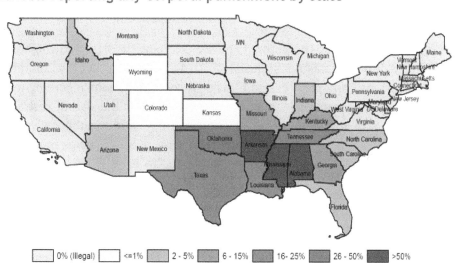

Gershoff & Font, 2013. Reprinted with permission

Some of the inconsistent policies regarding corporal punishment arise because it is regulated by individual state guideline. To view more specific areas where corporal punishment may still be in practice, see https:// www2.ed.gov/policy/gen/guid/school-discipline/images/2013-14-crdc-corporal-punishment-map-1200.png. Within a school district, schools can have different policies on the paddling, spanking and physical discipline (Sparks & Harwin, 2016). In some school systems, parents can opt out of corporal punishment.

As seen with violence statistics, the incidence of corporal punishment varies by race and disability status. The USDE reports,

> "What's more alarming is that the Civil Rights Data Collection (CRDC) shows that corporal punishment is used overwhelmingly on male students and is much more commonly administered to African-American students of all genders. In nearly all of the states where the practice is permitted, students with disabilities were subjected to corporal punishment at a higher rate than students without disabilities." (USDE, 2016, para 8.)

Students of color and with disabilities are more likely to experience corporal punishment than white and regular education students (USDE CRDC, 2016).

Public Health Issue: Why Is It Important to View School Violence, Including Seclusion, Restraint And Corporal Punishment, as a Public Health Issue?

School violence is a public health issue. Victims and witnesses of violence in schools experience short and long-term impacts including exacerbation of chronic illness, such as asthma, physical disabilities from injuries sustained, and behavioral/emotional challenges (Velsor-Fridrich et al., 2015; Wen & Goodwin, 2016). Restraint, seclusion and corporal punishment can also psychological and physical harm to both students and staff (Velsor-Fridrich et al., 2015; Wen & Goodwin, 2016). According to the Substance Abuse & Mental Health Services Administration (SAMHSA), studies have shown that restraints can be "harmful and often re-traumatizing for people, especially those who have trauma histories" (SAMHSA, 2015). The *Adverse Childhood Event Study* (ACES) conducted by Kaiser in the mid 1990's demonstrated a dose-response relationship between the number of negative childhood events within the family, e.g. abuse and neglect, and subsequent development of chronic physical and mental/behavioral health conditions (CDC, 2016e).

Students can be injured during staff use of restraint and seclusion in schools. Following review of legal cases of students injured or died during restraint or seclusion, a 2014 U.S. Senate Majority Committee of the Health, Education, Labor, and Pensions Committee issued 6 major recommendations regarding use of restraint and seclusion, the first of which was passing legislation that would "limit the use of restraints to emergency situations only, when there is an imminent threat of serious harm to students themselves or to others" (U.S. Senate, Health, Education, Labor, and Pensions Committee, 2014, p. 5). In a November 2016 letter sent to states, U.S. Education Secretary John B. King Jr. urged states to "to end the use of corporal punishment in schools, a practice repeatedly linked to harmful short-term and long-term outcomes for students" (USDE, 2016). Secretary King suggests a "safe, supportive school environment being critical to support effective teaching and learning" (USDE, 2016). Many professional groups such as National Association of School Nurses (NASN), American Academy of Pediatrics (AAP), National Education Association (NEA), American Psychological Association (APA), American Federation of Teachers (AFT) and many more want legislation in all states so that corporal punishment is banned for all students. Head Start programs do not allow corporal punishment (Gundersen Center for Effective Discipline, n.d.). For a full list of organizations against corporal punishment in schools, please see http://www.gundersenhealth.org/ncptc/center-for-effective-discipline/resources/organizations-against-corporal-punishment

According to the CDC (2015b), a public health approach uses an evidence-based, four-step process for effective outcomes that includes:

1. defining the problem
2. identifying risk and protective factors
3. developing and testing prevention strategies
4. assuring widespread adoption

A public health approach to this significant health and safety issue impacting student and adult populations in schools involves many disciplines, including education, law enforcement, nursing and psychology. School nurses are recognized as essential participants in public health as they work directly and indirectly, individually and collaboratively, to prevent health problems, including those caused by experienced or witnessed violence (AAP, 2016; USDE, 2016). As school nurses have an essential role in promoting population health of children and staff in the school setting, they must be knowledgeable and confident in their abilities to prevent violence in schools.

Prevention Efforts: How are Prevention Efforts Categorized?

The CDC identifies 4 levels of strategies in preventing school violence (CDC, 2016f).

Individual Level Strategies: include programs that are available for all students that address "emotional self-awareness, emotional control, self-esteem, positive social skills, social problem-solving, conflict resolution and teamwork" (para. 2).

Relationship Level Strategies: "include programs that generate positive connections between students, teachers and families" (para. 3).

Community Level Strategies: includes "supporting effective classroom management practices, promoting cooperative learning techniques, providing educators with train and support to meet the diverse needs of students, providing opportunities to actively engage families and creating open communication and decision-making processes" (para. 4).

Societal Level Strategies: includes "addressing social norms about the acceptability of violence in schools and ensuring that educational systems promote strong education growth for all students are additional strategies" (para. 5).

The school nurse can use this concept of strategy levels to prioritize efforts and to understand the various efforts her school community may be making to reduce violence.

IMPLICATIONS FOR SCHOOL NURSE PRACTICE

School nurses should be aware of their role in providing a safe and supportive school environment as described at the federal level within the *Every Student Succeeds Act* (ESSA), the federal educational law that specifies recommended activities and potential funding for specialized instructional support personnel to improve safety in schools (NASISP, 2016). Signed into law in 2015 under President Obama, ESSA is a reauthorization of the original *Elementary and Secondary Education Act* (ESEA) of 1965 under President Johnson aimed at promoting equity in access to educational opportunities and providing significant funding to states through Title 1 financial assistance. ESEA had been amended and reauthorized several times to ensure that Title 1 funds were going to the States to assist disadvantaged students as well as to increase accountability of States to demonstrate improving achievement by all students (Hunt Institute 2016; USDE, n.d.). During the 1980s and 1990s, ESEA was reauthorized with requirements for states to implement standards-based reforms in exchange for greater authority given to states and local education agencies for decision-making related to Title 1 programs. The *No Child Left Behind (NCLB) Act of 2001* required states to adopt standards for math, reading, science with regular assessments to be conducted and reported with student subgroups including those with disabilities, low-income, and across major racial and ethnic groups. NCLB did not address state and Local

Education Agency (LEA) efforts to provide a safe environment to support learning. With the passage of ESSA in 2015, the federal government provides funding under Title IV to states to use at their discretion:

- violence prevention
- activities that integrate and health and safety practices into school or athletic programs
- high-quality training for related to effective and trauma-informed practices in classroom management
- high-quality training for crisis management and conflict resolution techniques
- schoolwide positive behavioral interventions and supports (U.S. Government Publishing Office, 2015)

School nurses can and should take a leading, if not contributing, role in supporting the adoption and implementation of evidence-based programs that will support improved prevention and response to violence in schools.

NASN issued *"ESSA Talking Points for School Nurse"* in July 2016 that highlight the increased opportunity for school nurses to make an impact at their school and local levels on indicators such as data collected for ESSA required report cards on incidences of violence, bullying, harassment, and chronic absenteeism (NASN, 2016). NASN had previously issued several statements about the school nurse role related to school violence, including preventing school violence (NASN, 2013a), bullying (NASN, 2014), and the use of restraints, seclusion and corporal punishment in the school setting (NASN, 2015).

The school nurse's role related to violence in schools includes:

- assessment of school climate and student report of bullying and violence;
- gain and share knowledge about preventing and responding to violence;
- communication with school colleagues and safety teams about students at risk; and
- responding effectively as possible during and after a violent event; practicing self-care in the face of violence in schools (NASN, 2013a).

The following guidelines are found in these statements as well as other referenced resources:

Larry Altman, Esquire

Q: Do school nurses have any obligations with regards to student bullying?

A: The Federal Government, under the ESSA, and now some states require mandatory reporting of any bullying incident to those school staff members required to investigate bullying complaints. If a school nurse learns that the reason a student does not attend school is because the student is afraid because of being bullied, then the nurse often has an obligation, either under the school's anti-bullying policy or state law to immediately report that allegation to the person or persons charged by the school to investigate all allegations of bullying. For example, as of June 2016, Missouri has revised its school Anti-Bullying Statute that requires all staff to report allegations of bullying to the school's principal. Assuming that the school has adopted the mandated Missouri Statutory requirements, the principal starts an investigation into the allegation upon being notified by the nurse. As required by law, the nurse got the ball rolling by making the mandated report. So, not only did the nurse help the student, but they also assisted in making certain that the school complied with the law.

554

1. Assess school climate and student report of bullying and violence

School nurses should seek out youth risk behavior survey data to understand students' report of violence, bullying, mental health, and perception of adult support both in school and at home. School nurses should also determine how his/her school or district level data compares to other like communities as well as if the data is showing a trend over time. For example, the percent of students reporting carrying a weapon on school property may be lower than similar communities; however, data from the past three surveys may demonstrate an increase, suggesting need for a closer look at why more students are reporting weapon carrying.

Other risk factors identified by CDC Division of Violence Prevention, which may contribute to violence in youth are listed in Table 2 (adapted from CDC, 2016g):

Table 2. CDC Risk factors for violence

Individual	Family	Peer and Social	Community
History of violent victimization	Harsh, lax or inconsistent disciplinary practices	Association with delinquent peers	Diminished economic opportunities
History of early aggressive behavior	Parental substance abuse or criminality	Involvement in gangs	High concentration of poor residents
Involvement with drugs, alcohol or tobacco	Poor monitoring and supervision of children	Social rejection by peers	High level of transiency
Deficits in social, cognitive or information processing abilities	Low parental involvement	Poor academic performance	High level of family disruption
Anti-social beliefs and attitudes	Low parental education and income	Low commitment to school and school failure	Low levels of community participation
High emotional distress			Socially disorganized neighborhoods

School nurses should also be aware of protective factors, as nurses can have direct positive impact supporting attitudes and behaviors that reduce the risk of violence. Based on multiple studies, the CDC has proposed protective factors including the following listed in Table 3 (adapted from CDC, 2016g):

Table 3. Protective factors for violence

Individual	Family	Peer and Social
High academic achievement	Connectedness to family or adults outside the family	Close emotional relationships with those at school
Positive social orientation	Ability to discuss problems with parents	Commitment to school
Highly developed social skills/competencies	High parental expectations about school performance	Close relationship with non-deviant peers
Highly developed skills for realistic planning	Frequent shared activity with parents	Exposure to positive school climates
Religiosity	Parental modeling of constructive strategies for coping with problems	

School nurses may contribute to the development and maintenance of a positive climate by supporting supervision, clear behavior rules and consequences, as well as prioritizing interest and engagement in student activities. School nurses must partner with other school staff, family and community members to reduce the stigma of mental illness and to support families who are struggling (Rollins, 2013).

2. Communicate with school colleagues and safety teams about students at risk

School nurses should share concerns about students at risk for violence during student assistance and/or crisis intervention team meetings with administrators and counselors. It is important for school nurses to be present during these meetings to advocate for students about whom they may have concerns. For students exhibiting escalating behaviors, verbalizations of access to weapons and intent to harm, the school nurse would notify administration and law enforcement to protect the safety of the student and others. School nurses should be aware that, although student records are generally confidential under the *Family Education Rights and Privacy Act* ("FERPA"), FERPA provides an exception for the disclosure of otherwise-confidential information "to protect the health or safety of the student or other persons" in connection with an emergency (20 U.S.C. § 1232g(b)(1)(i)). In determining whether such emergency exists, the district "may take into account the totality of the circumstances pertaining to a threat to the health or safety of a student or other individuals." 34 C.F.R. § 99.36(c).

School nurses should be familiar with individual state laws pertaining to schools and bullying and stay abreast of any changes to state statutes. Most states have laws requiring schools to adopt bullying prevention policies or programs. *See, e.g.,* Ariz. Rev. Stat. § 15-2301 (requiring hazing prevention policy); Fla. Ed. Code. § 1006.135 (requiring hazing policy); Mo. Rev. Stat. § 160.775.1 (requiring antibullying policy); Ohio Rev. Stat. § 3301.22 (requiring harassment prevention policy). For questions, always consult with your school board attorney and follow your district policy on school violence and bullying. If necessary, nurses should determine the procedures for contacting district counsel so that the school nurse has access to school attorneys to seek legal advice.

3. Gain and share knowledge about preventing violence in schools

School nurses should assess if their schools have violence prevention programs, which often involve social-emotional curricula across multiple grades, which focus on building healthy relationships and managing challenging emotions such as anger, frustration, disappointment, and sadness. These programs have been shown to be successful in helping prevent violence at the individual and community level (CDC, 2016f). Additionally, school nurses can advocate for a welcoming physical environment, such as adequate natural lighting, cleanliness, and artwork that also contribute significantly to a positive school climate.

4. Respond effectively as possible during and after a violent event

According to the USDE, nurses and other school personnel have essential responsibilities related to school violence: "Learn the signs of a potentially volatile situation and ways to prevent an incident. Learn the best steps for survival when faced with an active shooter situation. Be prepared to work with law enforcement during the response" (USDE, 2013, p. 59). School nurses should know their school district policies about engaging law enforcement. As possible, school nurses should learn and practice de-escalation practices through crisis intervention trainings. According to the National Association of School Nurses, school nurses can be active members on crisis intervention teams, as well as participating on school safety committees and assisting with implementing violence prevention programs (NASN, 2014). School nurses should use strategies that may reduce a perceived threat, such as "maintaining a calm manner and using a calm tone of voice" as well as avoiding "touching, challenging, or arguing" with the person in crisis (Selekman et al., 2013, p.1092). School nurses can learn more about responding to a violent person in school from government and private organizations offering information and online videos, listed under Resources, such as: the U.S. Department of Homeland Security (2016), USDE (2013), Indiana State Police (2016), and ALICE Training Institute (2013-2016).

As with most emergency situations, being prepared for potential violence may lead to a more effective response. School nurses should collaborate as needed with key stakeholders, such as parents/guardians, teachers, school counselors, principals, local fire and police departments, to plan for students with special healthcare needs. For example, students with diabetes should have access at all times to necessary medications, testing supplies and food, especially if a lockdown might last more than several hours. When developing the Individual Healthcare Plan at the start of the school year, the school nurse should discuss with family members how medical needs might be addressed in the rare situation of a prolonged lockdown. Parents of students with special healthcare needs are encouraged to bring additional supplies to school in case their child is separated from them beyond the school/work day (AAP, 2015). The district should plan for special education students needing certain health services in the event of a lockdown. "School health services and school nurse services means health services that are designed to enable a child with a disability to receive FAPE as described in the child's IEP" (34 C.F.R. § 300.34(c) (13). An individualized plan should be developed and shared with school staff, in accordance with FERPA. School nurses should participate in school lockdown table top or practice scenario drills to identify gaps or updates needed to plans for students with special healthcare needs.

5. Practice self-care in the face of violence in schools

During and after an episode of school violence, the school nurse must be aware of how she or he is responding to the trauma. Students and staff may look to the school nurse for support after the event. Being patient and recognizing the impact of the violence on all involved will help the nurse cope effectively. It is important to debrief after an event with those who were involved. Outside agencies and their experienced, professional staff (EMS, local mental health organizations, etc.) will often lead a debriefing to assist those who witnessed a traumatic event. Getting enough quality sleep as well as healthy food, physical activity and relaxation activities are essential for helping to heal after trauma. For more suggestions on managing traumatic stress, please see the NASN document, *For the School Nurse: Caring for Yourself Following Traumatic Events at School* (NASN, 2013b).

Table 4. Summary of School Nurse Responses to Violence Types

TYPE	SCHOOL NURSE ACTIONS AND PRIORITIES
Bullying	Assess student, refer to administration/guidance, student support.
Cyber-bullying	Identify student(s), notify administration/guidance, student support.
Mental Health Crisis	Assess student. Follow district protocol (e.g. crisis response team) for de-escalation and contact behavioral health emergency services and/or activate EMS.
Physical assault	Assess and treat any physical injuries, including activating emergency medical services (EMS) if needed, report to administration, report to parents.
Sexual assault	Assess and treat student/staff, report to police, call Sexual Assault Nurse Examiner, and/or activating EMS.
Student on Student	Assess and treat any physical injuries, including activating emergency medical services (EMS) if needed, report to administration, report to parents.
Student on Staff	Assess and treat staff, report to administration, including activating emergency medical services (EMS) if needed.
Staff on Student	Assess and treat student, including activating emergency medical services (EMS) if needed, report to administration, report to child protective services.
Escalating Violence/Violent Intruder	Follow pre-planned district procedures, including lockdown, barricade, evacuation, and defensive/counter procedures. Make sure students with chronic conditions have access to what they will need. Maintain access to emergency equipment, student information, communication devices. In lockdown, remain in place until cleared by authorities according to district protocols.

6. Building resilience

School nurses should understand the importance of supporting the capacity of youth to recover from difficulties. According to the AAP, "resilience is critical to a child's ability to navigate through stressful events – even those that are traumatic – successfully. Resilience provides a buffer between the child and the traumatic event, mitigating the negative effects that could result, such as physical, emotional, and behavioral health issues that can last even into adulthood" (APA, 2017, para. 3). School nurses promoting the development of protective factors will assist students in building resilience even in the event of a violent incident (refer to table 4).

CONCLUSION

The national survey data show that, overall, different types of violence in school has decreased over the past 25 years. However, a small percentage of students continue to report carrying weapons and even more admit to engaging in physical fighting at school. Tragically, violence from individuals known and unknown to schools continues to take its toll on the physical and emotional well-being of members of the school community. As challenging as it may be to prepare, respond, and recover from violence in schools, the school nurse has the responsibility and capacity to save lives and support the primary mission of schools: helping students learn to be active, engaged citizens.

RESOURCES

ALICE Training Institute (2013-2016). *ALICE Training K-12 program*. https://www.alicetraining.com/ our program/alice-training/k12-education/

American Academy of Pediatrics. Promoting Resilience. (2017). https://www.aap.org/en-us/advocacy-and-policy/aap-health-initiatives/resilience/Pages/Promoting-Resilience.aspx

American Psychological Association for Parents & Educators, http://www.apa.org/helpcenter/resilience.aspx

Center for Disease Control and Prevention. School Associated Violent Death Study. https://www.cdc.gov/ violenceprevention/youthviolence/schoolviolence/savd.html

Centers for Disease Control and Prevention. About the CDC-Kaiser ACE Study (2016). https://www.cdc.gov/ violenceprevention/acestudy/about.html

Centers for Disease Control and Prevention. School-Associated Violent Death Study. https://www.cdc.gov/ violenceprevention/youthviolence/schoolviolence/savd.html

Centers for Disease Control and Prevention. Understanding School Violence: Fact Sheet http://www.cdc.gov/violenceprevention/pdf/School_Violence_Fact_Sheet-a.pdf

Centers for Disease Control and Prevention. School Violence: Prevention http://www.cdc.gov/violenceprevention/youthviolence/schoolviolence/prevention.html

Indiana State Police (2016). Unarmed Response to an In-School Active Shooter Event, retrieved from https://www.youtube.com/watch?v=zeoZmsXpc6k

PTA: Checklist to Help Prevent Violence in Schools http://www.pta.org/content.cfm?ItemNumber=984

Service Learning: A School Violence Prevention Strategy http://www.crf-usa.org/school-violence/school-violence-prevention-strategy.html

National Center for Education Statistics https://nces.ed.gov/fastfacts/display.asp?id=49

Selekman, J., Pelt, P., Garnier, S., Baker, S. (2013). Youth Violence. In J. Selekman (Ed.), *School Nursing: A comprehensive text*, 2nd ed., pp 1087-1117. Philadelphia, PA: F.A. Davis.

U.S. Department of Education. (2013). *Guide for developing high quality school emergency operations plans.* Retrieved from http://www2.ed.gov/about/offices/list/oese/oshs/rems-k-12-guide.pdf

U.S. Department of Homeland Security. (2016). *Active shooter preparedness.* Retrieved from https://www.dhs.gov/active-shooter-preparedness

REFERENCES

20 USC 1232g: Family educational and privacy rights. Retrieved from http://uscode.house.gov/view.xhtml?req=granuleid:USC-prelim-title20-section1232g&num=0&edition=prelim

34 C.F.R. § 300.34(c) (13) Retrieved from https://www.law.cornell.edu/cfr/text/34/300.34

American Academy of Child & Adolescent Psychiatry. (2014). *Corporal punishment in schools* (position statement). Retrieved from https://www.aacap.org/aacap/policy_statements/1988/Corporal_Punishment_in_Schools.aspx

American Academy of Pediatrics. (2015). *School safety during emergencies: What parents need to know.* Retrieved from https://www.healthychildren.org/english/safety-prevention/all-around/pages/actions-schools-are-taking-to-make-themselves-safer.aspx

American Academy of Pediatrics. (2016). *Role of the school nurse in providing school health services.* Retrieved from http://pediatrics.aappublications.org/content/early/2016/05/19/peds.2016-0852

American Academy of Pediatrics. (2017). *Promoting resilience.* Retrieved from https://www.aap.org/en-us/advocacy-and-policy/aap-health-initiatives/resilience/Pages/Promoting-Resilience.aspx

ALICE Training Institute (2013-2016). *ALICE Training K-12 program.* Retrieved from https://www.alicetraining.com/our-program/alice-training/k12-education/

Centers for Disease Control and Prevention (2015a). *Trends in the prevalence of behaviors that contribute to violence on school property. Retrieved from* https://www.cdc.gov/healthyyouth/data/yrbs/pdf/trends/2015_us_violenceschool_trend_yrbs.pdf

Centers for Disease Control and Prevention. (2015b). *The public health approach to violence prevention.* Retrieved from https://www.cdc.gov/violenceprevention/overview/publichealthapproach.html

Centers for Disease Control and Prevention. (2016a). *Understanding school violence (Fact Sheet).* Retrieved from http://www.cdc.gov/violenceprevention/pdf/school_violence_fact_sheet-a.pdf

Centers for Disease Control and Prevention. (2016b). *About school violence.* Retrieved from http://www.cdc.gov/violenceprevention/youthviolence/schoolviolence/

Center for Disease Control and Prevention. (2016c). *School associated violent death study.* Retrieved from https://www.cdc.gov/violenceprevention/youthviolence/schoolviolence/SAVD.html

Center for Disease Control and Prevention. (2016d). *School violence fact sheet.* Retrieved from https://www.cdc.gov/violenceprevention/pdf/school_violence_fact_sheet-a.pdf

Center for Disease Control and Prevention. (2016e). *About the CDC-Kaiser ACE Study*. Retrieved from https://www.cdc.gov/violenceprevention/acestudy/about.html

Centers for Disease Control and Prevention. (2016f). *School violence: Prevention.* Retrieved from http://www.cdc.gov/violenceprevention/youthviolence/schoolviolence/prevention.html

Centers for Disease Control and Prevention. (2016g). *Youth violence: Risk and protective factors.* Retrieved from https://www.cdc.gov/violenceprevention/youthviolence/riskprotectivefactors/html

Doe v. Clairborne County, Tenn., 103F.3d 495 (6th Cir. 1996). Retrieved from http://openjurist.org/103/f3d/495/doe-v-claiborne-county-tennessee-claiborne-county-board-of-education

Gersohff, E., & Font, S. (2016). Corporal punishment in U.S. public schools: Prevalence, disparities in use, and status in state and federal policy. *Society for Research in Child Development, 30(*1). Retrieved from http://www.srcd.org/sites/default/files/documents/spr_30_1.pdf

Gundersen Center for Effective Discipline. (n.d.) *Organizations against corporal punishment*. Retrieved from http://www.gundersenhealth.org/ncptc/center-for-effective-discipline/resources/organizations-against-corporal-punishment

Hunt Institute. (2016). *Evolution of the Elementary and Secondary Education Act: 1965-2016.* Retrieved from http://www.hunt-institute.org/wp-content/uploads/2016/09/Development-of-the-Elementary-and-Secondary-Education-Act-August-2016.pdf

Indiana State Police. (2016). *Unarmed response to an in-school active shooter event.* Retrieved from https://www.youtube.com/watch?v=zeoZmsXpc6k

King, K.K. (2014). Violence in the school setting: A school nurse perspective. *Online Journal of Issues in Nursing, 19.* doi: 10.3912/OJIN.Vol19No01Man04

Maness v. City of New York, 607 N.Y.S. 2d 325, 325 (N.Y. App. Div. 1st Dep't 1994). Retrieved from http://www.leagle.com/decision/1994548201AD2d347_2373/MANESS%20v.%20CITY%20OF%20NEW%20YORK

Mirand v. City of New York, 84 N.Y.2d 44,46 (N.Y. 1994). Retrieved from http://law.justia.com/cases/new-york/court-of-appeals/1994/84-n-y-2d-44-0.html

National Alliance for Specialized Instructional Support Personnel (NASISP). (2016). *Every Student Succeeds Act of 2015 (ESSA): References to specialized instructional support personnel. Retrieved from* http://www.nasisp.org/uploads/SISP_ESSA_References_2016.pdf

National Association of School Nurses. (2013a). *School violence: Role of the school nurse in prevention* (Position Statement). Retrieved from https://www.nasn.org/PolicyAdvocacy/PositionPapersandReports/NASNPositionStatementsFullView/tabid/462/ArticleId/566/School-Violence-Role-of-the-School-Nurse-in-Prevention-Adopted-June-2013

National Association of School Nurses. (2013b). *For the school nurse: Caring for yourself following traumatic events in school.* Retrieved from https://www.nasn.org/ToolsResources/ViolenceinSchools

National Association of School Nurses. (2014). *Bullying prevention in schools* (Position Statement). Retrieved from https://www.nasn.org/PolicyAdvocacy/PositionPapersandReports/ NASNPositionStatementsFullView/tabid/462/ArticleId/638/Bullying-Prevention-in-Schools-Adopted-January-2014

National Association of School Nurses (2015). *Use of restraints, seclusion and corporal punishment in the school setting* (Position Statement). Retrieved from https://www.nasn.org/PolicyAdvocacy/ PositionPapersandReports/NASNPositionStatementsFullView/tabid/462/ArticleId/725/Restraints-Seclusion-and-Corporal-Punishment-in-the-School-Setting-Use-of-Adopted-June-2015

National Association of School Nurses (2016). *ESSA talking points for school nurses.* Retrieved from https://www.nasn.org/portals/0/advocacy/2016_ESSA_Talking_Points.pdf

Rollins, J.A. (2013). The aftermath of December 14, 2014. *Pediatric Nursing, 39*, 10-11. Retrieved from https://www.pediatricnursing.net/interestarticles/3901_Rollins.pdf

Selekman, J., Pelt, P., Garnier, S., & Baker, S. (2013). Youth violence. In J. Selekman (Ed.), *School nursing: A comprehensive text* (2nd ed.) (pp. 1087-1117). Philadelphia, PA: F. A. Davis.

Substance Abuse & Mental Health Services Administration. (2015). *Alternatives to seclusion and restraint.* Retrieved from https://www.samhsa.gov/trauma-violence/seclusion

Sparks, S., & Harwin, A. (2016). Corporal punishment use found in schools in over 21 states. *Education Week.* Retrieved from http://www.edweek.org/ew/articles/2016/08/23/corporal-punishment-use-found-in-schools-in.html

U.S. Department of Education. (2012). *Restraint and seclusion: Resource document.* Retrieved from www.ed.gov/policy/restraintseclusion

U.S. Department of Education. (2013). *Guide for developing high quality school emergency operations plans.* Retrieved from http://www2.ed.gov/about/offices/list/oese/oshs/rems-k-12-guide.pdf

U.S. Department of Education. (2016). *King sends letter to states calling for an end to corporal punishment in schools.* Retrieved from https://www.ed.gov/news/press-releases/king-sends-letter-states-calling-end-corporal-punishment-schools

U.S. Department of Education. (n.d.) *Every Student Succeeds Act.* Retrieved from https://www.ed.gov/essa

U.S. Department of Education, Civil Rights Data Collection. (2016). *2013-2014 Civil Rights Data Collection: A first look.* Retrieved from https://www2.ed.gov/about/offices/list/ocr/docs/2013-14-first-look.pdf

U.S. Department of Homeland Security. (2016). *Active shooter preparedness.* Retrieved from https://www.dhs.gov/active-shooter-preparedness

U.S. Government Publishing Office. (2015). 'Every Student Succeeds Act'. *Sec. 4108 Activities to support safe and healthy students.* Retrieved from https://www.gpo.gov/fdsys/pkg/BILLS-114s1177enr/pdf/BILLS-114s1177enr.pdf

U.S. Senate, Health, Education, Labor, and Pensions Committee. (2014). *Dangerous use of seclusion and restraints in schools remains widespread and difficult to remedy: A review of ten cases.* Retrieved from https://www.help.senate.gov/imo/media/doc/Seclusion%20and%20Restraints%20Final%20Report.pdf

Velsior-Friedrich, B., Richard, M., Militello, L.K., Deane, K.C., Scott, D., Gross, I.M., & Romera, E. (2015). The impact of community violence on school-based research, *The Journal of School Nursing, 31*, 397-401, doi: 10.1177/1059840515605362

Wen, L.S., & Goodwin, K.E. (2016). Violence is a public health issue. *Journal of Public Health Management & Practice, 22*, 503-505, doi: 10.1097/PHH.0000000000000501

William G., 40 Cal. 3d 550, 221 Cal. Rptr. 118 (1985). Retrieved from http://scocal.stanford.edu/opinion/re-william-g-23395.

World Health Organization. (2017). *Violence*. Retrieved from http://www.who.int/topics/violence/en/

SCHOOL STAFF INTERACTIONS

Chapter 45

SCHOOL STAFF: PROVISION OF HEALTH SERVICE

Linda Caldart Olson, MS, BSN, RN, FASHA

DESCRIPTION OF ISSUE

School nurses are frequently asked to provide health services to staff. Schools, both public and private, employ large numbers of workers and must comply with the changing laws and regulations that concern worker health and safety. The increasing recognition of the correlation between school staff health and student health and academic achievement has increased the need for schools as employers to place a greater emphasis on staff health. Staff days away from work disrupt the educational process and add expense to school budgets. Most schools provide access to health insurance for staff and like other employers are burdened by more costs with less money. Increasingly, insurance companies provide incentives to enrollees to improve their health status as a means to lower insurance costs. Schools must also provide compensation to employees injured on the job. As a result, school nurses are being asked to increase services to school staff similar to those provided by occupational health nurses in industry. The expanded role challenges the school nurse to better understand the legal requirements and practice implications of providing health services to staff.

BACKGROUND

Historically, the focus of school nursing has been student health evolving from a public health model (National Association of School Nurses [NASN], 2013b). The changes in practice over the years resulted from a number of social, economic, legal and health issues of both students and school staff (NASN, 2016; Zaiger, 2013). The increasing health problems in the United States, especially obesity, have led to changes in policy and programing in an attempt to improve health status and decrease associated costs for all, often with a focus on prevention, health promotion and wellness.

School nurses report often being asked by school staff for health information, health monitoring, or first aid for illness and injury. In industry, occupational health nurses typically provide over-the-counter (OTC) medications for minor employee ailments with the goal of minimizing unnecessary absence. The practice of medication administration to school staff is inconsistent (Trano, 2016). School administrators may ask a nurse to determine an employee's fitness for duty or question if a staff person should be excluded for contagion, or engage the school nurse in other aspects related to staff health.

Federal agencies have encouraged the development of wellness programs and the concept of a comprehensive school health program (CSH) in schools beginning in the late 1980's (NASN, 2013a). School staff health is woven into the CSH program concept and subsequent models (ASCD, 2014); Lewallen, Hunt, Potts-Datema, Zaza, & Giles, 2015). In April 2016, the National Institute for Occupational Safety and Health (NIOSH) published the *National Occupational Research Agenda (NORA) National Total Worker Health Agenda (2016-2026)* to define and prioritize occupational safety and health research, practice, and prevention activities related to employees. NIOSH defines Total Worker Health as "...policies, programs, and practices that integrate protection from work-related safety and health hazards with promotion of injury and illness prevention efforts to advance worker well-being." (NIOSH, 2016, p. iv). Workers and worksites include schools. Scientific evidence now supports what many safety and health professionals, as well as workers themselves, have long suspected—that risk factors in the workplace can contribute to common health problems previously considered unrelated to work (NIOSH, 2016). Examples of risk factors range from the more obvious (frequent absence due to sinus infections related to poor indoor air quality) to more subtle (stress induced illness or negatively impacted well-being related to oppressive supervision) (NIOSH, 2016).

School nurses have been shown to save medical care costs as well as increase teacher productivity (Wang et al., 2014). Occupational health services in the business sector have saved a great deal of money (United States Department of Labor [DOL] Occupational Safety and Health Administration [OSHA], 2016). There are many common denominators in current school nursing practice, but also many differences in settings, roles, state laws and school employment practices. Although school nursing and occupational and environmental health nursing are very similar, the most obvious differences between school nurses and occupational nurses are in the target population and organizational mission. Poor employee health costs businesses nearly $1 trillion annually (American Association of Occupational Health Nurses [AAOHN], 2016). Business leaders are motivated to implement occupational health service programs to maximize productivity and reduce costs through improved absentee rates, fewer work related injuries, and lowered disability claims (AAOHN, 2016). The business bottom line is measured mostly in economic terms. Educational organizations also have an economic bottom line in addition to measuring student academic success, both of which can also be positively impacted by improved school staff health and safety. In business and education there is a greater emphasis on worker health and the provision of health services. For a school nurse, the increased emphasis on staff health has also increased questions of capacity, roles, responsibilities, and liability.

IMPLICATIONS FOR SCHOOL NURSE PRACTICE

Scope and Standards

While student health is the primary focus of school nurse practice, employee wellness is included in the school nurse's scope of practice. The scope and standards of nursing practice describe and measure a competent level of nursing practice and performance expected in all practice areas as well as in a particular specialty. The standards and correlating competencies may be used as evidence of a legal standard of care (American Nurses Association (ANA) & NASN, 2017). The school nursing scope and standards of practice are foundational to the school nurse role. Depending on the setting and role of the school nurse, the additional standards of occupational health, public health and advanced practice nursing as well as nursing administration standards may also provide the performance expectations.

Legal standards are those grounded in laws or regulations that inform what is needed to be done and serve as one criteria to determine, in the case of school nursing, if an action, the how, was negligent. The laws related to student health, safety, and education access are similar to laws related to worker health, safety and employment access (Americans with Disabilities Act [ADA], 1990; ADA Amendments Act [ADA AA], 2008; Individuals with Disabilities Improvement Act [IDEIA], 2004; Section 504 of the Rehabilitation Act, 1973; OSHA, 1970). The similarities allow for easier understanding, but each have nuances that must be addressed in policy and practice to avoid legal consequences.

The determination of liability in a practice situation is a complex set of variables that are applied to circumstances. The best preventive safeguard is to know the practice standards, laws, rules, and especially, the duty to provide a nursing service and under which circumstance.

The increasing focus on providing more comprehensive school staff health services beyond general wellness programs has raised many legal questions. It has also raised the issue of the school nurse's capacity to accomplish all that could be asked, especially since there is not a unique school nurse practice model to implement them. A school nurse working in a large urban school that employs multiple school nurses, has a school based health center, or staff whose only role is safety or human resources, will have exponentially different capabilities than the sole school nurse provider in a rural district with multiple buildings and administrators that wear multiple hats.

(Please see Chapter 3 for more information on scope and standards).

Liability, Negligence and Duty

Liability is in part determined by the standard of care, which is what an ordinary prudent professional with the same qualifications would provide under the same or similar circumstances. Negligence is failure to act to the standard. To be negligent, it must be proved the nurse had a duty to provide the care, the nurse failed to accomplish the duty, the failure caused harm, and the person was harmed or injured. There are a number of factors that may mitigate the outcome of a negligence claim, including whether the person harmed contributed to the harm by their action or inaction. For example, if the school nurse provides first aid to an injured staff person and advises that person to seek further medical treatment but the staff person refuses, it may not be considered negligence if the person is harmed (Scott & Bubert, 2013). However, in some states school nurses as school employees may be immune from suit for negligence, including malpractice, but even if there is such immunity from suit, the failure to adhere to the standard of care could be an ethical violation. As a result, school nurses are well advised to ensure that they are up to date on the proper standard of care for circumstances that they are likely to see in their practice.

The school nurse must be aware of the duty the school has in providing staff services, and the role, if any, he or she has in the provision of those services. Importantly, the nurse must determine if what might be asked is within the scope of practice, can be safely accomplished, and is what the law requires. For example, Title 1 of the Americans with Disabilities Act (ADA) makes it illegal for a school employer to discriminate against individuals with a disability in hiring practices. There are very specific requirements in the law and a breach can be costly. At a certain point in the process, a medical exam could be considered to certify if the potential hire is able to perform the requirements of the job with reasonable accommodations. Medical exam is not defined, but would indicate an exam by a healthcare provider or practitioner licensed to perform such exam (ADA, 1990).

Obligations of the school nurse as an employee are determined by several factors, but the most important is the school nurse's job description, especially since there is not a standard school nurse practice model for staff health services. The job description should include specific language of the school nurse role and purpose in provision of staff health services. For example, is the school nurse role in relation to staff health protection, health promotion, advocacy, or treatment?

Job functions are the duties and tasks that the employee is expected to perform in the position and may be essential or marginal (non-essential). All essential functions need to be included in the job description (National Law Review, 2011). If the school nurse is expected to monitor chronic health conditions of staff (for example, elevated blood pressure) it should be included as a formal part of the job description. The same would be true for care of staff illness and injury, including over-the-counter medication (OTC). Each job element should be prioritized and given a percentage of expected focus.

It is important that policy and procedures reflect the elements of the job description, including language to say what is not included. For example, if staff has authorized access to OTC but the school nurse will not dispense OTC medication to staff, a policy to that effect should be written. If the school nurse will provide OTC, all aspects of the nursing process should be articulated in policy and procedures, including medical standing orders if the nurse is not an advanced practice prescriber, assessment and monitoring, safe medication storage, documentation and records storage (Nursing Service Organization and CNA Insurance, 2016).

Other documents to consider in addition to the job description and standards of practice in the determination of negligence are the code of ethics, nurse practice act, requirements of professional malpractice insurance carrier, professional organization position papers and resolutions. Other documents to determine the school's duty include staff contracts, employee handbook, school board policies, health insurance carrier, and state health and labor laws.

Other State and Federal Provisions for Employee Health

The Occupational Safety and Health Act of 1970 (OSHA) is a standard which requires conditions, or the adoption or use of one or more practices, means, methods, operations, or processes, reasonably necessary or appropriate to provide safe or healthful employment and places of employment. One example of an OSHA safety requirement is staff blood borne pathogen training. The standard contains specific requirements for training content, targeted staff, frequency, and documentation. Most OSHA requirements contain preventive measures as well as specific steps to follow when an exposure or injury occurs. OSHA was originally written to cover private employers and federal employees. States have the option to develop their own plan and/or to have their plan approved by OSHA. Over half the States have an OSHA approved plan that basically covers all employers, private and public, including public schools. Other states have a similar law to cover public workers and are administered by a state agency. Specific coverage and agency oversight can be located at the OSHA. gov website or state websites (OSHA, 2016). It can be a confusing maze, but in general, OSHA is reader friendly and provides many options for information.

All employers are required to provide worker compensation insurance (OSHA, 1970; US Department of Labor [DOL], 2016). When an employee has a job-related injury, an employer must follow specific steps in reporting, record keeping, and determination of fitness for duty. A school nurse may be involved in aspects of the process, but must first know the laws and regulations, and have his or her role specified in his or her job description. For example, the school nurse would typically be the first person to provide care and initial disposition to an injured or ill worker (to seek further care or be sent home). The nurse would likely be involved in completing an incident report and possibly contribute to the Occupational Safety and Health Act (OSHA) log. However, if there is any question as to how long an employee must stay home, when they should return, or if they can return earlier, that disposition should be left to a medical or appropriately licensed healthcare professional.

Each state Workers' Compensation Program requirements vary and must be followed (DOL, 2016). Any dispute quickly becomes costly for anyone involved.

Wellness Programs

School nurses have long been involved in employee wellness (NASN, 2013a). Programs range from passive provision of general health promotion in the form of posters or brochures to more interactive group classes, immunization clinics, or to nursing interventions for individual health conditions.

Out of concern for potential discrimination in participation and privacy concerns surrounding the collection of medical information, the Equal Employment Opportunity Commission (EEOC) published the final rule in May 2016 to amend the regulations and interpretive guidance implementing Title I of the Americans with Disabilities Act (ADA). The amendments provide guidance on the extent to which employers may use incentives to encourage employees to participate in wellness programs that ask them to respond to disability-related inquiries and/or undergo medical examinations. This rule applies to all wellness programs whether they are offered:

- Only to employees enrolled in an employer-sponsored group health plan;
- To all employees regardless of whether they are enrolled in such a plan; or
- As a benefit of employment by employers that do not sponsor a group health plan or group health insurance (ADA, 2016).

Wellness programs that do not include disability-related inquiries or medical examinations (such as a class on healthy eating or heart health) are not subject to this final rule, although such programs must be available to all employees and must provide reasonable accommodations to employees with disabilities (ADA, 2016).

Many wellness programs obtain medical information from employees by asking them to complete a health risk assessment (HRA) and/or undergo biometric screenings (medical exams) for risk factors such as high blood pressure or cholesterol. Wellness programs that are part of or provided by a group health plan or by a health insurance issuer offering group health insurance in connection with a group health plan also must comply with the nondiscrimination provisions of the Health Insurance Portability and Accountability Act of 1996 (HIPAA), as amended by the Affordable Care Act. All of the provisions in this rule, including the requirement to provide a notice of privacy of information and limitations on incentives, apply to all employee health programs that ask employees to respond to disability-related inquiries and/or undergo medical examinations (ADA, 2016).

Regardless how staff healthcare information is collected in a wellness program, all employee health records are covered by HIPAA (HIPAA, 1996). The parallels of Family Educational Rights and Privacy Act of 1974 (FERPA) and HIPAA make understanding compliance easier, but importantly, the school nurse needs to work with administrators, especially human resource personnel, to determine where and how employee health records will be stored to allow practical use. Note that state law may create additional obligations in terms of maintaining and securing employment records.

CONCLUSION

Providing health services to school staff is within the standards of school nurse practice, but the extent of services is dependent on multiple variables, including the capacity of the school nurse to meet the demand. The best defense to a legal concern is preparation and knowledge. The school nurse must examine a number of issues to know if his or her practice is achievable and safe. The individual circumstances of employment will help determine what duty the nurse has to provide staff health services. Federal and state employment law, nurse practice acts, contracts, policy, handbooks, and roles of others in the school will guide the nurse, but the individual nurse is the best judge of capacity. It is imperative to gather data and meet with administrative decision makers, safety officers, human resource director, and the school's medical advisor to clarify responsibilities. In the process, document any discussions and decisions to protect your nursing practice.

RESOURCES

Legal References

- Amendment of Americans with Disabilities Act Tile II and Title III Regulations to Implement ADA Amendments Act of 2008, 29 CFR, Subtitle B, Chapter 14, Part 1630, § 1630.14
- Americans with Disabilities Act, 42 U.S.C. § 12101 (1990)
- Americans with Disabilities Act Amendments Act, 42 USCA § 12101 (2008)
- Equal Employment Opportunity Act of 1972, 42 U.S.C. §§2000e et seq. (1972)
- Family and Medical Leave Act of 1993 (FMLA), 29 U.S.C. §2601 et seq. (1993)
- Family Education Rights and Privacy Act (FERPA), 20 U.S.C. § 1232g, 34 C.F.R. (1974)
- Genetic Information Nondiscrimination Act of 2008 (GINA)
- Health Insurance Portability & Accountability Act of 1996 (HIPAA), 26 U.S.C. § 294, 42 U.S.C. §§ 201, 1395-b, (1996)
- Individuals with Disabilities Improvement Act (IDEIA), 20 USC et seq., 64 (2004)
- Occupational Safety and Health Act (OSHA) (1970)
- Regulations to implement the Equal Employment (EEOC) provisions of the Americans with Disabilities Act, 29 CFR, subtitle B, Chapter 14, part 1630, §1630.14(c) (2015, July)
- Section 504 *of the* Rehabilitation Act, 29 U.S.C. § 701 et seq. (1973)

Applicable/Related Case Law

- Nurses Service Organization & CNA Insurance. (2015). Nurses Medical Malpractice Case Study with Risk Management Strategies, "Failed to follow established policies..." Retrieved from http://www.nso.com/risk-education/individuals/Special-Edition-Legal-Case-Studies-for-Nursing-Professionals
- Leighton v. Three Rivers School District, 2014 U.S. District LEXIS 180736. Retrieved from http://www.osba.org/Resources/Article/Legal/ADA_Accommodations.aspxv
- Rider v. Lincoln County School District, 2015 U.S. District LEXIS 23128 Retrieved from http://www.osba.org/Resources/Article/Legal/ADA_Accommodations.aspx

Position Papers, Clinical Guidelines

- o ASCD, & Centers for Disease Control and Prevention. (2014). *Whole school, whole community, whole child: A collaborative approach to learning and health*. Alexandria, VA: ASCD. Available at: http://www.ascd.org/ASCD/pdf/siteASCD/publications/wholechild/wscc-a-collaborative-approach.pdf

- o National Association of School Nurses. (2013). Coordinated School Health (Position Statement). Silver Spring, MD: Author. Retrieved from http://www.nasn.org/PolicyAdvocacy/PositionDocuments/NASNPositionStatements

- o United States Department of Health and Human Services, Center for Disease Control and Prevention, National Institute for Occupational Safety and Health. (2016, April). *National Occupational Research Agenda, National Total Worker Health Agenda (2016-2026): A National Agenda to Advance Total Worker Health Research, Practice, Policy, and Capacity* (NIOSH Publication No. 2016-114).

- o United States Department of Labor, Occupational Safety and Health Administration. (2006). *Best practice guide: Fundamentals of a workplace first aid program* (OSHA Publication No. 3317-06N).

- o United States Department of Labor, Occupational Safety and Health Administration. (2015). *Guidelines for preventing workplace violence for healthcare and social services workers* (OSHA Publication No. 3148-04R)

REFERENCES

American Association of Occupational Health Nurses. (2016). *About us: What is occupational & environmental health nursing?* Retrieved from http://aaohn.org/page/about-aaohn

American Nurses Association & National Association of School Nurses. (2017). *School nursing: Scope and standards of nursing* (3rd ed.). Silver Spring, MD: Author.

Americans with Disabilities Act, 42 U.S.C. § 12101 (1990).

Americans with Disabilities Act Amendments Act, 42 USCA § 12101 (2008).

ASCD & Centers for Disease Control and Prevention. (2014). *Whole school whole community whole child: A collaborative approach to learning and health.* Retrieved from http://www.ascd.org/.../wholechild/wscc-a-collaborative-approach.pdf

Bubert, J. S., & Scott, L. R. (2013). Legal issues related to school nursing practice: The foundation. In J. Selekman (Ed.), *School nursing: A comprehensive text* (2nd ed.) (pp.196-204). Philadelphia, PA: F. A. Davis.

Code of Federal Regulations, Title 29, Subtitle B, Chapter XIV, Part 1630, § 1630, 14 (c) Medical examinations and inquiries specifically permitted. Retrieved from https://www.law.cornell.edu/cfr/text

Family Education Rights and Privacy Act (FERPA), 20 U.S.C. § 1232g, 34 C.F.R. (1974)

Individuals with Disabilities Improvement Act (IDEIA), 20 USC et seq., 64 (2004).

Lewallen, T., Hunt, H., Potts-Datema, W., Zaza, S., & Giles, W. (2015). The whole school, whole community, whole child model: A new approach for improving educational attainment and healthy development for students. *Journal School Health*, *85*, 729–739. doi:10.1111/josh.12310

National Association of School Nurses. (2013a). *Coordinated school health* (Position Statement). Silver Spring, MD: Author. Retrieved from http://www.nasn.org/PolicyAdvocacy/PositionDocuments/ NASNPositionStatements

National Association of School Nurses. (2013b). *Public health as the foundation of school nursing practice* (Position Statement). Silver Spring, MD: Author. Retrieved from http://www.nasn.org/PolicyAdvocacy/ PositionDocuments/NASNPositionStatements

National Association of School Nurses. (2016). *The role of the 21st century school nurse* (Position Statement). Silver Spring, MD: Author. Retrieved from http://www.nasn.org/PolicyAdvocacy/PositionDocuments/ NASNPositionStatements

Nurses Service Organization & CNA Insurance. (2016). *Case Study: Failed to follow established policies and procedures: Failed to perform a nursing assessment on a patient at high risk for a cardiovascular accident*. Retrieved from http://www.nso.com/risk-education/individuals/Special-Edition-Legal-Case-Studies-for-Nursing-Professionals

The Health Insurance Portability and Accountability Act (HIPAA), 42 U.S.C. § 300gg & 42 U.S.C. § 1301 (1996).

The National Law Review. (2011). *The importance of job descriptions.* Retrieved from http://www.natlawreview.com/article/importance-job-descriptions

Section 504 *of the* Rehabilitation Act, 29 U.S.C. § 701 et seq. (1973).

Trano, G. (2016, May 17). *Case example of legal risk giving staff OTC [Discussion of case study with risk management strategies from liability insurance company].* Retrieved from https://schoolnursenet.nasn. org/communities/community-home/digestviewer/viewthread?GroupId=205&MID=53310&CommunityK ey=36de3547-df3e-4be2-a8f9-e55bc3c8a09c&tab=digestviewer#bm18

United States Department of Health and Human Services, Center for Disease Control and Prevention, National Institute for Occupational Safety and Health. (2016, April). *National occupational research agenda, national total worker health agenda (2016-2026): A national agenda to advance total worker health research, practice, policy, and capacity* (NIOSH Publication No. 2016-114). Retrieved from http://www.cdc.gov/niosh/docs/2016-114/pdfs/nationaltwhagenda2016-1144-14-16.pdf

United States Department of Labor, Occupational Safety and Health Administration. (2016). *Safety and health topics, occupational health professionals.* Retrieved from https://www.osha.gov/SLTC/ healthprofessional/

United States Department of Labor, Occupational Safety and Health Administration. (n. d.). OSH Act of 1970. Retrieved from https://www.osha.gov/pls/oshaweb/owasrch.search_form?p_doc_type=OSHACT &p_toc_level=0&p_keyvalue=

United States Department of Labor, Office of Workers' Compensations Programs, Division of Federal Employees' Compensation (DFEC). (2016). *State Workers' Compensation Offici*als. Retrieved from https://www.dol.gov/owcp/dfec/regs/compliance/wc.htm

Wang, L., Vernon-Smiley, M., Gapinski, M., Desisto, M., Maughan, E., & Sheetz, A. (2014). Cost-benefit study of school nursing services. *Journal of the American Medical Association-Pediatrics, 168*(7), 642-648. doi: 10.1001/jamapediatrics.2013.5441

Zaiger, Donna, (2013). Historical perspectives of school nursing. In J. Selekman (Ed.), *School nursing: A comprehensive text* (2nd ed.) (pp. 2-24). Philadelphia, PA: F. A. Davis.

Chapter 46

SCHOOL STAFF TRAINING

Mary Blackborow, MSN, RN, NCSN

DESCRIPTION OF ISSUE

Advancements in medical technology and legislation have allowed children with severe disabilities to live and attend schools in their communities. More than 20% of students are at risk for chronic conditions that may require care management and collaboration with staff (National Association of School Nurses [NASN], 2016a). Staff training has emerged as a component to provide safe care for students in schools. The civil rights movement, Public Law 194-92, The Education of All Handicapped Children of 1975 (now known as the Individuals with Disabilities Education Improvement Act (IDEIA) (2004) and Section 504 of the Rehabilitation Act of 1973 (2000) have increased the demands on schools to provide a free appropriate education for all children in the least restrictive environment (Wolfe, 2013; NASN, 2015a). Since less than half of public schools have a full-time school nurse (for this discussion, this is a registered professional nurse) and large student to school nurse ratios exist; a need has arisen for non-medical personnel working in school districts to have a basic level of training about chronic medical conditions of students (NASN, 2015a; Biag, Srivastava, Landua, & Rodriguez, 2015).

BACKGROUND

In *Irving Independent School District v. Tatro (1984), the Supreme Court* ruled that a related service must be provided if it will assist the medically fragile student to be able to learn. The related service, in the Tatro case, was clean intermittent catheterization (CIC) that did not require the services of a healthcare provider, which are subject to a medical services exclusion. The court ruled that CIC could be performed by a nurse or a qualified lay person, and were deemed as school health services. In the *Cedar Rapids Community School District v. Garret F. (1999)*, the Supreme Court ruled that the district must pay for continuous nursing services for the ventilator dependent student. In this case, Garret would not be able to attend school unless the services were provided during the school day. Both these decisions resulted in school districts being required to provide nursing services, when it is needed, to support a medically fragile student being able to learn. This has also led to the expanded use of unlicensed assistive personnel (UAP), and delegation to help support students with complex healthcare needs due to the lack of nursing staff in many school districts.

The need for staff training is important in schools due to advances in medical care, and legislation, such as IDEIA and Section 504; adverse childhood experiences, social determinants of health and mental health issues have increased the numbers of students with chronic conditions, and make student management more complex (Wolfe, 2013; NASN, 2016a). School nurses have the knowledge and expertise to help the staff understand the impact that medical conditions have on academics, behavior and attendance (NASN, 2016a).

Teachers in the schools could be overwhelmed by the medical needs of students in their classrooms, especially if little information is provided to them. However, teachers are well-suited to facilitate efforts to improve students' health and well-being because they have direct contact with students (Biag et al., 2015).

Thus individualized healthcare plans (IHP) based on nursing process and emergency care plans (ECP) and are necessary for students with healthcare needs. Among other things, ECPs and IHP's assist teachers to recognize when their students are having a medical emergency (NASN 2015b).

Factors Influencing Staff Training

Federal, state and local school policies frequently mandate which health topics require staff training, for example, many states require that all staff be trained in asthma management. School nurses need to be familiar with these legislative requirements and the disease specific legislation in their individual states along with school policies that address the issues. In addition to national resources, some states have also created state-specific guidance based on legislation with accompanying resources.

Two national resources that provide guidance on the training required by assigned staff regarding diabetes and food allergies are found in the Resources section. While all staff would benefit from training about recognizing the signs and symptoms of diabetes and life-threatening allergies; not all staff would need training in how to administer glucagon or an epinephrine auto-injector.

Bloodborne Pathogen Training

A basic component of staff training includes education on how staff can protect themselves while safely providing care to their students. Schools are required to provide training and have available protective equipment for staff that may be exposed to blood borne pathogens as required by the Occupational Safety and Health Administration (OSHA) standards (Foley, 2013). Some states have developed state specific mandates. School districts should consider the intent of the guidelines since the implementation of the guidelines can benefit both staff and students.

Emergency Training

School staff may require additional training to respond to individual emergencies and to population-based emergencies at school. Preparation/mitigation, preparedness, response and recovery are the steps used in emergency management (U.S. Department of Education [USDE], 2013) that help provide a uniform response to emergencies. Identification of emergency plans, practice drills, development and communication of individual and emergency healthcare procedures for individual students, skills practice are necessary to evaluate effectiveness of response (NASN, 2014a). According to NASN (2014a), schools that are prepared to handle individual emergencies are more likely to be prepared for community disasters.

School-sponsored before and after care programs also will need to plan to respond to health-related emergencies, disaster preparedness, first aid, CPR, recognition of signs and symptoms of child abuse and neglect and procedures to manage blood-borne pathogens (NASN, 2014c).

Confidentiality

As the need for training evolved, there is a legitimate need to share more information about students' health needs with school staff. The Family Educational Rights and Privacy Act of 1974 (FERPA) (20 U.S.C. § 1232g; 34 CFR Part 99) provided guidelines about confidentiality of student records. The 1996 Health Insurance Portability and Accountability Act (HIPAA) (Pub.L. 104–191, 110 Stat. 1936) created an additional layer of confidentiality when sharing information outside of the schools. The publication "Joint Guidance on the Application of the Family Educational Rights and Privacy Act (FERPA) And the Health Insurance Portability and Accountability Act of 1996 (HIPAA) to Student Health Records" provides detailed information and answers to frequently asked questions about privacy records (U.S. Department of Health and Human Services, & USDE 2008). School nurses must be knowledgeable about sharing confidential medical information about students both within the healthcare and school settings.

IMPLICATIONS FOR SCHOOL NURSE PRACTICE

The Every Student Succeeds Act (2015) recognizes the school nurse as the care manager for students with chronic medical conditions at school. This requires that school nurses be knowledgeable about the health conditions of students and factors that can exacerbate or mitigate the impact on academic achievement.

School Nurse as an Educator

Clearly, there are many factors that influence the ability of school nurses to provide staff training. School nurse workloads, conflict between professional standards of care and local/state educational regulations, and ethical dilemmas are some of the challenges that school nurses encounter in schools (NASN, 2015c; NASN, 2016b). The American Nurses Association (ANA) and the National Association of School Nurses (NASN) School *Nursing: Scope and Standards of Practice* (2017) Standard 8: Education requires that the school nurse have knowledge and competence that reflect current nursing practice. School nurses as educators should attend professional development programs, read evidence-based peer reviewed journals and seek feedback on performance which help them remain current on latest trends and developments that can impact school health (Prager, 2013).

School nurses also need to be knowledgeable about the characteristics of an adult learner. Prager (2013) suggests that adults learn best when they perceive the education or training will help them perform or cope effectively with a current or immediate situation. Active participation should be encouraged when possible (Prager, 2013). As mandates and needs for training increase, technology can play a role in extending the reach of school nurses by providing virtual training, webinars and electronic communication for staff education which can be reinforced throughout the school year.

Confidentiality

FERPA does permit the sharing of confidential health information when necessary for "legitimate educational purposes". One way this can be handled with a generalized training for all staff on how to handle potential emergencies that might arise in the school setting (Foley, 2013). Staff members need to know how to intervene in an emergency, so, it is school nurses' responsibility to effectively communicate with staff about how to recognize the specific health condition and what to do to help maintain a safe environment for the student (Foley, 2013). This is a potential area of conflict between the school nurse and administration as "legitimate educational interest" is loosely defined. The USDE (2016) letter, clarifies that a school official would have a legitimate educational interest if he or she needed to review an educational record to fulfill his or her professional responsibility. (*See Chapter 11 for more information*).

Unlicensed Assistive Personnel

Unlicensed assistive personnel (UAP), where laws allow, have a valuable role to assist the school nurse in providing health services to students according to an individualized health plan (NASN, 2015c). Nurses are responsible for knowing about the Nurse Practice Act in their state and what nursing activities may be delegated. On occasion, there is conflict between the educational and health law which results in legal litigation to resolve the issues, such as the California case with insulin delegation (Zirkel, 2014). The California Supreme Court decision stated, "California law does permit trained, unlicensed school personnel to administer prescription medications, including insulin, in accordance with written statements of individual students' treating healthcare providers, with parental consent" which overrode the ANA's position that per the Nurse Practice Act, only nurses could administer insulin (*American Nurses Association v. Torlakson, 2013*).

Delegation

Delegation is defined by the ANA as transferring the responsibility of performing an activity to another person while retaining accountability for the outcome (ANA & National Council of State Boards of Nursing [NCSBN], 2006). Federal and state laws, rules and regulations, employer policies and procedures/agency regulations, and standards of professional school nursing practice hold school nurses accountable when delegating care in the school setting (NASN, 2014b). It is imperative that school nurses understand their state nurse practice act when delegating a nursing activity to a UAP. Delegation can help schools fulfill their obligations under Section 504, the Americans with Disabilities Act (ADA) and the IDEA (Bobo, 2014).

According to Resha (2010), school administrators and parents may not understand that school nurses are required to have and follow medical orders and are held to higher practice standards than parents when delivering care to students at school. The assessment for delegation takes into account the needs and condition of the student, the complexity of the task, potential for harm, the predictability of outcome, the competence of the UAP, the degree of supervision and parental consent (ANA, 2012; Bobo, 2014).

Many nurses express concerns about delegation but with education about how to use delegation, school nurses can develop those skills. School nurses may learn to view delegation as a positive tool and an opportunity for themselves to offer more health education for students, staff and families, and to provide more involved care for medically complex students (Resha, 2010).

Bobo (2014) noted that to reduce the risks associated with delegation, school nurses need to develop a written plan, become familiar with the state's Nurse Practice Act and learn more about delegation. They also need to develop a communication plan with UAP, provide ongoing supervision and evaluation, educate the school administrators about the process, and make sure that there is a school policy to support nursing delegation.

Since the school nurse is responsible for the outcome of delegated activities, it is important to follow, and document the steps in nursing delegation to reduce the risk of adverse outcomes and school nurses' liability concerns (Bobo, 2014).

The school nurse uses critical thinking and professional judgment when following the Five Rights of Delegation. This is necessary to be sure that the delegation or assignment is:

1. The right task;

2. Under the right circumstances;

3. To the right person;

4. With the right directions and communication; and

5. Under the right supervision and evaluation.

(ANA & NCSBN, 2006; NASN 2014b; Bobo, 2014)

Communication must be an open process that allows UAPs to ask questions and/or for clarification of what is expected of them and to decline delegation if it exceeds their knowledge or skills (ANA & NCSBN, 2006, NASN 2015c, Bobo, 2014).

"State law, regulations, standards and rules set by the state board of nursing may determine whether off-site supervision of UAP is an option in school settings within a particular state" (Schwab, Hootman, Gelfman, Gregory, & Pohlman, 2005, p. 148). This may require that a school nurse always be available for UAP to provide direction, supervision and immediate intervention as needed. However, when appropriate, technology has given us the means to expand the supervision capacity with the use of cell phones and video chats (Face Time, Skype, etc.) and to be able to provide timely consultation if off-site. (*See Chapter 4 for more information on delegation*).

Refusal to Accept Task

In the California Supreme Court decision, "volunteered" could mean assigned with the necessary training to administer the medication and may subject the refusing staff to discipline for insubordination (Zirkel, 2014). The "right" of the teacher to refuse has emerged in teacher contract negotiations through collective bargaining but many issues have not been decided judicially or legislatively (American Federation of Teachers [AFT], 2009; Zirkel, 2014). After the court's decision in California, the refusal of a school nurse to provide training may also result in insubordination, unless collective bargaining or local policy protects the school nurse in these circumstances (Zirkel, 2014). Collaboration is important to help resolve difficult issues.

CONCLUSION

Staff training is clearly an identified need to manage students with chronic health conditions, address federal mandates, such as blood-borne pathogen training, and to address the social determinant of health to keep students healthy, safe and ready

---

Strategies to Manage Staff Training

Be knowledgeable about current nursing practice

Understand the state Nursing Practice Act

Understand the ethical implications of nursing practice

Know the federal, state and local statutes that pertain to the educational and healthcare framework

Use the Scope and Standards of Practice: School Nursing to guide practice

Know school district policy as it pertains to nursing delegation issues and staff training

Understand state delegation rules

Utilize evidence-based guidelines for practice

Develop standards of practice for staff training across the school district to promote best practice

Learn how to use technology to help staff receive training and ask questions

Educate stakeholders (teachers, administrators, parents/guardians) about delegation, the school nurse's role and accountability

Incorporate practice drills into emergency and crisis planning and training

Collaborate with relevant stakeholders across disciplines to develop solutions to difficult problems

Document all staff training

Document unsafe staffing and unsafe practices in writing

Look to professional organizations to provide resources to promote optimal care of students

Consider purchasing malpractice insurance

to learn (NASN, 2016a). The school nurses are part of an educational team that can promote student success through collaboration and communication with students, families, administrators, educators, specialized instructional support staff and paraprofessionals.

School nurses must be knowledgeable about the school community and the resources that are available to meet the training needs for staff. The size of the school, the acuity of students, and the number of students, school nurses and staff are factors to consider when planning for training. Other considerations may include but are not limited to: are there before and after school programs, clubs and athletics taking place in the school or off school grounds, are the bus drivers district employees or contracted outside the school district?

The nursing process guides practice as outlined in the *School Nursing: Scope and Standards of Practice*: assessment, diagnosis, outcomes identification, planning, implementation and evaluation. Utilizing the Scope and Standards enables each school nurse to customize the staff training program for their school community. School nurses must be life-long learners and effective communicators with teaching skills to be able to train staff on the most current evidence-based care for their students. If available, technology can help outreach to staff by school nurses with the use of electronic communication and virtual trainings for staff.

Teachers want their students to succeed and view school nurses as a positive factor in helping them meet the needs of their students (Biag et al., 2015). Staff may require disease-specific information, planning for emergencies and specific training as UAP when care is delegated for a specific student. Communicating and collaborating with staff is important to recognize how school nurses can meet the staff and students identified needs and to discover any unrecognized needs that are not being met.

School nurses need to be knowledgeable about federal, state and local laws and policies that mandate training in order to be compliant with these regulations. In addition, school nurses need to understand their state Nurse Practice Act, FERPA and HIPAA confidentiality guidelines, evidence-based practice guidelines, delegation and the specific needs of their school community. There are many additional areas in which school nurses may contribute to educating staff about issues that impact student success including but not limited to bullying, violence prevention, social determinants of health and mental health.

Effective staff training by school nurses will help ensure the health and safety of all students.

RESOURCES

American Federation of Teachers, The Medically Fragile Child 2009
https://www.aft.org/sites/default/files/medicallyfragilechild_2009.pdf

Bobo, N. (2014). Principles for Practice: Nursing Delegation to Unlicensed Assistive Personnel in the School Setting. Silver Spring, MD: National Association of School Nurses

Centers for Disease Control and Prevention(CDC). (2013). Voluntary Guidelines for Managing Food Allergies in Schools and Early Care and Education Programs. http://www.cdc.gov/healthyyouth/foodallergies/pdf/13_243135_a_food_allergy_web_508.pdf

Diabetes, Helping the Student with Diabetes Succeed: A Guide for School Personnel (2016)
https://www.niddk.nih.gov/health-information/health-communication-programs/ndep/health-care-professionals/school-guide/section3/Documents/NDEP-School-Guide-Full.pdf

Joint Guidance on the Application of the Family Educational Rights and Privacy Act (FERPA) And the Health Insurance Portability and Accountability Act of 1996 (HIPAA) to Student Health Records. (2008).
http://www2.ed.gov/policy/gen/guid/fpco/doc/ferpa-hipaa-guidance.pdf

Joint Statement on Delegation. American Nurses Association (ANA) and the National Council of State Boards of Nursing (NCSBN) (2006). https://www.ncsbn.org/Delegation_joint_statement_NCSBN-ANA.pdf

National Association of School Nurses. Get Trained Tools to Manage Epinephrine Training at School.
http://www.nasn.org/ToolsResources/FoodAllergyandAnaphylaxis/GetTrained/TrainingTools

National Association of School Nurses. (2016). *Asthma resources*.
http://www.nasn.org/ToolsResources/Asthma

Nursing Delegation to Unlicensed Assistive Personnel in the School Setting.
http://www.nasn.org/Portals/0/positions/2014psdelegation.pdf

Nurse Practice Act Toolkit. https://www.ncsbn.org/npa-toolkit.htm

OSHA Training and Requirements and Guidelines for K-14 Schools.
http://www.nsta.org/docs/StroudRoy-OSHARequirementsforK-14Schools.pdf

Section 504 and Individuals with Disabilities Education Improvement Act
http://www.nasn.org/Portals/0/positions/2013ps504.pdf

Selekman, J. (2013) *School nursing: A comprehensive text* (2nd ed.). Philadelphia, PA: F.A. Davis Company.

Taliaferro, V. & Resha, C. (Eds.). (2016). School Nurse Resource Manual: A guide to practice (9th edition). Nashville:TN: School Health Alert.

U.S. Department of Education. Protecting Students with Disabilities:
Frequently Asked Questions About Section 504 and the Education of Students with Disabilities
http://www2.ed.gov/about/offices/list/ocr/504faq.html

U.S. Department of Education. Office for Civil Rights. (December 2016).
Parent and Educator Resource Guide to Section 504 in Public Elementary and Secondary Schools.
https://www2.ed.gov/about/offices/list/ocr/docs/504-resource-guide-201612.pdf

Voluntary Guidelines for Managing Food Allergies in Schools and Early Care and Education Programs
http://www.cdc.gov/healthyyouth/foodallergies/pdf/13_243135_a_food_allergy_web_508.pdf

REFERENCES

American Federation of Teachers. (2009). *The medically fragile child*. Retrieved from https://www.aft.org/sites/default/files/medicallyfragilechild_2009.pdf

American Nurses Association. (2012). *Principles for delegation by registered nurses to unlicensed assistive personnel (UAP)*. Silver Spring, MD: Nursesbooks.org.

American Nurses Association v. Torlakson (2013). Retrieved from http://www.cde.ca.gov/ls/he/hn/documents/anavtorlakson2013.pdf

American Nurses Association and National Association of School Nurses (2017). *School Nursing: Scope and standards of practice* (3rd ed.). Silver Spring, MD: Author.

American Nurses Association & National Council of State Boards of Nursing. (2006). *Joint statement on delegation*. Retrieved from https://www.ncsbn.org/Delegation_joint_statement_NCSBN-ANA.pdf

Biag, M., Srivastava, A., Landua, M., & Rodriguez, E. (2015). Teachers' perceptions of full- and part-time nurses at school. *The Journal of School Nursing, 31(3)*183-195. doi: 10.1177/1059840514561863

Bobo, N. (2014). *Nursing delegation to unlicensed assistive personnel in the school setting: Principles of practice*. Silver Spring, MD: National Association of School Nurses.

Cedar Rapids Community School District v. Garret F. (1999). Retrieved from https://www.oyez.org/cases/1998/96-1793

Every Student Succeeds Act of 2015 (ESSA), P. L. No. 114-95 § 114 Stat. 1177 (2015-2016).

Family Educational Rights and Privacy Act (FERPA) of 1974, 20 U.S.C. § 1232g (1974).

Foley, M. (2013). Health services management. In J. Selekman (Ed.), *School nursing: A comprehensive text* (2nd ed.) (pp.1190-1215). Philadelphia, PA: F.A. Davis Company.

Health Insurance Portability and Accountability Act (HIPAA) of 1996, Pub. L. No. 104-191 (1996).

Individuals with Disability Education Improvement Act (2004), 20 U.S.C. 1400 et seq.

Irving Independent School District v. Tatro (1984). Retrieved from https://www.oyez.org/cases/1998/96-1793

National Association of School Nurses. (2014a). *Emergency preparedness in the school setting - The role of the school nurse* (Position Statement). Silver Spring, MD: Author. Retrieved from https://www.nasn.org/PolicyAdvocacy/PositionPapersandReports/NASNPositionStatementsFullView/tabid/462/smid/824/ArticleID/117/Default.aspx

National Association of School Nurses. (2014b). *Nursing delegation to unlicensed assistive personnel in the school setting* (Position Statement). Silver Spring, MD: Author. Retrieved from http://www.nasn.org/PolicyAdvocacy/PositionPapersandReports/NASNPositionStatementsFullView/tabid/462/ArticleId/21/Delegation-Nursing-Delegation-to-Unlicensed-Assistive-Personnel-in-the-School-Setting-Revised-June-2

584

National Association of School Nurses. (2014b). *School-sponsored before, after and extended school year programs: The role of the school nurse* (Position Statement). Silver Springs, MD: Author. Retrieved from https://www.nasn.org/PolicyAdvocacy/PositionPapersandReports/NASNPositionStatementsFullView/tabid/462/smid/824/ArticleID/117/Default.aspx

National Association of School Nurses. (2015a) *School nurse workload: Staffing for safe care* (Position Statement). Silver Spring, MD: Author. Retrieved from http://www.nasn.org/PolicyAdvocacy/PositionPapersandReports/NASNPositionStatementsFullView/tabid/462/smid/824/ArticleID/803/Default.aspx

National Association of School Nurses. (2015b). *Individualized healthcare plans: The role of the school nurse* (Position Statement). Silver Spring, MD: Author. Retrieved from https://schoolnursenet.nasn.org/blogs/nasn-profile/2017/03/13/individualized-healthcare-plans-the-role-of-the-school-nurse

National Association of School Nurses. (2015c). *Unlicensed assistive personnel: Their role on the school health services team* (Position Statement). Silver Spring, MD: Author. Retrieved from http://www.nasn.org/PolicyAdvocacy/PositionPapersandReports/NASNPositionStatementsFullView/tabid/462/ArticleId/116/Unlicensed-Assistive-Personnel-Their-Role-on-the-School-Health-Services-Team-Adopted-January-2015

National Association of School Nurses. (2016a). *The role of the 21st century school nurse* (Position Statement). Silver Spring, MD: Author. Retrieved from https://schoolnursenet.nasn.org/blogs/nasn-profile/2017/03/13/the-role-of-the-21st-century-school-nurse

National Association of School Nurses. (2016b). *Code of ethics*. Retrieved from https://www.nasn.org/RoleCareer/CodeofEthics

Praeger, S. (2013). The school nurse's role as health educator. In J. Selekman (Ed.) *School nursing: A comprehensive text* (2nd ed.) (pp.109-141). Philadelphia, PA: F.A. Davis Company.

Rehabilitation Act of 1973, 29 U.S.C. § 504

Resha, C., (2010). Delegation in the school setting: Is it a safe practice? *Online Journal of Issues in Nursing, 15*(2). doi: 10.3912/OJIN.Vol15No02Man05

Schwab, N.C., Hootman, J., Gelfman, M.H.B.., Gregory, E.K., & Pohlman, K.J. (2005). School nursing practice: Professional performance issues. In N.C. Schwab and M.H. B. Gelfman (Eds.). *Legal issues in school health services: A resource for school administrators, school attorneys and school nurses* (pp.123-165). Lincoln, NE: Authors Choice Press.

U.S. Department of Education. (2016). *Dear colleague letter school officials at institutions of higher education.* Retrieved from http://familypolicy.ed.gov/sites/fpco.ed.gov/files/DCL_Medical%20Records_Final%20Signed_dated_9-2.pdf

U.S. Department of Education, Office of Elementary and Secondary Education, Office of Safe and Healthy Students (2013). *Guide for developing high-quality school emergency operations plans.* Washington, DC, 2013. Retrieved from http://rems.ed.gov/docs/rems_k-12_guide_508.pdf

U.S. Department of Health and Human Services, & U.S. Department of Education. (2008). *Joint guidance on the application of the family educational rights and privacy act (FERPA) and the health insurance portability and accountability act of 1996 (HIPAA) to student health records*. Retrieved from http://www2.ed.gov/policy/gen/guid/fpco/doc/ferpa-hipaa-guidance.pdf

Wolfe, L. C. (2013). The profession of school nursing. In J. Selekman (Ed.), *School nursing: A comprehensive text (2nd ed.) (pp. 25-47)*. Philadelphia, PA: F.A. Davis Company.

Zirkel, P.A. (2014). *Unlicensed administration of medication: The California Supreme Court decision. NASN School Nurse, 29*(5). doi:10.117/1942602X14540412

Chapter 47

EMPLOYMENT ISSUES AND CONFLICT RESOLUTION

Timothy E. Gilsbach, Esquire

DESCRIPTION OF ISSUE

School nurses are often times pulled in different directions, being called to serve both as a health professional and an educator. In addition, school nurses are often called upon to serve in the role of a leader in the school environment, although they are not typically in the formal chain of command. As a result, school nurses may have conflicts between their respective obligations and with other school employees they work with or to whom they report.

BACKGROUND

The role of school nurse is different than other school staff in a number of respects and those differences can create conflict. Among registered nurses, only about two percent (2%) serve in the role of school nurse and often they are often isolated from anyone else in the healthcare profession (American Nurses Association, 2011; Lechtenberg, 2009). School nurses, to a degree unlike most other staff in school buildings, are bound by two sets of laws, educational and health related laws (National Association of School Nurses [NASN], 2016a). The obligation to these two sets of laws, along with potential conflicts between professional nursing standards and school district policy, create conflicts for the school nurse which can result in conflict with other staff and employees (Lechtenberg, 2009; Solum & Schaffer, 2003).

IMPLICATIONS FOR SCHOOL NURSE PRACTICE

What Guides the Nature of the Employment Relationship?

School nurses may be employed by a school entity in a number of different ways and the manner in which they are hired will impact what guides the terms of their employment. In some circumstances the school nurse is employed through a direct contract with the school entity and under those circumstances that contract dictates the working conditions and duties of the nurse. Other places have school nurses as part of a collective bargaining unit and the conditions of employment are dictated by the collective bargaining agreement reached between the union and the school entity, although given the unique role a nurse plays the collective bargaining agreement may not provide much specificity in terms of the duties of the nurse. Lastly, in a number places school nurses are employed not by the school itself, but rather by an agency that enters into a contract with the school and under those circumstances the employment relationship is controlled by the contract that the school nurse has with the agency, although a separate contract between the school and the agency may also provide some conditions on what duties the school expects the nurse to perform.

Irrespective of what the nature of the employment relationship is between the school nurse and the school that he or she serves, the obligations of the school nurse must still be guided by the ethical guidelines and best practices of their profession (Lechtenberg, 2009; NASN, 2016b). In addition, to the extent that actions by the school entity are putting a student's health or safety at risk, a school nurse may have a duty to speak up in a way that does not apply to other staff members (Magnus Health, 2014). When the contractual obligations or the direction provided by supervisors appear to be in conflict with best practices or the ethical obligations of the school nurse, he or she is well advised to

raise that concern and, where appropriate, seek further guidance regarding the same from outside sources, consistent with confidentiality obligations. Such guidance may be sought from legal counsel, state or national professional associations that provide the same, or other practitioners. Belonging to professional organizations, especially those that focus on school nurses, will give nurses an avenue to discuss concerns with others in their profession and who may be facing similar issues.

Issues with Respect to Working Conditions

Given the unique role that school nurses play in the education agencies and schools that they serve; they are often treated differently than other employees. This is especially true given that school nurses are being expected to meet ever increasing needs but, given a lack of any uniform standards for the student to nurse ratio, may not have a reduced load of students (Brown, 2010). School nurses should carefully review the employment agreement they have with their school or agency to determine what their rights and obligations are with respect to their employment. In addition, if the employee is a member of a collective bargaining unit or union, they should be familiar with their union contract and discuss possible concerns with their union representative. However, school nurses should be careful in understanding that their contractual obligations do not alter their ethical ones and, to the extent these conflict, should comply with their nursing ethical obligations first and foremost. In addition, if such a conflict is found to exist, a school nurse may want to raise the issue before it impacts direct practice in order to avoid more significant conflicts.

Means of Addressing Issues with Other Staff

School nurses are in an unusual role within most school districts. While typically not administrators or supervisors, they play such a unique role in the school district that they are called upon to be leaders and to provide direction and expertise in the area of healthcare (NASN, 2016b). Some examples of this include:

Sharonlee Trefry, MSN, RN, NCSN

Q: How might you as a school nurse better respond to conflicts?

A: Consider taking a structured approach that you could apply to any conflict. Take the time to ask yourself if you have done your nursing assessment of the situation that lead to the conflict; what might be missing from your assessment? What is your nursing diagnosis, who are the appropriate stakeholders; what is the desired outcome and your plan of action for reaching that outcome? You are then ready to meet with the right people and discuss how you can, together, implement steps for addressing the concerns. Did you include plans for how you will document your actions and sustain a successful resolution?

Consider whether you have looked at the conflict from the perspective of others involved. For example, is the principal under pressure from the school board to address other issues on a deadline, is the secretary afraid of being left with a student with special needs, is there an existing protocol that needs revisiting or revision, does the family have more urgent health or security priorities? A strengths-based approach increases your chances for success; everyone wants what's best for students and to have a safe and healthy place to learn, to thrive, and to maintain their dignity.

- Being asked to provide direction to the school and staff on working with medically fragile students, which is on the increase (Brown, 2010).

- Being asked to take the lead in providing direction on working with students with a disability, who are mainstreamed into the least restrictive environment, and the drafting of the health components of these student's Individualized Education Plan (IEP) or Section 504 Plans (Brown, 2010; NASN, 2016b).

- Working in schools where the expectation is that schools are becoming, at least in part, a healthcare provider (Brown, 2010).

- Being an advocate for needs of individual students (NASN, 2016b).

- Being an advocate for systematic change for safety plans, promoting education, and healthcare reform (NASN, 2016b).

- Being asked to train other school staff members to provide tasks that in the past would have been done by a nurse, including administration of medication (Brown, 2010).

- Providing education to staff on the health needs of students, both individual students and the student body as a whole (NASN, 2016b).

However, these various roles along with the unique role that school nurses play can create some conflict between the school nurse and other staff in the school setting (Solum & Schaffer, 2003). One example of such a situation may be the dispute over what should be included in a student's IEP or Section 504 Plan with the school nurse taking one view and an administrator taking a different one. Another example of such conflicts may be a situation where a staff member is asking for medical information about a student and they are not entitled to that information under Family Education Rights and Privacy Act (Magnus Health, 2014).

As a result, school nurses may have to work carefully to defuse potential situations with staff. However, school nurses must ensure that despite any such disputes that they comply with their ethical obligations as a nurse (Solum & Schaffer, 2003). In addition, to the extent that a school nurse is being called upon to do something inconsistent with those obligations or is in conflict with other staff members they should work with their supervisors to address such conflicts. In addition, school nurses should consider discussing such disputes or ethical concerns, consistent with their confidentiality obligations, with other school nurses who may be able to help in addressing such concerns (Solum & Schaffer, 2003). School nurses may wish to look at possible means to proactively address such concerns prior to conflict arising including developing sound communication and conflict negotiation skills, using opportunities to train and educate staff on the obligations school nurses have, and by determining what the chain of command is for a nurse to voice concerns about such issues within the school or district that they work. Lastly, school nurses should consider networking with other school nurses and their professional organization (local and national) who can provide advice and support when such issues arise.

CONCLUSION

School nurses play an important but unique role in the school setting and, as a result, may have situations in which their obligations to the health profession and their obligation in education come in conflict and situations in which they come into conflict with other staff members. School nurses should remember that their first obligation is to their ethical duties and to the care of their patients. In addition, school nurses should learn about and use the process available to them to work to reduce conflict, when it arises and may wish to work with their local, statewide or national professional organizations to learn best practices for addressing the same.

RESOURCES

> ### See ADDENDUM: Q&A - Adverse Employment Actions

National Association of School Nurses Website - http://www.nasn.org/

Individual state School Nurses Association or Organization Website

Historic Leadership: One Courageous School Nurse's Heroic Journey
Ellen F. Johnsen, BA; Katherine J. Pohlman, MS, JD, RN
NASN School Nurse, Vol 32, Issue 1, pp. 19-24, January 2017
10.1177/1942602X16677742

Historic Leadership, Part 2
Ellen F. Johnsen, BA, Katherine J. Pohlman, MS, JD, RN
NASN School Nurse Vol 32, Issue 2, pp. 94 - 99 March-01-2017
10.1177/1942602X16688322

REFERENCES

American Nurses Association. (2011). Employment *and earnings, registered nurses, May 2010.* Retrieved
    from http://nursingworld.org/MainMenuCategories/ThePracticeofProfessionalNursing/workforce/
    -Employment-and-Earnings.pdf

Brown, M. D. (2010, Oct.). Today's school nurse: More than just bandaged knees. *Education World.*
    Retrieved from http://www.educationworld.com/a_admin/admin/admin146.shtml

Lechtenberg, J. (2009). Legal aspects of school nursing. *School Health Alert* (Apr. 2009). Retrieved from
    http://www.schoolnurse.com/public/images/Legal%20Aspects%20of%20School%20Nursing%
    2004-2009.pdf

Magnus Health. (2014). School nurse liability: 7 must-know legal facts. *Magnus Health Blog* (Apr. 17, 2009).
    Retrieved from http://web.magnushealth.com/insights/7-must-know-legal-facts-for-school-nurses

National Association of School Nurses. (2016a). *Code of ethics.* Retrieved from https://www.nasn.org/
    RoleCareer/CodeofEthics

National Association of School Nurses. (2016b). *The role of the 21ˢᵗ century school nurse* (Position
    Statement). Silver Spring, MD: National Association of School Nurses. Retrieved from
    https://www.nasn.org/PolicyAdvocacy/PositionPapersandReports/NASNPositionStatementsFullView/
    tabid/462/ArticleId/87/The-Role-of-the-21st-Century-School-Nurse-Adopted-June-2016

Solum, L. L., Schaffer, M. A. (2003, Dec.). Ethical problems experienced by school nurses. *The Journal of
    School Nursing ,19*(6), 330-337. doi: 10.1177/10598405030190060501

ADDENDUM

Q &A - Adverse Employment Actions

John E. Freund, Esquire and Steve M. Cohen, EdD with Erin D. Gilsbach, Esquire

Attorney John E. Freund, II, of King Spry Herman Freund & Faul in Bethlehem, PA, who has represented public schools in employment cases for over 30 years, identifies two specific rights to which school nurses may be entitled when adverse employment action is being taken or considered by a public school employer.

Q: My employer has called me in for a meeting, and I suspect that the meeting may involve some sort of disciplinary action. What rights do I have? What should I do?

A: School nurses are afforded the full panoply of applicable rights in cases where there is the potential for a serious deprivation of employment rights. Depending upon the jurisdiction and the nurse's specific employment circumstances, including whether or not he or she is a member of a collective bargaining unit, the nurse may have Weingarten rights, which refers to a 1975 U.S. Supreme Court case that established the right to have union representation present for any meetings that may involve a deprivation of rights. The nurse may also be entitled to what we call Loudermill rights in cases where the nurse has a protected property interest in continued employment. Loudermill rights are essentially due process rights guaranteed under the 14th Amendment that are required to be provided by employers where termination of employment is being considered for an employee who has a property interest in continued employment. Let's take a look at those two rights a little more closely:

Right to Union Representation

Where a school nurse is a member of a collective bargaining unit, or union, school nurses may be entitled to union representation at any meetings that may involve a deprivation of rights, pursuant to a U.S. Supreme Court Decision, NLRP v. j. Weingarten, Inc., 420 U.S. 251 (1975). This right has become such an important part of collective bargaining units that many state teachers' unions, such as the Pennsylvania State Education Association (PSEA) and other entities, provide Weingarten Rights printable cards for their members to carry in their wallets. The card handed out by PSEA states: WEINGARTEN RIGHTS - If this discussion could in any way lead to my being disciplined or terminated, or affect my personal working conditions, I respectfully request that my Association representative be present at the meeting. Without representation, I choose not to answer any questions.

Right to Due Process

School nurses may also be entitled to due process rights under the 14th Amendment. In 1972, the U.S. Supreme Court, in Bd. of Regents v. Roth, 408 U.S. 564 (1972), held that, where an employee has a property interest in their employment, public employers must provide their employees with due process protections before depriving them of such property interest.

In Loudermill v. Cleveland Board of Education, 470 U.S. 532 (1985), the Supreme Court held that employees with a Constitutionally-protected property interest in their public employment must be given notice and some kind of hearing prior to being terminated. The Court held that, at a minimum, employees must be provided with pre-termination notice of the charges, an explanation of the evidence that the employer has supporting the decision to terminate, and an opportunity for the employee to respond, which includes allowing for a reasonable amount of time for the employee to secure legal representation, if necessary/desired.

Not all public-school employees have a protected property right to their employment, such as to trigger the Loudermill rights, however. Property rights to continued employment are not established by the Constitution. Generally, either state law or specific contract language establishes whether or not a particular employee has a protected property interest in their employment.

Most states, for instance, have laws that grant protected property rights to tenured teachers. Employment contracts can also establish property rights. Employees who are terminable at will, such as non-tenured teachers, generally do not have a protected property interest in continued employment and may be dismissed/ terminated without due process protections. Bishop v. Wood, 426 U.S. 341 (1976). Even in situations where a school nurse may not have a legally-established right to due process and/or Loudermill rights, however, such process may always be requested.

So what should a school nurse do?

First, nurses should not be afraid to ASK whether the meeting will or may involve a deprivation of rights or consideration of a deprivation of rights. The nurse may be entitled to union representation during that meeting.

Second, where termination/dismissal action is being taken and Loudermill rights are not automatically provided, nurses should specifically invoke their rights under Loudermill. Depending upon state law and/or contractual rights, the nurse may be entitled to notice, a hearing, and the right to be represented by counsel. In some situations, even where the nurse is not legally entitled to those rights, the school may willingly afford them anyway.

Atty. Freund points out, many schools afford Loudermill rights to employees in an effort to be fair and transparent, even where they may not have a property right afforded to them under state law or their within specific contract

Q. If a nurse is aware of a practice by a district official, such as a building principal, that the nurse believes constitutes the unauthorized practice of nursing/medicine (i.e., an act that is expressly legally reserved for a nurse or other state-licensed medical practitioner), what should the nurse do?

A: This can be a very difficult situation, and the manner in which the nurse handles the situation can make all the difference. Attorney John E. Freund, III, chairman of the Education Law Practice Group at King Spry Herman Freund & Faul in Bethlehem, PA, has represented schools for over 35 years and offers some advice on the issue. "Nurses need to use a balanced approach in these types of matters. If a school nurse perceives a violation of the nurse practice act, they should make their concerns known to the building and/ or district-level administration. If the matter is serious enough that it poses a risk of harm to students that is not mitigated by informing the administration, the nurse may have an ethical and/or legal duty to report the violation to the state nursing authorities."

Steve M. Cohen, Ed.D, President and Managing Partner of the Labor Management Advisory Group located in Kansas City, who has an extensive background in both education and business, and whose wife and sister are both nurses, has some practical advice regarding how nurses could approach this sensitive topic with their employers. "The nurse should advise, in polite and professional terms, that the official has wandered into an area where the official is unauthorized to operate. The nurse should provide the administrator with documentation that supports the position that it is inappropriate and perhaps illegal to do what has been or is attempting to be done."

Dr. Cohen further advises, "I would point out that, by taking this action, the administrator is incurring liability for him/herself and for the District that is unnecessary and could be a job killer or even a career killer." Importantly, he urges nurses to come prepared not only with a message of potential liability but also potential solutions that will demonstrate that, while the nurse's foremost concern is for the safety of the students, they are also committed to finding practical solutions. "My suggestion is to not simply say 'no' but, rather, to seek to deploy a course of action that achieves a win / win. Anyone can say no and appear irksome and unaccommodating. The person that works toward getting to 'yes' without violating their fiduciary obligations demonstrates that they are trying to accommodate."

This approach is both practical and positive, and it achieves the desired goal: ensuring the safety and security of the students and preventing the unauthorized practice of nursing. Attorney Freund reminds nurses that, at the end of the day, "the most important factor in this decision-making is the health and safety of the students. All legal, regulatory, and employment requirements should be interpreted in light of their needs."

BEYOND THE PUBLIC SCHOOL WALLS

Chapter 48

SCHOOL-SPONSORED BEFORE, AFTER AND EXTENDED SCHOOL YEAR PROGRAMS

Elizabeth Clark, MSN, RN, NCSN

DESCRIPTION OF ISSUE

Local education agencies (LEA's) across the United States provide a variety of before and after school programs, extracurricular activities in athletics and the performing arts, as well as summer extended school year programs to support students' academic achievement and educational progress, as well as the health and wellness of students. In accordance with the American Disabilities Act (ADA) and Section 504 of the Rehabilitation Act of 1973 (Section 504), all students, including those with identified disabilities, must have **equal opportunity** to participate in (or equal access to) school-sponsored activities. The Individuals with Disabilities Education Improvement Act (IDEIA) (2004) mandates that a free and public education (FAPE) be provided for students with Individualized Education Programs, which also can include participation in before and after programs. School nurses need to be actively involved in supporting the health needs of students enrolled in these programs to enable this legal access and opportunity and understand their legal responsibility for the provision of support.

BACKGROUND

There are several factors that have created the need for school nurses to understand their role in addressing health needs for students in activities beyond the regular school day. In 2002, The No Child Left Legislation created 21st Century Community Learning Centers that included before, after, and summer school programs to improve the academic performance of low performing students. Currently there are over 1.6 million students participating in these programs across the U.S. (Afterschool Alliance, 2016). The Afterschool Alliance also reports that students receive not only academic support, but health education, art, counseling, music, and recreational programs. According to the American Institute for Research (2015), students participating in these programs have improved attendance, *classroom* behavior, and math and reading achievement.

Because of the increase of incidences of several common medical diagnoses in recent years, there are more students with chronic health needs attending school. The Centers for Disease Control and Prevention (CDC) National Statistics report (2016) reveals that 8.6 % of students have asthma, with the highest rates in the 5 to 14 age group, and in students living at 100% of the federal poverty level. The CDC (2014) also reported that there are over 200,000 students under the age of 20 with Type I Diabetes. Per Jackson, Howie & Akinbami (2013) the prevalence of food allergies has increased significantly in children from birth to 17 years of age. Russ, Larson & Halfon (2012) report there are approximately 460,000 children diagnosed with epilepsy. In addition, the National Center for Education Statistics (2014) describes that there is an increased number of students with: acute and chronic potentially life-threatening conditions; rare genetic disorders; transplants of heart, kidney, and lungs; and other medically complex conditions. Many of these students require specific nursing interventions, such as medication administration, gastrostomy tube feedings, catheterizations, and respiratory care, including suctioning, oxygen administration, and tracheotomy care. The National Association of School Nurses (NASN) (2014) clearly conveys the school nurse's role in the management of health care in an extended school day includes: direct nursing services; nursing accommodations; nutrition and food safety support; behavioral health care; environmental management; intervention in medical emergencies; and preparedness planning.

Federal law governs a school's provision and support of school sponsored events, before and after school programs, extended school year programs, and extracurricular activities, such as intramurals, sports, and the performing arts, as they must be offered to students regardless of race, economic status, or disability. It provides mandated legal protections and legal standards for accommodations, support, equal access and opportunity for inclusion of students with disabilities in school sponsored activities. The United States Department of Education, Office of Civil Rights states that students with disabilities, such as a severe life-threatening allergy or diabetes, may not be denied access to school sponsored events or services that are offered to other students (2000). Section 794 of the ADA states that LEA's receiving federal funds, must provide reasonable accommodations for students to participate in school activities (2004). In addition, IDEIA (2004) mandates a free appropriate public education (FAPE) in which school staff develops Individualized Education Programs for students that may require access to extended school day or school year activities under state specific guidelines (Zirkel, Fernan-Granthorn, & Lovato, 2012).

IMPLICATIONS FOR SCHOOL NURSE PRACTICE

School nurses are *essential* school employees to support health needs for students *participating in extracurricular activities*. They are leaders in the provision of health services and *in the training and support of educational professionals who are educating these students*. School nurses have the knowledge, skills, and expertise to assess, plan, and evaluate the health needs of students in programing and activities beyond the regular school day. They complete *individualized healthcare plans* and emergency care plans for students and provide expert health resources for accommodations to meet student health needs (NASN, 2016). School nurses manage complex health needs, including chronic disease management for students (Lineberry & Ikes, 2015).

Clear and timely communication within the local educational system is necessary as students enroll in extracurricular activities. For school-sponsored programs and activities beyond the regular school day, school nurse notification of a student's health need may be delayed, due to *a difference in the s*taff and administrators providing extended programs and activities, as compared to the regular school day. Program leaders, coaches, and administrators must have a system, with well-defined policies and procedures in place to obtain health information for enrolled students and notify school nurses of students' health needs, with respect to FERPA compliance in public education. School nurses are able to assist in the creation of policies and procedures to address a seamless process for enrollment and health service provision. Additionally, nursing accommodations must be planned, implemented, and evaluated by the school nurse. The implementation of health care delivered is dependent on the individual state Nurse Practice Act, which provides the guidelines for nursing tasks, training, and possible delegation of nursing tasks, if permitted. School nurses should continually monitor changes in local policies, as well as state, and federal legislation that may impact nursing practice.

LEA's should provide adequate financial compensation for school nurses that are required to provide nursing services beyond the regular school day or regular calendar year contract. The compensation received should be comparable to compensation teachers or other school staff that are providing extended school day or school year services. If direct nursing care or supervision is required by the nurse for medication administration, provision of a nursing task, or for emergency response, then an additional nursing position may be needed for the additional hours per week. Nursing services may be met by a nurse available on site, or on call in a location nearby for phone consultation, depending on the assessment by the school nurse of the student's health needs. A contract with a community nursing agency is also an option to meet this mandated requirement of support for equal opportunity and access for students to participate in activities occurring outside of the regular school day.

A variety of before and after school, extracurricular, and extended school year activities and programs have been developed across the county. These programs not only provide child care for elementary and middle school students, they provide supervised academic supports. They include school clubs and community and private programs located in school buildings, and often occur on student non-contact days, such as holidays and summer vacation. The programs focus on academics, as well as enrichment activities, clubs, social-emotional learning, physical education and sports. (After School Alliance, 2016). Programs may be district, community, or privately sponsored. Many programs fall under state child care rules and regulations, and school nurses must be knowledgeable of the requirements, which may be different than school regulations in their state or territory. School nurses should determine if the extended school day activities are sponsored by the LEA or are community or private agency sponsored with the activity located within or on the LEA's property. The LEA's legal counsel will be a valuable resource to assist in the determination of whether an activity is school sponsored versus community or privately sponsored. Community and privately sponsored activities located on the school district property, are not the responsibility of the local education agency. Therefore, the school nurse is not required to provide health services under this circumstance, and the duty of care would be the responsibility of the parent and the community agency.

Medication administration, including safe medication storage, is a significant issue that school nurses often address when children participate in before and after school programs. According to Foley (2013) policies and procedures for medication administration requirements should be based on state rules and regulations and include the acceptance of medications in the original pharmacy labeled containers, the obtainment of forms indicating consent from primary care provider and parent(s), and proper storage in a secure/locked cabinet or drawer (Foley, 2013, p. 1210). A parent or legal guardian may be requested to submit duplicate medication and permission consent forms to follow child care licensing requirements, which are in addition to the medication and permission forms received by the school for the regular school day. This request could potentially be a hardship for families, and school nurses may need to be innovative to address medication access issues for programs and sports beyond the school day.

Ideally, medication for after school programs should be used exclusively by the program and stored for the program. For example, nurses can request that parents obtain a separate labelled bottle of medication for the extended school program from the pharmacy. If shared medication between programs is the only available option, then it is important that nurses set up procedures for the return of medications to the school health room if there is an exchange in storage locations at the beginning and end of each day (i.e., medications stored in the health room during the school day and securely stored in the after-school location during that program). A mechanism for proper back and forth transfer is needed so that a nurse is not faced with failing to implement a medical order due to a lack of medication available during school day. If the before and after school staff have access to the school nurse's medication storage location, then procedures are needed to ensure no medications are missing (especially for any controlled substances that the nurse is accountable for ensuring an accurate count of those medications). The school nurse is paramount to ensure that state rules and regulations are followed for medication and other health issues, as the school nurse may be only school licensed staff to be knowledgeable of healthcare policies and regulations.

CONCLUSION

School nurses advocate for the health needs of their students in programs and activities beyond the regular school day. It is within the scope and practice of nurses to determine the health needs and accommodations for students (American Nurses Association [ANA] & NASN, 2017). Due to the legal requirements to meet the accommodation standards set forth in the IDEA, Section 504, and the ADA school nurses are necessary to address the health needs of students with identified nursing or health needs in activities and programs outside the regular school day.

School nurses are the experts in determining, in conjunction with a healthcare provider, the needed health care for students with identified health needs participating in before, after, and extended school year activities. The legal requirements of IDEA, Section 504, and the ADA mandates that students are not denied access to programs and activities based on their disability.

RESOURCES

U.S. Department of Education U.S., Office for Civil Rights. (2013). Dear Colleague Letter. January 25, 2013. Retrieved from https://www2.ed.gov/about/offices/list/ocr/letters/colleague-201301-504.pdf

REFERENCES

After School Alliance. (May 2016). *21st century community learning centers providing afterschool and summer learning support to communities nationwide.* Retrieved from http://afterschoolalliance.org/documents/21stCCLC-Overview-May2016.pdf

American Nurses Association & National Association of School Nurses. (2017). *School nursing: Scope and standards of practice* (3rd ed.). Silver Spring MD: Author.

American Institutes for Research. (2015). *Supporting social and emotional development through quality afterschool programs.* Retrieved from http://www.air.org/sites/default/files/Supporting-Social-Emotional-Learning-Through-Quality-Afterschool-ExecSum.pdf

Centers for Disease Control and Prevention. (2016). *Most recent asthma data.* Retrieved from http://www.cdc.gov/asthma/most_recent_data.htm

Centers for Disease Control and Prevention. (2014). *2014 National diabetes statistics report.* Retrieved from http://www.cdc.gov/diabetes/data/statistics/2014statisticsreport.html

Foley, M. (2013). Health services management. In J. Selekman (Ed.), *School nursing. A comprehensive text* (2nd ed.) (p. 1210). Philadelphia, PA: F.A. Davis Company

Jackson, K.D., Howie, L.D., & Akinbami, L.J. (2013). *NCHC data brief, no 121, Trends in allergic conditions among children: United States, 1997–2011*. Retrieved from http://www.cdc.gov/nchs/data/databriefs/db121.pdf

Lineberry, M. J. & Ikes, M. J. (2015). The role and impact of nurses in American elementary schools: A systematic review of the research. *The Journal of School Nursing, 31*(1), 22-23. doi: 10.1177/1059840514540940

National Association of School Nurses. (2014) *School sponsored before, after and extended school year programs: The role of the school nurse (*Position Statement). Retrieved from http://www.nasn.org/PolicyAdvocacy/PositionPapersandReports/NASNPositionStatementsFullView/tabid/462/ArticleId/643/School-Sponsored-Before-After-and-Extended-School-Year-Programs-The-Role-of-the-School-Nurse-Adopted

National Association of School Nurses. (2016). Framework for 21st century school nursing practice. *NASN School Nurse, 31(1), 45-53. doi: 10.1177/1942602X15618644*

National Center for Education Statistics. (2016). *Digest of education statistics, 2014 (NCES 2016-005).* Washington, DC: U.S. Department of Education, National Center for Education Statistics, Institute of Education Science. Retrieved from https://nces.ed.gov/pubs2016/2016006.pd

Nondiscrimination under Federal Grants and Programs. 29 U.S.C. § 794 Chapter 16, Subchapter V, Section 794. Retrieved from http://codes.lp.findlaw.com/uscode/29/16/29/V/794

Russ, S.A., Larson, K., & Halfon, N. (2012). A national profile of childhood epilepsy and seizure disorder. *Pediatrics 129*, 256- 264. doi: 10.1542/peds.2010-1371

U.S. Department of Education, (n.d.). Individuals with Disabilities Education Act of 2004. Retrieved from https://www.gpo.gov/fdsys/pkg/PLAW-108publ446/html/PLAW-108publ446.htm

U.S. Department of Education, Office for Civil Rights. (2000). *Laws & guidance. Civil rights. Regulations enforced by the Office for Civil Rights*. 34 C.F.R. §§ 104.4, 104.47. Retrieved from https://www2.ed.gov/policy/rights/reg/ocr/edlite-34cfr104.html

U.S. Department of Education, Office for Civil Rights. (2016). *Protecting students with disabilities. Frequently asked questions about Section 504 and the education of children with disabilities*. Retrieved from https://www2.ed.gov/about/offices/list/ocr/504faq.html

Zirkel, P.A., Fernan-Granthorn, M., & Lovato, L. (2012, December). Section 504 and student health problems: The pivotal position of the school nurse. *The Journal of School Nursing, 28*(6), 423-432. doi: 10.1177/1059840512449358

Chapter 49

HOMEBOUND SERVICES FOR REGULAR EDUCATION
AND SPECIAL EDUCATION STUDENTS

Suzanne Levasseur, MSN, APRN

DESCRIPTION OF ISSUE

"Homebound services" refers to the process of providing instruction to a student in the home, hospital or another agreed upon setting. Students may be eligible for homebound services for a variety of medical or mental health issues when the student is medically or physically unable to attend school. It can allow a student to stay current in their schoolwork and minimize the negative educational effects due to a serious or long-term illness. Homebound services can be provided under the provisions of the Individuals with Disabilities Education Improvement Act (IDEIA) (2004) and Section 504 of the Rehabilitation Act of 1973 as part of a general education program.

A distinction should be made between homebound services and home schooling. Often these two terms are confused by parents and staff. Homeschooling refers to parents who provide education to their children by themselves or through tutors in the home, outside of the public education system.

BACKGROUND

In November of 1975, Congress passed the *Education of all Handicapped Children Act* (Public Law 94-142 1975) which mandated that all school aged handicapped students receive a free appropriate public education (FAPE). When students cannot attend school due to a verified medical or mental health issue, homebound or hospital-based tutoring may be required as part of the student's FAPE or as a required by Section 504 of the Rehabilitation Act. Homebound services may also be appropriate for a medically complex student who has a serious, ongoing illness or chronic condition that may result in frequent absences or hospitalizations. It also may be provided for a student who is pregnant or has given birth and for extenuating medical reasons cannot attend school.

Policies and procedures related to homebound services are determined by the state statutes or at the local school district level. In general, a parent may request homebound services and documentation would be required from the treating healthcare provider (refer to state law for who can authorize treatment plans), which would include the medical condition or diagnosis, the anticipated duration of the absence, and the impact of the student's ability to receive the educational service. The school team or Individual Education Plan (IEP) team would then consider the request. Homebound tutoring is likely the most restrictive placement for a student. Students with disabilities have to be assured the least restrictive environment (LRE) (United States Department of Education, n.d.); therefore, careful consideration needs to be taken when considering (transportation)accommodations. If a student has an IEP, the IEP team should reconvene to consider the homebound request and if deemed necessary, the instruction should enable the student to continue to participate in the general education program and to make progress towards the student's IEP goals and objectives. At least one state makes every student on homebound service eligible for special education (Graff,

2013). In the case of a student not receiving special education or related services, the need for homebound services may prompt staff to review whether the student may have a disability and may require an eligibility referral to special education and/or related services or a Section 504 Plan.

In some instances, homebound services may be required for students with severe discipline problems, especially if there is an issue regarding safety that may affect other students. In these cases, schools should do a functional behavioral assessment and a behavior intervention plan with a goal of returning the student to the school as soon as possible.

CONSIDERATIONS

Location and Scheduling

Although the term "homebound" itself implies that the instruction is given in the home, it can be provided at other places such as the public library, the school itself or other locations. In general, student and staff availability can determine hours. The minimum number of hours would be determined by state law, regulation or district policy. Teachers often may be serving multiple students and occasionally rescheduling of the instruction must be done. Changing of times and locations generally does not require a change in the IEP or trigger an IDEA procedural safeguard provision (Graff, 2013). In the event that a student is in the hospital, the district may provide tutors to go to the hospital to give instruction or in some cases the hospital would provide the tutoring and bill the district for those services.

Staff Safety and Presence of an Adult

Although there is no legal mandate, most districts require the presence of an adult in the home when the instruction is taking place. There may also be challenging situations where staff do not feel safe during the instruction. Other alternatives such as distance learning could be considered. There should be solid documentation to support the perceived threat and compensatory services provided by the district may be necessary.

Related Services and Assistive Technology

If a student is receiving related services such as counseling, or physical or occupational therapy in the school setting, the services should also be included in the homebound setting. There is no distinction under IDEA between the two settings (Graff, 2013).

Parent Cooperation

For homebound services to be successful, parents need to be part of the process. Medical documentation including releases for exchange of information needs to be provided by the parent in order for the district to make a determination as to whether the student requires homebound services. In addition, schedules and appointments should be kept and parents need to make an adult available if the instruction is to be given in the home. A district cannot be held accountable if a parent does not make the student available for the tutoring. Documentation of the district's attempts to enable homebound instruction must be maintained.

Disputes

Occasionally disputes arise when the district may question the basis on which the treating healthcare provider has asserted the need for homebound instruction. In this case, the student should continue to receive the instruction pending the evaluation of additional information. The school nurse should utilize the district medical advisor if available for a case review and may also utilize another qualified healthcare provider to review and assess the information at the district's expense. Consent for exchange of information should be obtained prior to the consultation. Consultation may include a review of the educational and medical records, and where appropriate, a review of accommodations and school health services that can be provided so that the student can attend school safely.

Mental Health Issues

Homebound instruction as part of educational placements may be required for students with mental health issues or school refusal. Homebound instruction does not allow students to interact with their peers during the school day and has implications related to the least restrictive environment (LRE) laws. Often times an extended homebound instruction period makes it more difficult for the student to return to school and does not provide the student with the full experience of coming to school.

In the case of *Bradley v. Arkansas Department of Education, 45 IDELR 149, 443 F.3d 965 (8*[th]* Cir. 2006)* the courts found in favor of the district after the parent requested homebound based education on a diagnosis of school phobia and the district determined that home was not the appropriate placement and that in filing truancy the Principal did what state law required him to do (Martin, 2013).

IMPLICATIONS FOR SCHOOL NURSE PRACTICE

The school nurse will have an integral role in the homebound process. As the leader for health issues in the school setting, school nurses will be part of the team of professionals to help determine if a student has a disability or a diagnosis that prevents the student from attending school. An essential role of the school nurse is to be the liaison between the treating healthcare provider and the school team. Often the healthcare provider and /or parent may be unaware of the many accommodations that can be offered during the school day to the student to allow the student to attend at least some of the school day. This may include but not be limited to frequent rest periods, partial days, medication administration, or intermittent classes.

As homebound tutoring is a very restrictive environment, all accommodations should be explored prior to initiating the homebound services. It will also be the school nurse who helps determine if the student is well enough to receive the instruction. For example, a student recovering from a surgical procedure may not automatically be well enough for instruction immediately after the return from the hospital. The nurse should assess and plan for the homebound instruction to be implemented as soon as the student is medically ready. This should be incorporated into the Section 504 Plan, IEP or Individualized Healthcare Plan (IHP) as indicated.

Students with long-term healthcare needs or complex healthcare needs who may have repeated frequent absences can be especially challenging. The school nurse can be the case manager in these cases to monitor the student's attendance and quickly alert the school staff of absences. As part of these students' IEPs, homebound or hospital-based instruction may begin after a minimum time of missed school. State statute, regulation or district policy may dictate what this minimum time must be.

Although rare, a request may be made for homebound instruction based on the presence of a communicable disease such as tuberculosis. School nurses should work closely with their medical advisor and local public health authorities to ascertain the risk to others and the necessity of the restrictive environment.

When the student is ready to return to school, transition or return to school, a plan should be implemented. The school team, with the parents and student as appropriate, should be part of this team to determine what accommodations or services need to be put in place for the safe return of the student. For students with mental health issues this may include counseling or arrival monitoring with a pupil personnel or student services staff member. For a child with a medical condition it may include attendance for a partial day or rest periods during the day.

CONCLUSION

Providing FAPE when a student requires homebound or hospital-based instruction requires careful consideration of the whole team and especially the expertise of the school nurse. Many states offer guidance on homebound service policies and many districts develop their own policies and procedures. Home is the most restrictive environment in which a student can be provided instruction. The whole team must evaluate all aspects of the request. If the student is eligible for special education or Section 504, the IEP or accommodation should be revised to reflect the homebound instruction. If the student has not been previously identified the request itself may trigger an evaluation.

Communication and collaboration among the healthcare providers, school team and parents will be essential. The school nurse will often be the liaison between the stakeholders. With knowledge of healthcare, as well as an understanding of education and educational laws, the school nurse can help provide better understanding to all parties and be instrumental in assuring the most appropriate placement for a student with a medical or mental health condition.

RESOURCES

Selekman, J. (Ed.) (2013). School nursing: A comprehensive text (2nd ed). F.A. Davis Company, Philadelphia.

Bradley v. Arkansas Department of Education, 45 IDELR 149, 443 F.3d 965 (8th Cir. 2006)

REFERENCES

Bradley v. Arkansas Department of Education, 45 IDELR 149, 443 F.3d 965 (8th Cir. 2006). Retrieved from http://www.jstor.org/stable/42772958?seq=1#page_scan_tab_contents

Graff, H. (2013). Homebound services under the IDEA and Section 504: An overview of legal issues (p.vii). Palm Beach Gardens, FL: LRP Publications.

Individuals with Disability Education Improvement Act (2004), 20 U.S.C. 1400 et seq.

Public Law 94-142 - Education of All Handicapped Children Act. (1975). Retrieved from http://www.scn.org/~bk269/94-142.html

Rehabilitation Act of 1973, 29 U.S.C. § 504

United States Department of Education. (n.d.). *Building the legacy: IDEA 2004.* Retrieved from http://idea.ed.gov/

Zettel, J., & Ballard, J. (1979). THE EDUCATION FOR ALL HANDICAPPED CHILDREN ACT OF 1975 PL 94-142: Its history, origins, and concepts. *The Journal of Education, 161*(3), 5-22. Retrieved from http://www.jstor.org/stable/42772958

Chapter 50

PRIVATE AND PAROCHIAL SCHOOLS

Elizabeth Chau, SRN (UK), RN

DESCRIPTION OF ISSUE

Questions concerning legal issues are a recurring topic in discussion posts for the private and parochial school nurse (PPSN). To comply with current laws and regulations, nurses must be aware of standards that relate to school health within educational settings, and with an increase in number of medically fragile children attending all schools, legal acumen has become more important than ever.

School health issues are governed by federal, state and district laws, and as such, can be formidable to navigate, even for those who have some expertise in the legal arena. In most situations, the PPSN is employed in a school where the legal advisor may have little or no knowledge of health mandates, or the conflicts that can occur between federal and state laws. With or without direct and regular communication from their state or district department of health, the PPSN must resolve to become acquainted with laws, regulations, policies, and standards that affect delivery of health care to their students. The purpose of this chapter is to provide a brief overview of the five most frequently discussed topics, along with websites for additional exploration.

BACKGROUND

In the 2013-2014 academic year, 5.4 million elementary and secondary students were enrolled in private and parochial schools (National Center for Education Statistics [NCES], 2016). The first known record of collecting data on private schools goes back to 1890 (NCES, 2013), which coincides with a time when English and American nurses were entering schools to check on infectious diseases (Stanhope & Lancaster, 2014). In the 1920's, nurses were assigned by community health departments to go into schools, but by the 1940's, school districts began to employ their own school nurse (Stanhope & Lancaster, 2014). In 1974 the *Child Abuse Prevention and Treatment Act (CAPTA)* was enacted, marking the beginning of legislation affecting child health (Child Welfare Information Gateway, 2011).

Today, the two Acts that afford the greatest challenge to the PPSN are the Family Education Rights and Privacy Act (FERPA), and the Health Insurance Portability and Accountability Act (HIPAA). These and their associated documents are addressed in the next section, along with topics that have become of particular concern to nurses working in a non-public environment – health screenings, immunizations, the support of a school physician, and the administration of medications.

IMPLICATIONS FOR SCHOOL NURSE PRACTICE

Health mandates govern all public schools, and private and parochial schools must adhere to those directives that govern the jurisdiction in which their school is located. Using these mandates as a baseline, along with the incorporation of current evidence-based practice, the private or parochial school nurse is well-equipped to develop and implement policies and procedures applicable to their unique non-public school situation.

Unfortunately, private and parochial school nurses rarely have direct access to these local or regional public school health guidelines, and must resort to navigating an overwhelming maze of complex legislative material relating to child health; yet knowledge of these regulations is essential to establish school policies, procedures, and protocols that are in line with federal, state, and district laws. Supplemental to the laws that apply to the health and education of students in private schools, PPSNs must be aware of the regulations that apply to their nursing license. Disputes have arisen when practice standards have conflicted with regulations governing education, therefore thorough knowledge of the state Nurse Practice Act (NPA) is crucial. Working outside of the usual realm of a healthcare institution means administrative supervisors (often educators) and school lawyers, are not well versed in laws that apply to child health and nursing, therefore ready access to the-state NPA is essential. Some state nurse practice acts have a section on the duties of a school nurse, therefore be aware of legislative changes that may be under consideration by subscribing to updates offered by state boards of nursing. The National Council of State Boards of Nursing (NCSBN) gives a list of all states and their websites (see Resources below).

There is a long history of the US providing healthcare services to its citizens, particularly to those in need. Federal laws are established and implemented through state statutes and regulations (Stanhope & Lancaster, 2014). Over time, and with the introduction of electronic communication, concerns regarding confidentiality of have emerged, particularly the privacy of health information. Two regulations that directly affect school nurses are the Family Educational Rights and Privacy Act (FERPA) and the Health Insurance Portability and Accountability Act (HIPAA). There has been – and continues to be – much confusion over these pertaining to school health records. The National Association of School Nurses (NASN) has amassed a collection of facts about these that may be accessed on their website (see Resources below). This is a brief overview of how these affect private and parochial school nurses:

- FERPA - a federal law originally enacted in 1974 that is intended to protect the privacy of the educational records of a student, and limits access to those records except for parents, students of legal age, emancipated minors, or school officials with a justifiable interest in the student's educational record (US Department of Education [USDE]), Family Education Rights and Privacy Act, 2015). However, this applies only to schools that receive federal funds from any program managed by the Department of Education (USDE, 2015). As private and parochial schools generally do not receive such funding, they are not subject to these rules. Nevertheless, if a school district places a student with a disability in a private school, the records of that student *are* subject to FERPA laws; the records of the other students attending that school are not (US Department of Health and Human Services [USDHHS] & USDE, 2008).

- HIPAA – a privacy rule enacted in 1996 that prevents covered entities from disclosing protected health information (PHI) to others without written consent.

  A 'covered entity' is a health plan, healthcare clearinghouse, or any healthcare provider who transmits health information in electronic form... such as submitting claims for payment from a health plan. (Association of State and Territorial Health Officers, 2015, p.2).

Generally, that does not happen in private and parochial schools, but to be sure, contact your school administration to confirm that none of your enrolled students fall within the HIPAA and FERPA guidelines.

Obtaining immunization records from a student's healthcare provider continues to be problematic for some PPSNs. In 2013, because of the confusion and restrictions placed upon schools caused by the original HIPAA legislation, modifications were made to "increase flexibility" of the HIPAA, one of which applied to immunizations (USDHHS Federal Register, 2013, pp. 5616-5617). In this revision, a parent may give oral permission (instead of written permission) for the healthcare provider to share their child's immunization records. It was communicated to the Department of Health and Human Services that healthcare providers were unable to consistently obtain *written* permission from parents and guardians, thus causing a delay in sharing immunizations records. Now, permission may be received orally, and a written note made by the person receiving the oral directive placed in the student's health file at the time (USDHHS Federal Register, 2013). However, in states where immunizations are required for school entry, no such permission is necessary to provide this information to the state immunization registry. Permission – whether oral or written - is considered ongoing until a parent revokes such approval (USDHHS Federal Register, 2013).

Nevertheless, school nurses continue to encounter healthcare providers who will not share information, citing the HIPAA ruling. As a result, many PPSNs have found success in avoiding this complication by asking for parents' signature on their annual emergency information form to give permission for the school nurse to share healthcare information with their healthcare provider (Caldart-Olson & Thronson, 2013).

Health Screenings

In keeping with legislation, another frequent dilemma encountered by PPSNs, is the topic of student health screenings. Each state specifies how often health examinations should be completed, and checking with the State Department of Education (DOE) or Department of Health (DOH) will furnish this information. The approved health certificate is often available for downloading at the state website, and providing the link to families will ensure the correct documentation is completed when they take their child to their healthcare provider. Families of students coming from out-of-state or overseas will also benefit by having this information prior to arrival. A general list of state regulations may be found using the Centers for Disease Control and Prevention (CDC) website *Public Health Resources* (CDC, 2015).

Immunizations

Immunizations required for entry into school are mandated by each state, and the schedule of vaccinations to be administered along with the type of exemptions permitted may be found at each State DOH or DOE website. These sites include exclusion policies and, if allowed, how long a student may stay in school without an immunization record (e.g. District of Columbia permits 10 days, North Carolina, 30 days). Even for those states that allow a "grace period", there are policies and procedures for student exclusion if the school feels there is a health risk. Once retrieved, it is advisable a printed copy of these mandates is kept for use as a reference for clarification or in the event of a dispute where immunization laws may differ when a student lives in one state but attends school in another.

Electronic access to immunization records is becoming more frequent using state immunization registries. Access to these registries, along with their primary contact personnel, may be reached through the Immunization Information Systems (IIS) located at the Centers for Disease Control and Prevention (CDC) website (CDC, 2017). It is advisable to register with the state agency not only to verify the immunization history of a student, but to correct any discrepancies that may be present.

The promotion of immunizations as essential to preventing disease throughout life is a core tenet of the National Association of School Nurses (NASN, 2015a), and the school nurse is in a prime position to provide access to evidence-based, medically proven information, and to dispel myths that continue to circulate about the dangers of vaccines. Philosophical beliefs were the most common reason parents wished to have their children exempt (Luthy, Beckstrand & Meyers, 2013), and discussing these concerns will serve as an opportunity for the PPSN to educate parents on the importance of having their child immunized. One excellent resource on the history, signs and symptoms, schedule, and adverse reactions to all vaccine-preventable diseases may be found in the publication *The 13th Edition Epidemiology and Prevention of Vaccine-Preventable Diseases* (fondly known as "The Pink Book") presented by the CDC. This may be purchased as a bound copy or downloaded in its entirety from the CDC website (CDC, 2015b). For those schools who enroll students from overseas, this book also contains a section to help translate foreign immunization records.

States establish their immunization requirements for both public and private and parochial schools, and most allow exemptions (CDC, 2015c). In the event of a vaccine exemption, it is important for the RN PPSN to apprise these families – and the student - of the school policy in the event of an outbreak of a communicable disease for which the student has not been immunized, as most states require unvaccinated (or incompletely vaccinated) students to remain at home for a specific length of time. The applicable State Immunization Department will provide details, along with the procedure for reporting a communicable disease outbreak.

Medications

Most states will have written policies and statutes on the administration of over-the-counter (OTC) and prescription medications, along with identifying those who are permitted to administer them (National Association of State Boards of Education [NASBE], 2016). Many states now allow students to carry asthma inhalers and epinephrine auto-injectors with written permission from the student's healthcare provider, a completed individualized healthcare plan (IHP), and emergency care plan (ECP). However, be sure to check with your state DOE (or DOH) for the most current information.

The management of short-term prescription medications is generally straightforward, and schools should have written policies outlining the requirements for dispensation of these during the school day. Forms should be completed and signed by both the student's healthcare provider and the parent or guardian, and should specify a definitive beginning and end date. If it is a medication that the student will continue to take at home, it is recommended that the parent obtain two prescription bottles from the pharmacy – one for home and one for school. This eliminates the need for the student (or parent) to come in twice daily to deliver and collect the medication, and prevents the temptation for a "baggie" to be used – a practice that should not be permitted in school and discouraged at home. Upon receipt of any medication, note the amount received on the student chart and request the parent confirm and co-sign. All medications (except asthma inhalers and epinephrine auto-injectors) should be kept in a locked cabinet in the school nurse's office. Ideally, a separate double-locked metal cabinet for controlled substances should be used and kept in the school nurse's office. If a medication needs to be refrigerated, the temperature should be monitored on a regular basis and the refrigerator locked (Foley, 2013). This should also be located in the school nurse's office and be a medication-only refrigerator... not one that also houses drinks and snacks.

Student asthma inhalers, epinephrine auto-injectors, and diabetic supplies should be stored in easily retrievable containers with the student's name, photograph, date of birth, and expiration date of the medication clearly visible in the school nurse's office. Prior to the start of school, it is advisable for the RN PPSN to meet with the student (and family) to show where his or her medication is kept, and to ensure the student knows how to correctly use their medication. This would also be a suitable time to review school-wide and individual emergency action plans with the student and parent or guardian.

Providing OTCs in managing minor discomforts has shown to benefit student by keeping them in school (Wallace, 2016), yet their use continues to be controversial. The oversight of a healthcare provider in creating policies and procedures for their administration is strongly encouraged, where permitted by federal, state and district regulations. In addition, federal, state, and district laws must be considered when creating guidelines for the dispensation of medications, along with state NPA regulations, established safety procedures, and evidence-based practice (NASN, 2012). When trying to determine what stock OTC medication to keep on hand, an historical evaluation of the remedies that were most requested over the past three years should be made, then, after discussion and written authorization from the school physician, appropriate supplies may be ordered (Wallace, 2016). Annually, all students and their families should be provided with a health form indicating what OTC medications may be administered at the discretion of the school nurse during the school day. This form must be signed by the student's healthcare provider and parent. No OTC medication should be administered without these authorizations.

There will be instances (when permitted by state NPAs and state and district regulations) that administration of OTCs may be provided by unlicensed assistive personnel (UAP); the RN PPSN, has the knowledge and necessary expertise to decide whether a UAP is competent to perform this task, after taking into consideration the acuity and general status of the student to whom the medication will be given (NASN, 2014). Once all relevant criteria have been met, the RN PPSN, will create a student IHP that provides clear guidelines on the scope and limitations within which the UAP may function (NASN,2012, 2015b). These same standards apply in the event of on-and-off-campus school-sponsored field trips. If it is determined that care cannot safely (or legally) be delegated to a UAP during these events, the RN PPSN should - in conjunction with school administration - arrange for a substitute nurse to be brought in to either cover the health room while the RN PPSN accompanies the student on the trip (NASN, 2013), or escort the field trip in lieu of the PPSN. If the trip occurs in another state, the RN PPSN must verify whether that state is a member of the Nurse Licensure Compact (NLC), an interstate alliance that permits RN's located in one state to practice in another (NCSBN, 2017). If the state to be visited is not, the RN PPSN must receive permission from that state board of nursing to practice, and establish that permission to practice will include the ability to delegate to UAPs (NCSBN, 2016). In the event of an overseas trip, it is advised that communication with the embassy of the host country is made to determine their laws regarding prescription and OTC medications, and the guidelines for carrying and administering them to minors.

School Physician

One of the more difficult aspects of working as a registered nurse in a non-public school is the lack of inter-professional collaboration, with the absence of a consulting school physician presenting the greatest challenge. In general, many of the students are seen by a localized group of pediatricians, and with permission from parents, PPSNs are able to confer with these health professionals on individual students. Some school districts and local governments employ physicians to oversee school health services, but there is no national requirement to make such provisions available (American Academy of Pediatrics [AAP], 2013). To have such a partnership would be invaluable to the non-public school nurse. Apart from advising on policies and serving as consultant on the crisis management team, school physicians are able to collaborate on written standing orders for the administration of stock emergency medications and emergency treatment protocols, as well as provide confidential advice on issues of school health that may occur during the school year.

For those new to non-public school nursing, finding a healthcare provider may be a daunting task. Seasoned PPSNs propose the following options:

- Advise your school administration of your need and ask if you may be in touch with alumni who have entered the medical field for advice/referrals,
- Approach a parent of an enrolled student who is a pediatrician to ask if they would be willing to serve as consultant; they are usually happy to do so,
- Contact pediatricians who regularly see your enrolled students to ask if they would be willing to serve in the role of school adviser,
- Be in touch with other PPSNs in your jurisdiction to ask who they use,
- Get in touch with your state school nurse consultant to ask for referrals; if your state has no such person, make a direct call to your DOE, and
- Contact the American Academy of Pediatrics, the Society for Adolescent Medicine, and the American Academy of Family Physicians for local affiliates that may be able to help.

In some instances - and where permitted by federal, state, and local laws - a pediatric or family Nurse Practitioner (NP) may act as a school health consultant. These advanced nurse practitioners are registered nurses with master's or doctoral degrees in pediatrics or family practice. They provide several clinical practice resources for healthcare providers and families, and work in pediatric offices, departments of health, state boards of nursing, and outpatient clinics.

CONCLUSION

In the 2013-14 school year, almost 11% of students in the USA were enrolled in private and parochial schools (NCES, 2016). The percentage of those student who have chronic health conditions or are medically fragile is increasing (NASN, 2016) and many PPSNs will have these students in their community. As the sole healthcare provider in their educational setting, knowledge of laws pertaining to education, school health, and nursing must be implemented, and for those who have no access to administrative help (indeed the confidential nature of their role within the school makes such help unwise), the task for searching for legislative rulings falls to the PPSN. Membership in the Private and Parochial School Nurse Special Interest Group (PPSN SIG) of NASN will provide immeasurable help, advice, and support, and in many cases, easy access to legislative materials made available by other PPSNs. Find out more at www.nasn.org.

RESOURCES

> See APPENDIX: Are private schools required to comply with federal laws e.g. ADA?
> and ADDENDUM: Tort Claims Liability

Agency for Healthcare Research and Quality - http://www.ahrq.gov

American Academy of Pediatrics – https://www.aap.org

American Academy of Pediatrics – Healthy Children – https://www.healthychildren.org

American Nurses Association - http://www.nursingworld.org/

Asthma & Allergy Foundation of America - http://www.aafa.org/

Asthma & Allergy Network - http://www.allergyasthmanetwork.com/

Centers for Disease Control and Prevention - http://www.cdc.gov

Centers for Disease Control and Prevention Immunization Information Systems. (2017). https://www.cdc.gov/vaccines/programs/iis/contacts-registry-staff.html#dc

Centers for Disease Control and Prevention Morbidity and Mortality Weekly Report (MMWR) http://www.cdc.gov/mmwr/index.html

Centers for Disease Control and Prevention National Notifiable Diseases Surveillance System (NNDSS) https://wwwn.cdc.gov/nndss/

Healthy People 2020 - https://www.healthypeople.gov

Institute for Safe Medication Practices - http://www.ismp.org

National Association of Pediatric Nurse Practitioners - https://www.napnap.org

National Association of School Nurses: www.nasn.org

National Association of School Nurses HIPAA and FERPA - http://www.nasn.org/ToolsResources/DocumentationinSchoolHealth/HIPAAandFERPA

National Council of State Boards of Nursing - https://www.ncsbn.org

U.S. Department of Education - http://www.ed.gov

U.S. Department of Health and Human Services - https://www.hhs.gov

U.S. Department of Justice - https://www.justice.gov

U.S. Department of Justice Civil Rights Division - https://www.justice.gov/crt

United States Office of the Executive Branch Web Sites - http://www.loc.gov/rr/news/fedgov.html

U. S. Department of Justice, Civil Rights Division

REFERENCES

American Academy of Pediatrics (AAP). (2013). *The role of the school physician* (Policy Statement). *Pediatrics, 131*(1). doi:10.1542/peds.2012-2995

Association of State and Territorial Health Officers. (2015). *Public health and schools toolkit: Comparison of FERPA and HIPAA Privacy Rule for accessing student health data*. Retrieved from: http://www.astho.org/ programs/preparedness/public-health-emergency-law/public-health-and-schools-toolkit/comparison-of-ferpa-and-hipaa-privacy-rule/

Caldart-Olson, L. & Thronson, G. (2013). Legislation affecting school nurses. In Selekman, J. (Ed.), *School nursing: A comprehensive text* (2nd ed.) (pp. 225-256). Philadelphia, PA: F.A. Davis Company.

Centers for Disease Control and Prevention (CDC). (2015a). *Public health resources: State or territorial health departments*. Retrieved from http://www.cdc.gov/mmwr/international/relres.html

Centers for Disease Control and Prevention (CDC). (2015b). *Epidemiology and prevention of vaccine-preventable diseases. The pink book – 13th ed.* Retrieved from http://www.cdc.gov/vaccines/pubs/ pinkbook/index.html

Centers for Disease Control and Prevention (CDC. (2015c). *State school immunization requirements and vaccine exemption laws.* Retrieved from https://www.cdc.gov/phlp/docs/school-vaccinations.pdf

Child Welfare Information Gateway. (2011). *About CAPTA: A legislative history.* Washington, DC: U.S. Department of Health and Human Services, Children›s Bureau. Retrieved from: https://www.childwelfare.gov/pubs/factsheets/about/

Foley, M. (2013). Health services management. In Selekman, J. (Ed.), *School nursing: A comprehensive text* (2nd ed.) (pp. 1190-1215). Philadelphia, PA: F.A. Davis Company.

Luthy, K.E., Beckstrand, R.L. & Meyers, C.J. (2013). Common perceptions of parents requesting personal exemption from vaccination. *The Journal of School Nursing 29*(2), pp. 95-103. doi: 10.1177/1059840512455365

National Association of School Nurses (NASN). (2015a). *Immunizations* (Position statement). Retrieved from: https://www.nasn.org/PolicyAdvocacy/PositionPapersandReports/NASNPositionStatementsFullView/ tabid/462/ArticleId/8/Immunizations-Revised-January-2015

National Association of School Nurses (NASN). (2015b). *Unlicensed assistive personnel: Their role on the school health service team* (Position statement). Retrieved from https://www.nasn.org/PolicyAdvocacy/ PositionPapersandReports/NASNPositionStatementsFullView/tabid/462/ArticleId/116/Unlicensed-Assistive-Personnel-Their-Role-on-the-School-Health-Services-Team-Adopted-January-2015

National Association of School Nurses (NASN). (2017). *Medication administration in the school setting* (Position statement). Retrieved from https://schoolnursenet.nasn.org/blogs/nasn-profile/2017/03/13/ medication-administration-in-schools

National Association of School Nurses (NASN). (2013). *School-sponsored trips, role of the school nurse* (Position Statement). Retrieved from: http://www.nasn.org/Portals/0/positions/2013pstrips.pdf

National Association of School Nurses (NASN). (2014). *Nursing delegation to unlicensed assistive personnel in the school setting* (Position statement). Retrieved from: http://www.nasn.org/Portals/0/positions/2014psdelegation.pdf

National Association of State Boards of Education (NASBE). (2016). *State school health policy database. Administration of medicines*. Retrieved from: http://www.nasbe.org/healthy_schools/hs/bytopics.php?topicid=4110

National Center for Education Statistics (NCES). (2016). *Private school enrollment*. Retrieved from http://nces.ed.gov/programs/coe/indicator_cgc.asp

National Council of State Boards of Nursing (NCSBN). (2016). National guidelines for nursing delegation. *The Journal of Nursing Regulation, 7*(1), pp. 5-14. Retrieved from https://www.ncsbn.org/NCSBN_Delegation_Guidelines.pdf

National Council of State Boards of Nursing (NCSBN). (2017). *Nurse Licensure Compact.* Retrieved from https://www.ncsbn.org/nurse-licensure-compact.htm

Stanhope, M., and Lancaster, J. (Eds). (2014). *Public health nursing: Population-centered health care in the community* (8th ed.). Maryland Heights, MI: Elsevier.

U.S. Department of Education. (2015). *Family Education Rights and Privacy Act.* Retrieved from: http://www2.ed.gov/policy/gen/guid/fpco/ferpa/index.html)

U.S. Department of Health and Human Services. (n.d.) *HIPAA for professionals.* Retrieved from http://www.hhs.gov/hipaa/for-professionals/index.html

U.S. Department of Health and Human Services & US Department of Education. (2008). *Joint guidance on the application of the Family Educational Rights and Privacy Act (FERPA) and the Health Insurance Portability and Accountability Act of 1966 (HIPAA) to student health records.* Retrieved from: http://www2.ed.gov/policy/gen/guid/fpco/doc/ferpa-hipaa-guidance.pdf

U.S. Department of Health and Human Services, Federal Register. (2013). *Modification to the Health Insurance Portability and Accountability Act., 78(17),* pp. 5616-5617. Retrieved from https://www.gpo.gov/fdsys/pkg/FR-2013-01-25/pdf/2013-01073.pdf

Wallace, A.C. (2016). Managing use of over-the-counter medications in the school setting: Keeping kids in school and ready to learn. *NASN School Nurse, 31*(4), pp. 210-213. doi: 10.1177/1942602X16636123

APPENDIX

Are private schools required to comply with federal laws e.g. ADA?

Privately-run child care centers -- like other public accommodations such as private schools, recreation centers, restaurants, hotels, movie theaters, and banks -- must comply with title III of the ADA. Child care services provided by government agencies, such as Head Start, summer programs, and extended school day programs, must comply with title II of the ADA. Both titles apply to a child care center's interactions with the children, parents, guardians, and potential customers that it serves. The exception is child care centers that are actually run by religious entities such as churches, mosques, or synagogues. Activities controlled by religious organizations are not covered by title III) (U. S. Department of Justice, Civil Rights Division).

When a school is religious-based - i.e. a religious organization controls all aspects of the school's governance - they ARE exempt from federal laws. Having said that, of course, the school will need to check with their attorney who should know the specifics of their school, as even one child receiving any type of federal assistance will nullify that exemption.

Exemptions also apply to transportation. For example, if the transportation is owned by the wholly-run religious school, it does not have to comply with ADA requirements...e.g. a pneumatic lift or ramp to load a wheelchair. However, again, the school must check with their attorney (and it is advisable the school nurse get the attorney's response in writing to keep on file as they are the ones who initially deal with parents).

RESOURCES:

- **Overview from USDE on the role of Federal Government in Education**:
  https://www2.ed.gov/policy/landing.jhtml?src=pn

- **10 Facts about K-12 Education Funding:**
  https://www2.ed.gov/about/overview/fed/10facts/index.html

- **NAIS Americans with Disabilities Act and Independent Schools (2011):**
  http://www.nais.org/Articles/Documents/ADA_Pub_2011Final.pdf

- **Architectural and Transportation Barriers Compliance Board:**
  http://uscode.house.gov/statviewer.htm?volume=104&page=363

ADDENDUM: Tort Claims Liability

Erin D. Gilsbach, Esquire

The possibility of tort claims and malpractice actions, from which public schools are largely immune in most states, heightens the professional risk for school nurses and results in the need for additional protections for nurses. All states have some form of sovereign immunity tort claims limitation. The National Council of State Legislatures provides a helpful table of authority listing tort claims legislation by state. That resource can be found at: http://www.ncsl.org/research/transportation/state-sovereign-immunity-and-tort-liability.aspx

In most states, public schools fall within the full protection of their state's sovereign immunity laws due to the fact that they are local governmental entities. Sovereign immunity do not protect school officials against cases involving intentional harm, but they do provide varying degrees of protection for negligence and other non-intentional torts. Private and parochial schools, however, are not afforded this protection. While this fact is significant for the schools, themselves, it is even more important to the private school nurses. Medical malpractice or professional liability deals with professional negligence and is a sub-set of tort law from which public school nurses generally have immunity. The same is not true for a nurse in the private/parochial school setting. This type of liability has the potential to be very costly, and a legal finding of professional negligence can result in the loss of employment, difficulty obtaining future employment in that field due to the fact that court documents are public records, and potential action by the state against the nurse's license. The latter is, perhaps, the most damaging, due to the fact that the loss of licensure, for a nurse, equates to the complete loss of any potential employment in the field of nursing.

Due to the potential for liability, private and parochial school nurses need to take steps to ensure that they are protected from a devastating loss. The first thing that PPSNs should do is determine whether the school's insurance policy would cover a professional liability claim. Most insurance companies require schools to take out additional and specific professional liability policies (sometimes called "Errors and Omissions" policies). Where the school does have coverage for professional liability claims, the nurse should also verify whether such policies specifically include coverage for medical professional liability claims. In addition to determining whether coverage exists and is applicable to the nurse, it is also a good idea to determine the policy limitations, such as the amount of coverage and any specific exclusions. Where no coverage exists, or where the existing coverage is not sufficient, private/parochial school nurses will need to consider obtaining their own professional liability coverage. Where coverage does exist, school nurses should review the coverage to determine whether it provides licensure protection and will cover the costs of a nurse if they are required to defend his/her actions before the board of nursing or other licensure-issuing body.

Chapter 51

SCHOOL-SPONSORED FIELD TRIPS

Karen Erwin, RN, MSN
Sandra Clark, RN, ADN

DESCRIPTION OF ISSUE

School-sponsored field trips enhance the student's educational experience but may also create many challenges for the school nurse if the student requires health services during the field trip. Federal law requires equal access to school attendance and school-sponsored activities, which may require the provision of health services. Including the Nurse Licensure Compact (NLC) states, which is discussed later in this chapter, nursing practice laws and regulations vary from state-to-state. A critical issue of concern is delegation of nursing healthcare services to unlicensed assistive personnel (UAP) on school-sponsored trips. A review of state laws, regulations, and nursing scope of practice for school health services, in both the state of residence and the state where the field trip occurs, is critical when planning and problem solving for students requiring school health services on field trips.

Field trips offer a wonderful learning opportunity for students. The number of field trips offered to enhance learning during a school year is determined by the school and teacher. However, students attending school today include an increasing number of children with special healthcare needs. In order for these students to attend school or participate in school-sponsored activities, delegation of school health services may be necessary when a shortage of school nurses exists. Nursing Practice laws differ from state to state and may not allow for the delegation of school health services to unlicensed assistive personnel (UAP). Additionally, the home or destination state may have restrictions or mandates relative to the possession or administration of medications, particularly controlled drugs. For example, does the destination state nursing scope of practice allow for the administration or delegation of Intranasal Medazolam (Versed) or medical marijuana? An understanding of state laws, regulations and nursing scope of practice is essential when planning for the delivery of necessary student health services on both in- state and out-of-state field trips.

BACKGROUND

In order for students to participate fully on field trips, schools are obligated to provide any health service accommodation necessary for the student to have full access in the activity. Exclusion from participation is not an option. The location of the field trip may vary from a local site to a different city, state or country. Laws that protect students with special healthcare needs include: Section 504 of the Rehabilitation Act of 1973, Title II of the American Disabilities Act of 1990 (ADA) and the Individuals with Disability Education Improvement Act (IDEIA) reauthorized in 2004. All students, regardless of disability or special healthcare needs, have a right to attend and have full access to all school-sponsored activities (including field trips) (U.S. Department of Education [USDE],2011). School nurses must be included in the planning process for school-sponsored field trips that may include accommodations for healthcare needs, required medications and/or treatments and potential emergency care.

School nurses who provide healthcare to students know their own state's specific laws governing nursing. However, when a field trip occurs out-of-state or out-of-country, it is equally important to know and understand the laws and regulation for nursing practice in the state of countries where the care will be administered as well. School nurses should be particularly aware of the nursing practice regulations regarding delegation, medications, treatment and emergency care.

In-State, Out-of-State or Out-of- Country Field Trips and Nursing Scope of Practice

Federal law requires equal access to school-sponsored activities and field trip, including the provision of school health services on field trips (USDE, 2011). Students may not be denied access to these activities. While the school nurse is familiar with the nursing scope of practice in the state of residence, it is essential that the school nurse also understand the nursing practice laws where the field trip occurs. Nurses providing health services on out-of-state field trips must adhere to the state nursing law of the state they are visiting. If the field trip will occur out-of- country, the U.S. Embassy can provide information on whom to contact for that country.

Nurse Licensure Compact States

The Nurse Licensure Compact (NLC) is a mutual recognition model of licensure, similar to a driver's license that provides the privilege of driving in another state without the requirement of another drivers' license. The NLC is based on the nurse's license from their state of residence but provides the privilege to practice in another NLC member state. Nurses who work in a participating NLC member state do not have to obtain another nursing license to administer care. However, the nurse is obligated to follow the nurse practice laws of the destination state. Like a driver's license, the licensee is obligated to know and follow the rules for that particular state and not the state of residence.

Mutual Recognition

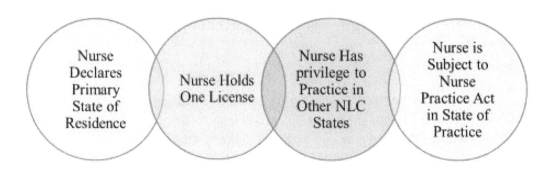

(Figure 1) Mutual Recognition of Nursing License (NLC). Reprinted with permission.

The Multi-State Licensure (MSL) follows the mutual recognition model of licensure.

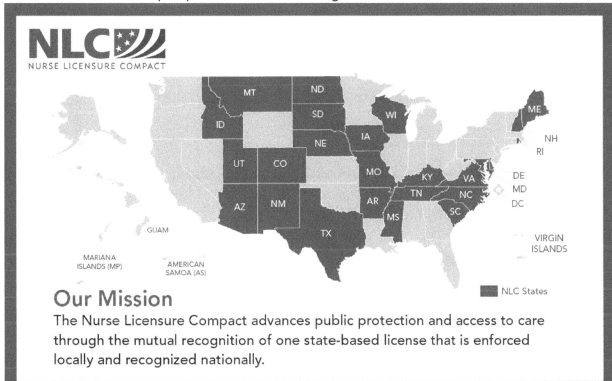

(Figure 2) Map of NLC membership. Reprinted with permission.

Not all states are NLC members that provide a Multi-State License (MSL). A nurse in a NLC non-member state has a single state license that limits practice to that specific state. Furthermore, a nurse whose primary state of residence is a non-compact state and who applies for a license in a compact state is issued a single-state license.

The NLC and the APRN Compact allow nurses to practice in other compact states with a single multistate license. The NLC provides multistate rights for registered nurses (RN) and licensed practical/vocational nurses (LPN/LVN) who reside in a member state. The APRN Compact provides the same rights to advanced practice registered nurses. When considering an out-of- state field trip, the school nurse must have a clear understanding of the nursing scope of practice and delegation regulation in the state where care will be provided. Some states do not allow for the practice of delegating nursing tasks to UAP while other states may limit the nursing tasks that may be delegated. The school nurse is responsible to the nurse practice laws where care will be administered. If the nurse may delegate a task that is permissible in the nurse's home licensing state, but not in the state where the field trip occurs, the nurse's actions are accountable to both state boards of nursing (NCSBN, 1998).

Considerations to include when planning an out-of- state field trip include:

- Do I hold a MSL?
- Is the state to be visited a member of the Nurse Licensure Compact?

- Does the state where the field trip will occur have the same scope of nursing practice? If no, what are the differences? Contacting the board of nursing in the state where the field trip will occur may be necessary to clarify nursing scope of practice.
- Are RNs permitted to delegate school health nursing services to UAPs in the state to be visited?
- If delegation is permitted, are there limitations to the delegation?
- If delegation is allowed, is training and competency verification required for the UAP?

IMPLICATIONS FOR SCHOOL NURSE PRACTICE

Not every school has a school nurse; not all state nursing laws and regulations are the same; and not all state laws allow for the delegation of nursing school health services to unlicensed assistive personnel (UAP). Therefore, when organizing plans for a field trip, the school nurse should be consulted for any health services that may be required.

Nursing health service considerations should include, but not limited to:

- What are the health services accommodations required by the students participating in the field trip (i.e. nursing assessment – see below)
- Are accommodations specified in Individual Health Plan (IHP), Individual Education Plan (IEP) or Section 504 Plan? Consider the activity and the student's limitations.
- Does the student have an Emergency Action Plan (EAP)?
- What are the school's policy and procedures for the provisions of school health services while on a school-sponsored field trip?
- What is the availability of trained staff to provide healthcare services?
- Where will the field trip occur (in-state, out-of-state, out-of-country)?
- If out-of-state, what are the nursing practice laws of the state the students will visit?
- Does the state where the field trip occurs allow for delegation of nursing health services to UAP?
- If out-of-state, is the state a Nurse Compact Licensure State? If not, what does the state where the field trip will occur require for the licensed registered nurse to provide care in that state? Is there a different requirement for LPN or LVN?
- If out-of-state, are there restrictions related to storage, possession, or administration of particular medications or substances?
- What options are available for alteration of the trip if not all students can be reasonably accommodated?

Use of Nursing Assessment

What is the level of care required for the student? Will medications or clinical procedures be required to be provided during the time for the field trip? Is the student able to provide self-care, self-monitoring and self-administration of medication? Regardless of the location of the field trip, the nurse must assess the healthcare needs of the students who will be participating in the field trip.

Student Accommodations

Does the student have an IHP, IEP or Section 504 Plan? What are the accommodations within the student's specific plan that must also be provided on the field trip? Are the accommodations reasonable, or can the accommodations be revised for the trip. e.g. MDs may write orders to forego glucagon on a day trip and use glucose gel and 911 depending on the location? Costs associated with any accommodation specified in the student's plan is the responsibility of the school and must be considered during the planning of any field trip.

The school nurse is already familiar with the healthcare services and accommodations the student requires to fully participate in school-sponsored functions. This familiarity gives the school nurse the unique position to coordinate care of the individual student's care needs on a field trip. Planning and coordination of what the student health services requirements may include:

- Assessing the method of transportation for the field trip, consulting with school food service personnel on the food to be served, determining the staff who will be present, the layout of the planned site, duration of the trip and emergency medical care proximity.
- Determining the medication and healthcare treatments or procedures that will need to be provided during the field trip, as well as potential for health emergencies (NASN, 2013).

Emergency Action Plan (EAP)

Does the student have asthma, diabetes, seizures, or a risk for anaphylaxis? A student Emergency Action Plan (EAP) is a plan written by the registered professional school nurse that is based on the Individual Health Plan (IHP) or used sometimes instead of an IHP. Using succinct terminology and the EAP should be written in clear action steps that can be understood by school unlicensed assistive personnel. The EAP should not only include how to treat the emergency, but also include the name of the student's healthcare provider and phone number as well as parent or legal guardian contact information. For the student who may have an undocumented risk of anaphylaxis, does the school provide the medication for emergency treatment? (NASN, 2015).

School Policies and Procedures

Does the school have specific policies and procedures/protocols in place for all students to be able to participate in school-sponsored activities? Does the school have a system in place to ensure that all school field trip responsible personnel have been consulted on the upcoming field trip? Furthermore, does the school allow the student to self-carry and self-administer their own medications while on the field trip? Some schools use a checklist that also includes the signature of the school nurse to ensure that all student accommodations have been arranged for the field trip and according to any existing accommodation plans of care.

> School Nurse Field Trip Checklist See **APPENDIX**

Trained Staff Availability

Before the school field trip occurs, it is essential for the school nurse to determine the availability of school staff to provide the necessary healthcare services during the field trip. What medications or supplies will be necessary to be provided on the field trip? If the school nurse is not attending the field trip, is there trained staff who can safely perform the health service?

"The level of nursing or healthcare services required for a student in the classroom is, at a minimum, the same level of care that the student requires during school programs outside the classroom" (Hootman, Schwab, Gelfman, Gregory, & Pohlman, 2005, p. 223). School districts should have procedures/protocols in place for the provision of health services, including acquiring medications and supplies from the student's parents or legal guardians, well in advance of the date of the trip so that the provision of health services for students while they are away from the school building is the same level of care received in the school building (Kentucky Department of Education, 2012). Parents may be invited to attend the trip to provide care for their child. However, schools may not mandate parents to accommodate their child (NASN, 2013).

Delegation of School Health Services

Delegation of nursing tasks in the school setting can be a valuable tool for school nurses, especially during field trips. Delegation of nursing services is defined as transferring the responsibility of performing a nursing activity to another person, while retaining accountability for the outcome (American Nurses Association [ANA] & National Council of State Boards of Nursing [NCSBN], 2006; National Association of State School Nurse Consultants [NASSNC], 2010). The nursing scope of practice in any state, including the delegation of nursing health services, is typically governed by the state's Board of Nursing and varies from state to state. State nurse practice acts, or equivalent state statues, define the legal parameters for nursing practice which may include delegation (ANA, 2012). Professional organizations such as the American Nurses Association (ANA) and the National Association for School Nurses (NASN) have developed standards of practice and policy statements to provide guidance on daily nursing practice and are utilized and referred to in a court of law (Erwin, Clark & Mercer, 2013).

Delegation of school nursing services is a complex skill requiring clinical judgement and final accountability of the client (NCSBN, 2006). The RN determines when a nursing service is appropriate to delegate to a UAP. "The RN may delegate components of care but does not delegate the nursing process itself. The practice pervasive functions of assessment, planning, evaluation and nursing judgment cannot be delegated" (ANA & NSCBN, 2006, p.1).

Determination of whether the delegation of a specific nursing task is appropriate in the school setting or on a field trip includes:

- RN assessment of the student health services needed
- Determined on a case by case basis
- Stability and acuity of the student's condition
- Potential for harm
- Complexity of task
- Predictability of outcomes
- Availability/competency of UAP
- Type and frequency of supervision required for UAP (ANA, 2012)

The decision to delegate and supervise a nursing task in schools is the responsibility of the registered nurse. For more guidance on determining appropriateness of delegating a school nursing health service, please refer to the ANA's *Principles for Delegation by Registered Nursed to Unlicensed Assistive Personnel (UAP)* and *Chapter 4,* which also includes a nursing delegation decision tree (ANA, 2012). Not all nursing practices are appropriate to delegate and some states do not allow for the delegation of nursing health services to a UAP. Therefore, when planning a field trip, particularly if out-of- state or out-of- country, the RN must determine the nursing laws for the state or country where the field trip will occur; including clarifying with the state's board of nursing whether alternative, natural medications are allowed.

According to NCSBN, the school nurse will need to contact the boards of nursing in the states where the fieldtrips occur in order to determine the practice allowances for the licensed nurse related to delegation of nursing function (NCSBN, 2012).

CONCLUSION

School-sponsored trips provide an opportunity for the student to expand their learning potential. Many variables must be considered when planning the field trip so that the student's healthcare needs are continued to be provided. The school nurse's knowledge and expertise to provide safe, optimal healthcare services is critical to the planning and collaboration with key school personnel, school administrators, families, and students attending the field trip. Pre-planning is of utmost importance, including the review of state nursing laws, regulations and nursing scope of practice in order to identify potential problems and ensure the safe delivery of school health services to each student participating in the field trip.

RESOURCES

Field Trips: Guidance for School Nurses. (2014). Connecticut State Department of Education, APPENDIX A Sample letters to out-of-state boards of nursing. Downloadable from
http://www.sde.ct.gov/sde/cwp/browse.asp?A=2663&BMDRN=2000&BCOB=0&C=21291

Massachusetts Field Trip Tool Kit. (2015). ESHS CQI Project. Downloadable from
https://neushi.org/student/programs/attachments/FieldTrip.pdf

NASN Position Statement: School-sponsored Trips, Role of the School Nurse. (2013).
https://www.nasn.org/PolicyAdvocacy/PositionPapersandReports/NASNPositionStatementsFullView/tabid/462/smid/824/ArticleID/567/Default.aspx

REFERENCES

American Nurses Association. (2012). *Principles for delegation by registered nurses to unlicensed assistive personnel (UAP).* Silver Spring, MD: Author.

American Nurses Association & National Council of State Boards of Nursing. (2006). *Joint statement on delegation.* Retrieved from https://www.ncsbn.org/Delegation_joint_statement_NCSBN-ANA.pdf

American with Disabilities Act of 1990 (2000). 42 U.S.C §§ 12101-12213

Erwin, K., Clark, S., & Mercer, S. (2014). Providing health services for children with special health care needs on out-of-state field trips. *NASN School Nurse, 29* (2), 85-88. doi: 10.1177/1942602X13517005

Hootman, J., Schwab, N.C., Gelfman, M.H.B., Gregory, E.K. & Pohlman, K.J. (2005). School nursing practice: Clinical performance issues. In M.H. Gelfman & N.C. Schwab (Eds.). *Legal issues in school health services* (pp. 167-229). Lincoln, NE: Authors Choice Press.

Individuals with Disability Education Improvement Act (2004). 20 U.S.C. 14 et seq.

Kentucky Department of Education. (2015). *Field trips and medication administration.* Retrieved from http://education.ky.gov/districts/SHS/Pages?Field-Trips-and-Medication-Administration.aspx

National Association of School Nurses. (2015). *Individualized healthcare plans: the role of the school nurse* (Position Statement). Silver Spring, MD: Author.

National Association of School Nurses. (2013). *School-sponsored trips, role of the school nurse* (Position Statement). Silver Spring, MD: Author.

National Association of State School Nurse Consultants. (2010). *Delegation of school health services* (Position Statement). Retrieved from http://www.schoolnurseconsultants.org

National Council of State Boards of Nursing. (1998). Nursing *license compact, adopted article V (original).* Retrieved from http://www.ncsbn.org./nlc.htm

National Council of State Boards of Nursing. (2015). *Nursing license compact.* Retrieved from http://www.ncsbn.org/nurse-licensure-compact.htm

Rehabilitation Act of 1973, U.S.C. § 504

U. S. Department of Education. (2011). Protecting *students with disabilities: Frequently asked question about Section 504 and the education of children with disabilities.* Retrieved from http://www2.ed.gov/about/offices/list/ocr/504 faq.html

APPENDIX

SCHOOL NURSE FIELD TRIP CHECKLIST

Trip Destination: _____ Date of Field Trip: _____

Field Trip Coordinator: _____

_____1) Review school district policy and follow plan accordingly.

_____2) Review district/school filed trip request form and develop list of all attending students.

_____3) Identify all health-related issues and concerns, including students with food allergies and accessibility for attending students.

_____4) Review Individual Healthcare Plans, Individual Education Plans, Section 504 Accommodation Plans and Emergency Action Plans (EAP)   for attending students.

_____5) Evaluate to determine whether student parent/guardian with medical need plans to accompany field trip.

_____6) Review nursing scope of practice and applicable state laws and regulations for in-state, out-of-state, and out-of-country field trips; including whether delegation to UAP and who may delegate (RN, LPN)? Is the destination state a MLS state?

_____7) Notify Field Trip Coordinator if a nurse is required for the field trip.

_____8) Prepare any necessary forms for documentation of medication administration, special healthcare procedures/ treatments, copies of EAP's, licensed prescribed orders, parent and physician contact information is to be included.

_____9) Prepare necessary equipment, medications and first aid supplies, including medications to be refrigerated, care plans, and treatment plans.

_____10) Review medical concerns, medication administration, treatment plans and emergency protocols with the nurse or staff member attending field trip.

_____11) Provide current cell phone number to attending nurse/staff/chaperone for on-going consultation for student health concerns if needed.

_____12) If a nurse is **NOT** accompanying field trip:

  • Notify parent/guardian the name of staff personnel who will be administering students medications and or/treatments. Obtain parenteral/guardian written consent.

  • Train staff members in medication administration, epinephrine and glucagon medication administration (as state practice act allows), Cardio Pulmonary Resuscitation and necessary healthcare treatments as indicated and document all trainings.

_____13) When the field trip is completed assure all medications, equipment, care plans, first aid supplies and other confidential information/forms are returned to the school nurse.

CHECKLIST COMPLETED:

School Nurse: _____ DATE: _____

Chapter 52

TRANSPORTATION OF STUDENTS WITH HEALTH CONCERNS

Suzanne Levasseur, MSN, APRN, CPNP, NCSN

DESCRIPTION OF ISSUE

Since 1939, school transportation safety experts have developed and revised safety standards for school buses (National Association of State Directors of Pupil Transportation Services [NASDPT]), 2000). Currently, it is estimated that approximately more than 25 million children ride school buses to and from school (National Center for Education Statistics, 2015). For school nurses, legal issues pertaining to transporting students generally involve bus accidents, transporting students via ambulances following an illness or injury at school and transporting students with disabilities.

Transporting students requires planning and often is monitored by the school transportation coordinator. Transporting students with disabilities requires more careful planning and preparation by the school team. The school nurse often takes the lead as the team member who is most equipped to understand the various considerations that are involved in a transportation plan. Traveling to and from school each day is only one component of the plan. It also includes traveling between schools and traveling within a school building as well as any specialized equipment needed to accomplish this, such as ramps, wheelchairs or lifts. Other considerations include specially trained staff and deciding what vehicle is best suited for the student's individual needs. The unique needs of the student need to be addressed on a case-by-case basis.

BACKGROUND

As mentioned, millions of children ride to and from school on school buses every day. Overall, due to safety standards and regulations, bus accidents are less common than other types of vehicular accidents; nonetheless, school districts should have policies and procedures in place for addressing transportation concerns in the general education settings.

Regulations for Part B of the Individuals with Disabilities Education Improvement Act (IDEIA) (2004) were first published on August 14, 2006 and went into effect in October 2006. Since then additional regulations were added and became effective in December 2008. In most states, transportation to and from school for students who do not live within a walking distance is provided by the district but this service remains up to the district policy. Under IDEA at 34 CFR 300.34(c) (16) (United States Department of Education[USDE], n.d.), transportation is listed as a related service and therefore is provided for all students with a disability if the student requires the transportation to take part in the educational program and it is part of the student's Individualized Education Program (IEP).

A student may live a short distance from school but because of a disability is unable to ambulate or a student may need specialized transportation such as a wheelchair accessible van. If it is determined the student's disability does not allow the student to get to school as do their nondisabled peers, the related service of transportation must be provided (Pfrommer, 2013). In addition, if a district does provide transportation to the general school population, it must also provide transportation to the disabled students in any special education program where the district has placed the student. It should also include any transportation needs for transition training or community placements which prepare the student for postsecondary needs.

Under Section 504 of the Rehabilitation Act (Rehabilitation Act of 1973 [§504], 2000), districts are also required to provide transportation to allow students with disabilities the same equal opportunity for participation as their nondisabled peers. As a student with health needs may require more specialized care in school, that student would also be eligible for that care during transportation.

In Macomb County Intermediate School District vs. Joshua S. (1989), the courts required the school district to provide tracheostomy care to a student during transportation to and from school in addition to the same care provided during the school day. Students with complex medical needs may also require the services of a trained paraprofessional, bus aide or a licensed nurse as part of their transportation requirements.

Students with disabilities should also have access to extracurricular activities and field trips as do their nondisabled peers to allow equal opportunity to participate. If the IEP team has determined that extracurricular activities or community placements are necessary to allow the student an equal opportunity for participation and is dependent on specialized transportation, then districts must provide this service (Pfrommer, 2013).

IMPLICATIONS FOR SCHOOL NURSE PRACTICE

School nurses are a vital part of the school team when addressing health needs during transport and deciding on transportation for disabled or medically complex students. As part of the general education team, IEP Team and Section 504 team, the school nurse will be instrumental in developing goals and objectives and accommodations related to transportation. For children with special healthcare needs, the nursing process should start with a comprehensive health assessment that would include functional nursing diagnosis and identification of student health status as well as any developmental issues. This assessment should be done with input from the healthcare provider, parent, and community resources involved with the student. After the assessment phase is complete, the school nurse can identify outcomes to begin to plan for the student transportation needs, which should be included in an individualized healthcare plan (IHP) and individualized transportation plan (ITP).

Any recommendations for necessary modifications, aids and nursing interventions involved in transportation should be shared with the school IEP or Section 504 team and decided during the evaluation process of the meeting and should be reflected in the student's IEP.

Considerations for Students with Health Concerns

Mode of Transportation

Decisions regarding the type of vehicle needed should be made by the school authorities in conjunction with the transportation coordinator, school nurse and parent, with the safe transportation of the student at the highest priority. Many different types of vehicles can be used including regular school buses, private cars, mini buses, taxis and when necessary ambulances with trained emergency personnel. It should be kept in mind that IDEA's least restrictive environment (LRE) requirement requires districts to transport students with a disability with their nondisabled peers as much as possible. For a student with a wheelchair, a bus with a ramp that can safely transport a wheelchair will be necessary.

Required Personnel

The school nurse will be the team member who determines if school health services or school nurse services are required during transportation. In general, the same level of health services needed in school may also be required in transportation. School nurses should be knowledgeable about their state statutes, Nurse Practice Acts and Standards and Scope of Practice regarding delegation to determine if the student's health services' needs can be safely met by Unlicensed Assistive Personnel (UAP). This would require appropriate training and supervision by the school nurse. It may also be determined that the student's needs require a licensed nurse to accompany the student on the bus. In some cases, the district may contract with an outside agency to provide the necessary personnel. The school nurse or nursing supervisor would be the appropriate person to communicate the student's needs to the outside agency to assure the appropriate level of care is provided. A back up plan including training of additional staff should also be in effect for the possibility of staff illness or absence.

Effective communication with transportation providers is important. Any potential problems or concerns of any student should be shared with transportation providers, monitors or any other staff members involved with the care of students on the bus. Any transportation worker that receives personally identifiable information about the student should also receive training regarding protecting the confidentiality of that information. The school nurse may be the most qualified school personnel to share that information with transportation staff.

Safety

Safety during transportation is always a concern and should be addressed in the student's IHP and/or ITP. Any needed emergency equipment such as oxygen, epinephrine and suctioning equipment must be with the student during transportation. This equipment or emergency medications should be safely stored and secured but also accessible in an emergency. The use of anything required for the student should be part of the comprehensive training program for the personnel responsible for the student on the bus.

In School Transportation

The definition of transportation also involves moving in and around the school building. The school nurse should be part of the planning for needed equipment such as ramps, lifts and wheelchairs. The district is responsible for providing, at no cost to the student and family, the needed equipment to navigate the school (Norlin, Pfrommer, & Pitasky, 2015). For some students an aide may be required in this process as well.

Field Trips/School-sponsored trips

A student with a disability cannot be denied access to a field trip/school sponsored trip due to transportation issues (Pfrommer, 2013). The student's individualized transportation needs must be met in the same way as transportation to and from school. School nurses should incorporate field trip planning in the student's IHP and ITP. *(See Chapter 51 for more information on school-sponsored trips).*

General Considerations for General Education Students

A review of the literature showed that there were few laws that pertain to transportation for general education students. District policy is generally the guiding principle and school nurses, as health experts in the school, should be involved in policy development for their district.

Bus Accidents

Some school nurses have been asked to attend bus accidents for their district. While the nurse may feel it is an important part of his or her role in an emergency, there are some other matters to consider. In an area where there is a quick emergency response time, the EMS provider would be the person in authority for medical care at their time of arrival and therefore, may not necessitate the need for the school nurse to go to the scene. Although a comforting person from the school that the children know may be warranted, a school administrator may be a better choice. If the school nurse leaves the building when EMS providers are available at the scene, there could be an issue of who would be available to address other health concerns or possible emergencies of children in the building.

Transportation of Students in Employee Owned Cars

Personally owned vehicles to transport pupils to and from school-related activities by school staff should be avoided for liability and safety concerns, unless specifically allowed by district policy and district and/or nurse auto liability insurance. Permission to use private vehicles should be obtained in writing from the administration and based on district policy. On occasion parents may be unable to pick up a sick child from school. The use of taxis or an unscheduled bus may be utilized for this purpose per school policy.

Minor Injuries on the Bus

On some occasions, a student will get off the bus and head to the school nurse for an injury obtained while riding the bus. Documentation of how and why the injury occurred should be thorough and shared with the building administrator if the injury was a result of an altercation with another student, as a result of misbehavior, or due to a safety issue on the bus. Parents should be notified and depending on the situation, an incident report should be completed.

Transportation via Ambulance

School nurses are often in the forefront when an ambulance is called for an injured or ill student. When EMS providers arrive, the transfer of health care is from school nurse to paramedic/EMT. If the student is transported to the hospital, one question that frequently emerges is who should accompany the student in the ambulance if a parent is unavailable. While district policy should dictate that responsibility, in general, it is not the school nurse but is someone from the school district who knows the student and can offer reassurance to the student until the parent/guardian is united with them. Again, there could be an issue of who would be available to address other health concerns or possible emergencies of children in the building if the school nurse left to accompany the student in the ambulance.

CONCLUSION

In order for a student with medical needs or a disability to receive a free and appropriate education (FAPE), it is often necessary for the Local Educational Authority (LEA) to provide specialized transportation. This can include transportation to and from school, between schools, transportation within the school building and any specialized equipment needed. School teams including IEP and Section 504 teams should give careful consideration to the needed accommodations when developing the student's IEP or Section 504 Plan. The school nurse will be essential in this planning and in the development of any IHP or ITP to be shared with the school team and other staff involved with the student's transportation needs.

RESOURCES

Mahoney, D. (2011). School Business Affairs. Know the risks: Transporting students in private vehicles. http://files.eric.ed.gov/fulltext/EJ966678.pdf

National Council on State Boards of Nursing. Nurse Practice Act Toolkit. https://www.ncsbn.org/npa-toolkit.htm

United States Department of Education. (n.d.). Building the Legacy of IDEA: 2004 http://idea.ed.gov/explore/view/p/,root,dynamic,QaCorner,12

United States Department of Education. (2015). Protecting Students with Disabilities. http://www2.ed.gov/about/offices/list/ocr/504faq.html

Letter to McKaig, 211 IDELR 161 (EHLR 211:161) (OSEP 1980)

Letter to Stohrer, 213 IDELR 209 (EHLR 213:209) (OSEP 1989)

REFERENCES

Individuals with Disability Education Improvement Act (2004), 20 U.S.C. 1400 et seq.

Macomb County Intermediate School District vs. Joshua S., 1989. Retrieved from http://www.leagle.com/decision/19891539715FSupp824_11367/MACOMB%20COUNTY%20INTERMEDIATE%20SCHOOL%20D.%20v.%20JOSHUA%20S

National Association of State Directors of Pupil Transportation Services. (2000). *History of school bus safety - Why are school buses built as they are?* (Position Statement). Retrieved from http://www.nasdpts.org/Documents/Paper-SchoolBusHistory.pdf

National Center for Education Statistics. (2015). *National digest of education statistics*. Retrieved from http://nces.ed.gov/programs/digest/d15/tables/dt15_236.90.asp?current=yes

Norlin, J., Pfrommer, J., & Pitasky, V. (2015). Transportation. In *The complete OSEP h*andbook, (2nd ed.) (pp. 1-20). Palm Beach Gardens, FL: LRP Publications.

Pfrommer, J. (2013). *Serving students with medical needs: Achieving legal compliance with 504,* (pp.32-34). Palm Beach Gardens, FL: LRP Publications.

Rehabilitation Act of 1973, 29 U.S.C. § 504.

United States Department of Education. (n.d.). *Building the legacy of IDEA: 2004*. Retrieved from http://idea.ed.gov/explore/view/p/,root,dynamic,QaCorner,12

INDEX

CPSIA information can be obtained
at www.ICGtesting.com
Printed in the USA
BVHW011626040921
615809BV00007B/535